Tafsīr al-Tustarī

Tafsīr al-Tustarī

by

Sahl b. ʿAbd Allāh al-Tustarī

Great Commentaries on the Holy Qurʾān

translated by

Annabel Keeler and Ali Keeler

Royal Aal al-Bayt Institute for Islamic Thought

FONS VITAE

First published in 2011 by

Fons Vitae
49 Mockingbird Valley Drive
Louisville, KY 40207

http://www.fonsvitae.com
Email: fonsvitaeky@aol.com

Great Commentaries on the Holy Qur᾽ān: ISSN: 1943-1821

Library of Congress Control Number: 2011922358

ISBN 9781891785191

This book was typeset by Neville Blakemore, Jr. and Muhammad Hozien

Printed in Canada

Contents

Plates follow page lx.

Acknowledgements

We would like to express our sincere gratitude to HRH Prince Ghazi bin Muhammad who first invited us to embark on the translation of a Sufi *tafsīr* for the Great Commentaries on the Qurʾān Project, and to the Royal Aal al-Bayt Institute, Amman, Jordan, for their generous patronage of our translation of the *Tafsīr al-Qurʾān al-ʿAẓīm* of Sahl b. ʿAbd Allāh al-Tustarī. We would also particularly like to thank the Series Editor, Yousef Meri, for his tireless support in overseeing the translation through all its different stages, for his careful perusal of the English translation against the Arabic original, and for his help and many suggestions regarding the referencing in the annotation of the translation.

We would also like to offer our thanks and appreciation to Samir Mahmoud, here in Cambridge, who has gone through the whole translation, both at an early stage, and in its final draft. Being a native speaker of Arabic and having fluency in English as well as a proficient knowledge of Sufism, his comments and suggestions on many details of the text, and his answers to our many queries, have been invaluable. Also here in Cambridge, we would like to thank Aziza Spiker, who has acted as proof reader and copy editor for the translation, and who has also made pertinent comments about the translation of some of the Qurʾānic verses. Our thanks are also due Sahra Ucar, who at short notice stepped in to help with compiling the Appendix, and to Lejla Demiri, who assisted with the sourcing of many *ḥadīth*s, and who acted as our guide at the Suleymaniye Library, whence we were able to obtain two of the manuscripts we used for the translation. In addition, we would like to thank Professor Paul Ballanfat of the Galatasaray University in Istanbul, with whom we have consulted on certain passages in the *Tafsīr*, and Professor Nasrollah Pourjavady of Tehran University and Harith Bin Ramli (the latter currently working on Makkī's *Qūt al-qulūb* at Oxford University), both of whom read through our Introduction to the Translation and made several helpful suggestions, though we should add that any and all mistakes are, of course, our own. We would also like to mention our gratitude to Robert Spiker and Ana Maria Giraldo for lending their expertise in design and graphics, and to Valerie Turner and Muhammad Hozien for the extraordinary, unstinting dedication they have shown in the final copy-editing, proofreading and typesetting of the manuscript.

Lastly, we would like to thank our families, and especially our spouses, Paul the husband of Annabel, and Mariam the wife of Ali, for their tremendous patience and encouragement during the completion of this work.

We would like to dedicate this translation to the master sitarist, Ustad Mahmud Mirza, whose pure and beautiful music first gave us a glimpse of Paradise, and has continued to inspire us ever since.

Preface

From the earliest centuries of Islam, Muslim mystics, or 'Sufis' as they are now mostly called, reflected upon the verses of the Qurʾān, expounding their insights and inspired comments to others who might benefit from them. These comments were not intended to contradict or stand in place of the literal readings of the Scripture; rather they were a way of going beyond them in order to draw out inner meanings that sprang from, and were informed by, states, stations and spiritual realities (*ḥaqāʾiq*) experienced by the mystics. This process of eliciting inner meanings from the Qurʾān, termed by some Sufis '*istinbāṭ*', meaning literally 'drawing up water from a well', might take the form of brief, elliptical and allusive comments, or lengthier and more detailed explanations. These early comments were eagerly memorised and passed on by the mystics' associates and followers, since they were seen not only as a profound way of understanding the Qurʾān, but also as a source of guidance and illumination for anyone aspiring to travel the spiritual path.

As with other religious sciences, the early esoteric interpretations of the Qurʾān were, to begin with, mainly transmitted through the oral tradition, and for the most part they appear to have remained as scattered comments preserved in disparate sources until the time when the fifth/eleventh-century Sufi, Abū ʿAbd al-Raḥmān al-Sulamī (d. 412/1021) compiled his anthology of Sufi Qurʾān commentary, the *Ḥaqāʾiq al-tafsīr* ('Realities' or 'Truths of Interpretation'). Sulamī arranged all the exegetical material he could gather, comments that had been attributed to many different mystics, in a verse-by-verse commentary on the Qurʾān.

The *Tafsīr al-Qurʾān al-ʿaẓīm* ('Commentary on the Great Qurʾān') of Sahl b. ʿAbd Allāh al-Tustarī (d. 283/896) is remarkable in having been compiled much earlier than this, by Tustarī's immediate disciples and within one generation of his death, and in having been preserved as a commentary on the Qurʾān through an authenticated chain of transmission, until it was first written down by a scribe in the mid-sixth/twelfth century. Thus it may claim to be the earliest extant Sufi Qurʾān commentary ascribed to a single author. What is more, Tustarī's disciples integrated within this exegetical corpus a large number of apposite sayings of their master as well as accounts of events in his life. This makes it possible to situate the interpretations within the compass of Tustarī's thought, and to gain a greater understanding of the profound connection between his mystical doctrines and his exegesis of the Qurʾān.

Tustarī was among the most important and influential mystics of the early, formative period of Islamic mysticism, and many later famous Sufis and thinkers drew upon his ideas and cited his sayings, including Abū Ḥāmid al-Ghazālī (d. 505/1111), Shihāb al-Dīn Yaḥyā al-Suhrawardī (d. 587/1191) and Muḥyī al-Dīn Ibn ʿArabī (d. 638/1240). The fourth/tenth-century Sufi author Abū Ṭālib al-Makkī (d. 386/996), who had fully imbibed Tustarī's teachings through contact with the circle of his followers in Basra, contributed to the promulgation of his thought and sayings through his treatise on Sufism, the *Qūt al-qulūb* ('Nourishment of Hearts'), which was freely used by Ghazālī in the composition of his celebrated *Iḥyāʾ ʿulūm al-dīn* ('Revival of the Religious Sciences'). Among Tustarī's significant contributions to the doctrines of Sufism are his emphasis on the remembrance of God (*dhikr*), on complete trust in God (*tawakkul*) and his discourse on the 'Muḥammadan Light'.

This volume represents the first translation into English of Tustarī's *Tafsīr*, and indeed of any complete Sufi commentary on the Qurʾān. The printed text we have used is the most recent edition published in Lebanon by Dār al-Kutub al-ʿIlmiyya, and edited by Muḥammad Bāsil ʿUyyūn al-Sūd.

This appears to be a replication of the Cairo edition published in 1911, and is not a critical edition of the text. However, we were fortunate in obtaining CDs of three manuscripts of the *Tafsīr*, and have consulted these manuscripts throughout the process of our translation. This has enabled us to fill in a number of lacunae, and correct numerous mistakes in the current published edition. All the additions that we have made on the basis of these manuscripts have been clearly marked between half brackets, thus: ⌜...⌝, and referenced in the footnotes along with the folio numbers of each manuscript, and likewise, any corrections we have made have been recorded in the notes. The corrections made to the text are not exhaustive, but have assisted, we hope, in clarifying many unnecessarily obscure passages. The manuscripts we have used are as follows:

MS Fātiḥ 638, dated 872/1468

MS Fātiḥ 3488, dated 965/1558

MS Ẓāhiriyya 515, dated twelfth/eighteenth or thirteenth/nineteenth century.

In the footnotes, we have referred to these as MSS Z515, F638 and F3488, and have cited them in this order, rather than in their chronological order, since it was the Ẓāhiriyya manuscript that was first available to us. The MSS Z515 and F3488 form part of the same manuscript tradition, whilst MS F638 represents the second manuscript tradition — Professor Gerhard Böwering, in his study of the manuscripts of Tustarī's *Tafsīr*, has identified two groups of manuscripts overall, and we have thus had access to representatives of both. A comparison of the manuscripts of the *Tafsīr* in general, and of the two manuscript traditions in particular, reveals only minor differences between them.[1]

As is the case with most Sufi commentaries on the Qurʾān, Tustarī's *Tafsīr* does not comprise interpretations of every single verse. Nonetheless there are comments on a selection of verses, or parts of verses, from all the *sūra*s of the Qurʾān, amounting to around 1000 verses in total. These comments, as they appear in both the published edition and the manuscripts, mostly follow the order of the Qurʾān itself, the main exception being sections of verse ordering in Sūras 2 and 3 (al-Baqara and Āl ʿImrān). In cases where there is a divergence from the verse order, we have not corrected it, unless such a change was warranted by the manuscripts. All citations of the Qurʾānic text are in italic. In accordance with the wishes of our patrons, we have used the Aal al-Bayt's official translation of the Qurʾān, with a few minor amendments which were often, though not always, required to comply with Tustarī's particular understanding of the meaning of a word in the verse. Indeed, any examination of a variety of Qurʾān translations will demonstrate the polysemy of its language.

The editor of the Dār al-Kutub al-ʿIlmiyya edition of Tustarī's *Tafsīr*, while not making any substantial changes to the earlier Cairo edition of the text, has sourced many of the *ḥadīth*s and traditions that are cited in the commentary. We felt it useful to include these as they are, even though we did not have access to the same editions of all the *ḥadīth* collections he was using, and were therefore not able to check all his references. Those that we were able to check, we found to be correct. We have additionally sourced quite a number of *ḥadīth*s for which the editor had not provided references, though we were unfortunately not successful in sourcing all those that are cited in the commentary. Where two editions of the same *ḥadīth* collection have been referred to, they are differentiated by the place and/or date of publication.

For a Sufi text that is so allusive in nature, and in which terms are used in subtly different ways in the various contexts, we decided that rather than providing a glossary of technical terms, it might be more useful to compile a detailed index, in which various meanings and applications of a particular term will be given along with the references to the relevant page and note numbers. The Introduction to the Translation presents detailed explanations and discussions of the salient doctrines presented in the *Tafsīr*, as well as some of the more unusual concepts and complex aspects of Tustarī's teachings.

It is worth explaining here the use of a few of the terms that occur frequently in this volume. As indicated above, the term 'Sufi', as a noun or adjective, is now generally used to denote either 'a

1 The manuscripts of Tustarī's *Tafsīr* are fully discussed in Gerhard Böwering, *The Mystical Vision of Existence in Classical Islam: The Qurʾānic Hermeneutics of the Ṣūfī Sahl at-Tustarī (d. 283/896)* (Berlin and New York, 1980), pp. 100–5.

proponent of mysticism in Islam', or 'related to, and associated with, Islamic mysticism', respectively. In the Introduction to the Translation, and in some of the notes to our translation, the word 'Sufi' has been used with this meaning. However, it is worth bearing in mind that this is a retrospective use of the term Sufi, which in the early period was mainly associated with mystics of Baghdad, and only gradually, from the sixth/twelfth century on, gained wider currency in the Muslim world. Tustarī never once uses the Arabic equivalent for 'Sufi' in his *Tafsīr* (that is, *taṣawwuf* or *ṣūfī*); instead, he speaks of the 'mystic' (*ʿārif*, pl. *ʿurafāʾ*) or the 'friend of God' (*walī*, pl. *awliyāʾ*). The second term that should be mentioned here is the word *maʿrifa*, a term applied by Sufis to mean a divinely-bestowed mystical or experiential knowledge of God that is beyond the level of knowledge attained merely through instruction or discursive reasoning. For this we have used the conventional English translation 'gnosis'. The word *nafs* (pl. *anfus* or *nufūs*) can be used to mean 'self', 'person' or 'soul', according to context. In the Qurʾānic verses translated in this volume, the word 'soul' has mostly been employed for *nafs*. In the translation of the passages of commentary we have translated *nafs* as 'soul' in those contexts where Tustarī seems to imply more generally the spiritual, immaterial and immortal part of the human being. However, we have used the word 'self' for *nafs* in the more numerous instances where Tustarī designates different levels and aspects of the *nafs* within the human being, as, for example, the 'spiritual self' (*nafs al-rūḥ*) 'natural self' (*nafs al-ṭabʿ*), 'evil-inciting self' (*nafs ammāra bi'l-sūʾ*) and so on. The all-important word *tawḥīd* meaning literally 'making or understanding as one', we have translated as either 'attesting to' or 'professing God's oneness', when Tustarī appears to imply an active commitment to belief in the oneness of God, or 'realising God's oneness', when he seems to imply by *tawḥīd* a more profound mystical experience of God's oneness.

We have retained the masculine gender in translating verbs and pronouns, assuming them to be intended inclusively. Likewise in the Introduction to the Translation, the use of the masculine gender or the terms 'man' or 'mankind' is intended to be inclusive of both genders.

The translation has employed the transliteration system used by the *International Journal of Middle East Studies* (*IJMES*). The *tāʾ marbuṭa* has been rendered *–a* in the presentation of Arabic equivalents, when the word is not in the construct state (e.g. *ḥaqīqa*), but *–at* in the construct form (e.g. *ḥaqīqat al-īmān*). Only the names of less well-known places have been transliterated. Standard abbreviations have been used for titles of encyclopaedias: e.g. *EI*[2] for the *Encyclopaedia of Islam* (Second edition); *EIr* for the *Encyclopaedia Iranica*; and *EQ* for the *Encyclopaedia of the Qurʾān*. The abbreviation of journal titles is as in the *Index Islamicus*. The honorific 'may God bless him and grant him peace' (*ṣalla' Llāhu ʿalayhi wa'l-salam*), which traditionally follows the mention of the Prophet, has been represented as (ﷺ) in the translation; while the honorific 'peace be upon him, or them' (*ʿalayhi/ʿalayhim al-salām*) following the mention of other prophets is represented as (عليه السلام, عليهم السلام). The traditional honorific for 'may God be pleased with him, her or them' (*raḍiya'Llāhu ʿanhu/hā/hum/humā*) following the mention of others is presented as (رضي الله عنه, رضي الله عنها, رضي الله عنهم). When cross-referencing in the footnotes, we have referred to the Introduction to the Translation as IT and the Introduction to the Commentary as IC; cross references to other notes appear by page and note number. Within Qurʾānic quotes, square brackets indicate a word or phrase (additional to the Qurʾānic text) that has been added to clarify the meaning; parentheses indicate that a part of the Qurʾānic text has been added that is not in the *Tafsīr* to provide necessary context for the reader.

In conclusion, we would like to add that the *Tafsīr al-Qurʾān al-ʿaẓīm* does not represent the entirety of Qurʾānic interpretations attributed to Tustarī; a large number of other comments in his name are included in Sulamī's *Ḥaqāʾiq al-tafsīr*, as well as in Sulamī's supplement to this work, the *Ziyādāt ḥaqāʾiq al-tafsīr*. We had considered the idea of including the translation of these comments as an appendix to the present publication, but decided that this, in itself no small undertaking, would be better attempted once Professor Böwering's critical edition of the *Ḥaqāʾiq al-tafsīr* has been published.

Introduction to the Translation

I. Sahl al-Tustarī's Spiritual Formation and his Teachers[1]

Sahl b. ʿAbd Allāh al-Tustarī was probably born in 203/818 in Tustar (pronounced in Persian as Shūshtar) in Khūzistān, south-western Iran, and it is here that he spent the early years of his life.[2] When still a young boy, he was introduced to Sufism by his maternal uncle Muḥammad b. Sawwār, and at the age of seven begged his uncle to allow him to wear the patched frock (*muraqqaʿ*) — an indication that he had been initiated into the mystical path.[3] Sahl would rise in the early hours and watch his uncle performing his nightly vigil.[4] It was his uncle who initiated Sahl into the Sufi practice of remembrance of God (*dhikr Allāh*), when one night he told him to recite inwardly without moving his tongue the words, 'God is with me, God is watching over me, God is my Witness (*Allāhu maʿī, Allāhu nāẓirī, Allāhu shāhidī*)'. To begin with, Sahl's uncle told him to recite these words three times. Then, when Sahl reported to him that he had done this, he instructed him to recite the words seven times every night, and when Sahl had accomplished this, he finally increased the number to eleven times each night, urging the young Sahl to continue this practice every day until he went to his grave, and explaining to him that he would derive great benefit from them in this world and the next. Tustarī relates that he soon experienced from this practice a sweetness (*ḥalāwa*) in his heart, and he states that after continuing the practice for two years, this sweetness was felt in his innermost being or 'secret' (*sirr*). His uncle later said to him, 'Sahl! If God is with someone, and beholds him and watches over him, can he then disobey Him? You should never do so.'[5] This teaching concerning the remembrance of God that his uncle had instilled in him had a profound influence on Tustarī, and was to become a cornerstone of his mystical doctrine, as we shall see. Muḥammad b. Sawwār also imparted to his nephew some instruction in Qurʾānic exegesis, and *ḥadīth*.[6] Little is known about Muḥammad b. Sawwār's spiritual background other than that he may have had some connection to Maʿrūf al-Karkhī (d. 200/815), whom, according to Tustarī, he once described as 'one of the significant masters and spiritual forbears'.[7]

1 For the first four sections of this introduction, I am indebted to the excellent study on Sahl al-Tustarī by Gerhard Böwering, *The Mystical Vision of Existence in Classical Islam: The Qurʾānic Hermeneutics of the Ṣūfī Sahl at-Tustarī (d. 283/896)* (Berlin and New York, 1980), as well as the PhD thesis of M. K. I. Gaafar, 'The Sufi Doctrine of Sahl al-Tustarī, with a Critical Edition of his *Risālat al-ḥurūf*' (Cambridge University, 1966). For the remaining sections of the Introduction, my main source has been the *Tafsīr* itself.

2 An alternative date of 200/815 is given in the sources, but both Böwering and Gaafar appear to favour the later date of 203/818 as more likely.

3 ʿAbd Allāh al-Anṣārī, *Ṭabaqāt al-ṣūfiyya* (Kabul, 1961), p. 116.

4 Abū al-Qāsim al-Qushayrī, *al-Risālat al-Qushayriyya fī ʿilm al-taṣawwuf* (Cairo, 1966) p. 83; trans. Alexander D. Knysh as *Qushayri's Epistle on Sufism* (Reading, 2007), p. 33.

5 Ibid, pp. 83–4.

6 In the *Tafsīr* Tustarī quotes quite a number of *ḥadīth* transmitted to him by his uncle Muḥammad b. Sawwār.

7 Abū ʿAbd al-Raḥmān al-Sulamī, *Ṭabaqāt al-ṣūfiyya* (Leiden, 1960), p. 74.

Even as a child, Tustarī showed a strong inclination to lead an ascetic, solitary and contemplative life.[8] He attended lessons with a Qurʾān teacher only on the condition that he should be allowed to return home after one hour lest his spiritual concentration (*himma*) be dissipated.[9] It was said that he lived on barley bread alone until the age of twelve.[10] At the age of thirteen, he experienced a spiritual crisis in the form of a profound question that persistently troubled him. He requested that he should be allowed to travel to Basra to discover whether any of the learned men of that city would be able to answer his question. Finding no one who was able to help him there, he travelled on to the island of ʿAbbādān (in present-day south-western Iran), where a famous *ribāṭ* or spiritual refuge and retreat is said to have been established by followers of Ḥasan al-Baṣrī. It was here that Tustarī met Abū Ḥabīb Ḥamza b. ʿAbd Allāh al-ʿAbbādānī, who was at last able to provide him with an answer to his question.[11] He remained with Abū Ḥabīb for some time, in order to benefit from his knowledge and become trained in the ways of Sufi *adab*, that is, the disposition and modes of conduct proper to the mystical path.[12] It was also in ʿAbbādān, Tustarī relates, that one night he saw the words: *God, there is no god save He, the Living, the Eternal Sustainer* [2:255], written in green light on one line across the sky from East to West.[13]

After this period of training under a spiritual master, Tustarī returned to his native town of Tustar, where for some twenty years he mainly lived a solitary life, subjecting himself to exceptionally rigorous ascetic disciplines with periods of sustained and severe fasting — indeed, he is cited many times in Sufi literature as exemplifying the benefits of hunger and fasting. The following account is taken from the *Risāla* of Qushayrī:

> Then I returned to Tustar. By that time, my diet had been reduced to the point that [my people] would buy barley for me for a dirham, grind it, and bake it into bread for me. Every night about dawn, I would break my fast with merely an ounce [of that bread], without salt or condiment. The dirham lasted a year for me. After that, I resolved to break my fast once every three days, then once every seven days, then once every twenty-five days. I continued this practice for twenty years.[14]

Although based in Tustar during this period, after a few years Tustarī did make another journey away from his home town, performing the pilgrimage to Mecca in the year 219/834. According to some reports, it was at Mecca that he first encountered Dhū'l-Nūn al-Miṣrī (d. 245/860).[15] It is not known whether or not Tustarī formally became a disciple of Dhū'l-Nūn, staying with him and remaining in service to him for a period of time, but there is little doubt that a strong spiritual association was established between the two mystics.[16] One report does state that Tustarī travelled to Egypt to visit Dhū'l-Nūn, where the latter taught him about the nature of true trust in God (*tawakkul*), which is in fact one of the key doctrines that Tustarī expounds in his Qurʾān commentary.[17] Moreover, a

8 Qushayrī, *Risāla*, p. 84. Farīd al-Dīn ʿAṭṭār, *Tadhkīrat al-awliyāʾ* (Tehran, 1992), p. 306.

9 Qushayrī, *Risāla*, p. 84; ʿAṭṭār, *Tadhkīrat al-awliyāʾ*, p. 305.

10 Qushayrī, *Risāla*, p. 84; ʿAṭṭār, *Tadhkīrat al-awliyāʾ*, p. 306.

11 According to Ibn ʿArabī, Tustarī's question related to the heart and whether or not it prostrated before God. The answer he was given was, 'Yes, it does, forever.' Muḥyī al-Dīn Ibn ʿArabī, *al-Futūḥāt al-Makkiyya* (Beirut, 2007), vol. 1, p. 101; vol. 2, p. 164; vol. 3, pp. 26 and 119–20.

12 Qushayrī, *Risāla*, pp. 84–5.

13 This is mentioned in Tustarī's commentary on 2:255.

14 Qushayrī, *Risāla*, p. 85; trans. Böwering, *Mystical Vision*, p. 55.

15 Sulamī, *Ṭabaqāt*, p. 199; Abū Nuʿaym al-Iṣfahānī, *Ḥilyat al-awliyāʾ* (Cairo, 1932–8), vol. 10, p. 190; Qushayrī, *Risāla*, p. 83.

16 Both Anṣārī, *Ṭabaqāt*, p. 113, and following him Nūr al-Dīn ʿAbd al-Raḥmān Jāmī, *Nafaḥāt al-uns min ḥaḍarāt al-quds* (Tehran, 1991), p. 66, refer to Tustarī as a disciple or pupil (*shāgird*) of Dhū'l-Nūn. While, as Böwering reports, Samʿānī and Ibn al-Athīr both describe Tustarī as having 'associated with' (*ṣaḥiba*) Dhū'l-Nūn. See Böwering, *Mystical Vision*, p. 50, who cites ʿAbd al-Karīm b. Muḥammad al-Samʿānī, *Kitāb al-Ansāb*, facsimile edition (Leiden, 1912), f. 106b and ʿIzz al-Dīn ʿAlī b. Muḥammad Ibn al-Athīr, *al-Lubāb fī tahdhīb al-ansāb* (Cairo, 1929–67), vol. 1, p. 176.

17 The report is to be found in a work compiled by Jalāl al-Dīn al-Suyūṭī on Dhū'l-Nūn's life and teaching, published by Arthur J. Arberry as 'A Biography of Dhul-Nūn Al-Miṣrī,' in M. Rām and M. D. Aḥmad, *ʿArshī Presentation Volume*

report in the *Kitāb al-Lumaʿ* of Abū Naṣr al-Sarrāj (d. 378/998) indicates that Tustarī certainly held for Dhū'l-Nūn a deference akin to that which a disciple would traditionally hold for his master, for when asked why in earlier years he had refrained from teaching, he answered: 'I did not like to engage in discourse concerning mystical knowledge as long as he [Dhū'l-Nūn] was alive, out of reverence and respect for him.'[18]

Later, both the philosopher/mystic Shihāb al-Dīn Yaḥyā Suhrawardī Maqtūl (d. 587/1191), and Ibn ʿArabī (d. 638/1240) were to assume in different ways a definite transmission of knowledge from Dhū'l-Nūn to Tustarī. Suhrawardī linked the two mystics not only to each other, but to the Hermetic tradition. He explained that of the two currents of ancient wisdom which together formed the basis of his 'Philosophy of Illumination' (*Ḥikmat al-ishrāq*), the current which he called the 'Pythagorean leaven', that is, the branch of Greek/Pythagorean wisdom that had been transmitted through Hermes, had come down to Dhū'l-Nūn and from him had passed to Tustarī and his 'party', whence it had been transmitted to the East.[19] According to Ibn ʿArabī, both Tustarī and Junayd had derived mystical teachings from Dhū'l-Nūn, as well as from other mystics.[20] A comprehensive study of the sayings and teachings of Dhū'l-Nūn al-Miṣrī, and a careful collation between these and the corpus of sayings collected from Tustarī is required before the extent and nature of influence of Dhū'l-Nūn on Tustarī's thought can be ascertained.

Suhrawardī was not alone in linking both Dhū'l-Nūn and Tustarī to the Hermetic tradition,[21] and there is at least some circumstantial evidence to support this. Dhū'l-Nūn was born and brought up in Ikhmīm, Upper Egypt, a major centre of Hermeticism in the Graeco-Egyptian world.[22] Ibn Nadīm names him as being among the philosophers who spoke about the art of alchemy, and two works on alchemy, now no longer extant, were said to have been written by him under the guidance of the famous alchemist, Jābir b. Ḥayyān (d. ca 200/815).[23] Yet the numerous sayings in the name of Dhū'l-Nūn that have been preserved in the works of Sufism are entirely concerned with the mystical path.[24] Dhū'l-Nūn was known as 'the leader (*imām*) among the Sufis',[25] and is said to have been the first mystic to have made a distinction between allusion (*ishāra*) and outward expression (*ʿibāra*), as well as devising the concept of mystical states and stations.[26] As for Tustarī, one anecdote certainly indicates that he had knowledge of alchemy,[27] and he included both alchemy and astronomy

(New Delhi, 1965), pp. 11–27.

18 Abū Naṣr ʿAbd Allāh b. ʿAlī (al-Ṭūsī) al-Sarrāj, *Kitāb al-Lumaʿ fī'l-taṣawwuf* (London and Leiden, 1914), p. 181.

19 The 'Khusrawan leaven', on the other hand, was transmitted into Islamic mysticism through Abū Yazīd Bisṭāmī (d. 261/874), Ḥusayn b. Manṣūr al-Ḥallāj (d. 309/922) and Abū al-Ḥasan Kharaqānī (d. 425/1029). See Shihāb al-Dīn Yaḥyā al-Suhrawardī, *Kitāb al-Maṣārī wa'l-mutāraḥāt*, in Henri Corbin, *Opera Metaphysica et Mystica* (Istanbul, 1945), vol. 1 p. 502f. For other references see Böwering, *Mystical Vision*, p. 52.

20 Ibn ʿArabī, *Futūḥāt*, vol. 1, p. 188.

21 For example, the philosopher and historian Abū al-Ḥasan al-Qifṭī (d. 646/1248), in his *Taʾrīkh al-ḥukamāʾ*, states that Dhū'l-Nūn was well-versed in alchemy and the secret hermetic sciences, and mentions both Sahl al-Tustarī and al-Ḥārith al-Muḥāsibī as being exponents not only of the esoteric knowledge associated with Sufis, but also of the legacy of the second/eighth-century alchemist and philosopher Jābir b. Ḥayyān (d. ca 200/815). See al-Qifṭī, *Taʾrīkh al-ḥukamāʾ* (Leipzig, 1903), pp. 160 and 185. For other examples see Böwering, *Mystical Vision*, pp. 53–4.

22 See Garth Fowden, *The Egyptian Hermes: A Historical Approach to the Pagan Mind* (Cambridge, 1996), and especially pp. 120–6 on Zosimus of Ikhmīm; and Peter Kingsley, *Ancient Philosophy, Mysticism and Magic* (Oxford, 1995), p. 389.

23 Ibn al-Nadīm, *Fihrist* (Leipzig, 1871–2), pp. 358 and 355; cf. Louis Massignon, *Essai sur les origines du lexique technique de la mystique musulmane* (Paris, 1922), p. 207.

24 See, for example, sayings of Dhū'l-Nūn cited in Annemarie Schimmel's *Mystical Dimensions of Islam* (Chapel Hill, NC, 1975), pp. 42ff.; and Margaret Smith, *Studies in Early Mysticism in the Near and Middle East* (London and New York, 1931), pp. 191ff. and 230ff.

25 Jāmī, *Nafaḥāt al-uns*, p. 28, citing Khwāja ʿAbd Allāh Anṣārī.

26 Ibid, pp. 27–8. It is also worth mentioning that Dhū'l-Nūn is said to have studied with Imam Malik. Moreover, under the rule of the Caliph al-Maʾmūn he was persecuted for his belief in the uncreated Qurʾān. Again, see *Nafaḥāt al-uns*, p. 27.

27 Sarrāj, *Kitāb al-Lumaʿ*, pp. 319 and 326ff.; Qushayrī, *Risāla*, p. 677. On the death of a person named Isḥāq b. Aḥmad (evidently an alchemist who had repented and then become Tustarī's disciple), Tustarī entered his cell and found some alchemical materials there, a lump of gold, a lump of silver and two bottles containing red and yellow liquids. Tustarī

or astrology in his categorisation of four branches of knowledge, comprising: *al-ṭibb* (medicine), *al-nijāma* (astronomy/astrology), *al-diyāna* (religion) and *al-kīmiyāʾ* (chemistry/alchemy).[28] Among the works attributed to Tustarī is an astrological chart, known as a *Zāʾirja* which, if it ever existed, has not survived.[29] An extant treatise on the significance of the letters of the alphabet is attributed to him, known as *Risālat al-ḥurūf*, and Tustarī is reported to have commiserated with another mystic, Abū ʿAbd Allāh al-Ḥusayn b. Makkī al-Ṣubayḥī, who was being persecuted for his knowledge of 'the divine names and attributes and of the science of the letters' (*ʿilm al-asmāʾ waʾl-ṣifāt wa ʿilm al-ḥurūf*).[30] However, the anecdote which shows Tustarī's knowledge of alchemy also implies that he did not see fit to practice it himself.[31] His treatise on letters is not concerned with the sciences of *jafr* or *abjad*,[32] but is concerned with the cosmological symbolism of the letters.[33] Again, it can be said that the examination of Tustarī's *tafsīr* and other works attributed to him, as well as the corpus of his sayings that have been preserved in the works of later Sufis, shows the essentially mystical nature of his thought.[34]

It is worth bearing in mind that during the second and third centuries of the Hijra, there was considerable interest in the different traditions of science and wisdom that had been preserved and were now being translated from Greek, Syriac and other languages into Arabic, especially in the Fertile Crescent.[35] Dhūʾl-Nūn had grown up in a centre of Graeco-Alexandrian learning, and Tustarī not far from Jundishapur, which had been a great centre for the translation of medical and other scientific texts. Thus it is no surprise that these two mystics should have been acquainted with, and possibly have drawn upon, the rich and diverse sources of knowledge that were accessible to them. It appears that at this time there may have been a particular intellectual fluidity, with boundaries of knowledge being less sharply drawn between Sufism other streams of thought. What is remarkable is not the fact that these early mystics should have been in contact with, or have drawn upon, such sources of knowledge, but rather the way in which aspects of this knowledge, and terms in which

threw the gold and silver into the River Tigris, and poured the bottles of liquid onto the ground, at the same time explaining to the disciple who was with him, Muḥammad b. Sālim, how the elixir of those liquids could transmute copper and lead into gold and silver.

28 *Kalām Sahl*, MS Köprülü, 727, f. 64a.

29 See Böwering, *Mystical Vision*, p. 54, citing Ibn Khaldūn's *Kitāb al-ʿIbar* (Beirut, 1961), vol. 1, p. 206f, and a much later work of Ismāʿīl Pāšā al-Bāghdādī (d. 1338/1920), *Hadiyat al-ʿārifīn* (Istanbul, 1951–5), vol. 1, p. 412.

30 This is recorded in Sarrāj's *Kitāb al-Lumaʿ*. See Arthur J. Arberry's publication of lacunae from the *Lumaʿ*, entitled *Pages from the Kitāb al-Lumaʿ* (London, 1947), p. 9.

31 As can be seen from the story related in n. 28 above. This is not to say that mystics in general, and Muslim mystics in particular, were necessarily opposed to alchemy, which was rich in symbolism and could even be practised as a spiritual discipline. On the spiritual dimensions of alchemy, see Fowden, *Egyptian Hermes*. On Sufism and alchemy, see Pierre Lory, *Alchimie et mystique en terre d'Islam* (Lagrasse, 1989). Tustarī's objection may have been to its practice purely in material terms. Interestingly, we find him using the language of alchemy in the *Tafsīr*.

32 On the science of divination according to the numerical values of the letters in the Qurʾān, see T. Fahd, 'Djafr,' *EI²*, vol. II, p. 375 (although Fahd does not make a clear distinction between *jafr* and the cosmological and metaphysical speculations on the letters made by mystics); Azartash Azarnoosh, 'Abjad', trans. R. Gholami, *Encyclopaedia Islamica*, vol. 1, p. 339.

33 See Gaafar's doctoral dissertation, which includes an edition, translation and commentary on Tustarī's *Risālat al-ḥurūf*. The treatise was subsequently published along with other works ascribed to Tustarī in idem (Muḥammad Kamāl Ibrāhīm Jaʿfar), *Min al-turāth al-Tustarī al-ṣūfī: dirāsa wa taḥqīq* (Cairo, 1974–), vol. 1. See also Pilar Garrido Clemente's article, 'El *Tradado de las Letras (Risālat al-ḥurūf)* del Sufí Sahl al-Tustarī', *Anuario de Estudios Filológicos* 29 (2006), pp. 87–100, which comprises a discussion and Spanish translation of the treatise; and idem, 'Estudio, Traducción y edición de las obras de Ibn Masarra de Córdoba: la Ciencia de las Letras en el Sufismo', PhD thesis (University of Salamanca, 2007).

34 That is to say, discussions of a theological and ethical nature are mainly centred on Tustarī's vision of the spiritual purpose of man's existence, as has been discussed by both Böwering and Gaafar in their comprehensive studies of the teachings of Tustarī.

35 On this subject see Richard Walzer, *Greek into Arabic* (Oxford, 1962); Franz Rosenthal, *The Classical Heritage in Islam*, translated from the German by Emile and Jenny Marmorstein (London, 1992); Dimitri Gutas, *Greek Wisdom Literature in Arabic Translation* (New Haven, CT, 1975); idem, *Greek Thought, Arabic Culture (2nd–4th/8th–10th centuries)* (London, 1998); and idem, *Greek Philosophers in the Arabic Tradition* (Aldershot, 2000).

they were expressed were assimilated, and integrated by them, so as to become part of the language they used to expound their doctrines.[36]

II. Tustarī as Spiritual Master, and his Disciples

According to Tustarī's own statement quoted above, he began teaching after the death of Dhū'l-Nūn, in the year 245/860. At this time he must have begun teaching publicly, that is, to a larger group of followers, though it is possible that he had already been imparting instruction to those of his disciples who were closest to him, such as Muḥammad b. Sālim (d. 297/909), who claimed to have been with him for his whole life.[37] Sometime between the years 262/876 and 263/877, Tustarī was forced to leave Tustar and flee to Basra along with his disciples.[38] Traditional sources are agreed that a local scholar, or at least someone claiming or purported to be a devout man of learning, roused the people against him. Both Sarrāj and Farīd al-Dīn ʿAṭṭār (d. before 617/1220) state that it was Tustarī's particular emphasis on the need for repentance (*tawba*) that was the focus of the scholar's disapproval,[39] while according to a report quoted from Sulamī, the antagonist made the accusation that Tustarī was claiming to be visited by angels, spirits and devils with whom he had conversed.[40] Tustarī was, according to the different accounts, accused either of committing evil acts or of heresy, and driven out of the city.[41]

Once he had settled in Basra, Tustarī's life was not entirely free of controversy, for on one occasion, he was challenged by two Shāfiʿī jurists, Abū Zakariyya al-Sājī and Abū ʿAbd Allāh al-Zubayrī, who took objection to his statement: 'I am the proof of God (*ḥujjat Allāh*) for you in particular and for the people in general', and went to question him as to whether he considered himself to be a prophet or a righteous saint. Tustarī's response to their objections eventually led them to acknowledge his spiritual superiority.[42] Tustarī made his home in Basra until his death in 283/896. He was apparently happily married and had at least one child.[43]

Tustarī had numerous disciples, some of whom remained with him for many years, while others stayed only a short time. Among his long-standing disciples, the most important were: Muḥammad b. Sālim and the latter's son Aḥmad b. Sālim (d. 356/967), both of whom transmitted and expounded numerous sayings and teachings of Tustarī; Abū Bakr al-Sijzī who received permission to transmit

36 One obvious example in the case of Tustarī's *Tafsīr* is his reference to red sulphur (*kibrīt aḥmar*) (*Tafsīr*, 19:61). Many other examples could be found, such as his definition of different dispositions or natures (*ṭabāʾiʿ*) within the human being (*Tafsīr*, 12:53). On the diverse sources of terms assimilated into the mystical language of Manṣūr b. al-Ḥallāj, see Massignon, *The Passion of al-Ḥallāj*, trans. Herbert Mason (Princeton, 1982), vol. 3, pp. 6ff.

37 According to Sarrāj, *Kitāb al-Lumaʿ*, p. 177, or 'many years,' according to Qushayrī, *Risāla*, p. 654; while he was his disciple for between thirty and sixty years according Anṣārī, *Ṭabaqāt al-ṣūfiyya*, p 258.

38 For a discussion of the likely dates of Tustarī's move to Basra see Böwering, *Mystical Vision*, pp. 58ff.

39 Sarrāj, *Kitāb al-Lumaʿ*, p. 407. This is also mentioned among the lacunae from Sarrāj's *Lumaʿ* in Arberry, *Pages*, p. 9, and in ʿAṭṭār, *Tadhkirat al-awliyāʾ*, p. 306. The objection was to the fact that Tustarī expressed the view that repentance (*tawba*) was a religious obligation (*farīḍa*), and that just as the sinner must repent of his sin, so also the obedient person (*muṭīʿ*) must repent of his acts of obedience.

40 Ibn al-Jawzī, *Talbīs Iblīs* (Cairo, 1950), p. 162. Perhaps this was a misrepresentation of Tustarī's account of his encounter with a jinn, which is discussed below.

41 Gaafar (dissertation, pp. 21–7) suggests other factors which may have aroused the opposition of the *ʿulamāʾ* in Tustar, such as the wide publicity concerning Tustarī's 'miracles' or charismata, some of his 'wild and ambiguous utterances (*shaṭaḥāt*) and his continuous criticism of various classes of religious scholars, Qurʾān reciters and ascetics. Böwering, however, conjectures that there may have been political reasons for his departure, for which see Böwering, *Mystical Vision*, pp. 59–63.

42 Böwering, *Mystical Vision*, p. 64, citing ʿAbd al-Wahhāb al-Shaʿrānī, *Ṭabaqāt al-kubrā* (Cairo, 1315/1897), vol. 1, p. 67; and Ibn al-Jawzī, *Talbīs Iblīs*, p. 204. Abū ʿAbd Allāh al-Zubayrī is also mentioned by Sarrāj as having persecuted al-Ṣubayḥī (see above p. xviii and n. 30), the mystic with whom Tustarī commiserated, and to whom he pointed out that people were not able to tolerate the knowledge they were speaking about. See Arberry, *Pages*, p. 9.

43 Gaafar (dissertation, p. 136) notes, without citing any sources, that from Tustarī's description of the way that she brought up their son, it appears that his wife was also something of an ascetic.

Tustarī's *Tafsīr* in the year 275/888; and ʿUmar b. Wāṣil al-ʿAnbarī, who narrated anecdotes about Tustarī and elucidated some of his Qurʾān interpretations. Others who are named by the sources as direct disciples of Tustarī include Ḥusayn b. Manṣūr al-Ḥallāj, who became his disciple at the age of sixteen and stayed with him only two years, perhaps moving to Basra with Tustarī, but then going on to join Junayd's circle in Bagdhad; Ḥasan b. Khalaf al-Barbahārī (d. 329/941), a well-known Ḥanbalī theologian and jurist of Baghdad; Abū Muḥammad b. Ḥusayn al-Jurayrī (d. 312/924), who went on to become one of of Junayd's foremost disciples, supervising his circle after his death; and Abū al-Ḥasan b. Muḥammad al-Muzayyin al-Tirmidhī (d. 328/939), who was also a disciple of Junayd.[44]

Tustarī's disciples not only transmitted his teachings and aphorisms, they also related their own observations about their master's spiritual states, as well as sayings in which Tustarī himself described his mystical experiences. Many of these are included in the text of the *Tafsīr*. Among them are reports of some miraculous events which Tustarī either described to them, or they themselves witnessed. Abū Bakr al-Sijzī assumes Tustarī's account of meeting a man who eats a pomegranate from Paradise, and his vivid description of how it tasted, to be an indication that Tustarī himself had tasted the fruit.[45] ʿUmar b. Wāṣil relates how one night Tustarī held his finger in the flame of a lamp for nearly two hours without feeling any pain.[46] Yet another anecdote tells of two men who came to visit Tustarī after the afternoon prayer, and then mysteriously vanished. When Muḥammad b. Sālim enquired where they had gone, he replied that one of them prayed the sunset prayer in the East, and the other in the West.[47] Tustarī himself describes his encounter and conversation with a jinn who was of such a great age that he had met both Jesus and Muḥammad.[48] He was also famed for his intimacy with wild beasts and birds. In the *Tafsīr* it is related that he kept a room in his house which he called the 'room for predatory beasts'. The beasts would approach him, and he would admit them into that room, offer them hospitality, feed them some meat, and then let them go free.[49] He warned one of his young disciples that if he was afraid of predatory beasts he should not keep company with him.[50] Many other anecdotes recount different miraculous occurrences involving Tustarī.[51]

However, Tustarī did not pay any particular regard to these 'miracles' or rather, charismata.[52] For example, when people remarked at having seen him walking upon water, he recounted to them an incident in which the muezzin of the mosque had rescued him from drowning once when he fell into a pool.[53] When asked how a person might reach the rank of such charismatic gifts, he replied, 'Whoever abstains from the world for forty days in true faith and sincerity, will have charismatic gifts (*karāmāt*) manifested to him from God, Mighty and Majestic is He. So, if [such gifts] are not manifested to a person, it is due to the lack of true faith and sincerity in his renunciation.'[54] Several anecdotes about Tustarī illustrate his humility. For example, one day someone remarked to him, 'O

44 Other disciples and associates of Tustarī are discussed in detail by Böwering, *Mystical Vision*, pp. 78–99.

45 *Tafsīr*, 2:25.

46 *Tafsir*, 21:69.

47 *Tafsir*, 114:4

48 *Tafsīr*, 72:1.

49 *Tafsīr*, 10:62; see also Sarrāj, *Kitāb al-Lumaʿ*, p. 316, where Sahl's house was called 'the house of predatory beasts' (*bayt al-sabuʿ*).

50 *Tafsīr*, 45:13. A similar anecdote (Qushayrī, *Risāla*, p. 447, ʿAṭṭār, *Tadhkira*, p. 309) relates that a young visitor found a viper in the house and became afraid, whereupon Tustarī warned him that no one reaches the reality of faith (*ḥaqīqat al-īmān*) as long as he fears anything on the face of the earth.

51 Other anecdotes about charismatic episodes connected with Tustarī are cited in Böwering, *Mystical Vision*, pp. 68–71.

52 The term 'charismatic gifts' or *charismata* (translating *karāmāt*, sing. *karāma*) is used here to distinguish it from other kinds of miracles defined in Arabic by the word (*muʿjizāt*, sing. *muʿjiza*). The former are associated with 'saints' or friends of God, while the latter are the preserve of prophets. On this subject see Josef W. Meri, *The Cult of Saints among Muslims and Jews in Medieval Syria* (Oxford, 2002), pp. 73–6 and *Kitāb Kasr al-shahwatayn*, trans. Timothy J. Winter, *Al-Ghazālī on Disciplining the Soul and on Breaking the Two Desires* (Cambridge, 1995), p. 97, n. A.

53 Qushayrī, *Risāla*, p. 703; ʿAṭṭār, *Tadhkira*, pp. 308–9.

54 *Tafsir*, 45:13; ʿAṭṭār, *Tadhkīra*, p. 314.

Abū Muḥammad! Look what [God] has done with you and how He has elevated you!' But he was totally unaffected by these words and said, 'It is He who is sought, He who is sought![55] Regarding his mystical knowledge, he is quoted as having said:

> Indeed, God willing, I have been granted wisdom and [knowledge of] the unseen which I was taught from His unseen secret (*min ghayb sirrihi*), and thus He sufficed me from the need for all other knowledge…and He completed what He had begun with me out of His grace and beneficence.[56]

This statement is an indication of Tustarī's constant awareness of his dependence on God, and of his perpetual consciousness of God's presence, precisely the teaching that had been instilled in him by his uncle. Thus it is related that he said, 'My state during the ritual prayer and before entering ritual prayer is the very same'.[57]

Mention has been made of Tustarī's apparently extreme imposition of hunger and fasting on himself. But the sources indicate that this practice was for him not a matter of self-mortification; it was rather that, as Böwering has observed, he was wholly sustained by God.[58] Thus it is reported that when questioned on the subject of provision, Tustarī stated that the believer's daily bread (*qūt*) is God, his sustenance (*qiwām*) is the remembrance of God, and his nourishment (*ghidhāʾ*) is religious knowledge (*ʿilm*).[59] He certainly extolled the spiritual benefits of certain ascetic practices, as when he said, 'God created the world and placed knowledge and wisdom in hunger, and ignorance in satiety'.[60] He also recommended that his disciples lead a life of simplicity, as when he advised them:

> Let your food be barley, your sweetmeat dates, your condiment salt and your fat yoghurt. You should let your clothes be of wool, your houses be mosques, your source of light the sun, your lamp the moon, your perfume water, your splendour be in cleanliness, and your adornment wariness (*ḥadhr*) [of God]…[61]

However, it is clear that he neither expected nor demanded that his disciples should attain the same level of abstinence as him. One of his disciples reports:

> Sahl used to intensify his ecstasy (*wajd*) for seventy days, during which he would not eat anything, while he would order his companions to eat meat once a week so that they would not become too weak for worship. However for him, when he ate he would become weak, and when he became hungry he would gain in strength. He would sweat during the severe cold of winter while wearing only one shirt.[62]

Tustarī explained the principle as follows:

> One should always adopt hardship for oneself, but when giving counsel to others, one should choose what is bearable and easy. To do this is to follow in the footsteps of the Prophet, who, when confronted with a particular matter concerning the community, used to choose what was light and gentle, but when the matter concerned himself, would apply that which is hardest and most severe.[63]

Moreover, Tustarī had some knowledge of medicine, yet it is reported that for thirty years he suffered from an illness which he used to treat in others, whilst not applying the treatment to himself.[64]

---

55 *Tafsīr*, 19:61.

56 *Tafsīr*, 2:3.

57 Sarrāj, *Kitāb al-Lumaʿ*, p. 293 .

58 Böwering, *Mystical Vision*, p. 56.

59 Ibid, citing Abū Ṭālib al-Makkī, *Qūt al-qulūb fī muʿāmalat al-maḥbūb*, 2 vols. (Beirut, 1997), vol. 2, p. 282.

60 *Tafsīr*, 7:31.

61 *Tafsīr*, 7:172.

62 *Tafsīr*, 15:3.

63 *Kalām Sahl b. ʿAbd Allāh*, MS Köprölü 727, 51a; ed. Gaafar (Jaʿfar), *Min al-turāth al-Tustarī*, vol. 2, p. 156. This was also the principle which Tustarī followed with regard to the practice of total trust in God (*tawakkul*) and earning (*kasb*), for which see, for example, his commentary on 25:58 in the *Tafsīr*.

64 *Muʿāraḍa*, MS Köprölü 727, f. 236b, 206; Sarrāj, *Kitāb al-Lumaʿ*, pp. 203–4. See also Qushayrī, *Risāla*, pp. 682, 704.

Towards the end of his life he became weakened both by this illness and by the effects of age, to the point that he could not get up from where he was sitting. Even so, Sarrāj reports that when it came time for prayer, he would stand upright like a pole in the prayer niche.[65] Concerning his qualities, Abū Bakr al-Sijzī relates:

> It was his way and his conduct to be full of gratitude and remember [God] a great deal. He was also constant in observing silence and reflection. He would dispute little and was of a generous spirit. He led people through his good character, mercy and compassion for them, and by giving good counsel to them...Truly God filled his heart with light, and made his tongue speak with wisdom...If it wasn't for the fact that nobody can be valued alongside the Companions because of their companionship and witnessing [of the Prophet ﷺ], then one would say that he was as one of them. He lived a praiseworthy life and died as a stranger in Basra, may God have mercy upon him.[66]

After his death, Tustarī's close circle of disciples divided broadly into two groups. Abū Muḥammad al-Jurayrī and Abū al-Ḥasan al-Muzayyin went to Baghdad and entered the circle of Junayd's disciples. Ḥasan al-Barbahārī and ʿUmar b. Wāṣil also went to Baghdad, and are known to have preached in the Ḥanbalī quarter of the city. The sources indicate that all these disciples eventually moved to, or spent a period in Mecca, where they would have disseminated Tustarī's teachings among the community of renunciants (*zuhhād*) and 'metics' (*mujāwirūn*) who chose to live close to the Sanctuary.[67] Muḥammad b. Sālim and his son Aḥmad b. Sālim, on the other hand, remained in Basra, where they assembled a group of associates (*aṣḥāb*) around them, who came to be known as the Sālimiyya. Some teachings of this so-called 'group of Sufi theologians',[68] were later denounced by the Shīrāzī Sufi Ibn Khafīf (d. 371/981),[69] the Ḥanbalī theologian, Abū Yaʿlā b. al-Farrāʾ (d. 458/1065),[70] and following the latter, the Ḥanbalī Sufi ʿAbd al-Qādir al-Jīlānī (d. 561/1167).[71] Some of these points may well amount to misreadings of sayings attributed Tustarī and his followers, such as the words:

> God has a secret; if He were to make it manifest, the divine providence would be rendered null. The prophets have a secret; if they were to make it manifest, prophethood would be rendered null. The learned have a secret; if they were to make it manifest, knowledge would be rendered null.[72]

---

65 Sarrāj, *Kitāb al-Lumaʿ*, p. 155; ʿAṭṭār, *Tadhkira*, p. 309.

66 *Tafsīr*, 10:62.

67 See Böwering, *Mystical Vision*, pp. 88ff. for sources.

68 According to the geographer al-Maqdisī (d. 380/990), the Sālimiyya were 'a group of popular preachers and ascetic Sufi theologians' at Basra. See ʿAbd Allāh Muḥammad b. Aḥmad al-Maqdisī (al-Muqaddasī), *Aḥsan al-taqāsīm fī maʿrifat al-aqālīm* (Leiden, 1877), pp. 126 and 130. They were also designated as 'a band of *kalām* scholars' by ʿAbd al-Qāhir al-Baghdādī in his *al-Farq bayn al-firaq* (Beirut, 1973), p. 247 (cited by Tobias Mayer, 'Theology and Sufism', in Timothy J. Winter, ed., *The Cambridge Companion to Classical Islamic Theology* [Cambridge, 2008], p. 262).

69 These were apparently compiled in a treatise that is no longer extant, *al-Radd ʿalā Ibn Sālim*, for which see Böwering, *Mystical Vision*, p. 93, citing Fuad Sezgin, *Geschichte des Arabischen Schrifttums* (Leiden, 1967), vol. 1, p. 663; Massignon, *Essai*, p. 319 and Abū al-Ḥasan ʿAlī al-Daylamī, *Sīrat-i Ibn-i Khafīf*, translated into Persian by Rukn al-Dīn Yaḥyā b. al-Junayd al-Shīrāzī, ed. Annemarie Schimmel (Tehran, 1984); see editor's introduction, p. 32.

70 In his *al-Muʿtamad fī uṣūl al-dīn* (Beirut, 1974), pp. 217–21. Böwering, *Mystical Vision*, pp. 94–5, has translated the eighteen objectionable points listed by Ibn al-Farrāʾ.

71 ʿAbd al-Qādir al-Jīlānī, *al-Ghunya li-ṭālibī ṭarīq al-ḥaqq* (Cairo, 1322/1904), vol. 1, pp 106ff. According to Böwering, *Mystical Vision*, p. 93, Jīlānī copied the list of Ibn al-Farrāʾ, omitting five of the points.

72 This, the fifth proposition in Ibn al-Farrāʾ's list, may be traced to a saying cited in Makkī's *Qūt al-qulūb*, vol. 2, p. 149; and ʿAbd al-Wahhāb al-Shaʿrānī, *Ṭabaqāt al-kubrā* (Cairo, 2005), vol. 1, p. 111. The saying as it appears in Makkī's *Qūt al-qulūb* is attributed anonymously to 'one of them', and might be translated as follows: 'The divine lordliness (*rubūbiyya*) has a secret which, if revealed, would render prophesy (*nubuwwa*) null; prophesy has a secret which, were it to be uncovered, would render knowledge (*ʿilm*) null; and the knowers of God (*ʿulamāʾ bi'Llāh*) have a secret which, were God to reveal it, would render the laws (*aḥkām*) null. The sustenance of faith and continual existence of the Law [is ensured] through the withholding of the secret. Through it [God's] management [of things] (*tadbīr*) is implemented and on its basis the command[s] and prohibition[s] are ordered.' I am grateful to Harith Bin Ramli both for locating this citation and for the translation of this extract, which is largely his. The statement is slightly reminiscent of part of Tustarī's comment on 12:108: 'For sure, the inner truth [or secret, *sirr*] has not been revealed to people, for if it were disclosed to them then they would have perceived it. Nor have they witnessed [it], for if they had witnessed it, the whole matter would be over,

Or:

> The [divine] volition (*irāda*) is a branch of the divine will (*mashīʾa*), and the divine will is the root of the divine volition. The divine will is eternal and the volition is originated.[73]

Other points may amount to distortions of sayings of Tustarī or his followers, or an exoteric, literalist reading of some esoteric sayings. The latter is likely, for example, in the case of the eighteenth proposition: 'God is present in every place, and there is no difference between the divine Throne and other places.'[74]

It was through the Sālimiyya that Tustarī's teachings reached Abū Ṭālib al-Makkī (d. 386/996). Makkī grew up in Mecca, where he is said to have studied with the Sufi Abū Saʿīd al-Aʿrabī (d. 341/952), who was of Basran origin and had been for a time in the circle of Junayd in Baghdad. Later Makkī went to Baghdad, where he studied for a while under Abū Naṣr al-Sarrāj, and then to Basra, where he spent time with the Sālimiyya, although it is not known whether or not he ever met Aḥmad b. Sālim in person. Eventually he returned to Baghdad, where he ended his days. Makkī's best known work, the *Qūt al-qulūb* ('Nourishment of Hearts'), was to become one of the most important sources for the transmission and propagation of Tustarī's sayings.[75] Böwering notes that Tustarī is quoted some two hundred times in the work, while there are also sayings of Aḥmad b. Sālim. He refers to the former as 'the master of our master' (*shaykh shaykhinā*), which would indicate that he regarded Aḥmad b. Sālim as his master.[76] The *Qūt al-qulūb* was later copiously used as a source by Abū Ḥāmid al-Ghazālī in the composition of his *Iḥyāʾ ʿulūm al-dīn*,[77] which has been described as 'an enlargement and popularisation of the *Qūt al-qulūb*',[78] and as 'a brilliant reworking of this often dense and at times abstruse compendium on piety'.[79] It has recently been argued that another work attributed to Makkī, bearing the title *ʿIlm al-qulūb* ('Knowledge or Science of Hearts') is in fact a composition of unknown authorship dating from the fifth/eleventh century.[80]

III. Tustarī's Works

Pre-modern bibliographical sources list some fourteen titles of different works ascribed to Tustarī.[81] However, only two of those listed works find equivalents of real significance among Tustarī's extant works, namely his commentary on the Qurʾān and a work on the stories of the prophets (*Qiṣaṣ al-anbiyāʾ*), though even then there is no precise correspondence between titles.[82] On the other hand,

---

and that is a grave matter.'

73 The thirteenth proposition in Ibn al-Farrāʾ's list, which may be compared to sayings of Tustarī cited in *Kalām Sahl b. ʿAbd Allāh*, ed. Gaafar, in idem (Jaʿfar), *Min al-turāth al-Tustarī*, Part 2, pp. 202 and 303; MS Köprülü 727, f. 72b and 142a. Gaafar has summarised this teaching as it appears in f. 72b, as follows: 'God's Will (or "Uncreated Will", *mashīʾa*), is associated with His Knowledge, while God's Volition (or "Creative Will", *irāda*) is associated with His Omnipotence. The *mashīʾa* is the gate of Knowledge (*bāb al-ʿilm*); the *irāda* is the gate of Omnipotence (*bāb al-qudra*).'

74 Compare the statement in Makkī's *Qūt al-qulūb* (vol. 2, p. 141), '…His proximity to the earth and to everything is as His proximity to the Throne…'

75 Makkī, *Qūt al-qulūb*. Translated into German with introduction and commentary by Richard Grämlich as *Die Nahrung der Herzen* (Stuttgart, 1992–5).

76 Böwering, *Mystical Vision*, pp. 25–7.

77 Abū Ḥāmid Muḥammad al-Ghazālī, *Iḥyāʾ ʿulūm al-dīn* (Damascus, 1417/1997).

78 Ali Hasan Abdel-Kader, *The Life, Personality and Works of al-Junayd* (London, 1947), p. xiv.

79 Ahmet T. Karamustafa, *Sufism: The Formative Period* (Edinburgh, 2007), p. 88. The influence of Makkī's work on Ghazālī's *Iḥyāʾ* is also discussed by Hava Lazarus-Yafeh, *Studies in al-Ghazzālī* (Jerusalem, 1975), pp. 34–5, and by Kojiro Nakamura, 'Makkī and Ghazālī on Mystical Practices', *Orient* 20 (1984), pp. 83–91.

80 See Nasrollah Pourjavady, 'Bāzmānda-yi kitāb-i *al-Ishārah wa'l-ʿibārah-i* Abū Saʿd Khargūshī dar kitāb-i *ʿIlm al-qulūb*', *Maʿārif* 15, no. 3 (1999) 34–41; now republished in idem, *Pazhūhishhā-yi ʿirfānī: just-u-jū dar manābiʿ-i kuhan* (Tehran, 2006), pp. 64–72.

81 For a full list of these see Böwering, *Mystical Vision*, pp. 8–12.

82 The only pre-modern bibliographical source to allude to the *Tafsīr* is the *Ṭabaqāt al-mufassirīn* of Shams al-Dīn Muḥammad al-Dāwūdī (d. 945/1538), who does not mention any title, but names Tustarī as the author of a Qurʾān

we find among extant works ascribed to Tustarī, titles of several works not listed among the early bibliographical sources. Important among these are three collections of Tustarī's sayings that are preserved in a manuscript in the Köprülü Library in Istanbul, MS, no. 727 (dated seventh century AH). They are entitled: *Kitāb al-Sharḥ wa'l-bayān li-mā ashkala min kalām Sahl* ('Explanation and Elucidation of Difficult Points in Sahl's Doctrine'); *Kitāb al-Muʿāraḍa wa'l-radd ʿalā ahl al-firāq wa ahl al-daʿāwā fī'l-aḥwāl* ('Remonstrance and Refutation of the People of Factions and of the People of Pretensions Concerning Mystical States'); *Kalimāt al-imām al-rabbānī Sahl b. ʿAbd Allāh al-Tustarī* ('Sayings of our Lordly Guide, Sahl b. ʿAbd Allāh al-Tustarī').[83] Another extant work attributed to Tustarī but not listed in the bibliographical works is the *Risālat al-ḥurūf* ('Treatise on the Letters'), which appears to have been preserved in one manuscript only, held in the Chester Beatty collection, CH. Beatty 3163/3. The treatise is a short work, most of which comprises a metaphysical and cosmological exposition of the relation between God, His names, His attributes and His creation, and the significance of the letters.[84]

Among those extant works ascribed to Tustarī that are also mentioned in bibliographical sources is the *Tafsīr al-Qurʾān al-ʿaẓīm*, which is preserved in six extant manuscripts and will be discussed in a separate section below. A work of not entirely unquestionable authenticity is the *Laṭāʾif al-qiṣaṣ* ('Subtleties of the Stories [of the Prophets]'), which comprises 17 chapters, 11 of which relate subtle reflections on a particular prophet, beginning with Adam and ending with Muḥammad, while the remaining three chapters consist of Sufi anecdotes and sections on ritual prayer and the *Basmala*.[85] Another title listed among Tustarī's works, the authenticity of which is less likely, is the *Risālat al-manhiyāt* ('Treatise on Illicit Acts'),[86] while the *Risāla fī'l-ḥikam wa'l-taṣawwuf* ('Treatise on Wisdom and Sufism'),[87] represents a collection of Tustarī's sayings gleaned from Qushayrī's *Risāla fī'l-taṣawwuf*.

Aside from these works in Tustarī's name, many of his sayings have been preserved in the works of Sufism, among the most important being the *Kitāb al-Lumaʿ* of Abū Naṣr al-Sarrāj and the *Qūt al-qulūb* of Abū Ṭālib al-Makkī (mentioned above). Both of these writers had direct contact with the second generation of Tustarī's followers. Other early sources for Tustarī's sayings include the so-called manuals of Sufism, such as those of Kalābādhī,[88] Hujwīrī[89] and Qushayrī; biographical or hagiographical works such as the *Ṭabaqāt al-ṣūfiyya* of Sulamī (d. 412/1021), and the *Ḥilyat*

commentary. The extant work on stories of the prophets bears the title *Laṭāʾif qiṣaṣ al-anbiyāʾ* and is preserved in MS Ṭalʿat, mag. 283, whereas Ḥājjī Khalīfa in his *Kashf al-ẓunūn* (Leipzig, 1835), vol. 4, pp. 303 and 518, and Ismāʿīl Pāshā in his *Hadiyat al-ʿārifīn*, vol. 1, p. 412, list a work entitled simply *Qiṣaṣ al-anbiyāʾ*.

83 The first and third of these collections of sayings are also preserved in the Asad Library, MSS, 1623 and 3527 respectively. The content of these works is discussed by Böwering, *Mystical Vision*, pp. 12–6, and by Gaafar, dissertation, pp. 41ff. As was noted above, Gaafar has also edited and published these works in Gaafar (Jaʿfar), *Min al-turāth al-Tustarī*.

84 Regarding the authenticity of this work, Böwering (*Mystical Vision*, pp. 17–8) expresses the view that 'the internal criteria do not go further than to prove a similarity of ideas'. Gaafar, however, argues for its authenticity in his dissertation, pp. 77–9, as does Pilar Garrido Clemente in her article, 'El *Tradado de las Letras*'. A critical edition of this work is included in her PhD thesis cited above, n. 34. On the question of authenticity, we might also refer again to the report in Sarrāj's *Kitāb al-Lumaʿ* mentioned above (Arberry, *Pages*, p. 9), where Tustarī's comments indicate that he was in sympathy with Ṣubayḥī who was known for his 'knowledge of God's names, attributes and the science of the letters', precisely the subject matter of the *Risālat al-ḥurūf*.

85 Böwering's view is that external evidence would confirm Tustarī's authorship of the work, since Ḥājjī Khalīfa not only lists a *Qiṣaṣ al-anbiyā* as among Tustarī's compositions, but also quotes the first sentence of the work, which exactly matches that of the manuscript. However, Böwering suggests that the internal evidence is not so strong, since, while some subject matter resembles that of the *Tafsīr*, there are no particular sayings or passages corresponding to any material in other works ascribed to Tustarī, or to his sayings in other Sufi sources. See *Mystical Vision*, pp. 16–17.

86 The treatise is held in Tehran, Tehran Faculty of Law, 251j.

87 This treatise is held in Istanbul, Ayasofia 4128/4.

88 Abū Bakr Muḥammad b. Isḥāq al-Kalābādhī, *Kitāb al-Taʿarruf li-madhhab ahl al-taṣawwuf* (Cairo, 1934); English trans., Arthur J. Arberry as *Doctrine of the Sufis* (Cambridge, 1935).

89 ʿAlī ʿUthmān Jullābī al-Hujwīrī, *Kashf al-maḥjūb* (Tehran, 2004); references in the text are to the Tehran, 2004 edition; English trans., Reynold A. Nicholson as *Kashf al-maḥjūb: The Oldest Persian Treatise on Sufism* (London, 1911).

al-awliyāʾ of Iṣfahānī (d. 430/1038);[90] and other treatises, such as the *Kitāb ʿAṭf al-alif al-maʾlūf* of Daylamī (fl. 400/1000).[91]

IV. The *Tafsīr al-Qurʾān al-ʿAẓīm*

Evidence suggests that Tustarī's *Tafsīr*, like many other Sufi works of this period, was not a written composition of Tustarī's hand, but was delivered orally by him to a circle of disciples, who preserved and transmitted it. At a later date the *Tafsīr* was then compiled and written down, with some additions.[92] Although the earliest extant manuscripts of the *Tafsīr* date to the ninth/fifteenth and tenth/sixteenth centuries,[93] the authorities cited by an anonymous scribe in the introduction of the original archetype of these manuscripts make it possible to date this archetype considerably earlier, to the mid-sixth/twelfth century.[94] However, since numerous comments cited in the name of Tustarī by Abū ʿAbd al-Raḥmān al-Sulamī in his *Ḥaqāʾiq al-tafsīr*[95] are identical word for word with comments in the *Tafsīr*, it is possible that the latter already existed in written form at least by the late fourth/tenth or early fifth/eleventh century. Since Sulamī includes some comments ascribed to Tustarī that are absent from the *Tafsīr*, it may be assumed either that the former had derived these comments from a separate written or oral source, or that he was drawing comments from a larger version of the text.[96]

In his detailed analysis of the history, structure and compilation of Tustarī's *Tafsīr*, Böwering has identified three structural layers in its composition, marking stages in its compilation: the first comprises Tustarī's actual comments on the verses; the second includes a number of Tustarī's aphorisms on mystical topics (usually those raised in the comments) as well as illustrative material taken from the stories of the prophets, probably added by Tustarī's disciples; the third level represents further insertions into the text by later hands, and includes exegetical proof texts taken from the Qurʾān and *aḥādīth*, the lengthy explanation of a poem, and anecdotes about Tustarī. Two of Tustarī's disciples who appear to have been the main compilers of the *Tafsīr*, and who are most often named in the *Tafsīr*, are Abū Bakr al-Sijzī and ʿUmar b. Wāṣil, while Muḥammad b. Sālim is also mentioned (as Ibn Sālim), though only three or four times.[97]

The *Tafsīr* includes comments on selected verses of all the *sūra*s of the Qurʾān, amounting to comments on some 1000 verses in all. As Böwering has suggested, it is likely that Tustarī's exegesis of the Qurʾān was delivered during sessions in which the Qurʾān was recited.[98] After the recitation of portions of the Qurʾān, he would have commented on certain verses, or parts of the verses, according to meanings that he was moved to expound. In its present written form, the comments follow on from the verses, and, with a few exceptions (most notably in Sūrat al-Baqara and Sūrat

90 Iṣfahānī, *Ḥilyat al-awliyāʾ*.

91 Abū al-Ḥasan ʿAlī al-Daylamī, *ʿAṭf al-alif al-maʾlūf ʿalāʾl-lām al-maʿṭūf* (Cairo, 1962); French trans. by Jean-Claude Vadet as *Le traité d'amour mystique d'al-Daylami* (Geneva, 1980); English trans. by Joseph N. Bell as *A Treatise on Mystical Love* (Edinburgh, 2005). For a detailed account of the respective importance of these works and many later Sufi works as sources for the Tustarī tradition, see Böwering, *Mystical Vision*, pp. 18–42.

92 For a detailed study of the history, authenticity, structure and compilation of Tustarī's *Tafsīr*, see Böwering, *Mystical Vision*, Chapter III.

93 MS Gotha 529 is dated 825/1422, MS Fātiḥ 638, 872/1422, while MS Ṣanʿāʾ 62 is dated 936/1530 and MS Fātiḥ 3488, 965/1558. A full discussion of the MSS is given in Böwering, *Mystical Vision*, pp. 100–5.

94 The two authorities mentioned are Abū Bakr al-Baladī (d. 504/1110) and his grandson Abū Naṣr al-Baladī (d. after 551/1156). See Böwering, *Mystical Vision*, pp. 107–8.

95 Abū ʿAbd al-Raḥmān al-Sulamī, *Ḥaqāʾiq al-tafsīr*, MS British Museum Or. 9433; ed. Sayyid ʿImrān (Beirut, 2001).

96 For a list showing the presence of comments on different verses of the Qurʾān ascribed to Tustarī in the *Ḥaqāʾiq al-tafsīr* of Sulamī, the *ʿArāʾis al-bayān fī ḥaqāʾiq al-Qurʾān* of Rūzbihān b. Abī Naṣr Baqlī (Lucknow, 1315/1898), *al-Muwāfaqāt fī uṣūl al-aḥkām* of Ibrāhīm b. Mūsā al-Shāṭibī (d. 790/1388), (Cairo, 1922), and *al-Shifāʾ bi-taʿrīf ḥuqūq al-muṣṭafā* of ʿIyāḍ b. Mūsā al-Qāḍī (d. 544/1149), (Damascus, 1972), as against Tustarī's *Tafsīr*, see Böwering, *Mystical Vision*, pp. 113–26.

97 See *Mystical Vision*, pp. 128–35.

98 Ibid, pp. 135ff.

Āl ʿImrān), are arranged according to their conventional numbering. The nature of the exegetical content is varied, and includes exoteric interpretations which either provide additional information and context for the verses, or explain and expand upon their literal meaning,[99] as well as comments that might be considered ethical in nature.[100] However, there is sufficient content of an esoteric nature for Tustarī's commentary to have been counted as part of the Sufi tradition of Qurʾānic exegesis.[101] It was, moreover, liberally used as a source for later Sufi commentaries, such as those of Sulamī, Maybudī (fl. sixth/twelfth century)[102] and Rūzbihān Baqlī (d. 606/1209). In addition to its exegetical content, the *Tafsīr al-Qurʾān al-ʿaẓīm* includes other material of a largely esoteric nature, such as discussions of mystical topics which arise in the interpretations, anecdotes about earlier mystics and about Tustarī himself, and numerous aphorisms of Tustarī concerning different aspects of the mystical path.

v. Tustarī's Approach to Qurʾān Interpretation

Tustarī's *Tafsīr* includes a number of traditions and statements which give us some idea of the principles underlying his interpretation of the Qurʾān. Several of these speak of different levels of meaning in the scripture, and among them are three quoted from Tustarī himself, all of which are presented in the Introduction to the Commentary.

The first is cited in the context of a discussion of the process of revelation:

> God sent down the Qurʾān in five instalments of five verses at a time: five clear verses (*muḥkam*), five ambiguous verses (*mutashābih*),[103] five concerning what is permissible (*ḥalāl*), five concerning what is prohibited (*ḥarām*), and five parabolic verses (*amthāl*). The believer who has gnosis (*maʿrifa*) of God, Exalted is He, adheres to what is clear in it, believes what is ambiguous, holds as permissible that which it has made permissible, holds as prohibited that which it has prohibited and comprehends its similitudes, as He has said: ...*but only those understand them [the similitudes] who know* [29:43] — that is, those who have knowledge (*ʿilm*) of God, Exalted is He, and especially those who have gnosis (*maʿrifa*) of Him.[104]

In the passage above, Tustarī has indicated an esoteric understanding or gnosis (*maʿrifa*) of the similitudes (*amthāl*) or parabolic verses of the Qurʾān. In a second statement he mentions knowledge of both the inner and outer levels of meaning in the Qurʾān, as when he states in the Introduction to the Commentary:

> ...God has said, Mighty and Majestic is He, *We have made it an Arabic Qurʾān* [43:3] — that is, we have expounded it in a clear Arabic tongue in the letters of the alphabet which God has clearly set forth for you, and by which you attain to knowledge of [its] inner (*bāṭin*) and outward (*ẓāhir*) [meanings].[105]

99 Comments of this type are too numerous to list, but we may cite here 5:83, 14:25, 42:7, 52:4 and 63:1 as examples.

100 As, for example, in the commentary on 3:159, 7:56, 7:68 and 15:85, though it should be borne in mind that it is often difficult to make a watertight distinction between the ethical and the mystical.

101 On Sufi hermeneutics see: Massignon, *Essai sur les origines,* trans., Benjamin Clark, *Essay on the Origin of the Technical Language of Islamic Mysticism* (Paris, 1997); Paul Nwyia, *Exégèse coranique et langue mystique* (Beirut, 1970); Böwering, *Mystical Vision*, esp. pp. 135–42; 'Sufi Hermeneutics and Medieval Islam', *Revue des études islamiques* 55–7 (1987–8); pp. 255–70; 'The Light Verse: Qurʾānic Text and Sufi Interpretation', *Oriens* 36 (2001), pp. 113–44; and 'The Scriptural Senses in Medieval Ṣūfī Qurʾān exegesis', in Jane D. McAuliffe et al., eds., *With Reverence for the Word* (Oxford and New York, 2003), pp. 350–1; Pierre Lory, *Les Commentaires ésotériques du Coran d'après ʿAbd al-Razzâq al-Qâshânî* (Paris, 1980); Kristin Z. Sands, *Ṣūfī Commentaries on the Qurʾān in Classical Islam* (London and New York, 2006); Annabel Keeler, *Sufi Hermeneutics: The Qurʾān Commentary of Rashīd al-Dīn Maybudī* (Oxford, 2006), especially ch. 3; and 'Sufi *tafsīr* as a Mirror: Qushayrī the *murshid* in his *Laṭāʾif al-ishārāt*', *JQS* 7 (2006), pp. 1–21.

102 Abū al-Faḍl Rashīd al-Dīn Maybudī, *Kashf al-asrār wa ʿuddat al-abrār* (Tehran, 1952–60).

103 The 'clear' (*muḥkam*) and 'ambiguous' (*mutashābih*) verses are mentioned in the Introduction to the Commentary and in 3:7. They will be discussed below, p. 4, n. 20.

104 IC, p. 6.

105 IC, p. 5.

Tustarī says more about the inner and outer levels of meaning in a passage earlier in his Introduction:

> Every verse of the Qurʾān has four senses: an outward (*ẓāhir*) and an inward sense (*bāṭin*), a limit (*ḥadd*) and a point of transcendency (*maṭlaʿ*). The outward sense is the recitation and the inward sense is the understanding (*fahm*) of the verse; the limit defines what is lawful and unlawful, and the point of transcendency is the heart's place of elevation (*ishrāf*) [from which it beholds] the intended meaning, as an understanding from God, Mighty and Majestic is He (*fiqhan min Allāh ʿazza wa jalla*). The outward knowledge [of the Qurʾān] is a knowledge [accessible to the] generality (*ʿāmm*); whereas the understanding of its inner meanings and its intended meaning is [for] a select few (*khāṣṣ*)...[106]

In this latter statement, Tustarī has indicated both that the inner meanings are intended for a select few, and that the understanding of these meanings comes 'from God'. A similar principle is expressed when he states:

> Truly God has not taken as a friend (*walī*) one of Muḥammad's nation (*umma*) without teaching them the Qurʾān, either in its outward or inner aspects. They said, 'We know about its outward aspect, but what is its inner aspect?' He replied, 'That is its understanding (*fahm*); and it is its understanding that is intended.'[107]

More than once in the *Tafsīr*, Tustarī warns against interpreting the Qurʾān according to one's own whims or desires (*ahwā*). Commenting on the words, *As for those in whose hearts is deviation, they follow the ambiguous part, desiring sedition and desiring its interpretation* [3:7], he glosses *sedition* as 'unbelief', and interprets the words *desiring its interpretation* as a reference to 'interpretation according to the desire of their lower selves'. Later in the commentary on this same verse [3:7], but this time on the words *those rooted in knowledge*, he cites a saying of ʿAlī b. Abī Ṭālib:

> [Those rooted in knowledge] are the ones whom knowledge has protected from plunging [into the interpretation of the Qurʾān] according to some whim (*hawā*) or with set argument[s] (*maḍrūba*), without [awareness of] the unseen [mysteries] (*dūn al-ghuyūb*). [This is] due to God's guidance of them, and His disclosing to them His unseen secrets (*asrārihi al-mughayyaba*) from within the treasure chests of knowledge.

Along with the sense that the esoteric meanings and 'unseen mysteries' of the Qurʾān are something precious that may be directly disclosed by God (to a certain chosen few, or His friends), Tustarī also conveys his awareness of the arcane, sometimes inexpressible nature of the inner meanings of the Qurʾān, and the humbling sense that the Qurʾān can never be fathomed. One example occurs in his commentary on the words, *Say, 'If the ocean were ink for [writing] the words of my Lord, it would run dry...'* [18:109]:

> His Book is part of His knowledge, and if a servant were given a thousand ways of understanding each letter of the Qurʾān, he would not reach the end of God's knowledge within it. This is because it is His pre-eternal speech, and His speech is one of His attributes, and there is no end to any of His attributes, just as He has no end. All that can be comprehended of His speech is as much as He opens to the hearts of His friends.

In another statement, he indicates that even were the mysteries of the Book to be fathomed, they are beyond expression or even allusion. The context is Tustarī's commentary on Abraham's request for an increase in certainty, related in 2:40:

> The one who is close (*qarīb*) [to God] has access to understanding (*fahm*), conjecture (*wahm*) and interpretation (*tafsīr*). But the one who is closest (*aqrab*) is beyond understanding, conjecture

---

106 IC, p. 2. An almost identical statement is cited by Sulamī as a tradition of ʿAlī b. Abī Ṭālib in the introduction to his *Ḥaqāʾiq al-tafsīr*. On this tradition and more generally on theories of four levels of meaning in the Qurʾān, see Böwering, 'The Scriptural Senses', pp. 346–75. On the levels of meaning in Qurʾānic exegesis, see also A. Keeler, *Sufi Hermeneutics*, pp. 69–81.

107 IC, p. 7.

and interpretation, and what is beyond that cannot be contained by expression (*ʿibāra*) or allusion (*ishāra*).[108]

The statements cited above go some way to explaining the varied nature of the content of the *Tafsīr*, and the often allusive, elliptical and even obscure style of the esoteric interpretations. However, some of this abstruseness may also be due to the fact that the comments were initially delivered orally as extemporary, inspired responses to the recited verses, such that the *Tafsīr* was eventually compiled from the notes of disciples who were themselves probably already familiar with the teachings that Tustarī was conveying through his exegesis. Indeed many of the aphorisms contained in the *Tafsīr*, which Böwering suggests were added later, may precisely have been added for the benefit of later aspirants in the circle of Tustarī's disciples, who did not have this familiarity with his doctrines.

The esoteric meanings which Tustarī elicits from the Qurʾānic verses and expounds through his commentary were clearly intended to convey spiritual guidance and illumination. For the most part, they provide direct guidance designed to assist the seeker with progress on the spiritual path, and include: discussions of qualities and virtues to which the seekers should aspire; vices which they should avoid; knowledge about the inner make-up of the human being; and descriptions of mystical experience. Other interpretations of an esoteric nature comprise Tustarī's metaphysical and cosmological discussions, such as those of the Muḥammadan Light, the covenant which God made in pre-eternity with all of humanity, known as 'the Covenant of *Alast*', and the miraculous Night Journey (*Isrāʾ*) and Ascension (*Miʿrāj*) of the Prophet.[109]

These interpretations appear to derive, or spring from, the verses in different ways.[110] Often they arise as metaphorical or allegorical interpretations, as in Tustarī's commentary on the words, *That you may warn [the people of] the mother of cities, and those around it…* [42:7], which he interprets in the following manner:

> In its outward meaning, *it* [the mother of cities] refers to Mecca. In its inner meaning it refers to the heart, while *those around it* refer to the bodily members (*jawāriḥ*). Therefore warn them, that they might safeguard their hearts and bodily members from delighting in acts of disobedience and following [their] lusts.

Another example of a metaphorical or allegorical interpretation occurs in his commentary on the words, *and the sun and moon are brought together* [75:9]:

> Its inner meaning is the following: the moon represents the light of the sight of the physical eye, which pertains to the natural self (*nafs al-ṭabʿ*), and the sun represents the light of the sight of the eye of the heart, which pertains to the spiritual self (*nafs al-rūḥ*) and the intellect (*ʿaql*).

Or again, his commentary on the words, *and the raised canopy* [52:5], which he glosses as:

> The pleasing and pure act, through which no reward is sought except God, Exalted is He.

In the first of these three comments, it is to be noted that Tustarī has juxtaposed his exoteric and esoteric interpretations. This he does in numerous contexts, as in the following example, which comprises firstly an explanation at the literal level and then an esoteric interpretation of the words, *By those sent forth in succession* [77:1]:

> By this is meant the angels who are sent with the good of His command…In its inner meaning it refers to spirits of the believers which are sent inspiration (*ilhām*) that is in accordance with the Book and the Sunna.

---

108 This saying occurs as part of the long commentary on a poem which is cited in the commentary on 2:40. It is possible, therefore, that these are the words of Abū Bakr al-Sijzī, or whoever was commenting on the poem. It may nonetheless be said to reflect Tustarī's teachings.

109 The content of these interpretations will be discussed in the section on Tustarī's mystical teachings below.

110 For a full discussion of Tustarī's 'method' of Qurʾān interpretation, see Böwering, *Mystical Vision*, pp. 135ff. For a discussion of the method of esoteric interpretation in Qushayrī's *Laṭāʾif al-ishārāt* (Cairo, 1968–71) and Maybudī's *Kashf al-asrār*, see Keeler, *Sufi Hermeneutics*, pp. 81–90.

Another mode of esoteric interpretation takes the form of a discussion of the spiritual or ethical significance of a word mentioned in a verse, as for example when he comments on the words, *So be forgiving with gracious forgiveness* [15:85]:

> [One should be] without resentment (*ḥiqd*) or censure (*tawbīkh*) after forgiving someone; this is to overlook [someone's misdeeds] graciously (*iʿrāḍ jamīl*).

Sometimes these comments constitute Tustarī's reply to a question put to him about a succinct interpretation he has given, as when he glosses Jacob's exhorting himself to *comely patience* [12:18] with the words 'patience and contentment', and when asked about the sign of this, replies, 'It is not to regret what has happened'. When further asked how a person can attain comeliness of patience, he explains:

> By knowing that God, Exalted is He, is with you, and by the comfort of [the concomitant sense of] well-being. Patience may be compared to a bowl which has patience at the top and honey underneath.

Another form of esoteric interpretation springs from what Böwering has termed 'Qurʾānic keynotes'.[111] This is where a particular word or expression sets off a train of mystical thought or associations in the commentator.[112] The resulting interpretation may or may not bear any obvious relation to the context in which the 'keynote' word appears. We find it exemplified, for example, in Tustarī's commentary on the words, *When God wishes to guide someone, He expands their breast to Islam* [6:125], where the verb *wishes* (*arāda*, from the root *r-w-d*) leads Tustarī into a discussion of the terms *murīd* and *murād*, both drawn from the same root. This subject may already have been in his mind since he refers to an earlier verse in the same *sūra* which mentions those who seek God's countenance, and therefore already indicates the 'aspirant' or 'one who seeks [God]' (*murīd*), while the 'one who is [divinely] sought' is picked up from the words, *God wishes* (or *seeks*):

> Truly God has distinguished between the one who seeks (*murīd*) and the one who is [divinely] sought (*murād*), even though they are both from Him (*min ʿindihi*). But He simply wanted to distinguish the elite (*khāṣṣ*) from the generality (*ʿumūm*), and so He singled out the one who is sought (*murād*) in this *sūra* and others. He also mentioned the one who seeks (*murīd*), representing the generality, in this *sūra* in His words, Exalted is He: *Do not drive away those who call upon their Lord, morning and evening, seeking His countenance* [6:52].

Another example of an interpretation arising from a 'keynote' or association of ideas occurs in Tustarī's commentary on the words, *If trouble should befall a man, he cries out to Us [in supplication], whether lying on his side…* [10:12], which in their Qurʾānic context refer to people who are heedless of God, and call on Him only when they are afflicted. However, here Tustarī is moved to speak of the true meaning of supplication, related to the verb translated as *he cries out* (*daʿā*):

> Supplication (*duʿāʾ*) is freeing oneself (*tabarrī*) of everything save Him, Exalted is He.

Given the complex nature of the doctrines expounded by Tustarī, the fact that they are sometimes allusively expressed, and the fact that they are scattered throughout the pages of his *Tafsīr*, the following sections will be devoted to a discussion of some of the key mystical teachings that are presented in the work. Striking in Tustarī's expositions is the extent to which he uses the imagery and metaphors of light, especially when discussing divinely-inspired knowledge and guidance.

---

111 See Böwering, *Mystical Vision*, pp. 136–7.

112 On this subject see also Nasrollah Pourjavady, 'Laṭāʾif-i Qurʾānī dar majālis-i Sayf al-Dīn Bākharzī', *Maʿārif* 18 (2001), pp. 3–24.

vi. Mystical Teachings

A. The Qurʾān and the Prophet

Throughout the *Tafsīr*, Tustarī emphasises the centrality and importance of the Qurʾān and the Sunna or exemplary practice of the Prophet. In his view, the Qurʾān and the Prophet together provide a complete source of guidance for humanity, as well as acting as mediators between God, the Ineffable and Transcendent One, and His creation. For example, in the Introduction to the Commentary, he draws on a Qurʾānic metaphor used in 3:103, when he states that the Qurʾān is 'a rope (*ḥabl*) between God and His servants', and when asked to explain this definition he says:

> This means that they have no way to Him save through the Qurʾān, and through understanding [all] that has been addressed to them therein concerning that which is required of them, as well as putting that knowledge into practice for God's sake with complete sincerity, and following the exemplary way (*sunna*) of Muḥammad ﷺ, who was sent to them.[113]

Tustarī cites numerous traditions concerning the nature of the Qurʾān, including a *ḥadīth* of the Prophet which states, 'The Qurʾān is God's wisdom (*ḥikma*) among His servants. Whoever learns the Qurʾān and acts according to it, it is as if prophethood were incorporated within him, except that he does not receive revelation…' He also repeatedly emphasises the importance of the Sunna, as when he says, 'Mindfulness of God (*taqwā*) signifies the Sunna, and no obligatory act (*farḍ*) is complete without the Sunna';[114] or again when he states, 'All action is futile except that which is done with sincerity (*ikhlāṣ*), and sincerity is not achieved except through adherence to the Sunna.'[115] The Sunna, he explains, has no limit, and this is explained as meaning:

> No one has fear like the fear of the Prophet ﷺ, and [the same goes for] his love (*ḥubb*), his longing (*shawq*), his abstinence (*zuhd*), his contentment (*riḍā*), his trust (*tawakkul*), and his [noble] characteristics (*akhlāq*). Indeed, God, Exalted is He, has said [of him]: '*Assuredly you possess a magnificent nature* [68:4].'[116]

Regarding the Qurʾān's role of mediation, Tustarī cites a *ḥadīth* according to which the Prophet describes the Qurʾān as 'an excellent intercessor whose intercession is accepted (*shāfiʿ mushaffaʿ*), and a truthful advocate (*māḥil muṣaddaq*)',[117] while of the Prophet's mediating role he states, '[God] has made the Emissary the most elevated and the greatest mediator (*wāsiṭa*) between you and Him'.[118]

In the Introduction to the Commentary, Tustarī shows how the Qurʾān and the Prophet are inextricably linked. For example, he states, 'God, Exalted is He, sent down the Qurʾān to His Prophet, and made his heart a mine of His oneness and of the Qurʾān'.[119] Both the Qurʾān and the Prophet are also linked in being identified with light. Regarding the Qurʾān, for example, Tustarī states 'God has made the Qurʾān a light and has said: *…but We have made it a light by which We guide whomsoever We wish of Our servants*' [42:52]; and he understands the words *…and [those who] follow the light which has been revealed with him* [7:157], to be a reference to the Qurʾān, 'of which the heart of the Prophet is the mine.'[120] Tustarī also describes the Prophet's breast (*ṣadr*) as a light, and Abū Bakr al-Sijzī explains this as meaning: 'it is a repository of light from the divine Substance (*jawhar*), which is the original locus of light within the breast.'[121] The *star of piercing brightness* [86:3] is interpreted

113 IC, p. 5.

114 *Tafsīr*, 5:2.

115 *Tafsīr*, 4:77.

116 *Tafsīr*, 18:30. The explanation is given by Mattā b. Aḥmad who, according to Böwering was also known as Aḥmad b. Mattā, and although not listed as one of Tustarī's disciples, appears to have been close to him.

117 IC, p. 3.

118 *Tafsīr*, 14:34.

119 IC, p. 3.

120 IC, pp. 4ff.

121 IC, p. 2.

by Tustarī as an allusion to the heart of the Prophet, 'resplendent with the realisation of God's oneness, the upholding of His transcendence, constancy in the practices of remembrance, and in the contemplative witnessing of the Omnipotent'; while in his commentary on the verse, *By the dawn* [89:1], Tustarī explains that its inner meaning refers to Muḥammad ﷺ, 'from whom the lights of faith, the lights of acts of obedience and the lights of the two worlds of existence gushed forth'.

Tustarī's teachings concerning the Qurʾān and the Prophet have theological and metaphysical, as well as cosmological, dimensions (as can be seen in the last quote above). At the beginning of the Introduction to the Commentary, he appears to associate the Qurʾān with God's pre-eternal knowledge, for when asked about whether God's knowledge about His servants was apparent to Him before or after He created them, he cites in answer the verse, *It is a Glorious Qurʾān* [85:21], and adds, 'that is, it is a Book [that was] fixed *in a Preserved Tablet* [85:22] before they were created.'[122] We have already seen above that he identifies the Qurʾān with God's knowledge and His speech, explaining that His speech is therefore (like His knowledge) one of His attributes. Not surprisingly, therefore, he also unequivocally asserts the uncreated nature of the Qurʾān, as when he comments on the words, *And there would never come from the Compassionate One any reminder that is new but that they used to disregard it* [26:5], and says:

> That is, whenever there came to them, through revelation, knowledge of the Qurʾān which was new to them and of which they had no prior knowledge, they would turn away from it. This is not to say that the Reminder (*dhikr*) [i.e. the Qurʾān] itself is created (*muḥdath*), however, for it is from among the attributes of the essence of God, and is therefore neither existentiated (*mukawwan*) nor created (*makhlūq*).[123]

In another context, Tustarī suggests that the Qurʾān 'contains' the Names and Attributes of God. In his commentary on the 'disconnected letters' at the commencement of Sūrat al-Baqara, *Alif lām mīm* [2:1], he observes, 'Each book that God, Exalted is He, sent down contains a secret and the secret of the Qurʾān is contained within the [disconnected] letters which open the *sūras*, because they are Names and Attributes [of God].' Before this, Tustarī's interpretation of the *Basmala* in the concluding section of the Introduction to the Commentary indicates more about the significance and mystery held in the letters of the Qurʾān:

> The '*bā*' stands for '*bahāʾ Allāh*' (the magnificence of God), Mighty and Majestic is He, the '*sīn*' stands for '*sanāʾ Allāh*' (the resplendence of God), and the '*mīm*' stands for '*majd Allāh*' (the glory of God), Mighty and Majestic is He. Allāh is the Greatest Name, which contains all His names. Between its '*Alif*' and '*Lām*' there is a cryptic letter, something of the unseen from an unseen to an unseen, a secret from a secret to a secret, a reality from a reality to a reality.[124]

B. The Muḥammadan Light

Tustarī was among the early Muslim mystics to have contemplated the idea of the Muḥammadan Light (*nūr Muḥammadiyya*).[125] The idea is twofold: firstly that Muḥammad had a special 'time' in pre-existence, alone with God; the second is that all of creation was created from the Muḥammadan Light.[126] These doctrines are first discussed in the context of 7:172, a verse which recounts the

122 IC, p. 1.

123 The doctrine of the majority of Sunni Muslims now is that the Qurʾān is uncreated and eternal. Among those who opposed this view were, to begin with, the Jahmites and then the Muʿtazilites. On this subject see Richard C. Martin 'Createdness of the Qurʾān', *EQ*, vol. 1, p. 467; Montgomery Watt, 'Early Discussions about the Qurʾān,' *Muslim World* 40 (1950), pp. 21–40 and 96–105; Wilferd Madelung, 'The Origins of the Controversy Concerning the Creation of the Qurʾān', in idem, *Religious Schools and Sects in Medieval Islam* (London, 1985), pp. 504–25; and Walter M. Patton, *Aḥmad b. Ḥanbal and the Miḥna* (Leiden, 1897).

124 IC, pp. 8–9.

125 He may well have been the earliest Sunni mystic to have formulated such a doctrine, although in Shīʿī and Imāmī circles the idea seems to have existed earlier. See, for example, Uri Rubin, 'Pre-existence and Light: Aspects of the Concept of *Nūr Muḥammad*', *Israel Oriental Studies* 5 (1975), pp. 62–119; and Arzina Lalani, *Early Shīʿī Thought: The Teachings of Muḥammad al-Bāqir* (London, 2004), pp. 80–2.

126 A similar doctrine in Sufism was that Muḥammad, the first in creation, was created for God, while the rest of creation

pre-eternal covenant which God made with humanity (the Covenant of *Alast*): *And, [remember] when your Lord took from the Children of Adam, from their loins their seed, and made them testify about themselves, [saying], 'Am I not your Lord?' They said, 'Yea, indeed, we testify'...*[127] In the following extract, Tustarī expounds his doctrine of the Muḥammadan Light:

> The seed (*dhurriyya*) comprise three [parts], a first, second and third: the first is Muḥammad ﷺ, for when God, Exalted is He, wanted to create Muḥammad ﷺ, He made appear (*aẓhara*) a light from His light, and when it reached the veil of divine majesty (*ʿaẓama*) it prostrated before God, and from that prostration God created an immense crystal-like column of light, that was inwardly and outwardly translucent, and within it was the essence of Muḥammad ﷺ.[128] Then it stood in service before the Lord of the Worlds for a million years with the essential characteristics of faith, which are the visual beholding of faith (*muʿāyanat al-īmān*), the unveiling of certainty (*mukāshafat al-yaqīn*) and the witnessing of the Lord (*mushāhadat al-rabb*). Thus He honoured him with this witnessing a million years before beginning the creation.[129]

Also in the context of 7:172, Tustarī discusses the creation of Adam and the descendants of Adam from the Muḥammadan light, and it can be seen that there are varying degrees of illumination in their creation:

> The second among the progeny is Adam ﷺ. God created him from the light of Muḥammad ﷺ. And He created Muḥammad ﷺ, that is, his body, from the clay of Adam ﷺ.
>
> The third is the progeny of Adam. God, Mighty and Majestic is He, created the seekers [of God] (*murīdūn*) from the light of Adam, and He created the [divinely-]sought (*murādūn*) from the light of Muḥammad ﷺ. Thus, the generality among people live under the mercy of the people of proximity (*ahl al-qurb*) and the people of proximity live under the mercy of the one brought near (*al-muqarrab*) [i.e. the Prophet] — *With their light shining forth before them and on their right* [57:12].

The Prophet's time alone with God is also alluded to in Tustarī's commentary on 53:13: *And verily he saw Him another time.* He states:

> That is, in the beginning when God, Transcendent and Exalted is He, created him as a light within a column of light (*nūran fī ʿamūd al-nūr*), a million years before creation, with the essential characteristics of faith (*ṭabāʾiʿ al-īmān*), in a witnessing of the unseen through the unseen (*mushāhadat al-ghayb biʾl-ghayb*).

The derivation of other creatures (or the light of other creatures) from the Muḥammadan Light is also referred to in a number of other passages, as in the following:

> He [God] made the gushing forth of the wellsprings of the heart of Muḥammad ﷺ, with the lights of knowledge of different kinds, a [sign of] mercy for his nation, because God, Exalted is He, honoured him with this honour. For the light of the prophets ﷺ is from his [Muḥammad's]

---

was created for Muḥammad. Later this idea became popularised and known simply as the doctrine of *law lāka*, being an abbreviation of 'If it were not for you We would not have created the spheres (*law lāka la-mā khalaqtuʾl-aflāk*)', on which see Annemarie Schimmel, *And Muḥammad is His Messenger* (Chapel Hill, NC, 1985), pp. 131–2.

127 In the so-called 'Covenant of *Alast*', the word *alast* is a reference to God's question, *alastu*, 'Am I not...?'

128 Interestingly, Tustarī speaks here of the 'essence' (*ʿayn*) of Muḥammad; later Sufis, especially after Ibn ʿArabī (d. 638/1240) would refer not only to the Muḥammadan Light (*nūr Muḥammadiyya*) but also to 'the Muḥammadan Reality' (*ḥaqīqa Muḥammadiyya*). See Michel Chodkiewicz, *Seal of Saints: Prophethood and Sainthood in the Doctrine of Ibn ʿArabī* (Cambridge, 1993), ch. 4.

129 A parallel passage is cited in both the *ʿAṭf al-alif* of Daylamī, p. 33, and the *ʿIlm al-qulūb* attributed to Makkī, *ʿIlm al-qulūb* (Beirut, 2004), p. 93, which according to Böwering's translation reads: 'When God willed to create Muḥammad, He made appear a light from His light and disseminated it. It spread in the entire kingdom [of pre-existence]. When it reached the majesty it bowed in prostration. God created from its prostration a mighty column of dense light like a crystal glass that is as thick as the seven heavens and outwardly and inwardly translucent.' On the Muḥammadan Light according to Tustarī, see Böwering, *Mystical Vision*, pp. 149–53; on the Muḥammadan Light in Sufi literature, see Schimmel, *Muḥammad*, ch. 7.

> light, the light of the heavenly dominions (*malakūt*) is from his light and the light of this world and the Hereafter is from his light.[130]

And the above-cited passage:

> *By the dawn* [89:1] refers to Muḥammad ﷺ, from whom the lights of faith, the lights of acts of obedience and the lights of the two worlds of existence gushed forth (*tafajjarat*).

C. Theology

The theological doctrines that Tustarī expounds in his *Tafsīr* are for the most part those that were adhered to by the majority of early Sunni traditionalist Muslims.[131] Among these doctrines, that of the uncreated Qurʾān has been discussed above. Another key theological doctrine that is presented early in the Introduction to the Commentary is that of God's pre-eternal knowledge of all human acts, and His decreeing everything in accordance with His knowledge:

> God's knowledge of His servants and what they would do was complete before He created them. [This does not imply] His forcing them into disobedience, coercing them into obedience, or leaving them out of His divine plan. Rather, it draws attention to that which those who deny His decree are promised, for He says: … *whoever will, let him believe, and whoever will, let him disbelieve* [18:29], in the way of a threat, since they [actually] have no power (*ḥawl*) or strength (*quwwa*) except in accordance with that which is contained in His pre-eternal knowledge concerning them, which will come to be, from Him, [but] through them and for them.[132]

Later in the course of his commentary, Tustarī adds that God's pre-eternal knowledge inevitably has to be manifested, 'since God's knowledge is a final decree that cannot change to other than that which the All-Knowing knows, Mighty and Majestic is He.'[133]

Tustarī's doctrine concerning the carrying through of the divine decree by human beings is interestingly nuanced. He teaches that God created both good and evil, and He commanded the good and forbade evil. However, as he indicates in the above passage, the compliance or otherwise to the divine command by human beings does not involve any coercion (*jabr*) on the part of God; rather, the matter of obedience depends upon His granting of protection (*ʿiṣma*), success (*tawfīq*) and help (*maʿūna*), while disobedience is the result of His withdrawing His protection from, or His abandonment (*khidhlān*) of, a person:

> Indeed, God, Exalted is He, has created good and evil and established the command and prohibition. He has made us worship Him through the good and linked that with success (*tawfīq*), while He has forbidden us from evil and linked the perpetration of it to the relinquishing of [His] protection (*ʿiṣma*), and abandonment (*khidhlān*) [by Him]. All of these are of His creation. Whoever is successful in [doing] good has a duty to show gratitude (*shukr*), and whoever has been left to do evil must repent and cry out for God's help, Mighty and Majestic is He.[134]

In another passage, the same principle is expressed slightly differently, and here he mentions the attribution of acts to human beings:

---

130 *Tafsīr*, 11:40.

131 On the development of Muslim theology see Josef van Ess, *Theologie und Gesellschaft im 2. und 3. Jahrhundert Hidschra: eine Geschichte des religiösen Denkens im frühen Islam* (Berlin, 1991–5); idem, *The Flowering of Muslim Theology*, trans. Jane Marie Todd (Boston, 2006); Montgomery Watt, *The Formative Period of Islamic Thought* (Edinburgh, 1973); Morris S. Seale, *Muslim Theology* (London, 1964); Robert Caspar, *A Historical Introduction to Islamic Theology: Muhammad and the Classical Period,* trans. P. Johnstone (Rome, 1998); Tilman Nagel, *The History of Islamic Theology: From Muhammad to the Present,* trans. Thomas Thornton (Princeton, 2000); Michael Marmura (ed.), *Islamic Theology and Philosophy* (Albany, 1984); Richard C. Martin, et al., *Defenders of Reason in Islam: Muʿtazilism from Medieval School to Modern Symbol* (Oxford, 1987); and Timothy J. Winter (ed.), *The Cambridge Companion to Classical Islamic Theology* (Cambridge, 2008).

132 IC, pp. 1–2.

133 *Tafsīr*, 2:41.

134 *Tafsīr*, 30:40.

> Affliction and well-being are from God, Mighty and Majestic is He. The command and prohibition are from Him; protection and the granting of success are from Him; and reward and punishment are from Him. However, actions are attributed (*manṣūba*) to the children of Adam, so whoever performs a good action must express gratitude to merit thereby an increase [in goodness]; and whoever performs a wicked act must seek forgiveness, so that he thereby merits forgiveness.[135]

In both these passages Tustarī is urging that human beings should recognise the omnipotence of God, who has predetermined all that they do, and whose help or abandonment is instrumental in their accomplishment of all predetermined acts of good or evil. Yet in addition, especially in the second passage, he is indicating that even God's predestination of wicked acts leaves a door open to salvation through repentance and forgiveness, and that through gratitude for good works, man may gain access to an increase in good works.[136]

The closely related doctrines of the divine decree, infallibly carried out in accordance with God's pre-eternal knowledge, of God's omnipotence, and of humanity's total helplessness and dependence on God, prevail throughout the *Tafsīr*. It could more specifically be called a 'mystical theology' since Tustarī shows how, as well as having profound implications for man's ultimate salvation, it can impact upon his inner spiritual states. He teaches that people should be aware not only that God controls all things, but also that He suffices for them in every way. Indeed, their downfall occurs precisely when they start to believe in their own power (*ḥawl*) and strength (*quwwa*), and try to rely on their own planning and management (*tadbīr*) of their affairs. He finds many opportunities to illustrate this principle. For example, in the continuation of the passage cited above from his commentary on 2:214, he states:

> Affliction from God is of two kinds: an affliction of mercy and an affliction of punishment. An affliction of mercy leads the afflicted person to show his utter need (*iftiqār*) for God, Mighty and Majestic is He, and leads him to the abandonment of devising (*tadbīr*). However, an affliction of punishment leads the afflicted person [to rely] on his own choice (*ikhtiyār*) and devising.

Another example of this teaching is to be found in his commentary on the words *those who believe in the unseen* (ghayb) [2:3], where Tustarī directly links believing in the unseen with disclaiming all power and strength:

> God is *the unseen* and His religion is *the unseen*, and God, Mighty and Majestic is He, has ordered them to believe in the unseen, to acquit themselves of [every claim] to power and strength concerning that which they have been commanded to do and prohibited from doing, in faith, speech and action, and to say, 'We have no power (*ḥawl*) to keep ourselves from disobedience save through Your protection (*ʿiṣma*), and we have no strength (*quwwa*) to obey You save through Your aid (*maʿūna*).'

Those who are 'damned from pre-eternity', however, are those who claimed their own power and strength, as exemplified by Pharaoh, who 'claimed to have power, strength and ability, and said, "Whenever I wish to believe I will believe", but when he actually came to believe [once he had seen the approach of his doom], it was not accepted from him, as God, Exalted is He, said, *Now — when hitherto you have disobeyed and been of those who do corruption?* [10:91]'[137]

One of the most interesting and unusual applications of this doctrine is in Tustarī's interpretation of the story of Adam's fall or 'slip' from grace in Paradise [2:30]. He describes how when Adam entered the Garden and saw all that was in it, he said, 'If only we could stay here forever; yet,

135 *Tafsīr*, 2:214. We might compare Tustarī's use of the concept of the 'attribution' of acts by human beings to the doctrine of 'acquisition' (*kasb*) which later came to be particularly associated with Ashʿarī theology. On the doctrine of *kasb* see W. Montgomery Watt, 'The Origin of the Islamic doctrine of Acquisition', *Journal of the Royal Asiatic Society* (1943), pp. 234–47; idem, *Free Will and Predestination in Early Islam* (London, 1948); Daniel Gimaret, *Théories de l'acte humaine en théologie musulmane* (Paris and Leuven, 1980).

136 Perhaps this statement may in part be intended to discourage a sense of fatalism. But it is also interesting how Tustarī emphasises the need for a spiritual response to predestination.

137 *Tafsīr*, 2:3.

indeed, we have an appointed time that extends to a known limit.' This, he explains, was Adam's heart's acquiescing in the 'whispering' or evil prompting (*waswasa*) of his lower self (*nafs*),[138] and it was thus that Satan could have access to him and offer to lead him to the 'tree of eternity that he longed for', which would be 'the means to attain immortality and everlastingness'. Further on in his interpretation of this primordial event, Tustarī observes that Satan had access to Adam because of the latter's preoccupation with his own devising and planning (*tadbīr*), and he adds:

> [Adam's] thought [for everlasting life] did not involve any considered reflection which might have made it a form of worship, but rather it was a kind of thinking that springs from a natural disposition (*jibilla*) in his lower self (*nafs*).

Thus Adam's reliance on his devising (*tadbīr*) represented, as Tustarī shows in his long commentary on this verse, a moment of forgetfulness and an absence of the remembrance of God, and we shall see later that remembrance of God is a touchstone of all Tustarī's teachings concerning the spiritual path.

The prophet Jonah is also shown by Tustarī to have succumbed, like Adam, to reliance on his own devising, this being his only sin, before he was *chosen by God and made of the righteous.*[139] Tustarī's general admonition on the basis of this doctrine is summarised in his commentary on the words *He directs the command from the heaven to the earth…*[32:5]:

> He reveals to His servants from His knowledge that which is a means of guidance and salvation for them. The person who is content with the destined provision resulting from God's management [of things] (*tadbīr*) for him, will have the evil of his own devising disposed of and removed from him. Thus [God] will have returned him to a state of contentment (*riḍā*) with the divine decree, and rectitude (*istiqāma*) in face of the unfolding of what is destined for him. [Such people] are among those who are brought into proximity [with Him] (*muqarrabūn*). Truly, God, Exalted is He, created people without any veil, and then made their devising [for themselves] (*tadbīr*) into their veil.

This last passage in particular illustrates the mystical dimension of Tustarī's theology, and its potentially transformative impact upon the inner life of the human being.

D. The Spiritual Destiny of Human Beings: Cosmology and Eschatology

The doctrine of the divine foreknowledge and decree is also to be found in Tustarī's interpretation of the pre-eternal covenant made between God and all of humanity (Covenant of *Alast*), as recounted in the Qurʾānic verse 7:172, which we shall again cite here:

> *And, [remember] when your Lord took from the Children of Adam, from their loins their seed, and made them testify about themselves, [saying], 'Am I not your Lord?' They said, 'Yea, indeed, we testify'…*

In his long interpretation of this verse, Tustarī not only expounds his doctrine of the Muḥammadan Light, as discussed above, but he also pays close attention to the Covenant itself, which in fact he understands as two covenants, taken separately, first from the prophets and then from all the progeny:

> God, Exalted is He, took the prophets ﷺ from the loins of Adam, and then He extracted from the back of each prophet his progeny in the shape of specks possessing intellects (*ʿuqūl*). Then he took from the prophets their pledge, as is stated in His words, *We took from the prophets their pledge: as (We did) from you and from Noah…* [33:7]. The Covenant that they were bound to was that they would convey from God, Exalted is He, His commandments and prohibitions. Then He called them all to affirm His lordship, with His words, Exalted is He: *'Am I not your Lord?'*, and He manifested His omnipotence [to them], so *they said: 'Yea, indeed, we testify.'* [7:172] … Then He returned them to the loins of Adam ﷺ, and subsequently He sent the prophets to remind them of His Pact and Covenant.

138 The word *waswasa*, derived from the onomatopoeic root *w-s-w-s*, means literally 'a whisper or whispering', but usually in religious texts in the sense of an evil prompting, incitement or temptation. Two derivatives from this verb are used in the final *sūra* of the Qurʾān, 114:4 and 5.

139 *Tafsīr*, 68:49.

As can be seen, Tustarī has here stated that the progeny were in the shape of specks 'possessing intellects (*ʿuqūl*)'. Later in the *Tafsīr*, in his commentary on the words, *O you who believe, fear God, and let every soul consider what it has sent ahead for tomorrow…* [59:18], he warns that on the Day of Resurrection everyone will be questioned about three things: 'that which he owes to himself, that which he owes to the knowledge between him and his Lord, and that which he owes to the intellect'. The believers, then, must be concerned in this life to fulfil the pre-eternal Covenant made with God, and to be among those who 'verify' the affirmation made in the response, 'Yes we testify', with the awareness that they will certainly be answerable for it in the Hereafter. This verifying is none other than the realisation of the oneness of God (*tawḥīd*). Thus he interprets *[those] who stand firm in their testimony* [70:33], as:

> [Those] who stand firm, upholding that to which they have testified, namely that there is no god except God, and who do not shirk with regard to it in any of their deeds, words or states.

Tustarī does not fail to remind those whom he is addressing of the accounting that they will inevitably face at the Resurrection,[140] and he also warns them not to be complacent, for they do not know in what state they will die. Thus when he comments on the words, *And no soul knows in what land it will die* [31:34], he says: '[It does not know] what its state (*ḥukm*) will be when it dies: [eternal] bliss (*saʿāda*) or wretchedness (*shaqāwa*)'. The use here of the word *ḥukm*, which can have the meaning of 'ordinance' or 'decree', is a reminder that the nature of our end is dependent on the divine decree, and for this reason, he follows his interpretation of the verse with two prayers of the Prophet Muḥammad, asking that God should make him die in His religion, as well as prayers of the prophets Abraham and Joseph asking that they should die in a state of submission to God.

Believers must, therefore, be aware that until their last breath they should be constantly renewing their pre-eternal Covenant by professing and realising the divine oneness, and, since they have no idea what is in God's pre-eternal knowledge, they should pray for His mercy and assistance in this. Tustarī must certainly have known that such awareness would be intensified by his many quite literal comments on the eschatological verses of the Qurʾān recounting the torments of Hell and delights of Paradise, to which he sometimes adds vivid details.[141] Again, he makes it clear that it is those who denied the divine oneness who will be consigned to Hell, whereas the reward for belief in God's oneness will be Paradise.[142]

However, Tustarī does not see Paradise as being confined to the delights that are portrayed in the Qurʾān. He understands there to be two Paradises: one, the Garden with all its delights, provides the rewards for the bodily members; the other, the reward for the realisation of God's oneness, contains 'the delight of the vision (*naẓar*) of God and the manifestation of the divine unveiling (*tajallī al-mukāshafa*), this itself being permanent subsistence with the Permanently Subsistent One (*baqāʾ maʿaʾl-Bāqī*).'[143] Moreover, those who have devoted themselves completely to God will have no desire for the delights of the Garden, but wish only to be with God. Commenting on the words, *And enter My paradise* [89:30], he says:

> It has been related in a report that the angels say to those solely devoted to Him (*munfaridūn*) on the Day of Resurrection, 'Proceed to your resting places in Paradise', to which they say, 'What is Paradise to us when we have devoted ourselves solely to [Him] because of a special understanding which has been [granted] to us from Him? We do not want anything save Him — that is the only good life (*ḥayāt ṭayyiba*).'

Whilst in his *Tafsīr* Tustarī shows the greatest and ultimate reward for the realisation of God's oneness to be the encounter with God, subsisting with Him and the beatific vision of Him, which

140 Examples of such comments occur in *Tafsīr*, 9:122; 16:55; 17:14; 19:83; 23:1 and 2; and 69:18.

141 As, for example, in *Tafsīr*, 57:13; 67:1 and 2, 69:32; 76:21; 81:7; Sūra 83; 84:9; Sūra 88 and 89:14.

142 e.g. *Tafsīr*, 83:18.

143 *Tafsīr*, 43:69 and 70. Tustarī also states in his commentary on 90:18 that those who perceived none other than God [in this world] will be rewarded with 'life with Life itself *(ḥayāt bi-ḥayāt)*, eternity with Eternity itself (*azaliyya bi-azaliyya*), and a mystery with Mystery itself (*sirr bi-sirr*)', while in his commentary on 92:21 he describes the reward as: 'a mystery with Mystery itself (*sirr bi-sirr*), life with Life itself (*ḥayāt bi-ḥayāt*), and eternity with Eternity itself (*azaliyya bi-azaliyya*).'

are to be anticipated and hoped for in the Hereafter, he does also indicate that mystics who have attained the highest states may taste in this life experiences of encounter with God, described as the unveiling (*mukāshafa*) and witnessing (*mushāhada*) of God. Thus in his commentary on the words, *As for the righteous, they will be in bliss* (naʿīm) [82:13], he states:

> The *bliss* of the elect among His servants who are the righteous (*abrār*) is the encounter with Him (*liqāʾuhu*) and the witnessing (*mushāhada*) of Him, just as their bliss in this world was in the witnessing of Him and proximity (*qurb*) with Him.

We find in the *Tafsīr* only a few glimpses into the nature of this experience. One of the best examples may be seen in the commentary on a mystical poem, probably composed by Tustarī, which is quoted in the context of the long commentary on 2:260. In this poem, the experience of 'face-to-face encounter with God' (*kifāḥ*) is compared to the spider's web which appeared over the entrance to a cave in which the Prophet and Abū Bakr were hiding when they were escaping from Mecca.[144] Commenting on this analogy, either Tustarī or one of his disciples explains:

> His saying: 'Like the spider's web covering the entrance of a cave', [is an allusion to] the cave of mystics (*ʿārifūn*) [which is] the[ir] innermost secret (*sirr*), and the[ir] beholding (*iṭṭilāʿ*) of the Lord of the Worlds, when they reach the station of face-to-face encounter (*maqām al-kifāḥ*), that is, the immediate vision of direct witnessing (*ʿiyān al-ʿiyān*) beyond what has been [verbally] elucidated (*bayān*). Then there is nothing between the servant and God except the veil of servanthood, due to his contemplation (*naẓar*) of the attributes of lordship (*rubūbiyya*), ipseity (*huwiyya*), divinity (*ilāhiyya*), and [God's being] eternally Self-Sufficing and Besought of all (*ṣamadiyya ilāʾl-sarmadiyya*), without any obstacle or veil.[145]

Tustarī draws from the words, *And brought him near in communion* [19:52], which allude to the special proximity accorded to the prophet Moses, a more general observation about the grace of unveiling (*mukāshafa*):

> That is, being secretly called for the unveiling (*mukāshafa*), [an unveiling] which is not concealed from hearts, in [intimate] conversation (*muḥādatha*) and loving affection (*wudd*), just as He said, Exalted is He, *Truly those who believe and perform righteous deeds — for them the Compassionate One shall appoint love* (wudd) [19:96], meaning that [through] this unveiling, the mysteries are received without any mediation. This is a station given by God to those who are true and faithful to Him both in secret and openly.

Parts of Tustarī's interpretation of the miraculous Ascension or *Miʿrāj* of the Prophet [53:1–18] also suggest that aspects of the Prophet's conduct are being presented to provide a model for the conduct of mystics in their experiences, as when Tustarī comments on 53:17, *The eye did not swerve, nor did it go beyond [the bounds]*:

> He did not incline to the evidences of his self (*shawāhid nafsihi*), nor to witnessing them (*mushāhadatihā*), but was totally absorbed in the witnessing (*mushāhada*) of his Lord, Exalted is He, witnessing (*shāhid*) the attributes [of God] that were being manifested [to him], which required firmness from him in that place (*maḥall*).

And when he comments on the words of the next verse, *Verily he saw some of the greatest signs of his Lord* [53:18]:

> That is, those of His attributes which became manifest through His signs. Though he saw them, he did not let slip [his gaze] from his witnessed Object (*mashhūd*), and did not withdraw from the vicinity of his worshipped Object (*maʿbūd*) but rather [what he saw] only increased him in love (*maḥabba*), longing (*shawq*) and strength (*quwwa*).

Aside from these glimpses into experiences of union or proximity with God or the mystical unveiling and contemplative witnessing of Him, most of the spiritual teachings in Tustarī's *Tafsīr* are concerned with outlining essential prerequisites of the Path, models to be emulated, qualities

144 The spider's web and a dove's nest next to the cave's entrance persuaded those among the Quraysh who were pursuing them that there was no point in entering, and so the Prophet and Abū Bakr were saved.

145 *Tafsīr*, 2:260.

to be aspired to and proprieties (*ādāb*) of spiritual conduct to be upheld, especially in relation to others. The spiritual aim of the mystical way is, as he indicates, to attain complete sincerity (*ikhlāṣ*) in the worship of God and in the attestation of His oneness, and the key to it is, as we shall see, the remembrance of God. Before outlining in more detail Tustarī's teachings about the principles and practice of the spiritual path, we shall look at his perception of the interior world of the human being and his teachings regarding the nature of, and relationship between, faith, knowledge and certainty.

E. Spiritual Psychology

1. *The inner make-up of the human being*

Sufis did not simply understand the human being to be made up of 'body, soul and spirit'; they developed a subtle and complex science of the inner human make-up, which one might call a 'spiritual psychology' or 'science of the soul'. The Qurʾān itself speaks of the human heart (*qalb*) upon which God inscribes faith [58:22], and which was able to take on the 'Trust' (*amāna*) [33:72];[146] the spirit (*rūḥ*) [e.g. 32:9; 15:29; 38:72]; the 'pith' or 'inner substance' (*lubb*, used in the plural, *albāb*) [e.g. 2:179, 197; 3:7, 190]; the 'breast' (*ṣadr*) [e.g. 7:2; 11:12; 15:97; 94:1]; and many times of the 'soul', 'self' or 'ego' (*nafs*).[147] Moreover, the Qurʾān speaks of different forms of the latter, namely, the 'evil-inciting self' (*al-nafs al-ammāra bi'l-sūʾ*) (alluded to in 12:53), the 'self-reproaching' or 'blaming self' (*al-nafs al-lawwāma*) [75:2] and the 'self at peace' (*al-nafs al-muṭmaʾinna*) [89:27]. These Qurʾānic designations no doubt inspired and informed the development of the Sufis' own ways of understanding the spiritual psychology of human beings.[148]

Tustarī was among the early Muslim mystics who expounded an understanding of the complexity of the inner human make-up.[149] In general terms, he seems to perceive two sides or propensities within the human being, one which tends toward earth and the physical and sensory pleasures, and the other which tends toward heaven and the spiritual realm. He expresses this overall scheme in different ways in the *Tafsīr* (see diagram, below). Most often, he contrasts two sides of the 'self' (*nafs*). There is on the one hand the 'self of man's basic nature' (*nafs al-ṭabʿ*, but also occasionally, *nafs al-jibilla*), which we have rendered as the 'natural self'; and on the other, the 'self of the spirit' (*nafs al-rūḥ*), which we have rendered as the 'spiritual self'.[150] The former is associated with darkness, and the latter with light, as when Tustarī interprets *the night when it enshrouds* [92:1] as 'the natural self' (*nafs al-ṭabʿ*) and *the day as it unveils* [92:2] as 'the spiritual self'.

In a few instances, Tustarī appears to employ the word *rūḥ* (spirit) on its own synonymously with *nafs al-rūḥ*. The term *ṭabʿ* on its own, however, is almost always used by him to designate man's basic nature, or his physical appetites and instincts, though in one context he speaks of four inborn natures or dispositions (*ṭabāʾiʿ*), which are all part of his basic nature (*ṭabʿ*). They are: the animal nature (*ṭabʿ al-bahāʾim*), the satanic nature (*ṭabʿ al-shayāṭīn*), the sorcerous nature (*ṭabʿ al-saḥara*) and the devilish nature (*ṭabʿ al-abālisa*). All of these are potentially negative forces within the

---

146 The 'Trust' (*amāna*) is discussed below, p. 219, n. 6.

147 On the different usages of the term *nafs* (pl. *anfus* or *nufūs*) in the Qurʾān, see Th. E. Homerin, 'Soul', *EQ*, vol. 5, p. 80.

148 On the connection between the development of Sufi concepts and terminology in relation to the Qurʾān, see Paul Nwyia, *Exégèse coranique* (Beirut, 1970) and Massignon, *Essai*.

149 Other early mystics to have developed such schemes are al-Ḥārith al-Muḥāsibī (d. 243/837), Abū al-Ḥusayn al-Nūrī (d. 295/907) and al-Ḥakīm al-Tirmidhī (d. between 295/905 and 300/910). On Muḥāsibī, see Josef van Ess, *Die Gedankenwelt des Ḥāriṯ al-Muḥāsibī* (Bonn, 1961); Gavin N. Picken, 'The Concept of *Tazkiyat al-Nafs* in Islam in the Light of the Works of al-Ḥārith al-Muḥāsibī', PhD thesis (University of Leeds, 2005). Nūrī is said to be the author of a work entitled *Maqāmāt al-qulūb*, ed. with introduction by Paul Nwyia in *Mélanges de l'Université Saint-Joseph* 44 (1968), pp. 117–54, while a comparable work on the inner make-up of human beings is ascribed to al-Ḥakīm al-Tirmidhī, entitled *Bayān al-farq bayn al-ṣadr wa'l-qalb wa'l-fuʾād wa'l-lubb* (Cairo, 1958); English trans. by Nicholas Heer, with Kenneth L. Honerkamp, *Three Early Sufi Texts* (Louisville, KY, 2003).

150 The use of this construct is unusual in Sufi texts, if not unique to Tustarī, and it may initially be tempting to understand the word *nafs* here in its idiomatic usage for emphasis in Arabic, as in *nafs al-shay*, meaning 'the thing itself'. However, we have discounted this interpretation partly because it occurs rather too frequently to be merely for emphasis, and partly for other reasons which will become apparent in the course of this discussion.

human being and should be combatted in different ways.[151] Thus Tustarī appears to distinguish man's 'natural self' (*nafs al-ṭabʿ*) from his 'basic nature' (*ṭabʿ*).

Twofold Inner Constitution of the Human Being					
nafs	[lower] self	*nafs*	spirit	*rūḥ*	*rūḥ*
	natural self	*nafs al-ṭabʿ/nafs al-jibilla*	spiritual self	*nafs al-rūḥ*	
	dense natural self	*nafs-al-ṭabʿ al-kathīf*	luminous spiritual self	*nafs al-rūḥ al-nūrī*	
ṭabʿ	basic nature / natural instinct	*ṭabʿ*	heart	*qalb*	*qalb*
	natures / dispositions	*ṭabāʾiʿ*	(discernment of the heart	*fiṭnat al-qalb*)	
	physical appetite / animal instinct	*ṭabʿ al-bahāʾim*			
	satanic nature	*ṭabʿ al-shayāṭīn*	intellect	*ʿaql*	*ʿaql*
	sorcerous nature	*ṭabʿ al-saḥara*	(understanding of the intellect	*fahm al-ʿaql*)	
	devilish nature	*ṭabʿ al-abālisa*			

Further Designations of the Self (*nafs*)			
evil-inciting self	*al-nafs al-ammāra bi'l-sūʾ*	self at peace	*al-nafs al-muṭmaʾinna*
self-reproaching / blaming self	*al-nafs al-lawwāma*	self of gnosis	*nafs al-maʿrifa*
lustful self	*al-nafs al-shahwāniyya*		

In fact, the term *nafs* on its own is frequently used by Tustarī to designate the darker, earth-bound side of the human being that is opposed to the spiritual self (or spirit). In these instances, we have translated the word *nafs* as 'lower self'. An example is the following passage:

> The lower self (*nafs*) desires the world because it comes from that, but the spirit (*rūḥ*) desires the Hereafter because it comes from that. Gain ascendancy over the lower self and open for it the door to the Hereafter by glorifying [God] (*tasbīḥ*) and seeking forgiveness for your nation.[152]

Here, Tustarī is indicating that the lower self can potentially be 'saved' through the glorification of God. Elsewhere, he shows that the natural self (*nafs al-ṭabʿ*) can be allied or brought into coalition with the spiritual self (*nafs al-rūḥ*) through the remembrance of God (*dhikr*). Thus he interprets *the forenoon* [93:1] as 'the spiritual self', and *the night when it is still* [93:2] as 'the natural self when it finds repose with the spiritual self in constant remembrance of God, Exalted is He.' In another context he emphasises the salutary role of both the remembrance of God (*dhikr*) and gratitude (*shukr*), as in his commentary on the words, *when souls shall be coupled* [81:7], where he states:

> The natural self and spiritual self will be joined together and will be mingled in [their partaking of] the bliss of Paradise inasmuch as they were allied in this world in keeping remembrance constantly and upholding a state of gratitude.

In an interesting passage, Tustarī contrasts the inner process which takes place at death with that which occurs during sleep. He explains that both the luminous spiritual self (*nafs al-rūḥ al-nūrī*) and the dense natural self (*nafs al-ṭabʿ al-kathīf*) have a subtle substance (*laṭīf*). When a person dies, God removes from him the subtle substance of the luminous spiritual self, separating it from the subtle substance of the dense natural self, 'and by this [luminous spiritual self] he comprehends things, and is given the vision (*rūʾyā*) [of God] in the heavenly kingdom (*malakūt*).' When a person sleeps, however, God removes from him only the subtle substance of the dense natural self, so that when he awakens, he is able to recover a 'subtle breath' from the luminous substance of the spiritual self, because it is 'by virtue of the light of the subtle substance of the spiritual self that the natural self has life'. Thus, the natural self derives life from the spiritual self, while the life

151 *Tafsīr*, 12:53.

152 *Tafsīr*, 110:2.

of the spiritual self, as Tustarī explains, is 'by virtue of the remembrance [of God] (*dhikr*), indeed its sustenance is remembrance, while the sustenance of the natural self is food and drink.' He then adds the observation:

> Whoever cannot reconcile these two opposites, I mean by that, the natural self and the spiritual self, so that the subsistence (*ʿaysh*) of the two together is by remembrance, and the endeavour [to accomplish] remembrance, is not a mystic (*ʿārif*) in reality.[153]

So far we have seen the 'natural self' (*nafs al-ṭabʿ* or *nafs al-jibilla*), the '[lower] self' (*nafs*) and basic nature (*ṭabʿ*) opposed to the 'spiritual self' (or the 'spirit'), but in his overall twofold scheme Tustarī sometimes contrasts the lower self (*nafs*) with the heart (*qalb*), as, for example, when he explains:

> If your lower self overpowers your heart, it will drive you to the pursuit of desire (*hawā*). But if your heart overpowers your lower self and your bodily members, it will tether them with propriety (*adab*), compel them into worship (*ʿibāda*), and then adorn them with sincerity in servanthood.[154]

He also interprets *the two seas* [55:19] as: 'the sea of the heart, full of gems, and the sea of the lower self. Between these two is *a barrier that they do not overstep* [55:20].' Likewise, in his interpretation of the words, *He knows what enters the earth* [57:4], he states: '*The earth* is the natural self, and thus He knows among the things which enters it that which is wholesome or corrupt for the heart.'

In many places in the *Tafsīr*, Tustarī presents a more complex twofold scheme of the inner constitution of human beings, comprising on one side the natural self (*nafs al-ṭabʿ*), or lower self (*nafs*), and on the other, the heart (*qalb*), the intellect (*ʿaql*) and the spiritual self (*nafs al-rūḥ*) — (again, see the diagram on p. xxxix) An example of such a scheme occurs in his commentary on the words, *By those that deliver the reminder* [77:5], which in its exoteric sense is understood to refer to the delivering of the revelation by the angels to prophets:

> This is the revelation (*waḥy*) through inspiration (*ilhām*) which the spiritual self (*nafs al-rūḥ*), the intellect (*ʿaql*) and the heart (*qalb*) cast upon the natural self (*nafs al-ṭabʿ*), and this is the hidden form of reminder (*dhikr khafīy*).

Sometimes Tustarī refines these definitions further, specifying 'the understanding of the intellect' (*fahm al-ʿaql*) and 'discernment of the heart' (*fiṭnat al-qalb*) as well as the spiritual self (*nafs al-rūḥ*),[155] or with minor variations, as when he speaks of 'the intuition of the spiritual self' (*dhihn nafs al-rūḥ*). One example is when he explains that the vision of God in the Hereafter will be the share of 'the intuition of the spiritual self, the understanding of the intellect and the discernment of the heart', since they were present *without* the natural self when God addressed human beings in molecular form in pre-eternity. He adds that the natural self will nonetheless receive some share of the beatific vision in Paradise, 'like a fragrant breeze, due to its being fused with those lights'.[156] These three faculties (heart, intellect and spirit or spiritual self) work together in different ways to overcome or transform the lower or natural self, as Tustarī shows, for example, when he explains the repetition of the words, *truly with hardship comes ease* [94:5]:

> God, Exalted is He, has magnified the state of hope in this verse out of His generosity and His hidden grace, and thus He mentions ease twice. Indeed, the Prophet ﷺ said, 'Hardship will not overwhelm the two 'eases'. By this he meant: the discernment of the heart (*fiṭnat al-qalb*) and the intellect (*ʿaql*) are the two 'eases' which overcome the natural self, and return it to the state of sincerity (*ikhlāṣ*).

---

153 *Tafsīr*, 39:42.

154 *Tafsīr*, 48:4.

155 *Tafsīr*, 18:21 and 19:61. The juxtaposition of these three in this form is a further indication that Tustarī is not using the word *nafs* in its emphatic meaning in the construct *nafs al-rūḥ*.

156 *Tafsīr*, 42:20. We may note here that Tustarī had stated in the passage on death and sleep cited above that 'the substance of the luminous spiritual self' is separated from 'the substance of the dense natural self at death', since it is through the former that man is able to comprehend things and enjoy the beatific vision in the Hereafter.

Interestingly, Tustarī does not, like later Sufis, suggest a particular hierarchy among these different faculties within the human being.[157] Neither does he include along with the heart, the intellect and the spiritual self, that important inner faculty so often mentioned in Sufism, the '[innermost] secret' (*sirr*), also translated as 'mysterium', 'mystery' or 'inmost being'.[158] However, he does mention the *sirr* separately, in a number of contexts. It seems that he understands the innermost secret (*sirr*) to be at the very deepest level of the human being. Most often, it is associated with the contemplative witnessing of God (*mushāhada*) and with certainty (*yaqīn*), and as such it will be seen in several extracts cited in Section 4 below. At other times he speaks of the innermost secret when he wishes to describe the deepest and most sincere attainment of a spiritual virtue, such as humility,[159] veracity,[160] neediness for God,[161] surrender to Him,[162] and fear of Him.[163] In one instance, he contrasts the 'innermost secret' (*sirr*) within the human being with the 'outer self' (*ẓāhir*). The life of the former is in God's remembrance, while the life of the latter is in praising and thanking God.[164]

2. *The nafs*

We have seen reference to man's natural self (*nafs al-ṭabʿ* or *nafs al-jibilla*), [lower] self (*nafs*) and also basic nature (*ṭabʿ*), being opposed to the heart, intellect and spiritual self or spirit. Describing the *nafs*, Tustarī states that when God created it, He made ignorance its nature and desire the closest thing to it,[165] and in another context he shows it to be in partnership with Satan.[166] When it is clearly in this role we have translated *nafs* as 'lower self', as noted above. But Tustarī, like other Sufis, also appears to understand the *nafs* to have a number of different levels according those mentioned above that are spoken of in the Qurʾān, namely the 'evil-inciting self' (*nafs ammāra bi'l-sūʾ*), the 'self-reproaching or blaming self' (*nafs lawwāma*) and the 'self at peace' (*nafs muṭmaʾinna*), though he refers to these only in one or two instances. About the evil-inciting self, he states that it 'is lust (*shahwa*), which itself is the role played by man's basic nature (*ṭabʿ*)'.[167] He identifies the self-reproaching or blaming self with the evil-inciting self.[168] Elsewhere, he speaks of the 'lustful self' (*nafs shahwāniyya*)[169] and the 'self of gnosis' (*nafs al-maʿrifa*),[170] which seem to be manifestations of the natural or lower self and the spiritual self, respectively. Moreover, in one context he identifies the self at peace (*nafs muṭmaʾinna*) with the spiritual self (*nafs al-rūḥ*).[171] In many Sufi texts, the different aspects of the *nafs*, such as those of the *nafs ammāra*, *nafs lawwāma*, and *nafs muṭmaʾinna* are understood as stages in its spiritual development. Without spiritual discipline, man remains enslaved to the dictates of the evil-inciting self, but through rigorous spiritual discipline and with the assistance of divine grace, the *nafs* may gradually be transformed into the self at peace (*nafs muṭmaʾinna*).[172] Tustarī, however, does not appear to see them as one *nafs* that is transformed, but

---

157 On these hierarchies, and levels within the inner world of the human being see Keeler, *Sufi Hermeneutics*, pp. 154ff.

158 The term *sirr* is used by different Sufi authors in various ways, but is generally used to define a subtle centre of perception or locus of mystical experience deep within the human being. On this subject see Shigeru Kamada, 'A Study of the Term *sirr* (secret) in Sufi *Laṭāʾif* Theories', *Oriens* 19 (1983), pp. 7–28.

159 e.g. *Tafsīr*, 5:6.

160 e.g. *Tafsīr*, 33:8.

161 e.g. *Tafsīr*, 35:15.

162 e.g. *Tafsīr*, 37:84.

163 e.g. *Tafsīr*, 23:1–2.

164 *Tafsīr*, 26:227. In this case, innermost secret (*sirr*) would appear to represent *nafs al-rūḥ*, and outer self (*ẓāhir*), the *nafs al-ṭabʿ*, here in coalition with the *nafs al-rūḥ* through the remembrance of God.

165 *Tafsīr*, 12:53.

166 *Tafsīr*, 22:52.

167 *Tafsīr*, 12:53.

168 *Tafsīr*, 75:1, 2.

169 *Tafsīr*, 33:4.

170 *Tafsīr*, 12:53.

171 *Tafsīr*, 89:27.

172 Or, according to the terminology of some schools of Sufism, beyond the *nafs muṭmaʾinna* to reach higher stages of the *nafs*.

as the twofold *nafs* (the natural and spiritual self), which can, through the remembrance of God, be brought into coalition, though they will not partake of the same experience in Paradise.[173]

3. The heart (qalb)

In his *Tafsīr*, Tustarī pays particular attention to the heart. Like other Sufis he sees the heart as the 'seat' or locus of faith within the human being, and this has its basis in the Qurʾān, for example in the words of 58:22: *...He has inscribed faith upon their hearts and reinforced them with a spirit from Him...* Commenting on these words, Tustarī states that this inscription on the heart is the work of God, not the work of the servant, and he describes it as a 'gift of faith (*mawhibat al-īmān*)'. He also speaks of the heart as being a locus of the realisation of God's oneness (*tawḥīd*) and of gnosis (*maʿrifa*), love (*maḥabba*) and intimacy (*uns*) with God. Interpreting the *Much-frequented House* (*Bayt Maʿmūr*) [52:4] in a metaphorical way, he states:

> In its inner meaning, it refers to the heart: the hearts of mystics are frequented (*maʿmūra*) by His gnosis (*maʿrifa*), His love (*maḥabba*), and intimacy (*uns*) with Him. It is to this [the mystic's heart] that the angels make pilgrimage, for it is the House of the Realisation of God's Oneness (*bayt al-tawḥīd*).

Tustarī states that God created the heart 'for Himself',[174] and in one instance interprets the House of God (i.e. the Kaʿba) esoterically to represent the heart. Thus when he comments on the words, *Purify My House for those who circumambulate it...* [22:26], he states: 'Just as God has commanded the purification of His House [at Mecca] from idols, so also He has commanded the purification of that house of His in which He deposited the mystery of faith (*sirr al-īmān*) and the light of gnosis (*nūr al-maʿrifa*), namely, the heart of the believer.' Tustarī again employs the symbolism of the house for the heart when he comments on *houses [lying] deserted* [27:52], and explains:

> *Their houses* are an allusion to hearts; for there are hearts which are inhabited (*ʿāmir*) through remembrance (*dhikr*), and there are those which are ruined (*kharib*) through heedlessness (*ghafla*). Whomsoever God, Mighty and Majestic is He, inspires with [His] remembrance, He has freed from oppression (*ẓulm*).[175]

Yet again showing the heart to be God's property, he states:

> Truly the heart is [like] a house: if it is unoccupied it goes to ruin, while if it is occupied by other than its owner, or by other than one whom the owner has settled there, it will also go to ruin. Therefore, if you wish your hearts to be in good repair, do not let your prayer in them be other than to God, Exalted is He.[176]

The heart, therefore, needs to be protected from heedlessness and from being occupied with other than God, and Tustarī shows that, although it is the seat of faith, it can be diverted from the true direction. As was seen above, Adam's banishment from Paradise was because his heart acquiesced in the desire and devising of his lower self. In one context he states that although the heart is the most beneficial part of the human being, it is also the most dangerous, due to its tendency to turn back and forth and fluctuate (*taqallub*) and its depth, and he compares it to a sea across which one must journey.[177] The heart has a light of insight, through which it can overcome desire and lust. But Tustarī warns:

> When the heart's sight is blind to what is within it, lust will overcome him and heedlessness will [afflict] him at regular intervals. Consequently his body will stray into sin without being guided to God under any circumstances.[178]

---

173 For example, the natural self will not be granted the vision of God.

174 *Tafsīr*, 19:85.

175 That is, the oppression of, or wrongdoing towards, their own selves.

176 *Tafsīr*, 22:26.

177 *Tafsīr*, 30:41.

178 *Tafsīr*, 22:46.

Interestingly, in his commentary on 22:46, he also speaks of an inner heart, which is 'the position from which the servant stands before his Master without being agitated or busied by anything, but in a state of tranquillity and stillness in Him'. It may be that what Tustarī is referring to here is that which he elsewhere describes as the function of the innermost secret (*sirr*).

The heart's locus is the breast (*ṣadr*), which acts as a medium of transmission between the heart and the body. The breast is itself described as the locus of Islam, so it can be said that just as *īmān* (faith) is situated within *islām*, so the heart is situated within the breast. (For references on breast or *ṣadr* see Index III).

4. *Knowledge, faith and certainty*

In the main, Tustarī speaks of three kinds of knowledge in the *Tafsīr*: 'knowledge' (*ʿilm*), 'gnosis' or 'mystical knowledge' (*maʿrifa*), and 'understanding' (*fahm*), although in a few contexts he also mentions 'wisdom' (*ḥikma*).

Gnosis (*maʿrifa*) differs from knowledge and understanding in that its locus is, as Tustarī consistently states, the heart (*qalb*). The 'light of gnosis' was, as we saw, a 'deposit from God' within the heart, along with faith. Conversely, he describes the nature of vengeance which God took on those who angered Him [43:55] as being: '[His] removal of the light of gnosis (*nūr al-maʿrifa*) from their hearts, the lamp of the realisation of [His] oneness (*sirāj al-tawḥīd*) from their innermost secrets (*asrār*), and entrusting them to their own selves.' Thus gnosis cannot be acquired through one's own efforts, but is granted by God. Like other Sufi authors, Tustarī understands *maʿrifa* to be the experiential, mystical apprehension of God or of the divine mysteries. He also extends gnosis to include the inner meanings of the Qurʾān,[179] and to the signs or portents of God in creation and within the human being. Thus in his commentary on the words *and in yourselves too [are signs], do you not see?* [51:21], he cites a tradition according to which God has created within the soul of the son of Adam one thousand and eighty portents, three hundred and sixty of which are apparent and three hundred and sixty of which are hidden, and revealed only to a prophet or veracious person, and he adds:

> Truly God, Exalted is He, has veiled the hearts of those who are heedless (*ghāfilūn*) from His remembrance due to their pursuance of lusts, which [prevent them] from perceiving these portents. However, He has unveiled them to the hearts of those who have gnosis of Him (*ʿārifūn*), thereby causing them to attain it [sincerity].

Tustarī shows gnosis (*maʿrifa*) to be beyond knowledge (*ʿilm*), as is indicated when he glosses the words, *but only those understand them [the similitudes] who know* [29:43] with the words, 'that is, those who have knowledge (*ʿilm*) of God, Exalted is He, and especially those who have gnosis (*maʿrifa*) of Him.' Moreover, he states that it is by granting gnosis that God elevates the rank of whomever He wills.[180] This principle is endorsed when he comments on the words, *And on the Heights are men* [7:46], and indicates that another dimension of gnosis is the knowledge of the inner states of men:

> The People of the Heights are the people of gnosis (*maʿrifa*). God, Exalted is He, said: ...*who know each by their mark* [7:47]. Their standing is due to the honour (*sharaf*) they enjoy in the two abodes and with the inhabitants of both...[God] honoured them by allowing them to see into the secrets of His servants and their states in this world.

Tustarī also teaches that the attainment of *maʿrifa* is associated with the experience of suffering and need. For example, he states, 'Truly affliction is a doorway between the people of gnosis (*ahl al-maʿrifa*) and God, Mighty and Majestic is He',[181] and exhorts his disciples:

> Say in your supplication (*duʿāʾ*): 'O my Lord, if you cook me, I'll bear it and if you roast me, I'll be happy. It is essential that You be known, so favour me with gnosis (*maʿrifa*) of You.'[182]

---

179 IC, p. 6.

180 *Tafsīr*, 40:15.

181 *Tafsīr*, 29:1, 2.

182 *Tafsīr*, 21:83. See also the commentary on 47:38, where Tustarī states that gnosis of the secret [divine] mystery is to be found entirely through a sense of neediness (*faqr*) [for God].

Understanding (*fahm*) is, like gnosis (*maʿrifa*), shown in the *Tafsīr* to be an aspect of esoteric knowledge, though unlike gnosis its locus is the intellect (*ʿaql*), as can be seen in the many cases when Tustarī speaks of the three allied tendencies of the spiritual self (*nafs al-rūḥ*), the understanding of the intellect (*fahm al-ʿaql*) and the discernment of the heart (*fiṭnat al-qalb*).[183] In this sense, understanding is among the pre-eternal gifts from God which assist the human being in overwhelming the natural or lower self:

> He [God] said, 'Truly, We gave ascendancy (*sallaṭnā*) over your dense natural self to the subtle [substances] (*laṭāʾif*) of your spiritual self, intellect, heart, and understanding (*fahm*), all of which pre-existed as a momentous gift (*mawhiba jalīla*) before the creation appeared by a thousand years, and thus did they subdue the natural self.[184]

Often, however, the term 'understanding' (*fahm*) is employed in a particular sense that is associated with the Qurʾān,[185] and indeed, in the Introduction to the Commentary there is a separate section devoted to those who 'seek the understanding of the Qurʾān (*fahm al-Qurʾān*)'. In this section, understanding is shown to be, on the one hand, a full and wholehearted grasping of the meanings of the Qurʾān, and particularly of its commands and prohibitions, as when Tustarī states: 'they have no way to Him save through the Qurʾān, and through understanding [all] that has been addressed to them therein concerning that which is required of them…';[186] On the other hand, understanding is often more specifically associated with the comprehension of the inner meanings of the Qurʾān. In the same section of his introduction, he speaks of God's teaching the Qurʾān to His friends, both in its outer and inner aspects, and as was mentioned above, when asked by his disciples what he means by its 'inner aspects', he replies, 'That is its understanding (*fahm*); and it is its understanding that is intended.'[187] It will also be recalled that in Tustarī's definition of four levels of meaning in the Qurʾān, he equated understanding (*fahm*) with the inward sense (*bāṭin*).[188] Like gnosis, understanding is granted as a grace from God. Thus, commenting on *the similitudes that We strike for the sake of mankind* [29:43], he states:

> The similitudes which God strikes for man are available for everyone [to see], since the evidences of [His] omnipotence (*qudra*) are [in themselves] proof of the [existence of] the Omnipotent. However, it is only His elect (*khāṣṣa*) who fully understand them. Thus, knowledge is rare and understanding granted by God (*fiqh ʿan Allāh*) even rarer.

However, the prerequisite for such a bestowal from God is fulfilment of what is commanded by Him, as Tustarī states:

> There are those who have been granted understanding by virtue of their maintaining the practice of what is commanded and the avoidance of what is forbidden, both inwardly and outwardly, and by their affirmation of it [the Qurʾān] with the light of the insight of certainty (*nūr baṣīrat al-yaqīn*)…[189]

Interestingly, Tustarī also points out that human understanding (*fahm*) has limits — as does the intellect (*ʿaql*), which will be discussed below, whereas he does not mention limits with regard to gnosis (*maʿrifa*). In the Introduction to the Commentary he states about the Qurʾān, 'It is that which is beautifully ordered in its outward form and profound in its inner meaning. It is, moreover, that before which all understanding (*fahm*) is powerless.'[190] As we saw above, he also describes a state that is beyond understanding:

---

183 See section 1 and diagram above.

184 *Tafsīr*, 94:5. Note that the understanding of the intellect was also present with the spiritual self and the discernment of the heart at the Covenant of *Alast*, without the presence of the natural self. See above, p. xl.

185 As, for example, in the commentary on 2:269, 3:7, 7:146, 29:43.

186 IC, p. 5. See also the commentary on 19:61.

187 IC, p. 7.

188 IC, p. 2.

189 IC, p. 3, as also is indicated in the commentary on the *Basmala*, IC, pp. 8–9. Conversely, acting arrogantly can result in a person's being deprived of the knowledge of the Qurʾān, as is shown in Tustarī's commentary on 7:146.

190 IC, p. 1.

> The one who is close (*qarīb*) [to God] has access to understanding (*fahm*), conjecture (*wahm*) and interpretation (*tafsīr*). But the one who is closest (*aqrab*) is beyond understanding, conjecture and interpretation, and what is beyond that cannot be contained by expression (*ʿibāra*) or allusion (*ishāra*).[191]

The term 'knowledge' (*ʿilm*) is employed in a number of ways in Tustarī's *Tafsīr*. In some instances, he uses it in a general way when it is opposed to ignorance, as when he comments on the words, *And He appointed darknesses and light* [6:1], and states that its inner meaning is that 'light is knowledge (*ʿilm*) and darkness is ignorance (*jahl*)';[192] or when he comments on 35:32, *Yet among them is the one who has wronged himself* (ẓālim), *the one who is moderate* (muqtaṣid) *and the one who is foremost in good deeds* (ṣābiq), where he interprets the *foremost* as the one who is learned (*ʿālim*); the *midmost* as the one who is learning (*mutaʿallim*), and the *one who has wronged himself* as the one who is ignorant (*jāhil*). In another context he uses the metaphor of life and death, when he contrasts people's knowledge with their ignorance of themselves (by which he means, perhaps, ignorance of their true human responsibility of realising the oneness of God):

> God, Exalted is He, created all creatures. Then He brought them to life by the name of life. Then He caused them to die by their ignorance of themselves. Those who live through knowledge are the living; otherwise they are dead through their ignorance.[193]

Usually, however, Tustarī applies the word *ʿilm* to an 'outer' knowledge of the oneness of God, of His commands and prohibitions and of the Sunna of the Prophet, as is evidenced by his admonitions concerning the need to put such knowledge into practice. Indeed, he repeatedly asserts that without being implemented, knowledge is not merely without benefit, it is detrimental, as when he states:

> This whole world consists of ignorance except for where knowledge is to be found. All knowledge is a testimony against [the one who possesses it], except for that which is acted upon.[194]

And again:

> Every possessor of knowledge (*ʿālim*) who has been given knowledge of evil but does not avoid it is not a [true] possessor of knowledge. Similarly, whoever has been given knowledge of the acts of obedience but does not practise them is not a [true] possessor of knowledge.[195]

In a number of contexts, he also warns of the uselessness or danger of knowledge that is attained for purely worldly reasons. Here he is contrasting two attitudes among those who have an understanding of the Qurʾān:

> There are but two [kinds of] men who understand the Word [of God]: the first wants to understand so he can speak about it from a position [of authority], and his lot is nothing but that; the other hears it and is occupied with acting upon it to the exclusion of all else. This person is rarer than red sulphur (*al-kibrīt al-aḥmar*) and more precious than all that is dear.[196]

In another context, it is related that a certain Abū Ḥamza al-Ṣūfī visited Tustarī and discussed with him the subject of intoxication. He informed Tustarī that he had heard it said that intoxication was of four kinds: 'The intoxication of drink, the intoxication of youth, the intoxication of wealth and the intoxication of authority.' To this Tustarī replies:

> There are two kinds of intoxication about which he did not inform you…: the intoxication of the scholar who loves this world, and the intoxication of the worshipper who loves to be noticed.[197]

The locus of knowledge is, according to Tustarī, the intellect (*ʿaql*):

---

191 *Tafsīr*, 2:260.

192 The verse is cited in his commentary on 3:106, in which he actually links knowledge to belief, and ignorance to disbelief.

193 *Tafsīr*, 16:21.

194 *Tafsīr*, 4:77.

195 *Tafsīr*, 11:88.

196 *Tafsīr*, 19:61.

197 *Tafsīr*, 16:67. See also his commentary on 23:17, where among seven veils which veil the believer from God, knowledge is named because of the vainglory it breeds among peers.

> Know that God, Exalted is He, when He wished to make His knowledge apparent, deposited His knowledge in the intellect (*ʿaql*). Then He ruled that no one could have access to any of it [His knowledge] except through the intellect. Thus whoever has been deprived of his intellect has also been deprived of knowledge.[198]

Tustarī's saying that no one can have access to God's knowledge 'except through the intellect' is an indication that he understands the intellect to be more than simply a repository of knowledge. In fact, the intellect has its own particular function, as can be seen in the many instances when the intellect or 'understanding of the intellect (*fahm al-ʿaql*)' is associated with the spiritual self and the heart.

It was seen that the heart should not be allowed to acquiesce in the desires of the lower self,[199] but this does not indicate a dual nature for the heart. The intellect, however, does have a dual nature, according to Tustarī. Included in the context of 33:4, *God has not placed two hearts inside any man*, is the following observation:

> [That is, he does not have] one heart with which he approaches God, and another heart with which he manages the affairs of this world. [On the other hand], the intellect (*ʿaql*) does have two natures (*ṭabʿān*): a nature which is orientated towards this world, and a nature which is orientated towards the Hereafter (*ākhira*). The nature which is orientated towards the Hereafter is in coalition (*muʾtalif*) with the spiritual self (*nafs al-rūḥ*), whereas the worldly-orientated nature is in coalition with the lustful self (*nafs shahwāniyya*).

The side of the intellect that is oriented towards the Hereafter, therefore, has a key role to play in relation to the heart. In another part of his commentary on 3:28, Tustarī explains:

> If [the servant] is involved in an act [motivated by] his lower self, and something comes to his heart which guides him to remembrance and obedience, that is the role played by the intellect (*mawḍiʿ al-ʿaql*).

This may be partly where the believer's answerability will lie, when at the Resurrection he is questioned in relation to what he owes his intellect.[200]

Yet, despite the important role of *ʿaql*, the servant must also recognise its limitations. In his discussion of the *locks on the heart* mentioned in 47:24, Tustarī explains that when God created the hearts He secured them with locks. The keys to those locks were the realities of faith, and the only ones who were vouchsafed the opening of their hearts through those realities were [God's] friends (*awliyāʾ*), messengers (*rusul*) ﷺ, and the veracious (*ṣiddīqūn*). The rest of people leave this world without the locks on their hearts being opened. He then adds:

> The renunciants (*zuhhād*),[201] devout worshippers (*ʿubbād*), and scholars (*ʿulamāʾ*) will leave this world with locked hearts because they sought the keys to them with the intellect (*ʿaql*), and thus strayed from the path. If only they had sought them by having recourse to divinely-bestowed success (*tawfīq*) and grace (*faḍl*), they would have attained them [the keys].

In his commentary on the words, *And He creates what you do not know [about]* [16:8], he states:

> The inner meaning of these words [is that] God, Mighty and Majestic is He, has taught you to restrain yourself when your intellect (*ʿaql*) fails to grasp the effects of His creation and the multifarious dimensions of [His] knowledge, so that it [your intellect] does not meet it with denial, for He has created what you do not know about, neither you nor anyone else among His creatures except those whom God has taught, Mighty and Majestic is He.

---

198 *Tafsīr*, 16:12.

199 As was discussed above in relation to Adam's banishment from Paradise, above p. xxxv.

200 See above, p. xxxvi.

201 The term *zuhd* is often translated as asceticism, though it is more precisely a renunciation and disdain for the world. Michael Cooperson, in his book *Classical Arabic Biography: The Heirs of the Prophets in the Age of al-Maʾmūn* (Cambridge, 2000), has coined the word 'renunciant' as a translation of the word *zāhid* (pl. *zuhhād*).

As can be seen from the two passages above, Tustarī teaches that there is a knowledge of unseen things or realities which God imparts not to all, but to a select few of His creatures.[202] In another context, when he is commenting on *those who are rooted in knowledge* (al-rāsikhūna fī'l-ʿilm), mentioned in 3:7, he discusses three categories of knowledge and four different ways in which God imparts knowledge (and here the term knowledge [*ʿilm*] is clearly not being restricted to an outer level). He observes that *those rooted in knowledge* are shown to be exceptional because of their saying, according to the verse: '*All is from our Lord*', and he then explains that they (the *rāsikhūna fī'l-ʿilm*) reveal three kinds of knowledge, since those who know may be designated in three ways: *rabbāniyyūn, nurāniyyūn* and *dhātiyyūn*. The precise nature of the connection Tustarī intends between each of these kinds of knowers and the divine lordliness, light and essence is not made clear by these allusive terms.[203] However, given that he has specified about these three kinds of knowers of God that they say, '*All is from our Lord*', we might render them somewhat freely as: 'those whose knowledge derives from, or is through, the divine lordliness, light and essence', respectively.[204] Another approach would be to interpret these three designations of knowledge as being manifestations of the divine lordliness, light and essence.[205] Tustarī discusses these three categories of knowers of God (*rabbāniyyūn, nurāniyyūn* and *dhātiyyūn*) once more in his commentary on 3:79, with a particular focus on the *rabbānī*. Here again the context suggests a kind of knowledge that is received directly from God, a knowledge through God's knowledge, which Tustarī here subtly compares to prophetic knowledge. Thus he cites the Qurʾānic words, *She asked, 'Who told you this?' He said, 'I was told by the All-Knowing, the Aware'* [66:3], and adds, 'Anyone who informs you of something which conforms to the Book and the Sunna, is 'an informant' (*munbiʾ*)'. Hence Tustarī is also suggesting that an aspect of the *rabbānī* knowledge is its transmission to others, and this is confirmed by a saying of ʿAlī b. Abī Ṭālib that he cites in this context, where the 'knower whose knowledge derives from the divine lordliness' (*ʿālim rabbānī*) is contrasted with 'the one acquiring knowledge' (*mutaʿallim*). Returning to his commentary on 3:7, we find that after Tustarī has discussed three of the highest modes of knowing, or of receiving knowledge from God, he then presents a different scheme comprising four modes of divinely-bestowed knowledge. These are: revelation (*waḥy*), theophany (*tajallī*), 'knowledge directly bestowed by God' (*ʿindī*) and 'knowledge from the divine presence' (*ladunnī*).

---

202 This was also mentioned above in relation to the understanding of the inner meanings of the Qurʾān. See above, p. xxvii.

203 Böwering's translation of the three designations in his *Mystical Vision* (pp. 227–9) reads: 'those who perceive God as Lord, those who perceive God as Light and those who perceive God as Essence'.

204 The idea of 'knowing' or 'perceiving' the essence of God is problematic, since not only theologians but most Sufis consider the divine essence to be unknowable. In other instances in the *Tafsīr*, when mentioning some connection with the divine essence, Tustarī appears to be cautious, as in his discussions of certainty (*Tafsīr*, 2:40 and 41), which will be discussed below. A passage quoted from Tustarī in the chapter on *Tawḥīd* in Qushayrī's *Risāla* may be helpful here: 'The essence of God may be characterised (*mawṣūfa*) through knowledge (*ʿilm*), not grasped through comprehension (*ghayr mudraka bi'l-iḥāṭa*), nor seen by human eyes (*marʾiya bi'l-abṣār*) in this world, though it is found (*mawjūda*) through the realities of faith (*ḥaqāʾiq al-īmān*), without any limit (*ḥadd*), comprehending (*iḥāṭa*) or indwelling (*ḥulūl*). In the Hereafter eyes will see it manifested in His dominion and omnipotence. He has veiled the creatures from gnosis (*maʿrifa*) of the profundity (*kunh*) of His essence, but He gives them an indication to it (*dallahum ʿalayhi*) by His signs…' Qushayrī, *Risāla*, p. 565.

205 In Chapter 58 of the *Kitāb al-Taʿarruf*, 'On Manifestation (or theophany, *tajallī*) and Veiling (*istitār*)', Kalābādhī opens his discourse with the following saying attributed to Tustarī: 'Manifestation has three 'degrees' (*aḥwāl*): a manifestation of [the] essence (*dhāt*), which is unveiling (*mukāshafa*); a manifestation of the attributes of the essence (*ṣifāt al-dhāt*), which is illumination (*mawḍiʿ al-nūr*); and a manifestation of the decree [or power] of the essence (*ḥukm al-dhāt*), which is the Hereafter and what it entails.' See also the *Qūt al-qulūb*, vol. 2, pp. 142–3, where Makkī states that God has 'elevated His essence above hearts (*qulūb*) and [modes of] thought (*afkār*); it can neither be imagined through the intellect (*ʿaql*) nor depicted through thought (*fikr*) lest fanciful supposition (*wahm*) should take hold of it.' He continues by saying that God's essence cannot be contemplated by any thought, understood by any intellect or perceived by any comprehension, unless or until it be by a manifestation (*tajallī*) through His beneficence (*iḥsān*), as in the first place He had manifested [it] through His loving compassion (*ḥanān*). This manifestation, Makkī states, may be to His friends today (i.e. in this life) through the lights of certainty (*anwār al-yaqīn*) in [their] hearts, whereas it will be a visual beholding of the eyes (*muʿāyanat al-abṣār*) tomorrow (in the Hereafter).

Tustarī speaks of divinely-bestowed knowledge in other contexts, often using the image of light, where knowledge is particularly associated with guidance from God. For example, in the Introduction to the Commentary he is quoted as saying, 'According to the measure of light which has been allotted to a person by God, Exalted is He, he will find guidance for his heart and insight (*baṣīra*).'[206] In his commentary on the words, *Those are upon guidance from their Lord* [2:5], he states:

> By the light of His guidance hearts witness Him in confident abandonment to Him due to a light from His light, by which He singled them out in His pre-eternal knowledge. Thus they do not speak except with guidance, and their inner perception is solely directed towards that guidance. So those who are guided by [this light] are never left by it. Thus they are [constant] witnesses to it because they are never absent from it.

Tustarī also speaks of his own experience of this direct guidance from God, as when he states, as noted above, 'Indeed, God willing, I have been granted wisdom and [knowledge of] the unseen which I was taught from the unseen of His secret (*min ghayb sirrihi*), and thus He sufficed me from the need for all other knowledge…'[207]

In these passages, Tustarī is indicating a profound and arcane connection between the depths of human consciousness and God, and he consistently employs allusive terms to describe such mystical experiences, as, for example in the following statement:

> In reality, the servant only beholds (*yanẓuru*) God by means of a subtle 'substance' (*laṭīfa*), through its connection to his heart. This subtle substance pertains to the attributes of the Essence of his Lord. It is neither brought into being (*mukawwana*), nor created (*makhlūqa*), neither conjunct [with God] (*mawṣūla*), nor cut off [from Him] (*maqṭūʿa*). It is a secret (*sirr*) from a secret to a secret, an unseen [mystery] (*ghayb*) from an unseen to an unseen.[208]

We find an analogous mode of expression in Tustarī's discussions of certainty (*yaqīn*). Thus in the continuation of the above passage, he states:

> Certainty (*yaqīn*) is through God, and the servant finds certainty due to a cause (*sabab*) that comes directly from Him to the servant, according to the measure of the gifts that God has apportioned him, and the wholeness of his innermost heart (*suwaydāʾ qalbihi*).

Tustarī discusses certainty in a number of passages in the *Tafsīr*, showing it to be beyond knowledge, and to be an advanced form of faith. Certainty also has degrees. Thus in the context of his commentary on Abraham's request that God show him how He gives life to the dead [2:260], Tustarī is asked if Abraham was in doubt concerning his faith, and was therefore making this request of God in order to restore his faith, he answers:

> His question was not out of doubt; he was merely asking for an increase in certainty (*ziyāda yaqīn*) to the faith he already had. Thus he asked for an unveiling of the cover of visual beholding with his physical eyes, so that by the light of certainty, his own certainty regarding God's omnipotence might be increased, and [his certainty] regarding His creative [power] might be consolidated... [Therefore] the request for profound peace of mind (*ṭumaʾnīna*) signified a request for an increase in his certainty.

A detailed explanation of the degrees of certainty and its relation to faith is outlined when Tustarī comments on the word *rahba*, meaning 'awe' in 2:40. He observes that endurance and struggle are part of faith when it is 'for the sake of' God (*īmān li'Llāh*). But when the heart ceases to have fear of any other than God, and is therefore in a state of true awe (*rahba*) towards Him, then the light of certainty is unveiled. Then the servant, who had been abiding in faith 'for the sake of' God, attains the level of faith 'through' God (*īmān bi'Llāh*). At this level, his affirmation of the oneness of God has reached a point of stability, and his heart is in a state of tranquil and confident repose with God. Then he is taken to a deeper realisation of certainty when, as Tustarī explains, 'the light of certainty (*nūr al-yaqīn*) unveils the knowledge of the eye of certainty (*ʿilm ʿayn al-yaqīn*) and

206 IC, p. 4.

207 *Tafsīr*, 2:3.

208 *Tafsīr*, 2:41.

this is the attainment of God.'[209] But this certainty that leads to the eye of certainty is not something that is brought into being (*mukawwan*) or created (*makhlūq*); it is rather 'a light from the light of the essence of God'. Here, lest he be misunderstood, Tustarī adds that what he means by this is not any 'indwelling (*ḥulūl*), conjoining (*jamʿ*) or conjunction (*ittiṣāl*) with God; rather it is due to the true realisation of God's oneness (*tawḥīd*) and obedience to God and His Prophet'. He further explains that according to the strength of the servant's perception (*baṣar*) of God (i.e. his certainty), he will attain both awe (*rahba*) and full awareness of God (*taqwā*). We also find that he associates the 'eye of certainty' with a wholeness, an 'all-ness' or entirety of perception — on three occasions when he speaks of *ʿayn al-yaqīn* he follows it with the words *wa kulliyyatihi*.[210] Tustarī sums up the importance of certainty at the end of this passage when he states:

> Know that human beings will vary in rank on the Day of Resurrection according to the measure of the light of certainty that they possess. The weightier the certainty a person has, the heavier will his scales weigh [in his favour], even though there might [otherwise] be less in his scales.

F. The Spiritual Path

1. Precepts and proprieties

In the preceding sections we have discussed some passages in which Tustarī shows glimpses of the experiences of certainty and mystical unveiling that might be encountered by those who are advanced on the spiritual path. But in the *Tafsīr* we also find numerous passages in which he presents instruction for aspirants, to guide them from the most elementary stages through to the highest attainments of the Way.

All important is, of course, the opposing and controlling of the lower self (*nafs*) and its desires, which was alluded to in some passages on spiritual psychology discussed above. The following is an example of a specific exhortation to control the self (or lower or natural self), which constitutes a metaphorical interpretation of the words, *It is He who has made the earth tractable for you…* [67:15]:

> God, Exalted is He, created the souls in a humble state. Whoever subdues (*adhalla*) his self by opposing it, actually saves it from temptations, tribulations and trials. However, whoever debases (*adhalla*) his self and follows it, will be brought to humiliation and destroyed by it.

In other passages, Tustarī interprets holy war (*jihād*) as the struggle or battle with the lower self. Thus, he states:

> All forms of obedience to God involve struggle with the lower self (*jihād al-nafs*). There is no struggle easier than the struggle with swords, and no struggle harder than opposing the lower self.[211]

When someone asked him, 'I have wealth and strength and I want to perform *jihād*. What do you command me to do?' he answered:

> Wealth is knowledge (*ʿilm*), strength is intention (*nīya*) and *jihād* is the struggle with the lower self (*mujāhadat al-nafs*).[212]

---

209 Here also Tustarī is clearly not using the term *ʿilm* in an outer sense. The juxtaposition of the 'knowledge of certainty' (*ʿilm al-yaqīn*) and the 'eye of certainy' (*ʿayn al-yaqīn*) have their origin in the Qurʾān 102:5 and 7, and in the latter verse the expression *ʿayn al-yaqīn* is actually used, and suggests a degree of certainty that is as direct and immediate as seeing with the eyes (see the passage cited above, p. xxxvii, regarding the meaning of the expression of *ʿiyān al-ʿiyān* derived from the same verbal root *ʿ-y-n*). In later Islamic mysticism a further degree of certainty was added, that of the 'truth of certainty' (*ḥaqq al-yaqīn*), an expression that is also to be found in the Qurʾān, 56:95 and 69:51. On the development of terminology denoting different levels of experienced or realised truth and certainty, see Nasrollah Pourjavady, 'Parvāna u ātash: sayr-i taḥawwul-i yik tamthīl-i ʿirfānī dar adabiyyāt-i Fārsī', *Nashr-i Dānish*, Year 16, no. 2 (1999), pp. 3–15.

210 *Tafsīr*, 2:40, 41; 102:7.

211 *Tafsīr*, 8:72.

212 *Tafsīr*, 16:110.

In another metaphorical interpretation, this time of the words, *O Prophet, struggle against the disbelievers and the hypocrites* [9:73], he states:

> Struggle against your lower self with the sword of opposition! Place upon its [back] the burdens of remorse (*nadam*), and guide it through the desert plains of fear (*khawf*), so that you may turn it back to the path of repentance (*tawba*) and contrition (*ināba*). Repentance is not acceptable save from one who feels perplexed at his concerns, and grief-stricken at heart due to what has befallen him.

In the latter passage Tustarī has associated opposing the lower self with repentance. Like other Sufis, he sees repentance (*tawba*) as an initial step on the way,[213] and so he says, 'The first thing that a novice is instructed to do is to change his reprehensible actions into praiseworthy ones, which is repentance.'[214] However, in his commentary on this same verse [9:112] he insists that repentance should be perpetual:

> Of the rights [due to God] in this world there is none whose fulfilment is more incumbent upon humanity than repentance. Indeed it is obligatory [for them] at every moment and instant, and there is no punishment severer on them than the lack of knowledge of repentance.[215]

In a similar vein, he emphasises the need for vigilance and self scrutiny. For example, he states:

> The real believer is the one who is not heedless of his lower self and his heart, but scrutinises his states (*aḥwāl*), and keeps a close watch over his moments (*awqāt*). He observes his increase [in a good state, distinguishing it] from his decline, and shows gratitude on seeing an increase, but when there is a decline devotes himself [to remedying it] and makes supplication.[216]

And elsewhere:

> The capital (*raʾs al-māl*) of wisdom consists of three things: the first is disciplining the lower self (*riyāḍat al-nafs*) concerning things which are reprehensible; the second is emptying one's heart of any love for carnal lusts (*shahawāt*); and the third is standing guard over one's heart by warding off [unwarranted] thoughts which occur to it (*khaṭarāt*). Moreover, whoever is mindful of God when [unwarranted] thoughts [come upon] his heart, will have [God] protect him in his bodily acts.[217]

Tustarī supplies numerous practical rules and guidelines for the spiritual life. Like many Sufis, he recommends fasting, seclusion and the night vigil, though he also advocates silence:

> All goodness comes together in four things: … an empty stomach, seclusion from people, the night vigil, and observing silence.[218]

He describes hunger as 'one of God's secrets',[219] and states, 'God, Exalted is He, created the world and placed knowledge and wisdom within hunger, and placed ignorance and transgression within satiety.'[220] Apart from these particularly rigorous disciplines, Tustarī generally advocates a simple life for aspirants. He warns against four traits that will prevent the aspirant from attaining anything: 'If he likes to eat tasty food, dress in fine clothes, see his commands executed and his possessions increase.'[221] When asked to define the proprieties of the Way he states:

---

213 In several Sufi manuals *tawba* is presented as the first stage on the Path, as for example in the *Risāla* of Qushayrī, where it is the first among the stations (*maqāmāt*), and the *Manāzil al-sāʾirīn* of ʿAbd Allāh al-Anṣārī (Cairo, 1962), where it is second only after awakening (*yaqẓa*).

214 *Tafsīr*, 9:112.

215 See above, p. xix, where Sarrāj, among others, suggested that it was Tustarī's insistence on the obligatory nature of repentance, to which the person who had him expelled from Tustar took objection.

216 *Tafsīr*, 48:25.

217 *Tafsīr*, 2:269.

218 *Tafsīr*, 10:62.

219 *Tafsīr*, 7:31.

220 ibid.

221 *Tafsīr*, 15:3.

> [It is that you should] let your food be barley, your sweetmeat dates, your condiment salt, your fat yoghurt. You should let your clothes be of wool, your houses be mosques, your source of light the sun, your lamp the moon, your perfume water, your splendour be in cleanliness and your adornment wariness (*ḥadhr*) [of God]. Moreover, you should let your work consist in being content (*irtiḍāʾ*) — or he said: contentment (*riḍā*) —, your journey's provision (*zād*) be piety, your eating be at night, your sleep in the day, your speech be remembrance (*dhikr*), your resolve (*ṣamma*) and your aspiration (*himma*) be for contemplation (*tafakkur*), your reflective thought (*naẓar*) be to take example (*ʿibra*), and your refuge (*maljaʾ*) and the one who helps you (*nāṣir*) be your Lord. Persevere in this until you die.[222]

In the above passage Tustarī has combined instructions for the practical side of life as well as giving guidelines for spiritual conduct. The *Tafsīr* also contains a great number of short passages presenting different prescriptions and formulae for the spiritual life. Just a few examples will be cited here:

> The backbone (*qiwām*) of religion and this world is in three things: knowledge (*ʿilm*), propriety (*adab*) and initiative (*mubādara*). However, the ruin of religion and this world comes from three things: ignorance (*jahl*), folly (*khurq*) and laziness (*kasal*).[223]
>
> There are four things which are among the buttresses (*daʿāʾim*) of religion: to uphold the truth even against your own self and others; to renounce falsehood in yourself or others; to love people who are obedient to God and to detest those who disobey Him.[224]

Here he lists six vices and six virtues:

> The servant will not get the taste of faith until he quits six vices [lit. character traits, *khiṣāl*]: he should quit what is forbidden (*ḥarām*), illegal possessions (*suḥut*), what is dubious (*shubha*), ignorance (*jahl*), intoxicant[s] (*muskir*), and ostentation (*riyāʾ*); [on the other hand] he should adhere to [six virtues]: knowledge (*ʿilm*), putting his actions right (*taṣḥīḥ al-ʿamal*), integrity of heart (*naṣḥ bi'l-qalb*), veracity of the tongue (*ṣidq bi'l-lisān*), correct conduct (*ṣalāḥ*) in associating with people, and sincerity (*ikhlāṣ*) in the way he deals with his Lord.[225]

And here he outlines the fundamentals of worship:

> The basis of worship is the profession of God's oneness (*tawḥīd*) along with living according to what is lawful, while avoiding the harm [of others] (*kaff al-adhā*). Furthermore, a person cannot accomplish living by what is lawful without abandoning the harm of others, and likewise he does not abandon causing harm save through living by what is lawful. If you know how to abide by what is lawful, how to abandon causing harm, and the [correct] intention (*nīya*) behind actions, as well as you know the *Fātiḥa*, then your faith will become pure, as will your hearts and bodily members. Indeed, these are the fundamentals.[226]

And here he defines three modes of excellence:

> The most ascetic (*azhad*) of people are those who have the purest source of food; the most devout (*abʿad*) of people are those who are most earnest in their effort to uphold His commandments and prohibitions; and the most beloved (*aḥabb*) of them to God are those who are the sincerest (*anṣaḥuhum*) towards His creatures.[227]

Noticeable among these precepts and guidelines is Tustarī's concern with correct conduct towards others, and avoidance of harm to them. In other passages he specifically focuses on this. For example, he states:

---

222 *Tafsīr*, 7:172.

223 *Tafsīr*, 4:171.

224 ibid.

225 *Tafsīr*, 48:25.

226 *Tafsīr*, 3:64. The *Fātiḥa* is the first *sūra* of the Qurʾān, which is recited in each *rakʿa* of the canonical prayer.

227 *Tafsīr*, 6:52.

> The earth will not consume the body of anyone who keeps the following three qualities: refraining from harming people, bearing the harm that comes from them and doing good to them.[228]

And here he states the same idea, this time using the earth as a simile.

> Know that the servant does not attain true faith (*ḥaqīqat al-īmān*) until he becomes as the earth for the servants of God — it endures the suffering that they [impose] upon it and they [derive] benefits from it.[229]

Tustarī also warns more than once against judging or criticising others. For example, he observes:

> No one looks upon the slips of [other] people except an ignorant wrongdoer, and no one [may] make known that which he has looked upon [of the faults of others] except God.[230]

In his commentary on the words *and shun much suspicion* [49:12], he further warns against holding a 'bad opinion' (*sūʾ al-ẓann*) of others, and when asked to explain in this context a *ḥadīth* of the Prophet, 'Be on your guard with people, [by holding a] bad opinion (*sūʾ al-ẓann*)', he replies:

> The meaning of this is [that protection from people] is [through holding a] bad opinion of yourself, not of other people. In other words, accuse your own self for not treating them fairly in your dealings with them.

He continues with an explanation of the psychology of 'bad opinion', in which he mentions not only holding a bad opinion of other human beings, but also of God:

> Bad opinion comes from ignorance and pertains to the natural self (*nafs al-ṭabʿ*). The most ignorant person is the one who estranges his heart [from God] without being aware of it. Indeed, God, Exalted is He, has said: *And that suspicion of yours which you held about your Lord has ruined you, so you have become among the losers* [41:23]. Certainly, the servant is deprived of blessed provision and prayer at night because of bad opinion.

The rewards for holding a 'good or beautiful opinion' (*ḥusn al-ẓann*) of God, however, are immense, as Tustarī shows. He discusses *ḥusn al-ẓann* in two quite different ways. The first occurs in the context of a discussion of God's forgiveness in the commentary on 4:48:

> If no one has any grievance against him, and his sins are only between him and God, Exalted is He, indeed He forgives those sins, for He is the Magnanimous, the Generous. It has been related from the Prophet ﷺ that he said, 'A servant may be brought forward on the Day of Resurrection and directed to the Fire, but then he will say, 'This is not in accordance with what I supposed [my outcome would be].'[231] Then God, Mighty and Majestic is He, will ask, 'What was your opinion of Me?' to which he will reply, 'That You would forgive me', upon which God, Mighty and Majestic is He, will say, 'Truly I have forgiven you', and He will direct him to Paradise.

Here, *ḥusn al-ẓann* is being shown as the means to salvation in the Hereafter, but in another context in the *Tafsīr*, *ḥusn al-ẓann* is shown to be the means to the most immediate experience of proximity with God. This particular, mystical understanding of *ḥusn al-ẓann* is presented in the poem which was already cited above, the first line of which indicates that 'good opinion' can be a means to 'direct or face-to-face encounter' (*kifāḥ*) with God, and that it traverses every veil. The first two couplets of this allusive and evocative poem may be rendered as follows:

> The abundant sufficiency (*kifāyāt*) of direct encounter [with God] (*kifāḥ*),
> [attained] through my good opinion of Him,
> Is like the spider's web covering the cave's entrance.
> Good opinion has traversed every veil,
> Good opinion has traversed beyond the light of fire[232]

---

228 *Tafsīr*, 76:5.

229 *Tafsīr*, 9:71.

230 *Tafsīr*, 83:1. See also the commentary on 49:12.

231 lit. 'This is not in accordance with my opinion (*mā kadhā ẓannī*).'

232 The poem follows the commentary on 2:260.

The meaning of *ḥusn al-ẓann* here is not clear, though it might be described as the soul's being predisposed for complete reliance upon, and confidence in, God. This may also be seen in another context where Tustarī links *ḥusn al-ẓann* with certainty (*yaqīn*).[233] When asked how one might know the soundness of a person's certainty he replies, 'By the strength of his confidence (*thiqa*) in God, Exalted is He, and his good opinion (*ḥusn al-ẓann*) of Him'.[234] *Ḥusn al-ẓann* is thus the soul's reaching a state of complete readiness, openness and receptivity, a state in which God may suffice for it in bringing it to Him. So Tustarī cites a tradition of the Prophet:

> 'Yesterday I saw an amazing thing; a servant between whom and God there was a veil, but then when his good opinion of God appeared, He drew him in from behind the veil'.[235]

2. *Emulation and aspiration*

Tustarī often speaks of the importance of emulation (*iqtidāʾ*) without always mentioning who is to be emulated and whose example is to be followed. Clearly, the first example to be followed is the Prophet through his Sunna, as Tustarī emphasises on many occasions, including the following:

> The believer has one face, without a reverse side; he makes repeated [advances] and never retreats. You will see him striving for the cause of God's religion and His obedience, upholding God's oneness and the following of His Prophet ﷺ, constantly making humble entreaty of God and seeking refuge in Him in the hope of connecting to Him through following [exemplary guidance] (*iqdidāʾ*).[236]

However, in the following passage he does not state who is to be followed:

> The livelihood (*ʿaysh*) of angels is in obedience (*ṭāʿa*); the livelihood of the prophets is in knowledge and waiting for relief; and the livelihood of the veracious (*ṣiddīqūn*) is in emulation (*iqtidāʾ*).[237]

While Tustarī shows the Prophet to be the supreme model for the believers, he also describes others whom he wishes to be seen as examples to be emulated. In some cases, he indicates their position in the spiritual hierarchy among successors to the Prophet, as when he observes that the veracious (*ṣiddīqūn*) are 'heirs to the secrets of their [the prophets'] sciences'.[238] They have attained the stage in which they speak only in four ways: 'in God, through God, for God and with God'. He understands *the foremost* mentioned in 56:10, as follows:

> They are those for whom God's election (*ikhtiyār*) and special friendship (*wilāya*) preceded them before they were even brought into existence. *The ones who are brought near [to God]* [56:11] are in stations of proximity (*manāzil al-qurb*), and [enjoy] the ease of intimacy (*rawḥ al-uns*). They are the ones who were the foremost (*sabaqū*) in this life. The prophets were the foremost in having faith in God. The veracious (*ṣiddīqūn*) and martyrs (*shuhadāʾ*) among the Companions and others were the foremost in having faith in the prophets.

In another passage it is those who are sincere and mindful of God (*al-mukhliṣūn al-muttaqūn*) who are portrayed as the best among the community:

> The best among people are the Muslims, the best among Muslims are the [true] believers, the best among believers are the scholars who act upon their knowledge, the best among those who act [upon their knowledge] are the fearful (*khāʾifūn*), and the best among the fearful are those who are sincere and mindful of God (*al-mukhliṣūn al-muttaqūn*), whose sincerity and mindfulness of God remains with them up until their death.[239]

---

233 And it is worth noting that the poem itself occurs as part of Tustarī's lengthy commentary on 2:260, which discusses Abraham's desire for an increase in certainty. See above, IT, p. xlviii.

234 *Tafsīr*, 2:40.

235 *Tafsīr*, 2:260.

236 *Tafsīr*, 22:11.

237 *Tafsīr*, 2:197.

238 *Tafsīr*, 58:22.

239 *Tafsīr*, 48:26.

A part of emulation is the desire to be close to those who have attained proximity with God, to whom Tustarī often refers as the 'friends' (*awliyāʾ*) of God. Thus, in his commentary on part of the prayer of Solomon, *and include me, by Your mercy, among Your righteous servants* [27:19], he explains:

> This means, 'Grant me proximity to Your friends (*awliyāʾ*) so that I may be among their company, even though I have not reached their station (*maqām*)'.

We have seen also that in his commentary on 7:172, Tustarī explains that the seekers (*murīdūn*) were created from the light of Adam ﷺ, while the [divinely] sought (*murādūn*) were created from the light of Muḥammad ﷺ. Following this statement he observes:

> Thus, the generality among people live under the mercy of the people of proximity (*ahl al-qurb*) and the people of proximity live under the mercy of the one brought near (*al-muqarrab*) — *With their light shining forth before them and on their right* [57:12].[240]

Apart from passages which exhort seekers to emulate, or keep close to, those who have attained spiritual perfection, friendship and proximity with God, there are also passages which describe qualities and virtues to which they should aspire, such as veracity (*ṣidq*),[241] patience or forbearance (*ṣabr*),[242] and humility. On the virtue of the latter he states that 'pure servanthood is self-abasement (*dhull*) and humble submission (*khushūʿ*)',[243] while in his commentary on the story of Korah (Qārūn) he states:

> The fortunate person (*saʿīd*) is he who averts his eye from [looking upon] his states and acts; to him is opened the way of receiving grace (*faḍl*) and being gracious to [others] (*ifḍāl*), whilst keeping sight of God's favour in [the accomplishment of] all acts.[244]

Closely related to humility is poverty (*faqr*), by which is not meant the outer poverty of not owning things (discussed above), but an inner sense of poverty or utter neediness (*iftiqār*) vis-à-vis God's infinite wealth, plenitude and lack of need (*istighnāʾ*). Thus when he comments on the words *O mankind! It is you who stand in need of God* [35:15], Tustarī states:

> That is, 'You [depend] upon Him in your very selves, for truly when God created all creatures, He imposed upon His servants neediness (*faqr*) for Him, while He is the Rich and Independent (*al-Ghanī*). Furthermore, whoever claims to be wealthy has been veiled from God, Mighty and Majestic is He. On the other hand, whoever shows his need for God, will find that He joins his need to His wealth.

In his commentary on the words: *You will not attain mindfulness of God until you expend of that which you love* [3:92], Tustarī finds an opportunity to discuss the quality or state of love, which he illustrates with a story about Jesus, who successively meets three groups of people. The first, with emaciated bodies and pale faces, when questioned by Jesus, explain that their state has been brought about through the fear (*khawf*) of God. He tells them that they will be granted safety from that which they fear. The second group of people he encounters are even more emaciated than the first. They inform him that their state is due to their yearning (*shawq*) for God, and he tells them that God has made it incumbent upon Himself to grant them that which they long for. Finally he comes across a group who are even more emaciated, but whose faces are radiant like full moons. When questioned by Jesus, they reveal that their condition is due to love (*ḥubb*). Jesus tells them three times that they are the people of proximity (*muqarrabūn*). Tustarī then adds, 'Thus, whoever loves God, Exalted is He, is one of the people of proximity, for if anyone loves something, they hasten towards it.'

240 The 'one brought near' being Muḥammad.

241 e.g. *Tafsīr*, 33:8 and 19:52.

242 *Tafsīr*, 103:3, for example.

243 *Tafsīr*, 35:15.

244 *Tafsīr*, 28:78.

3. Trust, mindfulness of God and sincerity

Three spiritual qualities or virtues which Tustarī particularly stresses in the *Tafsīr* are: trust, that is, complete trust in God (*tawakkul*); 'mindfulness' or 'full awareness of God' (*taqwā*); and sincerity (*ikhlāṣ*), which means making all one's actions purely for God, and freeing oneself from all other than Him. These three qualities are themselves often linked both to each other and to other qualities, as we shall see.

Tustarī defines trust (*tawakkul*) as the first of four pillars of faith,[245] and as the last of seven 'lines' of faith that God inscribes upon the hearts of His friends.[246] One of his longest discussions of *tawakkul* occurs in his commentary on the words, *So turn away from them, and put your trust in God* [4:81]. Here, he defines trust as 'a means of livelihood (*ʿaysh*) for those who possess it', and further states that the divine omnipotence (*qudra*) will not become apparent save to the one who has complete trust. In the section on mystical theology above, mention was made of Tustarī's teaching that the downfall of human beings lies in reliance on their own devising and management (*tadbīr*), and that they must therefore look only to God for the management of their affairs. This latter involves their realising that all power (*ḥawl*) and strength (*quwwa*) belongs to God. In this same discussion of trust in the context of 4:81, he explains that it involves three things: 'submission of the body in servanthood, attachment of the heart to the divine lordliness (*rubūbiyya*), and disclaiming all power and strength.' He also shows trust to be closely related to the state of *sukūn*, that is, the servant's tranquil reliance on God and complete acquiescence in what God has destined for him. He states that trust has a thousand ranks, the lowest of which is the ability to walk upon air.[247] When asked how that level might be reached, he states:

> The first thing is gnosis (*maʿrifa*), then affirmation (*iqrār*), then the profession of God's oneness (*tawḥīd*), then submission (*islām*), then the perfection of faith (*iḥsān*), then the committing of one's affairs [to God] (*tafwīḍ*), then trust (*tawakkul*), and finally the state of tranquil reliance (*sukūn*) on God, Mighty and Majestic is He, in every situation.[248]

Elsewhere Tustarī shows *tawakkul* to be connected to other qualities and capacities. For example, when asked about the reality (*ḥaqīqa*) of trust, he replies: 'It is to be at ease (*istirsāl*) with whatever God wants.'[249] Hence it is close to the quality of contentment (*riḍā*). This connection is clearly illustrated by the following statement:

> God is content with your performing for Him just a day's worship at a time, so be content with Him for the provision you receive a day at a time.[250]

A similar admonition is to be found when Tustarī discusses different ways in which the servants of God might worship, ending with the one who worships with equity or justice (*inṣāf*), that is, one who does full justice to worship. Asked to explain *inṣāf* in worship, he answers:

> It is that none of your bodily members moves unless it be for God. Furthermore, when you ask Him for the next day's provision your equity has left you, for the heart cannot bear two concerns (*hammayn*).[251]

In other words, Tustarī is here associating *tawakkul*, that is, not asking for the next day's provision, with equity, which is acting only for God and being concerned with none other than Him, and this, as we shall see, is also how he understands sincerity. Tustarī also links *tawakkul* with *taqwā* (mindfulness of God), when he states, 'Trust in God is not admissible from anyone except those

---

245 *Tafsīr*, 3:200. The other three pillars are complete submission (*istislām*) to God's commands; contentment (*riḍā*) with what God has preordained, and gratitude (*shukr*) for His blessings. These, Tustarī adds, are accompanied by mindfulness of God (*taqwā*).

246 *Tafsīr*, 58:22.

247 This is another indication that Tustarī did not attach any particular importance to charismatic gifts. See above, p. xx.

248 Again, this occurs in the commentary on 4:81.

249 *Tafsīr*, 12:67.

250 *Tafsīr*, 51:22.

251 *Tafsīr*, 36:11.

who are mindful of God, and mindfulness of God is not acceptable except with trust in God.'[252] In another context, Tustarī compares mindfulness of God (*taqwā*) and certainty (*yaqīn*) to the two pans of a pair of scales, while trust (*tawakkul*) is the pointer which indicates increase and decrease in the other two.[253]

Many passages in the *Tafsīr* emphasise the importance of *taqwā*, and the need to 'fear' or be fully aware and mindful of God. For example, in his lengthy commentary on the words, *So fear Me, O people of pith* [2:197] he states:

> Whoever hopes for God's favour (*karāma*), Mighty and Majestic is He, should be mindful of Him, for truly it is through mindfulness of God that [the servant] may attain His favour and admittance into Paradise, abide in His vicinity, and triumph with a tremendous victory.

Taqwā is, in Tustarī's words, 'the best travelling companion leading to the remembrance (*dhikr*) of God.'[254] Elsewhere, he links *taqwā* to sincerity (*ikhlāṣ*), as when he states in a passage cited above: 'the best among the fearful are those who are sincere and mindful of God (*al-mukhliṣūn al-muttaqūn*) whose sincerity and mindfulness of God remains with them up until their death.'[255]

The different resonances of the Arabic word used for sincerity, *ikhlāṣ*, which in its root (*kh-l-ṣ*) can have the meaning of both 'being pure and unmixed' and 'becoming free of', are illustrated in Tustarī's discussions of the term in his *Tafsīr*. The importance of this quality, state or station is emphasised in many contexts.[256] For example, among the list of aphorisms which appear at the end of the *Tafsīr* is the recommendation, 'You must have sincerity (*ikhlāṣ*) to keep you safe from [satanic] whispering.'[257] Elsewhere, he recommends, 'Seek sincerity with an [inner] intention, for only the sincere can recognise ostentation (*riyāʾ*).[258] In another context he warns that discernment (*fiṭna*) is not attained through effort, but by acting with sincerity for God.[259]

We have seen that sincerity (*ikhlāṣ*) is linked to mindfulness or full awareness of God (*taqwā*), but sincerity is also linked to both faith and certainty. For example, in his commentary on the words, *And they were only commanded to worship God, devoting religion purely to Him* [98:5], Tustarī states:

> All knowledge is concerned with acts, until the person attains sincerity (*ikhlāṣ*). Then when he reaches sincerity, he will attain profound peace (*ṭumaʾnīna*). For the one whose knowledge [has become] certainty (*yaqīn*) and whose works are [done in] sincerity will find that God removes from him three things: anxiety (*jazaʿ*), ignorance (*jahl*) and action (*ʿamal*), and will grant him patience (*ṣabr*) in exchange for anxiety, knowledge in exchange for ignorance, and the abandonment of choice in exchange for action — but this will only be the case for those who are fully aware of God (*muttaqūn*).

Or again in the following passage, where sincerity is shown to be a manifestation, fruit or branch of certainty:

> Certainty (*yaqīn*) is the heart of faith, patience (*ṣabr*) is the backbone of faith, and sincerity (*ikhlāṣ*) is the perfection of faith, for through sincerity the servant reaches true affirmation

---

252 *Tafsīr*, 65:2. See also 4:81.

253 *Tafsīr*, 67:2.

254 *Tafsīr*, 2:197

255 *Tafsīr*, 48:26.

256 Tustarī does not define these qualities or virtues as being either a 'state' (*ḥāl*) or 'station' (*maqām*), perhaps because the difference between these two as technical terms had not yet been generally or formally established in Sufism. On the emergence of a systemisation of states and stations in Islamic mysticism see Nasrollah Pourjavady, '*Nahj al-khāṣṣ* (atharī az Abū Manṣūr-i Iṣfahānī)', *Taḥqīqāt-i Islāmī*, Year 3 (1988–9), no. 2, pp. 94–149, and especially pp. 104ff. Two early mystics who are accredited with developing a scheme of stages in the spiritual path are Shaqīq Balkhī (d. 195/810), whose short treatise, the *Adab al-ʿibādāt*, concerned the waystations (*manāzil*) of the path, see P. Nwyia, *Exégèse coranique*, pp. 213–6; and Abū Saʿīd al-Kharrāz (d. 286/899 or earlier) who spoke of progress through different stations (*maqāmāt*), for which see Iṣfahānī, *Ḥilyat al-awliyāʾ*, vol. 10, p. 248.

257 See p. 321.

258 *Tafsīr*, 7:29.

259 *Tafsīr*, 19:61.

> (*taṣdīq*). Furthermore, through true affirmation he attains realisation (*taḥqīq*), and through realisation he reaches God (*al-Ḥaqq*). Sincerity is the fruit of certainty, for certainty is witnessing (*mushāhada*) in the innermost secret (*sirr*)...[260]

In his commentary on the words, *Then they pray to God, becoming sincere [in their] faith in Him* [10:22], Tustarī states:

> Sincerity (*ikhlāṣ*) is witnessing (*mushāhada*). The light of the heart is in two things: in its root, it is faith (*īmān*) and in its branch (*farʿ*), it is sincerity. Sincerity is a matter of great importance (*khaṭar*) and the one who possesses it is wary lest his sincerity should not prevail till death...

He presents a number of different definitions of sincerity, or the way that sincerity may be attained, some of which appear straightforward, as when he says, 'whoever subdues his lower self through propriety serves God, Mighty and Majestic is He, with true sincerity (*ikhlāṣ*).'[261] Other definitions may be less simple than they appear, as when he interprets the words, *Say 'Indeed I have been commanded to worship God devoting [my] religion purely to Him'* [39:11] thus:

> Sincerity (*ikhlāṣ*) is responding (*ijāba*), and whoever has no response has no sincerity.

Presumably the response is to God's command that worship should be devoted solely to him. Tustarī then explains what this implies:

> The astute (*akyās*) reflected upon sincerity and did not find anything except the following: that everything the servant does, whether done in secret or openly, is for God alone, Mighty and Majestic is He, and is mingled neither with desire nor with the self.

Similarly, commenting on the words *And they were only commanded to worship God, devoting religion purely to Him* [98:5], he states:

> Sincerity has three facets: worshipping purely for God (*ikhlāṣ al-ʿibāda li'Llāh*), acting purely for Him (*ikhlāṣ al-ʿamal lahu*), and [keeping one's] heart purely for Him (*ikhlāṣ al-qalb lahu*).

4. *Remembrance of God (dhikr)*

As can be seen, these virtues involve the seeker being wholly centred upon, aware of, and devoted to God, all of which are in fact aspects of the remembrance of God (*dhikr*). Tustarī not only shows the remembrance of God to be an essential key to the mystical path, he also describes it as the very 'sustenance of the spiritual self and the intellect, just as it is the sustenance of the angels.'[262] When discussing the nature of the 'provision' from God mentioned in 34:39, he states:

> Provision (*rizq*) is of two kinds: the provision that is remembrance for the spiritual self (*nafs al-rūḥ*), the intellect (*ʿaql*) and the heart (*qalb*), which is like the sustenance of the angels — their very life (*ʿaysh*) is in remembrance, and were this to be withheld from them they would perish. The other kind of provision is that which is eaten, drunk and so on for the benefit of one's physical nature.

Elsewhere, commenting on *[those who] remember God frequently* [26:227], he explains:

> God, Exalted is He, created the innermost secret (*sirr*) and made its life consist in His remembrance. He created the outward self (*ẓāhir*) and made its life consist in praising (*ḥamd*) and thanking (*shukr*) Him. He appointed for both of them duties (*ḥuqūq*), which are works of obedience (*ṭāʿa*).

This emphasis on the importance of remembrance of God may well have its roots in the instruction given to the young Sahl by his uncle Muḥammad b. Sawwār that he should recite to himself eleven times a day, 'God is with me, God is watching over me, God is my Witness'. We find this teaching

260 In a short section on faith at the end of his commentary on Sūra 3.

261 *Tafsīr*, 7:176.

262 *Tafsīr*, 78:11.

echoed more than once in the *Tafsīr*, as when, in the context of the words *and the men who remember God often and the women who remember God often* [33:35], he states:

> The one who observes true remembrance is he who is aware that God witnesses him. He perceives Him with his heart as being close to him, and therefore feels shame before Him. Then he gives Him priority over himself and over everything else in every situation.

Another instance is when Tustarī is asked to explain remembrance, and answers:

> It is the realisation (*taḥqīq*) of the knowledge that God, Exalted is He, witnesses you, and it is that you see Him close to you with your heart. Thus, you feel shame before Him and give Him priority over yourself in all your affairs.[263]

In these two cases, remembrance has an ethical dimension, or function, and this is also indicated when, in the context of this same verse, Tustarī is asked to explain the meaning of the Prophet's words, 'The world is accursed and what it contains is accursed, save the remembrance of God (*dhikr Allāh*), Exalted is He', and replies:

> His saying 'the remembrance of God' here means the abstinence from what is not lawful, that is, when something unlawful comes his way he remembers God, Exalted is He, and he knows that God is watching him, so he avoids that unlawful thing.[264]

However, remembrance also clearly has a contemplative dimension, as is shown when Tustarī explains the inner meaning of the command, *Glorify the name of your Lord Most High* [87:1]:

> It [means] to proclaim His transcendence above having rivals (*aḍdād*) and equals (*andād*). This is its outward meaning. In its inner meaning it is to witness Him through remembrance (*dhikr*) during the ritual prayer, without witnessing anything else.[265]

Of course, this is not intended to imply that remembrance should be limited to the occasion of ritual prayer. Tustarī advises that the remembrance of God should be with His servants at every moment, a point which he is at pains to emphasise when he gives his disciples the following admonishment:

> In truth I say to you without any falsehood, in certainty without a doubt, that any person who spends a breath in other than God's remembrance does so while being heedless of God, Mighty and Majestic is He.[266]

The same principle is here expressed in another way;

> There is not a servant who desired God with a genuine resolve, without everything vanishing from his [consciousness] besides Him.[267]

In the following passage Tustarī indicates the profundity of remembrance, employing different forms of the verbal root *dh-k-r*:

> The life of the spirit (*ḥayāt al-rūḥ*) is in the remembrance [of God] (*dhikr*), the life of remembrance is in the one who remembers (*dhākir*), and the life of the one who remembers is in the One who is remembered (*madhkūr*).[268]

Finally, Tustarī discusses the highest level of remembrance, which is purified of all other than God. Here he is taking up the word 'remember' as a keynote from a verse speaking of Abraham's *remembrance of the Abode* [38:46]:

---

263 *Tafsīr*, 7:205.

264 ibid. Again, this is reminiscent of the admonition given to Tustarī by his uncle. See above, p. xv.

265 One is reminded of the definition of spiritual virtue (*iḥsān*) in the famous *ḥadīth* of Gabriel, which is explained as 'To worship God as if you see Him, for if you do not, He surely sees You.' The *ḥadīth* is listed in Abū Zakariyya Yaḥyā al-Nawawī, *An-Nawawī's Forty Ḥadīth*, selected and translated by Ezzeddin Ibrahim and Denys Johnson-Davies (Lebanon, 1980), pp. 28–31, and also in the 'Kitāb al-Īmān' in the *Ṣaḥīḥ* collections of both Bukhārī and Muslim. Qushayrī discusses some spiritual implications of this *ḥadīth* in the twenty-fourth chapter of his *Risāla*, 'Bāb al-murāqaba' (Cairo, 1966), pp. 405–7; trans. Knysh, pp. 202–3.

266 *Tafsīr*, 7:205.

267 *Tafsīr*, 73:9.

268 *Tafsīr*, 58:22.

> He [God] purified Abraham, Ishmael and Isaac from the remembrance of this world through a remembrance of Him, purely for [His sake] (*khāliṣatan*), not for the attainment of recompense. Neither did they witness themselves in it [their remembrance]; rather, they remembered Him through Him and for Him. Furthermore, the one who remembers God through God is not like the one who remembers God through the remembrance of God.

The state which Tustarī is here describing, in which the mystic, represented by Abraham and his sons, is totally freed of himself to the point that it can be said that he remembers God *through* God, was defined by other mystics as the state of annihilation from self (*fanāʾ*) and subsistence in God (*baqāʾ*), and is now generally understood in Sufism as attainment of the ultimate state on the spiritual path.[269]

VII. Conclusion

It is hoped that the foregoing discussion will have given the reader some idea of the depth and scope of doctrines presented in Tustarī's *Tafsīr*. As can be seen, they range from theological discussions of the divine attributes, through cosmological reflections on the Prophet's time alone with God in pre-eternity and the derivation of the two worlds from the well-spring of the Muḥammadan Light, to eschatological portrayals of what is in store for those who are blessed and those who are doomed in the Hereafter; and from glimpses of the highest experiences of realised mystics, through descriptions of spiritual virtues, to practical guidelines for the way of life of intitiates, and instructions for their conduct on the path. Although the profoundest moments of illumination and intimacy with God are for the most part allusively expressed in the *Tafsīr*, we find that Tustarī articulates and expounds in a clear and precise manner his understanding of spiritual psychology and the workings of the inner world of the human being, with its two 'sides', the one tending toward the earth and the realm of darkness, namely man's lower self (*nafs*) along with his basic human nature (*ṭabʿ*), and the other tending toward heaven and the realm of light, namely man's spirit (*rūḥ*), heart (*qalb*) and intellect (*ʿaql*). Likewise he shows how these two sides can and should be brought into coalition through the remembrance of God.

During this period, knowledge of the states (*aḥwāl*) and stations (*maqāmāt*) of the spiritual path had not generally been subjected to any formal systematisation in Sufism,[270] yet Tustarī presents numerous discussions of topics such as repentance (*tawba*), spiritual poverty or neediness for God (*faqr*), patience (*ṣabr*), contentment (*riḍā*), complete trust in God (*tawakkul*), mindfulness of God (*taqwā*) and sincerity (*ikhlāṣ*), and in one or two instances incorporates some of these into a scheme of progress through spiritual stages.[271] Many of his sayings on these topics, which he regarded as necessary virtues or attributes for spiritual wayfarers, were to be cited in the manuals and treatises of later Sufi authors.

In the *Tafsīr*, Tustarī's teachings are inevitably dispersed through his interpretations of different Qurʾānic verses. However, when these fragments and gems of wisdom are brought together and collated, we find, as Böwering has noted, a 'mystical synthesis of ideas that is marked by its coherence and specific terminology', and we can get a clear impression of Tustarī's 'mystical world view'.[272] A thread that runs consistently through his teachings is the theme of light, which represents for him divine guidance at all its levels: the Qurʾān is light; the Prophet, in his primordial existence was light, and continues to be light, radiating the light of faith and guidance to believers and to the world, and it is a light from the light of the essence of God that brings the mystic to the highest level of certainty and the 'attainment' of God.

---

269 In his *Tafsīr*, Tustarī does not use these two terms *fanāʾ* and *baqāʾ* as they are frequently applied by Sufis to the concommitent states of 'annihilation from self' and 'subsisting in God'. However, he does use the term *baqāʾ* as a permanent subsisting with God in Paradise, as for example in his commentary on 43:69 and 70. See above, p. xxxvi, and n. 143. Abū Saʿīd al-Kharrāz is accredited with being the first mystic to have discussed *fanāʾ* and *baqāʾ* as mystical states.

270 See above, n. 256.

271 e.g. *Tafsīr*, 4:81.

272 Böwering, *Mystical Vision*, p. 265.

Tustarī's mystical world view, or perhaps we might call it his 'spiritual universe', is firmly framed within his theological, cosmological and eschatological beliefs, and this is, as he sees it, precisely the challenge which faces all human beings, and which he encourages aspiring mystics to take up. God is the Transcendent, the Unknowable, yet as he says, 'Truly behind the names and attributes are attributes which no comprehension can penetrate, for God is a blazing fire and is inaccessible. Yet we have no option but to plunge in [and try to reach Him].'[273] Our destiny is pre-determined for us by God, and it is actually and only through our knowledge that He is in control of all things, our acceptance of what He has destined for us with contentment (*riḍā*), and our complete trust (*tawakkul*) and tranquil acquiescence (*sukūn*) in Him, that we can be freed from the veil of our own management of things (*tadbīr*).[274] In the *Tafsīr*, Tustarī reminds us that at the Covenant of *Alast* all human beings bore witness to God's lordship, and that all human beings will definitely be answerable in the Hereafter for the extent to which they have kept that Covenant (i.e. the profession of God's oneness). The intense awareness of those two moments of encounter with God, one which took place in pre-eternity and the other that is to come, place the mystic in the immediacy of the present moment in which He stands before his Lord.

Annabel Keeler
November 2010

273 *Tafsīr*, 7:180. See the discussion of this saying in T. Mayer, 'Theology and Sufism', in T. Winter, *Cambridge Companion to Classical Islamic Theology*, p. 263.

274 *Tafsīr*, 32:5; also 7:33 and 16:97.

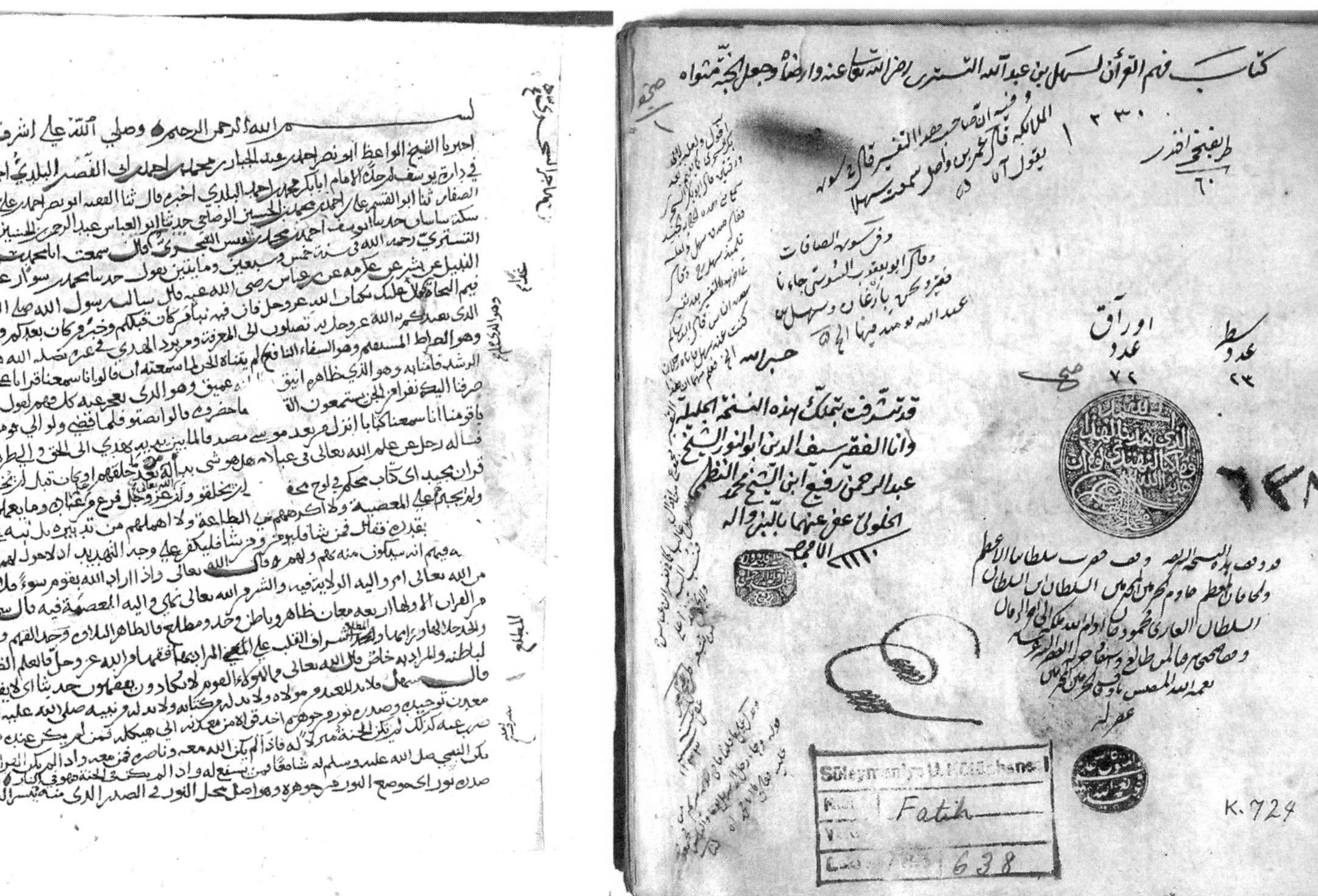

MS Fātiḥ 638, dated 872/1468, title and first pages (ff. 1a and b).

MS Fātiḥ 638, dated 872/1468, last page showing colophon (f. 72b).

MS Fātiḥ 3488, dated 965/1558, first and last pages (ff. 181b and 330a).

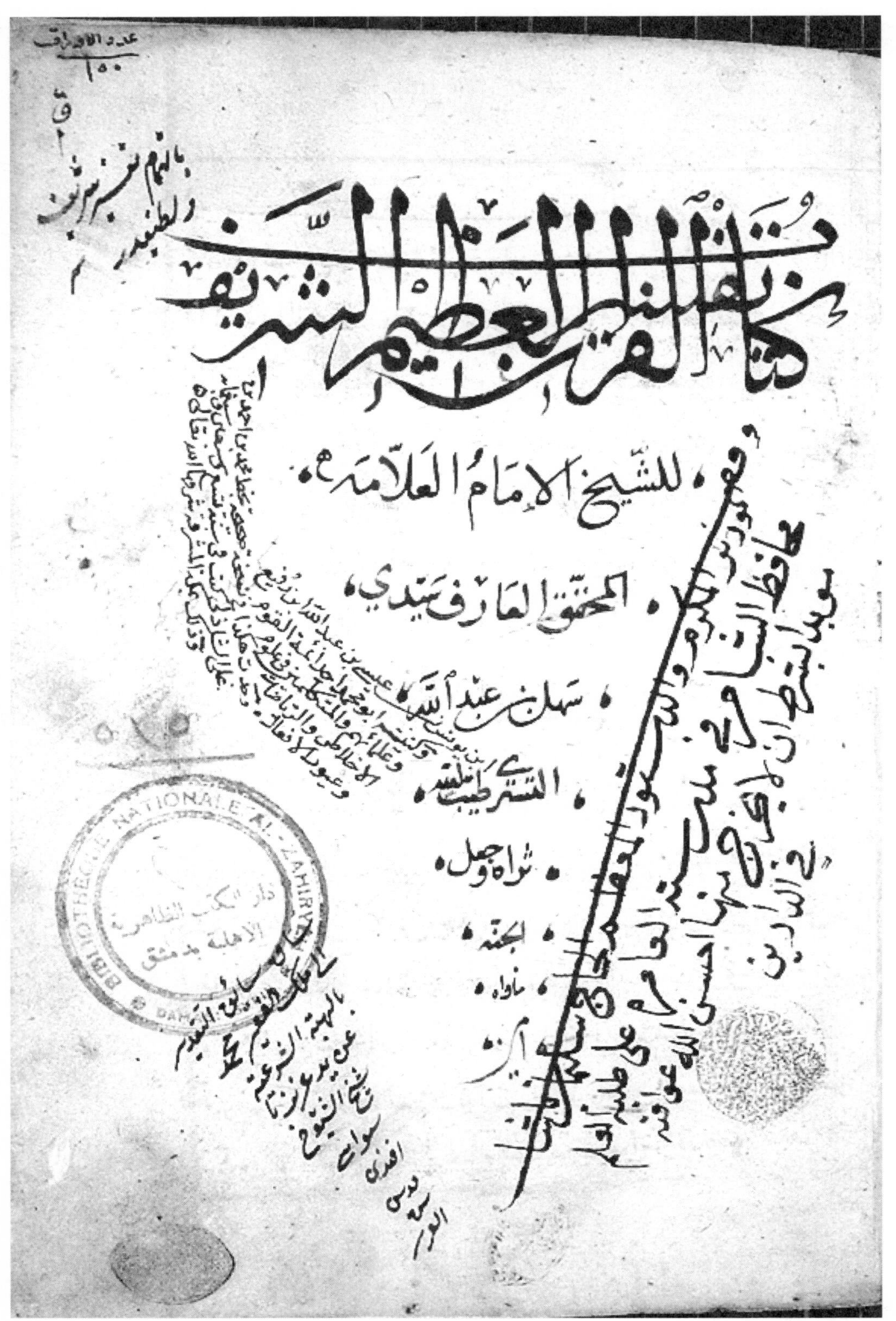

MS Ẓāhiriyya 515, dated twelfth/eighteenth or thirteenth/nineteenth century, title page (f. 1a).

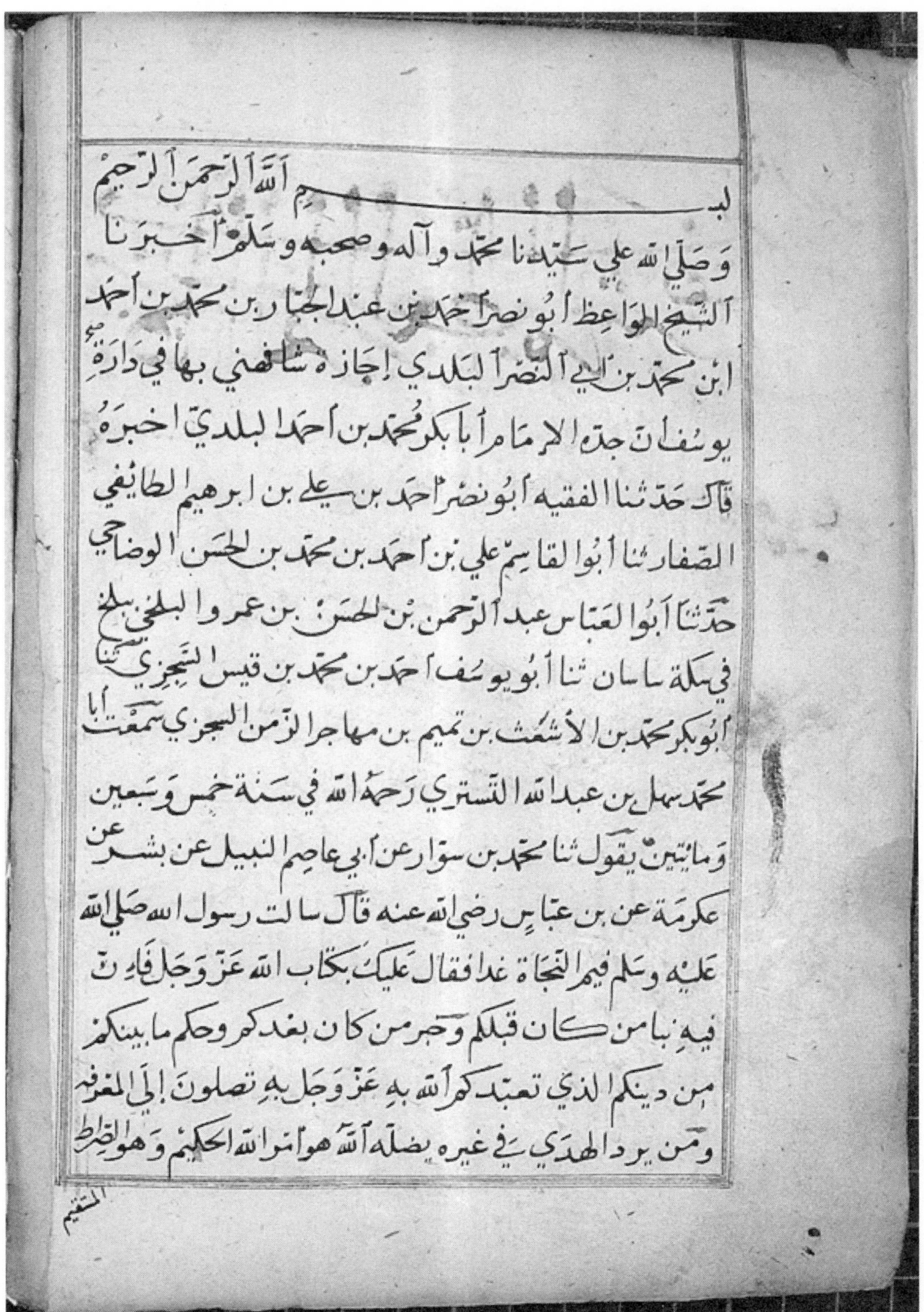

بسم الله الرحمن الرحيم
وصلى الله على سيدنا محمد وآله وصحبه وسلم أخبرنا
الشيخ الواعظ أبو نصر أحمد بن عبد الجبار بن محمد بن أحمد
ابن محمد بن أبي النصر البلدي إجازة شافهني بها في داره صح
يوسفان جده الإمام أبا بكر محمد بن أحمد البلدي أخبره
قال حدثنا الفقيه أبو نصر أحمد بن علي بن ابرهيم الطائفي
الصفار ثنا أبو القاسم علي بن أحمد بن محمد بن الحسن الوضاحي
حدثنا أبو العباس عبد الرحمن بن الحسن بن عمرو البلخي ببلخ
في سكة ساسان ثنا أبو يوسف أحمد بن محمد بن قيس السجزي ثنا
أبو بكر محمد بن الأشعث بن تميم بن مهاجر الزمن السجزي سمعت أبا
محمد سهل بن عبد الله التستري رحمه الله في سنة خمس وسبعين
ومائتين يقول ثنا محمد بن سوار عن أبي عاصم النبيل عن بشر عن
عكرمة عن بن عباس رضي الله عنه قال سألت رسول الله صلى الله
عليه وسلم فيم النجاة غدا فقال عليك بكتاب الله عز وجل فإن
فيه نبأ من كان قبلكم وخبر من كان بعدكم وحكم ما بينكم
من دينكم الذي تعبدكم الله به عز وجل به تصلون إلى المعرفة
ومن يرد الهدى في غيره يضله الله هو أمر الله الحكيم وهو الصراط
المستقيم

MS Ẓāhiriyya 515, dated twelfth/eighteenth or thirteenth/nineteenth century, first page (f. 1b).

وقال بن سالم كنت عند سهل رحمه الله فأتاه رجلان بعد صلاة العصر
وجلا يحدثانه فقلت في نفسي لقد أبطأ عنده وما أداما يرجعان في
هذا الوقت وذهبت إلى منزلي لأهيئ لهما عشاء فلما رجعت إليه لم
أر عنده أحدا فسألته عن حالهما فقال إن أحدهما يصلي المغرب بالمشرق ق
والآخر بالمغرب ولقد دخل علي رجل من عباد البصرة فرأى عنده بلبلة
في قفص فقال لمن هذه البلبلة فقال لهذا الصبي كان ابنا له قال
فأخرج سهل من كمه دينارا فقال بني أيما أحب إليك الدينار أم
البلبلة قال الدينار فدفع إليه الدينار وأطلق البلبلة قال فقعدت
البلبلة على حائط الدار حتى خرج سهل فجعل يرفرف فوق رأسه
حتى دخل سهل داره وكان في داره سدرة فسكنت البلبلة
الشجرة فلم تزل فيها حتى مات فلما رفعوا جنازته جعلت ترفرف فوق
جنازته والناس يبكون حتى جاؤوا بها إلى قبره فوقفت ناحية
• حتى دفن وتفرق الناس عن قبره فلم تزل تضطرب •
• على قبره حتى ماتت فدفنت بجنبه والله أعلم •
• كمل كتاب التفسير لسهل بن عبد الله التستري •
• نفعنا الله برحمته وأعاد علينا من •
وان وجدت عيبا فسد الخللا • بركاته وعلى كافة المسلمين آمين • جل من لا فيه عيب وعلا
وصلى الله على محمد وآله

MS Ẓāhiriyya 515, dated twelfth/eighteenth or thirteenth/nineteenth century, last page (f. 146a).

The Commentary

Introduction to the Commentary

In the Name of God, the Merciful, the Compassionate.

May God bless our master Muḥammad, his Family and Companions, and grant them peace.

In an authorised oral transmission in the house of Yūsuf, I was informed by the Shaykh and preacher Abū Naṣr Aḥmad b. ʿAbd al-Jabbār b. Muḥammad b. Aḥmad b. Muḥammad b. Abī al-Naṣr al-Baladī, that his grandfather the Imam Abū Bakr Muḥammad b. Aḥmad al-Baladī, had informed him: the jurist Abū Naṣr Aḥmad b. ʿAlī b. Ibrāhim al-Ṭāʾifī al-Ṣaffār related to us that Abū al-Qāsim ʿAlī b. Aḥmad b. Muḥammad b. al-Ḥasan al-Waḍḍāhī was told by Abū al-ʿAbbās ʿAbd al-Raḥmān b. al-Ḥasan b. ʿUmar al-Balkhī on the Sassanian Road in Balkh, that Abū Yūsuf Aḥmad b. Muḥammad b. Qays al-Sijzī ⌜related that Abū Bakr Muḥammad b. al-Ashʿath b. Tamīm b. Muhājir al-Zaman al-Sijzī⌝[1] said: 'I heard Muḥammad Sahl b. ʿAbd Allāh al-Tustarī, may God the Exalted have mercy on him, in the year two hundred and seventy five, say:

> It was narrated to us by Muḥammad b. Sawwār on the authority of Abū ʿĀṣim al-Nabīl, on the authority of Bishr, on the authority of ʿIkrima, [that] Ibn ʿAbbās, may God be pleased with them both, said, 'I asked the Messenger of God ﷺ how to attain salvation in the Hereafter, to which he replied: "You should keep to the Book of God, for in it there is information about those who came before you and news of those who will come after you. It is the arbiter between you in matters of your religion, by which God, Mighty and Majestic is He, has made you worship Him. Through it [the Qurʾān] you [may] attain gnosis (*maʿrifa*); and whoever seeks guidance another way, God will lead astray. It is the command of God, the Wise, it is the straight path, and it is the beneficial cure. No sooner did the jinn hear it than they exclaimed: …*We have indeed heard a marvellous Qurʾān. It guides to rectitude.* ۞ *Therefore we believe in it and we will never associate anyone with our Lord.* [72:1, 2]"'[2]

[He, Sahl, continued]:

> It is that which is beautifully ordered in its outward form and profound in its inner meaning. It is, moreover, that before which all understanding is powerless, according to the words of God, Exalted is He:
>
> *And when We sent a company of jinn your way to listen to the Qurʾān and when they were in its presence, they said, 'Listen carefully!' When [the reading] was finished, they returned to their people to warn [them].* ۞ *They said, 'O our people! Indeed we have heard a book revealed after Moses, confirming what came before it: it guides to the truth and to a straight path.'* [46:29–30]

Then a man asked him [Sahl] about God's knowledge of His servants, whether it was something that became apparent to Him after He created them, or before their creation. He replied:

> …*It is a Glorious Qurʾān* [85:21], that is, it is a book [that was] fixed *in a Preserved Tablet* [85:22] before they were created;[3] God's knowledge of His servants and what they would do was complete before He created them. [This does not imply] His forcing them into disobedience, coercing

1 Added on the basis of Z515, f. 1b and F3488, f. 181b.

2 Abū ʿĪsā Muḥammad al-Tirmidhī, *al-Jāmiʿ al-ṣaḥīḥ wa huwa Sunan al-Tirmidhī* (Cairo, 1937–65), 'Mā jāʾa fī faḍl al-Qurʾān'; Aḥmad b. al-Ḥusayn al-Bayhaqī, *al-Jāmiʿ li-shuʿab al-īmān* (Beirut, 1996), vol. 2, p. 836.

3 Here, Tustarī appears to be identifying the Qurʾān with God's pre-eternal knowledge.

them into obedience, or leaving them out of His divine plan. Rather, it draws attention to that which those who deny His decree are promised, for He says: *...whoever will, let him believe, and whoever will, let him disbelieve...* [18:29], in the way of a threat, since they [actually] have no power (*ḥawl*) or strength (*quwwa*) except in accordance with that which is contained in His pre-eternal knowledge concerning them, which will come to be, from Him, [but] through them and for them.[4] God, Exalted is He, says: *...And if God wills misfortune for a people there is none that can repel it* [13:11]. The good from God is a command for which He provides support (*wilāya*),[5] and the evil from God is a prohibition against which He provides protection (*ʿiṣma*).[6]

Sahl, may God be pleased with him, said:

Every verse of the Qurʾān has four senses: an outward (*ẓāhir*) and an inward sense (*bāṭin*), a limit (*ḥadd*) and a point of transcendency (*maṭlaʿ*). The outward sense is the recitation and the inward sense is the understanding (*fahm*) of the verse; the limit defines what is lawful and unlawful, and the point of transcendency is the heart's place of elevation (*ishrāf*) [from which it beholds] the intended meaning, as an understanding from God, Mighty and Majestic is He (*fiqhan min Allāh ʿazza wa jalla*). The outward knowledge [of the Qurʾān] is a knowledge [accessible to the] generality (*ʿāmm*); whereas the understanding of its inner meanings and its intended meaning is [for] a select few (*khāṣṣ*)...Thus God has said: *...What is wrong with this people that they fail to understand any words?* [4:78] That is, they do not understand what they are being told.

Sahl ﷺ, [further] said:

The servant cannot do without his Master, nor can he do without His Book, nor without His Prophet ﷺ, for his heart is a mine of God's oneness, and his breast (*ṣadr*) is a light from [His] 'substance' (*jawhar*). It [the breast] derives its strength from the mine of his heart, [transmitting it] to his frame.[7] He who has nothing by way of guidance that he has heard[8] or [has it] but ignores it, will likewise not have Paradise as his [final] abode, and if God is not with him as his succour, then who is? If the Qurʾān is not his guide, and the Prophet ﷺ is not his intercessor, then who is there to intercede for him? And if he is not in Paradise, then he must be in the Hellfire.

His [Sahl's] saying[9] that [the Prophet's] 'breast is a light' means that it is a repository of light 'from His [God's] substance', which is the original locus of light within the breast, whence light spreads throughout the rest of the breast. The attribution of 'substance' (*jawhar*) to God does not imply [a reference to] His essence (*dhāt*), but rather it is an indication of possession (*mulk*). 'It derives its

4 For Tustarī's teachings on divine preordination and decree, see Introduction to the Translation, pp. xxxiiiff. Henceforth abbreviated to 'IT'.

5 That is, patronage, guardianship or even friendship, all of which are meanings of the word *wilāya*, derived from the verbal root *w-l-y*, meaning to be near, from which is also derived the word *walī*, which will be discussed below. For a discussion of the different significations of the word *wilāya* and its variant *walāya*, see M. Izzi Dien and P. Walker, 'Wilāya', *EI*², vol. XI, p. 208–9; Hermann Landolt, 'Walāyah', *The Encyclopedia of Religion* (New York, 1987), vol. 14, pp. 9656–62; Chodkiewicz, *Seal of Saints*, chs. 1 and 2; Bernd Radtke and John O'Kane, *The Concept of Sainthood in Early Islamic Mysticism* (Richmond, 1996); and Bernd Radtke, 'The Concept of *Wilāya* in Early Sufism' in Leonard Lewisohn (ed.), *The Heritage of Sufism* (Oxford, 1999), vol. 1, pp. 483–96.

6 As can be seen here, Tustarī teaches that both good and evil come from God. As Böwering has explained, 'God lays down what is good through His command (*amr*), and He sets down what is evil through His interdiction (*nahy*).' Furthermore, 'God's command is accompanied by an act of divine help (*maʿūna*), [or, as above, *wilāya*] whereas His interdiction is accompanied by an act of divine protection (*ʿiṣma*).' See Böwering, *Mystical Vision*, pp. 176–80. See also IT, pp. xxxiiiff.

7 Lit. to his 'temple' (*haykal*). The question arises as to whether Tustarī intends here the heart of Muḥammad, or the human heart in a general sense. Böwering has taken it to mean the heart of Muḥammad, probably because of other similar passages. See his discussion of the heart of Muḥammad in *Mystical Vision*, pp. 162–3. However, Gaafar, in 'The Sufi Doctrine', p. 110, n. 7, has taken it to mean the heart of the human being in general. We have followed Böwering's interpretation, according to which Tustarī is here referring to the Prophet's heart.

8 MS F638, f. 1b has *samiʿa bihi* instead of *yatbaʿu bihi* which is in Z515, f. 2b, F3488, f. 182b and the published edition. The commentary which follows in the next paragraph would seem to favour the F638 version, which is what we have translated.

9 These words are a comment on the words of Tustarī, probably given by Abū Bakr al-Sijzī.

strength' means, the strength of light from his mine, 'it' being the breast and a truthful advocate (*māḥil muṣaddaq*).[10] 'To his frame' means [to] his limbs. What he meant by this is the light of acts of obedience [manifested] through the limbs. 'He who has nothing' means he [who does not have] any guidance, 'that he has heard', that is, understood.

[Sahl continued]:[11]

> The Prophet ﷺ said, 'The Qurʾān is an excellent intercessor whose intercession is accepted (*shāfiʿ mushaffaʿ*) and a truthful advocate (*māḥil muṣaddaq*). Whomsoever the Qurʾān intercedes for will be saved, and whoever acts evilly by it (*man maḥala bihi*) will be doomed.[12]

Sahl said:

> God, Exalted is He, sent down the Qurʾān to His Prophet and made his heart a mine of His oneness and of the Qurʾān, for He said: *It was brought down by the Trustworthy Spirit upon your heart...* [26:193]. He further charged him with its promulgation and explanation, so that through him the believers would be apprised of what had been sent down to them. Whoever believes in it, knows its explanation and acts upon its injunctions, will have perfected his faith in God, Exalted is He. But whoever believes in it and reads it, but does not act upon his knowledge of what it contains, will not receive his reward in full.
>
> People who recite the Qurʾān are of three ranks. There are those who have been granted understanding by virtue of their maintaining the practice of what is commanded and the avoidance of what is forbidden, both inwardly and outwardly, and by their affirmation of it [the Qurʾān] with the light of the insight of certainty (*nūr baṣīrat al-yaqīn*), which is [in effect] the heart's reliance on God, Exalted is He, in every state and in any situation. They attach no importance to melodies [in the recitation] or the delight that may be aroused by the charm of contrived vocal embellishments. Their only concern is with trying to understand, and asking God for an increase in such understanding with regard to His commands and prohibitions, and what is intended by the ordinances concerning that which He has made obligatory, and [that which is prescribed by] the Sunna of His Prophet ﷺ. Hence, these people act upon the knowledge they have of it, ever seeking God's aid, and are steadfast in carrying it out,[13] as He commanded them when He said: *...Pray for help from God and be patient...* [7:128], that is, 'Seek God's aid in fulfilling His command, in the obligatory way that is the way of God; and be steadfast in carrying it out both inwardly and outwardly, so that He may impart to you understanding, discernment and that which He wants from you, as a grace from Him.' [So, those whom I have described] do not pay attention to beautiful voices. It is to them that God has granted the understanding of the Qurʾān. They are the elect of God and His friends (*awliyāʾ*).[14] They have nothing to do with this world and the world has no claim on them, nor do they have any desire for what is in Paradise. He took the world away from them, but they did not mind, and when He gave it to

10 It is interesting to note that in the following paragraph Tustarī uses this same epithet for the Qurʾān, and later it will be seen that in one instance, he interprets the Preserved Tablet (*lawḥ maḥfūẓ*) as the breast in which the Qurʾān is preserved. See Tustarī's commentary on 85:22.

11 It is not quite clear here whether the speaker is Tustarī or Abū Bakr al-Sijzī.

12 That is, whoever finds respite in the Qurʾān, that is, a false sense of reassurance and ease, and therefore continues in error and disbelief will ultimately be doomed to perish in the Fire. We shall see later a similar doctrine in relation to the term *istidrāj*.

13 That is, translating *adāyihi* (for *adāʾihi*) according to MSS: Z515, f. 3b and F3488, f. 183a. F638, f. 3a has *ādābihi* the first time and *iddāyihi* (for *iddāʾihi*) the second. The confusion arises with some copyists who rendered *hamza* as 'yā'. Another example will be seen below.

14 *Awliyāʾ* is the plural of the word *walī*, which, like the word *wilāya* discussed above in n. 5, derives from the Arabic verbal root *w-l-y*. The *walī* can be a person in authority, a guardian, protector, or friend (especially of God). Concerning its latter meaning, Pierre Lory has stated ('Walī,' *EI*², vol. XI, p. 109): 'in some way the *walī* also acquires his Friend's, i.e. God's, good qualities and therefore he possesses particular authority, ... capacities and abilities.' In its meaning of 'friend of God', the word *walī* is often translated as saint, which is understandable given that there is no idiomatic equivalent for the word *walī* in English, but 'saint' does not really convey the Arabic sense, and can also be misleading since there is no canonisation in Islam.

them they refused it, just as their Prophet had refused it when it was presented to him.[15] They cast themselves before God in contentment and reliance on Him. They said: 'We cannot do without You. You are You, and we have no desire for other than You. They are the ones who have isolated themselves for God (*mutafarridūn*) mentioned by the Prophet ﷺ when he said 'Walk the way of those who are solely dependent (*mutafarridūn*) on the mercy of God, Exalted is He.' They inquired: 'Who are the *mutafarridūn*, O Messenger of God?' He replied: 'They are those who have become ecstatic (*ahtarū*) in the remembrance of God, Exalted is He.[16] They will come on the Day of Resurrection light [of load] for [their] remembrance will have lifted from them their burdens [of sin].'[17]

Sahl then said [concerning this *ḥadīth*]:

They are the shaykhs [or spiritual masters] who are ecstatic in the remembrance of God (*dhikr*), for which they are [constantly] assembled, as the Prophet ﷺ said: 'God, Exalted is He, says, "I keep company with the one who remembers Me. Whenever my servant seeks Me out, he will find Me."'[18] And He, Exalted is He, has said: ... *Whithersoever you turn, there is the Face of God...* [2:115]

A section on those who seek the understanding of the Qurʾān

God, Mighty and Majestic is He, has said:

'Truly it is a revelation from the Lord of the Worlds, ❁ *brought down by the Trustworthy Spirit,* ❁ *Upon your heart, that you may be [one] of the warners.'* [26:192–4]

Sahl said:

According to the measure of light which has been allotted to a person by God, Exalted is He, he will find guidance for his heart and insight (*baṣīra*). Lights from His light will be manifested in his characteristics. God, Exalted is He, has said: ...*For any to whom God has not granted light, there is no light.* [24:40] Thus the Qurʾān is God's rope (*ḥabl*) [linking] Him with His servants. Whoever holds fast to it is saved, for God has made the Qurʾān a light, and has said: ...*but We have made it a light by which we guide whomsoever We wish of Our servants...* [42:52].[19] The meaning of ... *We have made...* here is: 'We have expounded within it that which is clear (*muḥkam*) and ambiguous (*mutashābih*),[20] that which is lawful (*ḥalāl*) and unlawful (*ḥarām*),

---

15 This is a reference to one account of the Prophet's Night Journey and Ascension (*Isrāʾ wa Miʿrāj*), when, according to certain traditions, the whole world was presented to him in all its splendour and adornment, but he said that he had no need for it. See, for example, Abū al-Qāsim al-Qushayrī, *Kitāb al-Miʿrāj* (Cairo, 1964), pp. 44ff., who relates one such tradition on the authority of Ḍaḥḥāk. A lengthy traditional account of the *Miʿrāj* may be found in ʿAbd Allāh b. Masʿūd Ibn Isḥāq, *Kitāb al-Mubtadaʾ wa'l-mabʿath wa'l-maghāzī*, known as *Sīrat Ibn Isḥāq* (Rabat, 1976); English trans., Alfred Guillaume as *The Life of Muḥammad* (London, 1955), pp. 181–7. On the *Miʿrāj*, see also Abū ʿAbd al-Raḥmān al-Sulamī, *Bayān laṭāʾif al-miʿrāj*, English trans. with Arabic text by Frederick S. Colby as *Subtleties of the Ascension* (Louisville, KY, 2006).

16 Or it might be translated as crazed, for they appear incoherent and even insane, due to the ecstasy they experience in their remembrance of God. MS Z515, f. 3b and F3488, f. 183b both have *ihtazzū* and the corresponding *muhtazzīna* in the following sentence, meaning they quiver, tremble or are moved (by the remembrance). MS F638, f. 3a has *ihtadū* meaning they are guided and *muhtazzūna* in the following sentence.

17 Muḥammad b. ʿAlī (al-Ḥakīm) al-Tirmidhī, *Nawādir al-uṣūl fī maʿrifat aḥādīth al-rasūl* (Beirut, 1993), vol. 3, p. 64.

18 Bayhaqī, *Shuʿab al-īmān*, vol. 1, p. 451.

19 Tustarī has understood 'it' in this sentence to stand for the Qurʾān, though commentators point out that it could also be referring to the Spirit mentioned earlier in the verse: *and thus have We revealed to you a Spirit from Our command. You did not know what the Book was, nor faith...*

20 The *muḥkam* and *mutashābih* verses in the Qurʾān are mentioned in 3:7, which reads as follows: *'It is He who revealed to you the Book, wherein are verses [that are] clear* (muḥkam) *forming the Mother of the Book* (umm al-kitāb), *and others ambiguous* (mutashābihāt). *As for those in whose hearts is deviation, they follow the ambiguous part desiring sedition, and desiring its interpretation...'* The end of 3:7 reads: *wa mā yaʿlamu taʾwīlahu illā'Llāhu wa'l-rāsikhūna fī'l-ʿilmi yaqūlūna āmannā bihi kullun min ʿindi rabbinā wa mā yudhakkaru illā ūlū 'l-albāb.* There was a difference of opinion as to whether, grammatically, there should be a break between the word *Llāhu* and *wa* (underlined text). According to one opinion, held, for example, by Abū Jaʿfar al-Ṭabarī (d. 310/923) and Jalāl al-Dīn al-Suyūṭī (d. 911/1505), it should

and that which is commanded (*amr*) and forbidden (*nahy*)', as God has said, Mighty and Majestic is He: *We have made it an Arabic Qurʾān* [43:3] — that is, 'We have expounded it in a clear Arabic tongue in the letters of the alphabet which God has clearly set forth for you, and by which you may attain knowledge of [its] inner and outer [meanings]'.

God, Exalted is He, has said: *and [those who] follow the light which has been revealed with him* [7:157], referring to the Qurʾān, of which the heart of the Prophet is the mine.

He [Sahl] was asked the meaning of his saying that the Qurʾān is the 'rope' (*ḥabl*) between God and His servants. He replied:

This means that they have no way to Him save through the Qurʾān, and through understanding [all] that has been addressed to them in it concerning what is required of them, as well as putting that knowledge into practice for God's sake with complete sincerity (*mukhliṣūna fīhi*), and following the exemplary way (*sunna*) of Muḥammad ﷺ, who was sent to them. Thus He has said: *Whoever obeys the Messenger, verily obeys God* [4:80] — that is, whoever obeys the Messenger ﷺ in [keeping] his Sunna, has indeed obeyed God in those things that He made obligatory for him.

Ibn ʿAbbās ؓ has said, 'The Qurʾān was sent down all at once to the heaven of this world, and then God, Exalted is He, sent it down to the Prophet ﷺ in instalments of five verses at a time, or more or less than this'.[21] He has said, Glorified and Exalted is He: *Nay, I swear by the setting-places of the stars!* ❁ *— And that is indeed a tremendous oath, if you but knew —* ❁ *This is indeed a noble Qurʾān* [56:75–7].

And Ibn ʿAbbās ؓ said, 'The Qurʾān did not come down in one month or two, nor in a year or two; the time between the first revelation and the last was twenty years, or as [many] as God willed.' This is because Isrāfīl is stationed in the Throne with a lowered gaze,[22] and around him are the noble recording angels, and an emerald tablet. When God wills something, it is to be found on this Tablet, then that one [Isrāfīl] will knock his forehead on the Tablet so that he sees its contents, upon which he sends out the messengers [angels]. This is what is meant by His words: *[Sealed] in a Preserved Tablet* [85:22]. The Qurʾān was sent down all at once to the noble recording angels, then they in turn sent it down to Gabriel ؑ in instalments over the course of twenty years, and likewise did Gabriel bring it in instalments to the Prophet ﷺ. The idolaters said, 'If only the Qurʾān was sent down to him all at once', to which God, Exalted is He, responded: *Thus [is it revealed], that We may strengthen your inner heart with it* [25:32] — that is, so that it may be an answer to that about which they question you. For if We had sent it down all at once you would not have [to hand] the answers to their questions.

---

read: *and none knows its interpretation save only God. And those who are rooted in knowledge say, 'We believe in it; all is from our Lord'*, while according to the other, that held, for example, by Maḥmūd b. ʿUmar al-Zamakhsharī (d. 538/1144) and Abū Jaʿfar Muḥammad al-Ṭūsī (d. ca 460/1067), it should read: *and none knows its interpretation save only God and those who are rooted in knowledge, who say...*' Tustarī appears to hold the former view as will be seen below. On the *muḥkam and mutashābih* verses in Qurʾanic hermeneutics see Jane D. McAuliffe, 'Qurʾānic Hermeneutics: The Views of Ṭabarī and Ibn Kathīr', in Andrew Rippin, *Approaches to the History of the Interpretation of the Qurʾān* (Oxford and New York, 1988), pp. 46–62; Leah Kinberg, 'Muḥkamāt and Mutashābihāt (Q. verse 3/7): Implication of a Qurʾānic Pair of Terms in Medieval Exegesis', *Arabica* 35 (1988), pp. 143–72; Michel Lagarde, 'De l'ambiguité dans le Coran', *Quaderni di Studi Arabi* 3 (1985), pp. 45–62; Sahiron Syamsuddin, '*Muḥkam* and *Mutashābih*: An Analytical Study of al-Ṭabarī's and al-Zamakhsharī's Interpretations of Q. 3:7', *Journal of Qurʾanic Studies* 1/1 (1999), pp. 63–79; and Stefan Wild, 'The Self-Referentiality of the Qurʾān: Sura 3:7 as an Exegetical Challenge', in Jane D. McAuliffe et al., eds., *With Reverence for the Word* (Oxford and New York, 2003), pp. 422–36.

21 Bayhaqī, *Shuʿab al-īmān*, vol. 2, p. 331.

22 According to the Islamic tradition, Isrāfīl is one of the archangels, whose duty it is to read out the divine decrees from the Preserved Tablet (*lawḥ maḥfūẓ*) and transmit them to the other angels, and to blow the Trumpet signalling the coming of the Day of Judgement. Isrāfīl is said to be of an immense size, such that while his feet are beneath the seventh earth, his head reaches up to the pillars of God's Throne. He has four wings: one in the east, one in the west, one to cover his body, and one as a protection from the divine majesty. See A. J. Wensinck, 'Isrāfīl,' *EI*², vol. IV, p. 211.

Sahl said:

> God sent down the Qurʾān in five instalments of five verses at a time: five clear verses, five ambiguous verses, five concerning that which is permissible, five concerning that which is prohibited, and five parabolic verses. The believer who has gnosis (*maʿrifa*) of God, Exalted is He, adheres to what is clear in it,[23] believes what is ambiguous,[24] holds as permissible that which it has made permissible, holds as prohibited that which it has prohibited, and comprehends its similitudes (*amthāl*), as He has said: *but only those understand them [the similitudes] who know* [29:43] — that is, those who have knowledge (*ʿilm*) of God, Exalted is He, and especially those who have gnosis (*maʿrifa*) of Him.[25]

Sahl said:

> In the Qurʾān there are no two verses that are so harsh against those who dispute the Qurʾān as the following: [in the first,] God, Exalted is He, says: *None dispute the signs of God except those who disbelieve* [40:4], by which is meant the one who disputes God's verses, arguing in accordance with the whim[s] of his lower self (*hawā nafsihi*), and following his own mental disposition (*jibillat ʿaqlihi*). God, Exalted is He, has [likewise] said, *nor [should there be for them] disputing in the Hajj* [2:197], meaning, there shall be no quarrelling during Hajj. The second [of the two verses] is His saying: *But those who disagree about the Book are in a schism, far removed [from the truth]* [2:176].
>
> The Prophet ﷺ said: 'O fellow companions, do not dispute [with others] about what is in the Qurʾān. For while a believer who is guided may dispute with recourse to the Qurʾān and hit the mark, if a lying hypocrite disputes with recourse to the Qurʾān he will present his proofs based on analogy and selfish whims and will be far from correct.'[26] The Prophet ﷺ said: 'The worst of God's servants pursue the worst matters to test God's servants by provoking them.'[27] And God will be their opponent on the Day of Resurrection, as every questioner will be asked on the Day of Resurrection, 'What was intended by your question?'

Sahl said:

> How amazing it is that someone can read the Qurʾān, but then not act according to it, nor avoid what God forbids [in it]! Does such a person not feel shame before God for his contentiousness and rebellion against Him and against that which He has commanded and prohibited, even after having the knowledge of it? Is there anything of greater enormity than this contention? Has he not heard His promise and threat? Does he not listen to what God has promised him through admonishing examples, so that he might have compassion on himself and repent? Has he not heard His words, *Surely the mercy of God is near to the virtuous* [7:56], that he might strive to do good? Has he not heard His words, 'And My mercy has precedence over My punishment',[28] so that he might long for His mercy?

Then Sahl said:

> O God! You honoured them with this beautiful gift [the Qurʾān] and You privileged them with this favour. O God, pardon us and them!

---

23 The clear (*muḥkam*) verses are generally held to be unambiguous verses which inform believers of what is prescribed and proscribed by God.

24 The *mutashābih* verses mentioned in Q. 3:7 are often rendered in English as 'metaphorical' or 'allegorical', though they include other verses, the meanings of which are not readily understandable for other reasons.

25 Tustarī has here contrasted gnosis (*maʿrifa*) and knowledge (*ʿilm*), and indicated that the former goes beyond the latter. There are instances, however, when the word *maʿrifa* may simply mean knowledge. On the use of the term *maʿrifa*, see R. Arnaldez, 'Maʿrifa', *EI²*, vol. VI, pp. 568ff.

26 In other words, however correct the believer's argument might be, it is better not to enter into a dispute at all.

27 Aḥmad b. Shuʿayb al-Nasāʾī, *al-Sunan al-kubrā* (Beirut, 1991), vol. 2, p. 317.

28 This *ḥadīth qudsī* resembles a better-known *ḥadīth*, 'My mercy has precedence over My wrath (*raḥmatī sabaqat ghaḍabī*)', which is listed as *ḥadīth* no. 1 in Abū Zakariyya Yaḥyā al-Nawawī, *Forty Ḥadīth Qudsī*, selected and translated by Ezzeddin Ibrahim and Denys Johnson-Davies (Lebanon, 1980).

Then he said:

> Truly God has not taken as a friend (*walī*)[29] one of Muḥammad's nation (*umma*) without teaching them the Qurʾān either in its outward or inner aspects.
>
> They responded, 'We know about its outward aspect but what is its inner aspect?' He replied, 'That is its understanding (*fahm*); and it is its understanding that is intended.'

Abū Bakr al-Sijzī said:

> Junayd heard me relate the following story and said that Sahl spoke the truth. Once there was a man of a black complexion and foreign tongue with us in Baghdad. We would ask him about the Qurʾān verse by verse and he would answer us with the best response, without having learnt the Qurʾān by heart, and that was a clear proof of his friendship [with God] (*wilāya*). Sahl said, 'It was narrated on the authority of Ibn Masʿūd ﵁ that he [Ibn Masʿūd] said: "The one who knows the Qurʾān by heart [lit. bearer of the Qurʾān, *ḥāmil*] should be known for his vigil at night while people are asleep, for his fasting during the day while people are eating, for his sorrow while people are rejoicing, for his weeping when people are laughing, and for his silence when people are talking." Thus he who knows the Qurʾān by heart should be tearful, sorrowful, wise and learned, not hard-hearted and deceptive, that is to say, not dishonest.'

Sahl said:

> Muḥammad b. Sawwār informed me that when he performed the Hajj one year, he saw Ayyūb al-Sakhtiyānī, who had begun the first [part] of his recitation of the whole Qurʾān in his prayer (*ṣalāt*). [At the same time] he noticed another man from Basra facing the Kaʿba who had started reciting Sūrat al-Muṭaffifīn [83] and kept on repeating the verse, '*Do they not know that they will be resurrected?*' [83:4].

Sahl continued:

> Ayyūb al-Sakhtiyānī had reached two-thirds of the way through the Qurʾān when that man was still repeating this same verse. At the approach of dawn Ayyūb had reached the Sūrat al-Fīl [105], while the other man had reached God's words, *A day when (all) mankind will rise before the Lord of the Worlds?* [83:6].[30] Then that same man fell unconscious, and on approaching him we found him dead.
>
> Indeed people have differed in the way they seek the understanding of the Qurʾān. One group tries to understand the Qurʾān through repetitive study, so that they can derive an understanding of the outward meaning of its ordinances. Among these, some attain a little [understanding] and some attain abundant [understanding]. The latter are knowledgeable and [either] act for the sake of God, Exalted is He, [in the hope of attaining] the abodes of Paradise; or act for God, Exalted is He, in [pure] compliance (*ījāban*); or they are knowledgeable but do not act [on that knowledge].[31] Another group seek to understand the Qurʾān for the sake of memorising its recitation and teaching it to others. Among them, some are sound in their actions, while others are insolent before their Lord. Then there is the one who has studied it a great deal, but whose aim is to learn its melodies and be noticed. He gains [naught but] the ruin of this world and is the worst off out of the three groups in the eyes of God, Exalted is He.

Sahl said:

> I was informed by Muḥammad b. Sawwār who received it from ʿAmru b. Mirdās on the authority of Abū Hurayra ﵁, who related that the Prophet ﷺ said: 'Recite the Qurʾān with the melodies of the Arabs without extraneous affectation, and do not recite it using the tunes of churches, or of heretics or innovators. For verily I and the pious of my nation are free from affectation.

29 See above p. 2, n.5 and p. 3, n. 14 regarding the word *walī*. The word used of God in this context is *istawlā*, which usually means to take possession of, make oneself the master of, to overpower or to imprison; so there is a sense here of God's taking possession of His friends from among the nation of Muḥammad.

30 In other words, in all that time he had focussed his attention on three verses of the Qurʾān.

31 The printed edition has *ʿāmil lahu*, i.e. they do not act upon that knowledge 'for His sake'. However, the word *lahu* is absent from all three MSS.

> But people will come after me who will make their voices quaver in [their recitation] in the manner of female singers delivering their songs. Their hearts are beguiled and they beguile the hearts of their listeners. For sure, it is they who are the heedless.'[32]

Sahl said:

> I truly fear that by the year 300 [A.H.] onwards,[33] the Qurʾān will become effaced through people's preoccupation with tunes, poems and songs.

Then he was asked, 'How will that happen, O Abū Muḥammad?' He replied:

> It will come about because people only initiate these tunes, poems and songs in order to earn from it, and so Iblīs takes possession of their hearts, just as he took possession of the hearts of the poets of the Jāhiliyya,[34] depriving them of the understanding of the Qurʾān and of acting according to it for the sake of God. It was related by Muḥammad b. Sawwār from Ibn Abī Dhiʾb from Muḥammad b. ʿAbd al-Raḥmān on the authority of Thawbān that he heard the Prophet ﷺ say: 'Listening to songs makes you forget the Qurʾān and distracts you from the remembrance [of God].'

Abū Bakr [al-Sijzī] reported that Abū Saʿīd al-Kharrāz used to live in Mecca, and had the greatest love for listening to odes and love songs, and his servant Abū al-Udhnayn informed me that he saw him after his death in a dream and asked him, 'How did God deal with you, O Abū Saʿīd?', to which he responded: 'He forgave me after an upbraiding — I would have preferred to have been sent to the Hellfire rather than be upbraided by God!' When he [Abū al-Udhnayn] asked Abū Saʿīd why this was so, he replied, 'God (*al-Ḥaqq*) had me stand before Him behind the veil of fear and He said to me. "You assigned to Laylā and Suʿdā [feelings] that were My preserve, and if it was not for your taking up a standpoint for My sake from which you sought Me, I would have sent you to Hell." Then, when the veil of fear was changed to the veil of [His] good pleasure (*riḍā*), I said, "O God! I didn't find anyone who could bear what You have burdened me with except You, so I alluded to You."[35] He said, "You have spoken the truth", and He sent me to Paradise.' But God knows best.

A section on His words, *In the name of God, the Compassionate, the Merciful* [1:1][36]

Abū Bakr [al-Sijzī] reported that Sahl was asked about the meaning of [God's words], *In the name of God the Compassionate* (al-Raḥmān), *the Merciful* (al-Raḥīm). He replied:

> The '*bā*' stands for '*bahāʾ Allāh*' (the magnificence of God, Mighty and Majestic is He), the '*sīn*' stands for '*sanāʾ Allāh*' (the resplendence of God), and the '*mīm*' stands for '*majd Allāh*' (the Glory of God), Mighty and Majestic is He.[37] Allāh is the Greatest Name, which contains all His names. Between its '*Alif*' and '*Lām*' there is a cryptic letter, something of an unseen from an unseen to an unseen, a secret from a secret to a secret, a reality from a reality to a reality, of which no one can attain an understanding except those who are pure of all blemishes, and

32 Tirmidhī, *Nawādir al-uṣūl*, vol. 2, p. 255; Bayhaqī, *Shuʿab al-īmān*, vol. 2, p. 540.

33 912 C.E.

34 i.e. the period before Islam.

35 Presumably, his love was so great that no human could have borne it, so through his love-songs the poet/singer was alluding to God. The same can be said of much of the love poetry of later mystics who composed poetry.

36 We have followed the editor of the Dār al-Kutub al-ʿIlmiyya edition in numbering the words, *In the Name of God, the Compassionate, the Merciful* (*bismi'Llāhi'l-Raḥmān al-Raḥīm*), known as the *Basmala*, as the first verse of the first *sūra*. The inclusion of the *Basmala* as a verse of Sūrat al-Fātiḥa is obligatory according to the Shāfiʿī school, while more generally it is thought not to be incorrect to begin any *sūra* with the *Basmala* except Sūrat al-Tawba. Since the verses in the MSS are not numbered, it is not possible for us to know whether or not Tustarī considered it to be one of the verses of Sūrat al-Fātiḥa. In any case, it was customary for exegetes to devote a separate section to their commentary on the *Basmala*.

37 These being the three consonants forming the construct *bi ismi* meaning 'in the name of'.

who take what is permissible according to what is stipulated by their faith.[38] *Al-Raḥmān* is a name which contains a quality from the aforementioned cryptic letter between the *Alif* and *Lām*. *Al-Raḥīm* is the One who inclines to His servants in kindness by providing for them, this being a ramification (*farʿ*) [of the significance of this name], while in origin it is His initiation (*ibtidāʾ*) [of all things], as a mercy (*raḥmatan*), related to His pre-eternal knowledge.[39]

Abū Bakr added:

In other words, through the zephyr of His grace, God originated whatever He willed in the kingdom of creation, out of mercy because He is the Merciful. ʿAlī b. Abū Ṭālib ﷺ said: '*Al-Raḥmān* and *al-Raḥīm* are two names of compassion, one of which [signifies] greater compassion than the other;[40] by them God, Exalted is He, has expelled despair (*qunūṭ*) from the believers among His servants.'

38 This is probably the closest that Tustarī comes in his *Tafsīr* to the content of the cosmological treatise on letters that has been attributed to him, the *Risālat al-ḥurūf*. See IT, p. xxiv; the dissertation of Gaafar, ch. 4, and Garrido Clemente, 'El Tratado de las Letras'.

39 Alternatively, we might read it as: 'this being a ramification (*farʿ*), while in origin (*aṣl*) the initiation [of creation] is a mercy (*raḥma*) connected to His pre-eternal knowledge'. Either way, this passage indicates that Tustarī understands the creation as a manifestation of God's quality of being the Merciful, as is confirmed by the explanation that follows it.

40 lit. 'are two compassionate names (*ismān raqīqān*), of which one is more compassionate (*araqq*) than the other'. In his commentary on the *Basmala*, Ṭabarī explains that of the two forms derived from the verbal root *r-ḥ-m*, *al-raḥmān* denotes a stronger quality than *al-raḥīm*. According to a tradition narrated in Ṭabarī's commentary on the authority of al-ʿArzamī, '[the divine name] *al-Raḥmān* [denotes mercy] to all creatures, while the name *al-Raḥīm* [denotes mercy] to the believers.' According to another tradition narrated on the authority of Abū Saʿīd al-Khuḍrī, 'Jesus, the son of Mary, said: "*Al-Raḥmān* is the Merciful in the next world as well as in this world; *al-Raḥīm* is the Merciful in the next world."' See Abū Jaʿfar al-Ṭabarī, *Jāmiʿ al-bayān ʿan taʾwīl āy al-Qurʾān*, published under the title *Jāmiʿ al-bayān ʿan tafsīr al-Qurʾān*, ed. Maḥmūd Muḥammad Shākir and Aḥmad Muḥammad Shākir, vols. 1–16, incomplete (Cairo, 1955–69). vol. 1, pp. 148–9; trans. John Cooper, *The Commentary on the Qurʾān by Abū Jaʿfar Muḥammad b. Jarīr al-Ṭabarī* (Oxford, 1987), pp. 55–6.

1 Al-Fātiḥa

[1:2] ***Praise be to God***[1]

Sahl said:

The meaning of 'Praise be to God' (*al-ḥamdu li'Llāh*) is 'thanks be to God' (*al-shukru li'Llāh*), [for] gratitude towards God is obedience (*ṭāʿa*) to Him. Obedience to Him is guardianship (*wilāya*)[2] from Him, Exalted is He, and thus God, Exalted is He, has said: *'Your patron* (walī) *is God only, and His Messenger, and the believers...'* [5:55] God's patronage can only be fully attained by becoming free of all other than Him.

The meaning of *Lord of the Worlds* is: the Lord of all created beings and the One who rears and fosters them (*murabbī*); He is the One who presides over their affairs and who rectifies and orders things for them, even before they and their acts are brought into existence. He deals with them according to His pre-eternal knowledge of them, as He wills and for whatever purpose He wills, wishes, rules, and decrees, regarding that which is commanded and that which is forbidden, and they have no lord except Him.

[1:4] ***The Master of the Day of Judgement:***

That is, the Day of Reckoning.

[1:5] ***You [alone] we worship...,***

That is, we submit to, and humble ourselves before, You alone. We recognise Your lordship and we affirm Your oneness, and You do we serve. From this word (*naʿbudu*) is derived the word *ʿabd* meaning 'servant'.[3] *...And You [alone] we ask for help*, that is, in what You have charged us with, which is [rightfully] Yours, [and over which] You exercise Your will (*mashīʾa*) and volition (*irāda*).[4] Moreover, knowledge and sincerity are due only to You. We are incapable of [accomplishing that with which You have charged us] except through aid (*maʿūna*) and steadfastness (*tasdīd*) that come from You, for there is no power or strength except that which comes from You.

([1:6] ***Guide us to the straight path.***)[5]

He [Sahl] was asked, 'Has not God already guided us to the straight path?' He replied:

That is so, but this refers to seeking more from Him, as He has said: *and with Us there is yet more* [50:35]. [Thus] what is meant by His words *Guide us* is: 'Support us with Your aid (*maʿūna*) and empowerment (*tamkīn*)'.

---

1 See above, IC, p. 8, n. 36 concerning the numbering of the verses of Sūrat al-Fātiḥa.

2 That is, obedience is a way of manifesting our gratitude, and our gratitude is increased through obedience, while obedience itself is a manifestation of God's patronage and protection. See also above, IC, p. 2, and IT, p. xxxix. The relationship between gratitude and divinely bestowed increase is discussed again later, in Tustarī's commentary on 14:7.

3 Or 'slave'.

4 Gaafar (PhD thesis, p. 224) explains that in Tustarī's theology, God's Will (or 'Uncreated Will', *mashīʾa*), is associated with His Knowledge, while God's Volition (or 'Creative Will', *irāda*) is associated with His Omnipotence: 'The *mashīʾa* is the gate of Knowledge (*bāb al-ʿilm*); the *irāda* is the gate of Omnipotence (*bāb al-qudra*).' See also *Kalām Sahl ibn ʿAbd Allāh*, ed. Gaafar, in Jaʿfar, *Min al-turāth al-Tustarī*, Part 2, p. 202; MS Köprülü 727, f. 72b.

5 This verse (1:6) itself is not written out either in the printed edition or in the MSS, though the question and Tustarī's response which follow the comment on 1:5 clearly refer to 1:6.

On another occasion he said that *Guide us* (ihdinā) means:

> Guide us (*arshidnā*) to the religion of Islam, which is the way to You, through assistance from You, which is insight (*baṣīra*), for we cannot be guided except through You, just as he [Moses] said: '*Perhaps my Lord will show me the right way*' [28:22], that is, 'Guide me to pursue the path that leads to Him'.

I heard Sahl relate on the authority of Muḥammad b. Sawwār from Sufyān, who heard it from Salīm, who was told by Abū al-Jaʿd from Thawbān, who narrated that the Messenger of God ﷺ said:

> God says: 'I have divided the prayer between Me and My servant into two halves. Half of it is for Me and the other half is for My servant, and My servant gets what he asks for.' Thus, when the servant says, *Praise be to God, Lord of the Worlds,* God, Exalted is He, says, 'My servant has praised and thanked Me.' When he says, *the Merciful, the Compassionate*, [God says], 'My servant has extolled Me'. And when he says, *Master of the Day of Judgement*, [God says], 'My servant has glorified Me. These verses are for Me and for My servant is what he asks for [in the verses that come] after, as when he says, *You [alone] we worship, and You [alone] do we ask for help.* ۞ *Guide us to the straight path*, until the end of the *sūra*.' God, Mighty and Majestic is He, says: 'These verses are for My servant and My servant shall receive what he asks for.'[6]

Sahl said:

> The meaning of 'My servant has glorified Me' here is: 'He has attributed abundant beneficence (*iḥsān*) and munificence (*inʿām*) to Me'.

Sahl related on the authority of Mujāhid:

> *Āmīn* is one of the names of God, Exalted is He.[7] Ibn ʿAbbās ﷺ said, 'The Christians have never envied you anything as much as your saying *Āmīn*.'[8] Muḥammad b. Sawwār related from Ibn ʿUyayna from ʿAmr b. Dīnār on the authority of Jābir b. ʿAbd Allāh ﷺ, who related that the Messenger of God ﷺ said, 'Keep to the straight path, [though] you will not be able to encompass [all good actions]. Know that the best of your actions is prayer, and [indeed] only a believer observes ablution carefully. Whenever the imam says, *Nor [the path] of those who go astray* [1:7], you should say, '*Āmīn*', for God is pleased with the one who says it, and He accepts his prayer and responds to his supplication.'

Al-Zuhrī related from Ibn al-Musayyab on the authority of Abū Hurayra ﷺ that the Prophet said, 'When the imam says, *Nor [the path] of those who go astray*, say '*Āmīn*', for truly the angels say '*Āmīn*', and the one whose pronouncement of '*Āmīn*' is simultaneous with that of the angels will be forgiven for all his previous sins.'

6 Ibn Māja, *Sunan* (Beirut, 1995), 'Al-Adab: Bāb thawāb al-Qurʾān'; Abū Dāwūd al-Sijistānī, *Sunan* (Beirut, 1988), 'Kitāb al-Ṣalāt'; Tirmidhī, *Sunan*, 'Kitāb Tafsīr al-Qurʾān'.

7 *Āmīn* is traditionally said following the last verse of Sūrat al-Fātiḥa when it is recited during the canonical prayer, or as part of other prayers or invocations. When one person makes a supplication on behalf of and in the presence of others, it is likewise customary for the congregation to repeat *Āmīn* (Amen).

8 Regarding this saying of Ibn ʿAbbās, the editor of the Dār al-Kutub al-ʿIlmiyya edition cites here another version of the tradition, listed in ʿAbd al-Raʾūf al-Munāwī and ʿAbd al-Salām al-Suyūṭī, *Fayḍ al-qadīr: sharḥ al-Jāmiʿ al-ṣaghīr min aḥādīth al-bashīr al-nadhīr* (Cairo, 1938), vol. 5, p. 441, in which it is said to have been the Jews rather than the Christians who are envious of the Muslims' saying '*Āmīn*'.

2 Al-Baqara

[2:1] *Alif Lām Mīm*

Sahl said:

> *Alif Lām Mīm* is a name of God, Mighty and Majestic is He, and within it are meanings and attributes that people of understanding (*fahm*) know, not to mention the many meanings that it holds for the people of outward [knowledge].[1] If these letters are read separately, *Alif* stands for God's assembling [things in their creation] (*taʾlīf*), Mighty and Majestic is He, for He brought together all things as He willed. The *Lām* stands for His pre-eternal grace (*luṭfuhu al-qadīm*) and the *Mīm* stands for His great glory (*majduhu al-ʿaẓīm*).

Sahl said:

> Each book that God, Exalted is He, sent down contains a secret, and the secret of the Qurʾān is contained within the letters which open the *sūra*s, because they are names and attributes, such as when He says *Alif Lām Mīm* [2:1; 3:1; 29:1 and 31:1], *Ṣād* [38:1], *Alif Lām Rā* [10:1; 11:1; 13:1; 14:1 and 15:1], *Kāf Hā Yā ʿAyn Ṣād* [19:1], *Tā Sīn Mīm* [26:1 and 28:1], *Ḥā Mīm* [41:1], *ʿAyn Sīn Qāf*.[2] When these letters are brought together they make up the Greatest Name of God[3] — that is, if a letter is taken from each [group] of the opening letters of the *sūra*s, one after the other in the order that the *sūra*s were revealed, that is, *Alif Lām Rā, Ḥā Mīm,* and *Nūn*,[4] they form the divine name *al-Raḥmān*. Ibn ʿAbbās and Ḍaḥḥāk, on the other hand, said that *Alif Lām Mīm* means 'I am God and I know'; while ʿAlī said that these are names [in the form of] 'disconnected' [letters], but if a letter is taken from each of the opening groups of letters, on the condition that it is not the same as the letter adjacent to it, and then they are assembled, they form one of the names of the Merciful. If this name is known and used in supplication, it will be the mightiest name by which the prayer of the supplicant who uses it will be answered.

Sahl said:

> In the words *Alif Lām Mīm,* ❁ *That Book* [2:1–2], *Alif* stands for God (*Allāh*), *Lām* stands for the servant (*ʿabd*), and *Mīm* stands for Muḥammad. So, [through these letters] the servant may gain access to his Master from the position of affirming His oneness (*tawḥīd*) and by following the example of His Prophet.[5]

---

1 Note that above, IC, p. 2, Tustarī had connected understanding (*fahm*) to the inner meanings of the Qurʾān.

2 The 'disconnected letters' (*al-ḥurūf al-muqaṭṭaʿa*), also referred to in English as the 'mysterious letters', with which some of the *sūras* begin, have been the subject of many traditional interpretations as well as modern theories. Traditional interpretations include the view that they represent names of Qurʾānic *sūra*s, or names of God, as in the first tradition presented by Tustarī above, or that they have mystical significance, or a cryptic meaning, as in the second interpretation he presents above. They are also sometimes subject to interpretations based on the numerical values of the letters. See K. Massey, 'Mysterious Letters', *EQ*, vol. v, 412–4. For a discussion of one non-Muslim attempt to explain the significance of the detached letters, see Neal Robinson, *Discovering the Qurʾān: A Contemporary Approach to a Veiled Text* (Washington, D.C., 2003), pp. 260ff.

3 In this instance, the Greatest Name is said to be *al-Raḥmān*, but below it is said to be *Allāh*.

4 Sūra 68 (The Pen) commences with this letter.

5 See above, IC, p. 9, n. 38 and IT, p. xxiv, concerning Tustarī's *Risālat al-ḥurūf*. In that treatise Tustarī ascribes special cosmological significance to the letters *alif, waw* and *yā*, with *alif* being assigned to the rational power (*quwwa nāṭiqa*), *waw* being assigned to the 'animal force' (*quwwa ḥaywāniyya*), and *yā* being assigned to 'natural activity' (*quwwa*

Sahl further said:

> I received [a tradition] on the authority of Ibn ʿAbbās according to which he said: 'God, Exalted is He, has sworn that this Book which was revealed to Muḥammad ﷺ is the book from God's presence, Exalted is He. So He said: *Alif Lām Mīm, That Book...* [In these words], *Alif* stands for God (*Allāh*), *Lām* stands for Gabriel ﷺ and *Mīm* stands for Muḥammad ﷺ, thus God, Exalted is He, has taken an oath by Himself, by the angel Gabriel ﷺ and by Muḥammad ﷺ.'

He also said:

> God, Exalted is He, extracted from His Greatest Name [*Allāh*][6] the letters *Alif, Lām* and *Hāʾ* and said: *Indeed I am God, the Lord of the Worlds* [28:30],[7] and for [His creatures'] sake He derived a name from among His names and made it the name of His Prophet ﷺ, and He derived from the end of the name of His Prophet ﷺ the name of His prophet Adam ﷺ.[8] Thus He says: *That is because God is the Patron [or Friend] of those who believe, and those who disbelieve have no patron* [47:11] — except the Devil, that is, Satan.

[2:2] ***...In it there is no doubt* (rayb)...**

> This means that there is no uncertainty (*shakk*) in it. *A guidance for those who are mindful of God* (muttaqūn) — that is, an explanation (*bayān*) for those who are mindful of God.[9] The mindful of God are those who have freed themselves from the claim of possessing any power or strength except in God, Exalted is He, and who have resorted to taking refuge [in Him] and depending solely on His power and strength in every situation. So God has assisted them and provided for them whence they had no reckoning,[10] and made for them a source of relief and release from the trials to which He has subjected them.

Sahl [further] said:

> God's power (*ḥawl*) and strength (*quwwa*) are [manifest in] His act, His act is according to His knowledge, and His knowledge is among the attributes belonging to His essence.[11] The power and strength of the servant are but a temporary claim which lasts only until the last hour. The last hour is in the possession of God alone, Exalted is He.

[2:3] ***The [ones who are] mindful of God are those who believe in the unseen...***

> God is the unseen and His religion is the unseen, and God, Mighty and Majestic is He, has ordered them to believe in the unseen, to free themselves from [any claim] to power and

---

ṭabīʿiyya) (trans. Gaafar, PhD thesis, pp. 97–8).

6 See above, Tustarī's commentary on the *Basmala* and 2:1, and the accompanying notes.

7 These are among the words spoken to Moses from the burning bush.

8 i.e. when the last two letters, *mīm* and *dāl*, are taken in reverse order. Here is an allusion to the doctrine that in pre-eternity, the existence of the Prophet Muḥammad preceded all creatures and all the other prophets derived their light from him, although he was the last to appear in the sublunary world. This is discussed by Tustarī in his commentary on 11:40. On this doctrine see IT, pp. xxxiff. A later discussion is presented by Maybudī, *Kashf al-asrār*, vol. 10, p. 202.

9 The words *taqwā* and *muttaqī* are derived from the verb *w-q-y*, which means to 'be mindful, aware or wary of' something, though these two derivatives are often translated as 'fear of God' and 'God-fearing', respectively. However, there are various words for different forms of fear [of God], such as *khawf, khashy* and *waraʿ* (these are discussed later in the commentary by Tustarī), and therefore we are translating the word *taqwā* in cases such as this as 'mindfulness of God', and *muttaqī* as the one who is mindful of God. The expressions 'fear of God' or 'God-fearing' will only be used in our translation of these words in those contexts where a particular emphasis is placed on the sense of wariness and awe towards God. On *taqwā* in Tustarī's teachings see above IT, p. lvi.

10 That is, from a source which they had not taken into account.

11 We have seen above, p. 10, that God's Knowledge is the 'gate', hence 'prior' to His Uncreated Will (*mashīʾa*), which precedes His Creative Will and Omnipotence, not in their existence but in their effects. But, as Gaafar explains, Tustarī also suggests that the Uncreated Will of God is an immediate stage that *succeeds* His Knowledge. In his *Kitāb al-Muʿāraḍa*, MS Köprülü 727, f. 212a, Tustarī outlines the stages of creation as being firstly Knowledge (that is, the divine Omniscience); secondly, the Book, comprising all the decrees of God, which are susceptible of effacement or affirmation (*maḥw wa ithbāt*, through *mashīʾa*); thirdly there is *qaḍā*, the affirmed Decree of God (*ḥukm thābit*); and fourthly, there *is qadar*, the actual manifestation of that which has been decreed. See Gaafar, PhD thesis, pp. 223–5.

strength concerning that which they have been commanded to do and prohibited from doing, in faith, speech and action and to say, 'We have no power (*ḥawl*) to keep ourselves from disobedience save through Your protection (*ʿiṣma*), and we have no strength (*quwwa*) to obey You save through Your aid (*maʿūna*).' This is [a result of] of His compassion (*ishfāq*) towards them, and of His assisting them so that they do not claim power, strength and ability as did those who were damned from pre-eternity. When [these latter] saw the punishment with their own eyes, they disowned [their claim], but their disavowal did not avail them after they had actually seen the punishment. God has informed us about those who fit this description in His words *But their faith was of no benefit to them when they (actually) saw Our punishment* [40:85], and: *Their only plea when Our might came upon them, was to say, 'We were evildoers indeed'* [7:5]. Similarly, Pharaoh claimed to have power, strength and ability, and said, 'Whenever I wish to believe, I will believe', but when he actually came to believe it was not accepted from him, as God, Exalted is He, said, *Now — when hitherto you have disobeyed and been of those who do corruption?* [10:91]

[2:3] *...And spend out of what We have provided them:*

Sahl said:

Truly God, Exalted is He, has described in this way those whom He has moulded with a certain nature, who are connected to Him by a certain link, and who never lapse in their heedfulness (*murāqaba*) of Him. They are those who never made a choice and desired nothing other than Him. Their only choice is that He should choose for them, even as He has chosen them for Himself.[12] They desire nothing that has any relation to another which will remove them from their dependence solely on Him, for they have freed themselves from other than Him.

Abū Bakr relates that it was said to Sahl: 'Truly God has granted you wisdom (*ḥikma*)', to which he replied:

Indeed, God willing, I have been granted wisdom (*ḥikma*) and [a knowledge of] the unseen (*ghayb*) which I was taught from the unseen of His secret (*min ghayb sirrihi*),[13] and thus He sufficed me from the need for all other knowledge — *and that the ultimate end is toward your Lord* [53:42], and He completed what He had begun with me out of His grace and beneficence.

His words, Mighty and Majestic is He:

[2:5] *Those are upon guidance from their Lord...*

That is, a clear explanation (*bayān*) from their Lord: by the light of His guidance hearts witness Him in confident abandonment to Him due to a light from His light, by which He singled them out in His prior knowledge.[14] They do not speak except with guidance (*hudā*), and their inner perception is solely directed towards that guidance. So those who are guided by [this light] are never left by it; they are [constant] witnesses to it because they are never absent from it. If people were to ask them about it they would inform them, and if they were to will [something], it would quickly be brought about.[15] Thus ...*they are the ones who will prosper* [2:5], and they are directed to guidance and success through His guidance. [It is they who will] remain (*bāqūna*) in Paradise with the permanent subsistence (*baqāʾ*) of God, Mighty and Majestic is He.[16]

---

12 That is according to all three MSS (Z515, f. 10b, F638, f. 6a and F3488, f. 188b), which have: *kamā ikhtārahum lahu*, as opposed to *kamā ikhtārahu lahum*.

13 That is, perhaps, from the profound, secret link between man in his deepest being and God. This is explained by Tustarī in his commentary on 2:41. See also IT, p. xlviii.

14 There may be an allusion here both to 24:40 and to a *ḥadīth*, which reads 'Verily God created the creatures in darkness, and then He cast upon them some of His light. Whosoever was touched by that light found guidance and whomsoever it missed went astray.' Ibn Ḥanbal, *al-Musnad* (Cairo, 1895), vol. 2, pp. 176 and 197; Tirmidhī, *Sunan*, 'Kitāb al-Īmān', and *Nawādir al-uṣūl*, vol. 2, p. 413.

15 lit. 'things would hasten to [fulfil] their wish'.

16 We shall see later that Tustarī describes the grace which God grants to those who have found guidance and success, beyond the blessings and delights of Paradise, as being: 'life with Life itself', and 'permanent subsistence with Permanent Subsistence itself'.

Then Sahl said:

It was transmitted to me that God, Exalted is He, revealed to David ﷺ the words: 'Make sure that I do not pass you by, for in that case you would forgo everything. Verily I created Muḥammad ﷺ for My sake, and I created Adam ﷺ for his sake.[17] I created My believing servants for My worship, and I created all other things for [the service of] the son of Adam.[18] So if he preoccupies himself with that which I have created for his service, I will veil him from that [for] which I created [him] for My sake.'[19]

[2:22] *...So set not up compeers* (andād) *to God...*

That is, adversaries (*aḍdād*),[20] and the greatest adversary is the self that incites to evil (*al-nafs al-ammāra bi'l-sūʾ*), which is only bent on its own pleasures (*ḥuẓūẓ*) and cravings (*munā*), without having any regard for guidance from God.[21]

Sahl was asked about God's words:

[2:25] *...They shall be given it [the fruits] in perfect semblance; ...and there for them shall be spouses, purified...,*

He replied:

In Paradise there are no carpets, vessels, clothes, perfume, birds or plants, nor any fruits [as we know them]. Thus the semblance that the things of this world bear to those [mentioned in the verse] is no more than a coincidence in their names. So the pomegranate of this world does not in the least resemble the pomegranate in Paradise, except in name. The same is the case with resemblance of the date, the jujube and other such fruits [to those of Paradise]. What is intended in His saying *in [perfect] semblance* is only a likeness in colour, for there is a difference in taste. When in Paradise the angels bring an apple to the friends of God (*awliyāʾ*) during the day, and then they bring them another during the night, and they ask, 'Is this one [like the other]?' They are told, 'Taste it', and on tasting it they experience a different taste to that of the first one. It should not be discounted from God's ability, Exalted is He, that He could make an apple taste like a pomegranate, almond or quince.'

Sahl continued:

Indeed I know one of the friends of God (*awliyāʾ*) who saw on the seashore a man who had before him the biggest pomegranate that there ever was. The friend of God (*walī*) asked him what he had before him, to which he replied, 'It is a pomegranate that I saw in Paradise. I desired it so God granted it to me, but when He placed it before me I regretted my haste for having it while still in this world.' That man [the *walī*] asked, 'May I eat some of it?' and the man responded, 'If you have the capacity to eat it, then do so';[22] upon which he grabbed the fruit from him and ate most of it. When the man saw him eating the fruit he it was astounded and said, 'Receive glad tidings of Paradise, for I did not know your [spiritual] rank before you ate it; no one eats of the food of Paradise in this life except the people of Paradise.'

Then Abū Bakr asked Sahl if the one who had eaten the pomegranate had informed him of its taste, to which he replied:

He did, and its taste brings together the tastes of all fruits, and in addition it has a smoothness and coolness which is unlike any of the tastes [experienced] in this world.

---

17 That is, so that the Muḥammadan Reality could become manifest. Again, see above, IT, pp. xxxiff.

18 That is, humanity in general.

19 Or, 'from that which I created for My sake,' i.e. the Prophet.

20 The Qurʾānic word used is *andād*, which can mean 'peer', 'partner' or alternatively 'antagonist', 'rival'. Tustarī had clearly understood it to mean the latter here.

21 On the term *nafs ammāra*, or more fully, *al-nafs al-ammāra bi'l-sūʾ* and more generally on Tustarī's teachings concerning the *nafs*, see above, IT, pp. xxxviiiff, and especially pp. xliff.

22 If it is read in the passive (i.e. *qudirta* instead of *qadarta*), it could mean 'if you are foreordained to eat it', which is how Böwering translates it.

Then Abū Bakr commented, 'I have no doubt, nor does anyone who heard this story from Sahl, that he himself was in fact both the possessor of that pomegranate and the one who ate it.'

Sahl was asked about His words:

[2:30] *...I am appointing on earth a vicegerent...*

He answered:

> God, Exalted is He, before he created Adam ﷺ said to the angels *I am appointing on earth a vicegerent*, and He created Adam from the clay of might consisting of the light of Muḥammad ﷺ, and He informed him that his self which incites evil (*al-nafs al-ammāra bi'l-sūʾ*) would be his worst enemy,[23] and that He had created it so that he conduct it [on the path] to Him, according to his knowledge of it, regarding notions (*khawāṭir*)[24] and impulses (*himam*) [which arise in it], and that he [Adam] conduct it in such a way as to remain utterly dependent on Him, seeking refuge in Him.[25] If He shows it an act of obedience, it should respond by saying, 'O help me!', and if it is moved to an act of disobedience, it should cry out, 'O protect me!' If it is moved to a blessing, it should say, 'Grant me a share of it!' If He says to it, 'Be patient in the face of tribulation', it should respond saying, 'O, grant me patience!' His [man's] heart should not entertain the slightest whispering (*waswasa*) of the self without abandoning it and returning to its Lord. God, Exalted is He, made the natural propensity (*ṭabʿ*) of the self such that it is passive when faced with commandments and active when faced with prohibitions. However, He commanded it to respond with passivity when inclined to activity, and to be active when inclined to passivity, with the words, 'There is neither power nor strength except in God', that is, there is no power to resist disobeying Him except through His protection, and no strength to obey Him except with His aid.
>
> Then He ordered him [Adam] to enter the Garden and eat from it at ease wherever he wished, after which He decreed to him that he may not eat from the Tree. When he entered the Garden and saw what he saw there, he said, 'If only we could stay here forever; yet, indeed, we have an appointed time that extends to a known limit.' Then Satan approached him, on account of his heart's accommodating itself (*musākana*)[26] to the whispering of his lower self, and said, 'Shall I lead you to the tree of eternity that you long for in this abode, which is the means to attain immortality and everlastingness?', and he added, *Your Lord only prohibited you both from this tree, lest you become angels or immortals* [7:20]. His argument was just a form of deception. Thereby God, Mighty and Majestic is He, inflicted on [Adam] the Adversary's whispering, in accordance with His pre-eternal knowledge concerning him, and in fulfilment of what He had preordained and justly decreed for him.[27]

---

23 Here and in his commentary on 2:22 above, Tustarī is alluding to a *ḥadīth* of the Prophet in which he is reported to have said: 'Your greatest enemy is your lower self (*nafs*) which is between your two sides.' This *ḥadīth* is listed in Aḥmad b. al-Ḥusayn al-Bayhaqī's *Kitāb al-Zuhd al-kabīr* (Kuwait, 1983), p. 190. Ghazālī cites the *ḥadīth* in the *Iḥyāʾ ʿulūm al-dīn*, Book 21: *Kitāb Sharḥ ʿajāʾib al-qalb*.

24 The word *khāṭir* (pl. *khawāṭir*) has the sense of a thought which is stirred up in the mind, or occurs unexpectedly to a person. Kalābādhī explains that there are four kinds of *khaṭar*: one that comes from God; one that comes from an angel; one that comes from the *nafs*; and one that comes from the Enemy (i.e. Satan). See his *Kitāb al-Taʿarruf*, pp. 90–1; English trans. Arberry, p. 80.

25 That is reading *yuṣirrahā* on the basis of MSS Z515, f. 12a, F638, f. 7a and F3488, f. 190a, instead of *yaʾmurahā* as in the printed edition. It is also possible to read God as the subject throughout the sentence, in which case it would translate as: '...and He created it so that He might conduct it to Himself, according to His knowledge of it, regarding notions and impulses which arise in it, and that He might conduct it in the state of utter dependence on Him...'.

26 It will be seen that Tustarī uses the term *musākana* in a very particular way for the lower self's or heart's accommodating itself to, or acquiescing in, a desire that arises, or a suggestion that concerns, other than God, or the disobeying of His command.

27 Concerning Tustarī's doctrines of the dangers of the *nafs*, see Böwering, *Mystical Vision*, p. 258.

The first instance of forgetfulness (*nisyān*) that took place in Paradise was the forgetfulness of Adam, and it was a deliberate forgetfulness, not accidental, that is, it signified his abandonment of the Covenant.[28]

Sahl said:

I was informed in an account of one of the Followers (*tābiʿūn*)[29] that he [the Prophet] said that forgetfulness in the Book of God, Mighty and Majestic is He, is of two kinds. [One is] abandonment, as for example in Sūrat al-Baqara, *Or we cause to be forgotten* [2:106], when it means: 'We abandon it and we do not abrogate it'; and also in His words: *Forget not kindness between you* [2:237], meaning: 'Do not abandon kindness between yourselves'; and likewise in Sūrat Ṭā Hā, *but he [Moses] forgot* [20:88], meaning: 'He has abandoned the Covenant'. Another example occurs in Sūrat al-Sajda, in the words, *Taste [now], for your having forgotten the encounter of this day of yours, and We [too] shall forget you* [32:14], meaning: 'We shall abandon you to your punishment as We lifted Our protection from you when you persisted in committing sin.'

He continued:

The other meaning of forgetfulness is when someone cannot remember because the information leaves his memory, exemplified by his [Moses'] words [narrated] in Sūrat al-Kahf, *I did indeed forget the fish* [18:63], meaning: 'I couldn't keep it in my memory' — this is due to the fact that God, Exalted is He, has made Satan a partner with the natural self (*nafs al-jibilla*) regarding the desires that it has which have nothing to do with God, Exalted is He.[30] Another example is in Moses' words to Khiḍr, *Do not take me to task on account of that which I forgot* [18:73], meaning: 'That which escaped my memory'. Also He said in Sūra Sabbiḥ [Sūrat al-Aʿlā], *We will have you recite [the Qurʾān], so you do not forget.* [87:6] — that is: 'We shall have you memorise [the Qurʾān], so that you do not forget it'.

So this [Adam's forgetfulness and Satan's access to him] was because of his preoccupation with his own devising (*tadbīr*).[31] His thought [for everlasting life] did not involve any considered reflection which might have made it a form of worship, but rather it was a kind of thinking that springs from a disposition (*ṭabʿ*) in his self (*nafs al-jibilla*). God, Exalted is He, decreed when He created the heavens and the earth, that if He sees in a person's heart something in which he is acquiescing other than Himself, that person will be overpowered by Satan, who will whisper in his breast (*ṣadr*) to his lower self, by [generating] a desire, such that it [the *nafs*] will invite him to pursue it. Or he may turn back to his Lord seeking refuge in Him and clinging to His protection (*iʿtiṣām*). However, in his native land,[32] God concealed His remembrance from [Adam] until after he had committed that which was forbidden, so that His prior knowledge concerning that which He had forbidden him could be fulfilled; and Adam's act [of disobedience] then became a habit[33] among his progeny up until the Day of Resurrection. In reality, God did not mean by this the matter of eating [from the tree], but rather the acquiescence (*musākana*) of the desire (*himma*) in something other than Him. Phrased another way, [God

---

28 The covenant that is being referred to here is the pact that God took from Adam in Paradise that he would not eat of the tree (the Qurʾān does not, like the Bible, specify that it is the tree of the knowledge of good and evil), and Tustarī's words appear to be an allusion to 20:115: *And We made a covenant with Adam before, but he forgot, and We did not find any constancy in him.*

29 The *tābiʿūn* are the generation immediately after the Companions of the Prophet.

30 The construct here: *nafs al-jibilla* is similar to that of *nafs al-ṭabʿ* and Tustarī may here be using *jibilla* as more or less equivalent to *ṭabʿ*. On Tustarī's teachings concerning different levels of the *nafs*, see IT, pp. xliff.

31 i.e. his thinking about how much better it would be if he were to live forever in Paradise. In Sufi writings, human planning and contrivance (*tadbīr*) are often contrasted with divine determination and decree (*taqdīr*). The latter, of course, is always shown to overcome the former. In the course of his commentary, Tustarī frequently warns against having recourse to our own planning and attempts to manage our lives (*tadbīr*), which are both incompatible with true trust in God. On *tadbīr* and *taqdīr* see IT, pp. xxxivff.

32 i.e. Paradise.

33 That is a habitual practice or norm (*sunna*). The published edition has *ṣāra fiʿluhu ʿilm sunnatan*, whereas MS 515, f. 13a omits the word *ʿilm*, which in any case should have been in the accusative.

is saying]: 'He [man] should not concern himself with anything other than Me'. Adam ﷺ was not protected from the desire (*himma*) and the act (*fiʿl*) in Paradise, so what befell him, befell him for that reason. Similarly, he who claims what is not his, while his heart appeases him by entertaining the desire of his lower self, will be afflicted with God's abandonment (*tark*), Mighty and Majestic is He, notwithstanding the fact that God naturally disposed his lower self to it, unless He has mercy upon him by protecting him from his own devising (*tadbīr*), and helps him against his enemy, that is, his self that incites to evil.[34] The people of Paradise, when they are in Paradise, will be protected from the planning (*tadbīr*) that they were accustomed to in the abode of this world. Yet Adam, when he was placed in Paradise, was not protected from his heart's acquiescence in the planning of his lower self for immortality. Do you not see that calamity (*balāʾ*) befell him because of the reliance (*sukūn*) of his heart upon what his lower self whispered to him? And so desire (*hawā*) and lust (*shahwa*) overwhelmed knowledge (*ʿilm*), the intellect (*ʿaql*), lucidity (*bayān*) and the light of the heart (*nūr al-qalb*), on account of that which God, Exalted is He, had preordained. Thus the end of the situation was as the Prophet ﷺ foretold when he said: 'Truly passion and desire overwhelm knowledge and intellect'.[35]

[2:37] *Thereafter Adam received certain words from his Lord, and He relented towards him...*

Sahl was asked, 'What were the words that Adam learnt from his Lord?' He replied:

Muḥammad b. Sawwār informed me, [in a narration] from his father, from al-Thawrī, from ʿAbd al-ʿAzīz b. Rafīʿ, on the authority of ʿAbd Allāh b. ʿUmar ؓ, that he [the latter] said: 'When Adam ﷺ recalled his error he said: "O Lord, do you see the act of disobedience by which I disobeyed You as something that You preordained for me before You created me, or something that I initiated?" He replied: "Indeed, it is something that I preordained for you, that you would do as a consequence of My lifting My protection from you, fifty thousand years before creating you." Then Adam ﷺ asked, "As you preordained it for me, then forgive me, for indeed *We have wronged our own souls* [7:23], through carrying out the lower self's desire and relying on its devising, and we have repented from ever going back to that. *If You do not forgive us* — that is, in this life, *and have mercy upon us,* during what remains of our lives *we shall surely be among the lost* [7:23] — that is, among the damned and tormented in the Hereafter."' So these were the words which God, Exalted is He, was speaking about when He said: *Thereafter Adam received certain words from his Lord, and his Lord relented towards him, truly He is the Relenting, the Merciful.*

It was related from the Prophet ﷺ that he said: 'Adam asked Moses, (peace be upon them both), "How many years before my creation do you find that my sin was destined for me?" He replied, "Forty thousand years."' The Prophet ﷺ then said, 'Thus did Adam confute Moses (peace be upon them both).'[36]

Sahl was asked about God's words:

[2:30] *...Whilst we glorify You with praise and sanctify You...*

It means 'We purify ourselves for Your sake by saying what You inspired us to say through the favour that You bestowed upon us. Blessed are You, O our Lord!'

[2:40] *...And be in awe of Me.*

34 MSS Z515, f. 13a and F3488, f. 191a both have *nafs* while F638, f. 7b has *al-nafs al-ammāra biʾl-sūʾ*. None of the MSS has *Iblīs wa*, which is in the printed edition.

35 The editor of the Dār al-Kutub al-ʿIlmiyya edition notes that this is not a prophetic *ḥadīth*, but a saying of Ḥārith b. Asad, which is cited in Iṣfahānī, *Ḥilyat al-awliyāʾ*, vol. 10, p. 88.

36 This is part of a tradition which relates how the prophet Moses rebukes Adam for being the one who had humankind exiled from Paradise. Adam's response is to remind Moses that all this was predestined by God before his creation. For an account of this tradition, see Shihāb al-Dīn Aḥmad Samʿānī, *Rawḥ al-arwāḥ fī sharḥ asmāʾ al-Malik al-Fattāḥ* (Tehran, 1989), p. 156.

Sahl was asked, 'What is this awe (*rahba*) that He commanded them to feel towards Him?' He replied:

He meant by this, the [true] locating of the light of certainty (*mawḍiʿ nūr al-yaqīn*)[37] in relation to the heart's insight (*baṣar al-qalb*), and gnosis (*maʿrifa*) in relation to the entirety of the heart (*kulliyat al-qalb*). For endurance (*mukābada*) and struggle (*mujāhada*) are a part of faith ⌜for the sake of God (*īmān li'Llāh*)⌝. Then, when the heart ceases to have fear of all other than Him, the light of certainty is unveiled, and the servant who abides in faith for the sake of God, attains ⌜to faith in [or through] God (*īmān bi'Llāh*)⌝,[38] with an unshakeable realisation of His oneness (*tawḥīdan ʿalā tamkīn*), by which I mean, his heart is in a state of tranquil and confident repose with his Master (*sukūn qalbihi ilā mawlāhu*).[39] Consequently, the light of certainty unveils the knowledge of the eye of certainty (*ʿilm ʿayn al-yaqīn*),[40] and this is the attainment (*wuṣūl*) of God, Exalted is He. For this certainty, by virtue of the light of certainty (*bi-nūr al-yaqīn*) that leads to the eye of certainty, is not ⌜something that is brought into being (*mukawwan*)⌝,[41] nor is it something created (*makhlūq*); rather it is a light from the light of the essence of God (*dhāt al-Ḥaqq*), not in the sense of an indwelling (*ḥulūl*), nor of conjoining (*jamʿ*), or conjunction (*ittiṣāl*). Rather, the meaning of the servant's attainment (*ittiṣāl*)[42] of his Master refers to the [true] locating (*mawḍiʿ*) of his realisation of the divine oneness, and his obedience to God and His Messenger.

So, according to the strength of his perception (*baṣar*) of God, he will attain full awareness (*taqwā*) and awe (*rahba*) of Him. The root of full awareness of God is in relinquishing the lower self (*mubāyanat al-nafs*),[43] so let [the servant] relinquish [the lower self] for this, and not accommodate any of the pleasures [demanded by] its desire (*hawā*), nor any of those pleasures to which it [the lower self] is summoning him, and for which it has no excuse.[44] Know that human beings will vary in rank on the Day of Resurrection according to the measure of the light of certainty that they possess. The weightier the certainty a person has the heavier will his scales weigh, even though there might [otherwise] be less in his scales.

He [Sahl] was asked, 'How can you tell the soundness of someone's certainty?' To which he replied:

By the strength of his confidence (*thiqa*) in God, Exalted is He, and his good opinion (*ḥusn al-ẓann*) of Him.[45] Trust in God is witnessing (*mushāhada*) through certainty (*yaqīn*), the eye of certainty (*ʿayn al-yaqīn*), and the wholeness [of its vision] (*kulliyyatihi*). Its perfection and goal is the attainment of God, Mighty and Majestic is He.

---

37 The words 'light of certainty' have been substituted here for light of the self (*nūr al-nafs*) on the basis of Böwering's translation of this passage. We have found this only in MS F3488, f. 191b. The other two MSS (Z515, f. 14a, F638, f. 8a), as well as the printed edition, have *nūr al-nafs*.

38 These two additions were made with reference to MSS Z515, f. 14a and F638, f. 8a.

39 Tustarī appears to be teaching that endurance and struggle remain at the level of faith 'for God', that is, while the aspirant is in a state of separation from God, believing from the point of view of duality. However, once he reaches the level of *tamkīn* in *tawḥīd*, that is, firmly and unshakeably in the realisation of the divine oneness, he will have attained the level of faith in or through God. At this level also there can be no fear or awareness (*taqwā*) of other than God, because he is not conscious of anything other than God. On faith and certainty, see also IT, above p. xlviii.

40 The word *ʿayn* in this context was added from the MSS Z515, f. 14a and F3488, f. 192a. MS F638, f. 8a, however, has *ʿilm al-yaqīn*, like the published edition. On the expression *ʿayn al-yaqīn*, see above IT, p. xlix, n. 209.

41 'Brought into being or existentiated (*mukawwan*)' was added on the basis of the MSS: MS Z515, f. 14a, F638, f. 8a and F3488, f. 192a.

42 Sic in all the MSS as well as the published edition. Perhaps it should have been *wuṣūl* here, as earlier in the passage. Alternatively, the previous *ittiṣāl*, should perhaps have been *ittiḥād*.

43 Or it could mean 'separating the self [from the unreal]'.

44 Tustarī has returned in his discourse to the level of awareness of the separation of the slave and his Master, perhaps to remind his listeners on the one hand that, aside from those moments when the mystic experiences union with God, when he attains the realisation of *tawḥīd* through God, and the envisioning or 'eye' of certainty (*ʿayn al-yaqīn*), the awareness of man's slavehood and God's lordship must remain. On the other hand, it is a reminder that the way to *taqwā* and *rahba* requires the purification of the self from its desires and from other than God.

45 The subject of good opinion [of God] *ḥusn al-ẓann* is discussed further by Tustarī later in his commentary on this *sūra*, and is also discussed above, IT, pp. lii–liii.

[2:41] ***...And fear Me***[46]

When asked about this verse, Sahl replied:

> What He means by this is [their being aware] of His prior knowledge concerning them, that is, 'You should never feel secure from the [divine] ruse (*makr*),[47] nor of His act of giving respite (*istidrāj*),[48] such that your hearts become complacent in the observance of your security in this world while you persist in falling short [in good works]; nor should you rely upon My leniency towards you in the matter of [not] hastening your punishment, in that same [false] sense of security, and in your delusion (*ightirār*) and heedlessness (*ghafla*), lest you perish.'[49]
>
> The Prophet ﷺ said: 'Had Jesus the son of Mary ﷺ had greater certainty (*yaqīn*) he would have walked in the air as he walked on water.'[50] And truly our Prophet ﷺ traversed the air on the Night Journey (*Isrāʾ*) due to the strength of the light of his certainty, [a certainty] which God, Exalted is He, granted to him from His light, as an increase in light to the light that he already possessed from God, Exalted is He. The Prophet ﷺ also said: 'If gnosis (*maʿrifa*) had remained firmly rooted in the heart of David ﷺ and he had not slipped into negligence, he would not have fallen into disobedience.' By my life, truly gnosis (*maʿrifa*) was enclosed within its own abodes (*udrijat fī awṭānihā*),[51] in order that what was contained within God's prior knowledge concerning him would befall him. This is because it [God's prior knowledge] inevitably had to be manifested in his qualities, since God's knowledge is a final decree that cannot change to other than what the All-Knowing knows, Mighty and Majestic is He. Indeed God, Mighty and Majestic is He, concealed [from David] ﷺ in David's realm, the light of certainty (*nūr al-yaqīn*) by which he could have perceived [with] the eye of certainty (*ʿayn al-yaqīn*) and the wholeness [of its vision],[52] in order that His decree could thereby be fulfilled, Exalted is He. Do you not see that in reality the servant only beholds God by means of a subtle 'substance' (*laṭīfa*) from God, through its connection to his heart (*bi-wuṣūlihā ilā-qalbihi*). This subtle substance pertains to the attributes of the essence of his Lord. It is neither brought into being (*mukawwana*), nor created (*makhlūqa*), neither conjunct [with God] (*mawṣūla*), nor cut off [from Him] (*maqṭūʿa*). It is a secret (*sirr*) from a secret to a secret, an unseen [mystery] (*ghayb*) from an unseen to an unseen.[53] Certainty is through God, and the servant finds certainty due to a cause that comes directly from Him to the servant, according to the measure of the gifts that God has apportioned him, and the wholeness (*jumla*) of his innermost heart (*suwaydāʾ qalbihi*).
>
> Faith has two abodes (*waṭanān*),[54] and it is that which settles and does not leave. The light of certainty, [however] comes in momentary [flashes] and when it settles and takes root, it becomes faith. Thereafter certainty comes in flashes and increases in this manner indefinitely.

[2:42] ***And do not obscure the truth with falsehood, and do not conceal truth wittingly.***

---

46 Or we might translate this as 'Be fully aware' or 'mindful of Me'. The Qurʾānic words are *iyyāya faʾttaqūn*.

47 The word *makr* is used in Sufism to refer to an illusion created by God to test the spiritual wayfarer.

48 The word *istidrāj* here means God's drawing a person to destruction little by little, so that they are lulled into a sense of security and thinking that all is well.

49 Tustarī is here using *iltifāt*, the rhetorical feature of the Qurʾān, which involves shifts between the first person singular (or plural) and the third person singular.

50 Bayhaqī, *Kitāb al-Zuhd al-kabīr*, p. 357.

51 That is to say, God decreed that it (gnosis) should not be available to the prophet David at that moment, just as we see further down in this same passage that God concealed from him the light of certainty.

52 lit. and its 'entirety' (*kulliyya*). See above, IT, p. xlix, and the commentary on 102:7 below.

53 This passage is closely related to, and helps to clarify, the passage cited above on the previous verse (2:40), which discussed attainment of the eye of certainty (*ʿayn al-yaqīn*). Both passages use different words derived from the root *w-ṣ-l* (here *wuṣūl*, in the previous passage *ittiṣāl*), indicating an indefinable connection and closeness to God, that nonetheless does not imply any conjunction, or indwelling on the part of God.

54 Sic in the published edition and all three MSS. Tustarī does not say what these two abodes are, though elsewhere he states that the locus of faith (*īmān*) is the heart (*qalb*), on which see above IT, p. xlii.

Sahl was asked about this verse, to which he replied:

> This means, 'Do not cover up a matter of the Hereafter because of a worldly concern.' What [God] means is that it is not allowed for the people of truth to conceal the truth from the people of truth (*ahl al-ḥaqq*) in particular, or from those who long to be guided thereby to God. As for the people of truth, they will increase in insight (*baṣīra*) [through hearing it], and as for those who are not of the elite of the people of truth, the words of God are a source of guidance for them and of direction to God, Exalted is He.

[2:45] ***Seek help in patience and prayer…***

When asked about these words Sahl said:

> Patience here [means] fasting, while prayer [means] the bond (*waṣla*) of gnosis (*maʿrifa*). He whose prayer — this being his bond [with God] — is sound, will be exempt from accusation (*tuhma*) before God; for interrogation (*suʾāl*) is a form of accusation, but with this bond there remains no interrogation. Do you not take note of His words [in the second part of this verse], *It is hard indeed, except for the humble?*[55]

[2:48] ***…and no intercession shall be accepted from it [the soul], nor shall compensation be taken, neither shall they be helped.***

When asked about these words Sahl said:

> It means that even if it [the soul] were to bring the sum of all good actions great and small, in abundance or just a few, none of this will be accepted from it on its arrival on the Day of Resurrection, nor anything from him [the servant]. *Compensation* (ʿadl) here means equivalence [or like, *mathal*]. Do you not note His words: *Or its compensation in fasts* [5:95] — that is, its equivalence and reward?

[2:55] ***…and the thunderbolt took you even as you looked on***[56]

When asked about this verse Sahl said:

> The thunderbolt (*al-ṣāʿiqa*) signifies death, and it also signifies every destructive punishment that God sends down upon whomever He wills of His servants, which they behold with their own eyes, whereby He shows to others among them a lesson and an admonishment.

[2:71] ***…and without blemish…***[57]

When asked about this verse Sahl said:

> This means that there should be no mark on it which blemishes it, nor a patch of colour which differs from the colour of the rest of its body. In this there is wisdom from its Maker and a lesson for the one who takes heed by it, and grows in certainty because of his faith and his profession of God's oneness.

[2:72] ***And when you killed a living soul and disputed thereon…***

> That is, you fell into discord concerning it. *Why then did you slay them, if you speak the truth?* [3:183][58]

---

55 That is to say that it (prayer) is burdensome to those who lack humility, according to the commentary of Jalāl al-Dīn al-Suyūṭī and Jalāl al-Dīn al-Maḥallī, in *Tafsīr al-Jalālayn*, ed. ʿAbd al-Qādir al-Arnāʾūṭ and Aḥmad Khālid Shukrī (Damascus and Beirut: Dār Ibn Kathīr, 1998), trans. Feras Hamza (Louisville, KY: Royal Aal al-Bayt Institute for Islamic Thought and Fons Vitae, 2008).

56 This verse refers to Moses' people after they had been reprimanded for worshipping the calf in his absence (2:51–4). They then told him they would not believe him until they saw God openly, which is when they witnessed the thunderbolt.

57 This is among the qualities of the cow that was to be sacrificed by the Children of Israel, as commanded by God through Moses.

58 The relevance of the commentary on the verse introduced here is Tustarī's explanation that a matter may be addressed to a people concerning members of their community, even though what is being referred to may have occurred in the past. Likewise, a matter may be addressed to the community when it concerns the Prophet and vice versa.

Sahl said regarding these words:

This is a reproach from God, Mighty and Majestic is He, to them [the Jews] with regard to those of their forefathers who were murderers of prophets. As you know, those who are addressed in this verse had not killed a prophet at the time of the Prophet ﷺ, nor was there at that time any other Prophet but him. However, God addressed them with reference to those who came before them among their kin, as He addressed the Prophet ﷺ with what was in reality directed to his nation [as a whole] with His words: *O Prophet! When you [men] divorce women, divorce them by their prescribed period* [65:1] The same [principle applies] to His words: *About what are they questioning one another?* ۞ *About the awesome tidings* [78:1, 2], [by which is meant], 'For what reason do you question the Prophet ﷺ, when he is more knowledgeable concerning that'.[59]

[2:175] ***...Ah! What boldness [they show] for the Fire!***

When asked about these words, Sahl replied:

That is [boldness] in issuing legal ruling[s] (*fatwā*) without sufficient knowledge of the Sunna or the divine law (*sharᶜ*), and [boldness] in servitude to the practice of the people of the Fire.

[2:102] ***...But they could not thus harm anyone except by God's permission...***

That is, save that it be in God's prior knowledge, which precedes the occurrence of the act of the one doing it.

Concerning His words, Exalted is He:

[3:102] ***...Fear God as He should be feared...***

[Sahl said]:

That is, by the worship He has prescribed for you, and not by that which God merits in His essence (*fī dhātihi*).[60]

[2:59] ***...So we sent upon the transgressors a plague...***

He said:

the plague being punishment.

[2:112] ***Nay, but whoever submits his purpose to God, being virtuous...***

Concerning these words of God, Exalted is He, Sahl said:

That is, his religion, is as it is said in Sūrat al-Nisāʾ: *Who is fairer in religion than one who submits his purpose to God*? [4:125], meaning: 'Than a person who dedicates (*akhlaṣa*) his religion purely to God', that is, Islam and its laws.[61] This meaning is reiterated in Sūra Luqmān: *Whoever surrenders his purpose to God, and is virtuous* [31:22], which means [whoever] devotes himself in religion purely to God.

He was asked about His words, Exalted is He:

[2:78] ***...Who know not the Book, but only [see therein their own] desires...***

He said:

This means that they rest their hopes in God based upon falsehood, inclining towards the desire (*hawā*) of their lower selves without following guidance from God. This is referring to the Jews.[62]

---

59 According to the commentaries, these verses are being addressed to the Quraysh.

60 Or 'as He is in Himself', because that would be beyond the capacity of a human being, just as the Prophet is reported to have said at the end of a prayer: 'I cannot adequately encompass Your praise. You are as You have praised Yourself.' This prayer is reported in a *ḥadīth* which is listed in many collections, including Muslim, *Ṣaḥīḥ*, 'Kitāb al-Ṣalāt', and in Tirmidhī, *Nawādir al-uṣūl*, vol. 2, p. 384.

61 The fourth form of the verb *khalaṣa* here also has the meaning of sincerity, as in the title of Sūra 112 (Al-Ikhlāṣ).

62 Most of the traditions cited by Ṭabarī on this verse state that these were illiterate people among the Jews, perhaps because much of this part of Sūrat al-Baqara relates to the Jews. However, a couple of traditions simply state that they were illiterate people.

He was asked about His words:

[2:87 and 253] ***…and confirmed him with the Holy Spirit…***[63]

He replied:

> *The Holy* (al-Quddūs) refers to God, that is, the One who is sanctified above having children, partners or a spouse.

[2:128] ***…and of our progeny, a community submissive to You…***

> 'A community' (*umma*) refers to a group of people, and 'submissive' (*muslima*) means they submit to Your commandments and prohibitions, thereby attaining Your good pleasure and acceptance.

He was asked about His words:

[2:134 and 141] ***That is a community that has passed away. Theirs is what they have earned…***

He replied:

> That is to say, this was a community that passed away in accordance with God's prior knowledge concerning them.

[2:143] ***…a community of the middle [way]*** **(wasaṭan)*…***

> That is, they are just. In this way, a believer gives credence to God's servants in accordance with His words, *He believes in God, and has faith in the believers* [9:61], which means that he affirms [the truth of] God and ascribes truth to the believers.

His words, Exalted is He:

[2:143] ***…For God is gentle with people, merciful.***

> That is, He shows great [lit. intense, *shadīd*] mercy (*raḥma*) and kindness (*raʾfa*) towards them. This refers to the gentleness (*rifq*) and clemency (*ḥilm*) that He shows them due to His knowledge of their weakness and of the fact that they have no strength before Him, except through Him and from Him.

[2:148] ***Every person has a direction to which he turns…***

> He means by this that God, Exalted is He, turns people of each religion in the direction that He wills.

[2:155] ***…Yet give good tidings to those who are patient.***

He [Sahl] said:

> They are those for whom patience (*ṣabr*) has become a way of life (*ʿaysh*), a [source of] rest (*rāḥa*) and a homeland (*waṭan*). They find delight in practising patience for the sake of God, Exalted is He, in every situation.

[2:157] ***They are those on whom [descend] blessings from their Lord, and mercy; it is they who are truly guided.***

Sahl said:

> What is implied by blessings (*ṣalawāt*) upon them is the bestowal of mercy (*taraḥḥum*) upon them, that is, a bestowal of mercy from their Lord. The Prophet ﷺ said, 'May God bless the family of Abū Awfāʾ, when they brought him charitable donations, by which he meant '[May God] have mercy on them.'[64]

He also said:

> Muḥammad b. Sawwār told us on the authority of Abū ʿAmr b. ʿAlāʾ that he said: '*Ṣalāt*' has three meanings, one of which is the prescribed prayer with its bowings and prostrations, which is referred to when God says: *So pray to Your Lord and sacrifice* [108:2], that is, grasp your left arm with your right hand in prayer, in self-abasement and in awe before God, Exalted is He. This

---

63 The Arabic construction here is *rūḥ al-quddūs* meaning literally 'spirit of the holy'.

64 Bukhārī, *Ṣaḥīḥ*, 'Kitāb al-Zakāt'.

is also reported from ʿAlī ﷺ. The second meaning is to show mercy (*taraḥḥum*) [as discussed above], and the third meaning is supplication (*duʿāʾ*), as [for example] in the prayer over the dead. Indeed, the Prophet ﷺ said: 'If any of you are invited for a meal, you should [accept the invitation]. But if [the one invited] is fasting he should pray',[65] that is, he should make a supplication for them to be endowed with blessing. Furthermore, the Prophet ﷺ said in a *ḥadīth*, '...and may the angels pray over you', meaning pray for mercy to be bestowed upon you. In this [same] *ḥadīth* the Prophet ﷺ went on to say, 'And if someone eats at his house, the angels pray over him [the host] until eventide', meaning the angels supplicate for him.[66]

Sahl continued:

Ṣalāt carries two meanings: one is the seeking of forgiveness (*istighfār*), and the other is forgiveness itself (*maghfira*). As for the meaning of 'seeking forgiveness', it is referred to in His words, *And pray for them* [9:103], that is, ask forgiveness for them; [and in His words], *to [secure] the prayers of the Messenger* [9:99], meaning asking for the Messenger's supplication for forgiveness. As for its meaning of 'forgiveness', it is referred to in His words, Exalted is He, *He it is who blesses you* [33:43], meaning: 'He forgives you', and [again in His words]: *as do His angels...* [33:43], by which is meant: 'They seek forgiveness for you'. In the same vein are His words: *Indeed God and His angels bless the Prophet* [33:56], which mean: 'Truly God forgives the Prophet, and the angels seek forgiveness for him.' Then He says, *O you who believe, invoke blessings on him, and invoke peace on him in a worthy manner* [33:56], meaning: 'Seek forgiveness for him'. Also in Sūrat al-Baqara are His words: *Blessings from their Lord* [2:157], meaning: 'Forgiveness from their Lord.'

[2:161] *...Upon them shall be the curse of God...*

This means that their lot is banishment (*ṭard*) from the mercy of God, and alienation. In this manner, every accursed one is banished.

[2:166] *...and the cords are cut away before them*[67]

This refers to the ties by which they were connected to each other in this world. For the sake of [these ties] mutual affections were cemented, without obedience to God and His Messenger, and without seeking God's good pleasure.

[2:186] *...So let them respond to Me...*

He [Sahl] said,

[Let them respond] through supplication (*duʿāʾ*), *...and believe in Me...*, — that is, 'Affirm Me as True (*saddaqanī*), for I am there whenever someone calls on Me with sincerity (*mukhliṣan*), without despondency (*āyis*) or despair (*qanaṭ*).'

[2:197] *And take provision, but the best of provisions is mindfulness of God...*[68]

He [Sahl] said:

It [mindfulness of God, *taqwā*] is the [best travelling] companion (*rafīq*) leading to the remembrance (*dhikr*) of God, Exalted is He, in fear (*khawfan*); just as there is no [travelling] provision (*zād*) for the lover (*muḥibb*) save the Beloved (*maḥbūb*), and no provision for the possessor of mystical knowledge (*ʿārif*) save the Known (*maʿrūf*).[69]

---

65 Muslim, *Ṣaḥīḥ*, 'Kitāb al-Nikāḥ'; Tirmidhī, *Sunan*, 'Kitāb al-Ṣawm'.

66 Ibn Ḥanbal, *al-Musnad* (Egypt, n.d.), vol. 3, p. 137. Both these traditions of the Prophet are indications of the importance in Muslim culture of both giving and receiving hospitality. All references in the text are to this edition, unless another is mentioned.

67 In its outward meaning this verse refers to those who were leaders and misled their followers in denying God. At the Resurrection, they will disown all their followers, denying that they misled them.

68 This is part of the verse which describes some injunctions concerning the performance of the Hajj. Provision here firstly refers to bringing provisions (*zād*) to suffice for the journey.

69 Interestingly, Tustarī seems here to be alluding to three approaches to, or dispositions in, the mystical way, namely those of fear (*makhāfa*), love (*maḥabba*) and [mystical] knowledge (*maʿrifa*).

[Continuing on from this] Sahl explained that the words, *If he is able to make his way there* [3:97] are an allusion to the provision (*zād*) and the riding beast (*rāḥila*). He then asked, 'Do you know what the provision and riding beast are?' They replied: 'No.' So he said, 'The provision is remembrance (*dhikr*) and the riding beast is patience (*ṣabr*).' Then he went on to relate how a man had accompanied him on the road to Mecca, and for two days had not found anything [to eat], so he said, 'O teacher! I need sustenance!' to which he [Sahl] replied, 'Sustenance is God.' The other man then said, 'One cannot do without sustenance for the body to function.' To which he replied, 'All bodies exist [only] through God, Mighty and Majestic is He.' Then he recited the following lines [in the *basīṭ* metre]:

O Beloved, replenish [my longing]!
May the water of longing pour down upon you from the rain cloud,
Whose pouring increases my sorrows and anguish.
An anguish remains in my heart, consuming me,
Truly as love increases, with it will increase my rapture.[70]

After that, he said, 'It is the world[71] that severs those who are devoted to God from God, Mighty and Majestic is He.' Finally, he said, 'The livelihood (*ʿaysh*) of angels is in obedience (*ṭāʿa*); the livelihood of the prophets is in knowledge (*ʿilm*) and waiting for relief (*intiẓār al-faraj*);[72] and the livelihood of the veracious (*ṣiddīqūn*) is in emulation (*iqtidāʾ*).[73] As for the rest, their livelihood is in food and drink.'

[2:197] ...*So fear me,*[74] *O people of inner substance* (ulū'l-albāb)!

[Sahl said] that this means:

> 'O people of understanding (*fahm*)!'[75] That is, those who are possessed of sound intellects (*ʿuqūl salīma*). Truly God, Exalted is He, has commanded them to be aware of Him according to the capacity of their intellects, by virtue of that which He has specially allotted them, such as: the light of guidance by His essence;[76] [their] receptivity to [that light] from Him; His having singled them out by depositing something (*maʿnā*) within them; and His knowledge of them prior to their creation. So [in this verse], He reminded them of that bounty He had granted to them, and summoned them by this antecedent bounty to recognise a second bounty after their pre-eternal gift, which is the reality of gnosis (*maʿrifa*), and to accept [that] knowledge by dedicating their actions to Him.

It was asked [of him], 'What is the meaning and reality of mindfulness of God (*taqwā*)?' He answered:

> Its reality belongs to God, Mighty and Majestic is He, by virtue of the fact that you will be pressed on to death while in possession of few good deeds, and likewise [that you will be pressed on to the] punishment for your sins.[77] Thus [the one who is mindful of God] knows this and fears Him, and does not rely on anything save Him.

---

70 Some reference has been made to Gaafar's dissertation in the translation of these verses.

71 i.e. in this case, concern for physical sustenance.

72 i.e. from the suffering which they inevitably bear, according to the *ḥadīth*, 'Those who suffer the most are the prophets and those most like them' (*al-anbiyāʾ wa'l-amthāl wa'l-amthāl*). See Tirmidhī, *Sunan* 'Kitāb al-Zuhd'; Ibn Māja, *Sunan*, 'Abwāb al-fitan'; Ibn Ḥanbal, *al-Musnad* (Cairo, 1895), vol. 1, pp. 172 (the latter version of this *ḥadith* includes the virtuous (*ṣāliḥūn*) after the prophets), pp. 174, 180; vol. 4, p. 369. This teaching will be discussed by Tustarī again later.

73 Probably what is meant is emulation of the example of the Prophet. Tustarī often uses the term *iqtidāʾ* without specifying who is to be emulated. See IT above, pp. liiiff.

74 The word used is *ittaqūnī*, from the same root as *taqwā*, and therefore could also mean: 'Be fully aware, wary or mindful of Me!' See above, p. 13, n. 9, regarding the translation of words derived from the root *w-q-y*.

75 All the MSS (Z515, f. 18a, F638, f. 10a and F3488, f. 195a) have the plural here (*fuhūm*), corresponding to the plural in the following *ʿuqūl*, though the plural would not be idiomatic in English.

76 Note that earlier Tustarī states that the eye of certainty is a light from the light of the essence of God. See his commentary on 2:40 above.

77 Note that the MSS Z515, f. 18a only has the following: *wa kadhā khaṭāyā bi-asbāb al-ʿuqūba*.

Someone said to him, 'Truly, the reasons for people's mindfulness of God vary.' He affirmed this and added, 'Just as their deeds vary.' Abū Bakr [al-Sijzī] then said, 'I mentioned that it is confirmed in the Qurʾān that the awareness that every man [has of God] is according to his capacity.' He [Sahl] replied, 'Yes, indeed. God, Exalted is He, has said, *So be aware of God as much as you can; listen and obey...* [64:16].' Thus does He direct them to what is within their capability.' So I [Abū Bakr] then said to him, 'Truly God, Exalted is He, has said, *Fear God as He should be feared* [3:102]', to which Sahl replied:

> As for our companions, they say that this is addressed to a people distinguished by their eminence, because what was demanded of them was not [even] demanded of the prophets (ﷺ). And as both Abraham and Jacob said to their children: *'My sons, God has chosen for you the [true] religion; see that you do not die save in submission'* [2:132]. So truly God requires His creatures to worship Him according to their [individual] capacities. For those who were told, *'Fear God as He should be feared'*, awareness of God (*taqwā*) was demanded of them in the measure of their knowledge (*maʿrifa*) of Him. What is meant here is *'Fear God as He should be feared'*, as much as you can. This does not, however, constitute permission to abandon awareness of God. [Note that] in the context of Sūra Āl ʿImrān, the words: *See that you do not die save in submission* [3:102] mean: submitting to God's command in every condition and consigning [your affairs] to Him, while others are directed back to striving (*ijtihād*). So understand the difference between the two in this address, for although the wording is the same, the implication differs, the one [applicable] to the elect, and the other to the generality of people.[78]

Abū Bakr [al-Sijzī] then related that Sahl said:

> If those who are mindful of God (*muttaqūn*) had supplicated against the transgressors, (*musrifūn*), they [the latter] would have perished, both those who came first and those who come last. However God made the mindful of God as a mercy for the oppressors (*ẓālimūn*), that by means of them He might save them, and indeed the most noble (*akram*) of creatures before God, Mighty and Majestic, are those who are [fully] mindful and aware of Him. As He has said, *Truly the noblest of you in the sight of God is the one among you who is most mindful of Him.'* [49:13] So whoever hopes for God's favour (*karāma*), Mighty and Majestic is He, should be mindful of Him, for truly it is through mindfulness of God that a person may attain God's favour and admittance into Paradise, abide in His vicinity, and triumph with a tremendous victory. Indeed the Prophet ﷺ said, 'Whoever corrects his inner self [lit. secret, *sarīra*] will find that God puts right his public life and whoever fears God in his innermost secret, will find that God draws him nearer and brings him close [to Him].'[79]

[2:201] *...Our Lord, give us good in this world...*

> These words refer to knowledge and sincere devotion, *...and good in the Hereafter...*, refers to His good pleasure (*riḍā*), as He said: *God is well-pleased with them and they are well-pleased with Him...* [5:119].

[2:224] *Do not make God's [name] an excuse in your oaths not to be righteous...*

Sahl was asked concerning this verse, 'What is this righteousness (*birr*)?' He replied: 'This means that you do not maintain your family ties [just] because of an oath.' Then [in this connection] someone mentioned to him the verse: *It is not righteousness that you turn your faces towards East or West* [2:177], and he [Sahl] said:

---

78 This is because the first instance of the command that they should die in submission [to God] [2:132] comes in the context of Abraham and Jacob addressing their sons and telling them that God has chosen for them the true religion, whereas the second instance of the command to die in submission to God [3:102] follows the rigorous command to fear God as He should be feared, which is said to be possible only for an elect among the believers, and which, Tustarī has suggested, was not even demanded of the prophets (i.e. the sons of Abraham and Jacob).

79 Ibn Abī Shayba, *al-Muṣannaf* (Riyadh, 1988), vol. 7, pp. 162 and 217.

This means: it is not righteousness that you do nothing other than this; *[True] righteousness is [that of] the one who believes in God* [2:177], to the end of that verse.[80] Do you not notice how He says, *Do you bid others to righteousness, while you forget [to practise it] yourselves?* [2:44], which is a reference to Jews who were commanding their foster brothers to obey God, Exalted is He, and to follow the Prophet ﷺ, while they themselves did not do that.

[2:235] ***...But do not make arrangements with them secretly...***

That is, arrangements of marriage, *...and know that God knows what is within yourselves, so be wary of Him...*, by which is meant that He knew what was hidden within yourselves before He created you, namely, every single act[81] done in the way of goodness, that He was to command and the performance of which He would aid, and [likewise] every act [you would do], which He had forbidden, and from which He would not protect [you].[82] He abandoned whom He willed to his desire, so that the act which He had forbidden would become manifest from that person, and He did not grant His protection, out of His justice and decree. The meaning of His words, *what is within yourselves* refers to that which you have not yet done, and *within yourselves* refers to that which you will do. *So be wary of Him*, that is to say, humbly implore Him concerning it,[83] that He should be the one who takes care of your affairs by extending His aid and guaranteeing your success in the [realisation] of obedience, and by granting His protection from forbidden [acts] through [His] help and support. Do you not take heed of the words of ʿUmar and Ibn Masʿūd? ﷺ:

'O God! If in the Mother of the Book that is with You,[84] we are among those who are wretched and deprived, then erase that from [our destiny] and appoint us to be among those of felicity who are encompassed by Your mercy. Truly You erase what You will and establish [what You will] and the Mother of the Book is with You.'

His words:

[2:204] ***...Yet he is the most stubborn in altercation.***[85]

That is, [he is] extremely contentious [on the basis of] what is false. Indeed, ʿĀʾisha ﷺ narrated that the Prophet ﷺ said, 'The most abhorrent of men before God, Exalted is He, are those who are stubborn and antagonistic.'[86]

His words:

[2:214] ***...And were so shaken [in spirit]...***[87]

---

80 2:177 is a long verse which outlines the tenets of Muslim belief as well as other requisite virtues. It reads as follows: *It is not righteousness that you turn your faces to the East and to the West. True righteousness is [that of] the one who believes in God and the Last Day and the angels and the Book and the prophets, and who gives of his substance, however cherished, to kinsmen and orphans and the needy and the traveller and beggars, and sets slaves free, and who observes the prayer and pays the alms; and those who fulfil their covenant when they have engaged in a covenant, those who endure with fortitude misfortune, hardship and peril; these are the ones who are truthful, and these are the ones who are mindful of God.*

81 lit. every act (*fiʿl*) of motion (*ḥaraka*) and stillness (*sukūn*).

82 On this doctrine see above, IC, p. 2, and IT, pp. xxxiii–xxxiv.

83 i.e. the 'latent' acts of goodness and disobedience that are within us.

84 i.e. what is preordained, before it is even written on the 'Preserved' or 'Well-Guarded Tablet,' on which see above IC, p. 5, n. 22. The 'Mother of the Book' (*umm al-kitāb*) appears in around forty *ḥadīth*s and is interpreted in a number of ways. Most often it denotes the heavenly prototype of the Qurʾān, but it is also, as here, identified with the Preserved Tablet upon which the destiny of all creatures has been inscribed. In this meaning, it is found in the Qurʾān: *God effaces what He will and confirms [what He will]. With Him is the Mother of the Book* [13:39]. The term 'Mother of the Book' is also one of the many names given to Sūrat al-Fātiḥa, on account of the fact that it is said to contain the whole Qurʾān. See E. Geoffroy and F. Daftary, 'Umm al-kitāb', *EI*², vol. x, p. 854.

85 According to *Tafsīr al-Jalālayn* this refers to al-Akhnas b. Sharīq, while Ṭabarī cites this as one view along with others which consider that the verse concerns the hypocrites more generally.

86 Bukhārī, *Ṣaḥīḥ*, 'Kitāb al-Tafsīr'.

87 These words occur in the middle of a verse which describes a people (according to the commentaries, the early Muslim community in Mecca), who were suffering all sorts of trials and hardships.

That is, their willing was through Him, they were fearful because of Him, and were wary of God's ruse (*makr*), Mighty and Majestic is He; *...that the Messenger and those who believed with him said, 'When will God's help come?' Ah, but surely God's help is nigh.*

Sahl was asked concerning these words, 'Did they ask this because they found that help slow in arriving?' He replied:

No, but when they lost hope in their own devising (*tadbīr*) they said, *'When will God's help come?'* Hence, when God, Exalted is He, saw that they had given up on their own power (*ḥawl*), strength (*quwwa*) and devising (*tadbīr*), and saw their display of neediness for Him, and [their admission that] they had no means without Him, He responded to them with His words, *Ah, but surely God's help is nigh.*

Sahl further said:

Affliction (*balāʾ*) and well-being (*ʿāfiya*) are from God, Mighty and Majestic is He. The command and prohibition are from Him; protection and the granting of success are from Him; and reward and punishment are from Him. However, actions are attributed (*manṣūba*) to the children of Adam, so whoever performs a good action must express gratitude to merit thereby an increase [in goodness]; and whoever performs a wicked act must seek forgiveness, so that he thereby merits forgiveness. Affliction from God is of two kinds: an affliction of mercy and an affliction of punishment. An affliction of mercy leads the afflicted person to show his utter need (*iftiqār*) for God, Mighty and Majestic is He, and leads him to the abandonment of devising (*tadbīr*). However, an affliction of punishment leads the afflicted person [to rely] on his own choice (*ikhtiyār*) and devising.

Sahl was then asked, 'Which is more difficult, patience (*ṣabr*) in [a state of] well-being or patience during adversity?' He replied:

Asking for safety (*salāma*) in times of security is more difficult than asking for safety in [a state of] fear.

[On the same subject] Sahl said regarding His words, *And if anyone believes in God, [God] guides his heart [aright]* [64:11], '[Whoever] believes in God and that his affliction comes from God, will find his heart guided by God to the expectation of relief (*intiẓār al-faraj*) from Him'.

His words:

[5:2] ***...Help one another to righteousness and mindfulness of God...***

That is, to the performance of the obligatory acts, for righteousness (*birr*) is faith (*īmān*), and the performance of obligatory acts is a branch (*farʿ*) of faith. Mindfulness of God (*taqwā*) signifies the Sunna, and an obligatory act is not complete without the Sunna. He prohibited helping one another to sin (*ithm*) — which [is tantamount to] disbelief (*kufr*) and hypocrisy (*nifāq*) — and enmity, which [signifies] innovation (*bidʿa*) and controversy (*khiṣām*). Both the aforementioned are [derisive] play (*laʿbān*), and they have been forbidden from derisive play.[88] They have also been commanded to do [acts of] righteousness, which include both the obligatory acts and those which are Sunna, and to be steadfast in sincerely devoting themselves to God in all of this.

[Concerning] His words:

[2:246] ***Have you not seen the chiefs of the Children of Israel...***

Sahl was asked who *the chiefs* were. He replied:

He [God] means by this the leaders. Take note of the saying of the Messenger of God ﷺ when he heard a man after the Battle of Badr say, 'On the Day of Badr we only killed bald, old men', to which the Messenger of God ﷺ replied, 'They are the chiefs of Quraysh', meaning the notables and leaders.[89]

88 Several verses castigate the hypocrites and disbelievers for their derisive play (*laʿb*) and diversion (*lahw*); for example: 5:57 and 58; 6:32,70 and 91.

89 Tirmidhī, *Nawādir al-uṣūl*, vol. 1, p. 333.

Sahl was asked about His words:

[2:255] ***God, There is no god except Him, the Living, the Eternal Sustainer...***

He replied:

> This is the mightiest (*aʿẓam*) verse in God's Book, Exalted is He. Within it is God's Greatest Name, and it is written across the sky in green light in one line from East to West. This is how I saw it written on the Night of Great Merit (*Laylat al-Qadr*)[90] in ʿAbbādān: *There is no god except Him, the Living, the Eternal Sustainer.*
>
> *The Living, the Eternal Sustainer* is the One who oversees everything pertaining to His creatures: their life spans, their actions, and their provision. He is the One who requites goodness (*iḥsān*) with goodness, and misdeeds with forgiveness (*ghufrān*), but He requites hypocrisy, disbelief and innovation with punishment. Whoever pronounces the saying: 'There is no god except God' has made a pact with God, so it is unlawful for him, after making a pact with God, to disobey Him in any of His commandments or prohibitions, in secret or public, or to support His enemy, or to show enmity towards a friend of His.

...*No slumber can seize Him, nor sleep...* Slumber (*sina*) here means sleepiness.

He [Sahl] also said:

> Slumber is when the heart (*qalb*) is mingled with sleep.

[2:257] ***God is the protector of the believers...***

Concerning these words Sahl said:

> That is, [He protects them with] the protection of [His] good pleasure (*riḍā*). He is their protector due to the former guidance He granted them, and His knowledge concerning them, of their affirmation of His oneness. This is due to His knowledge that they have freed themselves from every cause except their Creator.[91] Hence they were taken out of the darkness into the light, and from disbelief, error, disobedience and innovation to faith, which is the light that God, Mighty and Majestic is He, established in their hearts. This is the light of the insight of certainty (*nūr baṣīrat al-yaqīn*) by which they seek inner perception of the divine oneness (*tawḥīd*), and obedience to Him in that which He has commanded and forbidden. *For anyone to whom God gives no light, there is no light!* [24:40]

His words, Mighty and Majestic is He:

[2:257] ***And the disbelievers — their protectors are false deities...***

> That is, Satan.

Sahl said:

> The head of all devils is the evil-inciting self (*nafs ammāra bi'l-sūʾ*), for Satan cannot overpower man except through the desire (*hawā*) of his lower self. So if he [Satan] senses something that it desires, he casts temptation at it.

[2:260] ***And when Abraham said, 'My Lord! Show me how You give life to the dead'...***

[Sahl] was asked whether or not Abraham was in doubt concerning his faith, and was therefore asking his Lord to show him a sign or miracle in order to restore his faith. He replied:

> His question was not out of doubt; he was merely asking for an increase in certainty (*ziyādat al-yaqīn*) to the faith he already had. Thus he asked for an unveiling of the cover of visual beholding with his physical eyes, so that by the light of certainty, his own certainty regarding God's omnipotence might be increased, and [his certainty] regarding His creative [power] might

---

90 *Laylat al-Qadr*, variously translated as the 'Night of Glory, 'Night of Power' 'Night of Ordainment', and here, 'Night of Great Merit', is mentioned in 97:1 as being the night during the holy month of Ramadan in which the Qurʾān was revealed in its entirety. Each year, *Laylat al-Qadr* is said to fall on an odd night during the last part of Ramadan, often the 27th night.

91 Both editions and MSS Z515, f. 20b and F3488, f. 197b have *khālif* here rather than *khāliq*, though it is difficult to understand what could be meant by *khālif* in this context. There are no visible diacritics in F638, f. 11b.

be consolidated. Do you not notice how when He asked [him], '*Why, do you not believe?*' he replied '*Yes.*' If he had been in doubt he would not have said 'Yes'. Furthermore, if God was aware of any doubt in him and had he given Him the answer 'Yes', [attempting to] conceal his doubt, God would definitely have disclosed that, Exalted is He, as such things cannot be concealed from Him. Therefore, this confirms that the request for [his heart's] reassurance (*ṭumaʾnīna*) signified a request for an increase in his certainty.[92]

Then it was asked, 'Surely the people of the "Table Spread"[93] sought profound peace of mind, through the sending down of the feast, and their [request] was out of doubt. So how does this correspond?' He replied:

Abraham ﷺ made it known that he was a believer, and he only asked for profound peace of mind in addition to faith in order to receive greater [certainty]. The people of the Table Spread, on the other hand, made it known that they would believe only after they had found calm reassurance in their hearts. As He said: *and that our hearts may be reassured, and that we may know that you have spoken to us truthfully* [5:113]. Thus they made it known that their knowledge of his [Jesus'] truthfulness, after they had been reassured by witnessing the feast, was to be the starting point of their faith.

Abū Bakr [al-Sijzī] said: I heard him say on another occasion:

...But so that my heart may be reassured... [2:260] — that is, 'I do not feel secure against one of Your enemies challenging me if I should say, *My Lord is He who gives life and death* [2:258], and then [one of them] should ask, "Did you see Him give life and death?" In this way my heart would be at ease in being able to answer "Yes" to him, once I had witnessed that.' This is why the Prophet ﷺ said: 'Hearing about something is not the same as seeing it.'

Sahl also said:

[Abraham's request] might also have another meaning: he might have asked God to show him the reviving of the dead so that he could feel sure that he had [truly] been chosen as the friend (*al-Khalīl*).[94]

Sahl then said:

Another aspect [of meaning] is the following: 'What I have requested of You, I have no right to, save [for] that which You will realise for me' — and this is the position of the elect of His creation — 'So my request for You to show me the reviving of the dead was in order to put my own heart at rest.' This was because he was called the 'intimate friend' (*al-Khalīl*) even in the 'Time of Ignorance' (*Jāhiliyya*).[95] And as we said, his words '*that my heart may be reassured*' mean '[that it may be reassured] of my friendship [with You]. This, because I know that You give life and death'.

Sahl was asked: 'If the servant reaches the face-to-face encounter of direct vision (*kifāḥ al-ʿiyān*), what signs of this will be manifest?' He replied:

He [the servant] triumphs by repelling Satan, and this is because the lower self is extremely weak;[96] there is no way for him, when it comes to [dealing with] the lower self and Satan, and

92 The words *ṭumaʾnīna* and *iṭmiʾnān* have the meaning of a calmness and tranquillity that is associated with a deep sense of confidence, reassurance, trust and, as can be seen in this context, a level of certainty.

93 This is an allusion to Sūrat al-Māʾida [5:112–5], which relates how Jesus' disciples asked if God would send a feast (lit. a table spread) down from heaven from which they could eat, so that this might act as a sign for them to know that what he was telling them was the truth. Jesus accordingly prayed to God to send down the feast. God agreed to do so, but warned that anyone who disbelieved after that would be punished.

94 Abraham is known by the honorary title 'Friend of God' (*Khalīl Allāh*) on the basis the words of 4:125, *...and God took Abraham for a friend.*

95 i.e. before the coming of Muḥammad and the revelation of the Qurʾān in which God's taking Abraham as a friend is mentioned.

96 This is according to the MSS Z515, f. 21b, F638, f. 12a and F3488, f. 198a, which have *bi-ghāyat al-hawān*, as opposed to *fī muʿāyanat al-hawān* as in the published edition.

cutting them both off,[97] save the protection of the All-Merciful.

He [Sahl] then recited a poem [in *wāfir* metre]:

The abundant sufficiency[98] of direct encounter [with God] [attained] through my good opinion of Him[99]
Is like the spider's web covering the cave's entrance[100]
Good opinion has traversed every veil,
Good opinion has traversed beyond the fire's light,[101]
The signs of the one brought near are clear,
Near or far it is the same to the night voyager,[102]
For the one who has beheld God directly,
There is no sleep to settle him until day.
Three times did God ask of them:
'Is there anyone to ask for the kindness of the Maker?'
When did the lapping [of a dog] defile an ocean of love?
So ignore the barking of that wretched creature at my porch
O ego along with Satan! Be off!
And likewise the falsity of incitement and trouble.

In his saying,[103] 'The abundant sufficiency of direct encounter (*kifāḥ*) [with God] [attained] through my good opinion of Him', it is as if he is alluding to His words: *Is it not sufficient that your Lord is witness to all things?* [41:53], to which the Messenger of God ﷺ replied, 'Yes it is, O Lord.' So it was, when the following verse was sent down: *Is not God the fairest of all judges?* [95:8], to which the Messenger of God ﷺ also replied, 'Yes, O Lord.' And from the way they understand the Qurʾān [this means]: *Is it not sufficient that your Lord*, O Muḥammad, has supported you in this world against your enemies through killing and defeating [them], and in the next life, by granting you the Praiseworthy Station (*maqām maḥmūd*) and the right to intercession, and in Paradise by granting you the encounter and the visitation (*ziyāra*)?[104]

His saying, 'Like the spider's web covering the entrance of a cave', [is an allusion to] the cave of mystics (*ʿārifūn*) [which is] the[ir] innermost secret (*sirr*), and the[ir] beholding (*iṭṭilāʿ*) of the Lord of the Worlds, when they reach the station of face-to-face encounter (*maqām al-kifāḥ*), that is, the immediate vision of direct witnessing (*ʿiyān al-ʿiyān*) beyond what has been [verbally]

---

97 In order to make sense of this passage, it was necessary to ignore the words *ʿan al-shayṭān*, which follow *bi-ʿazlihimā*, and which are found in all the MSS and the published edition.

98 *Kifāyāt*, sing. *kifāya* derived from the verbal root *k-f-y* means to be sufficient, but by extension can mean to suffice for protection, to guard or protect. Thus Tustarī compares it in the next line to the spider's web that protected the Prophet when he was hiding in the cave.

99 The expression *ḥusn al-ẓann* is usually rendered in English as 'good opinion', which is perhaps adequate when it involves relations between human beings. However, *ḥusn al-ẓann* towards God involves an unequivocal, wholehearted trust in His goodness. For a discussion of Tustarī's application of this term, see IT, pp. liiff.

100 This is an allusion to the time when the Prophet was fleeing Mecca, accompanied by Abū Bakr, pursued by a party of the Quraysh who were intent on killing him. The two of them hid in a cave, and when their pursuers came by the cave and were about to enter it, they found a spider's web over the cave's entrance (also a dove's nest, right next to the cave entrance), so they assumed that no one could be inside the cave and passed by without discovering its occupants. See Martin Lings, *Muḥammad* (Cambridge, 2005), p. 119.

101 This is an allusion to the stations of the prophets Abraham and Moses, as will be seen in the commentary on the poem which follows.

102 Here is another allusion to the *Miʿrāj*, the miraculous Night Journey and Ascension of the Prophet, as will also become clear from the commentary on the poem. For references on the *Miʿrāj*, see above IC, p. 4, n. 15.

103 If the poem was composed by Tustarī, then the lengthy commentary that follows it may be by his disciple and the main source of the *Tafsīr*, Abū Bakr al-Sijzī. However, if the poem was by some other anonymous author, then the commentary might be by Tustarī.

104 i.e. the visitation of God, His Throne. The 'Laudable or Praiseworthy Station' is, according to tradition, among the special blessings promised to Muḥammad in the Hereafter. It is said to be at the right hand of the Throne in Paradise. In the Qurʾān it is mentioned in 17:79.

elucidated (*bayān*).[105] Then there is nothing between the servant and God except the veil of servanthood, due to his contemplation (*naẓar*) of the attributes of lordliness (*rubūbiyya*), ipseity (*huwiyya*), divinity (*ilāhiyya*), and [God's being] Self-Sufficing and Besought of all, to eternity (*ṣamadiyya ilāʾl-sarmadiyya*), without any obstacle or veil. One similitude among many might be that of a spider's web when it encompasses his heart (*qalb*), his innermost secret (*sirr*) ⌜and⌝ his heart's core (*fuʾād*),[106] through the grace of lordship (*luṭf al-rubūbiyya*) and complete compassion (*kamāl al-shafaqa*), such that there is no veil between him and God, Exalted is He.[107] Just as through the spider's web, which covered the entrance to the cave of the Messenger of God ﷺ, God turned away all the enemies among the leaders of the Quraysh who were being directed by Iblīs against him, so in the case of the people of gnosis, when they reach the station of direct witnessing (*ʿiyān*) beyond elucidation (*bayān*), the provocations of Satan and the sultan of the lower self are cut off and repelled, and their scheming becomes ineffectual, as is expounded in His words, *Surely the plotting of Satan is ever feeble* [4:76], meaning, that it had become ineffectual against them, just as He also said, *Truly over My servants you [Satan] shall have no warrant...* [15:42]. This is because, if the servant traverses all veils through his good opinion [of God], such that there remains no veil between him and God, thereafter the lower self, Satan and the world can have no access to his heart and mind by means of provocation. Thus did the Prophet ﷺ say, 'Yesterday I saw an amazing thing; a servant between whom and God there was a veil, but then when his good opinion of God appeared, He drew him in from behind the veil'.

Regarding his saying [in the poem], 'Good opinion has traversed beyond the light of fire',[108] it is as if this is alluding to the honour of following the Messenger ﷺ, due to his being given preference [by God] over the Friend of God [Abraham] and the Interlocutor of God [Moses],[109] for in the station of perceiving fire and light prophets and saints are [accorded] different ranks (*maqāmāt*). The Friend [of God] saw the fire and it became for him a source of coolness and safety [21:69].[110] The Interlocutor [of God] saw the fire as light as is expounded in His words, *Wait, I see a fire in the distance'* [20:10; 28:29]. However, this [fire] was in origin light, as [is indicated] by His words, *Blessed is he who is in the fire* [27:8], which refer to Moses surrounded by [lit. in the midst of] light. But then [Moses] became preoccupied with the light, so God reprimanded him saying, 'Do not preoccupy yourself with the light, for truly I am the Illuminator of light', as expounded in His words, *Indeed, I am your Lord. So take off your sandals* [20:12]. However, when it came

105 The word *bayān* is derived from the root *b-y-n*, meaning to become separate (as in the preposition *bayn*, 'between') or, by extension, to become clear by being distinct. Lane lists numerous meanings for *bayān*, including: 'the means by which one makes a thing [distinct] apparent, manifest, evident clear or perspicuous', which may be either a circumstantial or verbal indication, and hence it can mean 'speech', or 'eloquent speech'. In this context, we may understand Tustarī to be using it to indicate that the mystic is taken beyond what he has come to know indirectly, for example through verbal communication, to experience it in a direct and unmediated way.

106 The *wāw* has been added on the basis of Z515, f. 22a, F638, f. 11b and F3488, f. 198b.

107 That is, the innermost secret of the mystic is at this moment enclosed and protected in its being completely with God.

108 This is an allusion to Moses' experience of hearing God speak from the burning bush, related in 20:10–66, 27:7–9 and 28:31–5.

109 While in Islamic tradition, Abraham has the honorific title of 'Friend of God' (*Khalīl Allāh*), Moses has the title of 'Interlocutor of God' (*Kalīm Allāh*), which is derived from the Qurʾānic words, '*kallama 'Llāhu Mūsā taklīman*' [4:164], which is usually translated as: 'God spoke to Moses directly'.

110 A reference to the story of Abraham, when his people (according to tradition, Nimrod and his followers) commanded that he should be thrown into a fire as a punishment for his destroying their idols, related in Sūrat al-Anbiyāʾ (21:51–70). God commanded the fire *Be coolness and safety for Abraham* (21:69). Some traditions concerning this verse relate that Abraham sat a while in the midst of the fire, where there appeared a garden. See for example Aḥmad b. Muḥammad al-Thaʿlabī, *Qiṣaṣ al-anbiyāʾ al-musammā biʾl-ʿArāʾis al-majālis* (Cairo, n.d.), p. 85; English trans. by William M. Brinner as *ʿArāʾis al-majālis fī qiṣaṣ al-anbiyāʾ or: Lives of the Prophets as recounted by Abū Isḥāq Aḥmad b. Muḥammad b. Ibrāhīm al-Thaʿlabī* (Leiden and Boston, 2002), p. 133, who relates one such tradition from Suddī. The same tradition is cited in Maybudī's *Kashf al-asrār*, vol. 6, pp. 267–8. The motif of the garden in the midst of a fire became a favourite motif in Persian mystic poetry.

to the Beloved [of God] [Muḥammad ﷺ],[111] God showed him the fire and the light, and took him beyond the veil of fire and light. Then He brought him near without fire or light until he saw in the closest proximity the Illuminator of lights, as is expounded in His words, *The heart did not deny what he saw* [53:11].[112] Thus did He elevate [His] Beloved [Muḥammad] above the station of [His] Friend [Abraham] and [His] Interlocutor [Moses], and the stations of all of the prophets who were brought nigh, until he was addressed by God without the means of any revelation (*waḥy*) or interpreter (*tarjumān*), as is expounded in His words, *Whereat, He revealed to His servant what He revealed* [53:10], meaning, 'The Beloved communicated with the beloved in secret, and taught him and honoured him by granting him the Opening of the Book (*al-Fātiḥa*) and the closing verses of Sūrat al-Baqara.[113]

When he says [in the poem], 'The signs of the one brought near are clear', he means that all the prophets and angels have proximity [with God], but Muḥammad ﷺ is the closest in proximity (*aqrab*), following the form of *afʿal*[114] — one says *qarīb* meaning close and *aqrab* meaning closer or closest. Now the one who is close (*qarīb*) [to God] has access to[115] understanding (*fahm*), conjecture (*wahm*) and interpretation (*tafsīr*). But the one who is closest (*aqrab*) is beyond understanding, conjecture and interpretation, and what is beyond that cannot be contained by expression (*ʿibāra*) or allusion (*ishāra*). Thus it was that Moses, when he heard the call of unicity (*waḥdāniyya*) from God, on the night of the fire, said, 'O God! Are You near that I may whisper to You, or far away that I should call out to You?'[116] Then He [God] called out to *Kalīm* from a place that was both near and far, telling him that He was near. This, however, was not how the Messenger was described when [God] brought him near, such that He greeted him saying, 'Peace be upon you!' Furthermore, God, Exalted is He, praised his nation when He said, *And the foremost, the foremost: ۞ they are the ones brought near [to God]*' [56:10, 11]. He did not say 'they were near' (*qarībūn*) [but they were 'brought near' (*muqarrabūn*)]. Thus the words [of the poem,] 'The signs of the one brought near are clear' refers to this nation.[117] The one who is near experiences bounty and honour from God, but the one who is far away experiences torment and punishment from Him. The one who is far away experiences from God veiling and severance [from Him], but the one who is brought near experiences from God the encounter [with Him] and [His] visitation (*ziyāra*).

As to his saying [in the poem], 'For the one who has beheld God directly [there is no sleep to settle him until the day]', [he is referring to] a sign of the people of longing (*mushtāqūn*), for they can enjoy neither sleep nor rest, by day or at night. Among those who were characterised by this trait are Ṣuhayb and Bilāl. Bilāl was one of the people of longing, and so was Ṣuhayb, for

111 Just as the prophets Abraham and Moses have their honorific titles (*Khalīl Allāh* and *Kalīm Allāh*) so the Prophet Muḥammad came to be known as *Ḥabīb Allāh*, the 'Beloved of God'.

112 This is another allusion to the *Miʿrāj*, or Night Journey and Ascension of the Prophet Muḥammad. See above, IC, p. 4, n. 15.

113 The importance of Sūrat al-Fātiḥa is evident because it is recited in every *rakʿa* of the canonical prayer (*ṣalāt*), and indeed the prayer is not acceptable without its recitation. But there are also *hadīth*s attesting to its importance, such as those that are listed in the *Ṣaḥīḥ* of Bukhārī, 'Kitāb al-Tafsīr', in which the honorifics 'Mother of the Book' and 'Seven Oft-repeated Verses' are given for Sūrat al-Fātiḥa. Other *ḥadīth*s mention the importance of reciting both al-Fātiḥa and the two last verses of Sūrat al-Baqara, such as one narrated on the authority of Ibn ʿAbbās, and listed in the *Ṣaḥīḥ* of Muslim, 'Kitāb al-Ṣalāt', which relates that an angel greeted the Prophet and gave him the message, 'Rejoice in two lights given to you which have not been given to any prophet before you: Fātiḥat al-Kitāb and the concluding verses of Sūrat al-Baqara. You will never recite any letter from them for which you will not be given a reward.' Another tradition narrated on the authority of Ibn Masʿūd states that if anyone recites the last two verses of Sūrat al-Baqara at night that will suffice him. The latter is also listed in the *Ṣaḥīḥ* of Muslim, 'Kitāb al-Ṣalāt', as well as in the *Ṣaḥīḥ* of Bukhārī, 'Kitāb al-Tafsīr'.

114 That is, the form of the adjective that makes it comparative, or in this case superlative.

115 lit. 'enters into' (*yadkhulu*).

116 The 'call of Unicity' is a reference to the words spoken to Moses from the burning bush: *Verily I am God, there is no God but Me* (20:14, 27:9 and 29:30).

117 i.e. the nation of Muḥammad.

neither of them could sleep or find rest. Indeed it was narrated that a woman who had bought Ṣuhayb [as a slave] saw him in this condition and said, 'I will not be satisfied until you sleep at night, for you are becoming so weak that you are not in a condition to perform the tasks you do for me.' Thereupon Ṣuhayb wept and said, 'Whenever Ṣuhayb thinks of the Fire, sleep flees from him, and when he thinks of Paradise, he is seized with longing, and when he remembers God his longing (*shawq*) is perpetuated.'

[When] he says [in the poem], 'Three times did God ask them "Is there (*hal*)…?", [the word] *hal* is an interrogative particle. Verily God, Mighty and Majestic is He, lifts the veil every night and says, 'Is there (*hal*) anyone asking, so that I may grant him his request? Is there (*hal*) anyone seeking forgiveness, so that I may forgive him? Is there (*hal*) anyone supplicating, so that I may respond to his supplication?'[118] However, if it is the Night of Great Merit (*Laylat al-Qadr*), God lifts the first condition and says, 'I have forgiven you even though you didn't seek forgiveness. I have granted [it] to you even though you didn't ask [it] of Me, and I have responded to you before you even supplicated to Me.'[119] This is the height of generosity (*karam*).

His saying [in the poem], 'When did the lapping [of a dog] ever defile an ocean of love?' is an allusion to the lapping of a dog in a vessel which [according to the divine law (*sharīʿa*)] then requires cleaning seven, or three, times [with water], depending on which of the different wordings of the sayings transmitted from the Prophet ﷺ are followed. However what if a thousand thousand [i.e. a million] dogs lapped [up water] from an ocean? There is no dispute within the community that in such a case the sea would not be defiled. So [it is] with the whisperings of Satan and his lapping in the hearts of the mystics and the lovers, for how can this cause defilement in the ocean of love (*baḥr al-widād*), when each time he laps there, a wave comes and washes over it.

Regarding his saying, 'So ignore the barking of a wretched creature at my porch', he means: 'Leave Iblīs in his wretchedness, yelling at the door of this world with all his different kinds of incitement (*wasāwis*), for he does not harm me.' As [God] says, *when a visitation from Satan touches them they remember…* [7:201] His oneness in accordance with His words, *And when you mention your Lord alone in the Qurʾān, they turn their backs in aversion* [17:46]. His saying: 'Be off!' means, 'Get far away from me!' 'Be off!' is said to dogs and signifies total expulsion and banishment. In this way did He punish them [the inhabitants of Hell] in the final punishment that He gave them. Thus He said, *Begone into it! And do not speak to me!'* [23:108].[120]

His words, Exalted is He:

[2:238] *Maintain the prayers…*

That is, 'Persist in upholding them'. However His words, *And establish prayer and pay the alms.* [24:56], have two aspects, one of which is establishing prayer without the affirmation [of faith], just as when He said in Sūra Barāʾa,[121] *if they repent,* [9:5] meaning, from idolatry (*shirk*), *and establish regular prayers'* [9:5], that is, committing themselves to prayer and almsgiving, *then let them be.* In this regard, He also said: *Yet if they repent, establish prayer, and pay the obligatory alms, then they are your brothers in religion* [9:11] [and comrades].[122] There is something similar

118 Reference is being made here to a *ḥadīth* listed in the *Ṣaḥīḥ* of Bukhārī in the 'Kitāb al-Ṣalāt', and in the *Ṣaḥīḥ* of Muslim, 'Kitāb al-Ṣalāt'. The *ḥadīth*, in a version narrated on the authority of Abū Hurayra, reads as follows: 'When half of the night or two thirds of it are over, God, Blessed and Exalted is He, descends to the lowest heaven and asks: "Is there any beggar to whom something might be given? Is there any supplicant that he might be answered? Is there anyone seeking forgiveness that he might be forgiven?" [And God continues asking this] till it is daybreak.' In other versions of this *ḥadīth* God's question begins with 'Who is there (*man*)…?'

119 Bukhārī, *Ṣaḥīḥ*, 'Kitāb al-Mutahajjid', 'Kitāb al-Daʿwāt', and 'Kitāb al-Tawḥīd'; Ibn Ḥanbal, *al-Musnad*, vol. 2, p. 433, vol. 4, pp. 81, 217, 218.

120 According to the commentaries, 'it' here refers to the Hellfire.

121 Sūra Barāʾa is otherwise known as Sūrat al-Tawba (or Repentance).

122 *Wa mawālīkum* is absent from the MSS.

to this in Sūrat al-Sajda.[123] The second aspect of establishing [the prayers] (*iqāma*) is referred to when He says in Sūrat al-Mujādala, *Then establish the prayer and pay the obligatory alms* [58:13], as in Sūrat al-Muzzammil [73:20],[124] and again with His words in Sūrat al-Māʾida,[125] *[believers who] establish the prayer* [5:55], meaning that they fulfil it [that duty] completely.

[2:238] *...especially the middle prayer...*[126]

[Sahl] was asked about these words, and the reason why [the middle prayer] is singled out. He replied:

> It is singled out due to a particular characteristic it possesses, even though it is not apart from the obligatory prayers as a whole, in the same way that Gabriel and others were singled out for mention among the host of the angels, due to a certain particularity.

He continued:

> There is another reason, namely, that the times of the rest of the prayers are known by both the knowledgeable and the ignorant, because their signs are obvious.[127] However, the time for the *ʿAṣr* prayer is less clear. Thus by mentioning [this prayer] in particular, He urged people to take care to observe it at its correct time.

His words [that follow in the same verse]:

...And stand before God in submission

> That is, 'Stand before God in prayer in a state of obedience, for many a worshipper is disobedient, such as the hypocrite and his like. The Prophet ﷺ was asked, 'Which prayer is the best?' He replied, 'The longest in devotion (*qunūt*), that is, the prayer [for which] one stands the longest (*ṭūl al-qiyām*).[128] And Zayd b. Arqam ؓ said that being devout (*qunūt*) is silence, for we used to speak during the prayer until God, Exalted is He, sent down the words, *And stand before God in submission* [2:238], after which we desisted from speaking [during prayer]. Muḥammad b. Sawwār said, 'The *qunūt* is the *witr*,[129] which was called a (*qunūt*) because of the supplication (*duʿāʾ*) which is offered in it whilst standing, aside from the recitation of Qurʾān.' This is a kind of magnifying (*taʿẓīm*) [of God] through supplication.

[2:268] *Satan promises you poverty and enjoins you to indecency...*

He was asked about these words and replied, '[He, Satan, does this] so that they should take something which is not lawfully theirs, and deposit it in other than its proper place.'[130]

[2:269] *...And he who is given wisdom has been given much good.*

He was asked about these words and he said:

> Abū Saʿīd al-Khudrī ؓ narrated from the Prophet ﷺ that he said: 'The Qurʾān is God's wisdom (*ḥikma*) among His servants. Whoever learns the Qurʾān and acts according to it, it is as if prophethood were incorporated within him, except that he does not receive revelation. He is called to account in the same way as the prophets except in the matter of conveying the message.'[131]
>
> And Muḥammad b. Sawwār reported to me from ʿAqīl, from Ibn al-Musayyab, on the authority of Abū Hurayra ؓ that he stated that the Prophet ﷺ said, 'The Qurʾān is wisdom, and

---

123 There is no obvious verse with this meaning in Sūrat al-Sajda.

124 The same words are also to be found in Sūrat al-Ḥajj [22:78].

125 Corrected by the editor of the Dār al-Kutub al-ʿIlmiyya from al-Baqara.

126 A term that is used for the *ʿAṣr* prayer, the time for which is between the middle of the afternoon and sunset.

127 For example, it is easy to see the time of the sun's rising and setting, and the moment when it is at its zenith.

128 Muslim, *Ṣaḥīḥ*, 'Kitab Ṣalāt al-musāfirīn wa-qaṣrihā'; Ibn Māja, 'Kitāb al-Ṣalāt'.

129 The *witr* is the prayer cycle (*rakʿa*) which makes the sum of supererogatory prayers an odd number. It is the late-night prayer prescribed by the Prophet for after the *ʿIshāʾ* prayers, and is usually prayed silently.

130 That is, Satan is trying to dissuade them from the almsgiving as prescribed in the previous verse [2:267]. The placing or depositing of something (probably wealth) in other than its proper place may mean avoiding giving it to those who have a right to it.

131 Ibn Abī Ḥātim, *ʿIlal al-ḥadīth* (Beirut, 1985), vol. 2, p. 65.

whoever learns the Qurʾān in his youth, it mingles with his flesh and blood.[132] And surely the Fire cannot touch a heart which contains the Qurʾān, nor a body which avoids that which it prohibits (*maḥārim*), and keeps to what it permits (*ḥalāl*), believes in that which is clear [in it] (*muḥkam*), refrains from judgement in that which is ambiguous [in it] (*mutashābih*), and does not make innovations regarding it.'[133] Mujāhid and Ṭāwūs said, 'Wisdom is the Qurʾān, as He says in Sūrat al-Naḥl, *Call to the way of your Lord with wisdom* [16:125], meaning the Qurʾān. Ḥasan said, 'Wisdom is the understanding of the Qurʾān, and wisdom is prophethood, as He says in Sūrat Ṣād, *and gave him wisdom*' [38:20], meaning prophethood (*nubuwwa*). And God said [concerning] David ﷺ, *And God gave him kingship and wisdom* [2:251] meaning prophethood, along with the Book.[134]

Qatāda said, 'Wisdom is understanding the religion of God, Mighty and Majestic is He, and following the Messenger of God ﷺ'; Suddī said: 'Wisdom is prophethood'; Zayd b. Aslam said, 'Wisdom is the intellect (*ʿaql*)'; while Rabīʿ b. Anas said, 'Wisdom is the fear of God, Exalted is He'. Ibn ʿUmar said, 'Wisdom is [to be found in] three things: a clear verse (*āya muḥkama*),[135] the Sunna put into practice and a tongue which is articulate with the Qurʾān.'

Abū Bakr stated that Sahl [himself] said, 'Wisdom is the integration of the sciences, and its origin is the Sunna. God, Exalted is He, has said: And recite what is rehearsed to you in your houses of the revelations of God and His wisdom [33:34]. The revelations are that which is obligatory [according to the religious law] and the wisdom (*ḥikma*) is that which is Sunna.' Sahl meant by this that the Arabs say that you restrain a man when you prevent him from falling into harm or leaving the truth.[136] [He was asked the meaning] of His words, *wisdom that is far-reaching* (bāligha) [54:5]. He replied:

It means perfect and complete (*tāmma*), as in His saying, *We gave him [power of] judgement* (ḥikma) *and knowledge* [21:74],[137] for it [wisdom] at that time was ⌜perfect and complete⌝[138] such that it reached those who were worthy of it without reaching others.[139] In every situation they speak according to it. They resort to its rulings and reveal its meanings.

It has also been said, 'Keep close to the wise, for certainly God revives dead hearts with wisdom just as He revives the barren land with a downpour of rain.'

Then he said:

The capital (*raʾs al-māl*) of wisdom consists of three things: the first is disciplining the lower self (*riyāḍat al-nafs*)[140] concerning things which are reprehensible (*makrūhāt*);[141] the second is emptying one's heart of any love for carnal lusts (*shahawāt*); and the third is standing guard (*qiyām*) over one's heart by warding off [unwarranted] thoughts (*khaṭarāt*) which occur to it.[142] Moreover, whoever is heedful (*rāqib*) of God when [unwarranted] thoughts [come upon] his heart, will have [God] protect him in his bodily acts.

---

132 Thus far, the *ḥadīth* is recorded in Bayhaqī, *Shuʿab al-īmān*, vol. 2, pp. 330 and 553; and in Tirmidhī, *Nawādir al-uṣūl*, vol. 2, p. 96.

133 See above IC, p. 6, nn. 23 and 24 regarding the categories of verses in the Qurʾān.

134 That is, reading *maʿaʾl-kitāb* as in all the MSS, Z515, f. 25b, F638, f. 13b and F3488, f. 201b, instead of *min al-kitāb*.

135 Given the interpretation that was made in the previous paragraph this probably means 'a clear (i.e. unambiguous) verse', as in the designation of the *muḥkam* and *mutashābih* verses given in 3:7, though it is also possible that it means a 'clear sign'.

136 It appears here that Sahl has attached to the meaning of wisdom the responsibility of commanding right and forbidding wrong.

137 Said of Lot.

138 *Tāmma* is added on the basis of all three MSS: Z515, f. 25b, F638, f. 13b and F3488, f. 201b.

139 Here again, what Sahl seems to imply by wisdom is the Revelation and the Sunna.

140 The MSS (Z515, f. 25b, F638, f. 13b and F3488, f. 201b) have the more likely *riyāḍa* instead of *riyāḍ* in the printed edition.

141 According to Islamic Law, the *makrūhāt* are things which, though not unlawful, are disapproved of, and should be avoided if possible.

142 As noted above, p. 16, n. 24; *khaṭar* is something that occurs to the mind or comes to the heart, which may be undesirable or even evil.

ʿUmar b. Wāṣil said: 'His words, Exalted is He, *He grants wisdom to whomsoever He pleases...* [2:269] mean that He bestows the correct understanding of His Book upon whomsoever He wills, just as He, Exalted is He, said while addressing the wives of the Prophet ﷺ, when they had been given bounties in abundance, *And recite what is rehearsed to you in your houses, of the revelations* (āyāt) *of God and His wisdom*' [33:34]. [In this verse] the revelations are the Qurʾān, and wisdom is that which the Messenger ﷺ had extracted from it (*mustanbaṭ*),[143] just as ʿAlī ﷺ said, 'The signs are [manifest in] a man to whom God has granted understanding of His Book.'[144]

He was asked about His words:

[2:273] *[Charity is] for the poor, who are constrained in the way of God...*

Sahl was asked about these words and the difference between the poor (*fuqarāʾ*) and the abject (*masākīn*).[145] He replied:

God, Exalted is He, described the poor (*faqīr*) in terms of destitution (*ʿadam*) due to their state of asking Him out of utter neediness (*iftiqār*) and resorting (*lijāʾ*) to Him. He also described them as having the qualities of contentment (*riḍā*) and satisfaction [with their lot] (*qunūʿ*), for He said, Exalted is He, ...*They do not beg from men importunately* [2:273].

These are the People of the Bench (*Ahl al-Ṣuffa*) of the Messenger of God ﷺ who were about forty men.[146] They did not have any dwellings in Medina nor [did they belong to] any tribes. These were the circumstances of a group of people whom God, Exalted is He, praised for the high degree of their dependence on Him. They had no ability (*istiṭāʿa*), nor any strength (*quwwa*) except in Him and from Him. He was their power (*ḥawl*) and strength (*quwwa*). He uprooted from them the power for their hearts to depend (*sukūn*) on anything other than Him, which is the incitement (*waswasa*) of the lower self towards that which is other than God, Exalted is He. Because of this [quality] they are elevated in their [spiritual] state. But [this is unlike] the one whom God turns back to the acquiescence of his lower self (*musākana nafsihi*), [about whom] He said, *It belonged to deprived people* (masākin) *who worked at sea* [18:79].[147] He returned them to the situation in which they had acquiesced. However, as regards the poor and needy person (*faqīr*), whose want has made him surrender himself to God, Exalted is He, his action involves

143 The word *mustanbaṭ*, or *istinbāṭ* meaning literally 'drawing water from a well' came to be used by some Sufis to designate their elicitation of inner meanings from the Qurʾānic verses. See, for example, the chapters on *mustanbaṭāt* in Sarrāj, *Kitāb al-Lumaʿ*, pp. 105ff, and in Abū Saʿd Khargūshī's *Tahdhīb al-asrār*, MS Ahlwardt 2819, fols. 2818ff; 98ff.

144 It should be borne in mind that the word *aya* (pl. *āyāt*) can mean a 'sign' or 'revelation' as well as 'verse'.

145 *Masākīn* is the plural of *miskīn*, which according to Lane can mean 'lowly, humble or submissive', although it can also take the meaning of 'low, abject, ignominious'. The word occurs in a *ḥadīth* of the Prophet: 'O God, make me live lowly, die lowly and gather me [on the Day of Resurrection] in the congregation of the lowly (*masākīn*).' The *ḥadīth* is listed in Ibn Māja, *Sunan*, 'Abwāb al-zuhd', and Khaṭīb al-Tibrīzī, *Mishkāt al-maṣābīḥ*, trans. by J. Robson (Lahore, 1975), vol. 2, Book 25, 'Words that Soften the Heart'. However, Tustarī appears in this passage to be using the word in a pejorative sense, as will be seen from the latter part of the commentary on this verse.

146 The *Ahl al-Ṣuffa*, usually translated in English as the 'People of the Bench', were a group of Companions of the Prophet who, according to tradition, chose to live their lives in a portico or vestibule of the mosque in Medina, only leaving when they were commanded by the Prophet to go and fight. For Sufis in particular, they exemplified the ideal of a life of simplicity, poverty and piety.

147 This is a reference to part of the story of Moses and Khiḍr, which is narrated in 18:60–82. Moses was on a journey to the 'meeting of the two seas' (*majmaʿ al-baḥrayn*). Having reached there, he and his servant find that the fish that they had brought in a basket for their breakfast miraculously swims away. Retracing their steps, they encounter a mysterious person who has been endowed with 'knowledge from the divine presence' (*ʿilm ladunnī*), and who is identified in Islamic tradition with Khiḍr (or Khaḍir). Moses asks if he may accompany Khiḍr on his way, and Khiḍr agrees, on the condition that he (Moses) does not question him about anything he does. Khiḍr then proceeds to carry out three apparently shocking acts, at each of which Moses is unable to restrain himself from expressing his objection. The first is the sinking of a ship with people aboard (referred to here in Tustarī's commentary); the second, is the killing of a youth; and the third is the rebuilding of a ruined wall without taking any payment. The third time Moses breaks the condition set for him, Khiḍr insists that they must part company, but not before he has given an explanation for the three actions he had carried out. Tustarī's identifying the people in the ship, whom the Qurʾān describes as *masākīn*, with his pejorative use of this term is interesting, since Khiḍr's explanation for the sinking of the ship and its company was that there was a king in pursuit of them, who was seizing every ship by force. Perhaps Tustarī is identifying the king with Satan.

[combatting] the desire (*hawā*) of his lower self,[148] and thus he is in a better state than the one who acquiesces in whatever state he is in, due to following his lower self.

ʿUmar b. Wāṣil said, 'If one needy of God (*faqīr ilāʾLlāh*), Mighty and Majestic is He, is satisfied, [yet] does not depend on[149] [his state of] contentment (*riḍā*) and self-surrender (*taslīm*), then both names are true for him: poverty (*faqr*) and lowliness (*maskana*).'[150]

Abū Bakr [al-Sijzī] said that he heard Sahl say:

The poor person is [one who is both] poor [and] helpless (*faqīr ʿājiz*). Poverty ⌜is honour (*ʿizz*)⌝[151] when it is the poverty of the heart's being agitated [in its need][152] for God, Mighty and Majestic is He, and the repose it finds in Him through obedience. Abjectness (*maskana*), however, is dishonour (*dhull*), for it is disobedience to God. Ḥasan related on the authority of Anas ﷺ from the Prophet ﷺ that when this verse was revealed he said, 'Treat the needy (*fuqarāʾ*) with kindness, until the day when they take possession.' He was asked, 'O Messenger of God! When is the day that they will take possession?' He replied, 'The Day of Resurrection.'[153]

[Sahl] was asked about His words:

[2:281] *And fear the Day wherein you shall be returned to God.*

He replied:

This was the last verse to have been revealed, and with it God, Exalted is He, brought the Qurʾān to a close. The Messenger of God ﷺ passed away eighty days after it was revealed.

Then he said:

When the night before the [trial] arrives when [justice will be demanded] by people of this world for crimes committed against them by others of this world, sleep and rest vanishes from those who are imprisoned [for those crimes]. They do not know what will be done with them due to My curse[154] on them, whether they will be killed or tortured, or let off and set free. This is the case for the offences committed by people of this world against others of this world, so how will it be for the people of the Hereafter when it comes to God's grievances [against them]?

Concerning His words:

[2:286] *God charges no soul save to its capacity...*

[Sahl said]:

That is, what it can bear; *...for it, is what it has merited...*, that is, its reward for righteous deed[s], *...and against it, is what it has earned...*, meaning, the burden of sins.'

Then he said:

Whoever is not concerned with his past sins will not be protected in the days that remain. Moreover, whoever is not protected in his remaining days will be among those who perish on their final return.

---

148 All the MSS (Z515, f. 26b, F638, f. 14a and F3488, f. 202a) here have *la-inna ḥarakatahu fī hawā nafsihi*. This would be in keeping with that which Tustarī advocated in his commentary on 2:30 above. The published edition, however, has: *ḥarakatahu fī mawt nafsihi*, that is: his action (lit. motion) is from the death of his lower self.

149 None of the MSS (Z515, f. 26b, F638, f. 14a and F3488, f. 202b) have *illā* as in the published edition. The latter would imply that they depend only on their contentment (*riḍā*) and self-surrender (*taslīm*). But Tustarī has just criticised those who depend on any state which they have.

150 Here *maskana* is evidently being taken in a positive sense of only acquiescing in God.

151 Added on the basis of all the MSS (Z515, f. 26b, F638, f. 14a and F3488, f. 202a).

152 There is a discrepancy between the MSS here, with Z515, f. 26b and F3488, f. 202a having *bi-lablabat al-qalb* (as in the printed edition) and F638, f. 14a having *inābat al-qalb* with the meaning of remorseful repentance.

153 Sulaymān b. Aḥmad al-Ṭabarānī, *al-Muʿjam al-ṣaghīr* (Beirut/Amman, 1985), vol. 2, p. 13. The *ḥadīth* is related to convey the principle that the rich should treat the poor with consideration and kindness, because they will be answerable to the poor on the Day of Resurrection.

154 Assuming that the *wāw* has dropped out here, as is often the case with copyists who were native Persian speakers, so that it should have been written as *daʿwatī*.

He was asked, 'When does a man know his own sins?' He replied:

> When he preserves the lights of his heart and does not allow anything to enter it or depart from it without [first] weighing it up, then he will know his own sins. Furthermore, whoever opens for himself a door to goodness, will find that God opens for him seventy doors to divinely-bestowed success (*tawfīq*). On the other hand, whoever opens for himself a door to evil, will find that God opens to him seventy doors to evil whence the servant will not know. Every heart that preoccupies itself with that which does not concern it will be punished immediately by missing out on that which is its [genuine] concern at that moment (*fī'l-ḥāl*).[155] No one knows this except those who know God.

[2:180] *...and leaves behind some good...*[156]

Concerning these words, he was asked, 'In your opinion what is this *good*?' He said:

> It refers to legitimate wealth, just as God, Exalted is He, has said, *Say, 'Whatever you spend that is good'* [2:215] — that is, out of legitimate wealth, for His purposes (*bi-wujūhihi*) and desiring His good pleasure; and [elsewhere] He said, *And whatever good you expend* of legitimate wealth, *shall be repaid to you in full* [2:272],[157] meaning that you shall receive, from God, Exalted is He, the return and reward for your deeds, and for your purpose in doing them.

He was asked about His words:

[2:177] *...those who show fortitude in misfortune and hardship...*

[Sahl said]

> This means that to begin with [they show fortitude] in upholding the Sunna; *and in hardship* means in avoiding that which is forbidden, both outwardly and inwardly, and in eating [only] that which is legitimate. The outward meaning of *misfortune* (baʾsāʾ) is poverty (*faqr*), and that of *hardship* (ḍarrāʾ) is adversity (*shidda*); *and times of peril*, that is, in battle.

He was asked about His words:

[2:206] *...he is seized by vainglory in his sin...*

He replied:

> This refers to [proud] fury (*ḥamīya*), just as He said in Sūra Ṣād, *in vainglory and defiance* [38:2], that is, in proud fury and dissension (*ikhtilāf*).

Concerning His words:

[2:165] *(Yet there are people who take to themselves idols), loving them as if loving God; but those who believe love God more ardently...*

He said:

> It means that they love idols (*andād*) in the way that they love God, Mighty and Majestic is He. Indeed, God, Exalted is He, described the intensity of their disbelief and their constancy (*ṣidq*) in the state of disbelief as ignorance (*jahl*). He then described the love of the believers and their constancy in the state of faith in God, as truth (*ḥaqq*). Then He accorded superiority to the believers due to their knowledge [or gnosis, *maʿrifa*],[158] saying, *those who believe love God more ardently*. This is due to their knowledge (*maʿrifa*), and all the other things that cause the believing servant to advance towards God and establish His remembrance. This is the level of

155 A reminder that the would-be mystic should be the 'son of the moment' (*ibn al-waqt*), and the word *waqt* is also used interchangeably with *ḥāl* to denote a person's state in the immediate present. Thus, preoccupation with what is past and what is to come is also, in a way, not the heart's business or concern.

156 Regarding the ordering of the verses in the *Tafsīr*, see above, Preface, p. xii.

157 Between these two phrases in verse 2:272 (*Whatever good you expend*, and *shall be repaid to you in full*) the following words intervene: *is for yourselves, for then you are expending, desiring only God's face*, which recalls Sahl's specifying that the spending should be for [God's] purposes and desiring His good pleasure, in his allusion to 2:215 below.

158 Note that the term *maʿrifa* is not necessarily being used here in the particular manner of the Sufis to designate mystical/experiential knowledge of God.

the loving mystics (*ʿārifūn muḥibbūn*), since love is the inclination (*ʿaṭf*) for the purest reality (*khāliṣat al-ḥaqq*), which God, Exalted is He, [produces] in them.

He was asked, 'What is the sign of love?' He replied:

It is the embracing of obedience and the relinquishing of [any sense] of need [for other than God] (*mubāyanat al-fāqa*). It has been related that God, Exalted is He, said in a revelation to Moses, 'Do you know why I cast my love upon you?',[159] to which he replied, 'No, O Lord.' He said, 'Because you sought My delight (*masarra*). O Moses, [always] keep Me in mind, and don't forget Me in any situation. Let your aspiration (*himma*) be for My remembrance (*dhikr*), for I will take care of your path.'[160] But God, Transcendent and Exalted is He, knows best.

159 An allusion to 20:39: *I cast upon you love from Me.*

160 That is to say, if a person takes care of the remembrance of God, He will take care of the outer, material concerns of their existence.

3 Āl ʿImrān

[3:1, 2] ***Alif, Lām, Mīm.* ❁ *God! There is no god except Him, the Living, the Eternal Sustainer.***

He [Sahl] said:

It [*Allāh*] is God's Greatest Name, which is written across the sky in green light from East to West.[1]

[3:4] ***…and He revealed the criterion…***

That is, the Qurʾān, wherein is the way out of all doubt and error.

[3:7] ***…As for those in whose hearts is deviation, they follow the allegorical part, desiring sedition…***

That is, disbelief; *…and desiring its interpretation,* refers to its interpretation according to the desire of their lower selves. *…But no one knows its interpretation except God.*

Ibn ʿAbbās said:

God sent down the Qurʾān according to four ways of reading (*aḥruf*):[2] the lawful (*ḥalāl*) and the unlawful (*ḥarām*), ignorance of which nobody is excused; the interpretation (*tafsīr*) according to which the Arabs have interpreted it; the interpretation according to which scholars (*ʿulamāʾ*) have interpreted it; and the ambiguous (*mutashābih*), which none but God, Exalted is He, knows, and whoever claims knowledge of it other than God, Mighty and Majestic is He, is lying.[3]

His words:

[3:7] ***…And those who are firmly rooted in knowledge* (rāsikhūna fiʾl-ʿilm)…**

[Sahl] said:

It was reported from ʿAlī that he stated, '[Those rooted in knowledge] are the ones whom knowledge has protected from plunging [into the interpretation of the Qurʾān] according to some whim (*hawā*) or with set arguments (*ḥujaj maḍrūba*) without [awareness of] the unseen [mysteries] (*ghuyūb*).' [This is] due to God's guidance of them, and His disclosing to them His unseen secrets from within the treasure chests of knowledge. Thus they said, *We believe in the Book; all of it is from our Lord* [3:7]. So God, Exalted is He, acknowledged them [in this verse], and made them among the people of profound and far-reaching knowledge, as an increase granted to them from Him. Just as God has said, Exalted is He, *But say: 'O my Lord! Advance me in knowledge* [20:114]'.

---

1 See the commentary on 2:255 above where Tustarī stated the words *God! There is no God but Him, the Living, the Eternal Sustainer* (Allāh lā ilāha illā hū al-Ḥayy al-Qayyūm) were written across the sky.

2 Ṭabarī has included in his commentary several *ḥadīths* concerning the revelation of the Qurʾān according to a certain number of *aḥruf* (sing. *ḥarf*). Most of these traditions speak of seven *aḥruf*. Ṭabarī presents two main interpretations of the word *ḥarf*: one meaning 'dialect' or 'tongue', and the other equivalent to 'aspect' (*wajh*, plur. *wujūh* or *awjuh*). The above tradition exemplifies the second understanding of the word *aḥruf*. See Abū Jaʿfar al-Ṭabarī, *Jāmiʿ al-bayān ʿan taʾwīl āy al-Qurʾān* (Cairo, 1955–69), *Tafsīr* Introduction, pp. 21–72; trans. Cooper, pp. 34ff.

3 A similar tradition, also attributed to Ibn ʿAbbās and included in the introduction to Ṭabarī's *Jāmiʿ al-bayān*, reads as follows: 'The *tafsīr* of the Qurʾān falls into four categories (*awjuh*): that which can be understood by the learned; that of which the Arabs have knowledge; that which it is unforgivable not to know; and that, the interpretation of which if anyone should claim to have knowledge, he is lying.' See Ṭabarī, *Jāmiʿ al-bayān*, vol. 1, pp. 29–30; trans. Cooper, pp. 16–34. Note regarding the above, in this tradition the word *awjuh* has been used instead of *aḥruf*.

Sahl also said:

God, Blessed and Exalted is He, showed those who are firmly rooted in knowledge to be exceptional because of their saying *all of it is from our Lord* [3:7], by which they mean, the abrogating and the abrogated, the clear and the ambiguous. They are the ones who reveal three [ways of] knowing (*ʿulūm*), since those who know (*ʿulamāʾ*) may be [designated in] three [ways], namely: those [whose knowledge derives from] the divine lordliness (*rabbāniyyūn*), those [whose knowledge derives from] the divine light (*nurāniyyūn);* and those [whose knowledge derives from] the divine essence' (*dhātiyyūn*).[4] [Those firmly rooted in knowledge reveal] in addition four [other kinds] of knowledge: revelation (*waḥy*), theophany (*tajallī*), knowledge directly bestowed by God (*ʿindī*) and knowledge from the divine presence (*ladunnī*),[5] just as God has said, *to whom We had given mercy from Us and We had taught him knowledge from Us* [18:65], [and when He said], *Yet none remembers but the people of inner substance* [2:269], that is, none reflects[6] save the people of understanding (*fahm*) and intellect (*ʿuqūl*), who say:

[3:8] ***Our Lord, do not cause our hearts to deviate after You have guided us…***

That is, 'Do not let our hearts turn away from faith after You have guided us with guidance from Yourself'; *…But grant us mercy from You,* ⌜that is, stability (*thabāt*)⌝[7] *…You are the One who bestows,* upon those who return to You in a state of neediness, entreaty and lowliness.

Then Sahl said:

The only stratagem (*ḥīla*) that the servant has is to establish the practice throughout his life of saying, 'My Lord! Protect me! Protect me! Keep me safe! Keep me safe! Help me! Help me!'[8] God, Exalted is He, has said, *As He brought you into being, so shall you return* [7:29].

Every person who affirms God's oneness should know for a certainty that not everyone who loves God (*Ḥaqq*) is loved by Him, for Iblīs encountered Him with the ⌜outward sign⌝[9] of love and said, '*Shall I prostrate before one whom You have created from clay* [17:61], when You are God, and it is not permissible to worship other than You?' Consequently God cursed him. Therefore, not all those who try to draw close to God are accepted by Him. Nor does God accept the obedience (*ṭāʿa*) of all who obey Him. Truly He perceives what is in the conscience (*ḍamīr*) [of all His creatures]. Thus, no one can feel secure that God will not deal with him in the same way that He dealt with Iblīs. God cursed him with the lights of His protection (*bi-anwār ʿiṣmatihi*) such that he was always in reality under His curse, but God veiled him from what had been foreordained [for him] from Him, up until the time when He punished him by bringing it to realisation through him.[10] Thus, the servant can do nothing except continually [implore] help (*ghawth*) from God. Indeed the Messenger ﷺ said, 'O You who make the steadfast firm, make me firm with Your firmness (*thabāt*)! O You whose oneness is unchanging, for there is no god except You, Glorified are You! Truly I have been among the wrongdoers.'[11] He would

4 Alternatively the terms *rabbāniyyūn, nūriyyūn* and *dhātiyyūn* might be translated as 'those whose knowledge manifests the divine lordliness, light and essence, respectively.' On these three designations in particular, see IT, pp. xlvii. On Tustarī's teachings on knowledge in general, see IT, pp. xlv–xlviii.

5 See Böwering's discussion of this passage *Mystical Vision*, p. 228 with reference to Baqlī's *ʿArāʾis al-bayān*. See also an almost identical passage cited from Tustarī in Makkī (attrib.), *ʿIlm al-qulūb*, p. 81.

6 That is, translating *lā yatafakkarūna*, as in the MSS Z515, f. 28b and F3488, f. 204a, instead of *mā yatadhakkaru* in the printed edition. F638, f. 15a has neither *lā yatafakkarūna* nor *yatadhakkaru*.

7 Added on the basis of MSS: Z515, f. 28b and F638, f. 15a. F3488 204a appears to have *thiyāb* which must be a copyist's error.

8 lit. 'Safety, Safety! Security, Security! Help, Help!'

9 That is, reading *ʿalāmat al-ḥubb* according to all three MSS: Z515, f. 29a, F638, f. 15a and F3488, 204a, instead of *aʿlā al-ḥubb* as in the printed edition. This makes more sense because later Tustarī goes on to say that God perceives what is in the conscience (*ḍamīr*).

10 Here we have an example of the divine ruse (*makr*) that was discussed earlier, whereby God can delude a person into believing that all is well with them (here the lights of divine protection), until the reality of that which has been foreordained for them is manifested. See above the commentary on 2:41, p. 20, n. 47 and n. 48 on *makr* and *istidrāj*.

11 Sulaymān b. Aḥmad al-Ṭabarānī, *al-Muʿjam al-awsaṭ* (Cairo, 1995), vol. 1, p. 206.

also say: 'O Lord and Protector (*walī*) of Islam and its people, make me firm in Islam until I encounter You!'[12]

[Sahl] said [on this matter], 'The place of faith in God, Exalted is He, is the heart and the place of Islam is the breast, and it is subject to increase and decrease.'[13]

His words:

[3:15] ***...with spouses pure...***

That is, purified from the defilements that they were subject to in this world, such as menstruation and the like. Do you not note His words, *And their Lord will give to them a pure drink to drink* [76:21], which means that He will purify them from the remaining blemishes of the world?

His words:

[3:18] ***God bears witness...***

He [Sahl] said:

That is, God knows and makes clear (*bayyana*) *...that there is no god but He.* He is witness to Himself by Himself; and this is particular to His essence. He called to witness those of His creatures whom He called to witness before their creation, according to His knowledge.[14] Consequently, the people possessed of His gnosis (*maʿrifa*) are made aware that He had full knowledge of everything that will be before it was actually brought into existence. Hence, [God's] oneness (*tawḥīd*) is independent of existentiated beings (*dūn al-akwān*), just as God was a witness to Himself by Himself before the existence of creation.

ʿAbd al-Wāḥid[15] said:

I was with Ayyūb al-Sakhtiyānī when he saw a porter carrying wood. I asked him, 'Do you have a Lord?' to which he replied, 'Is the likes of me questioned about his Lord?' So I said to him, 'If you have a Creator as you claim, why do you work with wood?' Then the man indicated to the sky, and lo and behold, the wood became gold! We were both amazed by him on account of this. Then he said, 'O God! I have no need for this', so the gold turned back to wood just as it was before. So we said to him, 'What led you to do this?', to which he replied, 'I am [God's] slave, so I carry this in order that I should not forget who I am.'[16]

His words:

[3:26] ***Say: 'O God! Master of the Kingdom, You give the kingdom to whom You will...***

That is, the [kingdom (*mulk*) of] gnosis, the profession of divine oneness (*tawḥīd*), the codes of law of Your religion of Islam, and a praiseworthy end. [All] this [depends on] God's taking care of the servant, and not relinquishing him to [reliance on] himself.

His words:

[3:103] ***And hold fast, all together to the rope of God and be not divided among yourselves...***

---

12 That is, according to all three MSS (Z515, f. 29a, F638, f. 15a and F3488, f. 204b), which do not have *bihi* following the *ḥattā alqāka.*

13 Which is why the Prophet prayed for stability (*thabāt*) in it. Other Sufis have spoken of the breast being the locus of Islam and the heart the locus of faith (*īmān*). See for example, Nūrī, *Maqāmāt al-qulūb*, p. 130; Maybudī, *Kashf al-asrār*, vol. 3, p. 557 and vol. 5, p. 333; and the treatise attributed to al-Ḥakīm al-Tirmidhī, *Bayān al-farq*, trans. Heer in *Three Early Sufi Texts*, pp. 24ff. On Tustarī's view of faith and its locus in the inner constitution of the human being, see IT, p. xlii.

14 A reference to the Covenant of *Alast*, on which see the commentary on 7:172, and IT, pp. xxxiff and xxxv–xxxvi.

15 This is most probably Ḥasan al-Baṣrī's student ʿAbd al-Wāḥid b. Zayd who died in the second century of the Hijra.

16 In other words, he wishes to be reminded of his subservience to God. It will be recalled above that the only veil remaining for the person who is in a state of the direct witnessing of face-to-face encounter (*ʿiyān al-kifāḥ*) is the veil of servanthood (*ʿubūdiyya*), though in effect, all veils were removed at that moment. See above, the commentary on Tustarī's poem, p. 32. See also the commentary on 2:41, p. 19, n. 44.

He said:

> That is, 'Adhere to your pact (*ʿahd*) with Him, which is that of professing His oneness (*tawḥīd*), just as He has said, Exalted is He, *Or has he made a covenant with the Compassionate One?* [19:78], meaning [a covenant of] professing His oneness. Hold fast to that which He has assigned to you, in terms of carrying out his obligations (*farḍ*) and the Sunna of His Prophet.'[17] Likewise is the meaning of His words, *Save a rope from God* [3:112], meaning a covenant from God and His religion. He called it a rope because whoever holds fast to it reaches that in which he put his faith.[18]

His words:

[3:28] *...God warns you to beware of Him...*

He said:

> That is, [beware of] His justice (*ʿadl*), because the Fire is His justice for the one that disobeys Him, and the Garden is His favour (*faḍl*) to the one who obeys Him. Have you not taken note of the words of the Prophet ﷺ 'O You, whose bounty alone is hoped for, and whose justice alone is feared!'?

His words:

[3:35] *When the wife of ʿImrān said: 'O Lord, I have consecrated what is in my womb solely to You...'*[19]

> That is, I have freed [what is in my womb], and emancipated it from enslavement to the world, from following its whim[s] and the desires (*murādāt*) of its lower self. I have committed it as a servant of the worshippers at the Temple of Jerusalem, and have dedicated it purely to God, Exalted is He.

His words:

[3:37] *Her Lord accepted her [the infant Mary] graciously...*

> That is, ⌜with [His] good pleasure (*riḍā*).⌝[20]

And he said:

> The Highest King took her into His special care, away from the shackles of the lower self and the world. *And He made her grow in goodness,* through righteous action, accompanied by the remembrance of God, Exalted is He, while all her bodily members were [engaged] in the service of God, and her heart was full of the knowledge of Him, Mighty and Majestic is He.

[3:43] *O Mary, be obedient to Your Lord...*

> That is, 'Pray to God and worship Him alone with sincerity. Bow in submission before Him, in supplication and humble entreaty.'

His words:

[3:47] *...'Even so. God creates what He will. When He decrees a thing, He says to it only: "Be" and it is.'*[21]

He [Sahl] said:

> When there is something in His pre-eternal knowledge that He wishes to bring to light, He says to it 'Be' and it is.[22] It has been said [in these lines of poetry]:

---

17 The word for God's assigning or granting possession to the believers used here (*malakakum*) derives from the same root as that for kingship used above in the commentary on 3:26, which went immediately before.

18 Note that in the Introduction to the Commentary (IC, p. 4), Tustarī identifies the Qurʾān as the 'rope (*ḥabl*) of God'.

19 The child in her womb was Mary, the mother of Jesus, as will become clear from verses 37 and 43.

20 Added on the basis of all three MSS: Z515, f. 30a, F638, f. 15b and F3488, f. 205a.

21 These words are said to Mary by one of the angels who bring her the tidings of the birth of Jesus, '*a Word from [God], whose name will be the Messiah, Jesus, the son of Mary.*' Mary asks, '*My Lord, how can I have a son when no man has touched me?*' and the verse above is the answer that is given to her.

22 These words are also to be found in Sūra Yā Sīn, 36:82.

He decreed, before creating the creation, all that He would create:
Created beings, none of whose affairs are hidden from Him, [nor]
Their desires, [nor their] intimate secrets, [nor] that which their hearts enclose.
And [He decreed] what was [in] their minds prior to their desire.

His words:

[3:61] *...then let us humbly pray* (nabtahil)

That is, 'Let us invoke [God's] curse, one upon the other.'[23] The one who beseeches (*mubtahil*) is the supplicant (*dāʿī*), and the [act of] beseeching (*ibtihāl*) is supplication (*duʿāʾ*). The one who glorifies (*musabbiḥ*) is the one who remembers (*dhākir*), and this is not written down by the recording angels,[24] for it is a witnessing of the One remembered in a remembrance that is *through* the One remembered.[25] This is the meaning of His saying, 'I keep company with the one who remembers Me, and when and wherever My servant seeks me out he will find Me.'[26]

His words:

[3:64] *Say: 'O People of the Scripture! Come to a word agreed upon* (kalimatin sawāʾin) *between us and you: that we worship none but God...'*

That is, '[Let us] seek a just [agreement] (*ṭamʿin ʿadlin*) between us and you.' This is because they affirmed that their Creator and the Creator of the heavens and the earth was God, Exalted is He, and [agreed]: 'Let us declare His oneness and not worship anyone except Him.'

The basis of worship is the profession of God's oneness (*tawḥīd*) along with living according to what is lawful, while avoiding the harm [of others] (*kaff al-adhā*). Furthermore, a person cannot accomplish living by what is lawful without abandoning the harm of others, and likewise he does not abandon causing harm save through living by what is lawful. If you know how to abide by what is lawful, how to abandon causing harm, and the [correct] intention (*nīya*) behind actions, as well as you know the *Fātiḥa* [Sūrat al-Fātiḥa], then your faith will become pure, as will your hearts and bodily members. Indeed, these are the fundamentals.

He continued:

Muḥammad b. Sawwār related from al-Thawrī that he said, 'The degree of importance within the servant of [the reality] of "There is no god save God" is as water to the world.[27] God has said, *And We produced from water every living thing* [21:30].' Thus, whoever is not benefited by his belief that 'There is no god save God' and his adherence to the Sunna of the Messenger of God ﷺ, is as a dead person.

Sahl added:

Truly I know a man among the friends of God, Exalted is He, who passed by a man who had been crucified (*maṣlūb*) with his head fixed in a direction away from the *qibla*. He said to him, 'Where is that tongue with which you used to pronounce with all honesty: "There is no god save God?"' Then he added, 'Oh God grant me his sins!'

Through God's Power [his head] was then turned towards the *qibla*.

His words:

[3:72] *...at the outset* (wajh) *of the day...*

---

23 According to the Qurʾānic context, Muḥammad has been ordered that if anyone disputes the knowledge that has been revealed to him, he should gather all of them together, and command them to invoke God's rejection upon whomsoever of them is lying. In his commentary, however, Tustarī focuses on the meaning of *ibtihāl* contrasting it with the act of glorifying God (*taṣbīḥ*).

24 That is, omitting the word *illā* before *al-ḥafaẓa*, since it is absent from all three MSS: Z515, f. 30a and F638, f. 15b. F3488, f. 205b does not have either the *lā* or the *illā*.

25 i.e. it is something that is between God and the one who remembers Him, and to which the angels are not privy.

26 Bayhaqī, *Shuʿab al-īmān*, vol. 1, p. 451. This same *ḥadīth* was cited earlier, in the Introduction to the Commentary when Tustarī was speaking of those who are 'crazed or ecstatic' in their remembrance of God.

27 This being the first of the two attestations of faith (*shahādatayn*), the second being 'Muḥammad is His Messenger'.

That is, at the beginning (*awwal*) of the day.

His words:

[3:73] ***And He is All-Embracing, All-Knowing.***

This means, He gives in abundance (*kathīr al-ʿiṭāʾ*). He is able, through His pre-eternal omnipotence (*qudra*), to give all that He is asked for. Furthermore He encompasses everything, as He has said [in the words of Abraham]: '*My Lord encompasses everything in His knowledge* [6:80]'.

He [Sahl] was asked about His words:

[3:79] ***...Rather [he should say], 'Be masters* (rabbāniyyūn) *by virtue of what you know of the Book and in what you study,***[28]

He related:

Muḥammad b. Sawwār said, 'The person [whose knowledge derives from the] divine lordliness (*rabbānī*) is the one who does not choose anyone over his Lord, and it [the name] is derived from the word *rubūbiyya*'.[29]

Sahl continued:

People whose knowledge derives from the divine lordliness (*rabbāniyūn*) are those who are elevated[30] in the degree of [their] knowledge by virtue of [that] knowledge, just as Muḥammad b. Ḥanafiyya said on the death of ʿAbd Allāh Ibn ʿAbbās ☙, 'Indeed, today one whose knowledge derived from the divine lordliness (*rabbānī*) in this community (*umma*) has died. Furthermore, he [the *rabbānī*] is associated with the Lord (*rabb*) because he is knowledgeable through His knowledge, just as He said, *She asked, 'Who told you this?' He said, 'I was told by the All-Knowing, the Aware'* [66:3].[31] He [the Prophet] related it to prophethood (*nubuwwa*),[32] because of that which God had taught him, Mighty and Majestic is He.[33] Thus, anyone who informs you of something which conforms to the Book and the Sunna, is 'an informant' (*munbiʾ*).[34]

---

28 Verses 60-84 of Sūra Āl ʿImrān speak about, and admonish the People of the Scripture (also known as the People of the Book, i.e. the Jews and Christians) concerning their conduct and their responses to the Scripture. In full it reads: *It belongs not to any mortal that God should give him the Book, the Judgement, prophethood, then that he should say to men, 'Be servants to me instead of God.' Rather, [he should say] 'Be masters, by virtue of what you know of the Book and in what you study'* [3:79].

29 See above, the commentary on 3:7, n. 34 below, and above IT, p. xlvii.

30 Translating *ʿālūn* according to all three MSS: Z515, f. 31a, F638, f. 16a and F3488, f. 206a, as opposed to *ʿālimūn* in the printed edition.

31 The context of these words is indicated by the beginning of the verse: *And when the Prophet confided a certain matter to one of his wives. However, when she divulged it and [then] God apprised him of it, he announced part of it [to her], and passed over part. So when he told her about it, she said, 'Who told you this?' He said, 'I was told by the Knower, the Aware'.* The commentaries name the person in whom the Prophet confided as Ḥafṣa, and the person to whom she divulged the confidence as ʿĀʾisha.

32 The word used in the verse for 'told you' is *anbā* from the root *n-b-ʾ*, from which the word for prophethood (*nubuwwa*) is derived.

33 In his *Qūt al-qulūb*, Makkī cites a tradition of ʿAlī on the authority of Kumayl b. Ziyād, in which he defines the *rabbānī* as one who knows the divine lordliness (*ʿālim biʾl-rubūbiyya*), or who knows through the divine lordliness. He then describes the *rabbāniyyūn* as being of three kinds, each of which is connected to a different verse of the Qurʾān. There are those who have knowledge of the Qurʾān and teach it, on the basis of 3:79: *Be masters* (rabbāniyūn) *by virtue of what you know* (taʿlamūn, also read as tuʿallimūn, 'you teach') *of the Book*. Another designation of *rabbānī* is the one who knows and acts and teaches people the good (*khayr*), and this is connected to 5:63: *Why do their rabbis* (rabbāniyyūn) *and priests not forbid them...* The third designation equates the *rabbāniyyūn* with *ribbiyyūn*, who are described in 3:146: *Many prophets have fought, with large bands of godly men* (ribbiyyūn) beside them..., and Makkī observes that they are as the rest of the verse describes them, in standing firm with what is commanded, and showing strength in the religion and forbearance in the face of God's decrees (i.e suffering that is destined for them). See Makkī, *Qūt al-qulūb*, vol. 1, pp. 257–8. We are grateful to Harith Bin Ramli for the reference to this citation.

34 Tustarī's use of words here is subtle, since the word *munbiʾ*, like the word *anbāʾ* in the verse, derives from the root *n-b-w*, and according to Muslim doctrine there can be no prophet after Muḥammad, he being the Seal of Prophets and prophethood (*Khatm al-Anbiyāʾ*). Nonetheless, Tustarī appears to have chosen this word in order to maintain the link

Those possessed of knowledge are of three kinds: there is the one whose knowledge derives from the divine lordliness (*rabbānī*), the one whose knowledge derives from the divine light (*nūrānī*), and the one whose knowledge derives from the divine essence (*dhātī*),[35] [who has] no intermediary between him and God most High; within him is a 'subsisting' (*baqiyya*) of God, Mighty and Majestic is He.[36] [On the other hand], ʿUmar b. Wāṣil said: those whose knowledge derives from the divine lordliness (*rabbāniyyūn*) are the collectivity of scholars. This resembles a saying of ʿAlī ﷺ, 'People are of three kinds: the knower whose knowledge derives from the divine lordliness (*ʿālim rabbānī*), the person acquiring knowledge (*mutaʿallim*) on the path to salvation, and the commoners and riff-raff, who follow every charlatan.[37]

His words:

[3:85] ***If anyone desires a religion other than Islam, it shall not be accepted of him...***

He [Sahl] said:

Islam means the committing of one's affairs [to God] (*tafwīḍ*) as in His words: *Do not die except as Muslims* [3:102], by which He means 'as ones who have committed their affairs [to Him].' The same is implied by His words: *The Religion before God is Islam* [3:19].

He was asked about His words:

[3:92] ***You will not attain mindfulness of God until you expend of that which you love...***

That is, he said:

It means, 'You will not attain full mindfulness of God until you go to war with your lower selves and expend some of what you love.' Furthermore, there is no spending (*infāq*) like consuming (*infāq*) the lower self by opposing it, and by seeking the good pleasure of God, Mighty and Majestic is He.

Then he related a story of Jesus ﷺ:

Once he passed by three people whose bodies were emaciated and faces pale. He asked them, 'What has brought you to this state I see you in?' They said, 'The fear (*khawf*) of our Creator and wariness (*ḥadhr*) of punishment for our disobedience.' He responded, 'God made it incumbent upon Himself to grant safety to the one who fears [Him].' Then he moved on until he came to three other people who were even more emaciated. He asked them, 'What has brought you to this state I see you in?' They answered, 'The yearning (*shawq*) for our Lord.' He replied, 'God made it incumbent upon Himself to grant you what you wish for.' Then he moved on until he came to three people who were even more emaciated, whose faces were like full moons. He asked, 'What has brought you to this state I see you in?' They replied: 'Love (*ḥubb*).' He said, 'You are the people of proximity [with God] (*muqarrabūn*)',[38] and he said it thrice.[39] Thus,

---

between the two words in the sense of knowledge coming directly from God, which is indicated by his citation of 66:3 and his comment on the Prophet's words.

35 Knowing here being perhaps a state of realisation, being, or manifestation as was discussed in the note to the commentary on 3:7 above, p. 42, n. 4, IT, p. xlvii and n. 205.

36 We may understand from this that Tustarī sees the level of knowing manifested by the *dhātiyyūn* to be in some way analogous to the state of *baqāʾ* (subsisting in God) that is concomitant with *fanāʾ* (annihilation from self), which may be implied by Tustarī's use of the the term *baqiyya*, though it should be added that in his *Tafsīr* he does not employ these two terms (*fanāʾ* and *baqāʾ*) as they are so often applied in later Sufism. Rather, he uses *baqāʾ* to refer to the everlastingness of Paradise. See above IT, p. lix, n. 269.

37 This saying appears in the *Nahj al-balāgha* of Imam ʿAlī b. Abī Ṭālib, at the commencement of a section of advice given privately to his disciple Kumayl b. Ziyad al-Nakhāʿī. The passage is discussed and translated in full by James W. Morris in idem, 'Surrender and Realisation: Imam ʿAli on the Conditions for True Religious Understanding', *Ruḥ ad-Din*, vol. 1 (2000). In the *Nahj al-balāgha*, the saying has, in addition to that which is cited by Tustarī: '... the riff-raff and rabble who follow every screaming voice; those who bend with every wind, who have not sought to be illuminated by the Light of Knowing and who have no recourse to solid support.' See the same article p. 27, n. 8 for a discussion of the word *rabbāniyyūn*.

38 lit. 'those who have been brought near'. See above, the commentary on the poem forming part of Tustarī's commentary on 2:241.

39 This story was popular among Sufi writers. It may be found narrated twice in Rashīd al-Dīn Maybudī's Qurʾān commentary,

whoever loves God, Exalted is He, is one of the people of proximity [with God], for if anyone loves something they hasten towards it.

So the first level is the rank of the repentant (*tawwābūn*); the second is that of the people of longing (*mushtāqūn*), and then the servant reaches the third rank which is that of love. Do you not see how they gave their all for the sake of the One who possesses all, turned their backs on all, and faced the direction of the One who possesses all?

[Concerning] His words:

[3:96] *The first House established for the people was that at Bakka, a blessed place...*

[He said]:

That is, 'The first house which was set down for men was the House of God, Mighty and Majestic is He, in Mecca.' This is the outward meaning [of the verse]. However inwardly it implies the Messenger. The one who believes in him [the Messenger] is the one in whose heart God has made firm the profession of His oneness (*tawḥīd*).[40]

His words:

[3:106] *On the Day when some faces are whitened...*

This means, the faces of the believers will become white through the light of their faith; *...and some faces are blackened...*, namely, the [faces] of the disbelievers, due to the darkness of their disbelief.

He was asked about His words, *Abasement and wretchedness were cast upon them* [2:61]. He replied:

The purpose of these bodies is in the 'deposits' (*waḍāʾiʿ*) that God has placed within them, by which He puts His creatures to the test. Among [these deposits] is one from which the obedient (*ṭāʾiʿūn*) should draw admonitory lessons, namely, disbelief (*kufr*). [On the other hand], there are those which are proof against the heedless (*ghāfilūn*), namely, gnosis (*maʿrifa*) and affirmation (*taṣdīq*) through speech and actions, just as He has said, *And He appointed darknesses and light* [6:1]. The inner meaning of this verse is that light is knowledge (*ʿilm*) and darkness is ignorance (*jahl*), in accordance with His words, *And he whom God has not granted any light has no light* [24:40], that is, the heart [of such a person] has not [the light] by which to perceive faith in God.[41]

The light of faith is one of the greatest blessings (*minan*) of God, Mighty and Majestic is He, and tokens of His generosity (*karāmāt*). The second [blessing] is the 'good word' which is referred to in His words, Exalted is He, *Come now to a word that is agreed upon between us and you* [3:64]. The third [great blessing] is obedience (*iṭāʿa*) that the bodily members carry out purely for God's sake, as when the prayers are maintained and obligatory alms (*zakāt*) are paid [in a spirit of] satisfaction (*qunūʿ*) and contentment (*riḍā*). Thus, [in this latter verse] He summoned them to the best speech, and the most excellent actions. If it had not been for faith in God and the Qurʾān, which is the knowledge of God, and which contains a call [for people] to affirm His lordship and to serve Him in fear, then the prophets, upon whom be blessings and peace, would not have known who among the people had responded to them.

His words:

[3:141] *And that God may prove the believers...*

---

the *Kashf al-asrār*, vol. 7, p. 78; vol. 9, p. 91, and it also appears in Ghazālī's *Iḥyāʾ ʿulūm al-Dīn*, Book 36: *Kitāb al-Maḥabba*, p. 182; idem., *Kīmiyāʾ al-saʿādat* (Tehran, 1985), vol. 2, p. 571.

40 See Böwering, *Mystical Vision*, p. 160, on Shāṭibī's citation of the correct reading of Tustarī's explanation 'that the hidden meaning of the house (*bāṭin al-bayt*) is the heart of Muḥammad', which may be found in Shāṭibī, *al-Muwāfaqāt*, vol. 3, p. 241.

41 The citation of these verses here seems to confirm that Tustarī sees disbelief (*kufr*) as well as gnosis (*maʿrifa*) and affirmation [of truth] (*taṣdīq*) as being deposits, and thus preordained by God.

This means their being purified (*takhlīṣ*)[42] from the blemishes of sins, just as they devoted themselves purely to Him (*akhlaṣū lahu*) in deed, which was [their] striving (*jihād*) in the way of God; *...and efface the disbelievers*. This means the destruction of the disbelievers through the affliction brought on by their sins.

His words:

[3:152] *...Yet now He has pardoned you...*

This refers to the defeated army on the Day of Uḥud, when He did not eradicate them all. *And God is bounteous to the believers*, by His pardoning them and accepting their repentance.

His words:

[3:155] *Truly, those of you who turned back the day the two hosts met, truly, it was Satan who caused them to slip, because of some of what they had earned...*

[Sahl] was asked about the meaning of that earning (*kasb*). He said:

It was the complacency that they felt because of their great numbers on the day of Ḥunayn and the glory they had gained on the Day of Badr.[43] This was due to Satan coming to associate with them, after [he saw] the acquiescence (*musākana*) of their hearts,[44] and their regard for themselves, because of the complacency (*iʿjāb*) that their own lower selves had seduced them into. So God lifted His protection (*ʿiṣma*) from them as a punishment. Indeed, when the Prophet ﷺ heard his Companions say on the Day of Ḥunayn, 'We shall not be overcome by so few', he warned them, 'Do not wish to encounter the enemy, rather ask for safety (*ʿāfiya*) from God, Exalted is He',[45] from dependency on your own devising (*tadbīr*) in any situation, and from [being unaware of your] neediness (*dūn al-iftiqār*) for God, Mighty and Majestic is He.

See how when David ﷺ asked his Lord to join him with the ranks of Abraham, Ishmael and Isaac, He replied, 'You are not on that level, O David.' He asked, 'Why is that O Lord?', to which God replied, 'Because I tested them and they showed patience. Furthermore, they did not know the world and the world did not know them. But you have known the world and it has known you, and you adopted it as your kin.' David ﷺ said, 'Show me one from among your servants who, if You tested him, would show patience.' Then God, Mighty and Majestic is He, said, 'I'm going to test you.' Thus he [David] became the first to request affliction (*balāʾ*), ⌜and the one who exposed himself to⌝[46] testing (*imtiḥān*) from God, Exalted is He. That is to say, this was [of course] in accordance with God's prior knowledge in the veiled unseen, which is solely known to Him. Then Iblīs came to him in the form of a pigeon and the story took place involving Uriah b. Ḥanān.[47] God did not protect [David] from desire, intent or action. However, He protected

---

42 The verb *khalaṣa*, from which is derived the word *takhlīṣ* (above) and the key Sufi term *ikhlāṣ*, has both the meaning of becoming pure, and becoming free or being delivered from something.

43 For an account of the Battles of Badr, Uḥud and Ḥunayn, see Lings, *Muḥammad*, pp. 138–52, 177–88 and 306–9; Guillaume, *Life of Muḥammad*, pp. 289, 370 and 566 respectively.

44 On the danger of the heart's (or lower self's) acquiescing (*musākana*) see above Tustarī's commentary on 20:30 and 2:273, p. 16, n. 26 and IT, pp. xxxiv–xxxv.

45 Bukhārī, *Ṣaḥīḥ*, 'Kitāb al-Jihād'; Muslim, *Ṣaḥīḥ*, 'Kitāb al-Jihād wa'l-sayr'.

46 That is translating *wa'l-mutaʿarriḍ* which is in Z515 f. 33a and F3488, f. 207b. F638, f. 17a has *al-taʿarruḍ* with more or less the same meaning.

47 The story relates how God warned David that He would test him on a certain day. On the said day, David shut himself in a room and began to read the Book of Psalms. Then Satan came to him in the form of a golden dove. David reached out to pick it up and it flew a little distance from him. He went after it, and again he tried to catch hold of it, but it flew away from him a little further. So it went on until the dove led him to a place where he caught sight of a beautiful woman bathing on a roof. When David inquired about her he discovered that her husband was Uriah, who was absent at war in a particular garrison which had defeated the enemy. David commanded that Uriah be sent to fight a stronger enemy, and again they were victorious, whereupon David commanded that they should go and fight an even stronger enemy and yet again they were victorious. Finally, after the army had been sent to fight an even mightier and more powerful enemy, Uriah was killed and David married his wife. Then two angels appeared before David and asked him to judge between two brothers, one of whom owned ninety-nine ewes and the other only one. The brother with ninety-nine ewes wished to take the one from his brother to make up a hundred. David could see the injustice of this, upon which

Joseph from action, though He did not protect him from desire and intent.[48]

His words:

[3:159] *It was by the mercy of God that you [Muḥammad] were lenient with them…*

This means, 'Due to an act of sympathy (*ʿaṭf*) from God you dealt gently with them', *And if you had been harsh*, with [your] tongue, *and fierce of heart, they would have dispersed from about you*, that is, 'They would have separated themselves from you'. *So pardon them*, that is, 'Overlook their faults', *and ask forgiveness for them*, for their defeat on the Day of Uḥud. *Consult them in the matter*, that is, 'Do not distance them from yourself because of their disobedience, but accommodate them through your graciousness (*faḍl*), for it is through Us that you pardon, through Us that you seek forgiveness, and to Us that you turn for guidance'. *Then, when you are resolved,* that is, 'If you wish to carry something out after consultation', *put your trust in God…*, that is, 'Rely on God notwithstanding that [consultation], consign all your affairs to Him, and depend on Him without regard for anyone else.' He [the Prophet] did not leave this world before God, Exalted is He, had disclosed to his heart realms of knowledge which were between him and God, Exalted is He, without any intermediary, due to his love of pondering and reflection, in reverent awareness (*iʿtibār*) of the omnipotence of his Lord, so that he attained an increase from God most High, just as He was commanded in the words of God, Exalted is He, *But say: 'My Lord! Increase me in knowledge'* [20:114]. Furthermore, he enjoined this upon his nation (*umma*), as is related from the Prophet ﷺ in his words, 'Consult those who are mindful of God (*muttaqūn*), who have preferred the Hereafter over this world, and who give you priority over themselves in your affairs.' And he also said, 'Consult the righteous scholars, and when you have made your resolve to carry something out, put your trust in God.'

He [Sahl] said [in this regard]:

Fraternise with brothers among the people who are mindful of God, and let the person whom you consult be one of those who fear God, Exalted is He. Let your word not be broken. And never be hostile to anyone until you know the states of his conduct with God, Exalted is He. If he has good conduct with God; then do not be hostile towards him, for certainly God, Exalted is He, will not forsake him for you. And if his conduct is bad, do not be hostile towards him [either] for his bad conduct will suffice him.[49]

He also said:

Whoever is consulted and then gives advice that is contrary to his own opinion, God most High will strip him of his opinion, that is, He will dupe him into [believing] what he advised. [Moreover], whoever consults, puts his trust in God, carries out what he has resolved to do, but afterwards regrets [what has happened] has reproached God, Exalted is He.

Concerning His words:

[3:160] *If God helps you, then no one can overcome you; but if He forsakes you, then who is there who can help you after Him?...*

He said:

To be forsaken (*khidhlān*) means to be utterly abandoned (*ghāyat al-tark*). As for abandonment itself (*tark*), that is for the sinner who recognises his sin. Being forsaken (*khidhlān*), however, is for the one who sins while believing that he is doing something good. This is God's punishment

---

it was pointed out to him that he had ninety-nine wives, whilst Uriah had had one wife, and that David had had Uriah killed in battle in order to take his one wife. David became deeply repentant at this. This version of the story appears in Ṭabarī, *History of al-Ṭabarī*, vol. 3, trans. William Brinner, *The Children of Israel* (Albany, 1991), pp. 145–7.

48 A reference to part of the story of Joseph narrated in 12:23–34, in which the wife of ʿAzīz, who is Joseph's master, attempts to seduce him. Verse 24 states: *And she certainly desired him, and he would have desired her, had it not been that he saw the proof of his Lord.* Tustarī was evidently among those commentators who considered that Joseph *did* desire her, and even added intent (*qaṣd*) to the desire, though unlike David, he was preserved though the divine protection (*ʿiṣma*) from committing the act. Again, see above regarding Adam, the commentary on 2:30, and IT, pp. xxxiv–xxxv.

49 Because it will inevitably bring its own punishment from God.

to the one who is forsaken, for He upholds him in sin, having the knowledge both of his sin and of his subsequent procrastination of repentance. Do you not see how Iblīs, when he refused [to obey], and persisted in that refusal was forsaken by God due to His prior knowledge about him? This is because He willed from him that which was in accordance with His knowledge; He did not will from him that which was in accordance with His command.[50] However Adam ﷺ, because he was not forsaken in his abandonment, confessed to his sin after committing it and returned to his Lord, Majestic and Mighty is He, and his repentance was accepted.

His words, Exalted is He:

[3:173] ***...God is sufficient for us; an excellent guardian is He.***

That is, He is the best guarantor of our provisions, and the best Lord. This is as in His words, Exalted is He, *Do not take any guardian beside Me* [17:2], that is, [do not take any] Lord [beside Me].

His words:

[3:187] ***...But they rejected it behind their backs...***[51]

That is, they did not act by the Book, *and purchased with it some miserable gain*, that is, they bought in exchange for the everlasting Hereafter, the goods of this transitory world.

His words, Exalted is He:

[3:191] ***Those who remember God, standing, sitting, and [reclining] on their sides...***

He [Sahl] said:

Whoever wishes to memorise the Qurʾān should complete three whole readings following the conditions stated in this verse: a reading completed while standing in prayer, a reading completed while sitting and studying it, and a reading completed while reclining on one's side. Then, he will not forget [it], God willing, Mighty and Majestic is He. Moreover, whoever occupies himself with seeking knowledge with the full awareness of God, and with the recitation of the Qurʾān, the remembrance (*dhikr*) of God, Mighty and Majestic is He, adherence to the Sunna, and avoidance of all frivolity (*lahw*), will not be afflicted by disease or sickness. Furthermore, whoever obeys God with knowledge and sincere intention (*nīya*) will not lose his mind [lit. intellect, *ʿaql*].

The Prophet ﷺ said, 'Whoever obeys God, Mighty and Majestic is He, has truly remembered Him, but whoever disobeys Him has truly forgotten Him.'[52]

His words:

[3:200] ***O you who believe, be patient, and vie in patience; be steadfast and fear God that you may prosper.***

He said:

Faith has four pillars. The first is trust (*tawakkul*) in God, the second is complete submission (*istislām*) to His commands, the third is being content and satisfied (*riḍā*) with what He has preordained (*qaḍāʾihi*), and the fourth is gratitude (*shukr*) for His blessings along with mindfulness of Him (*taqwā*).

A Section on Faith

Certainty (*yaqīn*) is the heart of faith, patience (*ṣabr*) is the backbone of faith, and sincerity (*ikhlāṣ*) is the perfection of faith, for through sincerity the servant reaches true affirmation (*taṣdīq*). Furthermore,

---

50 On the divine *mashīʾa* and *irāda*, see above notes to Tustarī's commentary on 1:5 and 2:2, and p. 10, n. 4.

51 This is a reference to the rejection by the Children of Israel of the covenant they had made with God, according to which they were to expound the scripture to people, and not conceal it.

52 ʿAlī Abū Bakr al-Haythamī, *Majmaʿ al-zawāʾid wa manbaʿ al-fawāʾid* (Cairo, 1933–4), vol. 2, p. 258; Sulaymān b. Aḥmad al-Ṭabarānī, *al-Muʿjam al-kabīr* (Mosul, 1983–90), vol. 22, p. 154. One is reminded of the admonition which Tustarī's uncle gave him when in his childhood. See above, IT, p. xv.

through true affirmation he attains realisation (*taḥqīq*), and through realisation he reaches God (*al-Ḥaqq*). Sincerity is the fruit of certainty, for certainty is witnessing (*mushāhada*) in the innermost secret (*sirr*).[53] Moreover, whoever does not experience witnessing in [his] innermost secret in the presence of his Lord ⌜and does not behold Him⌝,[54] has not made his actions sincere.[55] But God knows best.

53 On this level of certainty, and on the link between faith and certainty, see above Tustarī's commentary on 2:40 and 2:41, and accompanying notes. See also IT, pp. xlviii–xlix.

54 Translating *wa yarāhu*, as being governed by the preceding negative, as in all three MSS: Z515, f. 34b, F638, f. 17b and F3488, f. 209a. One is reminded here of the *ḥadīth* of Gabriel, in which the three levels of *islām*, *īmān* and *iḥsān* are discussed. On this *ḥadīth*, see above IT, p. lviii, n. 265.

55 Translating *lam yukhliṣ ʿamalahu*, on the basis of all three MSS: the MSS (Z515, f. 34b, F638, f. 17b and F3488, f. 209a). whereas the printed edition has *lam yukhliṣ ʿamalahu li'Llāh*, i.e. he has not dedicated his action, or made it sincerely for God.

4 Al-Nisāʾ

Sahl was asked about His words:

[4:4] ***And give women their dowries as a free gift...***

He said:

> It means, give them the dowry (*ṣadāq*) as a gift to them from God, Mighty and Majestic is He. Indeed dowry (*niḥla*) is religion (*diyāna*).[1]

He continued:

> The Prophet ﷺ said: 'The basest of sins before God, Exalted is He, is to prevent a worker from being paid, and to stop a woman receiving her dowry (*mahr*).'[2]

His words, Exalted is He:

[4:17] ***The repentance that God accepts is only of those who do evil in ignorance and repent shortly thereafter...***

He said:

> One who is repentant (*tāʾib*) keeps away from sin and observes obedience. One who is obedient (*muṭīʿ*) is wary of ostentation (*riyāʾ*) and persists in remembrance (*dhikr*). The one who is constant in remembrance (*dhākir*) is wary of conceit (*ʿujb*), and imposes upon himself [the sense of] his own deficiency (*taqṣīr*).

[Concerning this verse] he also said:

> God most High revealed to David ﷺ, 'The wailing of sinners is more beloved to Me than the clamour of the veracious (*surākh al-ṣiddīqūn*)'.[3]

His words:

[4:29] ***...And kill not yourselves...***

> Do not destroy yourselves through transgressions (*maʿāṣī*) and persistence [in transgression], and by neglecting repentance (*tawba*) after returning to rectitude (*istiqāma*). *Surely God is ever merciful to you* [4:29] in that He forbade transgression to you, so that you might not perish, which is further expounded in His words, Exalted is He:

---

1 The word *niḥla* can mean both a gift and a religion, so it is synonymous with *dīn* or *diyāna*.

2 In this passage, three different words for payments due to women upon their marriage have been used: *ṣadāq*, *niḥla* and *mahr*. There does not appear to be any practical difference in the application of these words, though it is interesting to note that the first is derived from the root *ṣ-d-q* meaning to be sincere, which is said to indicate that the man in giving the dowry is showing his sincere intentions towards the woman he is marrying, while the word *niḥla* is derived from the root *n-ḥ-l* meaning to give a gift.

3 This saying appears in Bayhaqī, *Shuʿab al-īmān*, vol. 5, p. 452. A variant form of the tradition, which has 'the murmuring of angels' (*zajl al-muqarrabīn*) instead of 'clamour of the veracious' (*surākh al-ṣiddīqīn*), is cited in Maybudī's *Kashf al-asrār*, vol. 3, pp. 21 and 640, while another version listed in Munāwī, *Fayḍ al-qadīr*, vol. 5, p. 331, has 'The groaning of sinners [is dearer] to God than the murmuring of those who glorify [Him]' (*anīn al-mudhnibīn [aḥabb] ilāʾLlāhi min zajl al-musabbiḥīn*). What is meant by the tradition is probably that the repentance and anguished remorse of sinners who acknowledge their sins and faults is dearer to God than the complacency of those who have confidence in their virtue and good works.

[4:31] ***If you avoid the grave sins that you are forbidden, We shall absolve you of your [minor] misdeeds…***

[Concerning that] he [Sahl?] said:

> It was related that Ibn Masʿūd said, 'The grave sins (*kabāʾir*) are those mentioned from the beginning of Sūrat al-Nisāʾ up to this verse.'

And Sahl added:

> The major sins are those that carry God's threat of the Fire within His Book, Exalted is He.

His words:

[4:36] ***…to the neighbour who is close, and the neighbour who is a stranger, to the companion at your side, and to the wayfarer…***[4]

He said:

> As for the outward meaning: the neighbour who is a stranger is the one who is not related to you and is foreign; the companion at your side is your fellow traveller, or it has also been said that it is your spouse; and the wayfarer (*ibn al-sabīl*) means the guest. As for its inner meaning: the neighbour who is near refers to the heart (*qalb*); the neighbour who is a stranger is the ⌜self in its natural state (*al-nafs al-ṭabīʿī*)⌝;[5] and the companion by your side is the intellect (*ʿaql*), which is guided by the *sharīʿa*. The wayfarer refers to the bodily members (*jawāriḥ*) which are in a state of obedience to God. This is the inner meaning of the verse.

His words:

[4:41] ***So how shall it be, when We bring forward from every community a witness, and We bring you as a witness against these?***

Sahl said:

> God, Exalted is He, has placed 360 angels in the service of each Muslim servant in accordance with the number of his veins.[6] When he wants to do something good they assist him in that, but if he wants to do something bad they chide him about it. If he acts upon any of those [intentions] they record that action for him until the Day of Judgement, when they show it to him, and apprehend him for it.[7] Then when he comes before God, Exalted is He, they will bear witness for him about the faithfulness of [his] obedience, and [against him] for the sins he committed. God said, Exalted is He, *And every soul will come accompanied by a driver and a witness* [50:21].

His words, Exalted is He:

[4:47] ***…Before We obliterate faces…***

> This means that God turns them back from guidance and insight to their natural disposition (*ṭabʿ al-jibilla*).[8]

---

4 The context of this verse is a command for the believers to worship God and be kind to parents, near kindred, orphans and the needy as well as to neighbours.

5 This is according to all three MSS: Z515, f. 35a, F638, f. 18a and F3488, f. 209b. The printed edition has simply 'nature' (*tabīʿa*). By *al-nafs al-ṭabīʿī* it is possible that Tustarī is referring to what he elsewhere terms the *nafs al-ṭabʿ* as opposed to the *nafs al-rūḥ*, and the use of these terms will be seen later in the commentary. These terms are also discussed in IT, pp. xxxviiiff.

6 Apparently the number of veins/arteries in the body was traditionally understood to be 360 (or some said 390). For example in the *Rasāʾil* of the Ikhwān al-Ṣafāʾ the body is compared to a kingdom in which there are 390 rivulets, corresponding to the veins and arteries. See Ikhwān al-Ṣafāʾ, *Rasāʾil Ikhwān al-Ṣafāʾ wa khullān al-wafāʾ* (Beirut, 1957), vol. 3, p. 380–2; and Seyyed H. Nasr, *An Introduction to Islamic Cosmological Doctrines* (London, 1978), p. 100. See also Ghazālī, *Kīmiyāʾ al-saʿādat*, vol. 1, p. 42. On the Muslim discussions of the numerical symbolism of parts of the body, see Seyyed H. Nasr, *Islamic Science: An Illustrated Study* (London, 1976), pp. 162–4.

7 Translating *awqafūhu* according to all three MSS (Z515, f. 35a, F638, f. 17a and F3488, f. 210a), instead of *wāfaqūhu* in the printed edition.

8 There is some discrepancy among the MSS here with MSS Z515, f. 35b having their 'natural disposition' (*ṭabʿ al-jibilla*), which is what we have translated, while F638, f. 18a has *ṭabʿ al-khaṭiyya*, 'sinful disposition', and F3488, f. 210a has *al-ṭabʿ*

His words, Exalted is He:

[4:48] ***God forgives not that anything should be associated with Him. But He forgives other than that, to whomsoever He wills…***

He said:

> If no one has any grievance against him, and his sins are only between him and God, Exalted is He, indeed He forgives those sins, for He is the Magnanimous (*al-Jawād*), the Generous (*al-Karīm*). It has been related from the Prophet ﷺ that he said, 'A slave may be brought forward on the Day of Resurrection and directed to the Fire, but then he will say, "This is not in accordance with what I supposed [my outcome would be]."[9] Then God, Mighty and Majestic, will ask, "What was your opinion of Me?"to which he will reply, "That You would forgive me", upon which, God, Mighty and Majestic, will say, "Truly I have forgiven you", and He will direct him to Paradise.'[10]

His words:

[4:63] ***…and say to them regarding their souls a penetrating word.***

> That is, 'conveying from Me with your tongue and with the best expression the essence of what is in your heart.'[11]

His words:

[4:76] ***Those who believe fight in the way of God, and those who disbelieve fight in the way of a false deity…***

He [Sahl] said:

> The believers are [with] God, adversaries against their lower selves, but the hypocrites are [with] their lower selves, adversaries against God, Mighty and Majestic is He. They hasten to question, and are not content with what God chooses for them. This is the way of Satan (*ṭāghūt*), for the lower self is the greatest of devils if the servant consorts with it because it will incite him to transgression.

His words, Exalted is He:

[4:77] ***Say: 'The enjoyment of this world is trifling…'***

He [Sahl] was asked, 'What is this world?' To which he replied:

> This whole world consists of ignorance except for where knowledge is to be found.[12] All knowledge is a testimony against [the one who possesses it], except for that which is acted upon. All action is futile except for that which is done with sincerity (*ikhlāṣ*), and sincerity is not achieved except through adherence to the Sunna.

Then he said:

> Your world is your lower self (*nafs*). Thus, if you annihilate it, there will be no world for you.[13]

His words, Exalted is He:

[4:81] ***…So turn away from them, and put your trust in God…***

He was asked, 'What is trust? (*tawakkul*)?' He replied:

> Trust is the submission of the body in servanthood, the attachment of the heart to the divine lordliness (*rubūbiyya*) and the disclaiming of all power (*ḥawl*) and strength (*quwwa*).

---

al-jahala which might be translated as 'foolish or licentious disposition' or it could also be *al-ṭabʿ al-jibilla* without any *tashdīd* being marked. The published edition has *ṭabʿ al-jahāla*.

9 lit.. 'This is not in accordance with my opinion (*mā kadhā ẓannī*).'

10 The point being that his good opinion (*ḥusn al-ẓann*) of God had saved him. On the spiritual function of good opinion, see above Tustarī's commentary on 2:241 and IT, pp. lii–liii.

11 That is, the Revelation.

12 lit. 'save for the locus of knowledge'. What is meant is: 'except for the people who have knowledge deposited in them'.

13 That is, the world will no longer take you away from God.

Then he was asked: 'What is the reality (*ḥaqīqa*) of trust (*tawakkul*) in principle?' He replied:

> At its root, the reality of trust is the realisation of God's oneness (*tawḥīd*), while its branch is the knowledge of the Last Day [lit. knowledge of the Hour] (*ilm al-sāʿa*); and through tranquil repose (*sukūn*) in it [trust] there is visual beholding (*muʿāyana*).

Then he said:

> Do not be anxious about trust, for truly it is a means of livelihood for those who possess it.

He was asked, 'Who are those who possess it?' He replied:

> They are those who have been privileged with a special quality.

Sahl was asked to clarify this further, and he said:

> Truly all the sciences are the lowest categories of worship (*taʿabbud*). The sum of all worship is only the lowest category of scrupulous piety (*waraʿ*). The sum of all renunciation (*zuhd*) is the lowest category of the manifestation of divine omnipotence (*ẓuhūr al-qudra*). Furthermore, the divine omnipotence does not become apparent to anyone except the one who has complete trust (*mutawakkil*). Trust is not susceptible of any categorical definition, nor does it have a limit that would make it susceptible of comparison,[14] nor does it have an utmost degree that can be reached.

Then he was asked, 'Describe something of it to us' and he replied:

> Trust has a thousand ranks, the first of which is the ability to walk on air.[15]

He was then asked, 'How does the servant reach that level?' He answered:

> The first thing is gnosis (*maʿrifa*), then affirmation (*iqrār*), then the realisation of God's oneness (*tawḥīd*), then submission (*islām*), then the excellence in faith (*iḥsān*), then the committing of one's affairs [to God] (*tafwīḍ*), then trust (*tawakkul*), and finally the state of tranquil repose (*sukūn*) in God, Mighty and Majestic is He, in every situation.[16]

And he added:

> Trust is not acceptable from anyone except one who is mindful of God (*muttaqī*).

He was asked, 'What is mindfulness of God?' He replied:

> It is to refrain from all harm [to others] (*adhā*).[17]

His words, Exalted is He:

[4:85] ***...Whoever intercedes with an evil intercession will receive a share of it...***

> That is, a portion of it. This is because it [the evil intercession] obstructs [that person's access to] God's good pleasure.

His words, Exalted is He:

[4:86] ***When you are offered a greeting, respond with a better one, or [at least] return it...***

> This means that you should surpass the greeting that issued [from that person] by acting with sincere friendship (*naṣḥ*) for God's sake, Exalted is He. The Prophet ﷺ said, 'Peace (*salām*) is one of the names of God which He made manifest on Earth, so spread it among yourselves.'[18]

His words, Exalted is He:

[4:88] ***...When God Himself has cast them back because of what they earned?...***

---

14 lit. so that similitudes might be coined for it. In other words, it cannot be compared to anything or explained by any metaphor.

15 This is another indication that Tustarī did not hold much store by miracles or charismatic gifts (*karāmāt*). See IT, p. xx.

16 It is worth keeping in mind that the expression *sukūn ilā* also has a sense of reliance upon. On *iḥsān*, see IT, p. lviii, n 265.

17 See above the commentary on 3:64 regarding the importance of not harming others (*kaff al-adhā*).

18 Bukhārī, *Ṣaḥīḥ*, 'Kitāb Ṣifat al-ṣalāt'; Ṭabarānī, *al-Muʿjam al-kabīr*, vol. 10, p. 82.

That is, He returned them to the state of ignorance of Him which was the natural constitution of their souls.[19] And the Prophet ﷺ also said: 'Do not clean yourselves [after defecation] with bones or animal droppings, for these [undergo] a reversal', meaning that these return from their former state to becoming the food of jinn. *What, do you wish to guide him whom God has left to stray?* Misguidance (*iḍlāl*) from God is His withdrawing His protection (*ʿiṣma*) [of a person] from that which is forbidden, and His withdrawing His assistance (*maʿūna*) [from a person] in what He has commanded.[20]

His words, Exalted is He:

[4:90] ***...Or those who come to you with their breasts constricted...***[21]

That is, 'They have become sick at heart because of fighting you and fighting their people, due to their love of safety, and their inclination towards their own well-being (*ʿāfiya*).' This refers to the Banū Madlaj.[22]

His words:

[4:105] ***...so that you may judge between people by that which God has shown you...***

That is, in accordance with the wisdom (*ḥikma*) that God, Exalted is He, has taught you within the Qurʾān and the laws of Islam.

His words, Exalted is He:

[4:117] ***What they pray to instead of Him are but females.***

That is, they [emit] sounds,[23] and they are of stone and iron.

His words Mighty and Majestic is He:

[4:121] ***...And will find no refuge from it.***

That is, no way out.

His words:

[4:139] ***...Do they desire power with them?...***

This refers to the hypocrites who were seeking power and protection from the Jews. Do you not [recall] the Prophet's words ﷺ, 'Nothing descended from the heavens mightier than certainty'?[24] That is, there is nothing more indomitable or formidable.[25]

His words:

[4:141] ***...Did we not gain mastery over you?...***

That is, conquer and overcome you.

His words:

[4:142] ***The hypocrites try to deceive God, but it is He who causes them to be deceived...***

This means that He hastens the recompense for their [outwardly] showing faith, and [inwardly] keeping secret their disbelief, by withdrawing His protection and grace from them, and by augmenting their wealth and offspring, and granting them access to the immediate [pleasures of] this world.[26] But, their final destination is the Fire. This is what is meant by His words, *[The*

---

19 lit. 'to that to which their souls were naturally disposed'.

20 On this aspect of Tustarī's doctrine, see above IC, p. 2 and n. 6, Tustarī's commentary on 2:3, and IT, pp. xxxiiiff.

21 These are among those who are excluded from being subject to the command in the previous verse (4:89): *slay them wherever you find them; and do not take any of them as a patron or as a helper.*

22 Reading 'Banū Madlaj', on the basis of MSS Z515, f. 37a, F638, f. 18b and F3488, f. 211a, instead of Banū Madraj in the printed edition. The Banū Madlaj were among the non-Muslim tribes to the south-west of Medina with whom the Prophet made a pact prior to the Battle of Badr.

23 A reference to the sound that came from the hollowed out idols.

24 Tirmidhī, *Nawādir al-uṣūl*, vol. 2, p. 169.

25 In other words, there could be no refuge for them outside what was certain, i.e. the truth.

26 Thereby lulling them into a false sense of well-being. Again this is an instance of *istidrāj*, on which see Tustarī's commentary on 2:41, p. 20, n. 48, his commentary on 3:8, and p. 42, n. 10.

hypocrites] try to deceive God, but it is He who causes them to be deceived. He meant by this the speed of delivering their recompense (*jazāʾ*) for what they perform and abstain from. This is as His saying, *Nay, but you marvel while they engage in ridicule* [37:12], by which He meant that He hastened their punishment for their persisting in denial [of the truth]. Thus were His words addressed in accordance with the name of their action. And indeed in [other] places He describes their being in a state of wonder (*ʿajab*); [for example,] in His words, *[Say, 'It has been revealed to me that a company of jinn listened and said], "We have heard a wondrous Qurʾān"'* [72:1]; and in Sūra Qāf, *Nay, but they [the disbelievers] think it strange* [50:2]; and in Sūra Ṣād: *What an astonishing thing!* [38:5]. So also [wonder] is mentioned in Sūra Ṣāffāt: *Nay but you marvel while they engage in ridicule* [37:12], that is, you see their recompense as immense (*ʿaẓīm*), And here He calls the immense recompense a marvel, for the one who marvels at something that has reached its utmost degree, and this is what is meant in His words, *you marvel.*

It has been related that Shaqīq read [the Qurʾānic words] to Sharīḥ as '*I marvel* (ʿajibtu)' to which Sharīḥ replied, '[It should be] *you marvel* (ʿajibta)', for truly God does not marvel at anything. The only one who marvels is one who does not know.' Then Shaqīq said, 'I informed Ibrāhīm of this, and he said, "For sure, Sharīḥ is pleased with his own knowledge. However, Ibn Masʿūd is more knowledgeable than him and he used to read it, *I marvel* with a *ḍamma* (ʿajibtu)."'[27]

[4:142] ***...When they stand up to pray they do so lazily...***

This is one of the signs of the hypocrites, and by this they betray the trust (*amāna*), which outwardly they appear to have taken upon themselves. Know that to God, Exalted is He, belong the trusts of your hearing, sight, tongue, private parts, your outward self and your inner self, which He presented to you. If you do not safeguard them, you betray God and *God does not love the treacherous* [8:58].

Ibn Ḥayyān[28] related that he journeyed to Mecca and went to Saʿīd b. Jubayr and said to him, 'I have come to you from Khurasan to ask you about the explanation of the words of the Prophet ﷺ, "The signs of a hypocrite are three: when he speaks, he lies; when he promises, he breaks his promise; and when he is entrusted with something, he is treacherous." I do not see any of these within myself.' Then Saʿīd smiled and said, 'The same thing occurred to my conscience that occurred to yours, so I went to ʿAlī b. Abī Ṭālib and ʿAbd Allāh Ibn ʿAbbās ﷺ at the time of the afternoon nap, and I found them at the [Holy] House, so I asked them about the explanation for this *ḥadīth*. They smiled and replied:

> We were also perplexed by what has perplexed you, so we went to the Prophet ﷺ at the time of the afternoon nap, and he gave us permission [to enter], so we mentioned this to him ﷺ, upon which he smiled and said, 'Do you not uphold the testimony that there is no god but God?' We replied, 'Yes, we do.' He said, 'Have you gone back on that?' We said, 'No, we have not.' He said, 'Indeed you have said it and confirmed it.' Then he said, 'Do you not uphold what you affirmed with regard to your belief in God, His angels, Books, messengers, Paradise, Hell and the Resurrection?' We said, 'Yes, as if we saw them with our own eyes.' He ﷺ said, 'This is a [great] achievement.' Then he said ﷺ 'Do you not pray and prostrate in prayer when you are alone?' We replied, 'Yes'. He said, 'That is true fidelity without a trace of treachery.'

---

27 This is an example of the debates which occurred in the science of the variant readings (*qirāʾa*) of the Qurʾān, which are often cited in exoteric commentaries on the Qurʾān, and on which independent works have been written, such as the *Muʿjam al-qirāʾāt al-Qurʾāniyya* of Aḥmad Mukhtār ʿUmar and ʿAbd al-ʿĀl Mukarram (Cairo, 1997), in which this disagreement between the two scholars of *qirāʾa*, Shaqīq and Sharīḥ, is recorded, vol. 4, p. 197.

28 Corrected from Abū Ḥibbān on the basis of MSS Z515, f. 27b and MSF638, f. 19a. MS F3488 has Abū Ḥayyān.

Sahl said:

> Truly, certainty (*yaqīn*) may be compared to mainstays (*awtād*) for the hearts of the mystics (*ʿārifūn*), and the souls of the yearning (*mushtāqūn*), just as the mountains of the world along with Mount Qāf, are the mainstays of the two earths (*ʿarḍīn*), and the backbone of the worlds.[29] However, He made your heart even stronger, for He said, Exalted is He: '*Had We sent this Qurʾān down upon a mountain, you would surely have seen it humbled, rent asunder by the fear of God* [59:21]. Indeed, I sent it down to their hearts that they may preserve it and upon you as a command. You will not be harmed by keeping it [the Qurʾān] within you, because of My protection, benevolence and My watching over you.'

Then he [Sahl] said:

> The intellects (*ʿuqūl*) of believers end up journeying to the Throne, where they are preserved and filled with the finest subtleties (*ẓarāʾif*) of His wisdom and diverse [manifestations] of His beneficence (*birr*). The intellects of the hypocrites on the other hand, journey until they reach [the threshold], and covet what is in the unseen, but are cast back rejected with heads bowed down (*munkasa*). *And he whom God sends astray, you will never find for him a way* [4:88, 143].

His words, Exalted is He:

[4:171] ***O People of the Scripture do not go to excess in your religion…***

> That is, do not exceed the limits in your religion through innovations (*bidaʿ*), or by deviating from the truth, which is the Book, the Sunna and consensus (*ijmāʿ*), by inclining towards the desire of your lower selves.

And he [Sahl] said:

> The backbone (*qiwām*) of religion and this world is in three things: knowledge (*ʿilm*), propriety (*adab*) and initiative (*mubādara*). However, the ruin of religion and this world comes from three things: ignorance (*jahl*), folly (*khurq*) and laziness (*kasal*).

On another occasion, I heard him say:

> There are four things which are among the buttresses (*daʿāʾim*) of the religion: to uphold the truth even against your own self and others; to renounce falsehood in yourself or others; to love the people who are obedient to God and to detest those who disobey Him.

29 Mount Qāf is the name of a mountain range which, according to Muslim cosmology, surrounds the earth. In mystical literature it came also to symbolise the end of the spiritual journey, as for example, in the epic poem of Farīd al-Dīn ʿAṭṭār, *Manṭiq al-ṭayr*, and the mystical-philosophical treatise of Shihāb al-Dīn Yaḥyā Suhrawardī, *Qiṣṣat al-ghurbat al-gharbiyya*, in *Oeuvres philosophiques et mystiques*, ed. H. Corbin (Tehran/Paris, 1952–77), vol. 2. See M. Streck [A. Miguel], 'Ḳāf' in *EI2*, vol. iv, pp. 400–2.

5 Al-Māʾida

He was asked about His words, Exalted is He:

[5:2] ***...Help one another to righteousness and mindfulness of God...***

He said:

> Righteousness (*birr*) is obedience to God and being on one's guard against disobedience.

His words, Exalted is He,

[5:3] ***...Yet fear them not, but fear Me...***

> That is, 'Do not fear the disbelievers with regard to obeying Me, but fear Me with regard to following them.'

Then he said:

> The weakest person is he who fears those who can neither benefit him nor harm him. However, the One in whose hand is the power to benefit and harm addresses him with His words, *Yet fear them not, but fear Me.*

His words, Exalted is He:

[5:5] ***This day the good things are permitted to you...***

[Sahl] said:

> The good things refer to the provision which is lawful.

His words, Exalted is He:

[5:6] ***When you prepare for prayer, wash your faces...***

[Sahl] said:

> Purification consists of four things: purity of the source of food, truthfulness of the tongue, avoidance of all sins, and the humility in one's innermost secret (*sirr*). In turn, each one of these four corresponds to the purification of the outer members of the body.

His words, Exalted is He:

[5:6] ***...But He wishes to purify you...***

> That is, to purify your state, your character and your actions, so that you return to Him in a state of true poverty (*ḥaqīqat al-faqr*) without being attached to any [secondary] cause.
>
> Purification is of seven kinds: the purification of knowledge from ignorance, the purification of remembrance from forgetfulness, the purification of obedience from disobedience, the purification of certainty from doubt, the purification of the intellect from foolishness, the purification of opinion from slander, and the purification of faith from anything which is alien to it.[1] Furthermore, each punishment constitutes a kind of purification, except the punishment of the heart, which is hardness.[2]

[Concerning] His words, Exalted is He:

[5:23] ***Two men among those who feared, whom God had blessed, said...***

---

1 A similar definition appears in Iṣfahānī, *Ḥilyat al-awliyāʾ*, vol. 10, p. 208, where only three kinds of purification are mentioned.

2 This is also cited in Iṣfahānī, *Ḥilyat al-awliyāʾ*, vol. 10, p. 208.

Sahl was asked, 'What was that blessing (*niʿma*)?' He replied:

God blessed them with fear (*khawf*) and vigilance (*murāqaba*), because fear, concern (*hamm*) and sorrow (*ḥuzn*) increase one's good deeds, whereas exuberance (*ashar*) and arrogance (*baṭar*) increase one's misdeeds.

His words:

[5:54] *...Stern towards the disbelievers...*[3]

That is, tough (*ghalīẓa*) on them.

His words:

[5:55] *Your patron is God only, and His Messenger, and the believers...*

[Sahl] said:

The patronage (*wilāya*)[4] of God is [His] choosing (*ikhtiyār*) for whomever He has taken under His patronage. Then He informed the Messenger that He is the Patron of the believers. Thus it became incumbent upon him to befriend those who had allied themselves to God, Exalted is He, and those who believed. Then He said:

[5:56] *As to those who ally themselves with God, His Messenger and the believers, it is the party of God that is certainly triumphant.*

That is, they are triumphant in vanquishing the desire of their lower selves.

His words:

[5:64] *Truly God's hands are extended wide. He expends however He wills...*

[Sahl] said:

This means that His rule, command and prohibition are operative in His dominion.

His words:

[5:66] *And had they observed the Torah and the Gospel and what was revealed to them from their Lord, they would surely have received nourishment from above them and from beneath their feet...*

That is, if they acted according to what God revealed to Muḥammad ﷺ, and if you acted according to it, you would attain this rank, just as those who acted according to it attained it. Furthermore, if you had turned to the Provider (*al-Razzāq*), your provision would have been taken care of.[5]

Then he said:

You are not greater than ʿAmr b. Layth, who would march with one thousand horsemen and one thousand foot soldiers in his charge, each one holding a mace of gold and silver. Eventually it came to pass that he was imprisoned in a house after being handed over to the Caliph, who subsequently deprived him of food and drink. When his door was opened they found him dead with his mouth full of straw and clay due to his intense hunger.[6] Then he [the Caliph] said, 'Truly I have advised you and truly I am among those who give you good counsel.'

It was related by Mālik b. Dīnār, from Ḥammād b. Salma and Ḥammād b. Yazīd, that these two came to visit Rābiʿa, and mentioned something concerning the matters of this world. So Rābiʿa said, 'You are talking about this world a lot. I think you must be hungry, so if you are hungry

---

3 These words are part of a warning from God to the believers that if they go back on their faith God will soon replace them with *people whom He loves and who love Him, who are humble towards the believers, stern towards the disbelievers and who strive in God's way without fearing anyone's reproach...* [5:54].

4 As stated above, IC, p. 2, n. 5, and p. 3, n. 14, *wilāya* can also mean friendship, and hence the *awliyāʾ* may be translated as 'friends [of God]'.

5 lit. 'you would have been spared the trouble of storing up, or maintaining, provisions [for yourself].'

6 ʿAmr b. Layth (d. 265/879) was the second ruler of the Ṣaffārid dynasty, founded in the Iranian province of Sīstān by ʿAmr's elder brother Yaʿqūb b. Layth (d. 253/867), the dynasty taking its name from the latter's trade of coppersmith (*ṣaffār*). The Ṣaffārid empire soon spread to include Khurasan and Fārs. ʿAmr tried to expand their empire by invading Transoxiana, but was defeated by the Sāmānid ruler, Ismāʿīl b. Aḥmad (d. 279/892), who had ʿAmr sent to the Caliph in Baghdad. There he was imprisoned and starved to death.

go over to that pot with the flour and make yourselves whatever takes your fancy.' Then, one of those who were with her remarked, 'If only we had some garlic.' Ḥammād continued, 'Then I saw Rābiʿa's lips moving and she had not even finished before a bird came with a clove of garlic in its beak which it cast down and then flew off.[7]

His words, Exalted is He:

[5:67] *...God will protect you from people...*

[Sahl] was asked, 'What is this protection (*ʿiṣma*)?' He replied:

> God, Exalted is He, promised him [the Prophet] that He would not put him through trials, as He had the rest of the prophets ﷺ, such as Abraham with the fire, Ishmael with the sacrifice, and others as well. Since he [Muḥammad] was not aware of what would happen to him — as He has related, *Nor do I know what will be done with me or with you* [46:9] — God, Exalted is He, informed him that He would protect him from people.

His words:

[5:83] *And when they hear what has been revealed to the Messenger, you see their eyes overflow with tears because of the truth that they recognise...*

[Sahl] said:

> These were the priests and monks from whom people would seek blessings and anointment due to their knowledge of the religion. They came to the Prophet ﷺ, and the Qurʾān was recited for them. They were deeply moved by it so that their eyes overflowed [with tears], and they were not haughty, due to God's protecting them from pride. Subsequently, they entered His religion because of the knowledge of God which He had deposited within them.

Then he said:

> The corruption of religion is in three things: when kings commit excess[es] and [follow] their lusts; when the scholars issue rulings based on concessions; and when the Qurʾān reciters worship without knowledge. Truly, people need the learned (*ʿulamāʾ*) for their life in this world and the Hereafter. Indeed, it was related by Jābir b. ʿAbd Allāh ﷺ from the Prophet ﷺ that he said: 'The people of Paradise need the learned just as much as the people need them in this world. They visit their Lord every Friday and it is said to them: "Desire anything you want", after which they head for the scholars, who tell them, "Desire such and such a thing", so they desire that thing.'[8]

His words:

[5:109] *The Day when God will assemble all the messengers and ask, 'What response did you receive?' They will say, 'We have no knowledge...'*

> That is, 'We do not possess knowledge of the faith in You that their hearts contained, nor knowledge of whatever else was [in their hearts]. Our knowledge is only of what they outwardly affirmed on their tongues. ...*You, only You are the Knower of things unseen.*'

[Sahl] was asked, 'Will He ask them about what was really in the hearts of [their] communities?' He replied:

> No, He only directed the question to them concerning their outward reality, which is in fact only an expression of their inner reality. They [the prophets] responded by indicating that [only He] possesses knowledge [of the answer]. It could also mean, 'We have no knowledge of the meaning of your question, since You already have knowledge of our reply — *You, only You, are the Knower of things unseen.*'

---

7 A similar story involving a bird bringing an onion required for the stew, is related in ʿAṭṭār's *Tadhkirat al-awliyāʾ*, pp. 77–8. The anecdote is translated by Margaret Smith in *Rābiʿa the Mystic and her Fellow Saints in Islam* (Cambridge, 1984), p. 34.

8 This *ḥadīth* is listed in Ismāʿīl b. Muḥammad al-ʿAjlūnī, *Kashf al-khafāʾ wa muzīl al-ilbās ʿammā ishtahara min al-aḥādīth ʿalā alsinat al-nās* (Beirut, 1979), vol. 1, p. 263; Aḥmad al-ʿAsqalānī, *Lisān al-mīzān* (Beirut, 1971), vol. 5, p. 15, as a fabricated *ḥadīth*.

His words:

[5:116] ...*You know what is in my self, though I do not know what is in Your Self...*[9]

That is, 'I do not know the hidden purport of Your question, while You have knowledge of it.'[10] It is also possible that what is implied is: 'You know what is in my human soul,[11] and I do not know the nature of the deposit (*mustawdaʿ*) [from] within Yourself that is in my innermost secret (*sirr*). This is because Your secret is between You and it [my innermost secret], and no one can have knowledge of it besides You.' It [that divine deposit] is the eye through which [the servant] sees God, the ear by which he hears God, and the tongue by which he calls Him. The evidence for it is in His words, Exalted is He, concerning the hypocrites, *Deaf, dumb and blind* [2:18]. This is because they do not have these deposits. But God knows best.

9 These words are part of the colloquy between God and Jesus. God asks Jesus if he had said to mankind that they should take him and his mother as gods besides Him. It is Jesus' answer that is the subject of Tustarī's interpretation.

10 i.e. 'You have knowledge of what I said, so there must be some other reason for Your asking the question.'

11 That is, according to all three MSS (Z515, f. 30b, F638, f. 20b and F3488, f. 214b) which have *fī nafsī al-bashariyya*, instead of *fī sirrī* in the printed edition.

6 Al-Anᶜām

He was asked about the words:

[6:52] ***Do not drive away those who call upon their Lord morning and evening, desiring His countenance...***

That is, they desire (*arādū*) the countenance of God and His good pleasure and they are not absent from Him for a moment.

Then he said:

The 'most ascetic' (*azhad*)[1] of people are those who have the purest source of food; the most devout (*aᶜbad*) of people are those who are most earnest in their effort to uphold His commandments and prohibitions; and the most beloved (*aḥabb*) of them to God are those who are the sincerest (*anṣaḥuhum*) towards His creatures.[2]

He was asked about life... He said, 'He who wastes his life...'[3]

His words, Exalted is He:

[6:54] ***...Your Lord has prescribed for Himself mercy. Truly, whoever of you does evil in ignorance, and repents thereafter and makes amends — truly He is Forgiving, Merciful.***

It has been reported that God, Exalted is He, revealed to David ﷺ, 'O David, whoever knows Me, desires Me;[4] whoever desires Me, loves Me; whoever loves Me, seeks Me out; whoever seeks Me out, finds Me; and whoever finds Me, preserves Me [in his heart] (*ḥafiẓanī*).' David ﷺ replied [by asking], 'O my Lord! Where can I find You when I wish to seek you out?' He said, 'With those whose hearts are broken from the fear of Me.'[5] David then said, 'O my Lord! I approached the doctors among Your servants for treatment, but they all directed me to You — Wretched are those who despair of Your mercy! Is there a chance of my being worthy of being cured by You?' God, Mighty and Majestic is He, asked him, 'Did all those you approached guide You to Me?' He answered, 'Yes', and God said, 'Then go and give the sinners good tidings, and give warning to the veracious (*ṣiddīqūn*).' David was baffled and said, 'Have I misunderstood or not?' He replied, 'You are not mistaken.' David asked, 'How is that?' He said: 'Give the sinners the good tidings that I am forgiving (*ghafūr*) and warn the veracious (*ṣiddīqūn*) that I am jealous (*ghayūr*).'[6]

---

1 *Azhad* being the superlative of *zāhid* which is often translated as 'ascetic', though it means more precisely 'one who renounces the world'. 'The most renunciant' would not quite be idiomatic here. On the term *zuhd* and its translation see above IT, p. xlvi, n. 201.

2 The verbal root *n-ṣ-ḥ* combines the meanings of being sincere and giving good advice, so this implies those who give good and sincere advice to God's creatures.

3 This appears to be incomplete in the printed edition and all the manuscripts.

4 The Arabic here is: *man ᶜarafanī arādanī*. The former verb (*ᶜarafa*) could also have the meaning 'has gnosis of', or 'recognises' or 'acknowledges' Me, while the second verb (*arāda*) could also imply 'aspires towards' God.

5 This tradition appears in Iṣfahānī, *Ḥilyat al-awliyā'*, vol. 4, pp. 31–2 and in the *Ṣifat al-ṣafwa* of ᶜAbd al-Raḥmān b. al-Jawzī [Ibn al-Jawzī] (Beirut, 1979), vol. 2, p. 293. In the *Ḥilya*, vol. 2, p. 364, God is asked the same question by Moses. The tradition also appears in Ghazālī's *Kīmiyā' al-saᶜādat*, vol. 1, p. 421, where Moses prays: 'O Lord! Where shall I seek Thee?' and God replies: 'With the broken-hearted' (without 'from the fear of Me').

6 According to Sufi tradition there are two kinds of jealousy (*ghayra*) on the part of God towards His lovers, mystics, and veracious servants. The first kind of jealousy arises if they should ever turn their attention to any other than Him; and

He [Sahl] was asked, 'Who are veracious?' He replied:

> They are those who combat their lower selves through the glorification (*taṣbīḥ*) and veneration (*taqdīs*) [of God]. Furthermore, they are those who keep their bodily limbs and senses in check. Hence, they become veracious in speech and action,[7] veracious outwardly and inwardly, veracious in their involvement in anything and likewise in their disengagement from anything. Consequently, their place of return is an abode of truth ⌜in the lofty rank of truth⌝[8] with the All-Powerful King.[9]

His words, Transcendent and Exalted is He:

[6:69] ***...but it is a reminder, so that they may be mindful of God***[10]

[Concerning these words] he said:

> Truly God, Exalted is He, placed on the shoulders of His friends (*awliyāʾ*) the duty of reminding His servants, just as He placed upon the shoulders of the prophets (may God's blessings be upon them all) the duty of conveying [the Message]. Thus, it is incumbent upon the friends of God to guide [people] to Him, and if they desist from doing so they are falling short of their duty.

It was put to him, 'Indeed, we have seen many who desist from doing this.' He replied:

> They only hold back from doing it when there is a lack of need for it, just as is the case with the commanding of what is right (*amr bi'l-maʿrūf*) and the forbidding of what is wrong (*nahy ʿan al-munkar*). There was a man with us in Basra who had a high [spiritual] station, and it was an imperative obligation on him that at a certain time he should do this [guide people]. When he set out to accomplish [this task] another man said to him, 'Truly God most High ordered me to what you are resolved to do, and has exempted you from [that duty].' So he returned home praising God, Exalted is He, for the goodness of that exemption. But God knows best.

His words, Mighty and Majestic is He:

[6:76] ***When the night descended upon him, he saw a star and said, 'This is my Lord...'***

> The whole of this speech is a form of allusion (*taʿrīḍ*) for the benefit of his people when their hearts are in a state of bewilderment, for he [Abraham] had already been granted *right guidance* (rushd) *before* [21:51], just as He said: *And so We showed Abraham the kingdom of the heavens and the earth.* [6:75][11]

He was asked about the meaning of His words:

[6:77] ***...If my Lord does not guide me...?***

---

the second is a protective jealousy, which shields their innermost secret or their love for Him from any unworthy or uninitiated person, or even from their own lower selves. This latter form of jealousy also has the function of protecting the mystics from complacency, or from lassitude. For a discussion of divine jealousy in Sufi doctrine, see A. Keeler, *Sufi Hermeneutics*, pp 196–7; 233; 297–8.

7 lit. 'their speech and acts become veracity'.

8 The words *qadam ṣidq*, lit. 'a foot of veracity or truth' were added on the basis of all three MSS: Z515, f. 41b, F638, f. 20b, F3488, f. 215b.

9 The words, *maqʿadi ṣidqin ʿinda Malīkin muqtadarin* are mentioned in 54:55, where they are translated by both Yūsuf ʿAlī and Muḥammad Asad as: 'In an Assembly of Truth in the presence of a Sovereign Omnipotent'; while *qadami ṣidqin* is mentioned in 10:2 where it is translated as: '...the lofty rank of truth...' However, in the *Tafsīr al-Jalālayn*, the words *qadami ṣidqin* are glossed with a different meaning of a preceding [or pre-existing] promise, i.e. understanding *qadam* in its other meaning.

10 According to the exoteric commentaries, the verse from which these words are taken and the preceding verse [6:68] concern a warning to believers that they should not sit and converse with those who mock God's signs. Those who are mindful (or fully aware) of God will not be accountable for such people; this is merely a reminder to them so that they should be wary of being involved in discourse with these people.

11 Probably, the lesson here is that although believers will from time to time experience bewilderment, they should be aware that it will pass, since they have previously been guided and will find guidance again. In the case of the prophet Abraham, he had been guided as a child, then later called the star, the moon and the sun in turn his lord, but then realised that *If my Lord does not guide me I shall surely be one of the folk who have gone astray* [6:77], on which Tustarī comments next.

He said:

It means: If my Lord does not continue to guide me *I shall be one of the folk who go astray.*[12]

Then he said:

The religion of Abraham ﷺ was generosity (*sakhāwa*), and [a state of] freedom (*tabarrī*) from everything save God, Exalted is He. Do you not see how when the angel Gabriel ﷺ asked him, 'Do you need anything?' He replied, 'From you, no.' He did not depend on anyone save Him, in any situation.[13]

His words, Exalted is He:

[6:98] *...Then gave you a dwelling place and a repository...*

A dwelling place, that is, in the wombs of women, *and a repository*, that is, as a drop in the loins of Adam ﷺ.

His words:

[6:120] *And avoid committing sin, whether openly or in secret...*

That is, give up the transgressions of the body, along with the desire for committing them within your heart, and [give up] persisting in doing them.

His words:

[6:125] *When God wishes to guide someone, He expands their breast to Islam...*

Sahl said:

Truly God has distinguished between the one who seeks (*murīd*) and the one who is [divinely] sought (*murād*), even though they are both from Him (*min ʿindihi*).[14] But He simply wanted to distinguish the elite (*khuṣūṣ*) from the generality (*ʿumūm*), and so He singled out the one who is sought (*murād*) in this *sūra* and others.[15] He also mentioned the one who seeks (*murīd*), representing the generality, in this *sūra* in His words, Exalted is He: *Do not drive away those who call upon their Lord morning and evening, seeking His countenance* [6:52].[16] This is the servant's being intent (*qaṣd*) upon God in his every moment of activity and stillness (*fī ḥarakātihi wa sukūnihi*),[17] just as He also said: *and those who hearken to their Lord and maintain the prayer...* [42:38]. Thus, whoever finds that he has the state of both the seeker and the sought, that is due to a grace (*faḍl*) from God to him. Do you not see how He has brought them together in His words, Exalted is He: *Whatever grace you have, it is from God* [16:53]?

---

12 In this comment and the previous one, Tustarī appears to be following the way of many commentators who did not believe that Abraham could have actually mistaken the star, the moon and the sun for his Lord. On this issue in the exegesis on 6:76–80, see Norman Calder, 'Tafsīr from Ṭabarī to Ibn Kathīr" in G. R. Hawting and A. K. Shareef, eds., *Approaches to the Qurʾān* (London and New York, 1993), pp. 101–40; and Keeler, *Sufi Hermeneutics*, pp. 74–9. On the doctrine of the prophets' (and in Shīʿism, the Imams') immunity from sin, see W. Madelung, "Iṣma', *EI²*, vol. v, pp. 182–5.

13 According to tradition, this exchange between Gabriel and Abraham took place when Abraham had been cast into the fire by his people (i.e. Nimrod and his followers). See above, p. 32, n. 110.

14 That is, both states, or conditions, are from Him. This topic has probably arisen because of the word *yurīdu* (He wants or wishes) used in the verse; the *murād* is the one who is desired [by God]. This is an example of the kind of Sufi interpretation that arises from what Böwering has termed a 'Qurʾānic keynote', a 'word or phrase of a particular verse which strikes the mind of the commentator' and 'is taken up as the focal point of the interpretation'. See *Mystical Vision*, p. 136 and IT, above p. xxix.

15 See Böwering, *Mystical Vision*, p. 232 for a discussion of Tustarī's use of the terms *murīd* and *murād*.

16 Here the wanting is on the part of the believers who 'seek' or desire God's countenance: *yurīdūna*, therefore Tustarī shows it to be a reference to those who are *murīds*. Many Sufis have defined the difference between the *murīd* and *murād*, in their treatises. For example, Kalābādhī defines the *murīd* as 'the man whose toiling (*ijtihād*) preceded his unveilings (*kushūf*)', whilst the *murād* is 'he whose unveilings preceded his toiling.' See *Kitāb al-Taʿarruf*, p. 107; English trans. Arberry, pp. 155–6, with a slight modification. Qushayrī, in his *Risāla*, p. 438, states that, according to the Sufis, the *murīd* is a novice (*mubtadiʾ*), whereas the *murād* is an adept (*muntahin*) and he goes on to observe that God's way with His seekers differs: 'most have to go through struggles and trials before they are brought to illumination, whereas some are given unveiling at the beginning, attaining to that which others do not reach even through their toiling. These latter nevertheless return from these graces to complete the disciplinary practices that they had passed by.'

17 This being a literal translation. However, it might simply be understood as: 'in everything he does'.

He was asked, 'Why are they [*murīd* and *murād*] separated then?' He said:

> The seeker who makes an effort to direct himself towards (*qaṣd*) God, Exalted is He, and to worship Him, and seeks the way to Him, is still in the state of seeking (*ṭalab*). As for the sought, it refers to the establishment of worship for him by God, Exalted is He.[18]
>
> Man has within himself that which [shows him] to be both a seeker (*murīd*) and one who is sought (*murād*). At one time, ⌜he enters into his acts of obedience [applying to them] struggle (*mukābada*) and striving (*mujāhada*), and this is [when he is] at the level of the seeker (*murīd*), when he may be stirred [into action] (*tuhayyijahu*) by the inducement of hope (*raghba*), or by fear (*rahba*). Then at another time⌝,[19] he finds himself carried through those acts without effort (*taklīf*) or striving (*jahd*),[20] [and this is] a solicitude from God, Exalted is He, towards him.[21] Then after that, he will move on to the highest stations (*maqāmāt*) and most elevated ranks (*darajāt*).

[At this point] he was asked about the meaning of the stations (*maqāmāt*), and he replied:

> They are mentioned in the Book of God, Exalted is He, in the story about the angels, *And there is not one of us but [that he] has a known station* [37:164]. He has also said, *All shall have degrees according to that which they have done* [6:132].

Regarding the characteristic of the seeker (*murīd*), he said:

> The occupation of the seeker is the performance of what is obligatory, seeking forgiveness for sins committed, and seeking safety (*salāma*) from people.

Sahl said:

> Truly, God, Mighty and Majestic is He, looks at the hearts and the hearts are with Him; those that He finds to be the humblest towards Him, He selects for what He wishes. Then after that, come those [hearts] that are the quickest in turning back [to Him]. These are the two qualities [of hearts].

And he said:

> Whenever God looks upon a heart and sees within it concern [or desire, *hamm*] for this world, He abhors it, and this abhorrence (*maqt*) is manifested through His abandoning it (*tark*) [the heart] along with [that person's] soul.[22] The heart is not owned by anyone except God most High, and it does not obey anyone except Him. So, if you are mindful [of] it, deposit your secret with God, for if you entrust it to anyone besides God, Mighty and Majestic is He, that person will divulge it.

His words:

[6:127] *Theirs shall be the abode of peace with their Lord…*

He said:

> That is, there he will be safe from the anxieties (*hawājis*) of his self and the whisperings (*wasāwis*) of his enemy.

His words, Exalted is He:

[6:129] *So, We let some evildoers have power over others because of what they were earning.*

---

18 Qushayrī appears to have alluded to this state in his *Laṭāʾif al-ishārāt* in the context of his commentary on 2:3. See Qushayrī, *Laṭāʾif al-ishārāt*, pp. 56–7. The passage is discussed in A. Keeler, 'Sufi *tafsīr* as a Mirror: Qushayrī the *murshid* in his *Laṭāʾif al-ishārāt*', pp. 4–5.

19 The addition is made with reference to all three MSS: Z515, f. 42b, F638, f. 21a and F3488, f. 216b.

20 lit. 'he finds or experiences that which carries him (*yaḥmiluhu*) through those acts'. Interestingly, Maybudī equates the position of *murīd* with 'bearing' (*mutaḥammil*), whereas he describes the state of the *murād* as 'being borne' (*maḥmūl*). See Maybudī, *Kashf al-asrār*, vol. 3, pp. 730–1. See also, Qushayrī, *Laṭāʾif al-ishārāt*, vol. 2, p. 406. This doctrine is explained in A. Keeler, *Sufi Hermeneutics*, pp. 260–1.

21 Compare with the passage above in Tustarī's commentary on 2:40 regarding different levels of certainty (*yaqīn*).

22 On abandonment by God, see above Tustarī's commentary on 3:160, also the latter part of his commentary on 2:30.

That is, God, Exalted is He, takes revenge on a wrongdoer by means of another wrongdoer, and then He Himself takes revenge on them.

His words, Exalted is He:

[6:147] ***If they deny you, say, 'Your Lord has all-encompassing mercy...'***

Sahl said:

It was reported from the Messenger of God ﷺ, 'Make whoever turns his back on you desirous of Me, for anyone who is desirous of Me is actually desirous of you, no other. Furthermore, give them hope of [My] mercy and do not cut your heart off from them — *say, "Your Lord has all-encompassing mercy."*'

His words, Exalted is He:

[6:151] ***...Do not draw near any acts of lewdness, whether openly or in secret...***

Whether openly refers to that which it has been forbidden to do with the external bodily members. *Or in secret* means the persistence (*iṣrār*) in committing that act, and this is of two kinds: the first is that a person commits a sin and persists in committing it; the other is that he persists in sin through desiring it in his heart, but he is not able to do it when he finds the opportunity because of a weakness in his bodily members, even though he is intent upon doing it. This is one of the most serious forms of persistence.

Then Sahl said:

Whoever eats what is permissible (*ḥalāl*) with gluttony is persistent (*muṣirr*), and whoever preoccupies himself with what the morrow may bring before the morrow arrives is persistent.

He was asked about the prophets ﷺ, regarding whether they thought about that which did not concern them. He replied:

An act with their bodily members was allowed to them, considering that they repented to God, Exalted is He, afterwards, let alone a mere thought.

He was asked, 'Is there a form of worship for the heart, which God requires of it, other than that which is performed by the bodily members?' He replied, 'Yes, it is the tranquil repose (*sukūn*) of the heart [in God].'[23] Then he was asked, 'Is such tranquil repose [in God] obligatory (*farḍ*)[24] or the knowledge by which it is attained?' He answered, 'It is a [kind of] knowledge, which I am calling tranquil repose, and that tranquil repose [in God] leads to certainty (*yaqīn*). Furthermore, tranquil repose accompanied with certainty is an obligation (*farīḍa*).'

His words, Exalted is He:

[6:152] ***...And if you speak, be just...***

He said:

The people of veracity (*ṣidq*) speak in four ways: they speak in God, through God, for God or with God. There are other people who speak to themselves and for themselves, and so they are preserved from the evil of speech. Yet other people speak about others and forget themselves,[25] and so they innovate and go astray. Wretched is that which they have produced for themselves! So abandon speech for knowledge, and then only speak when it is necessary, and you will be preserved from the ills of speech. What is meant [by 'when it is necessary'] is that you should not speak unless you are afraid that you will otherwise fall into sin.

---

23 As was seen above (4:81 and p. 56, n. 16), the word *sukūn* has a number of different meanings in Tustarī's commentary. Here it seems to mean a tranquil repose or acquiescence [in God], or serenity [with Him].

24 All the MSS (Z515, f. 43b, F638, f. 21b and F3488, f. 217b), clearly have *farḍ* rather than *gharaḍ* in the printed edition, and we may note that the word *farīḍa* is used in the Tustarī's response to this question.

25 That is, they are busy criticising others without attending to the faults in themselves, as is explained in the saying of Rabīʿ b. Khuthaym which follows.

Then he said:

> Whoever makes a [false] assumption (*ẓann*) will be deprived of certainty,[26] and whoever speaks about that which does not concern him will be deprived of veracity. Furthermore, whoever occupies his bodily members for other than the sake of God, Exalted is He, will be deprived of scrupulous piety (*waraʿ*). If a servant is deprived of these three he is ruined. Furthermore, he will be set down in the records as being among the enemies [of God].
>
> Truly, it was related from al-Rabīʿ b. Khuthaym, may God have mercy on him, ⌜that no one ever heard him speak about matters of the world (*amr al-dunya*). Someone asked him 'Why do you not mention people (*al-nās*), may God have mercy on you?'⌝[27] He replied, 'I am not satisfied with myself to the extent that I should be done with censuring myself, and turn to the the censure (*dhamm*) of others. [Yet people] fear God with regard to the sins of His servants, and leap into their own sins.'[28]

His words, Mighty and Majestic is He:

[6:153] ***And that this is My straight path*** **(ṣirāṭ)...**

He [Sahl] said:

> ⌜The path (*ṣirāṭ*) is⌝ the straight way (*ṭarīq mustaqīm*), and it is that which does not belong ⌜to the self which holds a share (*ḥaẓẓ*) or design (*murād*).[29]

His words, Exalted is He:

[6:159] ***As for those who have divided their religion and broken up into factions...***

He [Sahl] said:

> They are⌝[30] the people of whims (*ahwāʾ*) and innovations (*bidaʿ*) in religion. For them there is no form of repentance. Thus, has it been related from the Prophet ﷺ that he said, 'For every sin there is a form of repentance except for that of the people of whims and innovations, for truly I disown them just as they disown me, and God, Mighty and Majestic is He, has excluded them from repentance (*tawba*).'[31] That is, He has made the way to repentance difficult for them.

His words, Exalted is He:

[6:165] ***... Surely your Lord is swift in punishment, and surely He is Forgiving, Merciful.***

He [Sahl] said:

> This refers to the punishment of the heart which is a cover and veil, so that it [the heart] inclines to that which is other than Him. Furthermore, whenever God looks upon the heart of a servant and finds there that which is other than Him, He empowers his enemy over him. However, He is most forgiving to the one who repents for what he has done.
>
> No harm (*maḍār*) can be considered a punishment, because it [acts as] a purification and an expiation (*kaffāra*), except for hardness (*qaswa*) of the heart, for that in itself is a punishment. External punishments are a torment (*ʿadhāb*), but the punishments of the heart have different

---

26 The editor of the Dār al-Kutub al-ʿIlmiyya edition has added the words *ẓann al-sūʾ* following after *ẓann*, on the basis of *Ḥilyat al-awliyāʾ*, vol. 10, p. 196. However this addition does not conform to any of the MSS.

27 The section in brackets is added on the basis of all three MSS: Z515, f. 44a, F638, f. 21b and F3488, f. 217b–218a.

28 Referring back to those who criticise others instead of correcting themselves, and those who busy themselves with what is not their concern, also mentioned above. This tradition is cited in Iṣfahānī, *Ḥilyat al-awliyāʾ*, vol. 9, p. 52, and in Bayhaqī, *Shuʿab al-īmān*, vol. 5, p. 312, and vol. 6, p. 87, with the difference that in the *Ḥilyat al-awliyāʾ*, vol. 9, p. 52 and in *Shuʿab al-īmān*, vol. 6, p. 57, the tradition ends with the words 'they feel safe (*āminū*) regarding their own [sins]'. In *Shuʿab* vol. 5, p. 312, however, only the first part of the tradition is cited.

29 That is, the lower self, which wants to claim something (or everything) for itself. The term *ḥaẓẓ* could also be translated as 'pleasure', but Tustarī uses the pair of terms, *ḥazz* and *murād* below in the sense, perhaps, of the self having its own 'vested interest' in the heart.

30 The section in brackets is added on the basis of MS Z515, f. 44a, F638, f. 21b and F3488, f. 218a. This addition means that verse 159 precedes verse 165, whereas in the printed addition it follows it.

31 Tirmidhī, *Nawādir al-uṣūl*, vol. 2, p. 245; Iṣfahānī, *Ḥilyat al-awliyāʾ*, vol. 4, p. 138.

levels,[32] for the lower self holds a share and a design with regard to the heart.[33] [As for the one whose] heart is veiled, God empowers his enemy over him. His heart does not orbit the celestial dominions (*malakūt*), nor does the divine omnipotence (*qudra*) manifest itself to him, nor does he witness (*yushāhid*) God. But as for the one whose heart is hardened, God leaves him to his own devices and means. Truly the tendency of the heart may be compared to the tongue; when a person speaks, he can speak of only one thing [at a time]. Similarly if a heart is full of concern [for something] there is no room for anything along with that. But God knows best.

32 This section had to be rearranged on the basis of the MSS (Z515, f. 44b, F638, f. 22a and F3488, ff. 218a and b). Note that F638 has *mathal al-qalb* instead of *mathal mayl al-qalb*.

33 See above, p. 69, n. 29.

7 Al-Aʿrāf

His words, Mighty and Majestic is He:

[7:1] ***Alif Lām Mīm Ṣād***

[Sahl said]:

> This means, 'I am God, I divide up (*afṣilu*)[1] my servants with truth.' From these letters is produced the name of God, Exalted is He: *al-Ṣamad* (the Self-Sufficing, the One who is Eternally-Besought-of-All).[2]

His words, Exalted is He:

[7:16] ***Verily I shall sit in ambush for them on Your straight path.***

> [*Your straight path*] meaning the sacred laws (*sharāʾiʿ*) of Islam, after God, Exalted is He, has clearly expounded [those laws] to them, as is stated in His words, *Is it not an indication for them?* [32:26], meaning, 'Did We not clearly [distinguish] for them the path of goodness, which is what He has commanded, from the path of evil, which is what He has prohibited? Yet they inclined towards the desire of their lower selves, just as when *They [the messengers] said: "The evil omen is within yourselves* [36:19]."'

His words:

[7:20] ***Then Satan whispered to them…***

He said:

> The whispering [of Satan] is [his] mentioning [something] (*dhikr*) [firstly] in the natural [predisposition] (*tabʿ*), then in the lower self (*nafs*).[3] [This suggestion] then [becomes] the desire (*hamm*), and finally the devising (*tadbīr*). The whispering of the Enemy [i.e. Satan] has three possible situations (*maqāmāt*): the first is when he calls a person and whispers to him, the second is when he feels secure knowing that the person has accepted [the suggestion], but the third is when his lot is only to wait and hope, and this is [his situation] with the veracious (*ṣiddīqūn*).

His words, Exalted is He:

[7:29] ***…And call on Him, devoting your religion to Him…***

He [Sahl] said:

> Seek sincerity (*ikhlāṣ*) secretly with an [inner] intention, for it is only the sincere who can recognise ostentation. However, seek action openly through emulation, for truly whoever does not emulate the Prophet ﷺ in all his affairs is misguided. All other than these two [ways] are erroneous.

---

1 All three MSS (Z515, f. 44b, F638, f. 22a and F3488, f. 218b) have *afṣilu*, instead of *aqḍī* in the printed edition. The editor may have read this word in the text, because the implication is of God's allotting some of His servants happiness (*saʿāda*), and others wretchedness (*shaqāwa*) in His pre-eternal knowledge. This doctrine is alluded to in Tustarī's commentary on 7:172 below.

2 This is an example of a specific interpretation being given for the disconnected letters at the beginning of a *sūra*. See above, Tustarī's commentary on 2:1, and p. 12, n. 2.

3 On 'whispering' or 'evil incitement or suggestion' (*waswasa*), see above, IT, p. xxxv, n. 138.

His words, Exalted is He:

[7:31] ***...And eat and drink, but do not be excessive; He truly does not love those who are excessive.***

Eating is of five kinds: that which is a necessity [for subsistence] (*ḍarūra*); that which is a source of sustenance (*qiwām*); that which is a source of nourishment (*qūt*); that which should be of a determined [amount] (*maʿlūm*);[4] and that which one does without. [Beyond this], there is a sixth in which there is no good, and that is [wrongly] mixed (*takhlīṭ*).[5] Furthermore, God, Exalted is He, created the world and placed knowledge and wisdom within hunger (*jūʿ*), and placed ignorance and transgression within satiety (*shabʿ*). So, when you are hungry ask for satiety from the One who has afflicted you with hunger, and if you are satiated, ask for hunger from the One who has afflicted you with satiety, otherwise you will commit excesses and transgress.

Then he recited: *But man is wont to transgress* ❁ *when he thinks himself self-sufficient* [96:6, 7]. He also said:

Truly, hunger is a secret among the secrets of God, Exalted is He, on earth, which He does not entrust to anyone who will disseminate it.

His words, Exalted is He:

[7:33] ***Say: My Lord only forbids indecent acts, such of them as are apparent and such as are hidden...***

He [Sahl] said:

This refers to the envy (*ḥasad*) of a person's heart and the actions of his bodily members. If he were to give up the management (*tadbīr*) of both he would be one of the 'mainstays' (*awtād*) of the earth.[6] However, the servant is between two states: either he is managing with his heart that which is not his concern, or he is acting through his bodily members upon that which is not his concern. No one is saved from either of these two except through the protection (*ʿiṣma*) of God, Exalted is He. The source of life for hearts is certainty, and their darkness is brought on through [their own] devising and management (*tadbīr*).

He [Abū Bakr] said, 'We were with Sahl at sunset,[7] and he said to Aḥmad b. Sālim, leave off managing things, so that we may pray the *ʿĪshāʾ* prayer in Mecca.[8]

His words, Exalted is He:

[7:33] ***...And [forbids] that you say concerning God that which you do not know.***

Whoever speaks about God without permission, in a way which lacks reverence (*ḥurma*) or without maintaining the due propriety (*adab*), has rent the veil (*satr*). Indeed, God, Exalted is He, has forbidden anyone to say anything about Him of which he has no knowledge.

His words, Exalted is He:

[7:43] ***We shall strip away all rancour that is in their breasts...***

He said:

This refers to whims (*ahwāʾ*) and innovations (*bidaʿ*).

His words, Exalted is He:

[7:46] ***And on the Heights are men...***

---

4 Perhaps this is referring to the medicinal use of certain foods.

5 *Takhlīṭ* literally means 'confusion and disorder'. Since the root *kh-l-ṭ* can also have the meaning of infecting, it is possible that this could also mean contaminated.

6 According to Sufi tradition, the rank of the *awtād* (sing. *watad*) lit. 'mainstays' or 'props', is one of the ranks of spiritual hierarchy, which continue on from the time of the Prophet. These ranks will be discussed further below in Tustarī's commentary on 10:62 and p. 89, n. 5.

7 It is not clear whether the speaker here is Abū Bakr al-Sijzī or ʿUmar b. Wāṣil. ʿUmar b. Wāṣil transmits a saying of Tustarī soon after this in the commentary on 7:99.

8 Meaning that if he would only leave off his own attempt to manage things they might attain a miracle, such as being transported to Mecca in time to pray the *ʿĪshāʾ* prayer, when at the time it was sunset.

He said:

The People of the Heights are the people of gnosis (*maʿrifa*).[9] God, Exalted is He, said: ...*who know each by their mark* [7:47]. Their standing is due to the honour (*sharaf*) they enjoy in the two abodes and with the inhabitants of both, and the two angels[10] know them. Likewise [God] enabled them to see into (*ashrafahum*)[11] the secrets of His servants and their states in this world.[12]

His words, Exalted is He:

[7:56] *And work not corruption in the land, after it has been set right...*

He [Sahl] said:

[It means that] you should not spoil obedience with sin. This is because whoever persists in sinning, though it be of the smallest kind of prohibited act, will find all his good deeds alloyed by that transgression. Furthermore, his good deeds will not become pure as long as he maintains just one misdeed, until he repents and divests himself of that misdeed, thereby purifying them [his good deeds] from the defilement of sins [he commits], both in secret and openly.

His words, Exalted is He:

[7:68] *...I am your [sincere] truthful advisor.*[13]

Whoever is not sincere towards God within his own soul, and sincere towards Him with regard to His creatures, will be ruined. To act with sincerity (*naṣīḥa*) towards God's creatures is more difficult than being sincere within one's own soul. The lowest level of sincerity [towards God] within the soul is gratitude (*shukr*), which is not to disobey God by [abusing] the blessings He has bestowed [on you] (*bi-niʿamihi*).

On another occasion I heard him say:

Sincerity is not to involve yourself in anything which you do not have the power to put right.

His words, Exalted is He:

[7:94] *And We did not send a prophet to any city but that We seized its people with misery and hardship...*

He [Sahl] said:

This means they lost their hearts through their lack of knowledge, and because of severe hardship in their lives, such that they became preoccupied with their world[ly concerns] to the exclusion of their [concern for the] Hereafter.

[7:95] *Then We gave them in place of evil, good, until they multiplied...*

[He said]:

[The fact that] they multiplied does not signify a pardon (*ʿafw*) in the essential [meaning of that word].[14] God, Exalted is He, has said: *Indulge [people] with forgiveness* (ʿafw) [7:199], which

---

9 Note that the two words *aʿrāf* meaning 'the Heights' and *maʿrifa* meaning 'gnosis' are derived from the same verbal root *ʿ-r-f*.

10 Munkar and Nakīr are the two angels who question the dead in their graves concerning their faith.

11 Note the play on words here using the root *sh-r-f*. *Ishrāf* has the meaning of an elevated vantage point from which one has a commanding view over things, as was seen in Tustarī's explanation of the 'point of transcendency (*maṭlaʿ*)' in his discussion of four levels of meaning in the verses of the Qurʾān. See above IC, p. 2.

12 Mystics and men of great spirituality were said to be the 'spies of hearts' who had a penetrating spiritual perception or, more precisely, physiognomy (*firāsa*), that is, the ability to understand what is in a person's heart from their external appearance. Concerning *firāsa*, the Prophet said in a well-known *ḥadīth*: 'Beware the spiritual perception (*firāsa*) of the believer, for he sees with the light of God,' and then recited the verse: '*Therein lie portents for those who read the signs* (al-mutawaṣṣimīn)' (15:75). This *ḥadīth* is cited later by Tustarī in the context of his commentary on 15:75, where references for the *ḥadīth* are given.

13 The words used here are *nāṣiḥ amīn*. As was stated above, the verbal root *n-ṣ-ḥ* may convey both the meaning of advising and of being sincere towards others. This verse occurs as part of the story of the prophet Hūd, when he was trying to bring the message of the oneness of God to his people, the ʿĀd.

14 The verbal root *ʿ-f-w* has the meaning of being obliterated, or effaced, and hence the effacement of sin and being pardoned or excused, but it also has the meaning of becoming abundant in quantity, as here in this verse.

[actually] means, '[Take] the surplus (*faḍl*) of their wealth which is a deposit from God in their keeping, because God most High has purchased it from them.' And ⸢the believer⸣[15] possesses neither his soul nor his wealth.

He was asked, 'Where is [the believer's] soul?' He replied:

It has been placed under contract with God, Exalted is He. He said: *Indeed God has purchased from the believers their lives and their possessions, promising them Paradise in return.* [9:111]

His words, Exalted is He:

[7:99] *Do they feel secure from God's plotting?...*

He [Sahl] said:

The plotting (*makr*) belongs to His design (*tadbīr*) within His prior knowledge, and it pertains to His omnipotence,[16] hence no one should feel secure against His plotting, for feeling secure against it does not repel anything that has been preordained (*qadar*). No one can exit the [sphere of] His omnipotence, Exalted is He. No one should feel free of fear, even if they [think] they have experienced all [possible] fear. However, once someone recognises his station (*manzila*) with God, Exalted is He, his knowledge will increase and his desire (*raghba*) will be fulfilled. But as for the one who does not know his station, that will be a source of shame (*ʿār*) for him.

ʿUmar Wāṣil said that he then asked [Sahl], 'How does a person's station rise in accordance with his knowledge?' He answered:

There are two [kinds of] men: there is the man who rises [in his spiritual station] and asks for [further] elevation,[17] being avid for this; and then there is the man who is weaker than the other, whose [request] derives from gratitude, lest God should take back what He has given him.

His words, Exalted is He:

[7:128] *Moses said to his people, 'Seek help from God and be patient.'*

He [Sahl] said:

He ordered them to seek help from God in keeping God's commandments, so that they might enforce what is contained within them, take a firm hold on them and a firm stand against any breach of them, and show fortitude in this out of propriety.

His words:

[7:146] *I shall turn away from My signs those who behave arrogantly in the earth without right...*

He [Sahl] said:

It means that He will deprive them of understanding the Qurʾān, and following the Messenger ﷺ. It has been related from the Prophet ﷺ that he said, 'Whoever has been given understanding of the Qurʾān has been given abundant good. However, whoever has been denied understanding of the Qurʾān has been denied access to a great science (*ʿilm ʿaẓīm*).' Also, the Prophet ﷺ said: 'A part of magnifying (*taʿẓīm*) God is honouring (*ikrām*) the elderly in Islam, honouring the just leader, and honouring the person who has memorised the Qurʾān,[18] whilst not exceeding the proper bounds in this.'[19]

His words:

[7:146] *...[those who] if they see the way of error, adopt it as a way...*

He [Sahl] said:

He returned them to what He knew concerning them in His prior knowledge, which was that

---

15 Added on the basis of all three MSS: Z515, f. 46a, F638, f. 22b and F3488, f. 220a.

16 In other words, it is a manifestation of His prior knowledge (*ʿilm*) through His omnipotence (*qudra*).

17 lit. 'the man who grows [in his spiritual station] and asks for further increase.'

18 lit. 'bearer' (*ḥāmil*) of the Qurʾān.

19 That is to say, not being excessive in honouring them. The *ḥadīth* is listed in ʿAjlūnī, *Kashf al-khafāʾ*, vol. 1, p. 284.

they would do that [which is mentioned in the verse].[20] His forsaking (*khidhlān*) them is because of what they were directed to by their natural selves (*anfusuhum al-ṭabīʿiyya*), namely, being active regarding His prohibitions, and passive regarding His commandments, and [falsely] claiming to have the power and strength [to do] that which their souls had a propensity for, and their conceit (*ightirār*) in that.

His words, Exalted is He:

[7:148] ***In his absence, Moses' people made of their ornament a calf; a body, which lowed...***

He [Sahl] said:

The calf of each person is anything to which he devotes himself which diverts him away from God, be it a spouse or children. Furthermore, he will not rid himself of that until he has annihilated all the interests (*ḥuẓūẓ*) he has,[21] that are its [his calf's] means [of existence], just as the worshippers of the calf are not freed from its adoration except after slaying themselves.[22]

His words, Mighty and Majestic is He:

[7:149] ***And when they became at a loss...***[23]

He [Sahl] said:

That is, they regretted [what they had done]. You say that 'it falls into a person's hands' when he regrets something.

His words, Exalted is He:

[7:156] ***...We have turned to You...***

That is, We have repented to You.

His words, Exalted is He:

[7:163] ***...How they would transgress the Sabbath...***

He [Sahl] said:

They transgressed because they followed their desire (*hawā*) on the Sabbath.

His words, Exalted is He:

[7:169] ***...And they have studied what is in it...***

That is they gave up acting upon it.

His words:

[7:171] ***When we wrenched* (nataqnā) *the mountain [and held it above them]...***

That is, 'We rent it (*fataqnā*) and shook [it] violently, just as al-ʿAjjāj said: [*rajaz* metre]

They nurtured our great dreams,
And tore apart (*fataqnā*) our nightmares.[24]

His words, Exalted is He:

[7:172] ***And remember when your Lord took from the Children of Adam, from their loins, their seeds, and made them testify about themselves...***

20 The whole verse [7:146] reads: *I shall turn away from My signs those who behave arrogantly in the earth without right, and if they see every sign do not believe in it; and if they see the way of rectitude, do not adopt it as a way, but if they see the way of error, adopt it as a way. That is because they have denied Our signs and were heedless of them.* Thus God says that He will turn away from His signs those who have acted arrogantly on earth, and, according to Tustarī's interpretation, will forsake them because of His foreknowledge that they would do so.

21 *Ḥaẓẓ* (pl. *ḥuẓūẓ*) being either a [personal] interest, portion, share or pleasure.

22 A reference to Sūrat al-Baqara [2:54].

23 lit. when it 'fell into their hands'.

24 i.e., obliterated them. The editor of the Dār al-Kutub al-ʿIlmiyya states that this couplet is not by al-ʿAjjāj.

He [Sahl] said:

> God, Exalted is He, took the prophets ﷺ from the loins of Adam, and then He extracted from the back of each prophet his progeny in a molecular form [lit. in the shape of specks] possessing intellects (*ʿuqūl*). Then he took from the prophets their pledge (*mīthāq*), as is stated in His words, *We took from the prophets their pledge: as (We did) from you and from Noah* [33:7]. The Covenant that they were bound to was that they would convey from God, Exalted is He, His commandments and prohibitions. Then He called them all to affirm His lordship, with His words, Exalted is He: *'Am I not your Lord?'* Then He manifested His omnipotence [to them], so *They said: 'Yes, we testify'* [7:172].[25] Thus did God gather what He wanted (*murād*) from His creatures, and the beginning and end that was in store for them in their saying '*Yes*', since this was in the manner of a trial (*ibtilāʾ*).[26] Indeed, God, Exalted is He, said: *And His Throne was upon the water, that He might try you* [11:7]. He also made the prophets testify for themselves as a proof (*ḥujjatan*), as God, Exalted is He, has said, *and made them testify concerning themselves.* Then He returned them to the loins of Adam ﷺ, and subsequently He sent the prophets to remind them of His Pact and Covenant. Furthermore, within His knowledge on the day when they affirmed what they affirmed, were those who would deny it and those who would verify it,[27] and the last hour will not arrive until every person who made the Covenant has appeared.

He was asked, 'What are the signs of happiness (*saʿāda*) and wretchedness (*shaqāwa*)?'[28] He said:

> Truly, among the signs of wretchedness is the denial of His omnipotence, and truly among the signs of happiness is the expansiveness of your heart in faith,[29] your being provided with riches in your heart, protection in obedience, and success in renouncing [the world] (*zuhd*). Whoever is inspired with propriety (*adab*) in that which is between him and God, Exalted is He, will be purified of heart, and bestowed with happiness. There is nothing more exacting than preserving propriety.

He was asked, 'What is propriety?' [He answered]:

> [It is that you should] let your food be barley, your sweetmeat dates, your condiment salt, your fat yoghurt. You should let your clothes be of wool, your houses be mosques, your source of light the sun, your lamp the moon, your perfume water, your splendour cleanliness, and your adornment wariness (*ḥadhr*). Moreover, you should let your work consist in being content (*irtiḍāʾ*) — or he said contentment (*riḍā*) — , your journey's provision (*zād*) be mindfulness of God (*taqwā*), your eating be at night, your sleep in the day, your speech be remembrance (*dhikr*), your resolve (*ṣamma*) and your aspiration (*himma*) be for contemplation (*tafakkur*),[30] your reflective thought (*naẓar*) be to take example (*ʿibra*),[31] and your refuge (*maljaʾ*) and the

---

25 On the Covenant and Tustarī's interpretation of 7:172, see above IT, pp. xxxi–xxxii and xxxv–xxxvi.

26 The implication here seems to be that in this manifestation of the divine omnipotence, God had all His creatures testify (through Him) to His lordship, and within this testimony (their saying 'Yes'), was also their acknowledgment of their divinely decreed beginning and end. This was, moreover, a test and a trial (*ibtilāʾ*), for while it was testing them as to whether or not they would bear witness to His lordship, their very answering 'Yes', implied their acceptance of the trials of human existence.

27 According to the tradition that some made the affirmation willingly, others unwillingly. See for example, Daylamī, *ʿAṭf al-alif*, p. 53; English trans., Bell as *A Treatise on Mystical Love*, p. 133. For the numerous *ḥadīth*s commenting on 7:172 see Ṭabarī, *Jāmiʿ al-bayān*, vol. 13, pp. 222–50; also idem, *Tārīkh al-rusul wa'l-mulūk* (Cairo, 1960–9); English trans. of vol. 1 by Franz Rosenthal as *The History of al-Ṭabarī* I (Albany, 1989), pp. 304–7. On the development of the doctrines surrounding 7:172, according to Sunni and Shīʿī thought as well as in Sufism, see Nasrollah Pourjavady, "ʿAhd-i Alast: ʿAqīda-yi Abū Ḥāmid al-Ghazzālī wa jāygāh-i tārīkh-i ān', *Maʿārif* 7, no. 2 (1990), pp. 3–47, now expanded and republished as ch. 2 in *idem*, *Du mujaddid* (Tehran, 2002). On the Covenant of *Alast*, see references given in n. 25 above.

28 These two words, *saʿāda* and *shaqāwa*, are often used, as in this context, to denote our predestined and eventually eternal happiness or misery, hence felicity or wretchedness.

29 A reference perhaps to 6:125: *Whomever God desires to guide, He expands his breast to Islam.*

30 *Tafakkur* instead of *fikr* on the basis of all three MSS: MSS Z515, f. 48a, F638, f. 23b and F3488, f. 221b.

31 *ʿIbra* means the salutary lesson that can be drawn from things, often things which have happened to other people.

one who helps you (*nāṣir*) be your Lord. Persevere in this until you die.[32]

He also said:

Three of the signs of wretchedness (*shaqāwa*) are that a person misses the congregational prayer while he is close to the mosque; that he misses the congregational prayer while in Medina; and that he misses the Hajj while he is in Mecca.

[Returning to the interpretation of the verse 7:172], Sahl said:

The progeny (*dhurriyya*) comprise three [parts], a first, second and third: the first is Muḥammad ﷺ, for when God, Exalted is He, wanted to create Muḥammad ﷺ He made appear (*aẓhara*) a light from His light, and when it reached the veil of divine majesty it prostrated before God, and from that prostration God created an immense crystal-like column of light, that was inwardly and outwardly ⌜translucent⌝,[33] and within it was the essence of Muḥammad ﷺ. Then it stood in service before the Lord of the Worlds for a million years with the essential characteristics of faith (*ṭabāʾiʿ al-īmān*), which are the visual beholding of faith (*muʿāyanat al-īmān*), the unveiling of certainty (*mukāshafat al-yaqīn*) and the witnessing of the Lord (*mushāhadat al-Rabb*). Thus He honoured him with this witnessing, a million years before beginning the creation.

There is no one who is not overcome by Iblīs, may God curse him, or captured by him, save the prophets ﷺ, and the veracious (*ṣiddīqūn*), whose hearts bear witness to their faith according to their [different] stations (*maqāmāt*), and who know that God observes them in all their states. Furthermore, according to the measure of their witnessing (*mushāhada*), ⌜they experience trial[s] (*ibtilāʾ*), and according to the measure of their experience of trials, they seek protection. Likewise according to the measure of their poverty (*faqr*) and need (*fāqa*) for Him⌝,[34] they recognise harm (*ḍurr*) and benefit (*nafʿ*), and increase in knowledge (*ʿilm*), understanding (*fahm*) and reflective thought (*naẓar*).

Then he said:

God has not placed a burden of service (*khidma*) upon any of the prophets ﷺ as great as that which he placed upon our Prophet ﷺ. Furthermore, there is not a position of service in which God, Exalted is He, has been served by the children of Adam ﷺ up to the time when He sent our Prophet ﷺ, in which our Prophet ﷺ has not served God.

He [Sahl] was asked about a saying of the Prophet ﷺ, 'Truly, I am not like any of you, verily my Lord feeds me and gives to drink.'[35] He answered:

[He was not speaking about] food and water that he had, but he was mentioning his particular quality with God, Exalted is He, such that he was [in His presence] as someone who has eaten food and drunk water.[36] Indeed, had he had any food and water he would have given priority to his family and the People of the Bench (*Ahl al-Ṣuffa*) over himself.[37]

The second among the progeny, is Adam ﷺ. God created him from the light ⌜of Muḥammad ﷺ⌝.[38] And He created Muḥammad ﷺ, that is, his body, from the clay of Adam ﷺ.

The third is the progeny of Adam. God, Mighty and Majestic is He, created the seekers [of God] (*murīdūn*) from the light of Adam, and He created the [divinely]-sought (*murādūn*) from the light of Muḥammad ﷺ. Thus, the generality among people live under the mercy of the people

---

32 Bayhaqī, *Kitāb al-Zuhd al-kabīr*, vol. 2, p. 356.

33 That is, reading *yurā ẓāhiruhu wa bāṭinuhu* as in all three MSS: Z515, f. 48a, F638, f. 23b and F3488, f. 221b), to mean literally both its exterior and interior could be seen, i.e., as Böwering has translated, it was translucent, like a crystal.

34 The section between the brackets is absent from the MS Z515, but is present in F638, f. 23b and F3488, f. 222a, though the words *wa ʿalā qadri maʿrifatihim al-ibtilāʾ yaṭlubūnaʾl-ʿiṣma* are absent from F638.

35 Bukhārī, *Ṣaḥīḥ*, 'Kitāb al-Ṣawm'.

36 i.e. he received in a direct manner spiritual nourishment from God.

37 On the People of the Bench, see above Tustarī's commentary on 2:273 and p. 37, n. 146.

38 All the MSS (Z515 f. 48b, F638, f. 23b and F3488, f. 222a) have the words *Muḥammad ʿalayhi al-salām*, instead of *qāla ʿalayhi al-salām* in the printed edition.

of proximity (*ahl al-qurb*) and the people of proximity live under the mercy of the one brought near (*al-muqarrab*) — *With their light shining forth before them and on their right.* [57:12][39]

His words, Exalted is He:

[7:176] *Had We willed, We would have raised him up [with Our signs]...*

This refers to Balʿam b. Bāʿūrāʾ.[40] *But he was disposed to the earth and followed his [lower] desires.* He turned away [from God's signs] due to his following his [base] desire (*hawā*). God, Exalted is He, distributed desire among the bodily members such that each bodily member has a portion of it. If one of the bodily members inclines towards that desire, its harm will return to the heart. Know that the self has a secret which did not manifest itself except with Pharaoh when he said: *'I am your Lord most High'* [79:24].

Then [Sahl] was asked, 'How can we be preserved from [base] desire (*hawā*)?' He replied:

Whoever keeps himself in propriety (*adab*) will be preserved from it, for whoever subdues his lower self through propriety serves God, Mighty and Majestic is He, with true sincerity (*ikhlāṣ*).

He also said:

The self (*nafs*) has seven heavenly veils and seven earthly veils. The more the servant buries his [lower] self in the earth the higher will his heart soar heavenwards. Furthermore, if he [completely] buries his lower self beneath the earth his heart will reach the Throne. He also said about Kahmas that he used to pray a thousand *rakʿas* (cycles of prayer) during the course of the day and night. He would make the closing greetings of peace (*salāms*) between each pair of *rakʿas* then say to his lower self, 'Get up O refuge of evil, I am not satisfied with you.'

His words, Exalted is He:

[7:180] *And to God belong the Most Beautiful Names, so invoke Him by them.*

He [Sahl]said:

Truly behind the names and attributes are attributes which no comprehension can penetrate, for God is a blazing fire and is inaccessible. Yet we have no option but to plunge in [and try to reach Him]. *And leave those who blaspheme His names* [7:180], that is, those who are blasphemous with His names and deny [the truth].'

His words:

[7:182] *We shall draw on those who deny Our Signs, by degrees, in such a way that they will not perceive it.*

He [Sahl] said:

This means, 'We shall abundantly increase their bounties, and make them forget to show gratitude for them. Then when they are contented while veiled from the Bestower [of those

---

39 This is a description of the believing men and women on the Day of Resurrection. The 'one brought near' is an allusion to Muḥammad. See above, the commentary on the poem cited under 2:41, p. 33.

40 Balʿam b. Bāʿūrāʾ (Balaam son of Boer) is not mentioned by name in the Qurʾān, but he is said to be the subject of 7:175–6. According to Thaʿlabī, he was a Canaanite descended from Lot, who lived in the Syrian city of Balqāʿ, said to be inhabited by giants. As Moses was approaching their land, Balʿam, who knew God's Highest Name and whose prayers were answered, was approached by the people of that land, who, fearing that they would be driven out by the Israelites, importuned him to pray against Moses and his people. At first, Balʿam refused to curse one of God's prophets, but eventually he was persuaded to do so and ascended the mountain to pray against the Israelites. However, as he prayed against them his tongue was turned around so that his prayer was directed against his own people, and as he prayed for his own people, his tongue was turned around so that he prayed for the Israelites. When he returned to his people, they chided him for having prayed for the Israelites and against them. Balʿam then admitted that this was out of his control and his tongue stuck out so far that it fell on to his chest. He then devised a strategy whereby women would be sent among the Israelites to tempt them into fornication. This brought about a plague upon the Israelites. See Thaʿlabī, *ʿArāʾis al-majālis*, pp. 257–9; trans. Brinner, *ʿArāʾis*, pp. 392–6. See also Ṭabarī, *History*, vol. 3, *Children of Israel*, trans. Brinner, pp. 91ff. The Qurʾān compares Balʿam to a dog: *Therefore his likeness is as the likeness of a dog: if you attack it, it lolls its tongue out, and if you leave it, it lolls its tongue out.* As is the case in Tustarī's commentary, Balʿam is often shown in Sufi literature as a prototype of a man of religion or spirituality brought down by his own desires.

bounties] (*al-Munʿim*), they will be seized.'

His words:

[7:185] ***Have they not contemplated the dominion of the heavens and the earth...***

He [Sahl] said:

> [This is] God's reminder of His omnipotence (*qudra*) [manifested] in His creation, and a portrayal of their need for Him, Exalted is He. With regard to whatever He created that they have heard about but not seen, and those things that they have been deluded by, [He says], 'If only they had perceived them with their hearts, they would have believed in the unseen, and their faith would have led them to witness the unseen which was hidden from them. Then they would have inherited the ranks of the righteous (*abrār*) and become beacons of guidance.'

His words:

[7:187] ***He alone will reveal it at its proper time...***[41]

> That is, no one can reform the natural self (*nafs al-ṭabʿ*) from being ruled by passion (*hawā*) to obeying God, save He.[42] This is the inner meaning of the verse.[43]

His words:

[7:187] ***...They will question you as if you were eager to find it out... that is, as if you knew the time it would occur.***[44]

His words:

[7:188] ***I have no power to benefit or harm myself except as God wills...***

> So how can anyone benefit another when he does not have the power to benefit himself? That is for God alone, Exalted is He.

His words:

[7:198] ***...You see them staring at you, but they do not perceive.***

He [Sahl] said:

> It [refers to] those hearts that God, Exalted is He, has not adorned with His lights and with proximity, so that they are blind to the apprehension of realities (*ḥaqāʾiq*) and the recognition of great people (*akābir*).

His words:

[7:205] ***And remember your Lord inwardly, humbly and fearfully...***

[Sahl was asked], 'What is the true reality of remembrance (*ḥaqīqat al-dhikr*)?' He answered:

> It is the realisation (*taḥqīq*) of the knowledge that God, Exalted is He, witnesses you, and it is that you see Him close to you with your heart. Thus, you feel shame before Him and give Him priority over yourself in all your affairs.

Then he said:

> The one who claims to keep remembrance (*dhikr*) is not necessarily one who [truly] remembers [God] (*dhākir*).

He was asked, 'What is the meaning of the saying of the Prophet ﷺ: "The world is accursed and what it contains is accursed save the remembrance of God (*dhikr Allāh*), most High?"'[45] [He replied]:

---

41 In this verse the Prophet is being informed that he will be asked about the Hour and when it will come, and instructed what he should answer.

42 On Tustarī's use of the terms *nafs al-ṭabʿ* and *nafs al-rūḥ* see IT, pp. xxxviiiff. above, and Böwering, *Mystical Vision*, pp. 158–9, and 160–1.

43 The context for the words which Tustarī is commenting upon here is God's command to the Prophet regarding the answer he should give when he is questioned about the Hour (i.e., the Day of Resurrection).

44 Tustarī is returning here to the outer meaning of the verse.

45 Tirmidhī, *Nawādir al-uṣūl*, vol. 1, p. 255; Tirmidhī, *Sunan*, 'Kitāb al-Zuhd'.

> His saying 'the remembrance of God' here means renouncing what is unlawful (*zuhd ʿan al-ḥarām*), that is, when something unlawful comes a person's way he remembers God, Exalted is He, and he knows that God is watching him, so he avoids that unlawful thing.[46]

His words:

[7:205] ***...and do not be one of the heedless...***

Sahl said:

> In truth I say to you without any falsehood, in certainty without a doubt, that any person who spends a breath in other than God's remembrance does so while being heedless of God, Mighty and Majestic is He.

He also said:

> Heedlessness (*ghafla*) among the elite (*khāṣṣ*) is acquiescing (*sukūn*) in anything [other than Him]. Heedlessness among the generality (*ʿāmm*) is taking pride (*iftikhār*) in anything [other than Him], that is to say, it is [also] acquiescing (*sukūn*) [in other than Him].[47]

46 Again, this recalls the teaching imparted to Tustarī by his uncle. See above, IT, p. xv.

47 Note that Tustarī is here using the term *sukūn* in a pejorative way, in the same way he used the term *musākana* in his commentary on 2:30, above. It will be recalled that in his commentary on 4:81 and 6:151, he used the word *sukūn* in the positive sense of tranquil repose and acquiescence in God.

8 Al-Anfāl

His words, Exalted is He:

[8:1] ***...So have full awareness of God, and set things right between you...***

He [Sahl]said:

Having full awareness of God (*taqwā*) means abandoning everything which befalls one [which might impede that awareness]. Among the proprieties (*ādāb*), it refers to the noblest character traits. It means that even if one should be enticed [by reward] (*targhīb*), one does not reveal a secret, and even if one should be intimidated (*tarhīb*), one does not remain on the side of ignorance. Furthermore, full awareness of God is not acceptable except in the one who is a follower of the Prophet ﷺ and the Companions.

His words:

[8:2] ***The believers are those whose hearts tremble [with awe], when God is mentioned...***

He [Sahl] said:

Their [hearts] tremble from the fear of separation (*firāq*), and hence their bodily members humbly submit to God in [His] service (*khidma*).

His words, Exalted is He:

[8:11] ***Remember when He caused drowsiness to overcome you, as a reassurance from Him...***

He [Sahl] said:

Drowsiness (*nuʿās*) descends from the brain while yet the heart remains awake [lit. alive]. Sleep (*nawm*) [only descends] on the heart outwardly.[1] That is the rule (*ḥukm*) [for] sleep. However, the same rule [that applied to the heart] regarding drowsiness [applies to] the spirit (*rūḥ*).[2]

His words:

[8:19] ***If [O disbelievers] you were seeking a judgement, the judgement has now come to you...***

This is because Abū Jahl said on the Day of Badr, 'O God! Give victory to the best of the two religions with You, and the most pleasing of them to You.' Then the verse descended, *If you were seeking a judgement*, meaning, 'If you were seeking to be helped [to victory].'

It has been reported of the Prophet ﷺ that he would seek victory for the sake of the destitute (*ṣaʿālīk*) among the Emigrants, that is, he sought to be helped [to victory] for the sake of the poor (*fuqarāʾ*) among them.[3]

His words:

[8:23] ***For had God known any good in them, He would indeed have made them hear...***

That is, He would have opened the locks of their hearts with faith.

His words:

[8:29] ***...If you fear God, He will grant you a criterion* (furqān)...**

---

1 That is, the heart only appears to be asleep.

2 That is, the spirit remains 'awake' or 'alive'. The affect of sleep on the different parts of the inner make-up of the human being is discussed by Tustarī below in his commentary on 39:42. Again see IT, pp. xxxix–xl.

3 Ibn Ḥanbal, *al-Musnad*, vol. 3, p. 96; Ṭabarānī, *al-Muʿjam al-awsaṭ*, vol. 3, p. 348.

That is, a light in religion, by which [you can distinguish] between truth and falsehood in doubtful matters.

His words:

[8:37] ***In order that God may separate the wicked from the good…***

He [Sahl] said:

Wickedness (*khabīth*) takes different forms: it may be disbelief (*kufr*), hypocrisy (*nifāq*), or grave sins (*kabāʾir*). Likewise goodness (*ṭayyib*) is manifested in different forms: [that is to say], goodness is faith (*īmān*), within which are included the [different] ranks of the prophets (*anbiyāʾ*), veracious (*ṣiddīqūn*), martyrs (*shuhadāʾ*) and virtuous (*ṣāliḥūn*). God, Exalted is He, has informed us that He has separated them from one another [i.e. the good from the bad], and He then ranks the corrupt, one above the other, according to the measure of each of their sins, level upon level, just as He has said: *Verily the hypocrites will be in the lowest level of the Fire* [4:145].

His words:

[8:46] ***…[and lest] your strength* (rīḥ) *fade…***[4]

That is, your power (*dawla*).

His words:

[8:48] ***…He turned his back…***[5]

[That is], whence he came.

His words:

[8:53] ***Because God will never change a grace that He has conferred on a people, until they change that which is in themselves…***

He [Sahl] said:

Verily God most High has privileged the prophets ﷺ and some of the veracious (*ṣiddīqūn*) by acquainting them with the blessings (*anʿām*) He had bestowed upon them, before they disappear.[6] God showed clemency towards them.

His words:

[8:69] ***But [now] enjoy what you took in war, lawful and good…***

He said:

The lawful (*ḥalāl*) is that in which [a person] does not disobey God, and the good (*ṭayyib*) is that in which he does not forget God.

His words:

[8:72] ***Truly those who believed and emigrated and strove with their wealth and their lives in the way of God…***

He [Sahl] said:

All forms of obedience to God involve struggle with the lower self (*jihād al-nafs*). There is no struggle easier than the struggle with swords, and no struggle harder than opposing the lower self.

---

4 These words form part of an exhortation to the believers. The whole verse [8:46] reads: *And obey God and His Messenger, and do not quarrel with one another, lest you falter, and your strength fade; and be patient. Surely God is with the patient.* In *Tafsīr al-Jalālayn*, the word *strength* has been glossed as 'power and dominion'.

5 'He' here is Satan, who had been encouraging the army of the unbelievers on the occasion of the Battle of Badr. However, when he saw the two armies approaching each other, he disappeared whence he had come.

6 That is, they are able to appreciate the ephemeral blessings and graces before they inevitably disappear, perhaps also with an awareness of their transience.

9 Al-Tawba

Sahl said, 'Muḥammad b. Sawwār informed me from Mālik b. Dīnār from Maᶜrūf b. ᶜAlī from al-Ḥasan, from Maḥārib b. Dithār, from Jābir b. ᶜAbd Allāh (may God be pleased with them all), that he reported that when Sūrat Barāʾa was sent down, the Messenger of God ﷺ said, "I was sent to treat people with affability (*mudārāt*)."'[1]

His words, Exalted is He:

[9:2] ***Journey freely in the land…***

> That is, 'Travel through the land and while doing so learn the lessons [from what you see], whilst affirming (*iqrār*) God.'

His words, Exalted is He:

[9:2] ***…[neither bond of] kinship nor treaty…***[2]

> *Ill* means kinship, and '*dhimma*' means a treaty.

His words:

[9:16] ***…an intimate friend* (walīja)*…***[3]

ᶜUmar b. Wāṣil al-ᶜAnbarī said, 'A *walīja* is anything that you cause to enter or become part of something other than itself.'[4] Sahl said:

> This means that they[5] did not become heedless of Him by the inclining of their hearts towards their lower selves.

His words:

[9:29] ***…Nor do they practise the religion of truth…***

> That is, they do not obey [it]. And whoever is under the authority (*sulṭān*) of a man is also upon his religion (*dīn*), just as He has said: *He could not have taken his brother according to the king's law* [12:76], that is, under his authority. Likewise, if the self embraces sincerity (*ikhlāṣ*) before God, Exalted is He, it comes under the rule of the heart (*qalb*), the intellect (*ᶜaql*), the spiritual self (*nafs al-rūḥ*),[6] and the body in obedience, for the remembrance of God, Exalted is He.

---

1 Sūrat Barāʾa is an alternative name for Sūrat al-Tawba, taken from the word with which the *sūra* opens, meaning 'immunity from God and His Messenger', which is discussed in the first few verses. Repentance (*al-tawba*) is the subject of vv. 103, 112 and 118.

2 Referred to in this verse are the hypocrites, who give the appearance of making a pact, but when they gain the upper hand, have no regard either for the pact or for the bonds of kinship.

3 The context is that God is informing the believers that He has yet to know from them which of them has gone through the struggle and not taken any intimate friend besides Him, the Messenger and the believers.

4 According to Lane, *walījatuhum* means: 'an adherent to them', 'one who has entered, become introduced or been included among them'; 'a particular, intimate friend or associate'; or 'one whom a person takes to rely on or have confidence in, not being of his family'.

5 That is, those referred to in the verse as the ones who have been tested by God and found not to have resorted to any other than Him.

6 On *nafs al-rūḥ* and *nafs al-ṭabᶜ* in Tustarī's understanding of the inner make-up of the human being, see above IT, pp. xxxviiiff.

His words:

[9:32] ***They desire to extinguish God's light with their mouths...***

This means that they are intent upon destroying the Qurʾān with the lying of their tongues. *But God insists on bringing His light to its fullness*, that is, He will [fully] manifest His religion, Islam.

His words, Mighty and Majestic is He:

[9:67] ***...They have forgotten God, so He has forgotten them...***

He said:

This means that they have forgotten the bounties (*niʿam*) of God that they had, and He has made them forget to show gratitude (*shukr*) for those bounties.

His words:

[9:71] ***And the believers, both men and women, are protecting friends of one another.***

He said:

[A person's] protective friendship (*muwālāt*) towards the believers is [his] avoiding doing them any harm.

Then he said:

Know that the servant does not attain true faith (*ḥaqīqat al-īmān*) until he becomes as the earth for the servants of God — [it endures] the suffering that they [impose] upon it,[7] and they [derive] benefits from it.

He also said:

The fundamentals (*uṣūl*),[8] in our view, comprise seven things: adherence to the Book of God, following the Messenger of God ﷺ, abiding by what is lawful, refraining from harm [to others], the avoidance of sins, repentance and the observance of the rights [of others].

His words:

[9:73] ***O Prophet, struggle against the disbelievers and the hypocrites...***

He said:

Struggle against your lower self with the sword of opposition! Place upon its [back] the burdens of remorse (*nadam*), and guide it through the desert plains of fear (*khawf*), so that you may turn it back to the path of repentance (*tawba*) and contrition (*ināba*). Repentance is not acceptable except from one who feels perplexed at his plight, grief-stricken at his situation, and confounded in his heart at what has happened to him. God, Exalted is He, has said: *When the earth seemed straightened for them, for all its breadth* [9:118].[9]

His words:

[9:108] ***...In it are men who love to purify themselves...***

He [Sahl] said:

What He means by this purification (*ṭahāra*) is remembrance (*dhikr*) of God, Exalted is He, secretly and openly, and obedience to Him.

---

7 i.e. it passively endures whatever they do to it. According to the MSS (Z515, f. 51b, F638, f. 25a and F3488, f. 225a), an *alif* has been omitted in the published edition, which should read: *adhāhum ʿalayhā*.

8 Complying here with the printed edition and MS Fātiḥ 3488, f. 225a. Z515, f. 51b and F638, f. 25a, however, have *wuṣūl*, which might be translated as 'attainment'.

9 This is a reference to the three men who wavered and failed to support the Prophet on the expedition of Tabūk. Such was their sense of regret afterwards that not only did the earth feel constricted for them but also their own souls. So it was for them until, as the remainder of the verse relates, *they realised that there was no refuge from God except with Him. Then He turned [relenting] to them that they might also turn [in repentance]. Truly God is the Relenting, the Merciful* [9:118]. It is probably because of the emphasis in this verse and the previous one [9:117] on God's relenting towards the believers and those who wavered — and in Arabic the same verb is used (*tāba*) both for God's relenting towards humanity and for their repenting to Him — that the *sūra* is usually given the title al-Tawba. See above, p. 83, n. 1.

His words, Exalted is He:

[9:111] *Indeed God has purchased from the believers their selves and their possessions, so that theirs will be [the reward of] Paradise…*

That is, He has purchased [one's] self from the desires of this world and from all that distracts it from remembrance of Him, so that one's self and wealth may become solely devoted to Him. And how can anyone who has not sold his ephemeral life and fleeting desires to God, live with God, Exalted is He? Moreover how can he live a good life?

Then he said:

God has purchased from the believers their selves… notwithstanding the fact that there is no good in them, and He gave them in exchange that which is entirely good, even though all that is within the two realms of existence belongs to Him. Truly this is out of His utmost graciousness (*luṭf*) and generosity (*karam*) to His believing servants.

Mālik b. Dīnār has related that he passed by a palace under construction and asked the workers about their wages. Each one replied by telling him how much his wage was except for one of them. So he asked him, 'What is your wage?' He replied, 'I don't have a wage.' He asked, 'And why is that?' and he replied, 'It is because I am the servant of the owner of the palace.' Then Mālik ⌜cried out and⌝[10] said, 'O my Lord! How generous you are! All humanity are your servants, yet you have assigned them work to do and promised them a reward for it.'

His words:

[9:112] *Those who repent, those who worship…*

Sahl said:

Of the rights[11] [due to God] in this world there is none whose fulfilment is more incumbent upon humanity than repentance. Indeed it is obligatory [for them] at every moment and instant, and there is no punishment more severe on them than the lack of knowledge of repentance.

He was asked, 'What is repentance?' He answered, 'It is not to forget your sin.' Then he said:

The first thing that a novice is instructed to do is to change his reprehensible actions into praiseworthy ones, which is repentance. [However] his repentance is not complete until he imposes silence upon himself, and his silence is not complete until he forces himself to observe seclusion (*khalwa*). His seclusion is not complete unless his food is lawful. His consumption of what is lawful, however, is not complete unless he fulfils the right of God, Exalted is He, and his fulfilment of what is God's right is not complete unless he guards his bodily members and his heart. Moreover, none of that which we have described is acceptable unless [the novice] seeks God's aid at every stage.

He was asked, 'What is the mark of true repentance?' He replied:

Its mark is that a person gives up what is [rightfully] his in addition to what is not his.

Sahl was [then] asked about a man who repents and renounces a certain sin, but then it occurs to his heart, or he sees it or hears of it and finds sweetness in that vile sin. What is to be done in such a case? He replied:

The feeling of sweetness pertains to [his] nature (*ṭabʿ*) and is not susceptible of change, such that a thing which is loved could become something detestable. However, the heart's determination can be coerced so that he can return to God, Mighty and Majestic is He, and place his dilemma before Him. Then he should force on himself and on his heart a state of rejection [of that sin] which should never leave him, for if he becomes inattentive to that state of rejection for just the blinking of the eye, it is to be feared that he will not remain safe from it.[12]

---

10 The addition of *ṣāḥa* is in all three MSS: Z515, f. 52b, F638, f 25a and F3488, f. 225b.

11 The word *ḥaqq* (pl. *ḥuqūq*) means here the right or just claim which someone can claim from another. In this case, it is the right which God has to claim from human beings.

12 This saying is cited in Makkī, *Qūt al-qulūb*, vol. 1, p. 324.

He [also] said:

Give up all idle talk (*qāl wa qīl*). In this day and age, there are three things which you must do: repent to God, Mighty and Majestic is He, from what you are aware of between yourselves and Him; as far as you are capable, make amends for wrongs done to servants; and when morning comes do not preoccupy yourselves with the evening, nor when evening comes preoccupy yourselves with the morning [that has been or is to come]. Misfortunes have multiplied and the danger is great. So fear God and coerce yourselves into a state of repentance.

His words, Exalted is He:

[9:122] ... *a party from each group should go forth so that they may become learned in religion*

He said:

[That is], in order to learn what is necessary concerning their religion. It has been related from Ḥasan al-Baṣrī that he said, 'The erudite (*faqīh*) is the one who has renounced this world (*zāhid*), who is desirous (*rāghib*) of the Hereafter, and who has insight (*baṣīr*) into religious affairs. Sahl was asked about the words of the Prophet ﷺ, 'Seeking knowledge is an obligation (*farīḍa*) for every Muslim'.[13] He said, 'This refers to the knowledge of [one's] state (*ḥāl*).'

He was asked, 'What is the knowledge of [one's] state?' He replied:

Inwardly it is sincerity (*ikhlāṣ*) and outwardly it is emulation (*iqtidāʾ*).[14] Moreover, unless a person's outward [self] (*ẓāhir*) is leading his inner [self] (*bāṭin*), and his inner self is the perfection (*kamāl*) of his outward self, he will merely be fatiguing his body.[15]

He was asked, 'What is the explanation of this?' He said:

Truly God keeps watch over you, in what you keep secret and what you make known, in your [moments of] movement and stillness,[16] and you are never absent from Him even for the blinking of the eye, just as He has said, *Is He who stands over every soul [observing] what it has earned?* [13:33], and He has said, *There is not a secret consultation between three, but He makes the fourth among them* [58:7]. He has also said, *We are nearer to him than [his] aorta* (ḥabl al-warīd) [50:16]. This is the artery located deep inside the heart, and He has informed us that He is closer to the heart than that artery.[17] If you know this you should feel shame before Him. Furthermore, whenever some craving from the lower self stirs itself in the heart, and [at that moment] the servant remembers that God, Mighty and Majestic is He, is watching over him, and subsequently abandons [that craving], knowledge of his state will enter his heart, such that if what he is granted were to be distributed among the people of Medina, all of them would rejoice at it, and would triumph because of it. Mālik b. Anas ﷺ alluded to this point when he said, 'Knowledge is not just about how much you can relate [from memory] (*riwāya*) but rather knowledge is a light that God places within the heart.'

He [Sahl] was asked, 'How can a man recognise his state (*ḥāl*) and act upon it?'[18] He replied:

When you speak, your state is that of speech, and when you observe silence, your state is that of silence. When you stand your state is that of standing, and when you sit your state is that of

---

13 MS Z515, f. 53a only has 'every Muslim man and woman' (*muslim wa muslima*). The *ḥadīth* is listed in Ṭabarānī, *al-Muʿjam al-awsaṭ*, vol. 2, p. 289 and vol. 6, p. 97; Ṭabarānī, *al-Muʿjam al-ṣaghīr*, vol. 1, pp. 36, 58.

14 On *iqtidāʾ* see above IT, pp. liii–liv.

15 Tustarī is here emphasising the essential interdependence of outer practice and inner realisation in the mystical way.

16 Or, 'in everything that you do'. See above, p. 66, n. 17.

17 Although *ḥabl al-warīd* is customarily translated as 'the jugular vein', according to Lane (under *ḥ-b-l*) it is, 'a name applied to each of the two carotid arteries and sometimes to each of the two external jugular veins'. It is also applied to 'a vein between the windpipe and the two sinews, called the *ʿilbāwān*' or 'a certain vein in the neck' or throat (*ḥalq*). Lane elsewhere states, concerning *warīd* (under *w-r-d*), that it is applied to 'each of the two veins asserted by the Arabs to be from the aorta (*wartīn*)'. Since Tustarī states that the *ḥabl al-warīd* is 'deep inside the heart', he may understand it to be the aorta, this being the artery that issues from the heart. I am grateful to Aziza Spiker, who queried the conventional translation, 'jugular vein'.

18 That is translating *wa'l-ʿamal bihi* as in all three MSS (Z515, f. 53b, F638, f. 25b and F3488, f. 226b), instead of *ʿilm bihi* as

sitting. [To have] knowledge of your state you should see whether it is for God or for other than Him.[19] If it is for God you may settle in it, but if it is for other than Him you should abandon it. This is the act of taking account of oneself (*muḥāsaba*) which ʿUmar ﷺ enjoined when he said, 'Call yourselves to account before you are called to account, and weigh yourselves up before you are weighed up...'[20] Indeed, ʿUmar used to beat his chest while calling himself to account.

in the printed edition.

19 The use of the term *ḥāl* here is interesting, and different from its more technical usage in Sufism, when it denotes a spiritual state. What is being implied in this context is a kind of existential understanding of every action we do.

20 Tirmidhī, *Sunan*, 'Kitāb Ṣifat al-qiyāma'; Ibn Abī Shayba, *al-Muṣannaf*, vol. 7, p. 96.

10 Yūnus

His words, Exalted is He:

[10:2] ***...And give good tidings to those who believe that they have a sure footing with their Lord...***

He [Sahl] said:

> This refers to the preordained mercy that was deposited in Muḥammad ﷺ.

His words:

[10:3] ***...[He is] directing affairs...***

He said:

> He alone decrees every decree, and chooses for the servant what is best for him. Thus God's choice is better for him than his own choice for himself.

Sahl was asked on his death bed: 'What would you like to be shrouded in, where would you like to be buried and who would you like to pray over you after your death?' He replied:

> I [set about] arranging my affairs during my life and for [after my death], but found there was no need for me to attend to them due to the antecedent arrangements (*sābiq tadbīr*) that God, Exalted is He, made for His servant.

His words, Exalted is He:

[10:12] ***If trouble should befall a man, he cries out to Us [in supplication], whether lying on his side...***

He said:

> Supplication (*duʿāʾ*) is freeing oneself (*tabarrī*) of everything save Him, Exalted is He.[1]

His words, Exalted is He:

[10:22] ***...Then they pray to God, becoming sincere [in their] faith in Him...***

He [Sahl] said:

> Sincerity (*ikhlāṣ*) is witnessing (*mushāhada*). The life of the heart is in two things: in its root (*aṣl*) it is faith (*īmān*), and in its branch (*farʿ*) it is sincerity. Sincerity is a matter of great importance and the one who possesses it is wary lest his sincerity should not prevail till death, for actions are [judged] on the ones that come last — *Worship your Lord, until what is certain comes to you* [15:99].[2]

His words, Exalted is He:

[10:25] ***And God summons to the Abode of Peace, and He guides whomsoever He wills to a straight path.***

He [Sahl] said:

> The call (*daʿwa*) is universal (*ʿāmma*), but guidance (*hidāya*) is designated (*khāṣṣa*) [for a certain

---

1 This is another example of an esoteric interpretation springing from a 'keynote'. See above, p. 66, n. 14 and IT, p. xxix. In their Qurʾānic context these words are usually understood to refer to the unbeliever who only turns to God and petitions Him in times of trouble and difficulty, but when he is relieved of the misfortune, carries on as if he had never called out to Him.

2 What is certain being death.

number], and He refers His guidance back to His will (*mashīʾa*), this being what God, Exalted is He, has preordained (*sābiqat al-qadar*).

His words, Exalted is He:

[10:51] ***Is it [only then], when it has come to pass, that you will believe therein? Now when [until now] you have been hastening it on?***

That is, 'You hasten to deny Us and remember other than Us, but when you come before Us and behold with your eyes the punishment We had promised you, [only then] do you believe, when it is [no longer] of [any] benefit [to you].' For [indeed] all people [on that day] will inevitably affirm His oneness in the Hereafter, when the power of [His] essence (*ḥukm al-dhāt*) is made manifest, and all opposing and rival [deities that have been falsely set up] will be renounced, along with the [false] supplications made to them, due to the cessation of doubt and the fear of punishment.

His words, Exalted is He:

[10:58] ***Say: 'In the bounty of God, and in His mercy, in that let them rejoice...'***

That is, in the profession of His oneness and in His Prophet Muḥammad ﷺ, just as He said: *We did not send you except as a mercy to all the worlds* [21:107].

His words, Exalted is He:

[10:62] ***Assuredly God's friends, no fear shall befall them, neither shall they grieve.***

Sahl said:

They are those whom the Messenger of God ﷺ described, saying, 'When they are seen, God is remembered.'[3] They are those who strive in God's cause, who outstrip others in their [journeying] towards Him, and whose actions are constantly in conformity (*muwāfaqa*).[4] *Those are the true believers* [8:4].

And he [Sahl] said:

All goodness comes together in four things, and through these they [believers] become 'Substitutes' (*abdāl*):[5] an empty stomach, seclusion from people, the night vigil, and observing silence.

He was asked why the Substitutes (*abdāl*) are called Substitutes. He answered:

It is because they substitute their spiritual states (*aḥwāl*) [one for another]. They have submitted their bodies to the vigour (*ḥīl*) in their innermost secrets (*asrār*).[6] Then they move from state (*ḥāl*) to state, and from knowledge (*ʿilm*) to knowledge, so that they are constantly increasing in the knowledge of that which is between them and their Lord.

He was asked, 'Who are more excellent, the Mainstays (*awtād*) or the Substitutes (*abdāl*)?' He answered, 'The mainstays.' Then he was asked, 'And how is that?' He replied:

It is because the Mainstays have already arrived and their principles (*arkān*) are well established, whereas the Substitutes move from state to state.

---

3 Ibn Ḥanbal, *al-Musnad*, vol. 6, p. 459; Tirmidhī, *Nawādir al-uṣūl*, vol. 4, pp. 80, 86.

4 That is, in conformity with God's will.

5 According to Sufi tradition, the *abdāl* or *budalāʾ* (pl. of *badal* meaning literally 'substitute'), constitute one degree or rank in the spiritual hierarchy of saints or mystics after the time of the Prophet. They are said to be unknown to the generality of believers, but have a powerful influence in preserving the order of the universe. Sufi literature varies concerning both the different ranks that make up this hierarchy and the numbers within each of these ranks, but one that is generally agreed upon is as follows: at the apex of the hierarchy there is one 'Axis' or 'Pole' (*quṭb*), also known as 'Succour' (*ghawth*), who is the *axis mundi* or spiritual 'pole' of the universe; after the Pole come the two 'Foremost' or 'Assistants' (*imāmān*); below them come five 'Mainstays' (*awtād*) or 'Pillars' or 'Props' (*ʿumud*); then come the seven 'Incomparables' (*afrād*); then the Substitutes (*abdāl*); and so on down to ten ranks in total. The Substitutes in particular are mentioned in a number of *ḥadīths*, for which see: Ibn Ḥanbal, *al-Musnad* (Cairo, 1895), vol 1, p. 112; and Tirmidhī, *Nawādir al-uṣūl*, vol. 1, p. 165; vol. 2, p. 103. For a discussion of this hierarchy see, I. Goldziher, 'Abdāl,' *EI²*, vol. I, p. 94, and J. Chabbi, 'Abdāl' *EIr*, vol. III, pp. 173–4. The Mainstays are also discussed in Tustarī's commentary on 7:33, above.

6 That is, reading *akhrajū abdānahum ʿalāʾl-ḥīl* (MSS Z515, f. 54b, F638, f. 26a and F3488, f. 227b) instead of *ʿan al-ḥīl*, which is in the printed edition.

[On this subject] Sahl also said:

> I have met with one thousand five hundred veracious [servants of God] (*ṣiddīq*) among whom were forty Substitutes (*abdāl*) and seven Mainstays (*awtād*), and I found their way (*ṭarīqa*) and method (*madhhab*) to be the same as that which I follow.

Furthermore, he used to say, 'I am the proof of God (*ḥujjat Allāh*) against you in particular and against the people in general.'

It was [Sahl's] way and his conduct to be full of gratitude and remember [God] a great deal. He was also constant in observing silence and reflection. He would dispute little and was of a generous spirit. He led people through his good character, mercy and compassion for them, and by giving them good counsel. He held fast to the principle[s] (*aṣl*) [of religion] while putting into practice [the rules] that are derived from it (*farʿ*). Truly God filled his heart with light, and invested his speech with wisdom. He was among the best of Substitutes, and if we include him among the Mainstays he was the Axis (*quṭb*) around which the millstone [of the world] revolves.[7] Furthermore, if it were not for the fact that no one can be valued alongside the Companions because of their companionship and witnessing [of the Prophet ﷺ], then one would say that he was as one of them. He lived a praiseworthy life and died as a stranger in Basra, may God have mercy upon him.

There was a man who used to keep Sahl's company called ʿAbd al-Raḥmān b. Aḥmad.[8] One day he said to Sahl, 'O Abū Muḥammad! Sometimes I perform the ablutions for the prayer and the water runs between my fingers and becomes rods of gold and silver.' Then Sahl said:

> O my dear fellow, don't you know that when an infant cries he is given a rattle to distract himself with? So just consider what He is doing.[9]

And he said that he had within his house a room which he called the room for predatory beasts. The beasts would approach Sahl, and he would admit them into that room, offer them hospitality and feed them some meat, and then let them go free.[10]

His words:

[10:109] *And [Muḥammad] follow what is revealed to you, and be steadfast until God gives judgement, for He is the Best of Judges.*

He [Sahl] said:

> God imposed His rules upon people and assisted them in following them by His favour and His omnipotence. Furthermore He directed them to the right guidance (*rushd*) for them with His words, *And follow what is revealed to you, and be steadfast until God gives judgement, for He is the Best of Judges.* To be steadfast in following [what is revealed], is to abandon devising and self management (*tadbīr*), for in this [abandonment] there is now [i.e. in this world] deliverance from the vain caprices (*ruʿūnāt*) of the lower self, and later [i.e. in the next world] salvation from the shame of transgression.

7 On *quṭb* see n. 5 above.

8 Böwering identifies this person as ʿAbd al-Raḥmān b. Aḥmad al-Marwazī, who appears to have been one of three intimate disciples of Tustarī. See *Mystical Vision*, p. 84.

9 What is probably meant is that the disciple should not be amazed by this phenomenon, but rather he should see it as being analogous to a rattle that is given to a child merely to distract him. Thus the disciple should be concentrating on making the ablution, not being distracted by the appearance of the water. We have assumed the subject of the doing to be God, since this may be a test from Him, an example of the divine ruse (*makr*). See above p. 20, n. 47 and 3:8.

10 Regarding Sahl's relationship with wild animals, see above IT, p. xx. See also Tustarī's commentary on 45:13, regarding Shaybān's relationship with a lion and a wolf. Among other Sufis, Abū al-Ḥasan al-Kharaqānī was reputed to have used a lion as a beast of burden and to have tamed snakes. See ʿAṭṭār, *Tadhkirat al-awliyāʾ*, pp. 667–8, and Christiane Tortel, *Paroles d'un Soufie: Abû'l-Ḥasan Kharaqânî* (Paris, 1998), pp. 86–7.

11 Hūd

His words, Exalted is He:

[11:1] ***...then detailed from One Wise, Informed***[1]

That is, He has made clear His promise [of reward] for obedience and His threat of punishment for disobedience and for persistence therein.

His words:

[11:3] ***Ask forgiveness of your Lord, and turn to Him in repentance...***

He said:

Seeking forgiveness (*istighfār*) [entails] the response (*ijāba*), then contrition (*ināba*), then repentance (*tawba*), followed by the seeking of forgiveness. The response is [made] outwardly, the turning [to God] is through the heart, and repentance is through constantly seeking forgiveness for one's deficiency in these.[2] *...He will give you fair enjoyment.* He said, 'Renunciation (*tark*) of creatures (*khalq*) and drawing near (*iqbāl*) to God.'

His words:

[11:15] ***He who desires the life of this world and its adornment, We shall repay them their deeds...***

Whoever aspires by his actions (*ʿamal*)[3] to [attain] something other than God, will be granted by God the reward of his actions in this world, but there will remain nothing for him in the Hereafter. For such a person does not devote his actions purely to God, due to his desire for [having] a position in this world. If he but knew that God has placed the world and its people at the service of those who desire the Hereafter, he would not be ostentatious about his acts.

Sahl was asked, 'What is the hardest thing for the lower self (*nafs*)?' He replied, 'Sincerity (*ikhlāṣ*).' He was asked why this was so, and he said, 'It is because the lower self cannot have a share in it.' He was asked, 'Does ostentation (*riyāʾ*) penetrate the obligatory acts?' He replied:

Yes, it may even penetrate faith, which is at the root of obligatory acts, so that [faith itself] is falsified and becomes hypocrisy. So how then will the acts be? Anyone whose outward conduct is not found fault with by a single person but whose real state in his inner self God knows to be the contrary, is being ostentatious without a doubt.[4]

His words, Exalted is He:

[11:23] ***...and humble themselves before their Lord...***

That is, their hearts were humbled before their Lord, this being [an indication of] fear (*khashiya*). Thus humility is its outward [manifestation] and fear its inner state just as the Messenger ﷺ said, 'If his heart had become humble his bodily members would have been subdued.'[5]

---

1 The first part of this verse reads: *Alif Lām Rā, a Book whose verses have been set out clearly.*

2 A similar saying is cited in Makkī, *Qūt al-qulūb*, vol. 1, p. 335.

3 This correction was made on the basis of all three MSS (Z515, f. 55b, F638, f. 26b and F3488, f. 228b). In the published edition it is *bi-ʿilmihi* instead of *bi-ʿamalihi* in the manuscripts.

4 In other words, a person may appear to be impeccable as regards his outward conduct, but if God knows his inward intentions to be impure, then his conduct amounts to hypocrisy and ostentation.

5 Tirmidhī, *Nawādir al-uṣūl*, vol. 3, p. 210; vol. 4, p. 24.

It was related of Moses ﷺ that he was once castigating the Children of Israel, when a man from amongst them tore his shirt apart. Then God, Exalted is He, inspired Moses to say to him [on behalf of God], 'Do not tear your garment for Me; tear your *heart* for Me!'

His words, Exalted is He:

[11:40] ***...and the oven gushed forth...***[6]

It was an oven of stone, belonging firstly to Adam and then passing on to Noah, and God made the gushing forth of water from it a sign of His punishment.[7] However, He made the gushing forth of the wellsprings of the heart of Muḥammad ﷺ with the lights of knowledge of different kinds a [sign of] mercy for his nation, because God, Exalted is He, honoured him with this honour. For the light of the prophets ﷺ is from his [Muḥammad's] light, the light of the heavenly dominions is from his light and the light of this world and the Hereafter is from his light.[8] Whoever truly desires [God's] love must follow him. God said to His Prophet ﷺ: *Say: 'If you love God, follow me, and God will love you'* [3:31]. Thus has He made love [consist] of following him [the Prophet], and has made the reward for His servants who follow him His love, which is the highest honour (*aʿlā al-karāma*).

It is related on the authority of Abū Mūsā al-Ashʿarī that he said: 'While we were with the Messenger of God ﷺ, he approached us and [turned to] face us as if he wished to tell us something. Then he fell into prostration and we prostrated with him at the beginning of the day until around midday, such that some of us could taste the earth through our noses and we remarked to each other, "The Messenger of God ﷺ has died." But then he raised his head and said, "God is Great!", so we said, "God is Great!". Then someone said to him, "O Messenger of God, we thought you had died and if that had been the case we would not have cared if the sky fell onto the earth." He said, "My beloved, the Angel Gabriel ﷺ came to me and said to me, 'O Muḥammad, your Lord greets you with peace and gives you the choice between a third of your nation entering Paradise and the right to intercession.' As I hoped for more than a third, I chose intercession and then he rose up and I turned to face you and wanted to inform you of it, but he came to me again and said, 'Your Lord greets you with peace and gives you the choice between two thirds of your nation entering Paradise and the right to intercession.' As I hoped for more than two-thirds I chose intercession. Then he rose up and I turned to face you intending to inform you of it, but he came to me again and said to me, 'O Muḥammad, verily you Lord has granted you intercession for two thirds [of your nation] but has not responded to your request regarding the other third.' Upon this I prostrated in gratitude to God, Exalted is He, for what He had granted me."'[9]

Sahl said:

The aspirations (*himam*) of mystics reach the veils, where they stop and knock and are given admission. They enter and offer greetings, upon which He confers upon them His support (*taʾyīd*), and [a list] of exemptions are written for them on a parchment. However, the aspirations of the prophets ﷺ circle around the Throne and are bedecked with lights. Their ranks are raised and they are connected with the Compeller (*al-Jabbār*) who erases their own portions

---

6 According to Thaʿlabī, scholars interpreted *the oven gushed forth* in different ways. ʿAlī b. Abī Ṭālib stated that it meant, 'the dawn arose and filled the morning with light'; Ibn ʿAbbās identified the oven as the surface of the earth, since the Arabs call it 'oven' (*tannūr*). Ḥasan, however, said that it was an oven of stone which had belonged to Adam and was then passed on to Noah. Noah was told that when he saw water gushing from the oven, he should embark with his companions. See Thaʿlabī, *ʿArāʾis al-majālis*, p. 61; trans. Brinner, pp. 95–6. There is a belief among the inhabitants of Iraq that the Masjid of Kufa is the site of the oven, see ʿAlī al-Harawī, *Kitāb al-Ishārāt ilā maʿrifat al-ziyārāt* (Damascus, 1953), p. 78; English trans. J. W. Meri as *A Lonely Wayfarer's Guide to Pilgrimage* (Princeton, 2004), p. 200.

7 This is a reference to Noah's flood.

8 Regarding the light of other prophets being derived from Muḥammad's light, see also Maybudī, *Kashf al-asrār*, vol. 10, p. 202.

9 Al-Ḥākim al-Nīsābūrī, *al-Mustadrak ʿalāʾl-Ṣaḥīḥayn* (Beirut, 1996), vol. 1, pp. 60 and 137; Ibn Ḥanbal, *al-Musnad*, vol. 4, pp. 404 and 410, and vol. 6, pp. 23, 28 and 29.

(*ḥuẓūẓ*),[10] removes their will and makes them [entirely] at His disposal and for Him.

He also said:

> The endmost ranks of the veracious (*ṣiddīqūn*) are the initial states of the prophets ﷺ, and indeed our Prophet ﷺ worshipped God, Exalted is He, in all the states (*aḥwāl*) of the prophets. Furthermore, there is not a leaf among the leaves of the trees in Paradise that does not have the name Muḥammad ﷺ inscribed on it. It is with him that all things were initiated and it is with him that God brought them to a close, and thus he was called the Seal of the Prophets.

His words, Exalted is He:

[11:75] ***For Abraham was forbearing, tender-hearted, and penitent.***

He [Sahl] said:

> God, Exalted is He, gave him [Abraham] a view into the [moments of] activity and repose (*ḥaraka wa sukūn*) of the natural self (*al-nafs al-ṭabīʿiyya*),[11] but He did not give him a view of His knowledge, for he was either effaced from [the awareness of it] or abiding in it,[12] so that neither fear nor hope should leave his soul.[13] Thus, when he remembers it [that knowledge], he sighs, and keeps silent regarding the question of the knowledge of his end (*khātima*), since he has no [power of] choosing (*ikhtiyār*) with God, Mighty and Majestic is He.

Then Sahl said:

> Fear is male and hope is female, and if one iota of the fear of the fearful (*khāʾifūn*) were divided among the inhabitants of the earth, they would all attain eternal happiness by it.

Then he was asked, 'If that is so, how much fear do the fearful have?' He replied, 'It is like a mountain, a mountain!'

His words, Exalted is He:

[11:78] ***…Here are my daughters, they are purer for you…***[14]

> That is, they are more legitimate for you if you marry them, than [your] committing abominable acts.[15]

His words, Exalted is He:

[11:88] ***…And I do not desire to be different from you in what I forbid you to do…***[16]

He [Sahl] said:

> Every possessor of knowledge (*ʿālim*) who has been given knowledge of evil but does not avoid it is not a [true] possessor of knowledge. Similarly, whoever has been given knowledge of the acts of obedience but does not practise them is not a [true] possessor of knowledge.

---

10 That is, whatever pleasure or 'share' for themselves there might be in anything (other than God).

11 Or, 'everything that it does', as explained above, p. 66, n. 17.

12 i.e. subsisting through God's knowledge, that is, wholly in a state of oneness, beyond the duality that implies a knowing subject and object of knowing. Tustarī is here implying the concept of annihilation and subsistence, for which later Sufis would consistently use the terms *fanāʾ* and *baqāʾ*. However here Tustarī is not using these terms but rather the words *maḥw* and *muthbit*. See above, p. 47, n. 36 and IT, p. lix, n. 269.

13 It is common for Sufis to emphasise the need for the seeker to maintain a balance between fear and hope, for which the words usually used are *khawf* and *rajāʾ*. At a certain stage, the aspirant will continually alternate between these states. See for example Qushayrī, *Risāla*, p. 319; ʿAbd Allāh al-Anṣārī, *Ṣad maydān*, text and French translation in Serge de Laugier de Beaurecueil, 'Une ébauche persane des Manāzil as-Sāʾirīn: Le *Kitāb-e Ṣad maydān* de ʿAbdullāh Anṣārī', *Mélanges Islamologues d'Archéologie Orientale* 2 (1954), p. 61 [30], where Anṣārī describes fear and hope as the two wings of certainty (*yaqīn*), or as being the two pans of the scales of faith. Both Qushayrī and Anṣārī refer to the tradition that fear and hope are like the two wings of the bird of faith; unless it has both wings it cannot fly. In his commentary on 17:57 below Tustarī also cites a *ḥadīth* emphasising the need to balance fear and hope.

14 In reference to the Prophet Lot addressing his people.

15 In this case, it refers to homosexuality.

16 These are the words of the prophet Jethro (known in Islam as Shuʿayb), and they are generally understood to mean 'I do not wish to be inconsistent by doing myself what I have forbidden you to do.'

Somebody asked Sahl, 'O Abū Muḥammad, with whom do you instruct me to sit?' He replied, 'With one whose limbs [i.e. bodily actions] will guide you, not his tongue.'

His words, Exalted is He:

[11:91] ***...And were it not for your clan* (raḥṭ), *we would have stoned you...***

He said: 'Muḥammad b. Sawwār related on the authority of Abū ʿAmr b. al-ʿAlāʾ that he said, "A *rahṭ* is a group of people while a *nafr*, is a group of men among whom there are no women."[17]

His words, Exalted is He:

[11:113] ***And do not incline toward the evildoers...***

That is, 'Do not rely on anything regarding your religion except my Sunna.'

17 According to Lane's lexicon, both the *rahṭ* and the *nafr* would comprise between three and ten men.

12 Yūsuf

His words, Exalted is He:

[12:6] ***...And perfect His grace upon you...***

This means, 'By affirming the truth of the dream you had concerning yourself.'[1]

His words, Exalted is He:

[12:18] ***Yet, comely patience!***[2]

He said:

Patience with contentment (*riḍā*).

He was asked, 'What is the sign of this?' He replied, 'It is not to regret what has happened.' Then he was asked, 'How can one attain comeliness of patience (*tajammul bi'l-ṣabr*)? He said:

By knowing that God, Exalted is He, is with you, and by the comfort of the [concomitant sense of] well-being (*bi-rāḥat al-ʿāfiya*). Patience may be compared to a bowl which has patience at the top and honey underneath.[3]

Then he said:

I am amazed at the one who is not patient. How can he not show patience whatever the situation might be (*li'l-ḥāl*), when the Lord of Might says: *Surely God is with the patient* [8:46]?

His words, Exalted is He:

[12:21] ***...Give him an honourable place. Maybe he will be useful to us...***[4]

That is, 'Perhaps he will be an intercessor for us in the Hereafter.'

His words, Exalted is He:

[12:24] ***And she certainly desired him, and he would have desired her [too], had it not been that he saw the proof of his Lord.***

That is, with his natural self (*nafs ṭabīʿiyya*),[5] he desired and inclined towards her, but with his divinely supported and protected self (*nafs al-tawfīq wa'l-ʿiṣma*), he desired to escape from her and oppose her. This means that his Lord protected him, and if it had not been for the protection of his Lord, he would have desired her, inclining towards that to which his lower self called [him]. He was protected by witnessing the proof (*burhān*) of his Lord, Mighty and Majestic is He, this being that the angel Gabriel ﷺ came in the form of Jacob ﷺ biting on his finger, upon which Joseph headed for the door while seeking forgiveness.[6]

---

1 That is to say, that the dream came true.

2 The words said by Jacob when Joseph is taken from him by his brothers, who pretend he has been slain by a wolf.

3 In other words, patience comprises in itself the reward for patience, i.e. the honey, just as the knowledge that God is with us comprises in itself a sense of comfort and well-being.

4 The words said by Potiphar to his wife Zulaykhā after they have purchased Joseph as a slave.

5 It is possible that Tustarī is here referring to what he elsewhere defines as *nafs al-ṭabʿ*. See above, IT, pp. xxxviiiff.

6 An expression frequently used in Islamic literature is that a person 'bites the finger' of amazement, wonder, consternation or, in this case, horror. This is among several traditions relating the nature of *the proof of his Lord* that Joseph saw. See Ṭabarī's commentary on 12:24, for example.

His words, Exalted is He:

[12:42] ***'...Mention me to your lord...'***[7]

He [Sahl] said:

> It has been related that the angel Gabriel ﷺ visited Joseph in prison and said to him, 'O pure one, son of the pure one, verily God, Exalted is He, has honoured me through you and through your forefathers, and He says to you, "Joseph, did you not feel shame before Me for having sought intercession from someone other than Me? By My Might, I am going to make you remain in prison for several years more."' He [Joseph] asked Gabriel, 'Is He pleased with me?' He replied, 'Yes.' So he said, 'Then I do not mind.'
>
> ʿAlī b. Abī Ṭālib ؓ, used to say: 'I and my self are nothing but a shepherd and his flock, each time he gathers them in on one side, they disperse from the other.'

His words, Exalted is He:

[12:53] ***'Yet I do not exculpate my own soul; verily the soul is ever inciting to evil...'***[8]

He [Sahl] said:

> Truly, the [evil-]inciting self (*nafs ammāra*) is lust (*shahwa*), which is the role played by man's [basic] nature (*ṭabʿ*); *'...unless my Lord shows mercy'*, is the role played by the [divine] protection (*ʿiṣma*). The self at peace (*nafs muṭmaʾinna*) is the self of gnosis (*nafs al-maʿrifa*).[9] God, Exalted is He, created the self and made ignorance its nature (*ṭabʿ*) and made desire (*hawā*) the closest thing to it. He also made desire the door by which man's ruin enters.

Sahl was asked about the meaning of [a person's] nature (*ṭabʿ*) and how one might necessarily acquire protection from it. He said:

> Human nature (*ṭabʿ*) comprises four natural dispositions (*ṭabāʾiʿ*): the first is the animal disposition (*ṭabʿ al-bahāʾim*), that of the stomach and genitals; the second is the satanic disposition (*ṭabʿ al-shayāṭīn*), that of play (*laʿb*) and diversion (*lahw*); the third is the sorcerous disposition (*ṭabʿ al-saḥara*), that of delusion (*makr*) and deception (*khidāʿ*); and the fourth is the devilish nature (*ṭabʿ al-abālisa*), that of refusal (*ibāʾ*) and arrogance (*istikbār*). [Divine] protection (*ʿiṣma*) against the animal disposition is through faith (*īmān*). Safety (*salāma*) from the satanic disposition is through glorification (*tasbīḥ*) and sanctification [of God] (*taqdīs*), which is the natural disposition of angels. Safety from the sorcerous disposition is through truthfulness (*ṣidq*), sincere counsel (*naṣīḥa*), equity (*inṣāf*) and graciousness (*tafaḍḍul*). Safety from the devilish nature is through taking refuge (*iltijāʾ*) in God, Exalted is He, by humbly imploring him (*taḍarruʿ*) and crying out to Him (*ṣarākh*). The nature of the intellect (*ʿaql*) is to have knowledge but the nature of the lower self (*nafs*) is ignorance. The natural disposition of [human] nature is [to make] pretentious claims (*daʿwā*).

His words, Exalted is He:

[12:36] ***And there entered the prison with him two [chivalrous] youths*** **(fatayān)...**

He [Sahl] said:

> God, Exalted is He, said *[chivalrous] youths* because neither of them was excessive in his claim.[10] Rather they gave what was theirs over to their companion and for this He called them *fatayān*.

His words, Exalted is He:

[12:52] ***That is so that he may know that I did not betray him behind his back...***[11]

---

7 Said by Joseph to one of his fellow prisoners who was about to be released, *your lord* being a reference to the king.

8 These are words said by Joseph, after the king (on his insistence) has summoned the women of Egypt, who exonerate him. See also p. 96, n. 11 below.

9 For Tustarī's discussion of *nafs muṭmaʾinna* see his commentary on 2:260. On the different levels of the *nafs* again see above, IT, pp. xli–xlii.

10 The verbal root *f-t-w*, from which the word *fatayān* (dual form of sing. *fatā*) is derived, has the meaning 'to be youthful', but also 'to compete with or surpass another in generosity'.

11 These are the words spoken by Joseph, when he sets the condition before interpreting the king's dream, that the king

He [Sahl] said:

[That is], 'I did not breach my contract, nor did I disclose a secret [of his] that was concealed.'

His words, Exalted is He:

[12:67] *...On him I rely...*[12]

He [Sahl] was asked, 'What is the reality of complete trust [in God] (*tawakkul*)? He replied, 'It is to be at ease (*istirsāl*) with whatever God, Exalted is He, wants.' Then he was asked, 'What are the requisites of complete trust?' He said, 'The first is knowledge and its reality is acting [on it].' Then he said:

Truly the person who has complete trust [in God] (*mutawakkil*), when he attains it in reality (*ʿalā'l-ḥaqīqa*), does not eat any food in the knowledge that there is someone who has more of a right to it than himself.[13]

His words, Exalted is He:

[12:88] *...They said, 'O mighty Governor, misfortune has befallen us and our family.'...*[14]

That is, 'O great king', and its inner meaning is: 'O you, the one who has conquered himself, just as God, Exalted is He, has said, *And overpowered me with his words* [38:23], meaning, he conquered me through them.[15]

His words, Exalted is He:

[12:85] *...until you are consumed*[16]

It was related from ʿAlī ﷺ that he said, 'The word *ḥaraḍ* means affliction due to pain in the heart.'

Ibn ʿAbbās ﷺ said, '*Ḥaraḍ* is [severe sickness] close to death. Sahl said:

It means being impaired (*fāsid*) in body and in deed because of grief. His grief was only on account of Joseph's religion and not for the sake of [Joseph] himself, for he knew that if he died upon his religion he would be united with him in the Hereafter that is everlasting, but if he changed his religion they would never be united ever again.[17] It was related from Sufyān that he said, 'Verily when the one bringing good tidings [of Joseph] came to Jacob ﷺ, he asked him, "What was his religion when you left him?" He replied, "It was the religion of submission to God (*islām*)." So Jacob said, "Now the blessing is complete."'

His words, Exalted is He:

[12:86] *...I complain of my anguish and grief only to God...*

That is, 'My anxiety (*hamm*) and sorrow (*ḥuzn*)'.

Sahl said:

Jacob's grief was not over Joseph, but it [his grief] was an expression of the deep emotion (*wajd*) he felt in his heart after being separated from Joseph. For he asked himself, 'How great would

---

should first obtain the truth from the women of Egypt about what happened. The women then exonerate Joseph, while Zulaykhā admits that it was she who tried to seduce him, and that he was truthful.

12 These are words that are said by Jacob when he sends his sons to fetch back Benjamin, whom Joseph has detained in Egypt.

13 i.e. is more in need of it.

14 Joseph's brothers are appealing to him as the person in charge of the storehouse of Egypt on account of the famine they have been suffering in Canaan.

15 The word that has been translated in 12:85 as *mighty Governor*, in the Arabic *ʿazīz*, is variously translated as 'Ruler', 'Court Officer' and 'King'. In order to explain the esoteric significance of the use of the word *ʿazīz* here, Tustarī has drawn on 38:23, in which the words *wa ʿazzanī* have the meaning of 'he overpowered' or 'conquered me'.

16 These are the words of warning spoken by Joseph's brothers to Jacob, on account of the magnitude of his grieving over the absence of Joseph.

17 In other words, Jacob was not grieving for the loss of Joseph's soul, but for the [potential] loss of Joseph's religion. Tustarī is thus, among Sufi commentators, one of the early apologists for Jacob's intense grieving in separation from Joseph. Several of the early comments included in Sulamī's *Ḥaqāʾiq al-tafsīr*, for example, state that Jacob lost his sight because he was grieving for a human being. See A. Keeler, 'Joseph, in Exegesis' *EIr*, vol. xv, fasc. 1.

be the feelings I would experience if I were to be separated from God, Mighty and Majestic is He, when separation from a creature had caused me to act in such a way?' So he complained of his distraction and anguish to God, Exalted is He, and to no one else.

His words, Exalted is He:

[12:80] ***...The most senior of them said...***

That is, in intellect, not age.

His words, Exalted is He:

[12:87] ***...And do not despair of God's [gracious] spirit...***

The best and highest form of service (*khidma*) is waiting for relief (*intiẓār al-faraj*) from God, Exalted is He, as it has been related from Ibn ʿUmar ﷺ that the Prophet ﷺ said: 'Waiting for relief with patience is worship (*ʿibāda*).'[18] The relief for which one waits is of two kinds: one is close (*qarīb*) and the other distant (*baʿīd*). That which is close is in the secret that is between the servant and his Lord. That which is distant relates to [that which is between] people, and whoever looks to [relief that is] far away is veiled from what is close at hand.[19]

His words, Exalted is He:

[12:101] ***'...Take me [in death] in a state of submission [to You], and join me to the virtuous.'***[20]

Sahl said:

This entails three things: asking for what is necessary, manifesting one's poverty, and choosing what is obligatory.[21] What is meant is: 'Let me die as one who has committed his affairs over to You and handed over his concerns to You, so that I have no recourse to my lower self under any condition, and do not resort to managing things [for myself] (*tadbīr*) by means of any secondary cause (*sabab*) whatsoever.

His words, Exalted is He:

[12:106] ***And most of them do not believe in God without ascribing partners [to Him].***

He [Sahl] said:

This is referring to the association [of others with God] (*shirk*) by the self which incites to evil (*nafs ammāra*), as was [indicated] when the Prophet ﷺ said, 'Association [of others with God] (*shirk*) in my nation is more hidden than the creeping of an ant over a stone.'[22] This is the inner meaning of the verse. However, the outer meaning of the verse refers to the fact that the polytheists among the Arabs believe in God, just as He has said, *If you ask them, who created them, they will certainly say 'God'...*[43:87] Even so they are polytheists who believe in some of the messengers but do not believe in others.

His words, Exalted is He:

[12:108] ***I call to God being upon sure knowledge...***

That is, 'I convey the message, but I am not in possession of guidance. The guidance is up to You.'[23]

---

18 Bayhaqī, *Shuʿab al-īmān*, vol. 7, p. 204.

19 The meaning here appears to be that people who look for relief from [other] people, are waiting for relief from afar, whereas the relief that is from God within the innermost secret of the human being is close at hand. People will be veiled from the relief from God that is within them if they look for relief elsewhere.

20 This is part of Joseph's prayer, with which the narration of the story of Joseph in Sūra 12 finishes. Tustarī's comment appears to be referring more generally to prayer (supplication).

21 What Tustarī probably means here is: that we should ask only for what God deems necessary for us; that we should manifest our real situation of poverty and utter neediness for Him; and that we should choose only what is obligatory for us according to the religious law.

22 Nīsābūrī, *al-Mustadrak*, vol. 2, p. 319; Tirmidhī, *Nawādir al-uṣūl*, vol. 4, p. 147; ʿAbd al-ʿAẓīm al-Mundhirī, *al-Targhīb wa'l-tarhīb* (Beirut, 1996), vol. 4, p. 16.

23 That is, I am not in control of it.

Sahl was asked about the words of the Prophet ﷺ: 'The effort of a striving person cannot avail him against You.' He said:

> Whoever is assiduous in his quest, but finds his assiduity (*jidd*) is met by an impediment (*manʿ*) from You, will not be benefitted by striving in his quest.

And he said:

> For sure, the inner truth [or secret, *sirr*] has not been revealed to people, for if it were disclosed to them then they would have perceived it. Nor have they witnessed [it], for if they had witnessed it, the whole matter would be over, and that is a grave matter.[24]

Then he [Sahl] said:

> The People of 'There is no God but God' are many but the sincere among them are few. But God knows best.

24 This saying recalls one of the statements included in Ibn al-Farrāʾ's refutation of the Sālimiyya, for which see above, IT, p. xxii, n. 72.

13 Al-Raʿd

His words, Exalted is He:

[13:11] ***For him are attendants* (muʿaqqibāt) *in front of him and behind him, guarding him by God's command…***

The meaning of *muʿaqqibāt* is the angels of the night and day, which come one after the other in succession.[1] *Guarding him by God's command…*, that is, [preserving] all the good and evil things that He has determined for His servant.[2] Furthermore, they bear witness for [the servant] with fidelity (*wafāʾ*), and against him with severity (*jafāʾ*) on the Day of Resurrection.

His words, Exalted is He:

[13:12] ***It is He that shows you the lightning [inspiring] fear and hope…***

He [Sahl] said:

The following saying is related from Ibn ʿAbbās ﷺ: 'Thunder is an angel and it is his voice that you hear.[3] As for the lightning, it is a whip of light by which the angel drives the clouds.' Mujāhid also said this. It is reported that ʿAlī b. Abī Ṭālib ﷺ said: 'Lightning is that with which the angels drive [the clouds] (*makhārīq*), and thunder is the voice of an angel.' Qatāda said: 'Thunder is the sound of the clouds.'

His words, Exalted is He:

[13:13] ***And the thunder proclaims His praise, and so too the angels are in awe of Him…***

Thus does He make special mention of the angels. ʿIkrima said: 'Thunder is an angel who has been put in charge of the clouds; he drives them along just as a camel herder would do his camels.'

Kaʿb reported from ʿUmar ﷺ that he said, 'I heard the Messenger of God ﷺ say: "Truly, God creates clouds so they speak with the most excellent speech and laugh with a most excellent laugh. Their speech is thunder and their laughter is lightning."' Abū Bakr said that he asked him ﷺ, 'What would you say regarding a day on which there is a heavy downpour and the sound of the thunder is violent?' He replied, 'This is a report of God's good pleasure (*riḍā*), Mighty and Majestic is He, so how must be the report of His wrath (*ghaḍab*). Let us seek refuge in God from His wrath.'

His words, Exalted is He:

[13:28] ***…Truly, it is in the remembrance of God that hearts find peace.***

[In] remembrance (*dhikr*) with knowledge (*ʿilm*) there is tranquil repose (*sukūn*), and [in] remembrance with intellect (*ʿaql*) there is profound peace (*ṭumaʾnīna*).[4]

---

1 Thus the word *muʿaqqibāt* is related to the idea of one angel's 'watch' succeeding the other as day succeeds night and night day (see Lane regarding meanings of the root *ʿ-q-b*). On angels according to Islamic tradition, see D. B. Macdonald and W. Madelung, 'Malāʾika', *EI*², vol. VI, p. 216.

2 Perhaps in the sense that they administer what is conferred on them by Isrāfīl from the Guarded Tablet (*lawḥ maḥfūẓ*). For which see above IC, p. 5 and n. 22.

3 The MSS Z515, f. 60b and F3488, f. 233a have *yasmaʿūna*, whereas F638, f. 28b and the printed edition have *tasmaʿūna*.

4 As was stated above (p. 30, n. 92), the word *ṭumaʾnīna* or *iṭmiʾnān* has the meaning of a calmness and tranquillity which is associated with a deep sense of confidence, reassurance and trust. In the context of 2:260, it was discussed regarding Abraham's request for his heart to find reassurance through certainty. On Tustarī's view of *ʿaql*, see IT, p. xlv.

He [Sahl] was asked, 'And how is that?' He replied:

> If a servant is maintaining [true] obedience to God, he will be in a state of remembrance (*dhākir*), but when something occurs to his mind, he will be in a state of severance (*qāṭiʿ*) [from God]. If he is involved in an act [motivated by] his lower self, and something comes to his heart which guides him to remembrance and obedience, this is the role played by the intellect (*mawḍiʿ al-ʿaql*).

Then he said:

> Anyone who claims to practise remembrance falls into one of two types. There are those whom the fear of God, Mighty and Majestic is He, never leaves, but who also experience love (*ḥubb*) and fervour (*nashāṭ*) in their hearts. They are truly people of remembrance and they live for God, the Hereafter, knowledge and the Sunna. Then there are those who claim to be in a state of fervour, joy and happiness in every situation. They are living for the enemy, this world, ignorance, and innovation and they are the worst of people.

His words, Exalted is He:

[13:36] ***...Say, 'I have been commanded to worship God, and not to associate anything with Him...'***

Sahl was asked: 'When does the servant prove true in the station of servanthood (*ʿubūdiyya*)?' He replied:

> When he gives up his own management (*tadbīr*) and becomes satisfied with the management of God, Exalted is He, for him.[5]

His words, Exalted is He:

[13:39] ***God erases whatever He will and He fixes whatever He will, and with Him is the Mother of the Book.***

He [Sahl] said:

> God erases what He wills in the realm of [secondary] causes (*asbāb*), and fixes what is decreed. *And with Him is the Mother of the Book.* It is the irrevocable decree (*qaḍā*) to which nothing may be added and from which nothing may be taken away.[6]

His words, Exalted is He:

[13:43] ***And he who possesses knowledge of the Book.***

Sahl said:

> The Book is noble (*ʿazīz*), and knowledge of the Book is even nobler, as is acting by it [that knowledge]. Action is noble, but sincerity in action is nobler still. Sincerity (*ikhlāṣ*) is noble, but witnessing (*mushāhada*) in [the state of] sincerity is nobler. Being in conformity (*muwāfaqa*)[7] is noble, but intimacy (*uns*) in conformity is even nobler. Intimacy is noble, but the proprieties (*ādāb*) which are appropriate to intimacy are nobler still.[8] And God, Transcendent and Exalted is He, knows best.

---

5 On the danger of relying on one's own devising, planning and management of things (*tadbīr*), see Tustarī's commentary on 2:30, 3:155 and 7:20 above. For a broader discussion of this doctrine in Tustarī's *Tafsīr*, see IT, pp. xxxiv–xxxv.

6 On the Mother of the Book, see above Tustarī's commentary on 2:235 and p. 27, n. 84.

7 That is according to all three MSS: Z515, f. 61a, F638, f. 29a and F3488, f. 233b, as opposed to *murāfaqa* in the printed edition.

8 What may be meant here is that the person who is in a state of intimacy [with God] does not lose their sense of awe at His transcendence and glory. See the comment on 13:28 above concerning those whom the fear of God never leaves, even though they have love and longing in their hearts, and whom Tustarī sees as truly being the people of remembrance.

14 Ibrāhīm

His words, Exalted is He:

[14:7] ***If you are thankful then assuredly I will give you more...***

He [Sahl] said:

> Gratitude (*shukr*) for knowledge is acting (*ʿamal*) [on this knowledge].[1] Gratitude for acting [on this knowledge] increases [one's] knowledge.[2] This is how it always is, and this is its condition.

He also said:

> Gratitude is that you should acknowledge [that] increase.[3] Otherwise gratitude is flawed. The true realisation of weakness (*ḥaqīqat al-ʿajz*) is in acknowledging it. It is reported that David, ﷺ said, 'How can I thank You when through my gratitude I receive renewed bounty from You?' God replied, 'Now you have shown true gratitude towards me.'[4]

His words, Exalted is He:

[14:11] ***...But God favours whomever He will of His servants...***

> That is, [He favours them] with [the ability to] recite (*tilāwa*) His Book and understand (*fahm*) it.

His words, Exalted is He:

[14:19] ***Have you not seen that God created the heavens and Earth in truth?...***

He [Sahl] said:

> He created all things through His omnipotence (*qudra*), adorned them through His knowledge (*ʿilm*), and governed them through His wisdom (*ḥikma*). Thus, to the one who contemplates the Creator through the creation, the wonders of the creation will become apparent. But to the one who contemplates the creation through the Creator, the traces of His omnipotence, the lights of His wisdom and the extent and profundity (*balīgh*) of His workmanship (*ṣanʿa*) will be unveiled.

His words, Exalted is He:

[14:25] ***It produces its fruit every season* (ḥīn), *by leave of its Lord...***

He [Abū Bakr al-Sijzī] said, 'Ibn al-Musayyib used to say the word *ḥīn* is six months. A man posed the question: "I have sworn an oath that my wife will not visit her family for a *ḥīn*. So what is a *ḥīn*?" Saʿd said, "The *ḥīn* lasts from the time that the date palm flowers until the time that its dates

---

1 Lit. 'Gratitude for knowledge is action'. That is, either that gratitude is manifested by our acting according to our knowledge, or that by having gratitude we are granted 'gratitude's increase' through the ability to act according to our knowledge.

2 That is, gratitude for having acted according to our knowledge, which is only by the grace of God. This statement recalls the tradition that whoever acts according to their knowledge will be given knowledge that they did not have, a tradition which is cited by Makkī in his *Qūt al-qulūb*, vol. 1, p. 217.

3 Translating *al-shukr an tarā al-mazīd* according to all three MSS Z515, f. 61b, F638, f. 29a and F3488, f. 233b, instead of *al-shukr an turīda'l-mazīd*. The former seems more plausible in the context. It is worth bearing in mind that the word *raʾā* can have the meaning of seeing in the sense of experiencing as well as seeing in the sense of recognising, acknowledging.

4 David's recognition that his state of gratitude is necessarily accompanied by increase thus demonstrates both his true gratitude, and his true awareness of humanity's incapacity to experience or express gratitude that is free of God's favour and infinite bounty.

ripen, or from the time that its dates ripen until it blossoms." Ibn ʿAbbās ﷺ said, "*Kulla ḥīn* means morning and night." He is of the same view as Sahl Ibn ʿAbd Allāh who said, "God coined this similitude referring to the people who have gnosis (*maʿrifa*) of God with regard to their performing His obligations night and day.'"

Sahl was asked about the meaning of His words:

[14:24] ***Have you not seen how God has coined a similitude? A goodly saying is as a goodly tree; its roots set firm and its branches in heaven.***

He replied:

> It was related from Ibn ʿAbbās ﷺ that the Prophet ﷺ went out to his Companions while they were discussing the 'goodly tree', and he ﷺ said: 'That is the believer whose root is in the earth and whose branch is in heaven.' This means that his works are raised to the heavens and accepted. This is the similitude that God coined for the believer and the disbeliever. So He said, *A goodly saying*, that is, a saying of sincerity (*ikhlāṣ*), *is as a goodly tree*, that is, the date palm; *its roots set firm and its branches in heaven,* that is, its branches rise up to heaven. Likewise the root of the works of a believer are in the saying [which attests to] God's oneness (*kalimat al-tawḥīd*), which is a firm root whose branches, his works, are raised up to the heavens and accepted, unless there is some deficiency or ill-effect (*iḥdāth*) in them. However, even then the root of his actions, namely the saying which attests to God's oneness, is not removed, just as the winds shake the branches of the date palm, but its root remains firmly in place.
>
> He likened the actions of a disbeliever to a foul tree (*shajara khabītha*), saying *but an evil saying is as a bad tree* [14:26], meaning the colocynth tree (*ḥanẓal*). It is the foulest on the earth, for it has no roots at all beneath it. Just so is disbelief and hypocrisy, which have no endurance in the Hereafter. Thus, in the treasure houses of God, there is nothing greater than the attestation of God's oneness (*tawḥīd*).

Sahl was asked about the meaning of 'There is no god save God' (*lā ilāha illā'Llāh*). He said: 'There is no bestower of benefit (*nāfiʿ*) and no defender (*dāfiʿ*) except God, Exalted is He.'

He was asked about *islām*, *īmān* and *iḥsān*.[5] He answered:

> *Islām* is the law (*ḥukm*), *īmān* is the bond [with God] (*waṣl*) and *iḥsān* is the reward (*thawāb*); and for that reward there is a reward. *Islām* is the affirmation (*iqrār*), and that is outward, *īmān* pertains to the unseen; and *iḥsān* is devotion (*taʿabbud*) — or he might have said: *īmān* is certainty (*yaqīn*).

He [Sahl] was also asked about the code of laws of Islam and he said:

> The scholars have spoken about it, and at great length too. However it can be summarised in two precepts (*kalimatān*): *And take whatever the Messenger gives you, and abstain from whatever he forbids you* [59:7].

Then he said:

> It can be summarised in one precept: *Whoever obeys the Messenger verily obeys God* [4:80].

His words, Exalted is He:

[14:34] ***...If you tried to enumerate God's favour[s] you could never calculate them...***

> due to the fact that He has made the Emissary the most elevated, and the greatest mediator (*wāsiṭa*) between you and Him.

5 The three levels of *islām*, *īmān* and *iḥsān* are raised in the so-called 'Ḥadīth of Gabriel' (*ḥadīth Jibrīl*). On this *ḥadīth* see above IT, p. lviii, n. 265.

15 Al-Ḥijr

His words, Exalted is He:

[15:3] ***Leave them to eat and enjoy [themselves]. Let them be diverted by [false] hope; for they will come to know.***

He [Sahl] said:

> If four [traits] come together in a servant, it will be said to him, 'Truly, you will not attain anything in this affair':[1] if he likes to eat tasty food, dress in fine clothes, see his command executed and his possessions increase. Of such a one it will be said, 'Alas, this is the one who was cut off from God, Exalted is He, by the creation.' It has been related that God revealed to David ﷺ the following: 'Caution and warn your companions about the gratification [lit. consuming, *akl*] of one's carnal desires (*shahawāt*), for verily if hearts are attached to the desires of this world, their intellects (*ʿuqūl*) will be veiled from Me.'[2]

Sahl [then] said:

> Hope (*amal*) is the soil of every transgression (*maʿṣiya*); cupidity (*ḥirṣ*) is the seed of every transgression, and procrastination (*taswīf*) is the water of every transgression. Strength (*qudra*) is the soil of every act of obedience (*ṭāʿa*), certainty (*yaqīn*) is the seed of every act of obedience and action (*ʿamal*) is the water of every act of obedience.

He [probably Abū Bakr al-Sijzī] said:

> Sahl used to intensify his ecstasy (*wajd*) for seventy days, during which he would not eat anything, while he would order his companions to eat meat once a week so that they would not become too weak for worship. However for him, when he ate he would become weak, and when he became hungry he would gain in strength. He would sweat during the severe cold of winter while wearing only one shirt. If they asked him a question on knowledge he would say, 'Don't ask me questions, for you cannot benefit from my speech at this time.' ʿAbbās b. ʿIṣām came one day while Sahl was saying, 'For thirty years I have been speaking to God while people imagine that I'm speaking to them.'[3]

His words, Exalted is He:

[15:40] ***[All] except those servants of Yours who are sincerely devoted to You. He [Sahl] said:***

> All people are dead, except the learned (*ʿulamāʾ*) among them; all the learned are asleep, except those among them who act; all those who act are deluded, except the sincere (*mukhliṣūn*) among them, and the sincere are in great danger.[4]

---

1 i.e. in the spiritual path.

2 This saying appears in Iṣfahānī, *Ḥilyat al-awliyāʾ*, vol. 5, p. 382.

3 In his *Mathnavī-yi maʿnavī*, Rūmī attributes a similar saying to the third/ninth-century mystic Abū Yazīd al-Bisṭāmī (commonly referred to in the Persian form of his name as Bāyazīd Basṭāmī): 'During all these years, I have never spoken to any creature or heard any creature speak to me; but people fancy (*pindārand*) that I am speaking to them, because they do not see the Great Speaker, of whom they in relation to me are only the echo.' See Jalāl al-Dīn Rūmī, *Mathnavī-yi maʿnavī*, Bk. 5, title preceding line 1683, trans. Reynold A. Nicholson. The saying appears in a different form attributed to Bāyazīd in Maybudī's *Kashf al-asrār*, vol. 8, p. 520: 'Bāyazīd said, "For forty years I have not spoken to people; whatever I said was to God, and whatever I heard was from God."'

4 Maybudī provides some sort of explanation for this saying: *al-mukhliṣūna ʿalā khaṭarin ʿaẓīmin*, in a passage in which

His words, Exalted is He:

[15:72] ***…In their drunkenness they were bewildered.***

That is, in their ignorance (*jahl*) and error (*ḍalāla*) they disobey. Know that all acts of disobedience may be attributed to ignorance, and [all] ignorance may be attributed to intoxication [with the world]. It is said that it [the world] is just like [an] intoxicating drink (*muskir*).

His words, Exalted is He:

[15:75] ***Indeed, in that there are signs for those who take note*** **(mutawassimīn).**

He [Sahl] said:

That is, those of spiritual perception (*mutafarrisīn*). Indeed, it was related from Abū Saʿīd al-Khuḍrī ‹› that the Prophet ‹› said: 'Beware of the spiritual perception (*firāsa*) of the believer, for verily he sees with the light of God.' Then he recited, '*Indeed in that there are signs for those who take note*.'[5] His meaning was those who can see into (*mutafarrisūn*) the secrets (*sarāʾir*), and an example of this is when ʿUmar ‹› said to Sāriya: 'The mountain, the mountain!'[6]

His words, Exalted is He:

[15:85] ***…So be forgiving with gracious forgiveness.***

He [Abū Bakr al-Sijzī] said, 'Muḥammad b. Ḥanafiyya related from ʿAlī ‹› that regarding His words, *So be forgiving with gracious forgiveness*, he said: "It is contentment (*riḍā*) without reproval (*ʿitāb*)."' And Sahl said:

[One should be] without resentment (*ḥiqd*) or censure (*tawbīkh*) after forgiving someone; this is to overlook [someone's misdeeds] graciously (*iʿrāḍ jamīl*).

His words, Exalted is He:

[15:91] ***Those who have reduced the Recitation*** **(Qurʾān)** ***to parts.***

He [Sahl] said:

The outward meaning of the verse is as the commentators have explained.[7] However, its inner meaning concerns the rules (*aḥkām*) that God, Exalted is He, sent down regarding our hearing, sight and heart[s] (*fuʾād*), [referred to] in His words, Exalted is He: *Indeed, the hearing, the sight and the heart, each of these it will be asked* [17:36]. Thus, they turned away from acting by it, inclining towards the demands of their natural self (*nafs al-ṭabʿ*).[8]

His words, Exalted is He:

[15:92] ***By your Lord, We will question them all,***

---

he contrasts those who are *mukhliṣ* (the active participle), i.e. purifying themselves, and those who are *mukhlaṣ* (the passive participle), i.e. those who are liberated [from themselves by God], and he compares the situation of the former to the one who is in *sulūk* (making his way) and the latter to the one who is in *jadhb* (or *jadhba*) drawn by a rapture from God. As long as a person is making their own way, and not freed from themselves, they are in great danger. See Maybudī, *Kashf al-asrār*, vol. 6, p. 62, and for an explanation of this doctrine, Keeler, *Sufi Hermeneutics*, pp. 219–23.

5 Tirmidhī, *Nawādir al-uṣūl*, vol. 3, p. 86; Tirmidhī, *Sunan*, 'Kitāb Tafsīr al-Qurʾān'; Ṭabarānī, *al-Muʿjam al-awsaṭ*, vol. 3, p. 312 and vol. 8, p. 23. *Firāsa* often manifests itself as a form of 'physiognomy', the ability to understand a person's feelings or disposition from their outward appearance — the Sufi shaykh's being a 'spy of hearts'. But it may also have the meaning of being able to perceive things over long distances, as will be seen in the example Tustarī cites below. On *firāsa*, see also Tustarī's commentary on 7:46 and p. 73, n. 12.

6 According to tradition, ʿUmar b. al-Khaṭṭāb was delivering the sermon at Friday prayer, and was able to perceive great danger facing the commander Sāriya, who was leading the Muslim army thousands of miles away in Persia: the enemy were about to assault them from behind the mountain, so he cried out, 'O Sāriya, the mountain, the mountain!'

7 The word *qurʾān* here is understood by commentators to refer to the revelations of the Christians and Jews, which were recited out loud as was the Qurʾān. According to traditions cited in the commentary on 15:91 in Ṭabarī's *Jāmiʿ al-bayān*, they (specified either as People of the Book, or as Christians and Jews) divided the scripture in parts, believing in some and disbelieving in others.

8 Thus they selected from the scripture what they wanted, and followed only that which suited their lower desires. We have already seen mention of the natural self (as *nafs al-ṭabʿ*, *nafs ṭabīʿiyya* or *nafs al-jibilla*) in Tustarī's commentary on 2.30, 4:36, 4:47, 7:187, 11:75, 12:24 and 15:91; and of the spiritual self (*nafs al-rūḥ*) in his commentary on 9:29. He discusses the respective roles of these two aspects of the self later in the *Tafsīr*.

He said:

In this verse there is specificity (*khuṣūṣ*) [within the *all*]. For indeed there are among this nation (*umma*) those who are gathered up from their graves [and taken] directly to Paradise, who do not attend the reckoning (*ḥisāb*), or experience any of the horrors [of the day]. They are those of whom God, Exalted is He, says, *they will be kept away from it* [21:101].[9] And indeed the Prophet ﷺ said: 'Verily, the friends of God (*awliyāʾ Allāh*) leave their graves for Paradise and they do not stop for the reckoning, nor do they fear the length of that day. They are the first to reach Paradise. *God is well-pleased with them and they are well-pleased with Him. That is the great triumph* [5:119].'

His words, Exalted is He:

[15:94] *So, proclaim what you have been commanded…*

That is, 'Recite the Qurʾān openly in the prayer, as We have revealed it to you.'

He was asked: 'What is revelation (*waḥy*)?' He said:

It is clandestine [speech] (*mastūr*).[10] God has said, Exalted is He: *They suggest alluring words to each other* [6:112], that is, they confide in one another. It can also carry the meaning of inspiration (*ilhām*), just as when God, Exalted is He, says: *And your Lord revealed to the bee* [16:68], meaning: He gave it inspiration.[11]

His words:

[15:97, 98] *And verily We know that your heart is [at times] oppressed by what they say,* ۞ *But celebrate the glory of your Lord…*

That is, 'Pray to God, Exalted is He, and remember Him', for it is as if God, Exalted is He, had said to him: 'If your heart is weighed down because of your proximity to the disbelievers and the calumny of that which they are ascribing to Us in the way of adversaries, rivals and partners through their ignorance and envy, then return to the state of witnessing Us (*mushāhada*) and proximity to Us (*qurb*) through remembering Us, truly it is with Us that you have proximity, and it is in remembering and witnessing Us that your happiness [lies]. Furthermore, have forbearance with this [suffering], for in it [that forbearance] is My good pleasure (*riḍā*).[12]

It was related that Moses ﷺ said: 'O my Lord! Guide me to an action by which I will gain Your good pleasure.'

He continued:

Then God sent the revelation to him: 'O son of ʿImrān, truly My good pleasure is in [subjecting you to] what you detest, [but] you will not be able to bear that.'

He then said:

Then Moses ﷺ fell down in prostration, weeping and said: 'O Lord! You privileged me with [hearing] Your speech, for You did not speak to any human being before me, yet You have not guided me to an action by which I can gain Your good pleasure.' Then God, Exalted is He, revealed to him saying: 'Verily My good pleasure is in your contentment with My decree (*riḍāʾī fī riḍāka bi-qaḍāʾī*).'

9 The whole of this verse reads: *Indeed those to whom [the promise of] the best reward went beforehand from Us, they will be kept away from it.*

10 i.e. concealed from all save those who are designated to receive it.

11 On *waḥy*, see A. J. Wensinck. 'Waḥy,' *EI²*, vol. xi, p. 53; and on *ilhām*, see D. B. Macdonald, 'Ilhām', *EI²*, vol. iii, p. 1119.

12 That is, translating *riḍāʾī fīhi* according to all three MSS: Z515, f. 64b, F638, f. 30a and F3488, f. 236b, instead of *riḍāʾī fīka* in the published edition.

16 Al-Naḥl

He was asked about His words, Exalted is He:

[16:8] ***...And He creates what you do not know [about].***

He said:

Regarding the outward meaning of the verse, it is as Ibn ʿAbbās ﷺ related, that the Prophet ﷺ said: 'Among the things which God, Exalted is He, has created is an earth (*arḍ*) made from white pearl with a length of a thousand years and a width of a thousand years.[1] There is a mountain on it made of red ruby and that planet is surrounded by a sky. On it there is an angel who has filled its space from East to West, who has 660,000 heads, each head having 660,000 mouths and each mouth having 660,000 tongues, and each of these tongues praises God, Exalted is He, 660,000 times a day. When the Day of Resurrection arrives he [that angel] will behold the greatness (*ʿaẓama*) of God, Exalted is He, and say: "By Your might and majesty, I have not worshipped You as You deserve to be worshipped."' God has said, Exalted is He: *And He creates what you do not know [about].* The inner meaning of these words [is that] God, glorified be His majesty, has taught you to restrain yourself when your intellect (*ʿaql*) fails to grasp the effects of [His] creation and the multifarious dimensions of [His] knowledge (*funūn al-ʿilm*), so that it [your intellect] does not meet them with denial (*inkār*),[2] for He has created what you do not know about, neither you nor anyone else among His creatures, except those whom God has taught, Mighty and Majestic is He.[3]

He was asked about His words:

[16:11, 12] ***...and all kinds of fruit...❁ [And He disposed for you the night and the day and the sun and the moon and the stars.] Surely in that there are signs...***

He said:

This is because the crops [mentioned] are of one species [i.e. fruit], whereas the night and day are two kinds, and likewise are the sun and moon. And He said: *...signs in this for people who understand* (yaʿqilūn) [16:12]. Know that God, Exalted is He, when He wished to make His knowledge apparent, deposited His knowledge in the intellect (*ʿaql*). Then He ruled that no one could have access to any of it [His knowledge] except through the intellect. Thus whoever has been deprived of his intellect has also been deprived of knowledge.[4]

His words:

[16:21] ***They are dead, not living, and they are not aware...***

Sahl said:

God, Exalted is He, created all creatures. Then He brought them to life by the name (*ism*) of

---

1 Presumably this indicates that it would take a thousand years to go from one end to the other and the same time to go across it.

2 According to MS F638, f. 30a it is *an tuqābilahu inkāran* meaning that you should restrain *yourself* from meeting this with denial.

3 See above the commentary on 3:7 regarding different kinds of knowledge granted by God.

4 Tustarī's teachings concerning knowledge and the role of the intellect are discussed above in IT, pp. xlivff.

life.[5] Then He caused them to die by their ignorance of themselves. Those who live through knowledge are the living; otherwise they are dead through their ignorance.

His words, Exalted is He:

[16:36] ***And verily We sent forth among every community a messenger, [to say] 'Worship God...'***

He said:

Worship (*ʿibāda*) is the adornment of mystics (*ʿārifūn*). Furthermore, the best that one who is knowledgeable can do in the fields of worship [or servanthood, *ʿubūdiyya*] and service (*khidma*) is to give up that which is his [right] (*mā lahu*) for that which is his duty (*mā ʿalayhi*).[6]

His words:

[16:53] ***Whatever grace you have, it is from God. Then when misfortune befalls you, to Him you cry for help.***

Sahl said:

If God put to task the bearers of the Throne, and the angels below them [in rank], along with the prophets and messengers, concerning something they had disregarded among the blessings that He had bestowed upon them, He would punish [even] them for that, for God is not unjust.

Sahl was asked: 'What does God do with His servant when He loves him?' He said:

He inspires him to seek forgiveness for his shortcomings and show gratitude for blessings he has received. Truly, they desired with a [wholehearted] intention that they should come to know of the blessings that God, Exalted is He, had bestowed on them, that [their state of] gratitude might endure, and the increase [resulting from that gratitude] might continue.[7]

[16:53] ***...Then when misfortune befalls you, to Him you cry for help.***

That is, to Him alone do you call in times of deprivation (*faqr*) and affliction (*balāʾ*). [Moreover] this may [itself] be a blessing from God upon you, for if He so wished He could have afflicted you with something severer than that, so in comparison to a severer affliction, it is a blessing, for [under a severer affliction] they would recoil in fear from it, and neither exercise patience (*ṣabr*) nor show gratitude.

It came to our knowledge that God, Exalted is He, revealed to David ﷺ the words: 'Be patient with the provisions (*maʾūna*) you have [from Me], and you will be granted help (*maʿūna*) from Me'.[8]

His words, Exalted is He:

[16:55] ***...So enjoy, for soon you will know.***

He said:

This is a promise from God, Exalted is He, to the disbelievers of Mecca that for their denial, in spite of the blessings that God had bestowed upon them in this world, they will come to know the penalty for that [disbelief] in the Hereafter. This verse is also a severe warning to those who are heedless (*ghāfilūn*), in accordance with the saying of the Messenger ﷺ: 'Whoever gratifies his insatiable desire (*nahma*) in this world, will, in the Hereafter, be separated from [the object

---

5 Here Tustarī is alluding to the power of the divine word, as when it is said in 36:82, *His command, when He wills a thing, is just to say to it 'Be' and it is.* There may also be in this comment an indication of the connection between the knowledge of things and their names, as is already indicated in 2:31: *And He taught Adam the names of things, all of them*, which commentators have usually understood to mean 'He was taught the knowledge of things', and also the connection between knowledge and life, as indicated by the next sentence. The power of the divine word is also discussed in Tustarī's *Risālat al-ḥurūf*.

6 Compare Tustarī's recommendation that we should give up that which is rightfully ours as well as that which is not, in his commentary on 9:112.

7 See the comment on 14:7 above.

8 Thus patience, which is often associated with gratitude, also brings increase. Again, see above, the commentary on 14:7 regarding gratitude's increase.

of] his desire. For that which was legitimate, there will be an accounting (*ḥisāb*), and for that which was forbidden, there will be punishment (*ʿiqāb*).'[9] Indeed, the believers are made to account for what they enjoyed legitimately in excess of their needs. Whoever takes of what is legitimate [only] that which suffices him, falls under the category mentioned by the Prophet ﷺ when he said, 'Worldliness is not in the consumption of a piece of dry bread by which a person abates his hunger, a garment by which he covers his private parts and carries out what is legally binding upon him, or a house which shelters him from the sun and cold in winter.'[10]

His words, Exalted is He:

[16:67] ***And of the fruits of date-palms and vines from which you draw wine and goodly provision.***

He [Abū Bakr al-Sijzī] said, 'This verse was abrogated by the verse on wine (*khamr*).[11] Ibrāhīm[12] and Shuʿabī also said this.' Sahl said:

As far as I am concerned, wine (*sakar*)[13] is anything which intoxicates the lower self (*nafs*) in this world, and for which it [the *nafs*] does not believe it will be punished in the Hereafter.

Abū Ḥamza al-Ṣūfī[14] visited Sahl and he asked him: 'Where have you been, Abū Ḥamza?' He replied, 'We were with such and such a person who informed us that intoxication is of four kinds.' He said, 'Tell me what they are.' [Abū Ḥamza continued], 'The intoxication of drink, the intoxication of youth, the intoxication of wealth and the intoxication of authority.' Sahl replied, 'There are two kinds of intoxication which he did not inform you about.' He asked, 'What are they?' and Sahl answered, 'The intoxication of the scholar who loves this world, and the intoxication of the worshipper who loves to be noticed.'

His words, Exalted is He:

[16:72] ***…And made for you out of your mates, children* (banūn) *and grandchildren* (ḥafada)…**

He said:

The following saying is transmitted from Ibn Masʿūd ؓ: '*Ḥafada* are the in-laws.' According to Ibn ʿAbbās ؓ, *children* (banūn) refers to the children of the children, and *grandchildren* (ḥafada) refers to those among them who help their father in his work.

According to Ḍaḥḥāk, *ḥafada* are the servants devoted to God in willing compliance (*ījāban*), without their asking of anyone except Him.

His words:

[16:88] ***… We shall add torment upon torment …***

He said:

Jābir b. ʿAbd Allāh ؓ related that he asked the Prophet ﷺ about what this increase [in torment] was. The Messenger of God ﷺ replied: 'The increase is in five rivers which come out from beneath the Throne and fall upon the heads of those among the people of the Hellfire who reject God and His Messenger. Three of them are proportionate to the night in measure, and two of them proportionate to the day in measure. They flow with fire forever, as long as they abide there.'

His words, Exalted is He:

[16:90] ***Indeed, God enjoins justice* (ʿadl) *and benevolence* (iḥsān) *and giving to kinsfolk, (and He forbids you indecency* (faḥshāʾ), *abomination* (munkar) *and aggression. He admonishes you so that you may take heed*).**

---

9 Bayhaqī, *Shuʿab al-īmān*, vol. 7, p. 125.

10 Mundhirī, *al-Targhīb*, vol. 4, p. 77, (with different wording); Ṭabarānī, *al-Muʿjam al-awsaṭ*, vol. 9, p. 136.

11 The verse concerning intoxicating drinks is 2:219.

12 It is not clear who the person named as Ibrāhīm is, though the editor of the Dār al-Kutub al-ʿIlmiyya edition states that this is Ibrāhīm b. Adham (d. 161/777), for which he gives no evidence.

13 The word *sakar*, derived from the root *s-k-r* meaning to become intoxicated, can mean an intoxicant, or by extension, wine.

14 Böwering has identified him as Abū Ḥamza Muḥammad b. Ibrāhīm al-Bazzāz (d. 289/902), a Sufi of Baghdad.

He said:

Justice is professing 'There is no god but God and Muḥammad is the Messenger of God', and adhering to the Sunna of His Prophet ﷺ; *and benevolence* is that you do good to each other; *and giving to kinsfolk* means that whoever God has provided for in abundance should give to those among his relatives for whom God has made him responsible; *indecency* (faḥshāʾ), refers to calumny (*kadhb*), backbiting (*ghayba*), slander (*buhtān*) and all other offences of the tongue; and *abomination* (munkar), refers to the committing of transgressions in the form of actions. *He admonishes you*, means He instructs you in the finest conduct (*adab*), and draws your attention to the highest awareness (*intibāḥ*), *so that you make take heed,* that is, receive admonishment and refrain [from sins].

Sahl [also] said:

People are asleep and when they die they awaken.[15]

His words:

[16:97] *Whoever acts righteously, whether male or female, and is a believer, him verily, We shall revive with a good life, a new life...*

He said:

Life (*ḥayāt*) is in the removal from the servant of his contrivance and management [of things] (*tadbīr*), and his turning back to God's management of things for him.

His words:

[16:110] *Then indeed your Lord — towards those who emigrated after they were persecuted, and then struggled and were steadfast [will be most Forgiving and most Merciful].*

Sahl said:

They emigrated means they left behind the evil company [they had been keeping] after it became clear to them that associating with them was a source of corruption for them. Then *they struggled* to keep themselves in the company of the people of goodness (*khayr*). Subsequently, *they were steadfast* in this and did not go back to the situation they were in at the beginning of events.

Once a man asked Sahl, 'I have wealth and strength and I want to perform *jihād*. What do you command me to do?' Sahl answered:

Wealth is knowledge (*ʿilm*), strength is intention (*nīya*) and *jihād* is the struggle with the lower self (*mujāhadat al-nafs*). No one is assured safety concerning what God has forbidden except a prophet or veracious person (*ṣiddīq*).

Abū ʿUthmān was asked the meaning of his [Sahl's] saying, 'Except a prophet or veracious one (*ṣiddīq*).' He replied, 'He does not enter into anything whose safety [or benignity] (*ʿāfiya*) is in question.

His words:

[16:119] *But towards those who did wrong out of ignorance, and afterwards, repent and make amends, your Lord is Forgiving and Merciful.*

Sahl said:

No one ever disobeyed God, Exalted is He, save through ignorance, yet many an act of ignorance gives rise to knowledge. Knowledge is the key to repentance. Making amends (*iṣlāḥ*) is [a sign of] a sound repentance. Whoever does not make amends as ⌜a part of (*fī*)⌝[16] his repentance, [will find] his repentance is soon ruined, for God, Exalted is He, has said, *and afterwards, repent and make amends.*

---

15 The editor of the Dār al-Kutub al-ʿIlmiyya edition notes that a variant of this saying is attributed to Tustarī in Bayhaqī, *Kitāb al-Zuhd al-kabīr*, vol. 2, p. 207, while in ʿAjlūnī, *Kashf al-khafāʾ*, vol. 2, p. 525, it is attributed to ʿAlī b. Abī Ṭālib, in Munāwī, *Fayḍ al-qadīr*, vol. 5, p. 56 it is said to be a *ḥadīth* of the Prophet, and in Iṣfahānī, *Ḥilyat al-awliyāʾ*, vol. 7, p. 52 it is attributed to Luqmān.

16 Added on the basis of all three MSS: Z515, f. 66b, F638, f. 31a; Fātiḥ 3488, f. 239a.

Sahl was asked about the ignorant person [referred to in the verse]. He said:

> He is the one who takes himself as his guide (*imām*), and has no virtuous guide (*imām ṣāliḥ*) whom he follows.

His words:

[16:127] ***So be patient: and your patience is only by [the help of] God...***

Sahl said:

> Be patient and know that there is no helper (*muʿīn*) in your affairs except God, Exalted is He. ⌜And God, Exalted is He, knows best⌝.[17]

17 The last sentence is present only in MS F638, f. 31a.

17 Al-Isrāʾ

His words, Exalted is He:

[17:8] ***...but if you revert, We too revert...***

Sahl said:

> It means, 'If you revert to transgression, We revert to forgiveness; and if you revert to turning your backs on Us, We revert to advancing towards you; and if you revert to fleeing from Us, We revert to barring the ways [of escape] for you. Return to Us for the way (*ṭarīq*) is taken care of by Us.'[1]

His words:

[17:11] ***And man prays for ill as [avidly] as he prays for good...***

Sahl said:

> The soundest of supplications is the remembrance (*dhikr*) [of God], and relinquishing the choice [that is made] through petitioning and supplication, for remembrance [itself] suffices. For it may be that when a person supplicates, he asks for something that will lead to his ruin without realising it. Do you not see that God, Exalted is He, says, *And man prays for ill as [avidly] as he prays for good*? The one who remembers [God] constantly, and who abandons choice (*ikhtiyār*), supplication (*duʿāʾ*) and petitioning (*suʾāl*), will be granted the best that could be desired, and the ills of petitioning and choice will fall away from him. For this reason the Messenger of God ﷺ said, 'To those whose remembrance of Me kept them from petitioning Me, I will grant the best that petitioners ask for.'[2]

His words, Exalted is He:

[17:13] ***And We have attached every person's omen to his neck...***

He said:

> [This means] his action[s],[3] that is, of whatever came to be of good or evil.

His words:

[17:14] ***Read your record! This day your own soul suffices as your own reckoner.***

He said:

> The following saying is related from Ḥasan al-Baṣrī: 'Prepare for the questioning with an answer, and [be ready] to respond with what is correct. Or else, prepare to have the Fire as your cloak.' ʿUmar ؓ said: 'Call yourselves to account before you are called to account. Weigh yourselves up before you are weighed up, and prepare for the great [Day of] Exposure before you are exposed.'[4]

---

1 lit. the way (*ṭarīq*) is incumbent upon Us (*ʿalaynā*).

2 Tirmidhī, *Nawādir al-uṣūl*, vol. 3, p. 64 and 259; Muḥammad b. Salāma al-Quḍāʿī, *Musnad al-Shihāb* (Beirut, 1986), vol. 1, p. 34, vol. 2, p. 326.

3 All the MSS (Z515, f. 67a, F638, f. 31b and F3488, f. 239b) have *ʿamalahu* here instead of *ʿilmahu*.

4 i.e. the Day of Resurrection, when humanity will be 'exposed' or 'presented' (the verb *ʿ-r-ḍ* can have both these meanings), before God, as for example in 17:83.

Sahl was asked about the calling to account (*muḥāsaba*) and the weighing up (*muwāzana*). He said:

> The calling to account is of two kinds: the accounting that concerns those matters which are between the servant and his Lord, and this is in secret; and the accounting that concerns matters that are between him and other people, and that is done openly. The weighing up is when you have before you [the possibility of] two obligatory acts, two Sunna acts, or two supererogatory acts (*nafl*). After reflecting on which of them will bring you closer to God and is weightier with Him, you start with that act.[5]

His words:

[17:25] *Your Lord knows best what is within your souls* (nufūsikum)...

> That is, what is in your hearts (*qulūb*), because the heart includes the intellect (*ʿaql*), the self (*nafs*) and desire (*hawā*).[6]

His words:

[17:25] *...If you are righteous, then truly He is Forgiving to those who keep turning [to Him] in repentance.*

> Ibn al-Musayyib said: 'The one who turns again and again in penitence (*awwāb*) is the one who sins, then repents, then sins, then repents, and dies in a state of repentance'. Ḥasan al-Baṣrī said, 'The *awwāb* is the penitent who repents without delay.[7] Indeed he is ready (*muhayyaʾ*) for repentance at every instant and moment.' It was related on the authority of Ḍamra b. Ḥabīb that the Prophet ﷺ said: 'He for whom a door to goodness has been opened should seize [the opportunity] as he does not know when it will close on him.'[8] This means that he should seriously consider his present moment (*waqt*) and not procrastinate.

His words, Exalted is He:

[17:36] *And do not pursue* (lā taqfu) *that of which you have no knowledge.*

> That is, 'Do not desire (*lā tabghī*) that about which you have no knowledge', just as the Prophet ﷺ said, 'We are of the [tribe] of Banū al-Naḍīr b. Kināna. We do not try to trace our origins through our mother, nor do we deny our father.'[9] That is, the father of the Arabs.

His words, Exalted is He:

[17:57] *...and they hope for His mercy and fear His chastisement...*

He said:

> The outer meaning of *His mercy* is His Paradise, and its inner meaning is the reality of gnosis (*ḥaqīqat al-maʿrifa*).[10]

Then he said:

> Truly, fear and hope are two restraining ties (*zamāmān*)[11] for mankind. If they have equal [sway], a person's condition [lit. states *aḥwāl*] will be stabilised, but if one of them preponderates, the

---

5 It appears that in this passage, Tustarī is applying these two terms differently: the calling to account (*muḥāsaba*) here appears to refer to that to which the slave will be subjected in the Hereafter, whereas the weighing up (*muwāzana*) is referring to something to be done in this world. However, Tustarī clearly recommends an accounting (*muḥāsaba*) for this world, since he cited the saying of ʿUmar.

6 For a discussion of Tustarī's understanding of the inner constitution of the human being, again see IT, pp. xxxviiiff. However, in this sentence it is possible that Tustarī is using the word 'hearts' (*qulūb*) more generally to refer to man's inner world or soul.

7 lit. 'He doesn't have two moments for this', i.e. he does not imagine he has two opportunities for it.

8 Quḍāʿī, *Musnad al-Shihāb*, vol. 1, p. 268.

9 lit. 'We do not ask about our mother'. The *ḥadīth* is listed in Ibn Ḥanbal, *al-Musnad*, vol. 5, pp. 211–2; Ṭabarānī, *al-Muʿjam al-kabīr*, vol. 1, p. 235 and vol. 2, p. 286; and Ibn Māja, *Sunan*, vol. 2, p. 871.

10 Substituted for *ḥaqīqat al-maʿrūf*, on the basis of all three MSS: Z515, f. 68a, F638, f. 31b and F3488, f. 240a. Tustarī's comment is in accordance with the Sufi teaching that true mystics do not have any hope or desire for the delights of Paradise; their only desire is to attain the unmediated experiential knowledge or beholding of God, otherwise expressed as union with God.

11 Substituting the dual for the singular, on the basis of all three MSS: Z515, f. 68a, F638, f. 31b and F3488, f. 240a.

other will be cancelled out. Notice how the Prophet ﷺ said: 'If a believer's hope and fear were weighed they would balance each other.'[12]

His words, Exalted is He:

[17:67] *And when distress befalls you at sea, those whom you are wont to invoke are no longer present, except Him…*

That is, those other than Him from whom you ask relief. Then [eventually] you give up all dependency on your own power (*ḥawl*) and strength (*quwwa*) and recognise His power and His strength. This verse is a refutation of the Qadarīs, who claim to have ability for themselves without [the need for] God, Exalted is He.[13] God, Exalted is He, has said, *Do you feel secure that He will not cause a slope of land to engulf you, or unleash upon you a storm of pebbles?* [17:68] And He said, *or unleash upon you a shattering gale to drown you* [17:69]. So, if they really have ability (*istiṭāʿa*), let them repel the punishment from themselves.

His words, Exalted is He:

[17:72] *And whoever has been blind in this [world] will be blind in the Hereafter…*

That is, whoever is blind of heart in this world such that he does not show gratitude for the blessings, both outward and inward, that God, Exalted is He, has bestowed upon him, will be blind in the Hereafter such that he is prevented from seeing the Bestower of blessings (*al-Munʿim*).

His words:

[17:80] *And say, 'My Lord make me enter with veracity…'*[14]

That is, 'Make me enter, by virtue of my conveying the Message (*risāla*), by an entrance of veracity. This signifies that I will not incline to anyone, and that I will not fall short in observing the limits and conditions in conveying it. Also grant me a safe exit [from this world], seeking Your good pleasure in [upholding] it with conformity (*muwāfaqa*) [to Your will]. *And grant me from Yourself a supporting authority* (sulṭānan naṣīran).' That is, 'Adorn me with the adornment of Your dominion (*jabarūt*), so that the authority of truth prevails over them and not the authority of desire.'

And on another occasion I heard Sahl say:

…*And grant me from Yourself a supporting authority* [refers to having] a tongue which speaks on the authority of (*ʿan*) You and no one else.

His words, Exalted is He:

[17:107] *…Those who were given knowledge before it, when it is recited to them, fall down on their faces in humble prostration.*

Sahl said:

There is nothing which affects [man's] innermost secret (*sirr*) like listening to the Qurʾān. This is due to the fact that when the servant listens, his innermost secret is humbled in submission (*khashaʿa*), and his heart is illuminated by this with truthful proofs (*barāhīn ṣādiqa*). Furthermore his bodily members are adorned with self-abasement (*tadhallul*) and obedient submission (*inqiyād*). But God knows best.

12 Ibn Abī Shayba, *al-Muṣannaf*, vol. 7, p. 178; Bayhaqī, *Shuʿab al-īmān*, vol. 2, p. 12. See above Tustarī's commentary on 11:75 and p. 93, n. 13 on the need to retain both fear and hope and keep them in balance.

13 The term Qadarīs or Qādirites (*Qādiriyya*) was commonly applied to a group of theologians in early Islam who were advocates of free will. The term *qadar* means 'power', and therefore conversely, the term was also occasionally applied to those who held the opposite view and maintained the divine omnipotence, insisting that God was the Creator of all human acts. Tustarī is clearly applying the term in its former designation.

14 Verses 72–80 are directly addressed to the Prophet.

18 Al-Kahf[1]

His words:

[18:7] ***...that We may try them, as to which of them is best in conduct.***[2]

He said:

> That is, as to which of them is best in their relinquishing of this world and all that leads to distraction (*ishtighāl*) from God, Exalted is He, and in their humbling themselves (*ikhbāt*) before Us, their tranquil reliance (*sukūn*) on Us, their complete trust (*tawakkul*) in Us, and their advancing (*iqbāl*) towards Us.

He was asked about His word:

[18:9]*...the inscription* (al-raqīm)...

He said:

> *Al-Raqīm* is their leader who is called 'the dog' but they do not actually have a dog.[3] God, Exalted is He, said *Their dog [lay] stretching his two forelegs on the threshold* [18:18]. That is, stretching his two forelegs in command and prohibition. ʿIkrima said, '*al-raqīm* is the word for inkwell in the Byzantine tongue.' Ḥasan said, '*al-Raqīm* is the valley in which the Cave is situated', while Kaʿb[4] said, '*al-raqīm* is a lead tablet on which is inscribed their names, their genealogies, their religion and from whom they fled.'[5] *Al-waṣīd*, however, is the threshold.

---

1 Sūrat al-Kahf takes its title from the story of the 'Companions of the Cave' (*aṣḥāb al-kahf*), which is narrated from 18:9–26. The story, which is terse, almost cryptic in its telling, is referred to in 18:9 as *a marvel from among Our signs*, and is therefore to be reflected on. It tells how a group of believing young men take refuge in a cave. There they pray for God's mercy and to be granted [guidance to] the correct course of conduct (*rashad*) from Him in their affair or situation [18:10]. God makes them sleep in the cave for a number of years [18:11], then rouses them, and strengthens their hearts so that they can attest to the oneness of God, and denounce the calling upon other gods besides Him [18:14]. It becomes clear that the Companions of the Cave have isolated themselves from their people, who have become polytheists [18:15]. We are told of the dog, as it were standing guard at the entrance of the cave [18:18]. One of the young men is eventually sent to the city by the others to procure the purest food and bring them a supply of it, but is warned that he should do it in such a way that no one is made aware of him [18:19]. The reason for this caution is then given: *For indeed if they should come to know of you, they will [either] stone you, or make you return to their creed, and then you will never prosper* [18:20]. The story of the cave has been a subject of particular interest in Sufi exegesis, since the Companions of the Cave are seen as prototypes of the spiritual wayfarer, both in their retreat from worldliness and in their dependence upon God's guidance.

2 The verse in full reads: *Truly We have made all that is in the earth as an adornment for it, that We may try them as to which of them is best in conduct.*

3 Interestingly, Tustarī follows this statement with a citation of 18:18, and he does later speak of the dog of the Companions of the Cave in his commentary on 31:15. Perhaps his meaning is that they did not own a dog. According to Thaʿlabī, the dog belonged to a shepherd who joined the Companions of the Cave and led them to the cave on the mountain where they hid. To begin with, the young men drove the dog away, being afraid that its bark would reveal their whereabouts, but then the dog got up and spoke to them, and made the attestation of divine oneness and they let him alone. Thaʿlabī includes a number of views about the dog's appearance and its name. See Thaʿlabī, *ʿArāʾis al-majālis*, pp. 452–3; trans. Brinner, pp. 695–6.

4 Kaʿb al-Aḥbār.

5 These interpretations of '*al-Raqīm*' are among those which Ṭabarī presents in his commentary on 18:9 in his *Jāmiʿ al-bayān*. Other opinions are that it was the name of a village (*qarya*) or the name of the mountain (*jabal*) on which the cave was situated. He does not include the view that *al-Raqīm* is the name of the dog. In his long commentary on 18:9,

His words, Exalted is He:

[18:10] ...*'Give us mercy from Yourself...'*

That is, 'Keep us in the state of Your remembrance (*dhikr*).'

His words, Exalted is He:

[18:13] ...*They were indeed young men who believed in their Lord...*

Sahl said:

He called them young men (*fitya*) because they believed in Him without [the aid] of any intermediary (*wāsiṭa*), and they devoted themselves to Him by ridding themselves of all other attachments (*ʿalāʾiq*).[6]

His words, Exalted is He:

[18:13] ...*And We increased them in guidance.*

That is, in insight (*baṣīra*) concerning faith.

His words, Exalted is He:

[18:17] ...*whomsoever He leads astray, you will not find for him a guiding friend.*

If God wishes to manifest His [prior] knowledge of a person's ill-fortune (*shaqāwa*) by lifting His protection (*ʿiṣma*) from them, you will not find for that person anyone who can protect them from that.

His words, Exalted is He:

[18:18] ...*If you had observed them you would have turned away from them in flight, and would have been filled with awe...*

This means: 'If you had observed them through your self, you would have run away from them in fear, but if you had observed them through God, you would have come to know (*waqafta*) in them the realities of unicity (*ḥaqāʾiq al-waḥdāniyya*) from Him.'

His words, Exalted is He:

[18:21] ...*Those who prevailed regarding their affair said...*

He said:

Its outward meaning is a reference to authority [and the power of those who held sway] (*wilāya*), and its inner meaning refers to the spiritual self (*nafs al-rūḥ*), the understanding of the intellect (*fahm al-ʿaql*) and discernment of the heart (*fiṭnat al-qalb*) [which hold sway] through the remembrance of God, Mighty and Majestic is He.

His words, Exalted is He:

[18:28] ...*And do not obey him whose heart We have made oblivious to Our remembrance...*

He said:

Heedlessness (*ghafla*) is wasting time with futile things (*biṭāla*).[7]

And he further said:

The heart has a thousand deaths, of which the ultimate is being cut off (*qaṭīʿa*) from God, Mighty and Majestic is He; and the heart has a thousand lives, of which the ultimate is the encounter (*liqāʾ*) with God, Mighty and Majestic is He. Furthermore, with each sinful act the heart undergoes a death, and with each act of obedience it receives [new] life.

His words, Exalted is He:

[18:30] ...*Indeed, We do not let the reward of those of good deeds go to waste.*

Ṭabarī does, however, include the view that there was a dog which lay at the entrance to the cave.

6 On the word *fitya* see also Tustarī's commentary on the word *fatayān* (12:36) and p. 96, n. 10.

7 According to Lane, *biṭāla* can mean 'being diverted from that which would bring profit in this world or in the life to come'. Thus we have translated it as 'wasting time with futile things'.

He said:

Goodness of conduct (*ḥusn al-ʿamal*)[8] is maintaining rectitude (*istiqāma*) [in one's conduct] by [adhering to] the Sunna. The similitude of the Sunna in this world is that of the Garden in the Hereafter. Whoever enters the Garden is safe. Likewise whoever adheres to the Sunna in this world is preserved from all ills. Mālik b. Anas ﷺ said, 'If a man had committed all the enormities (*kabāʾir*), but then harboured no desire for any of them nor any innovation,[9] I would be hopeful for him.' Then he said, 'Let whoever dies following the Sunna be of good cheer', three times over.

Sahl said:

The veils will not be lifted from the servant until he buries his lower self in the earth.

He was asked, 'How does he bury his lower self?' He replied:

He slays it through the Sunna, and also buries it by adhering to the Sunna. This is because every station of the worshippers, such as fear, hope, love, longing, abstinence, contentment and trust, has a limit (*ghāya*) except for the Sunna, for it has no limit or end.

Mattā b. Aḥmad was asked about the meaning of the words: 'The Sunna has no limit.' He said, 'No one has fear like the fear of the Prophet ﷺ, and [the same goes for] his love (*ḥubb*), his longing (*shawq*), his abstinence (*zuhd*), his contentment (*riḍā*), his trust (*tawakkul*), and his [noble] characteristics (*akhlāq*). Indeed, God, Exalted is He, has said: *Assuredly you possess a magnificent nature* [68:4].'

He [Sahl] was asked about the meaning of the words of the Prophet ﷺ, 'Make yourselves hungry and denude yourselves.'[10] He replied:

Make yourselves hungry for knowledge and denude yourselves of ignorance.

His words:

[18:39] ...*What God has willed.*[11] *There is no power except in God...*

That is, whatever God has willed in His prior knowledge, with which no one is acquainted except God, Exalted is He. *There is no power except with God* means, 'We have no power (*quwwa*) to perform what You commanded us in principle (*fī'l-aṣl*), nor do we have success in its practical application (*farʿ*), nor [can we be sure of having] a praiseworthy end, except with Your aid (*maʿūna*).[12] This is also a commentary on the words of the Prophet, 'There is neither power nor strength except in God',[13] — that is: 'There is no means of security against ignorance concerning the principle, or against persistence [in transgression] resulting from that [ignorance], save through Your protection. Likewise, we have no power to perform what You have commanded us in principle (*aṣl*), nor security in putting that into practice (*fī'l-farʿ*), nor of a praiseworthy end except through Your aid'.

---

8 *Ḥusn* also has the meaning of beauty, because what is good is fair and beautiful.

9 By not having any innovation, he would be conforming to the Sunna.

10 This saying appears in an extended form in Iṣfahānī, *Ḥilyat al-awliyā*ʾ, vol. 2, p. 370, attributed to Jesus ﷺ, who says, 'Make yourselves hungry, and thirsty, denude yourselves and wear yourselves out, that your hearts may come to know God.'

11 *Mā shāʾaʾLlāh*, which according to Islamic tradition, should be said when encountering or remarking on beauty or virtue, especially in a person, child or personal possession. The beginning of this verse makes it clear that these words should have been uttered on entering the garden. This verse is part of the story of two men, one of whom possesses two gardens which have abundant yield and are watered by a gushing stream. The latter boasts to the other that he has greater wealth and is stronger with respect to men. Then that same man looks at his garden, and expresses the view that it will never perish, and that the Hour will never come, and that even if it does, he will surely find an even better resort than this garden. In response, his companion reminds him of his lowly origin and that God has fashioned him, and he then expresses the admonition of the above verse, continuing by warning the man that God might grant him (the speaker) a better garden, or unleash on his companion's garden [thunder] bolts, so that it becomes a barren plain.

12 The words *aṣl* and *farʿ* here are probably allusions to the two aspects of the sacred law: its principles: (*uṣūl*) and its practical applications (*furūʿ*), lit. branches.

13 Bukhārī, *Ṣaḥīḥ*, 'Kitāb al-Tahajjud'.

Sahl was asked, 'What is the best thing that a servant can be given?' He said:

> Knowledge by which he increases in his sense of utter neediness (*iftiqār*) for God, Mighty and Majestic is He.

His words:

[18:55] *What has prevented people from believing, when the guidance has come to them?*

He said:

> Guidance (*hudā*) came to them but the ways of guidance (*ṭuruq al-hidāya*) had been blocked (*masdūd*) for them, for guidance (*hudā*) and faith (*īmān*) were barred from them by the pre-eternal decree (*ḥukm*) over them.

His words:

[18:109] *Say, 'If the ocean were ink for [writing] the words of my Lord, it would run dry…'*

> That is, in recording the knowledge of my Lord and His wonders.

Then he said:

> His Book is part of His knowledge, and if a servant was given a thousand ways of understanding each letter of the Qurʾān, he would not reach the end of God's knowledge within it. This is because it is His pre-eternal speech, and His speech is one of His attributes, and there is no end to any of His attributes just as He has no end. All that can be comprehended of His speech is as much as He opens to the hearts of His friends.

His words:

[18:110] *So whoever hopes to encounter his Lord, let him do virtuous work and not associate anyone with the worship of his Lord.*

He said:

> A virtuous act is that which is free of ostentation (*riyāʾ*), and bound (*muqayyad*) by the Sunna. But God, Transcendent and Exalted is He, knows best.

19 Maryam

His words, Exalted is He:

[19:13] ***and compassion from Us...***[1]

That is, 'We did this out of mercy for his [John's] parents', *and purity…*

'We purified him of the false opinions (*ẓunūn*) that people hold with regard to Him.'[2] *And he was God-fearing*, that is, 'He advanced towards Us, shunning all other than Us.'

He also said:

The states (*aḥwāl*) of the prophets are all pure (*maḥḍa*).[3]

His words:

[19:31] ***And He has made me blessed wherever I may be...***[4]

That is, I [Jesus] command what is right, forbid what is wrong, guide aright those who are astray, support the oppressed, and give relief to the anxious.

His words, Mighty and Majestic is He:

[19:32] ***…He did not make me arrogant and wretched.***

That is, ignorant of His commandments, and disdainful of His worship out of pride. The Prophet ﷺ said, 'Pride (*kibriyāʾ*) is the cloak of God, and whoever contests with God over it, He will cast face-first into the Fire…'[5]

He was asked about His words, Mighty and Majestic is He:

[19:26] ***…I have vowed to the Compassionate One abstinence* (ṣawm)…**

He said:

'I have abstained from all [speech] save Your remembrance, [as] when the person observing abstinence asks for comfort in You, and his heart finds repose in You, and no one else. *…so I will not talk to any human today.*'

---

1 The first part of Sūrat Maryam (vv. 2–11) relates the story of Zachariah praying to God for an heir, since his wife is barren, and God's reassuring Zachariah that this would be easy for Him. Zachariah is told that the sign of the accomplishment of this would be that he would be unable to speak for three days and nights. Verse 12 then speaks of the young boy John being commanded by God to hold firmly to the scripture, and in the same verse, we are informed that while still a boy he was granted wisdom. Verse 13, with which Tustarī commences his commentary, relates that John was also granted compassion (*ḥanān*) from God, that is to say, he was given to be compassionate in nature (19:13), as well as pure, and that he was God-fearing.

2 In that, according to the commentaries, he was an upholder of the divine oneness (*tawḥīd*).

3 That is, according to MSS F638, f. 32b and F3488, f. 242b and the printed edition, with the verb *m-ḥ-ḍ* being taken in its meaning of 'to be pure, unalloyed, untainted'. MS Z515, f. 70b, however, has *muḥaṣṣana* meaning guarded, protected. Either would be possible in this context.

4 These are words spoken by Jesus while still in the cradle. Thus he, like John, was endowed with the miracle of speaking as an infant.

5 Ibn Māja, *Sunan*, 'Bāb al-barāʾa min al-kibr'; Abū Dāwud, *Sunan*, 'Bāb mā jāʾa fī'l-kibr'; Ibn Ḥanbal, *al-Musnad*, vol. 2, pp. 248, 376, 414, 427 and 442.

His words:

[19:52] ...*And brought him near in communion.*[6]

That is, being secretly called for the unveiling (*mukāshafa*) from God, [an unveiling] which is not concealed from hearts, in [intimate] conversation (*muḥādatha*) and loving affection (*wudd*), just as He said, Exalted is He, *Truly those who believe and perform righteous deeds — for them the Compassionate One shall appoint loving affection* (wudd) [19:96], meaning that [through] this unveiling, the mysteries (*asrār*) are received without any mediation (*wāsiṭa*). This is a station given by God to those who are true and faithful (*ṣadaqū*) to Him both in secret and openly.

His words, Exalted is He:

[19:61] *Gardens of Eden, which the Compassionate One has promised to His servants in the unseen...*

This means the 'visual' beholding (*muʿāyana*) of God, in the sense of nearness which He appointed between Him and them, so that the servant sees his heart in the proximity of God, witnessed (*mashhūd*) in the unseen of the unseen (*ghayb al-ghayb*). The unseen of the unseen is the spiritual self (*nafs al-rūḥ*), the understanding of the intellect (*fahm al-ʿaql*), and the discernment of meaning by the heart (*fiṭnat al-murād bi'l-qalb*).[7] The spiritual self is the seat of the intellect (*ʿaql*), which is the seat of the Holy (*al-Quds*). This Holy is linked with the Throne (*ʿarsh*), and is one of the names of the Throne. God, Exalted is He, apportioned for the self one part in a thousand parts [i.e. one thousandth] of the spirit (*rūḥ*) — or rather, even less than that. When the will (*irāda*) of the spirit becomes the will of the self (*nafs*) [as in the spiritual self], they are given between them discernment (*fiṭna*) and intuition (*dhihn*). Discernment is the guide (*imām*) of understanding (*fahm*),[8] and understanding is the guide of intuition (*dhihn*). Discernment (*fiṭna*) is life (*ḥayāt*) and understanding (*fahm*) is livelihood (*ʿaysh*).

There are but two [kinds of] men who understand the Word [of God]: the first wants to understand so he can speak about it from a position [of authority] and his lot is nothing but that; the other hears it and is occupied with acting upon it to the exclusion of all else. This person is rarer than red sulphur (*al-kibrīt al-aḥmar*) and more precious than all that is dear. He is among those who love one another for God's sake (*al-mutaḥābbūn fī'Llāh*).[9] Trying to understand (*tafahhum*) is an exertion of effort (*takalluf*), yet discernment (*fiṭna*)[10] cannot be attained through effort, but rather by acting in sincerity (*al-ʿamal bi'l-ikhlāṣ*) for Him. Truly God, Exalted is He, has servants in Paradise who, if they were veiled from the encounter (*liqāʾ*) [with their Lord] for a blinking of the eye, would cry out for help against it, just as the inhabitants of the Hellfire plead for help against the Hellfire. This is because they have come to know Him (*ʿarafūhu*). See how God's Interlocutor [Moses][11] ﷺ could not wait to see Him on account of

---

6 Verses 51–53 allude briefly to the story of Moses' communing with God (i.e. his hearing Him speak), both from the burning bush and at Mount Sinai. The former incident is narrated more fully in 20:10–6, 27:7–9 and 28:29–30, while the theophany at Mount Sinai is recounted in 7:142–6.

7 A similar configuration of the spiritual psychology of the mystic is given in the commentary on 18:21 with the difference that the earlier passage has 'discernment of the heart' (*fiṭnat al-qalb*) instead of 'discernment of what is intended or meant by the heart' (*fiṭnat al-murād bi'l-qalb*). On Tustarī's different discussions of the inner make-up or spiritual psychology of the human being, again see IT, pp. xxxviiiff.

8 Translating *al-fiṭna imām al-fahm* according to all three MSS: Z515, f. 71a, F638, f. 33a and F3488, f. 243a, not *dhihn* as in the published edition.

9 This is probably an allusion to a *ḥadīth* narrated on the authority of Abū Hurayra or Abū Saʿīd al-Khuḍrī in which the Prophet includes 'those who love each other for the sake of their Lord' among seven who will be given God's shelter on the Day of Judgement. Another similar *ḥadīth* mentions those who love each other for the sake of God's greatness. They are listed in Ibn Mālik, *al-Muwaṭṭaʾ*, trans., Muhammad Rahimuddin (Damascus, 2003), ch. 522, 'On those who keep friendship for the sake of Allāh'.

10 That is, according to the published edition and MSS F638, f. 33a. However, both MSS Z515, f. 71a and F3488, f. 243b appear to have *al-ghibṭa* meaning a state of happiness or well-being.

11 As stated above, the 'Interlocutor' [of God] (*Kalīm Allāh*) is the honorary title given to Moses on account of his conversing with God directly, and on the basis the words *kallama'Llāhu Mūsā taklīman*, 'God spoke to Moses directly' [4:164].

the sweetness he had experienced in communion with Him, so that he said, 'O my Lord what is that Hebrew voice[12] from You which has seized my heart so! Indeed, I have heard the voice of the caring mother, and the sound of birds in flight, but I have never heard a sound more alluring to my heart than that voice.' Henceforth, whenever Moses saw a mountain he would rush towards it and climb it, yearning [to hear] His speech, glorified be His majesty. There was a man from among the Children of Israel who would walk in the footsteps of Moses wherever he went, and would sit wherever he sat, until Moses ﷺ became annoyed with him. Someone said to him, 'You have offended the prophet of God.' He replied, 'All I desire is to look at the mouth which spoke to God.'

Then he [Moses] said, *My Lord! Show me [Yourself], that I may behold You!* [7:143], and God replied, 'O Moses! No creature will see me on earth without dying.'[13] So he said, 'O Lord! Let me behold You and die, for that is preferable to me than not seeing You and remaining alive.' Thus, whoever gives his heart solely to God and longs for Him, will reach Him.

Abū ʿUbayd Allāh al-Khawwāṣ used to shout in Baghdad: 'Your remembrance (*dhikr*) has given me a hunger that I cannot satisfy. Your remembrance has given me a thirst that I cannot quench. Oh, how I long for the One who sees me, but whom I see not!' Then he came to the Tigris river and threw himself in the river with his clothes on, plunging into the water at one place and emerging in another, shouting all the while: 'Your remembrance has given me a hunger that I cannot satisfy. Your remembrance has given me a thirst that I cannot quench. Oh, how I long for the One who sees me but, but whom I see not!' Meanwhile, all the people on the banks of the river wept.

One day a man came to Sahl while people were gathered around him and said, 'O Abū Muḥammad! Look what He has done with you and how He has elevated you!'[14] However, this did not affect Sahl and he said, 'It is He who is sought, He who is sought!'

His words, Exalted is He:

[19:76] *And God increases in guidance those who found [right] guidance…*

He said:

This means that God will increase the insight (*baṣīra*) of those who are guided due to their faith in Him and their emulation (*iqtidāʾ*) of Muḥammad ﷺ, and this is an increase in guidance (*hudā*) and clear light (*nūr mubīn*).

His words, Exalted is He:

[19:85] *[Mention] the day on which We shall gather those who are mindful of God to the Compassionate One, [honoured] on mounts* (wafdan).

That is, mounted (*rukbānan*). The mindful of God (*muttaqūn*) are those who are wary of all besides God, Mighty and Majestic is He.

And he said:

Nothing will be complete for the servant until he fortifies[15] his work[s] (*ʿamal*) with fear [of God] (*khashiya*), his deed[s] (*fiʿl*) with scrupulous piety (*waraʿ*), his scrupulous piety with sincerity

12 Sic in all MSS, whereas the printed edition has *ʿayrānī*, which may well be a misprint.

13 This was the reason given by God for His refusal to allow Moses to see Him in Exodus, 34:18–20. This traditional explanation was probably derived from among the 'Isrāʾīliyyāt', that is, traditions concerning the stories of the Biblical prophets that were derived either from Jewish converts to Islam or early Muslims who had contact with the Jews and Christians of the Arabian peninsula. For this and other definitions of the 'Isrāʾīliyyāt' see *EI*², vol. IV, pp. 211–2. The Qurʾān does not give any reason for God's denying Moses the vision of Him, though the tremendous and devastating effect of the divine theophany is demonstrated to Moses through the mountain, which is 'levelled to the ground', when God reveals Himself to it [7:143].

14 That is, substituting *aysh yarfaʿu laka* as in MSS Z515, f. 71b and F3488, f. 244b, for *aysh yaqaʿu laka* in the published edition. MS F638, f. 33a is faded and not entirely clear, but appears to read *rafaʿa laka*.

15 MSS Z515, f. 72a and F3488, f. 243b appear to have *yaḥṣula* here, while MS F638, f. 33b has *yuḥassila*, either of which might be translated as 'achieves'. However, we have translated *yuḥaṣṣina* as in the printed edition.

> (*ikhlāṣ*), his sincerity with contemplative witnessing (*mushāhada*), and his contemplative witnessing with wariness (*taqwā*) of all besides God.

And he said:

> Their hearts are too precious to them than that they should see within them anything other than God, Mighty and Majestic is He. Indeed, when God created the heart He said, 'I have created you especially for Me.' Thus, these hearts are wanderers (*jawwāla*); they either circumambulate the Throne, or they wander [aimlessly] in the dry fodder (*ḥashsh*) [of the desert wilderness.][16]

His words, Exalted is He:

[19:83] *Have you not seen that We unleash the devils against the disbelievers to urge them on impetuously?*

He said:

> They arouse them, stirring them up to acts of disobedience (*maʿāṣī*) and they call them to those transgressions by means of that which their lower self desires, due to the abandonment of God's protection,[17] just as God, Exalted is He, has said in the story of the Accursed One [Satan] (*al-Laʿīn*): *I had no power over you except to call you, and you responded to my call* [14:22]. His calling is at different levels. It may be to what is evil or it may be to what is good, just as the Prophet ﷺ said, 'Truly Satan will show one of you seventy doors to goodness just in order to make him enter one door to evil and thereby ruin him.'

He [Sahl] continued:

> Indeed, the Accursed One whispers to all those who perform acts of worship (*ahl al-ʿibādāt*) and strive [for the good] (*aṣḥāb al-jahd*), but he has no concern for them; his concern is rather for the one who does not enter into anything without knowing whether it is [spiritually] to his benefit or detriment.[18] It is only with regard to knowledge[19] that worshippers and renunciants (*zuhhād*) fall into errors, not because of their striving, for [regarding the latter] they do not possess a state in which they might discern [errors] in their relationship with God. When God, Exalted is He, calls a servant to account on the Day of Resurrection, his intellect will remain firm with regard to every action that was done with the knowledge of whether he was in a state of obedience or transgression. However, he will fall into confusion (*taḥayyur*) and bewilderment (*dahsha*) on account of whatever he did in a state of ignorance (*jahl*). This is because, when he knows what state (*ḥāl*) he is in, his obedience and repentance (*tawba*) will be acceptable through God's proof (*ḥujja*).[20] However, if he does not know [his state] he will fall into confusion and bewilderment, because he acted without anything that could act as proof [for him before God].[21]

Sahl was asked concerning the man who is in a state of remembering God, and the thought (*khaṭar*) 'God is with you' occurs to his heart. He said:

---

16 According to Lane, the word *ḥashsh* meant a garden or more specifically, a garden of palm trees, though it also came to mean a privy, because it was the place in the garden where people relieved themselves. If we simply assume the word *ḥashsh* to mean a garden or a remote, forgotten part of the garden, then perhaps Tustarī's meaning is that hearts are made for God, and they either reach their potential station and roam about the Throne, or they remain at a lower level roaming in the garden (the neglected corner of the garden) of this world.

17 According to Tustarī's earlier comments, we would assume this to be God's removing His protection from them, rather than their abandonment of His protection.

18 lit. whether it is for or against him, i.e. will weigh for or against him in the Hereafter. Satan is therefore more concerned to tempt those who have awareness of their state, than with those who are worshipping without consciousness of their state. This is explained in the continuation of Tustarī's commentary on this verse.

19 That is, their deficiency in knowledge.

20 That is, will be found to be true or sound according to the proof (*ḥujja*) that God requires.

21 In this passage Tustarī is showing that what is desirable is the knowledge of whether one is obeying or disobeying God, and he is connecting this to knowledge of one's state, which he elsewhere defines as a person's knowing whether each act that he does is for God or not. See above, Tustarī's commentary on 9:122.

It [the thought] is one of three things: it is either an enemy who wishes to cut him off [from God], or his lower self wanting to betray him, or his lower self trying to deceive him. In this case, he should not pay any attention to such thoughts (*khawāṭir*).[22]

22 On *khaṭar* see above Tustarī's commentary on 2:30, 2:269, and p. 16, n. 24.

20 Ṭā Hā

His words, Exalted is He:

[20:7] ***...He knows [that which you keep] secret and that which is yet more hidden* (akhfā).**

He said:

> *That which is yet more hidden* than a secret is something which the servant does not [consciously] think about, but thinks about in his sleep [unconsciously].

His words, Exalted is He:

[20:18] ***...I also have other uses for it.***[1]

> The first one to own the staff was Adam. It came from a myrtle tree in Paradise. Then it was passed down from prophet to prophet until it came to Shuʿayb. Subsequently, when [Shuʿayb] gave Moses his daughter in marriage, he presented the staff to him. Moses ﷺ used to lean on it, drive his sheep with it, scatter leaves for his sheep with it; then he would take from the tree whatever he wanted with it, and he would send it after lions, wild beasts and the vermin of the earth and it would strike them. If the heat became intense, he would stick it in the ground upright and it would provide shade. When he slept, it would guard over him until he awoke, and if the night was pitch dark, it would light up for him like a torch. When it was a cloudy day and he could not tell the time for prayer, it would give off rays from one of its sides. If he became hungry he would plant it in the earth and it would bear fruit immediately. These were the uses of his staff.[2]
>
> Moses ﷺ mentioned the benefits and uses of the staff that had appeared to him, but God, Exalted is He, intended [to draw his attention to] uses and benefits [of the staff] that were, as yet, hidden from him, such as its turning into a snake, or [Moses'] striking the rock with it so that the springs gushed forth from it, or his striking the sea with it, and other such uses. It was through this that He showed him that the knowledge of people, even when they are supported by prophecy (*nubuwwa*), is deficient when compared to God's knowledge regarding the universe of created things.

His words, Exalted is He:

[20:39] ***...I cast upon you love from Me...***[3]

He said:

> God made apparent his bequest of knowledge to him [Moses] before any works [were done].[4] He bequeathed for him love (*maḥabba*) in the hearts of His servants.[5] Thus, there

---

1 Referring to the staff of Moses, about which God has just inquired.

2 In his *ʿArāʾis al-majālis,* Thaʿlabī has devoted a chapter to traditions describing the many uses and miraculous powers of Moses' staff. See Thaʿlabī, pp. 190–1; trans. Brinner, pp. 294–6.

3 The context of these words is when Moses' mother is commanded by God to place him into an 'ark' and cast him into the river. Thus the love cast by God upon Moses was when he was still an infant. But interestingly, in his interpretation Tustarī refers to the bequest of knowledge before he speaks of the bequest of love, as will be seen in the commentary that follows.

4 By Moses, or even required of him.

5 Sufis teach that God rewards his prophets and saints by causing people to love them. However, possibly what is meant

are hearts that are rewarded before any action and punished before they have even considered [such an action] (*qabl al-raʾy*), just as a person may experience joy within his soul without knowing the reason for it, or experience sadness without knowing the reason for it.

His words, Exalted is He:

[20:40] ***...And We tried you with various ordeals...***[6]

That is, 'As trials for your natural self (*li-nafsika al-ṭabīʿiyya*),[7] and explained them [the tests] to you (*bayannāhā*) ⌜so that⌝ you should never feel secure from God's ruse'.[8]

His words, Exalted is He:

[20:41] ***And I chose you for Myself.***

That is, 'Devote yourself solely (*tafarrad*) to Me through the stripping away (*tajrīd*) [of all other], [so that] nothing diverts you from Me.'[9]

His words, Exalted is He:

[20:42] ***...And do not flag in remembrance of Me***[10]

That is, 'Do not keep abundant remembrance on [your] tongue, whilst being negligent concerning vigilance (*murāqaba*) in [your] heart.'

His words, Exalted is He:

[20:44] ***And speak to him gentle words...***

He said:

It was related from Ibn ʿAbbās ﷺ that he said, 'Moses ﷺ, when he visited Pharaoh, would say to him, 'O Abū Musʿab say: "There is no god except God and I am the Messenger of God"'.[11]

Sahl said:

Truly God, Exalted is He, invested Moses ﷺ with the robe of those who possess refined manners (*mutaʾaddibūn*),[12] and He removed from him the hastiness of those who impulsively rush in (*mutahajjimūn*),[13] due to the bounty (*faḍl*) and empowerment (*tamkīn*) that he found [from God].[14]

---

here is simply that Pharaoh's wife was moved with love for him, rescued him from the river and adopted him.

6 In verses 20:38–40 God is recounting to Moses episodes in his past life. The nature of the ordeals mentioned are not specified in the Qurʾān, although it is evident from the context that they occurred after his slaying of an Egyptian and his being hired by Shuʿayb: *...Then you slew a soul, whereupon We delivered you from [great] distress, and We tried you with various ordeals. Then you stayed for several years, among the people of Midian. Then you came [hither] as ordained. O Moses!*

7 The printed edition has *fitanan li-nafsika al-ṭabīʿiyya*, and this differs from all three MSS (Z515, f. 73a, F638, f. 34a and F3488, f. 245b), which read: *fatannā li-nafsik al-ṭabīʿī wa bayyannāhā ḥattā...*, with the variant: *fatannā nafsaka al-ṭabīʿī*. The latter simply takes *nafs* as a direct object of *fatanna*. Tustarī seems to use the terms *nafs al-ṭabʿ* and *nafs ṭabīʿiyya* interchangeably (see the commentary on 12:24). The masculine form of the adjective following the feminine noun (*nafs*), which appears here in the MSS, and in other contexts, in the printed edition, is puzzling. We have followed the printed edition in this case, since *bayyannāhā* appears to refer back to the trials (*fitan*).

8 On the divine ruse, see above Tustarī's commentary on 2:41 and p. 20, n. 47. See also 3:8 and p. 42, n.10.

9 In Sufism, the technical term *tajrīd*, lit. 'stripping away', means the purification of the self from all other than God. It is usually paired with the term *tafrīd*, lit. 'making single', which is to isolate the self for and in God. In this comment Tustarī has used the fifth form verbal noun from the root *f-r-d* (*tafarrud*), instead of the second form (*tafrīd*). On these two terms see, for example, Kalābādhī, *Kitāb al-Taʿarruf*, ch. 52, and Anṣārī, *Manāzil al-sāʾirīn*, chs. 97 and 98.

10 Both Moses and Aaron are being addressed here.

11 According to Ṭabarī's history, the name of the Pharaoh of Moses' day was Qabūs b. Musʿab b. Muʿāwiya, though Tustarī has here referred to him as 'Abū Musʿab. See Ṭabarī, *History*, vol. 3, *Children of Israel*, trans. Brinner, p. 31.

12 Substituting *mutaʾaddibūn* for *mutaʾawwibūn* in the published edition, on the basis of Z515, f. 72b; F638, f. 34a; and F3488, f. 245b.

13 Moses earlier had the reputation of being easily angered, as for example in 28:18. See also Ṭabarī, *History*, vol. 3, *Children of Israel*, trans. Brinner, p. 42.

14 MS Z515, f. 72b has *limā arāhu* instead of *limā raʾāhu*, which comes to the same, in that Moses was seeing what God showed him.

However, He did not will for him [Pharaoh] faith (*īmān*), for had He willed it, He would have said, 'So he may believe.'[15] Rather, God, Mighty and Majestic is He, intended by this [command] that Moses ﷺ should show graciousness (*mulāṭafa*) through the most beautiful discourse and gentlest speech, for this moves the hearts of all people, just as the Prophet ﷺ said, 'Hearts have been created with the disposition to love those who are good to them and to hate those who do wrong to them.'[16] This was to pre-empt his [Pharaoh's] argument (*ḥujja*), and to awaken interest in those among the sorcerers and others whom God knew would be guided.

His words, Exalted is He:

[20:46] ***He said, 'Do not fear, for I shall be with the two of you, hearing and seeing'.***

He said:

God informed them [Moses and Aaron] that He was with them through His regard (*naẓar*), witnessing every predicament they experience, [and] through His strength (*quwwa*), aid (*maʿūna*) and support (*taʾyīd*). So [He said], 'Do not be afraid of conveying the message under any circumstances.'

[**[20:81]** ***Eat of the good things We have provided for you, but do not transgress regarding them...***][17]

His words, Exalted is He, concerning this are [an admonition] that you should eat from them [the good things provided by God] in order to sustain yourselves, and should not satiate yourselves to the extent that you reach a state of intoxication (*sukr*) in which you are diverted from the remembrance [of God], for intoxication is forbidden.

And he said:

Whoever forces hunger upon himself, his blood will decrease in proportion to that, and in proportion to how much his blood decreases, evil suggestions (*waswasa*) will be blocked from entering his heart. If a mad person forced hunger upon himself he would become sane. The Prophet ﷺ said, 'There is not a vessel more detestable to God than a stomach filled with food.'[18]

His words, Exalted is He:

[20:111] ***And faces shall be humbled before the Living, the Eternal Sustainer...***

He said:

It means: They are humbled before Him in accordance with their station in gnosis (*maʿrifa*) of God and their being empowered (*tamkīn*) for receiving success (*tawfīq*) from Him.

His words:

[20:123] ***...then whoever follows My guidance will not go astray, nor fall into misery.***

He said:

That is, following and adhering to the Book and the Sunna. [Such a person] will not deviate from the path of guidance, and will not fall into wretchedness either in the Hereafter or in the present life.

His words, Exalted is He:

[20:131] ***Nor extend your gaze to what We have given to some pairs among them to enjoy [as] the flower of the life of this world...***

---

15 The verse actually says: '*that perhaps he may be mindful*' [20:44].

16 Tirmidhī, *Nawādir al-uṣūl*, vol. 1, p. 149; ʿAjlūnī, *Kashf al-khafāʾ*, vol. 1, p. 395; and Quḍāʿī, *Musnad al-Shihāb*, vol. 1, p. 350.

17 Tustarī appears in his commentary to have moved ahead to the next verse (20:81), which we have added in square brackets. All the MSS (Z515, f. 72b, F636, f. 34a and F3488, f. 346a) have *qawluhu taʿālā fīhi an kulū minhā*, which may indicate that the words of 20:81, which would have followed the words *qawluhu taʿālā*, may have been omitted. But the editors of both published editions have assumed the words: *kulū minhā* to be the words of the verse Tustarī is commenting on, with the editor of the Dār al-Kutub al-ʿIlmiyya edition adding the reference for 2:58, since the words for that verse also read: *kulū min ṭayyibāt mā razaqnākum*.

18 Bayhaqī, *Sunan al-kubrā* (Beirut, 1994), vol. 4, p. 177 and ʿAjlūnī, *Kashf al-khafāʾ*, vol. 2, p. 260.

He said:

> That is, 'Do not direct your attention to that which results in the whispering of Satan, opposition (*mukhālafa*) to the All-Merciful, cravings (*amānī*) from the lower self, or acquiescence (*sukūn*) in what is familiar to one's [basic] nature (*ṭab*ʿ)'; for each one of these is among the things which cut a person off from the remembrance (*dhikr*) of God, Mighty and Majestic is He.

21 Al-Anbiyāʾ

His words, Exalted is He:

[21:7] ***...Ask the People of Remembrance, if you do not know.***

He said:

> That is, the people who possess understanding of God and those who have knowledge of God, His commands and His days (*ayyām*).[1]

They said: 'Describe them for us.' He replied:

> Those possessed of knowledge are of three [kinds]. There are those who have knowledge of God but do not know His commandments or His days; they are the generality of the believers. There are those who have knowledge of God and His commandments but not of His days; they are the learned scholars. Then there are those who have knowledge of God, His commandments and His days; they are the prophets and veracious (*ṣiddīqūn*).

His words, Exalted is He:

[21:10] ***And now We have sent down [as revelation] to you a Book in which is remembrance that is yours...***

> That is, '[You will find] life (*ḥayāt*) through acting according to it.'

His words, Exalted is He:

[21:27] ***They do not [venture to] speak before He speaks, and they act according to His command.***

He said:

> Verily God, Exalted is He, has assigned every token of honour (*karāmāt*)[2] [firstly] to those among His servants who are mindful of Him (*muttaqūn*), and then to novices (*mubtadiʾūn*). Then he described them saying *They do not [venture to] speak before He speaks*, meaning: There is no choice for them along with His choice; *they act according to His command*, which is outwardly following the Sunna, and inwardly, maintaining vigilence (*murāqabat*) concerning God.

His words:

[21:35] ***...We test you with ill and good by way of a trial...***

He said:

> Ill (*sharr*) is the following of the lower self and desire (*hawā*), without guidance. Good (*khayr*) is [being granted] protection (*ʿiṣma*) from disobedience, and assistance (*maʿūna*) in obedience.

His words, Exalted is He:

[21:83] ***And [mention] Job, when he called out to his Lord, 'Indeed, harm has befallen me...'***

He said:

> Suffering (*ḍurr*) is of two kinds: outward suffering (*ẓāhir*) and inward suffering (*bāṭin*). The inward kind is a commotion (*ḥaraka*) and perturbation (*iḍṭirāb*) [within] the soul (*nafs*) in

---

1 On these levels of understanding see *Mystical Vision*, pp. 226–7. According to Makkī, the 'Days of God' refer to 'God's hidden blessing and His concealed punishments'. See Makkī, *Qūt al-qulūb*, vol. 1, p. 254; Makkī (attrib.), *ʿIlm al-qulūb*, p. 64.

2 Verse 26 speaks of God's *honoured servants*, so that Tustarī is here taking up the concept of honour or favour.

response to a moving emotional experience (*wārid*). The outward kind is when [the emotion] that is concealed in a person becomes outwardly apparent. [However], when what is being suffered inwardly settles [within a person, his] exterior becomes still and does not show it, and he patiently endures those pains. But when the interior (*bāṭin*) becomes unsettled (*taḥarraka*) under the influence of the [emotional] experience, the person's exterior will be shaken into weeping and loud cries. His [Job's] plea to God, Mighty and Majestic is He, is that He grant him assistance in finding acceptance (*riḍā*) in his heart for that experience. This is because as long as the heart is accepting of God's command, the servant will not be harmed by his outward reaction.[3] Just consider the instance of the Prophet's weeping ﷺ. Note that when he ﷺ wept on the death of his son Ibrāhīm, he wept for him out of compassion in accordance with his human nature. Yet his physical response did not harm him because his heart was accepting (*rāḍin*) of it.

Sahl used to say to his companions:

> Say in your supplication (*duʿāʾ*): 'O my Lord, if you cook me, I'll bear it and if you roast me, I'll be happy.[4] It is essential that You be known, so favour me with gnosis (*maʿrifa*) of You.'

He was asked about the abode (*dār*), whether it was an abode of Islam or disbelief.[5] He replied, 'The abode is the abode of tribulation (*balāʾ*) and testing (*ikhtibār*).'[6]

ʿAbd al-Raḥmān al-Marwazī asked Sahl, 'What do you say of a man whose lower self has been calling him to satiate it on the leaves of a lotus tree (*sidr*) for eighteen days?' Sahl answered, 'What do you say of a man whose lower self has been calling him to let him just catch the scent of the leaves of a lotus tree ⌜for twenty-five days⌝?'[7] He[8] said, '"ʿAbd al-Raḥmān started at this and became indignant.'[9]

His words, Exalted is He:

[21:69] ***We said: 'O Fire! Be coolness and safety for Abraham.***[10]

He said:

> Fire is [generally] authorised to burn; even so it will not burn anyone whom it is not authorised to burn.

ʿUmar b. Wāṣil al-ʿAnbarī said, 'I was with Sahl one night and removed the wick from the lamp, but in the process a small part of the flame touched my finger, causing me pain. Then Sahl looked at me and put his finger [in the flame] for nearly two hours without feeling any pain and without it having any effect on his finger, saying all the while, "I take refuge in God from the Fire."'

His words, Exalted is He:

[21:105] ***Indeed the land shall be inherited by My righteous servants.***

He said:

> He associated them with Himself and He graced them with the adornment of virtue (*ṣalāḥ*). What is implied by this is: 'Nothing is acceptable to Me except that which is done solely for Me without a trace within it for anyone besides Me.' They are those who have put their

---

3 lit. the acts of his bodily members, *jawāriḥ*.

4 That is, substituting *masʿūd* from MS Z515, f. 74b and F3488, f. 247a for *maḥnūdh* meaning thoroughly cooked in the published edition. MS F638, f. 34b appears to have *suʿūd*.

5 What is meant by *dār* in their question is this world.

6 Perhaps this question and the preceding comment has been inserted here on account of Tustarī's answer, which is relevant to the subject of being tested (cooked or roasted) by God in this life, and the need to be accepting of the suffering we experience.

7 Inserted on the basis of MSS Z515, f. 74b, and F3488, f. 247b. MS F638, f. 34b has the last part of ʿAbd al-Raḥmān's question and all of Sahl's reply missing.

8 Probably either Abū Bakr al-Sijzī or ʿUmar b. Wāṣil al-ʿAnbarī.

9 A similar tradition is related in Makkī, *Qūt al-qulūb*, vol. 2, pp. 292–3.

10 On this story of Abraham, see above, p. 32, n. 110. See also, 6:77 and p. 66, n. 13.

innermost secret (*sarīra*) in a good state with God, Exalted is He, and have detached themselves wholeheartedly from all besides Him.

His words, Exalted is He:

[21:106] ***...Indeed there is in this [Qurʾān] a proclamation for people who are devout...***

He said:

He did not make it a proclamation (*balāgh*) for all His servants. Rather, He made it especially for the group of people who are [true] worshippers (*ʿābidūn*). They are those who worship God, Exalted is He, and give their entire being (*muhaj*) to Him, not for a recompense, nor because of Paradise or Hell, but out of love (*ḥubb*) [for Him], and taking pride in the fact that He has made them worthy of worshipping Him. But God knows best.

22 Al-Ḥajj

His words, Exalted is He:

[22:3] ***And among mankind are those who dispute about God without any knowledge…***

That is, they dispute about religion as their whim (*hawā*) [dictates], or through analogical [reasoning] (*qiyās*), without following [exemplary guidance] (*iqtidāʾ*).[1] By doing this they lead people astray and produce innovation.

His words, Exalted is He:

[22:11] ***And among mankind there is the one who worships God, as it were, on a knife edge…***

The believer has one face, without a reverse side; he makes repeated [advances] and never retreats. You will see him striving for the cause of God's religion and His obedience, upholding God's oneness and the emulation of His Prophet ﷺ, constantly making humble entreaty (*taḍarruʿ*) of God and seeking refuge in Him in the hope of connecting to Him through following [exemplary guidance]. Zayd b. Aslam related from the Prophet ﷺ that he said: 'Every person of my nation (*umma*) will enter Paradise, save the one who refuses.' We said, 'O Messenger of God who will refuse that?' He said, 'Whoever obeys me will enter Paradise, and whoever disobeys me has refused to enter Paradise.'[2]

His words, Exalted is He:

[22:11] ***…if good [fortune] befalls him, he is reassured by it…***

That is, whoever follows [his] desire, if his heart is satisfied and his lower self is happy in its worldly share, he will feel reassured by it. Otherwise he will return to the disbelief that his desire calls him to.[3]

His words:

[22:14] ***Truly God shall admit those who believe and perform righteous deeds into gardens…***

He said:

They are those who were faithful to God in secret as well as in public, and followed the Sunna of the Prophet ﷺ and did not innovate in any situation.

His words:

[22:18] ***…the sun and the moon…***[4]

He said:

The prostration of these things consists of their recognition (*maʿrifa*) of God [manifested] through their abasing themsleves (*tadhallul*) and submitting (*inqiyād*) to Him.

---

1 The nature of this exemplary guidance is not specified here, but it could refer to the Prophet's Sunna, guidance of the pious predecessors (*salaf*), or of a spiritual teacher. See above. IT, pp. liii–liv.

2 Bukhārī, *Ṣaḥīḥ*, 'al-Iʿtiṣām bi'l-Kitāb wa'l-sunna.'

3 'Otherwise' meaning if an ordeal befalls him he will return to unbelief, as it says later in the same verse: *…he makes a turn about, losing this world and the Hereafter. That is the manifest loss.*

4 The context of these words is: *Have you not seen that to God prostrate whoever is in the earth, together with the sun and the moon, and the stars and the mountains, the trees and the animals…*[22:18].

His words:

[22:26] *...Purify My House for those who circumambulate it...*

That is, 'Purify My House from idols, for those among My servants whose hearts are pure from doubt (*shakk*), misgivings (*rayb*) and hardness (*qaswa*). Therefore, just as God has commanded the purification of His House [at Mecca] from idols, so also He has commanded the purification of that house of His in which He deposited the mystery of faith (*sirr al-īmān*) and the light of gnosis (*nūr al-maʿrifa*), namely, the heart of the believer. God, Exalted is He, has commanded the believer to purify himself from rancour (*ghill*), deceit (*ghishsh*), inclination towards the lusts of the lower self (*shahawāt al-nafs*) and heedlessness (*ghafla*). For those who circumambulate it [the Kaʿba], as also for those who uphold the lights of faith, there will be manifold increase in [God-given] success (*tawfīq*).

[22:26] *...And those who bow and prostrate themselves*

in fear and hope. Truly the heart ⌈is [like] a house⌉[5]: if it is unoccupied it goes to ruin, and [likewise] if it is occupied by other than its owner, ⌈or by other than one whom the owner has settled there⌉, it will also go to ruin. Therefore, if you wish your hearts to be in good repair, do not let your prayer in them be other than to God, Exalted is He;[6] ⌈if you want to keep your breasts (*ṣudūr*) in good repair, let not anything be in them other than [awareness of] the Hereafter⌉;[7] if you want to preserve your tongues, do not let your prayer on them be other than truthfulness (*ṣidq*); and if you wish to preserve your bodily members, do not allow them to become engaged with anything other than what is in accordance with the Sunna.

His words:

[22:27] *And announce among the people the [season for] Pilgrimage. They shall come to you on foot...*

Verily God, Exalted is He, has servants among whom some go to mosques on thrones (*sarīr*), and some ride on conveyances of gold covered with silk and drawn by angels.

Aḥmad b. Sālim said, 'I was working on a piece of land to improve it, when I saw Sahl on a couch above the water of the Euphrates River.' He also said, 'One day I entered Sahl's house, the door of which was very small, and I saw a horse standing there. Then I left in fright, wondering how it could have entered through such a small door. Sahl saw me and told me to come back, so I returned and saw nothing there.'[8]

It has been related that ʿUmar b. al-Khaṭṭāb ﷺ was gazing down on the congregation at ʿArafāt and said, 'If only the congregation in this plain knew [the hosts] who have descended, they would have rejoiced at His bounty (*faḍl*) after [receiving tidings of] being forgiven (*maghfira*)'.[9]

His words:

[22:28] *...And celebrate God's name, on specified days, over the livestock He has provided for them...*

[By which] is meant the gifts and sacrifices. It was related of Fatḥ al-Mawṣilī that on the day of Eid he looked down over the city of Mosul and could see smoke rising from many houses, so he said, 'O my Lord! How many people are drawing closer to You through sacrifice (*qurbān*) this night! I have also tried to draw closer to You through sacrifice,' that is to say, through prayers (*ṣalawāt*). 'What will You make of it, O Beloved One?'[10] It was related of ʿAdī b. Thābit

5 Added on the basis of MS F638, f. 35a only, but the addition of the word *bayt* here really makes better sense and completes the analogy.

6 Who, as we saw above, is the Owner of hearts.

7 The other additions in the passage were made on the basis of all three MSS: Z515, f. 76a, MS F638, f. 35a and MS F3488, f. 248b.

8 On some charismatic gifts (*karāmāt*) attributed to Tustarī, see IT, above p. xx.

9 As part of the Hajj, pilgrims gather on the plain of ʿArafāt and stay there from after the dawn prayer until sunset.

10 Ibn al-Jawzī, *Ṣifat al-ṣafwa*, vol. 4, p. 188; Ibn Ḥanbal, *Kitāb al-Waraʿ* (Beirut, 1983), p. 92.

al-Anṣārī that he said, 'The sacrifice of those who are mindful of God (*muttaqūn*) is prayer.'[11] But God knows best.

His words:

[22:29] *...And perform the circumambulation of the Ancient House.*

He said:

People have differed concerning this. Ḥasan said, 'He called it Ancient (*ʿatīq*) to honour it, just as the Arabs speak of an "ancient" body, and an "ancient" horse if it is noble.'[12]

My maternal uncle, Muḥammad b. Sawwār,[13] related on the authority of al-Thawrī that he said, 'It is called this because it is the oldest (*aqdam*) and most ancient (*aʿtaq*) place of worship belonging to God, just as He said: *The first House (of worship) to be established for people was that at Bakka, a blessed place* [3:96].'

Some have said, 'He [God] called it *ʿatīq* because no tyrant ever headed for it with an evil design without God's destroying him and freeing (*aʿtaqa*) His House from him. Some have said, 'It is because it was saved (*uʿtiqa*) from being submerged during the great flood and raised to the sky.' Just as God has freed His House, so He has also freed the heart of the believer from other [than Him]. It [the Kaʿba] is older than anything else that God, Exalted is He, erected on His earth as a sign (*ʿalam*), and He placed it within the Sacred Mosque (*al-Masjid al-Ḥarām*). Likewise the heart has [within it] another heart, which is the position from which the servant stands before his Master without being agitated or busied by anything, but in a state of tranquil repose in Him (*sākin ilayhi*).

His words, Exalted is He:

[22:46] *...Indeed, it is not the eyes that become blind, but it is their hearts that become blind within the breasts.*

He said:

Is it not true that with the light of the heart's insight (*nūr baṣar al-qalb*) a person can overcome desire and lust? But when the heart's sight is blind to what is within it, lust will overcome him and heedlessness (*ghafla*) will [afflict] him at regular intervals. Consequently his body will stray into[14] sin without being guided to God under any circumstances.

His words, Exalted is He:

[22:52] *We did not send before you any Messenger or prophet but that when he recited [the scripture] Satan cast [something] into his recitation...*

He said:

That is, if he recites [the Scripture] and his lower self notices the recitation,[15] Satan casts [something into it], for he[16] has a partnership with the lower self in this, and that noticing of the recitation comes from the desire of the lower self and its lust. However, if [the person reciting] then witnesses the One remembered (*madhkūr*) instead of the remembrance [itself] (*dhikr*), the heart will become oblivious of it [the recitation], and he will not witness anything besides his Master. Consequently Satan will become one of his captives. Do you not see how if a servant is inattentive (*sahā*) in his recitation (*qirāʾa*) or in his remembrance of his Lord, Mighty and

11 Ibn Abī Shayba, *al-Muṣannaf*, vol. 2, p. 159.

12 The word *ʿatīq* can mean excellent, when associated with being old.

13 Translating 'my maternal uncle Muḥammad b. Sawwār' (*khālī Muḥammad b. Sawwār*), on the basis of MS F638, f 36a. MSS: Z515, f. 76a and F3488, f. 249a have 'Muḥammad b. Sawwār's maternal uncle' (*khāl Muḥammad b. Sawwār*), while the printed edition has 'his maternal uncle' (*khāluhu*).

14 MS F638, f. 35b has *mutakhabbiṭan*, meaning 'blunder or stray into', instead of *mutakhaṭṭiyan*, meaning 'err'.

15 In a vain manner. On the manner in which the Qurʾān should and should not be recited, see Tustarī's comments above, IC, pp. 3–4 and pp. 7–8.

16 The published edition has 'into his ear' (*alqā fī udhnihi*) before the words *idh lahu*. However these words do not appear in any of the MSS. MS Z515, f. 76a has *adhalla ʿālāʾl-nafs*, which could easily be a misreading of *idh lahu*.

> Majestic is He, his heart acquiesces in the basest pleasures (*ḥuẓūẓ*) of his lower self and thus can the Enemy [Satan] get at him. Ḥasan said, 'The whispering (*waswās*) is of two kinds, one of which is from the lower self and the other from Satan. That which persists in coming is from the lower self, and assistance against it is sought through fasting, prayer and propriety (*adab*). However, that which [comes, but then] withdraws (*nabdhan*) is from Satan, and assistance against it is sought through the recitation of the Qurʾān and remembrance [of God] (*dhikr*).'

His words:

[22:54] ***...so that they may believe therein and their hearts may be humbled to Him...***

He said:

> True faith (*ṣidq al-īmān*) and its [true] realisation (*ḥaqīqa*) produce humility (*ikhbāt*) within the heart, which consists of tenderness (*riqqa*), fear (*khashiya*) and humble submission (*khushūʿ*) in the heart, and results in long periods of reflection (*fikr*) and silence (*ṣamt*). These are among the results of faith, for God, Exalted is He, has said: *So that they may believe in it and their hearts may be humbled to Him.* And God knows best.

23 Al-Muʾminūn

His words, Exalted is He:

[23:1–2] ***Indeed, prosperous are the believers, ۞ those who in their prayers are humbly submissive* (khāshiʿūn),**

[Sahl was asked], 'What is humble submission?' He replied:

Humble submission (*khushūʿ*) is openly [manifested] (*ʿalāniyya*). It is to stand before God, Exalted is He, while maintaining the conditions for the finest conduct (*ādāb*) required by the One who commands (*al-Āmir*), which is to purge your [moments of] activity (*ḥarakāt*) and stillness (*sukūn*) from anything other than Him. The root of this is fear (*khashiya*) within the innermost secret (*sirr*). If a person is given fear, humble submission will manifest in his exterior and this is one of the conditions of [true] faith.

It has been related of Ḥasan b. ʿAlī ﷺ that when he finished his ablutions, the colour of his face would change and he was asked about that. He said, 'It is appropriate that the face of the one who intends to enter the presence of the Master of the Throne [God] should change colour.' It is related of the Prophet ﷺ that he said to Muʿādh, 'Truly, the Qurʾān has curbed (*qayyada*) the believer from much of what his lower self desires, and by God's permission has come between him and his being ruined by that desire. Indeed, the believer is a captive to whomsoever has a rightful claim over him. O Muʿādh! The believer strives to liberate himself. O Muʿādh! Truly a believer's fear will not abate, nor his unrest be stilled until he leaves behind him the Traverse over Hell.[1] O Muʿādh! Truly the believer knows that there are observers keeping watch over his hearing, sight, tongue, hands, feet, stomach and genitals, and even the blinking of his eye, the particles of mud on his fingers, the kohl in his eyes and every movement he makes. Mindfulness of God (*taqwā*) is his companion (*rafīq*), the Qurʾān is his guide (*dalīl*), fear (*khawf*) is his way (*maḥajja*), longing (*shawq*) is his riding beast (*maṭiyya*), dread (*wajl*) is his emblem (*shiʿār*), prayer (*ṣalāt*) is his cave [of refuge] (*kahf*), fasting (*ṣiyām*) is his garden [or Paradise] (*janna*), charity (*ṣadaqa*) is his source of liberation (*fikāk*), truthfulness (*ṣidq*) is his vizier, shame (*ḥayāʾ*) is his emir, and behind all of these, his Lord is on the look out (*bi-mirṣād*). O Muʿādh! I wish for you what I wish for myself. I have forbidden you that which Gabriel ﷺ forbade me. I do not know anyone at all who will join me on the Day of Resurrection and who will be happier than you at what God has granted you.'[2]

His words:

[23:17] ***And verily We created above you seven paths…***

That is, the seven veils (*ḥujub*) which veil [a person] from his Lord, Mighty and Majestic is He: the first veil is his intellect (*ʿaql*), the second his knowledge (*ʿilm*), the third his heart (*qalb*), the fourth his fear (*khashiya*), the fifth his self (*nafs*), the sixth his wish (*irāda*) and the seventh his will (*mashīʾa*). The intellect [is a veil] in its preoccupation with the management of the affairs

1 The 'Traverse' (*ṣirāṭ*) is traditionally described as a bridge stretched over the gulf of Hell, sharper than a sword and thinner than a hair, which all the believers are made to cross at the Resurrection. It is described in Ghazālī's *Iḥyāʾ ʿulūm al-dīn*, Book 40: *Kitāb Dhikr al-mawt wa-mā baʿdahu*, trans. Timothy J. Winter, as *The Remembrance of Death and the Afterlife* (Cambridge, 1989), pp. 205–10.

2 Ṭabarānī, *al-Muʿjam al-awsaṭ*, vol. 8, p. 176; Iṣfahānī, *Ḥilyat al-awliyāʾ*, vol. 1, pp. 26–7, and vol. 10, p. 31.

of this world (*tadbīr al-dunyā*); knowledge because of the vainglory (*mubāhāt*) [it breeds] among peers; the heart in its heedlessness (*ghafla*); fear because of its disregard for influxes [of grace from above] (*bi-ighfālihā ʿan mawārid al-umūr ʿalayhā*)[3]; the self because it is the haven (*maʾwā*) for every tribulation (*baliyya*); the will because it is directed towards this world and turned away from the Hereafter; the wish due to its pursuance of sins.

His words:

[23:51] ***...Eat of the good things and perform righteous acts...***

That is, 'Eat what is legitimate to sustain yourselves whilst keeping propriety.' Sustenance (*qiwām*) is that which you need to maintain your body while preserving your heart. Propriety in this is to show gratitude (*shukr*) to the Bestower of blessings (*al-Munʿim*). The least amount of gratitude a person should show is not to disobey Him by [abusing] any of the blessings [He has bestowed upon him].

His words:

[23:57] ***Surely those who are in awe of their Lord are apprehensive,***

He said: Fear (*khashiya*) is broken-heartedness (*inkisār al-qalb*) which comes from constantly standing (*intiṣāb*) before Him.[4] After this level comes fearful apprehension (*ishfāq*), which is a milder (*araqq*) state than fear and more subtle (*alṭaf*).[5] Fear is milder than dread (*khawf*) and dread is milder than terror (*rahba*), but for each one there is a particular characteristic and a place.

His words:

[23:76] ***...Yet they did not humble themselves to their Lord, nor do they devote themselves to prayer.***

They did not devote themselves solely to their Lord in worship nor did they abase themselves before Him in His unicity (*waḥdāniyya*).

3 Note the use of *ʿalayhā*, feminine referring back to fear (*khashiya*), and thus suggesting a direct connection between these divine influxes of grace from God and the state of fear. As Tustarī has indicated a number of times, fear is a condition of true faith, yet in itself it can become a veil.

4 That is, maintaining a reverential awareness of His presence.

5 The printed edition has *al-luṭf* instead of *alṭaf*, which is clearly written in MSS: Z515, f. 78a and F3488, f. 251a. MS F638, f. 36a appears to have the extra 'lām' of *al-luṭf* partially erased.

24 Al-Nūr

His words, Exalted is He:

[24:1] ***[This is] a sūra which We have revealed and prescribed…***

That is, We compiled it and expounded within it what is lawful and unlawful.

His words, Exalted is He:

[24:22] ***…Let them forgive and excuse…***

That is, 'Let them pardon the wrong done to them by people.' It is related from Sufyān al-Thawrī that he said, 'God sent the revelation to ʿUzayr:[1] "If you are not good natured such that you are like a morsel in the mouths of the children of Adam, I will not record you among the humble (*mutawāḍiʿūn*)." ʿUzayr replied, "O my Lord, what is the hallmark of the one whom You have chosen for Your love (*mawadda*)?" He replied, "I make him content with a meagre provision, and I activate him to [prepare for] the momentous and tremendous [event].[2] [His hallmark is also that he] eats little and weeps much; he seeks My forgiveness before dawn, and detests the licentious (*fujjār*) for My sake."'

His words:

[24:26] ***Vile women are for vile men…***

Women who have corrupted hearts are for men with corrupted hearts, and men who have corrupted hearts are for women with corrupted hearts.

His words:

[24:30] ***Say to the believing men to lower their gaze…***

That is, avert your gaze from that which God, Exalted is He, has forbidden you. This means to avoid any look that lacks a sense of honour. It is related from ʿUbāda b. Ṣāmit that the Prophet ﷺ said, 'If you can safeguard six things, I will guarantee for you entry into Paradise: be truthful when you speak; fulfil whatever you promise; carry out what has been entrusted to you [to do]; keep your chastity; lower your gaze; and refrain from doing harm to anyone.'[3]

It is reported that Ibn ʿUmar ؓ was asked, 'Did the Messenger of God ever look around during the prayer?' He answered, 'Not even outside the prayer [did he look around].'

His words:

[24:31] ***…And rally to God in repentance, O believers…***

---

1 ʿUzayr is mentioned only once in the Qurʾān [9:30], *The Jews say: ʿUzayr is the son of God; and the Christians say: The Messiah is the son of God.* Muslim commentators have usually identified ʿUzayr with Ezra, or occasionally with the man who slept for a hundred years, referred to in 2:259. However, modern scholars have variously identified him with Enoch, Azazel and even Osiris. See H. Lazarus Yafeh, 'Uzayr', *EI²*, vol. x, p. 960. According to Muslim tradition, God caused the Jews of ʿUzayr's time to forget the Torah, due to their sinning. ʿUzayr grieved over this loss, and was consequently enlightened by a divine flame and taught the entire Torah by God. Once it was confirmed that what he had received was indeed the Torah, people started to revere him as the son of God. We can see in Tustarī's comment above that ʿUzayr is regarded as a recipient of divine revelation.

2 i.e. the Resurrection.

3 Bayhaqī, *Shuʿab al-īmān*, vol. 4, pp. 206 and 230.

[Sahl] was asked: 'What is repentance (*tawba*)?' He replied:

It is that you exchange your ignorance for knowledge, your forgetfulness for remembrance and your disobedience for obedience.

His words, Exalted is He:

[24:35] ***God is the light of the heavens and the earth…***

That is, the One who has adorned the heavens and earth with lights.[4] *The likeness of his light* means the likeness of the light of Muḥammad ﷺ. Ḥasan al-Baṣrī said, 'He intended by this the heart of the believer and the luminescence (*ḍiyāʾ*) of professing the divine oneness (*tawḥīd*), for the hearts of the prophets ﷺ are far too brilliant in their light to be described in terms of the likeness of these lights. He said,[5] 'The similitude of the light of the Qurʾān is a lamp (*miṣbāḥ*), a lamp whose candle (*sirāj*) is gnosis (*maʿrifa*), whose wick (*fatīl*) is the religious obligations (*farāʾiḍ*), whose oil (*duhn*) is sincerity (*ikhlāṣ*) and whose light (*nūr*) is the light of [spiritual] attainment (*ittiṣāl*).[6] Whenever the sincerity increases in purity, the lamp increases in brightness (*ḍiyāʾ*); and whenever the religious obligations increase in [inner] realisation (*ḥaqīqa*), the lamp increases in light (*nūr*).

His words:

[24:37] ***…They fear a day when hearts and eyes will be tossed about,***

That is, the Day of Resurrection, when hearts and eyes will turn over, in one state after another, and will not remain constantly in one state.[7] The believer is the one who fears that Day. According to a saying related from Ḥasan [al-Baṣrī], someone mentioned in his presence, 'There is a man who will leave the Hellfire after a thousand years', to which Ḥasan responded, 'If only I were him.'[8] It was related from ʿAwn b. ʿAbd Allāh that he said, 'Luqmān counselled his son, saying: "Have hope in God without feeling secure from His ruse (*makr*) and fear God without despairing of His mercy."[9] He responded [by asking], "How can I do that when I only have one heart?" He replied: "O my son, the believer has two hearts, one with which he carries hope in God and the other with which he fears Him."'[10] And God knows best.

4 On Sufi interpretations of the Light Verse (24:35), see Gerhard Böwering, 'The Light Verse: Qurʾānic Text and Sufi Interpretation', *Oriens* 36 (2001), pp. 113–44.

5 All three MSS (Z515 f. 79a; F638, f. 36b and F3488, f. 252a) have *qāla al-Thawrī*, while the published edition has *qāla al-nūr*. The latter, which is what we have translated, seems more likely.

6 This is on the basis of Böwering's translation.

7 Commenting on the words, *They fear a day when hearts and eyes will be tossed about*, Ṭabarī writes that hearts will be tossed or turned about in terror (*hawl*) at it (the Day or what they are to experience), while eyes are turned about to see from which direction they will be seized, or in which hand their book will be given to them, the right or the left.

8 Ḥasan al-Baṣrī was known for his austerity and fear of God.

9 On the divine ruse see above Tustarī's commentary on 2:41 and p. 20, n. 47. See also p. 42, n. 10.

10 Though elsewhere, Tustarī accords with 33:4 (*God has not placed two hearts inside any man*), when he contends that man has only one heart. On this, see IT, p. xlvi above.

25 Al-Furqān

His words, Exalted is He:

[25:1] ***Blessed is He who revealed the Criterion…***

Sahl said:

> That is, Majestic and Exalted is He who privileged Muḥammad ﷺ by revealing to him the Criterion (*furqān*), that he may distinguish truth from falsehood, friend from foe, and the one who is close [to God] from the one who is remote [from Him]; *to His servant,* that is, to His purest servant, His most privileged Prophet, His closest beloved, and the foremost of His elect; *that he may be to all the worlds a warner*, that is, so that he may be a lamp (*sirāj*) and a light (*nūr*), by which We guide people to [follow] the rulings of the Qurʾān, so that they can proceed thereby according to the path of truth (*ṭarīq al-ḥaqq*) and the way of veracity (*minhaj al-ṣidq*).

His words:

[25:20] ***…And We have made some of you a trial for others, will you be steadfast? Your Lord is ever Watchful.***

He said:

> Verily, God, Exalted is He, has commanded steadfastness (*ṣabr*) in the face of that in which He has placed a test (*fitna*) for mankind. From this [steadfastness] comes a diminishing in one's coveting (*iṭrāq*) what [other] people possess. Abū Ayyūb related concerning the Prophet ﷺ that a man came to him ⌜and said 'Give me a sermon, in a few words⌝',[1] so he said, 'When you stand for prayer, perform the prayer of one who is bidding farewell;[2] do not say anything which you will be sorry for saying tomorrow; and resolve to give up hope of [attaining] that which other people possess.'[3]
>
> Indeed our predecessors used to take full advantage of this [admonition], such that it is related of Ḥudhayfa that he said, 'Truly, the most delightful day for me is the day on which I return home and my family complains to me of their need. This is because I heard the Messenger of God ﷺ say: "Verily God has kept the world from his believing servant, just as the family of a sick person keeps food and drink from him. Indeed, God promises the believer affliction (*balāʾ*) just as the father promises good things (*khayr*) for his son."'

His words, Exalted is He:

[25:28] ***Oh woe is me! Would that I had not taken so and so as a friend!***

He said:

> The soundest friendship is that which does not lead to regret (*nadāma*), and that is nothing less than intimacy (*uns*) with God, Exalted is He, and seclusion from people. The Messenger of God ﷺ used to observe seclusion (*khalwa*) for the sake of the knowledge that God had opened to his heart, for he liked to reflect upon it.

---

1 Added on the basis of Z515, f. 79b and F638, f. 36b.

2 i.e. bidding farewell to this world, that is, with the care you would take if it were the very last prayer you were able to make.

3 Ibn Māja, *Sunan*, 'Bāb al-Ḥikma'; Ibn Ḥanbal, *al-Musnad*, vol. 5, p. 412.

Everything will befriend the person whose prayer is good. Such a person will be stirred during sleep at the prayer times so that he awakes. This is done by his brothers among the jinn who have befriended him. They may also accompany him when he travels and give him priority over themselves. The angels may even befriend him.[4] Once a man made a request from Sahl saying, 'I really want to keep your company.' He said, 'When one of us dies, let whomsoever keeps company with the one who survives, keep his company from then on.'[5]

Al-Rabīʿ b. Khaytham was sitting on his porch one day when a stone came flying at him and struck his forehead making a gash in it, upon which he said, 'Truly, you have been admonished, O Ibn Khaytham!' Then he entered his home, shutting the door behind him and was not seen seated in that same position up to his death.[6]

His words:

[25:58] *Put your trust in the Living One who does not die…*

Ibn Sālim was asked about trust (*tawakkul*) and earning (*kasb*), and through which of these [two] people should serve [God]. He said:

Trust (*tawakkul*) was the state of being (*ḥāl*) of the Messenger of God ﷺ and earning was his Sunna. He only established the Sunna of earning for them due to their weakness, after they fell from the rank of trust (*tawakkul*), which was his state of being. However he did not demote them from the rank of seeking a living through earning, which is his Sunna. Furthermore, had it not been for that [the Sunna of earning] they would have perished.[7]

Sahl said:

Whoever defames earning (*kasb*), has defamed the Sunna and whoever defames trust (*tawakkul*) has defamed faith.[8]

His words:

[25:63] *…And when the ignorant address them they say [words of] peace…*

That is, they say that which is correct and appropriate. Ḥasan al-Baṣrī said: 'This was their way during the day. However, during the night they were as God describes them in the next verse, *Those who spend the night [in adoration of] their Lord prostrating and standing* [25:64].

His words:

[25:70] *Except for him who repents…*

He said:

The repentance of not one of you is acceptable until he abstains from much of that which is permissible for fear that it will lead him into something which is not permissible, just as ʿĀʾisha said, 'Put between you and what is forbidden (*ḥarām*), a screen of that which is permissible (*ḥalāl*). It was the practise of the Messenger of God ﷺ to keep away from us for three days after our purification [after menstruation or childbirth] until any possibility of renewed bleeding (*fawra*) had gone.'

---

4 All three MSS (Z515, f. 80a, F638, f. 37a and F3488, f. 253a) have *bihim* here instead of *bihi* in the published edition. However, the flow of the text suggests *bihi*.

5 It appears, then, that when two righteous people become companions, one of them will inherit on the death of the other, all the jinn who had kept company with his companion. But Tustarī is here suggesting that they should benefit from the company of each other's jinn even before either one of them dies.

6 This was evidently a sign to him that he had not been enjoying the protection of the jinn. The tradition is listed in Bayhaqī, *Shuʿab al-īmān*, vol. 6, p. 264, and in Ibn al-Jawzī, *Ṣifat al-ṣafwa*, vol. 3, p. 67.

7 Iṣfahānī, *Ḥilyat al-awliyāʾ*, vol. 10, pp. 378–9; Sulamī, *Ṭabaqāt al-ṣūfiyya*, p. 431.

8 The saying is cited in Makkī, *Qūt al-qulūb*, vol. 2, pp. 4 and 9–10. The latter citation has the variant: 'discredited the oneness of God (*tawḥīd*)' instead of 'discredited faith (*īmān*)'. See also Iṣfahānī, *Ḥilyat al-awliyāʾ*, vol. 10, p. 195.

His words:

[25:72] ***And those who do not give false testimony…***

He said:

False testimony (*zūr*) is the tribunal of the [heretical] innovators.[9] But God knows best.

9 i.e. it is what they share.

26 Al-Shuʿarāʾ

His words, Exalted is He:

[26:3] ***It may be that you kill yourself with grief that they will not become believers.***

He said:

> That is, that you would destroy yourself in pursuing what is required for the sake of their guidance, but the decree (*ḥukm*) has preceded from Us concerning the faith of every believer, and disbelief of every disbeliever, and there will be no change or substitution [in that decree]. The inner meaning of these [words] is: 'You have been distracted from Us through your preoccupation with them, out of a desire that they should believe. But you are only responsible for conveying [the Message], so do not let your grief concerning them distract you from Us.'

His words:

[26:5] ***And there would never come from the Compassionate One any reminder[1] that is new, but that they used to disregard it.***

He said:

> That is, whenever there came to them, through revelation, knowledge of the Qurʾān which was new to them and of which they had no prior knowledge, they would turn away from it. This is not to say that the Reminder (*dhikr*) itself is created (*muḥdath*),[2] however, for it is from among the attributes of the essence of God, and is therefore neither existentiated (*mukawwan*) nor created (*makhlūq*).[3]

His words:

[26:78] ***'...[He] who created me, it is He who guides me,'***[4]

He said:

> 'He who created me for His adoration guides me to proximity (*qurb*) with Him.'

His words:

[26:79] ***and provides me with food and drink,***

He said:

> 'He feeds me with the joy of faith and gives me to drink from the draught of trust (*tawakkul*) and of being sufficed (*kifāya*).'[5]

---

1 Commentators gloss the word *reminder* here as 'revelation'.

2 This caveat has been inserted because Tustarī has used the word *aḥdatha* in the sense of the coming of something new, but the verbal root *ḥ-d-th* can also be used to imply something that is temporal or an 'accident', in philosophical and theological terminology.

3 Tustarī is here indicating his belief that the Qurʾān is the uncreated word of God, on which see above IT, p. xxxi. Tustarī's doctrine of the divine speech as one of the attributes of God is discussed in his *Risālat al-ḥurūf*, which is edited and analysed in the dissertations of Gaafar and Garrido Clemente.

4 Verses 72–89 of Sūrat al-Shuʿarāʾ relate words of Abraham, firstly his reasoning with his father and his people over the falsity of their worship of idols and his description of his Lord (vv. 72–82), and then his prayer to God for salvation for himself and for forgiveness for his father (vv. 83–9).

5 On the term *kifāya* and its connection to *ḥusn al-ẓann*, see above Tustarī's commentary on 2:260.

His words:

[26:80] ***and when I am sick, it is He who cures me,***

He said:

> This means: 'If I am stirred into acting by other than Him for other than Him, He protects me [from carrying out that action], and if I incline towards a worldly desire He averts it from me.'

His words:

[26:81] ***Who will make me die and then give me life [again],***

He said:

> 'He causes me to die through heedlessness (*ghafla*), and then gives me life again through remembrance (*dhikr*).'

His words:

[26:82] ***'And who, I hope, will forgive my iniquity on the Day of Judgement.'***

> He [Abraham] expressed his words according to the requisites of propriety (*adab*) [before God], [poised] between fear and hope, and did not [assume] that forgiveness had been predetermined for him.[6]

His words, Exalted is He:

[26:84] ***'And confer on me a worthy repute among posterity,'***

He said:

> 'Grant me the praise of all nations and hosts.'

His words, Mighty and Majestic is He:

[26:89] ***except him who brings to God a heart that is sound.***

He said:

> [This refers to] the one who is preserved from innovations (*bidaʿ*), who commits his affairs to God and who is content with God's decree (*qadar*).

His words, Exalted is He:

[26:212] ***Truly they are barred from hearing [it].***

He said:

> This means [they are barred] from listening (*istimāʿ*) to the Qurʾān and understanding (*fahm*) [where] the commandments and prohibitions [are applicable].

His words:

[26:214] ***Warn the nearest of your kinsfolk,***

He said:

> Put fear into those who are closest to you and lower the wing of [gentleness] over those who are distantly related to you. Guide them to Us [kindly] with the finest proofs (*alṭaf al-dalālāt*),[7] and inform them that I am Magnanimous (*al-Jawād*) and Generous (*al-Karīm*).

His words, Exalted is He:

[26:227] ***Save those who believe and perform righteous deeds and remember God frequently...***

He said:

> God, Exalted is He, created the innermost secret (*sirr*) and made its life consist in His remembrance. He created the outward self (*ẓāhir*) and made its life consist in praising (*ḥamd*) and thanking (*shukr*) Him. He appointed for both of them duties (*ḥuqūq*), which are works of obedience (*ṭāʿa*).

---

6 On balancing fear and hope see Tustarī's commentary on 11:75 and p. 93, n. 13 above.

7 The word *alṭaf*, superlative or comparative of *laṭīf* could also mean delicate, subtle or gracious.

27 Al-Naml

His words, Exalted is He:

[27:10, 11] ...*Surely in My presence the messengers do not fear,* ❁ *except he who has wronged [others]...*

He said:

> There was never among the prophets and messengers an oppressor. However, this address to them is actually indirectly referring to their people, just as when He said to the Prophet ﷺ: *If you associate others [with God], your work shall surely fail* [39:65], those who are intended are his nation (*umma*), for when they hear this admonition being addressed to the Prophet ﷺ, they will be even more cautious [concerning themselves].

His words, Exalted is He:

[27:19] ...*[And he said] 'My Lord, inspire me to be thankful for the blessings You have granted me...'*[1]

He said:

> The servant has no right to speak except with the command of his Master, nor strike except with His command, nor walk except with His command, nor eat, sleep or reflect except with His command. This is the best form of gratitude and it is the gratitude of servants to their Master.

His words, Exalted is He:

[27:19] ...*and include me, by Your mercy, among Your righteous servants.*

He said:

> This means, 'Grant me proximity to Your friends (*awliyāʾ*) so that I may be among their company, even though I have not reached their station (*maqām*).'

His words, Exalted is He:

[27:52] *So those, then, are their houses [lying] deserted because of the evil that they did...*

He said:

> *Their houses* are an allusion to hearts;[2] for there are hearts which are inhabited (*ʿāmir*) through remembrance (*dhikr*), and there are those which are ruined (*kharib*) through heedlessness (*ghafla*).[3] Whomsoever God, Mighty and Majestic is He, inspires with [His] remembrance, He has freed from oppression (*ẓulm*).[4]

His words, Exalted is He:

[27:59] *[Say] 'Praise be to God and peace be on His servants whom He has chosen...'*

---

1 These words are spoken by Solomon after he hears one of the ants warn the other ants to enter their homes lest Solomon and his army crush them. The Qurʾān relates that Solomon smiles on hearing these words and then thanks God for the blessings he and his family have been granted — including, presumably, his ability to hear the language of the birds and other creatures.

2 Translating the plural, *qulūb*, on the basis of MS F638, f. 38a.

3 See above, Tustarī's commentary on 22:26, for an explanation of how houses that are unoccupied, especially by their owners, go to ruin, the point there being that the only occupant of the heart should be its Owner, namely God, whereas the emphasis here is on remembrance of God, which really comes to the same.

4 That is, the oppression of, or wrongdoing towards, their own selves.

He said:

> Peace from God attaches itself to the people of the Qurʾān in this life according to His saying, *peace be on His servants*; while peace [for them] in the next life [is indicated by] His saying *'Peace!' the word from the Lord [who is] Merciful* [36:58].

His words, Exalted is He:

[27:62] *Or [is] He who answers the destitute one when he calls to Him [better]...?*[5]

[Sahl] was asked, 'Who is *the destitute one* (muḍṭarr)?' He replied:

> It is the person who, when he raises his hands [in prayer], does not see himself having any good deeds other than the profession of [God's] oneness (*tawḥīd*), and even considers himself in danger [of losing that].[6]

On another occasion he said:

> The destitute person (*muḍṭarr*) is the one who has washed his hands of all power (*ḥawl*), strength (*quwwa*) and reprehensible means (*asbāb madhmūma*).[7] Supplication (*daʿwa*) from mankind is of two kinds, and is answered, without doubt, whether it be from a believer or unbeliever: the supplication of the destitute (*muḍṭarr*) and the supplication of the oppressed (*maẓlūm*);[8] for God says, Exalted is He: *Or [is] He who answers the destitute one when he calls to Him... [better]?*, and He also says, *and who provides for you from the heavens and [from] the earth* [27:64]. The supplication of the oppressed is raised above the veil, and God, Exalted is He, responds with the words; 'By My glory and majesty, I will come to your aid though it may be after a while.'[9]

His words:

[27:65] *Say, 'No one in the heavens or on earth knows the unseen, except God...'*

He said:

> He [God] has concealed His unseen [mystery] (*ghayb*) from creatures (*makhlūqūn*) in His [realm of] dominion (*jabarūt*), lest any of His servants feel secure from His ruse (*makr*). Thus, no one knows what has been predestined for him by God, lest their concern be with deluding themselves (*īhām*)[10] concerning the final outcomes (*ʿawāqib*) and predestined events (*majārī al-sawābiq*), and, lest they claim for themselves that of which they are not worthy, such as claims of [having attained the station of] love (*maḥabba*), gnosis (*maʿrifa*) and so on.

He said:

> There were in Jerusalem (*Bayt al-Maqdis*) a hundred thousand veracious ones (*ṣiddīqūn*) publicly known to people, such that the sound of water flowing from the roof gutters could not be heard due to the [noise] of those who were making their spiritual devotions at night [lit. spiritually striving (*mujtahidūn*)]. But when two things appeared [from them] they asked God, Exalted is He, and He caused them to die. They were: the claim to love (*maḥabba*) and claim to have trust [in Him] (*tawakkul*).[11]

---

5 This is one of the (rhetorical) questions that the Prophet is commanded to ask of the unbelievers, e.g. *Is God better or the partners they ascribe [to Him]?* [27:59].

6 A similar saying is cited in Makkī, *Qūt al-qulūb*, vol. 2, p. 9.

7 Since to rely on secondary causes and means is to rely on other than God.

8 The word order is changed here according to MS Z515, f. 82a, F638, f. 38a and F3488, f. 255b.

9 On God's responding to supplications, see also the commentary on 40:60.

10 This is according to MS Z515, f. 82a. The published edition has *ibhām*, which might be translated as 'obscuring', and F638, f. 38a, *ittihām*, which would translate as doubt, suspicion or uncertainty, either of which would be feasible in the context. F3488, f. 255b, however, has *ījāb*, which would translate as 'compliance' or 'necessity', which would not really fit the context. We have followed MS Z515 in this instance.

11 Presumably their request was that God should cause them to die, because they feared the consequences of their making any claim for themselves.

He was asked about the saying of al-Ḥārith,[12] who stated, 'I stay up at night and thirst during the day.' He replied:

> He means, 'I have no need for disclosure (*kashf*) for this is the lot of the disbelievers in this life, and I do not share with them their lot. This is why I said, "I am a believer"'.[13]

He [Sahl] was asked about those who say something similar to that which was said by al-Ḥārith. He replied:

> Their claim is false. How can their claim be acceptable when Abū Bakr and ʿUmar ﵄ did not allow themselves to do such a thing, and a hair on their chests is better than al-Ḥārith. However, al-Ḥārith did not say that by himself, rather God brought that out [of him] as a test (*fitna*) for all those pretentious people (*muddaʿūn*) who came after him. So how then is it acceptable for these people to claim such things for themselves?

His words, Exalted is He:

[27:73] ***And surely your Lord is bountiful to mankind...***

He said:

> His withholding (*manʿ*) is a bounty (*faḍl*), just as His giving (*ʿaṭāʾ*) is a bounty, but it is only the elite among the friends [of God] (*awliyāʾ*) who know the situations in which deprivation is a bounty.

His words, Exalted is He:

[27:88] ***And you see the mountains, supposing them to be fixed...He said:***

> Truly God, Exalted is He, has drawn the attention of His servants to the passing of time and their heedlessness of it. He made the mountains as a representation of the world (*dunyā*), which appears to the observer to be standing in support of him, when in actual fact it is taking its share from him. When time has run out, nothing will remain except sighs of regret over what is lost to the one who perceived it as standing in support of him, while in reality it was taking [its share from him].[14]

12 The editor of the Dār al-Kutub al-ʿIlmiyya edition identifies him as al-Ḥārith b. Mālik b. Qays, known as Ibn al-Barṣāʾ al-Laythī, a Companion of the Prophet and transmitter of *aḥādīth*.

13 The editor of the Dār al-Kutub al-ʿIlmiyya edition has noted that the following tradition is listed in the *Muṣannaf* of Ibn Abī Shayba (vol. 6, p. 170), narrated from Zubayr: The Prophet ﷺ asked, 'How did you start the day, O Ḥārith b. Mālik?' He replied, 'I began my day as a true Muslim (*musliman ḥaqqan*)'. The Prophet then asked him, 'Verily, every word has a reality (*inna li-kulli qawl ḥaqīqa*). What is the reality of that (which you claimed)?' He replied, 'I began the day turning myself away from the world; I kept a vigil at night and I thirsted during the day. It was as if I were looking at the Throne of my Lord and had been brought forth for the reckoning...'

14 MS Z515 f. 81b, ends the commentary on this *sūra* with the words: 'God knows best what is right' (*wa'Llāhu aʿlam bi'l-ṣawāb*).

28 Al-Qaṣaṣ

His words, Exalted is He:

[28:11] ***...So she watched him from a distance, while they were not aware.***[1]

That is, at a distance from Our observance of him.[2]

His words, Exalted is he:

[28:8] ***...that he might become an enemy and a [cause of] grief for them...***

That is, they[3] raised him up to be a [cause of] joy and happiness for them, without knowing what the divine omnipotence had concealed within him which would make him become *an enemy and a [source of] grief for them.*

His words, Exalted is He:

[28:10] ***The next day, Moses' mother [felt] a void in her heart...***

That is, she was void of remembrance of other than God, [since she had] reliance on God's promise, *We shall restore him to you* [28:7].

His words:

[28:24] ***...My Lord, I am in dire need of whatever good thing You may send me.***[4]

He returned to God in a state of utter neediness (*iftiqār*) and humble entreaty (*taḍarruʿ*) and said, 'Truly since You have accustomed me to Your favourable beneficence (*iḥsān*), I am in need of Your compassion (*shafaqa*), and of Your looking upon me with the [watchful] eye of [Your] care and protection. So bring me back from the grief and solitude of those who oppose [You] (*mukhālifūn*) to the intimacy (*uns*) of those who are in conformity [with You] (*muwāfiqūn*).' Then God provided for him the companionship of Shuʿayb ﷺ and his children.

His words, Exalted is He:

[28:60] ***Whatever things you have been given are only the [short-lived] enjoyment of the life of this world and an ornament thereof...***

He said:

Whoever takes [something] from the world out of his own lust for it, will find that God deprives him of what is better than it both in this world and the Hereafter. Whoever takes from it [the world] out of a necessity [that arises] within himself or to fulfil a duty that is required of him, will not be deprived of what is better in this world, namely, the joy of worship (*ʿibāda*) and the

---

1 This is relating the story of Moses as an infant, when his mother had been commanded to put him into the river, and when Pharaoh's wife took him up and requested of Pharaoh that they adopt him. Moses' mother sent his sister to follow her brother and so, as this verse relates, she kept watch at a distance.

2 Because God was constantly keeping watch over him.

3 'They' being Pharaoh's kinsmen.

4 These are the words of Moses' prayer. Having killed a man in Egypt, he escaped in fear for his own life and came to Midian. Here, he assisted two women who were holding back from watering their flocks, because a group of shepherds watering their own sheep were impeding their access to the well. Moses watered their sheep for them and then retired to the shade and made the prayer related in this verse for assistance from God. His prayer was immediately answered because one of the women then took him to her father (Shuʿayb), who married her to him, and put him in charge of his flocks for ten years.

love of God, Mighty and Majestic is He, and in the Hereafter of the highest ranks (*al-darajāt al-ʿulā*).[5]

Someone said to ʿĀmir b. ʿAbd al-Qays, 'You have contented yourself with just a little from this world.' He replied, 'Shall I not inform you of someone who has contented himself with even less than myself?' [Those present] said, 'Please do!' He answered, 'He who has contented himself with having his share of this world in the Hereafter!'[6]

His words:

[28:76] ...*'Do not gloat, for God does not like people who gloat...'*[7]

He said:

Whoever rejoices without good reason, will draw upon himself sorrow without end. There is no comfort [or rest] for the believer, save in the encounter with God, Mighty and Majestic is He.

It was related of al-Aʿmash that he said, 'We were witness to a funeral procession and did not know to whom we should offer our condolences due to the grief of all the people [present].'

His words, Exalted is He:

[28:78] *[He said] 'In fact I have been given it [this wealth] because of knowledge I possess...'*

He said:

No one who has regard for himself will triumph; nor a state come into being for anyone who claims to possess it. The fortunate person is he who averts his eye from [looking upon] his states and acts; ⌜to him is opened⌝[8] the way of receiving grace (*faḍl*) and being gracious to [others] (*ifḍāl*), whilst keeping sight of God's favour in [the accomplishment of] all acts.[9] The wretched person, on the other hand, is the one who makes himself, his states (*aḥwāl*) and his deeds beautiful [in his eyes], to the point where he becomes proud of them, and then claims [responsibility for] them himself. His disgrace will ruin him one day if it does not ruin him in the present. See how God spoke of Korah with His words: *I have been given it [this wealth] because of knowledge I possess,* that is, merit (*faḍl*).[10] This was because he was the most learned among them with regard to the Torah. He claimed merit for himself and so God made the earth beneath him swallow him up. This is the outer meaning [of the verse]. But just how many a person has sunk low through vices (*ashrār*), whilst being quite unaware of [what he is doing]. Sinking low [through] vices means a person's being deprived of [divine] protection (*ʿiṣma*) and being left to his own power (*ḥawl*) and strength (*quwwa*), so that his tongue is loosened and he starts to utter great claims. It also means he will be blind to God's favour, and fail to show gratitude for what he has been given. At this point it will be time for [his] demise.

---

5 A similar saying is to be found in Tirmidhī, *Nawādir al-uṣūl*, vol. 4, p. 186. See above Tustarī's commentary on 16:55 regarding the avoidance of excess.

6 Ibn Abī ʿĀṣim al-Ḍaḥḥāk al-Shaybānī, *Kitāb al-Zuhd* (Cairo, 1988), p. 228; but it is found attributed to al-Ṭāʾī in Iṣfahānī, *Ḥilyat al-awliyāʾ*, vol. 7, p. 353.

7 These are words spoken to Korah by his people. The context is given in note 10 below.

8 The addition is made on the basis of all three MSS: Z515, f. 83b, F638, f. 38b and F3488, f. 257a, all of which have: *wa futiḥa lahu* before *sabīl*.

9 On Tustarī's doctrine that acts of obedience are only accomplished through God's favour and assistance, while disobedience is through God's withdrawing His protection, see IC, p. 2, and Tustarī's commentary on 2:3, 2:30, 2:235, 3:160, 18:17 and 18:39. See also IT, pp. xxxiii–xxxv.

10 Korah (Ar. Qārūn) is mentioned in both the Bible and the Qurʾān. According to the Qurʾānic account [28:76–82], he lived at the time of Moses, but oppressed Moses' people. He owned such wealth that even the keys to his treasures would have weighed down a whole company of strong men. However, when he was advised not to gloat over his wealth, but to think of the life to come and to do good to others, he made the claim that his wealth was given to him on account of the knowledge he possessed. Eventually, God caused the earth to swallow up both him and his house.

29 Al-ʿAnkabūt

His words, Exalted is He:

[29:1, 2] ***Alif Lām Mīm ❁ Do people suppose they will be left to say, 'We believe,' without being put to the test?***

He said:

> That is, without their being beset by affliction (*balāʾ*). Truly affliction is a doorway between the people of gnosis (*ahl al-maʿrifa*) and God, Mighty and Majestic is He. It has been related that the angels say, 'O Lord! Your disbelieving servant has had [the goods of] this world made available to him in abundance, while affliction has been kept away from him.'[1] Then He says to the angels, 'Reveal his [the unbelieving servant's] punishment to them [the other angels?].' When they see it they say, 'What he gets from the world is not a blessing for him.' Then they say, 'O Lord! You keep the world away from Your believing servant and expose him to affliction!'[2] And He says to the angels, 'Reveal to the others his [the believing servant's] reward.' When they see his reward they say, 'Whatever he suffers in this world will not harm him.'[3]

He [Tustarī] said:

> Let your prayer (*ṣalāt*) be forbearance (*ṣabr*) in the face of suffering (*baʾsāʾ*), your fasting (*ṣawm*) be to observe silence (*ṣamt*), and your charity (*ṣadaqa*) be to refrain from doing harm [to anybody] (*kaff al-adhā*). Furthermore, forbearance in [times of] well-being (*ʿāfiya*) is more difficult than forbearance in [times of] affliction (*balāʾ*).[4]

This saying is also related from him:

> Seeking safety (*salāma*) is not exposing yourself to affliction.

His words:

[29:17] ***...So seek your provision from God...***

He said:

> Seek provision (*rizq*) through trust (*tawakkul*) not through earning (*kasb*), for seeking provision through earning is the way of the generality (*ʿawāmm*).[5]
>
> It was related of Jesus son of Mary ﷺ that he said, 'Truly I say to you, neither do you want the world, nor the Hereafter.' They said, 'Please explain that to us, O prophet of God, for we previously thought that we only wanted one of them.' He said, 'If you obey the Lord of the world, in whose hands are the keys to its coffers, He will give it to you. Likewise, if you obey the Lord of the Hereafter He will give it to you. However, neither do you want the latter nor the former.'[6]

---

1 The use of the passive here is according to all three MSS: Z515, f. 84a, F638 f. 39a and F3488, f. 257b.

2 The MS F638, f. 39a only maintains the passive construction here.

3 Ibn Abī Shayba, *al-Muṣannaf*, vol. 7, p. 166; Iṣfahānī, *Ḥilyat al-awliyāʾ*, vol. 4, pp. 118, and 123.

4 *Ṣabr* here has the meaning of patient perseverance.

5 See the commentary on 25:58 above for a discussion of *tawakkul* versus *kasb*, the former being the state of being (*ḥāl*) of the Prophet, and the latter being his Sunna.

6 This principle, namely that the true mystic and lover of God should desire neither this world nor the Hereafter, but only God Himself, was taken up and developed in later Sufism. Indeed, the person who obeyed God for the sake of salvation from the Fire and the rewards of Paradise was known in Persian mysticism as a 'mercenary' (*muzdūr*). See Keeler, *Sufi*

His words, Exalted is He:

[29:21] ***He chastises whomever He wishes…***

by [abandoning him] to follow innovation, *and has mercy on whomever He wishes* by [assisting him] in adherence to the Sunna.

His words, Exalted is He:

[29:43] ***And such similitudes We strike for [the sake of] mankind, but none understands them except those who know.***

He said:

The similitudes which God strikes for man are available for everyone [to see], since the evidences of [His] omnipotence (*qudra*) are [in themselves] proof of the [existence of] the Omnipotent. However, it is only His elect (*khāṣṣa*) who fully understand them. Thus, knowledge is rare and understanding granted by God (*fiqh ʿan Allāh*) even rarer.[7] Whoever becomes acquainted with the knowledge ⌜of Him through the knowledge [acquired by]⌝ his natural self (*bi-ʿilm nafsihi al-ṭabīʿiyya*), will experience Him in a delusory manner.[8] But regarding the one who becomes acquainted with [God] through the knowledge of God, God knows what He willed from him for Himself (*faʾLlāhu ʿarafa murādahu minhu li-nafsihi*).[9] The creature has no knowledge of God beyond that. This allusion (*ishāra*) [to similitudes in the verse] was made due to the fact that their hearts are truly far away from knowledge [of God]. Take note of ⌜his words, ﷺ 'If you knew God with a true knowledge of Him (*ḥaqq maʿrifatihi*) then the mountain would cease to exist by [the power of] your supplication'⌝.[10]

His words:

[29:45] …*Truly prayer guards against lewd acts and indecency…*

This verse refers to the adornment (*tazyīn*) that [is derived from] shunning all lewd acts and indecency, and this [is attained] through one thing, namely, sincerity (*ikhlāṣ*) within the prayer (*ṣalāt*). Every prayer that does not restrain shameful and unjust deeds, and is devoid of the adornment of shunning of these deeds, is defective, and it is incumbent upon the person [in this case] to purify it [his prayer].

His words, Exalted is He:

[29:56] ***…My earth is [indeed] vast, so worship Me and Me [alone].***

He said:

This means: If transgressions and innovations are the practice in a particular land, then leave it for a land of obedient servants. Indeed the Prophet ﷺ said: 'He who flees for [the sake of] his religion at a time when the community is in a state of corruption, will receive the reward of seventy martyrs in the cause of God, Mighty and Majestic is He.'

Hermeneutics, pp. 167–8, 194. The tradition is cited in Iṣfahānī, *Ḥilyat al-awliyāʾ*, vol. 6, pp. 57–8.

7 lit. 'even more of a special privilege', i.e. for a select few (*akhaṣṣ*).

8 Several corrections have been made on the basis of the MSS (Z515, f. 84b, F638, f. 39a; F3488, f. 258a), which have: *fa-man ʿarafa ʿilmahu bi-ʿilm nafsihi al-ṭabīʿiyya* instead of *fa-man ʿarafa ʿilm nafsihi al-ṭabīʿiyya* in the published edition. Also all MSS have *wahman* instead of *wahm*, and MS F638 has *wajadahu* which would then make sense of the accusative case for *wahm*. If, on the other hand, we follow the published edition and read it as: *ʿilm nafsihi al-ṭabīʿiyya waḥda* then it would be followed by the verb and translated as: 'according to the knowledge [acquired by] his natural self alone, has deluded [himself]'.

9 In other words, the extent of knowledge that is revealed by God is a matter of that which He has destined for that mystic.

10 This *ḥadīth*, present in all three MSS (Z515, f. 84b, F638, f. 39a; F3488, f. 258a), is absent from the published edition. The *ḥadīth* is listed in Tirmidhī, *Nawādir al-uṣūl*, vol. 2, p. 103.

30 Al-Rūm

His words, Exalted is He:

[30:4] ***...To God belongs the command, before and after...***

This means, before everything else [existed], and after everything else [ceases to exist]. This is because He is the One who initiates [everything] (*al-Mubdiʾ*) and brings it back [to its source] (*al-Muʿīd*). His arrangement (*tadbīr*) of [the affairs of] His creatures was antecedent [to them] (*sabaqa*), for He knows them in their origin (*aṣl*) and what will proceed from them (*farʿ*).

His words:

[30:40] ***God is the One who created you, then provided for you...***

He said:

The most excellent provision (*rizq*) is tranquil reliance (*sukūn*) upon the Provider (*al-Rāziq*).

His words:

[30:40] ***...then makes you die.***

That is, He will destroy you.

He said:

Indeed, God, Exalted is He, has created good and evil and established the command and prohibition. He has made us worship Him through the good and linked that to success (*tawfīq*), while He has forbidden us from evil and linked the perpetration of it to the relinquishing of [His] protection (*ʿiṣma*), and abandonment (*khidhlān*) [by Him]. All of these are of His creation. Whoever is successful in [doing] good has a duty to show gratitude (*shukr*), and whoever has been left to do evil must ⌜repent and⌝[1] cry out for God's help, Mighty and Majestic is He.

His words, Exalted is He:

[30:41] ***Corruption has appeared on land and sea...***

He said:

God, Exalted is He, has made the land a similitude of the bodily members and the sea a similitude of the heart. It [the sea, and therefore the heart] is more widely beneficial (*aʿamm nafʿan*), and much more dangerous (*akthar khaṭaran*).[2] This is the inner meaning of the verse — do you not see that the heart (*qalb*) was thus named due to its tendency to turn (*taqallub*), and due to the extent of its depth (*ghawr*). This is why the Prophet ﷺ said to Abū al-Dardāʾ ؓ, 'Overhaul the ship, for the sea is deep.' In other words, 'Make afresh your intention (*nīya*) for God, Exalted is He, from your heart, for the sea is deep.'[3] Therefore [with this renewed intention (*nīya*)], when the trafficking (*muʿāmala*) goes on in the hearts, which [as we have seen] are [like] seas, the self will leave its place at the centre, and the bodily members will come to

1 This word *tawba* appears in all three MSS: Z515, f. 85a, F638, f. 39b and F3488, f. 259a.

2 That is, translating *wa huwa* (for the sea or the heart) according to MSS F638, f. 39b and F3488, f. 259a, instead of *wa hum* in the published edition and MS Z515, f. 85a.

3 According to the *Firdaws bi-maʾthūr al-khiṭāb*, of Shīrawayh b. Shardār al-Daylamī (Beirut, 1986), vol. 5, p. 339, this *ḥadīth* was addressed by the Prophet to Abū Dharr al-Ghifārī.

> rest.[4] Thereafter, with each day, the possessor of [the sea of the heart] will find himself closer to its ultimate depth and further away from his self until he reaches ⌜Him⌝.[5]

He was asked about the meaning of the [saying of] the Prophet ﷺ, 'Whoever humbles himself before a person of wealth will lose two thirds of his religion.'[6] He replied:

> The heart has three stations: the principal part (*jumhūr*) of the heart; the station of the tongue in relationship to the heart, and the station of the bodily members in relationship to the heart. His words, 'has lost two thirds of his religion' means that two out of the three were involved, the tongue and the rest of the bodily members, but the principal part of the heart remained in its place, for no one can reach that because it is the seat of his faith (*īmān*) within the heart.

Then he said:

> Truly, the heart is delicate (*raqīq*) and everything affects it, so guard over it carefully, and fear God with it.

He was asked, 'When does the heart become purified of all corruption (*fasād*) ?' He replied:

> It does not become purified until it abandons all conjecture (*ẓann*) and scheming (*ḥiyal*) — for it is as if scheming in the eyes of your Lord is [as bad] as a major sin to our eyes. Indeed, the Prophet ﷺ said: 'Righteousness (*birr*)[7] is what causes an expansion within your breast, and iniquity (*ithm*) is what sows intrigue (*ḥāka*) in your breast, even if those who are authorised to give out legal rulings provide you with [legal] *fatwā* upon *fatwā* [to the contrary].[8]

Then he [Sahl] said:

> If the heart is perturbed, that will be evidence (*ḥujja*) against you.

His words:

[30:50] ***So behold the effects of God's mercy…***

> In its outer meaning it refers to the rain, and in its inner meaning it alludes to the life of hearts through remembrance (*dhikr*). But God, Transcendent and Exalted is He, knows best.

---

4 The meaning of this passage is not entirely clear, but following Tustarī's comparison of the heart to a sea, with its tendency to turn, along with its depth, we have assumed that the renewed [spiritual] intention, alluded to in the saying of the Prophet, eventually causes the [lower] self to leave its domination of the heart (its being at the centre), after which neither the self nor the limbs will disturb the heart, and it come to will reach its utmost depths, ultimately attaining God.

5 All three MSS (Z515, f. 85a, F638, f. 39b and F3488, f. 259a) have *ilayhi* following *yaṣilu*.

6 Bayhaqī, *Shuʿab al-īmān*, vol. 6, p. 298.

7 Not *al-kabīra* as in the published edition.

8 Ibn Ḥanbal, *al-Musnad*, vol. 4, p. 194; Tirmidhī, *Nawādir al-uṣūl*, vol. 1, p. 239.

31 Luqmān

His words, Exalted is He:

[31:6] ***But among people there is he who purchases idle talk, without knowledge, to mislead...***

He said:

This refers to disputing in [matters of] religion and plunging into falsehood (*bāṭil*).

His words:

[31:15] ***...and follow the way of him who returns to Me [in penitence]...***

This means that anyone who has not been guided to the path [that leads] to God, Mighty and Majestic is He, should follow in the footsteps of the virtuous (*ṣāliḥūn*), so that the blessing (*baraka*) of following them may lead him to the path of God. Do you not see how the dog of the Companions of the Cave benefitted by following those virtuous ones, to the point that God, Exalted is He, repeatedly mentioned it in a good light?[1] Indeed, the Prophet ﷺ said in a *ḥadīth* in this regard, 'Anyone who keeps their company will not be among the wretched.'[2]

His words:

[31:19] ***...for the most abominable of all voices is the braying of an ass.***

⌜Sufyān al-Thawrī said, 'The voice[s] of all things glorify [God] except for the voice of the ass (*ḥimār*),⌝[3] for it screeches on account of seeing Satan, and this is why God, Exalted is He, calls it abominable (*munkar*).

[31:20] ***...and He has showered His favours upon you, [both] outwardly and inwardly...***

Outwardly it refers to the love of the virtuous and inwardly it refers to the heart's tranquil repose (*sukūn*) in God, Exalted is He.

His words:

[31:22] ***And whoever surrenders his purpose to God and does good* (muḥsin)...**

He said:

[That is,] whoever purifies (*akhlaṣa*) his religion for God, Mighty and Majestic is He,[4] and accomplishes well the propriety (*adab*) of sincerity (*ikhlāṣ*) *[has certainly grasped] the firmest handhold,* this being the Sunna.

His words:

[31:18] ***Do not turn your cheek disdainfully from people...***

That is, 'Do not turn your back on one who seeks from you guidance on the path to Us. Acquaint them of My grace and goodness towards them.'

---

1 See Sūra 18 (al-Kahf) vv. 18 and 22.

2 Bukhārī, *Ṣaḥīḥ*, 'Kitāb al-Daʿwāt'; Muslim, *Ṣaḥīḥ*, 'Kitāb al-Dhikr wa'l-duʿāʾ wa'l-tawba.'

3 The section in brackets is added on the basis of all three MSS: Z515, f. 85b–86a, F638, f. 40a and MS F3488, f. 259b and F638 has *tasbīḥ* whereas the other two MSS have *yusabbiḥu*.

4 As stated before, *akhlaṣa* has the meaning of making one's religion solely for God, freeing it for Him alone, and of making it pure and sincere for His sake, as is found in the verbal noun derived from it, *ikhlāṣ*. See IT, pp. lvi–lvii.

His words:

[31:34] *...No soul knows what it will reap tomorrow...*

That is, [no soul knows] what [counts] for and against it in the preordainment of the unseen (*maqdūr al-ghayb*). So, be wary of [what has been preordained] by upholding His remembrance and crying out to Him for help, until He takes it upon Himself to take care of your affair,[5] just as He has said: *God erases and confirms whatever He will.* [13:39]

His words, Exalted is He:

[31:34] *...And no soul knows in what land it will die...*

He said:

[It does not know] in what state (*ḥukm*)[6] it will be when it dies: [eternal] bliss (*saʿāda*) or wretchedness (*shaqāwa*). This is why the Messenger ﷺ said: 'Do not be deceived by your great [accumulation of] works, for works are [judged] according to the last ones.'[7] He also used to say, 'O Protector of Islam and its people! Hold me fast to[8] Islam so that I meet You in Islam'.[9] And he would say, 'O Turner of hearts and eyes, make my heart firm[ly rooted] in Your religion',[10] despite the fact that God had secured for him his end.

In actual fact, he said this by way of instruction (*taʾdīb*), so that they might follow his example, make known their poverty and need for God, Mighty and Majestic is He, and give up their reliance on being secure from His ruse (*makr*). It was for this reason that Abraham ﷺ said, *'Preserve me and my sons from idolatry'* [14:35], and Joseph said, *'Let me die in submission to You, and join me to the righteous'* [12:101]. This was by way of disclaiming all power (*ḥawl*) and strength (*quwwa*) and showing neediness for Him. Likewise, God has said, *'were it not for your supplications'* [25:77],[11] that is, [were it not for your] dissociating yourselves from everything besides Me, verbally (*qawlan*). And He said: *O mankind! You are the ones who are in need of God* [35:15], Mighty and Majestic is He.

---

5 The MSS (Z515, f. 86a, F638, f. 40a and F3488, f. 260a) all have *shaʾnikum* instead of *shaʾnihim*, which agrees with the 2nd person plural of the verb used earlier.

6 Or 'in what decreed state'.

7 Ibn Ḥanbal, *al-Musnad*, vol. 5, p. 335; Mundhirī, *al-Targhīb wa'l-tarhīb*, vol. 4, p. 48.

8 Correcting *thabbitnī* in the published edition to *massiknī* as is written in all three MSS: Z515, f. 86a; F638, f. 40a and F3488, f. 260a.

9 Ṭabarānī, *al-Muʿjam al-awsaṭ*, vol. 1, p. 206; Haythamī, *Majmaʿ al-zawāʾid*, vol. 10, p. 136.

10 Tirmidhī, *Sunan*, 'Kitāb al-Qadar' and 'Kitāb al-Daʿwāt'; Haythamī, *Majmaʿ al-zawāʾid*, vol. 6, p. 325 and vol. 7, p. 210.

11 The words in context are as follows: *Say [Muḥammad], 'My Lord would not be concerned with you were it not for your supplications'.*

32 Al-Sajda

His words, Exalted is He:

[32:5] ***He directs the command from the heaven to the earth…***

He said:

> He reveals to His servants from His knowledge[1] that which is a means of guidance (*hudā*) and salvation (*najāt*) for them. The person who is content with the destined provision (*rizq al-qaḍāʾ*) resulting from God's management [of things] (*tadbīr*) for him, will have the evil of his own devising (*tadbīr*) disposed of and removed from him. Thus [God] will have returned him to a state of contentment (*riḍā*) with the divine decree (*qaḍāʾ*), and rectitude (*istiqāma*) in the face of the unfolding course of what is destined for him. [Such people] are among those who are brought into proximity [with Him] (*muqarrabūn*). Truly, God, Exalted is He, created people without any veil, and then made their devising [for themselves] (*tadbīr*) into their veil.[2]

His words, Exalted is He:

[32:13] ***If it had been Our will, We would have given every soul its [means to] guidance…***

He said:

> If it had been Our will, We would have brought to fulfilment all that the people of truth call for, and invalidated the arguments of the people of falsehood (*mubṭalūn*).

His words, Exalted is He:

[32:15] ***Only those believe in Our signs, who, when they are reminded of them, fall down in prostration…***

He said:

> The servant will not experience the joy of faith until his knowledge vanquishes his ignorance, ⌜his [awareness of] the Hereafter dominates⌝ his heart, his compassion ⌜rules over his anger, and mercy is upon his heart.⌝[3]

His words, Exalted is He:

[32:16] ***Their sides withdraw from their beds…***

> Verily, God, Exalted is He, bestowed on a people a gift (*hiba*), which is that He brought them close to Him to call upon Him [in intimate proximity] (*munājātihi*). Then he made them the people who are a means (*wasīla*) and connection (*ṣila*) [to] Him,[4] and then He praised them ⌜for this,⌝[5] as a manifestation of [His] generosity,[6] in that He granted them success in what He assisted them in doing. So He said, *Their sides withdraw from their beds.*

---

1 That is translating ʿ*ilmihi* according to all three MSS (Z515, f. 86b, F638, f. 40a and F3488, f. 260b) instead of *amrihi* in the published edition.

2 The saying is also cited in Makkī, *Qūt al-qulūb*, vol. 2, p. 9.

3 The additions are made on the basis of all three MSS (Z515, f. 86b, F638, f. 40a and F3488, f. 261a), which have: *wa yakūnu al-ghālib* ʿ*alā qalbihi* ʿ*ākhiratuhu* and *taghallaba raḥmatuhu sakhṭahu wa yakūnu* ʿ*alā qalbihi al-raḥma.*

4 Perhaps what is meant are people who, through their spiritual qualities, act as agents of God in the creation, and help to connect people with Him. We shall see an example of this described later in the commentary on 57:20.

5 Added on the basis of all three MSS: MSS Z515, f. 87b, F638, f. 40a and F3488, f. 260b.

6 Translating *iẓhāran li-karamihi* according to MSS Z515, f. 87a and F3488, f. 260b, or *iẓhāran li-karāmatihi* according to

His words, Exalted is He:

[32:16] ***...[while] they supplicate their Lord in fear and in hope...***

He said:

> That is, in fear of being separated (*hijrān*) from Him, and in the hope of meeting (*liqāʾ*) Him.

His words, Mighty and Majestic is He:

[32:17] ***No person knows what delights of the eye are kept hidden [in reserve] for them...***[7]

He said:

> Their eyes ⌜delight⌝ at the outward and inward realities that they witness, which are revealed to them in the way of ⌜knowledge (*ʿulūm*)⌝[8] of unveiling (*mukāshafa*). So they behold them and hold on to them such that their eyes delight and their hearts find tranquil repose in them. Others, however are unaware of what is hidden [in reserve] for them. But God, Glorified and Exalted is He, knows best.

F638, f. 40a, instead of *iẓhār al-karam* according to the published edition.

7 Among the rewards of Paradise.

8 Both additions have been made on the basis of all three MSS: Z515, f. 87a, F638 f. 41a and F3488, f. 261a.

33 Al-Aḥzāb

His words, Exalted is He:

[33:4] ***God has not placed two hearts inside any man…***

He said:

> The one who has directed himself to God, Mighty and Majestic is He, and is intent upon (*qaṣdan*) [Him], [does not] avert his gaze (*iltifāt*) [from Him]. For whoever pays attention to anything other than God is not truly intent upon his Lord. Indeed God, Exalted is He, says, *God has not placed two hearts inside any man…*

It has been said:

> [That is, he does not have] one heart (*qalb*) with which he approaches God, and another heart with which he manages the affairs of this world. [On the other hand], the intellect (*ʿaql*) does have two natures (*ṭabʿān*): a nature which is orientated towards this world, and a nature which is orientated towards the Hereafter. The nature which is orientated to the Hereafter is in coalition (*mūʾtalif*) with the spiritual self (*nafs al-rūḥ*), whereas [the intellect's] worldly-orientated nature is in coalition with the lustful self (*nafs shahwāniyya*). It was due to this that the Prophet ﷺ [prayed], 'Do not leave me to my self for the blinking of an eye.'[1] For truly the servant, ⌜as long as he is occupied with God, will be veiled from himself, and⌝[2] as long as he is occupied with himself will be veiled from God, Mighty and Majestic is He.

His words, Exalted is He:

[33:6] ***The Prophet is closer to the believers than their [own] souls…***[3]

He said:

> Whoever does not see himself [or his soul] as belonging to the Messenger ﷺ and does not see the patronage (*wilāya*) of the Messenger ﷺ in every situation, has in no way tasted the sweetness of his Sunna.[4] This is because the Prophet ﷺ is the closest to the believers, and the Prophet says, 'None of you believes until I am dearer to him than his soul, his wealth, his children and everyone else.'[5]

His words, Exalted is He:

[33:8] *so that He may question the truthful* (ṣādiqīn) *about their veracity. And he has prepared for those who disbelieve a painful chastisement.*[6]

---

1 Bayhaqī, *Sunan*, vol. 6, pp. 147 and 167; Haythamī, *Majmaʿ al-zawāʾid*, vol. 10, pp. 117, 137 and 181; Ibn Ḥanbal, *al-Musnad*, vol. 5, p. 42.

2 The section in brackets is added on the basis of MS, F638, f. 40b. However, the first part of the saying differs in MSS Z515, f. 87a and F3488, f. 260b, which have: 'Truly the servant who does not cease to be occupied with God (*mā zāla mushtaghilan bi'Llāh*), will be veiled from himself.'

3 Or the verse could be translated, *The Prophet has a greater right* [*or greater authority,* awlā] *over the believers than they have over their own selves.*

4 See above, IC, p. 2, n. 5 and p. 3, n. 14 regarding the different meanings of *wilāya*.

5 Bukhārī, *Ṣaḥīḥ*, 'Kitāb al-Īmān'; Muslim, *Ṣaḥīḥ*, 'Kitāb al-Īmān'.

6 This verse relates part of the covenant that was taken by God from the prophets at the same time that He took the covenant from the seed of all the children of Adam. On the Covenant of *Alast* see above Tustarī's commentary on 7:172 and IT, pp. xxxi–xxxii and xxxv–xxxvi.

ʿAbd al-Wāḥid b. Zayd said:

Veracity (*ṣidq*) is being faithful (*wafāʾ*) to God in your act[s].

Sahl was asked about veracity and said:

Veracity is fear concerning [our] end (*khātima*), and patience (*ṣabr*) is the proof [lit. witness (*shāhid*)] of veracity. Truly, veracity is hard for the veracious (*ṣiddīqūn*), sincerity (*ikhlāṣ*) is hard for the sincere (*mukhliṣūn*), and repentance (*tawba*) is hard for the repentant (*tāʾibūn*), for these three[7] require [extraordinary] exertion of the spirit (*badhl al-rūḥ*).[8]

Aḥmad b. Mattā was asked about its meaning [*ṣidq*] and said:

It is that there no longer remains a share for a person's lower self.

Sahl said:

No one will get a whiff of the fragrance of veracity as long as he panders to his lower self or to others. Rather, veracity is that a person feels in his innermost secret (*sirr*) that there is no one on the face of the earth from whom God has demanded servanthood besides him. Furthermore, his hope is his fear,[9] and his fear is [of] his demise (*intiqāl*).[10] Then when God, Exalted is He, sees them [the veracious] in this state, He takes upon himself the care of their affairs (*tawallā umūrahum*) and suffices for them (*kafāhum*), and every hair on their bodies speaks [as one] with God (*maʿa'Llāh*) in gnosis (*maʿrifa*). Thereafter God, Exalted is He, says to them on the Day of Judgement, 'For whom did you work, and what did you desire?' They will reply, 'We worked for You, and You alone did we desire.' He will say to them, 'You have spoken the truth.' And by His Might, His words of testimony affirming their veracity are a greater source of joy to them than the bliss of Paradise.

Aḥmad b. Mattā was asked about the meaning of his [Sahl's] saying, that the hope of veracity is his fear, and that his fear is [of] his demise (*intiqāl*). He said:

It is because veracity (*ṣidq*) is their hope and what they seek, but they fear that they are not veracious in their quest (*ṭalab*), so that God will not accept it from them. He has said regarding this: *and [those] who give what they give while their hearts tremble [with awe]* [23:60], meaning that they are in trepidation while doing acts of obedience, for fear that they will suffer rejection.

His words:

[33:35] ***For Muslim men and women…***

He said:

Faith (*īmān*) is superior to surrender (*islām*), but mindfulness of God (*taqwā*) within faith is superior to faith. Certainty (*yaqīn*) within mindfulness of God is superior to mindfulness of God, but veracity (*ṣidq*) within certainty is superior to certainty. Truly, you have taken a firm hold on the lowest (*adnā*) [of these],[11] so you must not by any means let that escape from you.

He also said:

Faith in God is established (*thābit*) in the heart, and certainty is firmly rooted (*rāsikh*) [in it] through veracity (*ṣidq*). Veracity of the eye is refraining from looking at all that is forbidden. Veracity of the tongue is relinquishing engagement in that which is meaningless. Veracity of the hand is not extending it to seize what is forbidden. Veracity of the feet is refraining from

7 That is translating *hādhihi'l-thalātha* according to MS Z515, f. 87b, F638, f. 40b and F3488, f. 262a, instead of *al-talbiya* in the published edition.

8 Reading *badl* as *badhl*, while MS F638, f. 40b has *nuzūl al-rūḥ*, which also might be translated here as 'surrender of the spirit'.

9 That is, presumably, that his hope is accompanied by fear. This is explained by Aḥmad b. Mattā below.

10 That is, perhaps his fear is concerned with his state of veracity at his passing, which would be in accordance with his statement shortly before, that 'Veracity is fear concerning [our] end (*khātima*)'. Another possibility might be: 'his fear is of veracity's disappearance from him, or his moving away from (*intiqāl*) veracity'. The meaning of *intiqāluhu* does not become clear from Aḥmad b. Mattā's explanation either.

11 i.e. Islam. MS 3488, f. 262b only has *awlā* instead of *adnā*.

walking in quest of indecent acts. The truth of veracity (*ḥaqīqat al-ṣidq*) in ⌜the heart⌝[12] is that it constantly reflects on the past and refrains from regarding what is to come. Verily, God, Exalted is He, has granted the veracious (*ṣiddīqūn*) so much knowledge that if they spoke of it, the ocean would dry up with their speech.[13] They are hidden and do not appear in public before people, except when it is [absolutely] necessary for them, and until a virtuous [servant] (*ṣāliḥ*) appears, at which point they make themselves known, and teach the learned (*ʿulamāʾ*) from their different branches of knowledge.

His words, Exalted is He:

[33:35] ***...and the men who remember God often and the women who remember God often...***

The one who observes true remembrance (*al-dhākir ʿalāʾl-ḥaqīqa*) is he who is aware that God witnesses him. He perceives Him with his heart as being close to him, and therefore feels shame before Him. Then he gives Him priority over himself and over everything else in every situation.

On another occasion Sahl was asked, 'What is remembrance (*dhikr*)?' He said, 'Obedience (*ṭāʿa*).' Then someone asked, 'What is obedience?' He replied, 'Sincerity (*ikhlāṣ*).' Then he was asked, 'What is sincerity?' and he answered, 'Witnessing (*mushāhada*).' Someone then asked, 'What is witnessing?' He replied, 'Servanthood (*ʿubūdiyya*).' Then they asked: 'What is servanthood?' He answered, 'Contentment (*riḍā*).' Then they asked, 'What is contentment?' He replied, 'Neediness (*iftiqār*).' He was asked: 'What is neediness?' and he said, 'It is humble entreaty (*taḍarruʿ*) and seeking refuge [in Him] (*iltijāʾ*). Submit! Submit, until death!'

Ibn Sālim said:

Remembrance is of three kinds: remembrance of the tongue, and that is a good deed (*ḥasana*) which is rewarded tenfold; remembrance of the heart, and that is a good deed which is rewarded seven-hundred fold; and a form of remembrance whose reward is beyond being weighed, and that is being filled with love [of God] (*maḥabba*).

His words:

[33:38] ***...and God's commandment is an inexorable destiny,***

That is, it is known before it befalls you. Is anyone able to avoid what is determined [for him]? ʿUmar ﷺ said after he was stabbed, '*...And God's commandment is an inexorable destiny*. Indeed, the Messenger of God ﷺ informed me that they would do this to me.' It was related from al-Ḍaḥḥāk that two angels descend from heaven, one of them carrying a scroll with writing on it and the other one carrying a scroll without any writing on it. [The latter] records the servant's actions and what he leaves behind. When he [the latter] intends to ascend again, he says to his companion [carrying the scroll with writing on it], 'Show me [what is in your scroll]' and he shows him, [and he sees] that there are no mistakes, not even as to a letter.[14]

His words:

[33:71] ***He will rectify your deeds for you and forgive you your sins...***

He said:

When God gives someone success in enabling him to perform good deeds, this is a sign that he is forgiven, for God, Exalted is He, has said: *He will rectify your deeds for you and forgive you your sins.* But God, Transcendent and Exalted is He, knows best.

---

12 Added on the basis of all three MSS: Z515, f. 88a, F638, f. 41a and F3488, f. 262b.

13 Sic in all the MSS as well as the published edition. Perhaps it means that the ocean would dry up in shame at the depth and breadth of their speech, an analogous metaphor to that of the sun and moon hiding their faces before the luminous beauty of the beloved, which one finds in Persian poetry. There may also be an allusion here to Sūra 18 (al-Kahf) verse 109: *Say: 'If the ocean were ink for the words of my Lord, the ocean would be dried up before the words of my Lord were exhausted.'*

14 The point being made here is that there is no contradiction between what God has predestined and what we do.

34 Saba᾽

His words, Exalted is He:

[34:39][1] ***Say, 'My Lord extends provision to whomever He wills of His servants, and restricts it for him…'***

He said:

> Provision (*rizq*) is of two kinds: a provision that is remembrance [providing nourishment] for the spiritual self (*nafs al-rūḥ*), the intellect (*ʿaql*) and the heart (*qalb*), which resembles the sustenance of the angels — their very life (*ʿaysh*) is in remembrance, and were this to be withheld from them they would perish. The other kind of provision is that which is eaten, drunk and so on for the benefit of one's [physical] nature (*ṭabʿ*). It is this kind which falls under what is permitted (*ḥalāl*) or prohibited (*ḥarām*). The legitimate is that which God, Exalted is He, has provided for us, and commanded us to partake of. The prohibited, on the other hand, is what God, Exalted is He, has provided but forbidden, and this is the portion of the Fire. And I do not know anything more difficult than averting the harm [of others] (*kaff al-adhā*) and adhering to what is permitted.

His words, Exalted is He:

[34:37] ***Nor is it your wealth or children that will bring you nearer to Us in proximity* (zulfā)…**[2]

He said:

> *Al-zulfā* is proximity to God, Exalted is He.

His words, Exalted is He:

[34:39] ***'…and whatever thing you may expend [for good] He will replace it…'***

He said:

> There will be a replacement (*khalaf*) of what has been spent, along with the intimacy (*uns*) of living with God (*ʿaysh maʿa'Llāh*), Exalted is He, and delighting in that.

His words:

[34:46] ***Say, 'I will give you [one] admonition: that you stand before God, in twos and singly…'***

He said:

> The reckoning on the Day of Resurrection is [an appraisal of] four things: veracity (*ṣidq*) in speech, sincerity (*ikhlāṣ*) in actions, rectitude (*istiqāma*) with God in all affairs, and heedfulness (*murāqaba*) of God in every situation. But, God, Glorified and Exalted is He, knows best.

---

1 The order of the verses in the commentary is thus in the MSS.

2 Verses 36–9 comprise things which the Prophet is commanded to say to the disbelievers, particularly those who have been corrupted by their wealth, and assume that their having wealth and children will protect them from punishment.

35 Al-Malāʾika (or Fāṭir)[1]

His words, Exalted is He:

[35:6] ***...He [Satan] only summons his adherents...***

That is, Satan summons to him those who obey him among the people of whims (*ahwāʾ*), innovations (*bidaʿ*) and abberations (*ḍalālāt*), along with those who listen to such things from one who propounds them.

His words:

[35:10] ***...To Him ascends the good word, and as for righteous conduct, He raises it up...***

He said:

Its outer meaning is supplication (*duʿāʾ*) and charity (*ṣadaqa*), and its inner meaning is remembrance (*dhikr*), while acting upon what you know and advancing through [following] the Sunna. *He raises it up* means, He makes it reach [Him] due to the presence within it of sincerity towards God, Exalted is He.

His words:

[35:15] ***O mankind! It is you who stand in need of God...***

He said:

That is, 'You [depend] upon Him in your very selves, for truly when God created all creatures He imposed upon His servants neediness (*faqr*) for Him, while He is the Rich and Independent (*al-Ghanī*). Furthermore, whoever claims to be wealthy has been veiled from God, Mighty and Majestic is He. On the other hand, whoever shows his need for God, will find that He joins his need to His wealth. The servant should feel the need for Him in his innermost secret (*sirr*), cutting himself off from all other than Him, so that his servanthood (*ʿubūdiyya*) becomes pure (*maḥḍa*); for pure servanthood is self-abasement (*dhull*) and humble submission (*khuḍūʿ*).

He was asked, 'How does one show one's need for Him?' He said:

The neediness takes three [forms]: [the servants'] showing [awareness] of having been needy from pre-eternity (*faqruhum al-qadīm*); their showing need in their state (*faqr ḥālihim*), and their showing neediness through the death of the self to its [own] devising and managing [of things] (*tadbīr*). Whoever does not come up to [these standards] is false in his claim to neediness.

He also said:

The truly needful [person] (*al-faqīr al-ṣādiq*) is the one who does not ask [for things except from God] (*lā yasʾalu*), does not turn down [that which has been granted to him by God] (*lā yaruddu*), and does not hold back [from giving in the path of God when asked] (*lā yaḥbisu*).

ʿUmar b. ʿAbd al-ʿAzīz ﷺ said that the friends of God can be described [as having] three characteristics [lit. things]: confidence (*thiqa*) in God, Exalted is He, in everything; showing neediness for Him (*faqr ilayhi*) in everything; and taking refuge in Him (*rujūʿ ilayhi*) from everything.

1 The *sūra* bears the title 'al-Malāʾika' in all three MSS. The printed edition has the alternative title: Fāṭir.

His words:

[35:32] ***Then We gave the Book as inheritance to those of Our servants whom We chose. [Yet among them is the one who has wronged himself, the one who is in the middle position and the one who is foremost in good deeds…]***

ʿUmar b. Wāṣil stated that he heard heard Sahl say:

> The *one who is foremost* (sābiq) is the one who is learned; *one who is in the middle position* (muqtaṣid) is the one who is learning (*mutaʿallim*), and the *one who has wronged himself* (ẓālim) is the one who is ignorant (*jāhil*).

He also said:

> The *one who is foremost* is he who is only preoccupied with his Hereafter; the *one who is in the middle position* is the one who is preoccupied with his Hereafter and his life in this world; but the wrongdoer is he who is preoccupied only with his worldly life, without any concern for his Hereafter. Ḥasan al-Baṣrī (may God have mercy on him) said the foremost are those whose good deeds outweigh their misdeeds, those who are in the middle position are the ones whose good deeds and misdeeds balance each other, while the wrongdoers are those whose misdeeds outweigh their good deeds.

His words:

[35:34] ***…Praise be to God, who has removed from us* (all) *sorrow…***

> That is, the sorrow of being cut off [from God] (*ḥuzn al-qaṭīʿa*). …*Truly our Lord is Forgiving, Appreciative*, that is, He forgives abundant sins, and shows appreciation for insignificant works.

36 Yā Sīn

His words, Exalted is He:

[36:11] ***You can only warn him who follows the Remembrance, and fears the Compassionate One in secret…***

He said:

> The one who worships God in his innermost secret (*sirr*), will be endowed with certainty (*yaqīn*) by God. The one who worships God with a truthful tongue, will find his heart ascends to the very Throne.[1] The one who worships God with equity (*inṣāf*),[2] will have the heavens and the earth weigh [in his favour].[3]

He was asked, 'What is equity (*inṣāf*) [in worship]?' He replied:

> It is that none of your bodily members moves unless it be for God. Furthermore, when you ask Him for the next day's provision (*rizq*), your equity has left you, for the heart cannot bear two concerns (*hammān*).[4] Equity between you and other people is when you take from them with the attitude that you are receiving a favour. However, if you demand to be treated justly, that means you are not being equitable.[5]
>
> It was related of John the Baptist and Jesus ﷺ that they went out walking, and John bumped into a woman, upon which Jesus said to him, 'O son of my maternal aunt! Today you have committed a grave sin for which I do not think God will forgive you.' He responded, 'And what is that?' He said, 'You bumped into a woman.' He said, 'By God, I did not notice her.' Jesus said 'Glory be to God! Your body is with me but where is your heart?' He said, 'It is attached to the Throne, and if my heart were to find rest with the angel Gabriel ﷺ for just a blinking of the eye, I would consider myself as not having known God, Mighty and Majestic is He.'

His words:

[36:22] ***'And why should I not worship the One who created Me…'***[6]

He [Sahl] was asked about the best form of worship and replied:

> It is sincerity (*ikhlāṣ*), in accordance with His words, *And they were only commanded to worship God alone, devoting religion purely to Him* (mukhliṣīna lahu al-dīn) [98:5]. No one's actions become truly sincere, nor his worship whole, as long as he tries to evade four things: hunger (*jūʿ*), nakedness (*ʿury*), poverty (*faqr*) and abasement (*dhilla*). Indeed, God, Exalted is He, made his servants worship Him through the following three: the intellect (*ʿaql*), the spirit (*rūḥ*) and [physical] strength (*quwwa*). If he is afraid of [losing] two of these, the loss of intellect and the

---

1 lit. 'his heart will not stop until it reaches the Throne.'

2 *Inṣāf* can have the meaning of 'doing justice to something' or 'giving it its due'.

3 lit. 'in his scales'. That is, they will weigh in his favour on Judgement Day.

4 In other words, if your mind is on your next day's provision, it is not on God.

5 This is because if someone receives something from another person, they should have the awareness that it has been destined for them by God. But if they demand something from others, then they are not having true trust in what He has planned for them.

6 These words are said by a man unnamed in the Qurʾān *who came from the furthest part of the city* [36:20]. His warning to people that they should follow the messengers runs from vv. 20–25 of Sūrat Yā Sīn. Ṭabarī identifies him as Ḥabīb b. Marī, or according to one tradition, as Ḥabīb b. Zayd b. ʿĀṣim. In the *Tafsīr al-Jalālayn* he is said to have been a carpenter.

loss of the spirit, then he should take pains to perform well [the acts of worship]. As for [the loss of] physical strength, then there is no taking pains to perform them or learn them well, even if he prays seated.[7]

His words, Exalted is He:

[36:66] ***If it had been Our will, We could have taken away their sight...***

He said:

This means: 'If We so willed We could gouge out the eyes of their hearts by which they perceived disbelief (*kufr*) and its path, so that they could only perceive Islam and nothing else.' *...but how would they have seen?* the path of Islam if He did not do that.

His words:

[36:69] ***...It is just a Reminder and a Qur'ān that makes things clear,***

He said:

It is a reminder (*dhikr*) and a [source of] contemplation (*tafakkur*). But God, Glorified and Exalted is He, knows best.

7 The only apparent difference to note is that MS F638 has *takallafa lahumā* instead of *takallafa lahā*. Perhaps what is meant here is that a person can address any deficit or shortcomings in his intellectual and spiritual life through worship, while in the case of a loss of physical strength, it may not be possible to regain it.

37 Al-Ṣāffāt

His words, Exalted is He:

[37:84] ***when he came to his Lord with a sound heart* (qalb salīm).**[1]

That is, in a state of self-surrender (*mustaslim*), having committed his affairs to his Lord, resorting [to Him] through his innermost secret (*sirr*) in every situation.

His words, Exalted is He:

[37:88, 89] ***And he cast a glance at the stars* (nujūm) ❁ *And he said, 'Indeed I feel sick.'***

He said:

It is narrated from Muḥammad b. Sawwār from ʿAmr b. al-Aʿlāʾ who said, 'Its meaning is that he looked at the plants (*nabāt*), as in His words, *and the plants* (najm) *and trees* (shajar) *bow in prostration* [55:6], intending by the word *najm*, plants which have no trunk,[2] and by the word *shajar*, those which have a trunk.'[3]

His words:

[37:107] ***Then We ransomed him with a mighty sacrifice.***[4]

He said:

When Abraham ﷺ loved his son with a natural human [love], God's favour (*faḍl*) and protection (*ʿiṣma*) corrected him, such that He commanded him to sacrifice his son, though the intention [of this command] was not the realisation of the sacrifice, but rather the aim was to purge his innermost secret (*sirr*) from the love of other than Him by the most effective means. Then when He had purified his innermost secret for Himself, so that he desisted from following his natural habit (*ʿādat al-ṭabʿ*), He *ransomed him with a mighty sacrifice*.

His words:

[37:106] ***Truly this was indeed a clear test.***

He said:

That is, a trial of mercy (*balāʾ al-raḥma*).[5] Do you not see how God sent him [Abraham] in a state of contentment (*riḍā*)?[6]

---

1 The verse is speaking about Abraham.

2 The word *najm* (plur. *nujūm*) can mean 'star' while the word *najm* is a collective noun for 'herbs' or 'plants'.

3 This is an exoteric interpretation, through which Muḥammad b. Sawwār possibly intends to make it clear that Abraham was not worshipping the stars, as did his ancestors, while other commentators point out that Abraham was deliberately giving his father and others the impression that he still depended on the stars. See, for example, the *Tafsīr al-Jalālayn* on this verse. See also p. 66, n. 12 above.

4 This a reference to the ram which God commanded should be sacrificed in place of Abraham's son, once he (Abraham) had proved his readiness to sacrifice his son out of obedience to God.

5 The reason for its being called a trial of mercy is explained in the paragraph which follows in Tustarī's commentary.

6 That is, the prophet Abraham manifested the quality of contented acceptance of whatever trials God had decreed for him. See above Tustarī's commentary on 15:97, 98.

He said:

> We have heard that the following is written in the Psalms, 'I did not decree anything for a believer which he either liked or detested without its being good for him.' And it is related that God, Exalted is He, revealed the following to Abraham ﷺ, 'There is no one [whose provision in this world] I have increased, but that I have decreased by the same proportion [his provision] in the Hereafter, and that goes for you also, My true friend.'[7]

Abū Yaʿqūb al-Sūsī[8] relates, 'A *faqīr* came to us while we were in Arrajān and Sahl b. ʿAbd Allāh happened to be there also on that day.[9] He [the *faqīr*] said, "You are the people of [God's] special care (*ahl al-ʿināya*). Indeed, a severe trial and affliction (*miḥna*) has descended upon me." Sahl said to him, "In the registry of afflictions, it descended only after you exposed yourself to this matter.[10] So what is it?" He replied, "Something of this world opened itself up to me, so I took possession of it to the exclusion of my family and thus lost my faith and my [spiritual] state (*ḥāl*)." Sahl said, "What do you say concerning this, O Abū Yaʿqūb?" I replied, "The affliction was more intense [for him] regarding [the loss of] his state than regarding [the loss of] his faith." Sahl responded, "A person like you would say that O Abū Yaʿqūb."'[11]

Sahl was asked about the [spiritual] state (*ḥāl*). He replied:

> The state of remembrance (*dhikr*) [at the level of] knowledge (*ʿilm*) is tranquil repose [in God] (*sukūn*), and the state of remembrance [at the level of] the intellect (*ʿaql*) is profound peace (*ṭumaʾnīna*). The state of mindfulness of God (*taqwā*) [at the level of] Islam [consists of observing] the limits [of the law] (*ḥudūd*), and the state of mindfulness of God [at the level of] faith (*īmān*) is profound peace (*ṭumaʾnīna*).[12]
>
> If the servant has a state, and an affliction visits him, and he then asks for relief through a state lower than the one he is in, that counts as a defilement (*ḥadath*) from him.

He was asked, 'Why is that?', and he said, 'It is like someone who is hungry asking for satiation, because the rank of the hungry is higher.'[13]

His words:

[37:143] *And had he not been one of those who glorify God,*[14]

He said:

> That is, among those who upheld the rights (*ḥuqūq*) of God, Exalted is He, before affliction (*balāʾ*) came. But God, Glorified and Exalted is He, knows best.

---

7 Compare the commentary on 29:1, 2 above, regarding suffering and the reward of the Hereafter.

8 Abū Yaʿqūb Yūsuf b. Hamdān al-Sūsī (d. end third/ninth century). Böwering (*Mystical Vision*, p. 80) understands Sūsī to be among the visitors to Tustarī who benefited from his teaching for a short time.

9 Arrajān is an ancient town built by the Sassanians, which is now a ruin. It is situated in Khūzistān, southern Iran, close to Behbahān.

10 That is exposing himself to the matter of the affliction.

11 This discussion is related in Sarrāj, *Kitāb al-Lumaʿ*, p. 193. See Böwering, *Mystical Vision*, pp. 78–9. Böwering understands from this encounter that both Tustarī and Abū Yaʿqūb are in agreement in their disapproval of the *faqīr*'s being more distressed about the loss of his state than the loss of his faith.

12 On the significance of the levels of *islām* and *īmān*, as well as *iḥsān* see above Tustarī's commentary on 14:25.

13 The state of hunger is higher in the spiritual ranks than that of satiation, so if the aspiring mystic who is hungry asks for satiation, then that is tantamount to 'defilement'. On the virtue of hunger, see above Tustarī's commentary on 7:31 and IT, p. xvi, and p. xxi.

14 This is part of a brief account of the story of Jonah in the whale [37:139–48]. The following verse completes the conditional sentence, so the two verses read as follows: *And had he not been one of those who glorify God,* ۞ *he would have tarried in its belly until the Day when they are raised* [37:143–4].

38 Ṣād

His words, Exalted is He:

[38:1] ***Ṣād. By the Qurʾān endowed with the Remembrance!***

He said:

That is, endowed with healing power (*al-shaʾn al-shāfī*) and sufficient admonition (*al-waʿẓ al-kāfī*).

His words:

[38:6] ***…'Walk away! And stand by* (iṣbirū) *your gods'…***[1]

He said:

This is the reprehensible form of forbearance (*ṣabr*),[2] for which God has reprimanded the disbelievers.

Indeed, I heard him [Sahl] say:

Forbearance (*ṣabr*) is on four levels: forbearance in obedience (*ṭāʿa*), forbearance with suffering (*alam*), forbearance with pain (*taʾallum*), and lastly, the reprehensible kind of forbearance, which is that of persistence (*iqāma*) in opposing [the truth] (*mukhālafa*).[3]

His words:

[38:20] ***And We strengthened his kingdom, and gave him wisdom and decisive speech* (faṣl al-khiṭāb).**[4]

He said:

God only gave him [David] this when he asked Him to raise his rank to the rank enjoyed by Ishmael and Isaac. He said, 'You are not on that level, O David. However, I am giving you a high rank for your wisdom, and articulation in speech (*fāṣila*)'[5] — this being the saying: *ammā baʿd* (to proceed), which he was the first to say. Quss b. Sāʿida was the one who followed the precedent of saying this [*ammā baʿd*].[6] It has also been said *decisive speech* (faṣl al-khiṭāb) is lucidity (*bayān*) and faith (*īmān*).[7]

---

1 These words were said by a group of Quraysh, who used to go round discouraging people from listening to the words of the Prophet.

2 Note that the word used in the Qurʾān for to 'stand by' is from the same root, *ṣ-b-r*, as the word for patience, endurance, forbearance.

3 See also the discussion of forbearance in Tustarī's commentary on 29:1, 2.

4 Verses 17–26 of this *sūra* relate a story of the prophet David, and are said to allude to his acquisition of another man's wife to add to the numerous wives he already had. David realised that this had been a test from God and repented (v. 24). God then forgave him (v. 25), but with an admonition (v. 26). See above p. 49, n. 47 for a brief account of this story.

5 We have used the word 'articulation' here for *fāṣila*, because it has the dual meaning in English of something which both links two things while keeping them separate, as in a joint — the same meaning attaches to the Arabic root *faṣala*, from which is derived *mafṣal*, meaning both a joint, and something which is clearly enunciated in terms of language.

6 The expression *ammā baʿd*, which is given as an example of *fāṣila*, serves the purpose of maintaining continuity of discourse, while also making a clear division of one topic from another.

7 That is translating *faṣl al-khiṭāb al-bayān waʾl-īmān*, according to all three MSS, Z515, f. 91b, F638, f. 41b and F3488, f. 267a, instead of *faṣl al-īmān li-khiṭāb al-bayān*.

His words:

[38:20] ***We strengthened his kingdom…***

He said:

> That is, with justice (*ʿadl*) and with virtuous ministers to rule over it with goodness, just as the Messenger ﷺ said, 'Truly, if God, Exalted is He, wills good for a ruler, He grants him a truthful minister (*wazīr ṣadūq*) who reminds him when he forgets, and assists him when he remembers.'

His words:

[38:24] ***…He fell down on his knees and repented.***

He said:

> Turning often to God in contrition (*ināba*) is returning from heedlessness to remembrance with a broken heart (*inkisār al-qalb*) and the anticipation of [His] loathing (*intiẓār al-maqt*).

His words:

[38:26] ***…and do not follow [your] desire, lest it then lead you astray from the way of God…***

He said:

> That is, the darkness of desire which obscures the lights of the intuition of the self (*dhihn al-nafs*), the spirit (*rūḥ*), the understanding of the intellect (*fahm al-ʿaql*), and the discernment of the heart (*fiṭnat al-qalb*).[8] Similarly, the Prophet ﷺ said: 'Truly, [when followed], desire (*hawā*) and lust (*shahwa*) overwhelm the intellect, knowledge,'[9] and lucidity (*bayān*), due to the pre-eternal ordainment of God, Exalted is He.[10]

His words:

[38:32] **(He [Solomon] said)** ***'Lo! I have preferred the love of the good things [of this world] over the remembrance of my Lord…'***

He said:

> [Over] the afternoon prayer and its [prescribed] time.[11]

His words:

[38:35] ***…'O my Lord! Forgive me, and grant me a kingdom which shall not belong to anyone after me…'***

He said:

> God, Exalted is He, inspired Solomon to ask for a kingdom which would not be attainable by anyone after him, that He might shatter thereby the tyrants, the unbelievers, those who transgress against their Lord, and those among jinn and men who claim to possess power by themselves.[12] Thus, the question was posed by Solomon ﷺ, in accordance with God's choice for him, and not following his own choice for himself.[13]

His words:

[38:46] ***Assuredly We purified them with a pure [thought]: the remembrance of the Abode.***[14]

---

8 For a discussion of these terms used by Tustarī to explain the inner make-up of the human being see IT, pp. xxxviiiff.

9 The first part of this *ḥadīth* was quoted earlier in Tustarī's commentary on 2:30, and is cited as being among the sayings of al-Ḥārith b. Asad in Iṣfahānī, *Ḥilyat al-awliyāʾ*, vol. 10, p. 88.

10 This is according to MS F638, f. 41b, which has *li-sābiq al-taqdīr*, while Z515, f. 91b, F3488, f. 267a and the published edition have *li-sābiq al-qudra min Allāh taʿālā*. However in a later citation of this same tradition in the commentary on 91:4 Z515 has *li-sābiq al-qadar*.

11 This is also the reason given by various authorities in Ṭabarī's commentary on this verse in the *Jāmiʿ al-bayān*.

12 Solomon was granted dominion over jinn, men, birds and the wind. For the story of Solomon see Ṭabarī's *History*, vol. 3, *Children of Israel*, trans. Brinner, pp. 152ff.; Thaʿlabī, *ʿArāʾis al-majālis*, trans. Brinner, pp. 490ff.

13 Because he was inspired by God to request it.

14 i.e. the Hereafter. This verse refers to Abraham, Isaac and Jacob, who are mentioned in the previous verse.

He said:

> He purified Abraham, Ishmael and Isaac from the remembrance (*dhikr*) of this world through a remembrance of Him, purely for [His sake] (*khāliṣatan*), not for the attainment of recompense (*jazāʾ*). Neither did they witness themselves in it [their remembrance]; rather, they remembered Him through Him and for Him. Furthermore, the one who remembers God through God (*bi'Llāh*) is not like the one who remembers God through the remembrance of God (*bi-dhikri'Llāh*). But God, Glorified and Exalted is He, knows best.

39 Al-Zumar

His words, Exalted is He:

[39:7] ***…If you give thanks He will approve…***

He said:

> Gratitude (*shukr*) begins with obedience (*ṭāʿa*) and ends with the vision of Paradise (*ruʾyat al-janna*).[1]

His words:

[39:9] ***…Say: 'Are those who know equal with those who do not know?…'***

He said:

> Knowledge [comes from] the Book and emulation (*iqtidāʾ*) [of the Prophet's example], not [from] reprehensible suggestions (*khawāṭir madhmūma*). Any knowledge that the servant does not seek from the position of emulating [the Prophet's example] will be a curse (*wabāl*) to him because he will make false claims on account of it.[2]

His words:

[39:11] ***Say: 'Indeed I have been commanded to worship God devoting [my] religion purely to Him.'***

He said:

> Sincerity (*ikhlāṣ*) is responding (*ijāba*), and whoever has no response has no sincerity.[3]

And he said:

> The astute (*akyās*) reflected upon sincerity and did not find anything except the following: that everything the servant does, whether done in secret or openly, is for God alone, Mighty and Majestic is He, and is mingled neither with desire nor with the self.

His words:

[39:17] ***Those who steer clear of [the worship of] false deities…***

He said:

> Evil (*ṭāghūt*)[4] is the world, its root is ignorance (*jahl*), its branch is what is eaten and drunk, its adornment is hubris (*tafākhur*), its fruits are transgressions (*maʿāṣī*) and [in] its scales [of recompense] (*mīzān*) are severity (*qaswa*) and punishment (*ʿuqūba*).[5]

His words:

[39:38] ***[Say] '…If God should desire some harm to befall me, would they [be able] to remove the harm imposed by Him?'…***

---

1 By which Tustarī may mean the vision of God in Paradise. See above the commentary on 2:214 and 14:7, and Tustarī's words on gratitude vis-à-vis acting upon one's knowledge, which could also be seen as obedience.

2 For Tustarī's teachings regarding emulation (*iqtidāʾ*) see IT, pp. liii–liv.

3 With this elliptical comment Tustarī is indicating that all that is required for sincerity is to devote our religion purely to God, which is the only worthy response to the divine command. What is implied by the [true] response is explained in the statement that follows.

4 *Ṭāghūt* is a word for idols or Satan, but by extension it has come to mean evil.

5 That is, according to MSS Z515, f. 91b, F3488, f. 268a and the published edition, whereas MSF638, f. 43a, has *mīrāth* instead of *mīzān*, which might be translated as 'legacy'.

He said:

That is, 'If God removed from me protection against acts of opposition (*mukhālafāt*), or the knowledge (*maʿrifa*) of acts of conformity (*muwāfaqāt*), could anyone bring them back to me? *Or if He should desire some mercy for me,* that is, in granting me forbearance (*ṣabr*) in avoiding what He has forbidden, and assistance (*maʿūna*) in carrying out what He has commanded, and in granting me full reliance (*ittikāl*) on Him at the end [of my life], [*could they withhold His mercy?*].

And he said:

Mercy (*raḥma*) is well-being (*ʿāfiya*) in one's religion, in this world and in the Hereafter. In other words, it is [God's] taking charge and taking care (*tawallī*) [of His creatures] from the beginning to the end.

His words:

[39:41] ***Truly, We have revealed the Book to you for [the sake of] mankind with the Truth...***

That is, He revealed it for them so that they may be guided by the Truth to the Truth (*bi'l-ḥaqq ilā'l-ḥaqq*),[6] and that they may find illumination through Its [His] lights.

His words:

[39:42] ***God takes the souls at the time of their death, and those that have not died, in their sleep...***

He said:

When God takes the souls (*anfus*) to Himself, He extracts the luminous spirit (*rūḥ nūrī*) from the subtle substance (*laṭīf*) of the dense natural self (*nafs al-ṭabʿ al-kathīf*). The taking up [of souls] (*al-tawaffī*) in God's Book is of three kinds: the first is death (*mawt*), the second, sleep (*nawm*), and the third, ascension (*rafʿ*). Death is as we have just mentioned. Sleep is as [described] in His words: *and those that have not died, in their sleep*, which means that He also takes unto Himself (*yatawaffā*) those who have not died, in their sleep (*manām*). [God also] said, *It is He who takes you at night* [6:60] meaning, in sleep. Ascension (*rafʿ*) is mentioned in relation to Jesus ﷺ, to whom God said, *'O Jesus, I am gathering you and raising you to Me'* [3:55]. Thus when a person dies, He [God] removes (*yanziʿu*) from him the subtle substance (*laṭīf*) of the luminous spiritual self (*nafs al-rūḥ al-nūrī*) [separating it] from the subtle substance (*laṭīf*) of the dense natural self (*nafs al-ṭabʿ al-kathīf*), and by this [luminous spiritual self] he comprehends things (*yaʿqilu al-ashyāʾ*), and is given the vision (*rūʾyā*) in the heavenly kingdom (*malakūt*).[7] However, when a person sleeps, He extracts from him the subtle substance of the dense natural self, not the subtle substance of the luminous spiritual self. Therefore, when the sleeping person awakens, he recovers a subtle breath (*nafas laṭīf*) from the subtle substance of the spiritual self, for if this were to part from him, it would leave him without motion (*ḥaraka*), and lifeless (*mayyit*). Thus, the dense natural self has a subtle substance (*laṭīfa*) and likewise the spiritual self has a subtle substance (*laṭīfa*).[8] The life of the subtle substance of the natural self is by virtue of the light of the subtle substance of the spiritual self (*nūr laṭīf nafs al-rūḥ*). The spiritual life of the subtle substance of the spiritual self (*ḥayāt rūḥ laṭīf nafs al-rūḥ*)[9] is by virtue of remembrance [of God] (*dhikr*), just as He has said: *rather they are living with their Lord, provided for [by Him]* [3:169], that is, they are sustained by remembrance, due to what they attained through the subtle luminous self.[10] The life of the dense nature (*ṭabʿ kathīf*) is

---

6 Or it might be translated as 'by God to God' since the name *al-Ḥaqq* ('the Absolute Truth') has often been used to refer to God.

7 For a discussion of this passage in the context of Tustarī's 'spiritual psychology', see IT, pp. xxxix–xl.

8 All three MSS (Z515, f. 93a, F638, f. 43b and F3488, f. 269a) have *laṭīfa* here instead of *laṭīf* in this sentence, though Böwering (*Mystical Vision*, p. 245) has in any case read them as *laṭīf* as in the rest of the passage.

9 Or more precisely we might translate this as 'the life of the spirit of the subtle substance of the spiritual self'. MS F638, f. 43b, however, has *ḥayāt rūḥ nafs al-rūḥ* without the word *laṭīf*, which would read literally as 'the life of the spirit of the spiritual self'.

10 In its outward meaning, this verse [3:169] describes the situation of those who became martyrs in the Battle of Uḥud.

through eating, drinking and [physical] enjoyment (*tamattuʿ*).

Whoever cannot reconcile these two opposites, by which I mean, the natural self and the spiritual self, so that the two together are sustained by remembrance (*dhikr*) and by the endeavour [to accomplish] remembrance,[11] is not a mystic (*ʿārif*) in reality.

ʿUmar b. Wāṣil said, 'The grammarian al-Mubarrad used to say that the spirit (*rūḥ*) and the soul [or self, *nafs*] are two interconnected things; the one cannot subsist without the other.' He continued, 'I mentioned this to Sahl and he said':

He is mistaken. The spirit subsists by His grace (*bi-luṭfihi*) within its own essence (*bi-dhātihi*), independent from the dense natural self. Do you not see that God, Exalted is He, addressed everyone while still in a molecular form,[12] by virtue of the existence of the spiritual self, the understanding of the intellect, the intuition of the heart, and the presence of a subtle kind of knowledge, without the presence of [man's] dense nature (*ṭabʿ kathīf*).

His words:

[39:43] ***Or have they taken intercessors besides God?...***

He said:

Have they followed the path of innovation in religion as a way of drawing closer to God through their religion, on the basis that this would benefit them?

His words:

[39:45] ***And when God is mentioned alone, the hearts of those who do not believe in the Hereafter shrink [with aversion]...***

⌜He said:

That is,⌝[13] their hearts disavow the gifts of God that they possess (*ʿindahā*).

His words:

[39:53] ***Say [that God declares]: 'O My servants who have been prodigal against their souls! Do not despair of God's mercy...'***

He said:

God, Exalted is He, has given his servants respite, out of His bounty, up to their last breath, and He says to them, 'Do not despair of My mercy; even if you came back to Me in your last breath, I would receive you.'

He said:

This verse is the most far reaching in conveying the compassion (*ishfāq*) shown by God, Exalted is He, to His servants; because, in accordance with His knowledge, He does not deprive them of that which He bestows on others, rather He showers mercy upon them to the point that He admits them to the very essence of [His] generosity (*ʿayn al-karam*), by virtue of [His] eternal remembrance of them.[14]

There were those who had stayed behind, who urged their brothers not to go, saying: *'Had they obeyed us, they would not have been slain'* [3:168], at which the Prophet was commanded to give the reply, in the same verse, *Then avert death from yourselves, if you speak the truth*, which is an ironic answer, indicating that they have, in any case, no power to avert death when it is decreed for them. There follows the admonition: *Count not those who are slain in battle as dead, but rather living with their Lord, provided for [by Him]* [3:169]. As is often the case in his esoteric interpretations, Tustarī has widened the application of the meaning of the verse here so that it refers to the spiritual life of the subtle substance of the spiritual self.

11 lit. 'so that the sustenance of the two together is remembrance and the endeavour (*saʿī*) for remembrance.'

12 An allusion to the Covenant of *Alast*, for which see the commentary on 7:172, and IT, pp. xxxi–xxxii and xxxv–xxxvi. In connection with this passage see also IT, p. xl, n. 156 and p. xliv, n. 184.

13 The addition was made on the basis of all three MSS: Z515, f. 93b, F638, f. 43b and F3488, f. 269b.

14 This may mean that He has remembered them in this very verse, which is the word of God and in its essential form, eternal (*qadīm*).

> It was related of the angel Gabriel ﷺ that he heard Abraham ﷺ pray, 'O You who are Most Generous in pardoning!' Then Gabriel ﷺ said to him, 'O Abraham! Do you know what the generosity of His pardon (*ʿafw*) [implies]?' He answered, 'No, O Gabriel.' He continued, 'It is that when He pardons a misdeed, He converts it into a good deed.'[15]

Then Sahl said:

> Witness this of me: it is part of my religion that I do not disown the sinners among the nation of Muḥammad ﷺ, nor the wicked, the murderers, the adulterers or the thieves, for truly, the extent of the generosity, bounty, and beneficence that God, Exalted is He, shows, especially to the nation of Muḥammad ﷺ, cannot be fathomed.

His words:

[39:54] ***'And turn [penitently] to your Lord, and submit to Him….'***[16]

> That is, 'Return to Him through supplication (*duʿāʾ*), and by humbly beseeching (*taḍarruʿ*) and petitioning (*masʾala*) [Him]'; '*and submit to Him*'. That is, 'Commit all your affairs to Him'.

His words:

[39:56] ***Lest any soul should say, 'Woe is me for what I have neglected of [my] duty to God!...'***

He said:

> [That is, lest any soul should say], 'I was preoccupied by the present world (*ʿājil al-dunya*), the pleasure of passion (*ladhdhat al-hawā*) and with going the way of the lower self. I neglected *[my] duty to God*, that is, with regard to God's person (*dhāt Allāh*), [and I neglected] being intent upon Him (*qaṣd ilayhi*), and dependent upon Him (*iʿtimād ʿalayhi*), on account of my neglecting to observe His rights (*ḥuqūq*) and adhere to His service (*khidma*).'

His words, Exalted is He:

[39:63] ***To Him belong the keys of the heavens and the earth…***

> That is, in His hand are the keys to hearts. He gives success to whomever He wills, so that they obey him and serve Him with sincerity, and He turns away from His door whomever He wills.

His words:

[39:67] ***And they do not esteem God as He should be esteemed…***

> That is, they did not come to know Him as He deserves to be known (*ḥaqq maʿrifatihi*), [either] in the fundamental[s of His knowledge] (*aṣl*),[17] or in its branch[es] (*farʿ*).[18]

His words:

[39:68] ***…when whoever is in the heavens and earth will swoon...***[19]

He said:

> The inner [meaning] of the verse is that [this will happen] when the angels are commanded to desist from remembrance, and not due to the Trumpet's blast, nor Azrāʾīl's removal [of the souls of all living creatures].[20] This is because He gave them life through His remembrance just

---

15 Bayhaqī, *Shuʿab al-īmān*, vol. 5, p. 389. The tradition appears in Makkī, *Qūt al-qulūb*, vol. 1, pp. 376–7, where it is the Prophet Muḥammad instead of Abraham who is spoken to by Gabriel.

16 This is a further exhortation that the Prophet has been commanded to give to those mentioned in the previous verse.

17 i.e. knowledge of Him.

18 The fundamentals of religion (*uṣūl al-dīn*) and its branches (*furūʿ*) being the two main categories of religious sciences: theology and substantive law, that is, the positive rules of law, including worship (*ʿibādā*) and transactions (*muʿāmalāt*).

19 That is, on the Day of Resurrection, when the Trumpet will be blown for the first time. The latter part of this same verse states that when it is blown again *they will rise up, looking on*.

20 The complete verse reads: *The Trumpet will be sounded when whoever is in the heavens and earth will swoon*. According to tradition, on the last day Isrāfīl will blow the Trumpet and the Angel of Death, Azrāʾīl, will capture the souls of all living creatures, including the other angels and himself. What Tustarī is saying here is that the real cause of the end is not the Trumpet or the Angel of Death, but God's commandment that the angels should stop praising and remembering Him.

as He gave the children of Adam life through their breathing.[21]

God, Exalted is He, has said: *They glorify [Him] night and day and do not falter* [21:20] But when He withholds remembrance from them they perish.

His words:

[39:69] ***And the earth will shine with the light of its Lord…***

He said:

The hearts of the believers will shine on the Day of Resurrection with the light of [their realisation] of the oneness of their Lord,[22] and their following of the Sunna of their Prophet ﷺ.

His words:

[39:74] ***[And they will say,] 'Praise be to God who has fulfilled His promise to Us…'***

He said:

Indeed, their praise (*ḥamd*) in Paradise does not take the form of an act of worship (*taʿabbud*), since they are exempted from that, just as they are exempted from the fear (*khawf*) related to the [need for] earning (*kasb*) and the [possibility] of alienation (*qaṭʿ*). What remains, though, is the [reverential] fear [that accompanies] the exaltation (*khawf al-ijlāl*) and magnifying (*taʿẓīm*) of God, Mighty and Majestic is He. So their praise is simply a delight for the natural self (*nafs al-ṭabʿ*), the spiritual self (*nafs al-rūḥ*), the intellect (*ʿaql*) ⌜and the heart (*qalb*)⌝.[23] But God, Glorified and Exalted is He, knows best.

21 See the discussion above in Tustarī's commentary on 39:42.

22 That is according to MS F638, f. 43b, which has: *bi-nūr tawḥīd sayyidihim*, while the published edition and MSS Z515, f. 94b and F3488, f. 270b have *bi-tawḥīd sayyidihim* which might be translated as 'they shine or are radiant due to [their knowledge] of the unity of their Master'.

23 Added on the basis of all three MSS Z515, f. 94b, F638, f. 44a and F3488, f. 270b.

40 Al-Muʾmin (or Ghāfir)[1]

His words, Exalted is He:

[40:1, 2] *Ḥā Mīm.* ❁ *The revelation of the Book is from God, the Almighty, the All-Knowing,*

He said:

> That is, the Living (*al-Ḥayy*), the King (*al-Malik*),[2] who sent down the Book to you. He is ⌜God⌝,[3] who turns thereby [by the Revelation] the hearts of mystics (*ʿārifūn*). He is Almighty (*al-ʿAzīz*) beyond the grasp of created beings, the All-Knowing (*al-ʿAlīm*) with regard to what He has produced and ordained.

[40:3] *Forgiver of sins…*

> That is, He conceals the sins of whomever He will; *and Accepter of repentance* from the one who repents to Him and devotes his actions purely to Him with knowledge (*ʿilm*); *One of [infinite] bounty*; Possessed of a richness [which makes Him] Independent from all (*al-Ghanī ʿan al-kull*).

[40:4] *None dispute the signs of God…*[4]

> That is, [they do not dispute] concerning His essence (*dhāt*), or omnipotence (*qudra*), or concerning the Qurʾān, or the Sunna, out of some whim of the lower self. Just as He said, *And argued with falsehood* [40:5], meaning: following [their] own whim (*hawā*) without referring to guidance from God, and just as He also said, *Why do you then dispute concerning that of which you have no knowledge?* [3:66] — *[None dispute]…save those who disbelieve* and create innovations that do not belong to the truth.

His words:

[40:7] *…So forgive those who repent…*

He said:

> They are those who repent from heedlessness, find intimacy in remembrance and follow the Sunna of Muṣṭafā ﷺ.[5]

His words:

[40:10] *Indeed [to] those who disbelieve it will be proclaimed, 'Surely God's abhorrence is greater than your abhorrence of yourselves…'*

---

1 The published edition gives Ghāfir as the title to this *sūra*. However, all three MSS use the title al-Muʾmin.

2 Tustarī has here interpreted the letters *ḥā* and *mīm* of *Ḥā Mīm* as *al-Ḥayy* and *al-Malik*, respectively. Sometimes, as in this case, these 'disconnected letters' with which some of the *sūras* begin, are interpreted individually as representing something for which they stand as the initial letter. But it is also the custom to interpret the combination of letters, as was seen above in the commentary on *Alif, Lām, Mīm*, at the beginning of Sūrat al-Baqara. On the 'disconnected letters' see above, Tustarī's commentary on 2:1, and p. 12, n. 2.

3 Present in all three MSS: Z515, f. 94b, F638, f. 44a and F3488, f. 270b.

4 The verse continues: *except those who disbelieve, so do not be deceived by their bustle in the towns.* The next verse gives examples of those, beginning with the people of Noah, who sought to dispute the truth brought by the messengers.

5 Muṣṭafā is one of the honorific titles of the Prophet, meaning 'the Chosen One [of God].'

He said:

Abhorrence (*maqt*) is the most extreme form of alienation (*ibʿād*) from God, Mighty and Majestic is He. [Furthermore], when the disbelievers enter the Fire they abhor themselves. However, God's abhorrence of their deeds is even severer [for them] than their entry into the Fire.

His words:

[40:15] ***The Exalter of rank, Lord of the Throne, He casts the Spirit of His command…***

That is, He is the Raiser of ranks, and He elevates the ranks of whomever He wills by [granting him] gnosis (*maʿrifa*) of Him. *He casts the Spirit of His command…*That is, He sends the Revelation from the heavens to the earth by His command.

His words:

[40:60] ***And your Lord has said, 'Call on Me and I will respond to you…'***

He said:

[It is a requirement of] chivalry (*muruwwa*), that supplication (*duʿāʾ*) should be answered, without doubt. It [supplication] is a quiver of arrows.[6] A believer does not supplicate God, Exalted is He, without His either answering him by granting him exactly what he asked for, even though that servant may not be aware of it, or repelling thereby something evil from him, or recording for him a good deed because of it.

He was asked, 'What is the meaning of the saying: "Supplication is the best of deeds?"' He replied:

It is because it [supplication] is a way of humbly imploring [God] (*taḍarruʿ*), taking refuge (*iltijāʾ*) [in Him], and showing one's poverty (*faqr*) and neediness (*fāqa*) [for Him].

His words:

[40:81] ***And He shows you His signs; then which of the signs of God do you reject?***

He said:

God, Exalted is He, has made His signs (*āyāt*)[7] manifest to His friends (*awliyāʾ*), and He has made happy those among His servants who believe in them, [affirming the truth of] their charismatic gifts (*karāmāt*).[8] However, He has made the eyes of the damned blind to seeing them, and has turned their hearts away from Him. Whoever denies the charismatic gifts of the friends [of God] denies the omnipotence of God, Exalted is He. For the omnipotence [of God] manifests [itself] at the hand of the friends [of God], and they cannot by themselves cause their manifestation, in accordance with His words *And He shows you His signs; then which of the signs of God do you reject?*

His words:

[40:85] ***…[This is] God's way* (sunna) *with His slaves, which has its precedent…***

He said:

[The word] *sunna* is derived from some of the names of God, Exalted is He: the letter 'sīn' stands for *sanāʾūhu* (His resplendence), the *letter* 'nūn' stands for *nūruhu* (His light) and 'hā' stands for *hidāyatuhu* (His guidance).[9] His saying: *God's way* means: ⌜His 'primordial nature' (*fiṭratuhu*) upon which He moulds (*jabala*) the elite among His servants, out of His guidance for them⌝, and thus they are [already disposed towards] the norms (*ʿalā sunan*) of the clear path to Him.[10]

But God, Glorified and Exalted is He, knows best.

---

6 That is, the arrows will hit their target.

7 'Signs' in this context represent the miracles that are accorded by God to His friends, or the saints (*awliyāʾ*).

8 The term charismatic gift is used here to translate *karāma*, designating the miracle of a mystic or friend of God, as opposed to *muʿjiza*, which is applied to the miracles of prophets. On this subject, see above IT, p. xx, n. 52.

9 The 'ha' here refers to the *tāʾ marbūṭa* at the end of the word *sunna* for which reason the convention is sometimes to write it as *sunnah*. See below the commentary on 69:1, 2 and p. 244, n. 1.

10 The addition is made on the basis of all three MSS, Z515, f. 94b, F638, f. 44b and F3488, f. 271b.

41 Al-Sajda (or Fuṣṣilat)[1]

His saying:

[41:1] ***Ḥā Mīm***

That is, He decreed [everything] upon the Preserved Tablet (*lawḥ maḥfūẓ*), in which was inscribed all that exists [and will come into existence] (*kāʾin*).

His words:

[41:4] ***[bearing] good tidings and a warning...***[2]

He said:

Giving the good news of Paradise to those who obey Him and follow what is within it [the Book], and a warning of the Fire for those who disobey Him, turn away from what God intends within it, and oppose it.

His words, Exalted is He:

[41:5] ***And they say, 'Our hearts are veiled against that to which you call us...'***

He said:

That is, [veiled] with coverings of neglect (*ihmāl*), such that they inclined towards lust (*shahwa*) and desire (*hawā*), and could not comprehend the summoning (*daʿwa*) of God; '*and in our ears*, [the ears] which are in our hearts, *there is a deafness*', that is, deafness to the good, so they do not hear the calls (*hawātif*) of God; '*And between us and you is a partition*', that is, 'a veil of desire and of [our] natural disposition (*jibillat al-ṭabʿ*), so we do not see you as others see you.'

His words:

[41:24] ***So if they endure, the Fire will [still] be their abode...***[3]

That is, if they seek release they will not be released, and if they apologise they will not be pardoned.

His words:

[41:30] ***Truly, those who say, 'Our Lord is God.' And then remain on the straight path...***

He said:

That is, they do not associate partners along with Him. This is as in the saying narrated from the Prophet ﷺ, 'They are my nation and, by the Lord of the Kaʿba, they remained on the straight path and did not commit association (*shirk*) like the Jews and the Christians.'[4]

ʿUmar said, 'They did not evade [the truth] with the evasiveness of foxes'.[5]

---

1 The MSS have the title al-Sajda. The published edition gives two titles for the *sūra*.

2 Verses 3 and 4 describe attributes of the *Revelation from the Merciful, the Compassionate* mentioned in v. 2.

3 This verse is part of the description (vv. 19–24) of what happens to God's enemies when they are gathered up and sent to the Fire, and their unremitting punishment therein.

4 This tradition is cited in Muḥammad b. Aḥmad al-Qurṭubī, *al-Jāmiʿ li-aḥkām al-Qurʾān*, known as *Tafsīr al-Qurṭubī* (Beirut, 1985), vol. 15, p. 358.

5 This saying, presumably of ʿUmar b. al-Khaṭṭāb, is cited in the *Kitāb al-Zuhd waʾl-raqāʾiq* of ʿAbd Allāh Ibn Mubārak (Beirut, 1971), p. 110.

His words:

[41:30] ***...the angels descend to them and say, 'Do not fear nor grieve...'***

That is, at the time of death. Indeed, the Prophet ﷺ said, 'God, Exalted is He, says: "I have never hesitated over anything as much as I have hesitated over snatching (*qabḍ*) the soul (*rūḥ*) of the believer"',[6] by which He means, 'The angels never hesitate over anything as much as they hesitate over snatching the soul of My believing servant, which they do while giving him good tidings (*bashāra*) and treating him with honour (*karāma*) saying, "Do not fear for your souls and do not grieve about the Day of Gathering"', just as He has said, *The Supreme Terror shall not grieve them* [21:103].

He said:

[He is] the One who takes you all into His care (*al-mutawallī li-jumlatikum*)[7] with [His] good pleasure (*riḍā*), protecting your hearts, and delighting your eyes with the [divine] manifestation (*tajallī*), in reward for your profession of His oneness and as a favour (*tafaḍḍul*) from your Lord.

His words:

[41:33] ***Who is better in speech than one who summons [others] to God...***

That is, than one who guides [people] to God, His worship and the Sunna of His Messenger ﷺ, and to the avoidance of all that is forbidden; [and who guides] to perseverance (*idāma*) in rectitude (*istiqāma*) with God, steadfastness in this for fear of one's end (*khātima*); and to the middle way (*ṭarīqa wusṭā*),[8] and the straight path (*jādda mustaqīma*), upon which whoever travels will be safe, but away from which whoever deviates (*taʿaddā*) will be filled with regret (*nadam*).

His words:

[41:49] ***Man never wearies of supplicating for good...***

He said:

He does not weary of remembering His Lord, nor of thanking Him, praising Him, or extolling Him.

His words:

[41:51] ***And when We bestow graces upon man he shows disregard and turns away...***

He said:

That is, [he turns away] from supplication, and from showing gratitude for what God has bestowed upon him. He becomes preoccupied with the bounties [themselves] and takes pride in that which is not worthy of any pride.

His words:

[41:53] ***We shall show them Our signs on the horizons and in themselves...***

That is, death.

He said:

Death has a specific (*khāṣṣ*) and a general (*ʿāmm*) meaning.[9] The general [meaning of] death is the death of the physical body (*khilqa*) and [its] natural form (*jibilla*). The specific [meaning]

6 Bukhārī, *Ṣaḥīḥ*, 'Kitāb al-Riqāq'; Tirmidhī, *Nawādir al-uṣūl*, vol. 2, p. 232.

7 The second person plural pronoun in the expression *jumlatikum* here may be referring back to 21:92, where *ummatukum* is mentioned, i.e. *Truly this nation (or religion) of yours* (pl.) *is one nation,* and in his translation of the Qurʾān Muhammad Abdel Haleem has understood this as being addressed to the messengers altogether. Or maybe the expression simply means all of you. M. Abdel Haleem, trans. *Qur'an* (New York, 2008).

8 The Muslims are described as *a midmost nation* (umma wasaṭa) in 2:143. According to Ṭabarī, being the 'middle' or 'midmost' means their being on the one hand free of extremism (*ghuluww*), and on the other, just (*ʿudūl*).

9 i.e. a meaning that is understood by the elect (*khāṣṣ*), that is, an inner meaning, and a meaning more widely understood by the generality (*ʿāmm*), namely its literal meaning, as is clear by the interpretation that Tustarī presents. Note that in the Introduction to the Commentary, p. 2, he stated that the understanding of the inner meanings of the Qurʾān are for

is the death of the lusts of the lower self (*shahawāt al-nafs*).[10] But God, Glorified and Exalted is He, knows best.

a select few.

10 That is, according to MS F638, f. 44b and the published edition. MS Z515, f. 96a and F3488, f. 272b, have *shahawāt al-nufūs*.

42 Al-Shūrā (or Ḥā Mīm ʿAyn Sīn Qāf)[1]

His words, Exalted is He:

[42:7] ***...That you may warn [the people of] the Mother of Cities, and those around it...***

He said:

> In its outward meaning, it [the Mother of Cities] refers to Mecca. In its inner meaning it refers to the heart, while *those around it* refer to the bodily members (*jawāriḥ*). Therefore warn them that they might safeguard their hearts and bodily members from delighting in acts of disobedience and following [their] lusts.

His words:

[42:7] ***...and that you may warn [people] about the Day of Gathering...***

He said:

> That is, the Day when the inhabitants of the earth will be gathered for His remembrance, just as the Hosts of the Heavens are assembled [for His remembrance].

His words:

[42:7] ***...[whereupon] some will be in the Garden and some will be in the Blazing Fire.***

He said:

> Whoever plants thorn trees will not reap grapes. So do what you will, for indeed there are just two paths, and whichever one of those paths you [choose to] tread, you will end up with its folk.

His words:

[42:8] ***And had God willed, He would have made them one community...***

He said:

> The outer meaning [of the verse] refers to disbelief (*kufr*),[2] and its inner meaning refers to the servant's [moments of] activity (*ḥarakāt*) and passivity (*sukūn*).[3] If God so willed He would have placed them all in obedience to Him; *but He admits whomever He will into His mercy*, that is, into His obedience. *And the evildoers*, who claim to possess the power (*ḥawl*) and strength (*quwwa*), *have neither guardian nor helper* in [their being] contrary (*khilāf*) [to the state they should be in], that is, they are in a state of passivity (*sukūn*) with regard to [His] commandments (*amr*) and activity with regard to that which is forbidden (*nahy*).

His words:

[42:9] ***...He revives the dead...***

> In its inner meaning, it refers to the hearts of the people of truth, which He revives through remembrance (*dhikr*) and the contemplative witnessing (*mushāhada*) of Him.

---

1 The former title is used in the published edition and in Z515, f. 96a and the latter in the two Fātiḥ MSS.

2 *One community* here being understood to mean, 'If God willed He could have made everyone part of a community of believers'. The second part of this verses reads: *but He admits whomever He will into His mercy, and the evildoers have neither guardian nor helper.*

3 In other contexts, we have translated these words as '[moments of] activity or stillness', when, as stated above (p. 66, n. 17), it might also be understood to mean 'every single thing that we do'. However, the translation here of *sukūn* as 'passivity' seems to be required by the context. Relevant to this passage is Tustarī's commentary on 2:30.

He [also] said:

Souls cannot gain [real] life until they die.[4]

His words:

[42:13] *He has prescribed for you as a religion that which he enjoined upon Noah…*

⌜He said⌝[5]

The first [prophet] to have made it unlawful [to marry] one's daughters, mothers, and sisters was Noah ﷺ. Hence, God has legislated for us [Muslims] the best of the laws that the prophets brought.

His words:

[42:13] *…and that which We have revealed to you, and which We enjoined on Abraham and Moses and Jesus…*

[is] that they should uphold obedience (*ṭāʿa*) to God,[6] maintain sincerity (*ikhlāṣ*) in that, and manifest [goodness in their] moral character (*akhlāq*) and states (*aḥwāl*).

His words:

[42:20] *And whoever desires the harvest of the Hereafter, We will enhance for him his harvest…*

He said:

The *harvest of the Hereafter* is being satisfied [with one's lot] (*qanāʿa*) in this world, and [finding] contentment (*riḍā*) in the Hereafter. The *harvest of this world* is that which is sought other than Him.

He [also] said:

Another shade of meaning is that he who acts for the sake of God, Mighty and Majestic is He, in a state of compliance (*ījāban*), without seeking a reward, [will find that] everything which is sought other than God, Mighty and Majestic is He, becomes diminished in his sight. Thus, he desires neither the world, nor Paradise, but desires only the vision (*naẓar*) of Him, this being the share (*ḥaẓẓ*) of the intuition of the spiritual self (*dhihn nafs al-rūḥ*), the understanding of the intellect (*fahm al-ʿaql*), and the discernment of the heart (*fiṭnat al-qalb*), as when He addressed them [before] (*ka-mā khāṭabahum*); for conformity [lit. imitation, *iqtidāʾ*], on that occasion was without the presence of the natural self (*nafs ṭabīʿiyya*).[7] Notwithstanding the fact that the [natural] self receives a share [of the beatific vision in Paradise], like a fragrant breeze, due to its being fused with those lights.[8]

[However,] whoever acts for the sake of this world, …*We will give him of it, but in the Hereafter he will have no portion* (naṣīb), for his ⌜natural⌝ self will be occupied with the enjoyment (*tanaʿʿum* or *naʿīm*) of Paradise, which itself is its share (*ḥaẓẓ*), [while forgoing] its *portion* in the Hereafter, namely the vision of God for eternity (*ruʾyat al-Ḥaqq ʿalāʾl-abad*).[9]

---

4 This accords with the well-known saying attributed to the Prophet 'Die before you die', which is listed in, among other sources, Muḥammad al-Sakhāwī, *al-Maqāṣid al-ḥasana fī bayān kathīr min al-aḥādīth al-mushtahira ʿalaʾl-alsina* (Beirut, 1979), p. 436 and ʿAjlūnī, *Kashf al-khafāʾ*, vol. 2, p. 291.

5 Added on the basis of Z515, f. 96b, F638, f. 45a and F3488, f. 273a.

6 MSS Z515, f. 96b and F3488, f. 273a precede this clause with *an aqīmū al-dīn*, 'that they should uphold religion…'

7 For the natural self was absent at the Covenant of *Alast*, see above Tustarī's commentary on 7:172 and IT, p. xliv, n. 184. By *iqtidāʾ*, Tustarī is presumably referring to the answer *'Yes, we testify'* to God's question, *'Am I not your Lord'*?

8 That is, due to its connection to the three modes of man's spiritual being: *nafs al-rūḥ*, *ʿaql* and *qalb*. On the joining of the natural self and spiritual self in the life of this world see below the commentary on 57:6 and 85:3. See also Böwering, *Mystical Vision*, p. 249.

9 The published edition has: 'Whoever acts for the sake of the world' (*man ʿamila li-ajliʾl-dunyā*), presumably because these words are followed by the Qurʾānic words: *We will give him of it, but in the Hereafter he will have no portion.* This is what has been translated here. However, all three MSS have the word *janna* in place of *dunyā*, so that the passage reads: 'whoever acts for the sake of Paradise (*man ʿamila li-ajliʾl-janna*)' followed by the Qurʾānic words: …*We will give him of it, but in the Hereafter he will have no portion* (nasīb). After this, there is a slight variation between the MSS in terms of wording, though not a significant one in terms of meaning: Z515, f. 97a and F3488, f. 273b have *yashghalu nafsahu*

His words, Exalted is He:

[42:23] ***...Say 'I do not ask of you any reward for it, except the affection due to [my] kinsfolk'...***

He said:

The inner meaning of the verse refers to the link between the Sunna and obligatory acts (*farḍ*). It is related regarding this verse that Ḥasan [al-Baṣrī] said, 'Whoever draws closer to God through obedience to Him, [will find that] God's love becomes obligatory [for Him].'[10]

His words:

[42:23] ***...If anyone acquires a good deed, We shall enhance for him his goodness...***

He said:

It refers to the cognisance (*maʿrifa*) [that a person should have] of his state relating to an act, before entering upon it, and after its completion, as to whether it is unhealthy (*saqīm*) or sound (*ṣaḥīḥ*).[11]

His words, Exalted is He:

[42:24] ***...For if God so wishes, He can seal your heart...***

He said:

He could place the seal of longing (*shawq*) and love (*maḥabba*) on your hearts, so that you would cease to notice people and you would not occupy yourselves with love for them and visiting them anymore.

His words, Exalted is He:

[42:52] ***...And verily you guide to a straight path.***

That is, you summon [people] to your Lord with the light of His guidance.

al-ṭabīʿiyya tanaʿʿum al-janna, while MS F638, f. 45a has: *yashghalu nafsahu al-ṭabīʿiyya bi-naʿīm al-janna*, both of which would translate as 'he occupies his natural self with the pleasure of Paradise', as was indicated in the previous paragraph. Note the MSS also have *janna* instead of *dunyā* following the word *tanaʿʿum* or *naʿīm*, and we have complied with the MSS here, because it seems that Tustarī is explaining that those who desired a share in this world (or in Paradise) will be denied the *naṣīb*, which he interprets here and in the previous passage to be the eternal beatific vision of God. This latter will be experienced in the Hereafter by those who desired neither the world nor Paradise.

10 i.e. it will be incumbent upon God to love him.

11 On this subject, see above Tustarī's commentary on 9:22 and 19:83.

43 Al-Zukhruf

His words, Exalted is He:

[43:1, 2] ***Hā, Mīm* ❁ *By the Book that makes things clear.***

That is, within it He clearly distinguished guidance from error, good from evil, and expounded the bliss of the fortunate (*suʿadāʾ*) and the misery of the wretched (*ashqiyāʾ*).

[43:4] ***And it is indeed (with Us) in the Mother of the Book…***

He said:

This is the Preserved Tablet.[1]

[43:4] ***…[and it is] indeed exalted, wise.***

He said:

That is, it is elevated and dominant over all the other scriptures.

His words, Exalted is He:

[43:13] ***that you may sit upon their backs and then remember your Lord's grace when you are settled upon them…***[2]

He said:

Truly, God has privileged the prophets ﵈ and some of the veracious (*ṣiddīqūn*) with the cognisance (*maʿrifa*) of the blessings (*niʿam*) that God, Exalted is He, has bestowed upon them, before their disappearance, as well as the knowledge of God's clemency (*ḥilm*) with them. However, the blessings of God, Exalted is He, are indeed diminished in the eyes of the person who does not recognise the blessings that God has granted him, other than those pertaining to his eating, drinking and riding [a beast of burden].

His words, Exalted is He:

[43:15] ***Yet they assign to Him a part from among His servants…***[3]

⌜He said⌝:

That is, a part in their[4] worship. Do you not notice how the Prophet ﷺ says, 'Truly, some of you when they pray only gain from their prayer a third or a quarter of it'?[5]

His words:

[43:32] ***…and [We have] raised some of them above others in ranks…***

---

1 On the Mother of the Book and its association with the Preserved Tablet, see above Tustarī's commentary on 2:235 and p. 27, n. 84.

2 Verse 12 mentioned the ships and cattle on which human beings are able to ride.

3 The 'part' (*juzʾ*), is usually understood by commentators to mean 'offspring', that is to say that in pre-Islamic times, the Arabs believed that angels were the daughters of God. However, Tustarī frees the word from that traditional association in his comment on this verse.

4 Translating *ʿibādatihim* according to all MSS: Z515, f. 97b, F638, f. 45b and F3488, f. 274a, as opposed to *ʿibādatihi* in the published edition.

5 Muḥammad Shams al-Ḥaqq al-ʿAẓīmābādī, *ʿAwn al-maʿbūd: sharḥ li-Sunan Abī Dāwud* (Beirut, 1998), 'Kitāb al-Ṣalāt'.

He said:

> We raised some of them above others in gnosis (*maʿrifa*) and obedience (*ṭāʿa*) [this being their source of] subsistence (*ʿaysh*) in this world and in the Hereafter.

His words:

[43:32] ***...and the mercy of your Lord is better than what they amass.***

> That is, than an abundance of works done seeking reward.[6]

His words, Exalted is He:

[43:36] ***We assign a devil as a companion for whoever turns away from the remembrance of the Compassionate One.***

He said:

> God has decreed that any servant who turns away from His remembrance, which is to say that he sees in his heart anything besides Him, and acquiesces in[7] that thing, will not do so without God putting a devil (*shayṭān*) in power over him, who will divert him from the path of truth and subject him to temptation.[8]

His words, Exalted is He:

[43:55] ***So when they had angered Us, We took vengeance on them...***

He said:

> That is, 'When they enraged Us by persisting in their transgression against [Our] commandments, by their exhibition of innovations (*bidaʿ*) in the religion, their abandoning of the traditional ways [of the Prophet] (*sunan*), due to their pursuit of [their own] opinions[9] and desires, We removed the light of gnosis (*nūr al-maʿrifa*) from their hearts, the lamp of the realisation of [Our] oneness (*sirāj al-tawḥīd*) from their innermost secrets (*asrār*), and We entrusted them to their own selves, and to whatever they chose [for themselves]. Consequently they went astray and misled [others].

Then he said:

> Following (*ittibāʿ*) [is the key], following! Emulation (*iqtidāʾ*) [is the key], emulation! For sure, that was the way of the predecessors (*salaf*). He who follows [their guidance] will not go astray, but he who innovates will not be saved.

His words, Exalted is He:

[43:69, 70] ***Those who believed in Our signs and submitted themselves [to Us will be told], ❁ 'Enter Paradise, you and your spouses, to be made joyful',***

> with the delight of the vision [of God] (*naẓar*), as a reward for the realisation of His oneness (*tawḥīd*), with which He blesses His friends, when they experience the manifestation of the [divine] unveiling (*tajallī al-mukāshafa*), this being subsistence with the Subsistent One (*baqāʾ maʿaʾl-Bāqī*). See how He privileges them with faith on the condition that they submit to His command and acquiesce [in a state] of tranquil repose before Him (*sukūn bayna yadayhi*).

His words, Exalted is He:

[43:71] ***...and therein will be whatever souls desire and eyes delight in...***

He said:

---

6 See above, the commentary on 29:17 and p. 149, n. 6, and regarding those who do good works for the sake of the rewards of Paradise (or of this world), 42:20 and p. 181, n. 9.

7 Translating *musākinan* according to all three MSS: Z515, f. 97b, F638, f. 45b and F3488, f. 274b, instead of *sākina* in the published edition. On *musākina* see above Tustarī's commentary on 2:30 and 273, and p. 16, n. 26.

8 See the commentary on 2:30 above.

9 Translating *al-ārāʾ* according to all three MSS: Z515, f. 97b, F638, f. 45b and F3488, f. 274b, instead of *wujūd* in the published edition.

> That is to say, *whatever souls desire* is[10] the reward for their works, whereas *whatever eyes delight in* is the empowerment (*tamkīn*)[11] which God bestows on them at the time of the encounter (*liqāʾ*) [with Him] as a reward for their realisation of His oneness (*tawḥīd*).

[Then] he said:

> Paradise is the reward for works performed by the bodily members. The encounter is the reward for the realisation of God's oneness (*tawḥīd*). Note how God, Exalted is He, has said:

[43:72] *And that is the Paradise which you have been given to inherit [as a reward for] what you used to do.*

10 Translating *hiya*, according to MS F638, f. 45b, instead of *min*, according to the published edition, MS Z515, f. 98a and F3488, f. 274b.

11 Or *tamkīn* could be translated as 'stability'. In Sufi manuals, the term *tamkīn* (stability) is often contrasted with *talwīn* (vacillation). See, for example, Hujwīrī, *Kashf al-maḥjūb*, p. 486; trans. Nicholson, p. 372; Qushayrī, *Risāla*, p. 232.

44 Al-Dukhān

His words, Exalted is He:

[44:3] ***Indeed We revealed it on a blessed night…***

He said:

> God sent the Qurʾān down as a whole on the Night of Great Merit (*Laylat al-Qadr*) to the House of Might (*bayt al-ʿizza*) in the heaven of this world, from the Preserved Tablet in the hands of the recording angels (*malāʾik safara*). It was then sent down to the spirit (*rūḥ*) of Muḥammad ﷺ, which is the blessed spirit (*rūḥ mubārak*), and thus He called the Night of Great Merit a blessed night (*layla mubāraka*) due to the [spiritual] link between one [descent of] blessing and the other.[1]

His words, Exalted is He:

[44:10] ***…the day when the heaven will produce a visible smoke…***

He said:

> The smoke in this world is hardness of the heart and heedlessness of (His) remembrance,[2] and there is no punishment severer in this world than the corruption of the heart.
>
> It was related of Uways al-Qaranī and Haram b. Ḥayyān that they met one day and Haram said to Uways, 'Make a supplication to God [for me]'. So he prayed, 'May He make your intention (*nīya*) and your heart (*qalb*) sound, for there is nothing more seriously in need of curing than these two. For while your heart [seems to be] going towards [God] (*muqbil*), it may [in fact] be going away [from Him] (*mudbir*), and while your heart [seems to be] going away, [it may, in fact] be going towards [Him]. Do not consider the insignificance of a misdeed, but rather consider [the greatness of] the One whom you have disobeyed.[3] If you deem it [the misdeed] as great, verily you have magnified God, Exalted is He, whereas if you belittle it, for sure you have belittled God, Exalted is He.'

His words, Exalted is He:

[44:8] ***There is no god except Him. He gives life and brings death…***

He said:

> In reality, there is no god except the One who has the power to bring into existence that which was not in existence, and bring to extinction that which was in existence.

His words:

[44:24] ***And leave the sea behind you, at rest…***[4]

---

1 i.e. the coming together of the descent of the blessed Qurʾān from the Preserved Tablet to the House of Might, and then to the blessed Prophet. The image is one of a cascade of blessings streaming down to the heart of the blessed Prophet.

2 This may mean literally the remembrance of God, but it could also mean His Reminder (*dhikr*) in the sense of the Revelation.

3 The published edition has the addition of the word *ʿaẓama* here, which is nicely symmetrical, although it does not accord with the MSS.

4 This is part of God's command to Moses that he should lead the Children of Israel to escape Egypt by crossing the Red Sea (vv. 23–32).

[That is], a calm pathway (*ṭarīq sākin*) [for you to cross]. Its inner meaning is: 'Make your heart acquiesce in (*sākin*) My management (*tadbīrī*) [of your affairs].'[5] …*Indeed they will be a drowned host*, that is, those who are opposed to consigning the management (*tadbīr*) of themselves [to God].

His words:

[44:42] ***…except for him on whom God has mercy…***

That is, whomever God knows from His prior knowledge to be one of those who will receive mercy, [so that] in the end, the grace of that mercy will reach him, by virtue of His making the believers intercessors (*shufaʿāʾ*) for one another.

5 It may be recalled that in his commentary on 30:41, Tustarī interprets the sea as the heart.

45 Al-Jāthiya

His words, Exalted is He:

[45:3] ***Truly in the heavens and the earth there are signs*** (āyāt) ***for those who believe.***

He said:

> The signs (*ʿalāmāt*) are for the one who has certainty (*yaqīn*) in his heart, and who is guided by their existence (*kawn*) to the One who has brought them into existence (*mukawwin*).

His words:

[45:13] ***He has put at your disposal all that is in the heavens and the earth, [as a gift] from Him...***

He said:

> When the heart of the servant finds tranquil repose (*sukūn*) in its Master, the state of the servant becomes strong.[1] Subsequently everything is subjected to him, and indeed everything is on intimate terms with him, even the birds and the beasts.
>
> It was related of al-Thawrī that he said, 'I set off with Shaybān al-Rāʿī towards Mecca and on the way a lion appeared before us, so I said, "O Shaybān, do you not see this dog?" He replied, "Do not fear! It's only that the lion heard the speech of Shaybān al-Rāʿī so he started to wag his tail." Then Shaybān approached him and proceeded to take hold of his ear and twist it. Then I said, "O Shaybān what is this fame you have?" He answered, "And what sort of fame is it that you see, O Thawrī? I swear by God that if it wasn't for the fear of fame I wouldn't have carried my provisions for the journey to Mecca other than [loaded] on its back."[2] Shaybān was on his way to the Friday prayer when he caught sight of a wolf with his sheep, so he said to it, "Sit with the sheep until I return and I will give you a lamb." When he returned from the Friday prayer, he found the wolf sitting down looking after the sheep, so he gave him a lamb to take away.'[3]

Sahl used to say to a youth who kept his company, 'If you are afraid of predatory beasts then do not keep my company.' And he was asked, 'How does a man reach the rank of charismatic gifts (*karāmāt*)?'[4] He replied:

> 'Whoever abstains from (*zahada*) the world for forty days in veracity and sincerity (*ṣādiqan wa mukhliṣan*), will have charismatic gifts (*karāmāt*) manifested to Him from God, Mighty and Majestic is He. But if [such gifts] are not manifested to a person, it is due to the lack of true faith and sincerity in his renunciation' — or words to that effect.

His words, Exalted is He:

[45:17] ***and We gave them clear signs of the commandment...***

---

1 There is always, as has been seen in Tustarī's comments above, a combined sense in the expression *sakana ilā* or *sukūn* of being peaceful or at rest with, and depending upon, God, especially His management of our affairs (*tadbīr*).

2 This story is related in Ibn al-Jawzī, *Ṣifat al-ṣafwa*, vol. 4, p. 377, and in Iṣfahānī, *Ḥilyat al-awliyāʾ*, vol. 7, pp. 68–9. Shaybān's fear of fame could be seen as an early example of the teachings associated with the 'School of Blame' (*malāmatiyya*) in Islamic mysticism. The principle source work on the *Malāmatiyya* is Abū ʿAbd al-Raḥmān al-Sulamī's *Risālat al-malāmatiyya wa'l-ṣūfiyya wa ahl al-futuwwa*, ed. Abū al-ʿAlāʾ Afīfī (Cairo, 1945). Qushayrī's *Risāla* and Hujwīrī's *Kashf al-maḥjūb* also have chapters on *malāma*.

3 See also the commentary on 10:62 and p. 90, n. 10 above regarding the relationship between mystics and wild beasts.

4 On charismatic gifts (*karāmāt*) see above IT, p. xx, n. 52.

He said:

We opened their ears so that they could understand Our discourse (*khiṭāb*), and We made their hearts (*afʾida*) as vessels (*wiʿāʾ*) for Our speech (*kalām*). We gave them true physiognomy (*firāsa*),[5] by which they can make certain and truly-informed judgements concerning Our servants. These are the ...*clear signs of the commandment*... on the inner path (*ṭarīq al-bāṭin*).

His words, Exalted is He:

[45:18] ***Then We set you [Muḥammad] on a [clear] course* (sharīʿa) *of the commandment, so follow it...***

He said:

That is, a way (*minhaj*) consisting of the established norms (*sunan*) of the prophets who came before you, for they [were following] the way of guidance; and the Law (*sharīʿa*) is the clear thoroughfare that extends to the path of salvation (*ṭarīq al-najāt*) and the way of right guidance (*sabīl al-rushd*).

His words, Exalted is He:

[45:19] ***Assuredly they will not avail you in any way against God...***

Whoever becomes wealthy without recourse to God will become needy through his wealth; and whoever gains honour without recourse to Him will be humiliated through his honour. Take note of how God says: *Assuredly they will not avail you in any way against God...*

His words, Exalted is He:

[45:21] ***Do those who have perpetrated evil acts suppose that We shall treat them as those who believe and perform righteous deeds, equally in their life and in their death?...***

He said:

The one who has been seated on the carpet of conformity (*bisāṭ al-muwāfaqa*) is not like the one who has been made to stand in the station of opposition (*maqām al-mukhālafa*); for the carpet of conformity brings the person [stationed] upon it to the 'seats' of true faith (*maqāʿid al-ṣidq*), whereas the station of opposition will plunge the person who holds it into a blazing fire.

His words, Exalted is He:

[45:23] ***Have you not seen him who has taken as his god his [own] desire...?***

He said:

That is to say, have you considered the one who is submersed in the delights that his lower self [is deriving] from this world, being neither scrupulous (*wariʿ*) nor mindful of God (*taqī*)? Hence, he pursues his own will (*murād*), and does not take the path of emulation (*iqtidāʾ*),[6] but prefers the lusts of this world over the bliss of the life to come. So, how will he be able to attain the high ranks and sublime stations (*manāzil saniyya*) in the Hereafter?

[45:23] ***...and whom God led astray knowingly...?***

He said:

That is, with God's prior knowledge [concerning him] that He would withdraw from him His protection and aid.

His words:

[45:26] ***Say: 'God [is the One who] gives you life, then makes you to die, then gathers you to Day of Resurrection...'***

He said:

He gives you life in the bellies of your mothers, then He causes you to die through ignorance, and then without doubt He gathers you together from the first to the last of you.

5 On *firāsa* see above p. 73, n. 11 and p. 105, n. 5.

6 i.e. emulating the example of the Prophet and pious predecessors.

His words, Exalted is He:

[45:28] ***And you will see every community crouching…***[7]

He said:

> [Crouching] on their knees, each [community] contending for itself in the presence of [its] escort (*murāfaqa*). The one who is true in faith (*ṣādiq*) will strive to prove his veracity (*ṣidq*), and the denying unbeliever (*jāḥid*) will strive to defend himself. Each one will be judged according to what he recorded [for himself], his ink being his saliva, his pen his tongue and his parchment his bodily members.

His words:

[45:37] ***To Him belongs all grandeur in the heavens and the earth…***

He said:

> Exaltedness (*ʿuluww*), omnipotence (*qudra*), majesty (*ʿaẓama*), power and strength (*ḥawl wa quwwa*) belong to Him in the entire dominion of creation (*mulk*). He will support with His power and strength whoever seeks His protection, whilst He will consign whoever relies on himself to his own care. But God, Glorified and Exalted is He, knows best.

7 That is, on the Day of Resurrection.

46 Al-Aḥqāf

His words, Exalted is He:

[46:6] ***And when mankind are gathered, [at the Resurrection], they will be enemies to them...***[1]

He said:

> [This] concerns their lower selves, which led them into following them, [they will be turned against them] as a penalty for their allowing their desire to rule [over them], for they [their lower selves] will bear witness against them. Indeed, the Messenger of God ﷺ said: 'Truly, the severest foe of man is his self that is between his two sides.'[2]

His words, Exalted is He:

[46:9] ***Say, 'I am nothing new among God's messengers...'***

He said:

> That is, 'There were messengers before me who commanded what I command [you] and forbade what I forbid [you]. I am not peculiar (*ʿajab*) among the messengers. I do not call you to anything except the profession of God's oneness (*tawḥīd*), and I do not guide you to anything other than the noblest of ethics (*makārim al-akhlāq*). It was with this that the prophets before me were sent.'

His words, Exalted is He:

[46:15] ***...[So that] he may say: 'Lord, inspire me to be truly grateful for the favour with which You have blessed me...'***

He said:

> That is, 'Inspire me to repent and do works of obedience.'

His words:

[46:15] ***'...Invest my offspring with righteousness...'***

He said:

> 'Make them Your true servants and faithful heirs for me.'

His words:

[46:30] ***'...It guides to the truth and a straight way.'***[3]

He said:

> That is, it shows the path of truth, [as that] by which one leaves dealings (*muʿāmalāt*) and formalities (*rusūmāt*) behind, [and endeavours] to realise the truth (*taḥqīq al-ḥaqq*), which is the straight path (*ṣirāṭ mustaqīm*).

His words:

[46:31] ***'O our people! Respond to God's summoner...'***

---

1 It the context of the previous Qurʾānic verse, 'they' are those whom mankind has called upon besides God.

2 ʿAjlūnī, *Kashf al-khafāʾ*, vol. 1, p. 148 and 160, and vol. 2, p. 222.

3 The subject of this verse being the Qurʾān. The speakers are the jinn who had listened to the Qurʾān being recited and then went back to their people to inform them about it.

He said:

> None can respond to the one who summons, except he who has heard the call (*nidāʾ*), and then has been granted success to do good things, and has attained certainty (*yaqīn*). Otherwise, who can respond well to the call?

And he further said:

> Truly, in the heart of every believer there is one who summons him to his right course (*rushd*). The fortunate person is he who is attentive to the call of that summoner, and follows it up.

His words, Exalted is He:

[46:35] ***So endure [with patience] like those messengers of firm resolve…***

He said:

> It means, 'Be patient with the patience (*ṣabr*) of the people of gnosis (*ahl al-maʿrifa*), just as those of firm resolve (*ūlū'l-ʿazm*) among the messengers showed patience, a patience which is [one of] contentment (*riḍā*) and submission (*taslīm*) without complaint (*shakwā*) or impatience (or anxiety, *jazaʿ*).' Abraham, God's friend ﷺ, was afflicted with the fire, and the sacrifice of his son, but accepted it with contentment (*riḍā*) and submitted. Job ﷺ was afflicted by sickness, and Ishmael with the sacrifice and [likewise] showed contentment. Noah [was tested] with denial but remained steadfast (*ṣabara*), while Jonah [was placed] in the belly of the whale, but called on God and sought refuge in Him. Joseph, God's blessings be upon him, [was afflicted with] prison and the well, but he did not alter; and Jacob was tested by the loss of his sight and his son, but he complained of his grief only to God and did not complain to anyone else.[4] There are twelve prophets, God's blessings be upon them, who remained steadfast in the face of what befell them, and they are known as 'those of firm resolve (*ūlū'l-ʿazm*) among the messengers'.[5] But God, Transcendent and Exalted is He, knows best.

4 An allusion to 12:86: *I complain of my anguish and grief only to God.*

5 The most widely accepted tradition is that the *ūlū'l-ʿazm* are not twelve but five in number mentioned in Sūrat al-Aḥzāb, 7–8 and al-Shūrā, 13: Noah, Abraham, Moses, Jesus and Muḥammad. Tustarī has not mentioned here Moses, Jesus or Muḥammad, but has mentioned Job, Jonah, Joseph and Jacob.

47 Muḥammad

His words, Exalted is He:

[47:1] ***God will bring to naught the deeds of those who disbelieve and bar others from the way of God.***

He said:

He brought them to naught because of their utterance of words that had no reality (*ḥaqīqa*) behind them.

His words:

[47:5] ***He will guide them and dispose their minds aright.***

He said:

This means that He will guide them in their graves to answer Munkar and Nakīr correctly; *and dispose their minds aright*, that is, He will bring about the commencement[1] of the reward in their hearts [in the grave] (*jazāʾ*), and in the Hereafter, the delight of the meeting [with Him] (*ladhdhat al-liqāʾ*) at the moment of the manifestation (*tajallī*) of unveiling (*mukāshafa*), as a face-to-face encounter (*kifāḥan*), and thereupon, [His] taking care (*tawallī*) of them, as when He says:

[47:11] ***That is because God is patron* (mawlā) *of those who believe…***

That is, by His good pleasure, love and His keeping them in the station of proximity (*qurb*).

His words:

[47:15] ***…and forgiveness from their Lord.***[2]

He said:

Forgiveness from their Lord in Paradise is the lights of God which cover them at their vision of Him.[3]

His words:

[47:19] ***…And ask forgiveness for your sin and for the believing men and women…***

He said:

That is, 'Seek forgiveness for the desire (*himma*) of the natural self (*nafs al-ṭabʿ*).' The Prophet ﷺ said, 'There is not one among us who has not had the desire [to do something] and then transgressed.'

This means that a [person's] lower self (*nafs*) intended something,[4] overwhelming the heart (*ʿalāʾl-qalb*), for the immediate [gratification of its share of] lusts (*ʿājil al-shahawāt*), but then that

1 That is, translating *yashraʿu* in all three MSS: Z515, f. 100b, F638, f. 47a and F3488, f. 277b, instead of *yasraʿu* in the published edition.

2 Here, forgiveness is being described as one of the rewards of Paradise.

3 Because otherwise they would be annihilated at the vision of God. Above, in his commentary on 43:71, Tustarī spoke of empowerment (*tamkīn*) being given to those who realise the divine oneness at the moment of encounter (*liqāʾ*) in Paradise.

4 The word used is *hamma*, which has a number of meanings including to entertain the desire for something, consider, or be on the point of doing something, apart from its meanings of being concerned about or of importance, which are

person turned away from that [intent] and sought forgiveness from God, just as the Prophet ﷺ said: 'Truly, my heart becomes clouded, and truly I ask forgiveness from God, Exalted is He, seventy times every day.'[5]

His words:

[47:24] ***...or is it that they have locks on their hearts?***

He said:

God, Exalted is He, created the hearts, and secured them with locks. Then He made the realities of faith (*ḥaqāʾiq al-īmān*) the keys to hearts. With those keys, the only hearts He opened to realisation (*taḥqīq*) were those of His friends (*awliyāʾ*), messengers (*rusul*) ﷺ, and the veracious (*ṣiddīqūn*). The rest of people leave this world without the locks on their hearts being opened. The renunciants (*zuhhād*), devout worshippers (*ʿubbād*), and scholars (*ʿulamāʾ*) will leave this world with locked hearts because they sought the keys to them with the intellect (*ʿaql*), and thus strayed from the path. If only they had sought them by having recourse to God-given success (*tawfīq*) and grace (*faḍl*), they would have attained them [the keys].[6]

The key is to know that God is taking care of you (*qāʾim ʿalayka*), and watching over (*raqīb*) your bodily members, and to know that works are not complete without sincerity (*ikhlāṣ*) accompanied by heedfulness (*murāqāba*) [of God].

His words:

[47:13] ***And how many a town, mightier in power than your town, which expelled you, have We destroyed and they had none to help them.***

In this verse there is proof of his [Muḥammad's] ﷺ superiority over Kalīm [Moses], because he did not leave out of fear of them in the way that Moses ﷺ did,[7] but he left in the way that God, Exalted is He, said in the words: *which expelled you.* He did not say 'you left', nor ⸢'you fled'⸣, nor 'you felt afraid', for he [acted] by God and for God at all times,[8] and it never happened that his attention was diverted to other [than Him] in any particular situation.

His words:

[47:14] ***Is he who follows a clear sign from his Lord...?***

He said:

The believer has a clear explanation (*bayān*) from his Lord and whoever has a clear proof (*bayyina*) from his Lord adheres to following the established ways of the Prophet (*sunan*).

His words, Exalted is He:

[47:19] ***Know, then, that there is no god but God...***

He said:

All people are dead except those who know (*ʿulamāʾ*), and for this reason He summoned His Prophet ﷺ to the abode of life (*maḥall al-ḥayāt*), through knowledge (*ʿilm*), with His words: *Know...*

His words:

[47:33] ***...Obey God and obey the Messenger...***

That is, in revering (*taʿẓīm*) God. ...*Do not render your own works void*, that is, by seeing them as coming from yourselves and by seeking recompense (*aʿwāḍ*) from your Lord, for sincere works are those that are done without seeking recompense.

---

not relevant here. Note that the saying of the Prophet cited in the previous paragraph used the word *himma* from the same verbal root, *h-m-m*.

5 Bukhārī, *Ṣaḥīḥ*, 'Kitāb al-Daʿwāt', Ibn Ḥanbal, *al-Musnad*, vol. 4, p. 211.

6 On Tustarī's teachings concerning the limitations of *ʿaql*, see IT, pp. xlvff.

7 A reference to Moses' fleeing Egypt in fear, after he had killed an Egyptian, related in 28:15–21.

8 The insertion of the words *wa lā fararta*, and a change of word order from *lillāh wa bi'llāh*, to *bi'llāh wa lillāh*, has been made on the basis of all three MSS: Z515, f. 101b, F638, f. 47b and F3488, f. 278a.

His words, Exalted is He:

[47:38] ***...God is the Self-Sufficient One, while you are the needy....***

Gnosis (*maʿrifa*) of the secret [divine] mystery (*sirr*) is [attained] entirely through neediness (*faqr*), and that is God's secret (*sirr Allāh*). The knowledge of [one's] neediness for God, Exalted is He, is the corrective to the knowledge that [one has] richness (*ghinā*) through God, Mighty and Majestic is He. But God, Glorified and Exalted is He, knows best.

48 Al-Fatḥ

His words, Exalted is He:

[48:1] ***Verily, We have given you a clear victory,***

He said:

> That is to say, '[We have opened] the secrets of the sciences (*asrār al-ʿulūm*) within your heart, so that their traces have become manifested upon you.'[1] They are the signs of [His] love and the fulfilment of [His] bounty.

[48:2] ***that God may forgive you what is past of your sin and what is to come...***[2]

He said:

> That is, *what is past*, of the sin that your father Adam ﷺ [committed] while you were in his loins, and *what is to come*, of the sins of your community, as you are their leader (*qāʾid*) and guide (*dalīl*).

His words:

[48:4] ***It was He who sent down the spirit of peace* (sakīna) *into the hearts of the believers...***

> That is, profound peace (*ṭumaʾnīna*). For God first of all discloses to His servants gnosis (*maʿārif*), then forms of mediation (*wasāʾil*),[3] then the spirit of peace (*sakīna*), and lastly intuitive insights (*baṣāʾir*). And one to whom God discloses intuitive insights, knows things according to their essences (*jawāhir*),[4] as did Abū Bakr al-Ṣiddīq ؓ who never erred in speech.

His words:

[48:4] ***And to God belong the forces of the heavens and the earth...***

He said:

> His forces (*junūd*) are of different kinds: His forces in heaven are the prophets (*anbiyāʾ*), and on earth, [His] friends (*awliyāʾ*). His forces in heaven are hearts (*qulūb*), and on the earth, souls (*nufūs*). Whatever God empowers (*sallaṭa*) over you, [may be counted as being] among His forces. If He empowers your lower self over you, your lower self will itself destroy you; and likewise, if He empowers your bodily members over you, they themselves will destroy you. If your lower self overpowers your heart, it will drive you to the pursuit of desire (*hawā*). But if your heart overpowers your lower self and your bodily members, it will tether them with propriety (*adab*), compel them into worship (*ʿibāda*), and then adorn them with sincerity in servanthood (*ikhlāṣ fiʾl-ʿubūdiyya*). All of these together amount to God's forces.

His words:

[48:8] ***Indeed We have sent you as a witness, and a bearer of glad tidings and a warner.***

---

1 The verbal root *f-t-ḥ* means to open, therefore, literally the meaning of the verse is *We 'opened' a clear victory for you.* Note that Tustarī's interpretation brings out the idea of opening. *Fatḥ* (pl. *futūḥ* or *futūḥāt*) is also used in Sufism to mean a spiritual opening, hence the title of Ibn ʿArabī's work *al-Futūḥāt al-Makkiyya*.

2 These words are addressed to the Prophet.

3 Böwering has 'means of communication.' Note, above in his commentary on 32:16, Tustarī spoke of them being favoured with *wasīla*. On this term see p. 155, n. 4. An example of *waṣīla* will be seen in Tustarī's commentary on 57:20.

4 lit. 'substances', and we might understand it to mean: 'knows things according to their true meaning or significance'.

He said:

As a witness to them of the divine oneness (*tawḥīd*), bringing glad tidings to them of help (*maʿūna*) and support (*taʾyīd*), and warning them against falling into innovations (*bidaʿ*) and errors (*ḍalālāt*).

His words:

[48:9] *...and that you may honour Him, and revere Him...*

He said:

That is, revere Him with the utmost reverence (*taʿẓīm*) in your hearts and obey Him with your bodies. This is why reverence (*taʿzīr*) is so called, because it is the greatest [thing for] disciplining [the self] (*taʾdīb*).[5]

His words:

[48:10] *...the Hand of God is above their hands...*

He said:

That is, the power (*ḥawl*) of God and His strength (*quwwa*) is above their strength (*quwwa*) and their action (*ḥaraka*).[6] This is in their saying to the Messenger ﷺ at the time of the pledge (*bayʿa*), 'We have pledged to you that we will not flee, and we will fight for you.' There is another possible meaning of *the Hand of God is above their hands*, which is, the grace (*minna*) of God is above them in their being guided to take the pledge, and His reward (*thawāb*) for them is above their pledge and their obedience for you.

His words:

[48:11] *... 'Our possessions and our families kept us occupied...'*[7]

They tried to excuse themselves with this, and God related it to you so you would know that the way to approach God (*iqbāl ʿalāʾLlāh*) is through leaving behind the world and what it contains, for certainly that is what distracts [you] from God. Take note of how the hypocrites excused themselves by saying: *'Our possessions and our families kept us occupied...'*

His words:

[48:25] *...And were it not for [some of] the believing men and believing women whom you did not know — lest you should trample them...*[8]

---

5 The verb *ʿazzara* (2nd form of the root *ʿ-z-r*) has a variety of meanings, including 'to discipline', 'chastise', 'to give religious instruction' and 'to honour' or 'revere'. Likewise, the verb *addaba* (2nd form of *ʾ-d-b*) can mean 'discipline' in the sense of punishment, and also 'discipline' in the sense of training, refining, educating, hence the noun *adab*, meaning 'culture', 'propriety' or 'manners', comes from this verb. What Tustarī may be implying here is that through a true sense of reverence for God, a person is inwardly disciplined and groomed.

6 Tustarī here shows that he is ready to interpret the anthropomorphic verses metaphorically. Others believed that anthropomorphic expressions in the Qurʾān (or *ḥadīth*), such as the 'hand(s) of God' (Q. 5:64; 36:70; 38:76; 48:10), or His 'mounting' or 'being established on the Throne (7:54; 10:4; 13:2; 20:5; 25:59; 32:4; 57:4) should be accepted as they are, without seeking to interpret them, an approach known as *bi-lā kayf*, meaning literally 'without how'. This doctrine, which is said to go back to Mālik b. Anas (d. 179/795), became particularly associated with the Ashʿarī school of theology, though it was adopted with a passion by many Ḥanbalīs and traditionalist Shāfiʿīs. The Muʿtazilīs condemned this approach as being *tashbīh*, literally likening God [to creatures] and insisted on interpreting the anthropomorphic verses metaphorically. On this subject see: B. Abrahamov, 'The *bi-lā kayfa* Doctrine and its Foundation in Islamic Theology', *Arabica* 42 (1995), pp. 165–79; W. Williams, 'Aspects of the Creed of Aḥmad ibn Ḥanbal: A Study of Anthropomorphism in Early Islamic Discourse', *IJMES* 36 (2002), pp. 441–63; Merlin L. Swartz, *A Medieval Critique of Anthropomorphism* (Leiden, 2002); Richard C. Martin, 'Anthropomorphism', *EQ*, vol. 1, p. 103; Josef van Ess, 'Tashbīh wa Tanzīh', *EI²*, vol. x, p. 341.

7 The first part of this verse states that these words were said by the Bedouins who stayed behind and did not accompany the Prophet on his journey to Mecca.

8 The verse continues: *and thus incur sin on account of them without knowing [it]*. That is to say, if they unwittingly slew believers along with the disbelievers.

He said:

> The real believer (*al-muʾmin ʿalāʾl-ḥaqīqa*) is the one who is not heedless of his lower self and his heart, but scrutinises his states (*aḥwāl*), and keeps a close watch over his moments (*awqāt*).[9] He observes his increase (*ziyāda*) [in a good state, distinguishing it] from his decline (*nuqṣān*), and shows gratitude on seeing an increase, but when there is a decline, devotes himself [to remedying it] and makes supplication.
>
> It is through these [real believers] that God repels calamity (*balāʾ*) from the inhabitants of earth. The [true] believer is never lax (*mutahāwin*) with the slightest shortcoming, for laxity with a little will inevitably lead to [laxity in] a lot.

He further said:

> The servant will not get the taste of faith until he abandons six vices [lit. character traits, *khiṣāl*]: he should abandon what is forbidden (*ḥarām*), illegal possessions (*suḥut*), what is dubious (*shubha*), ignorance (*jahl*), intoxicant[s] (*muskir*) and ostentation (*riyāʾ*); [on the other hand] he should adhere to [six virtues]: knowledge (*ʿilm*), putting his actions right (*taṣḥīḥ al-ʿamal*), integrity of heart (*naṣḥ biʾl-qalb*), veracity of the tongue (*ṣidq biʾl-lisān*), correct conduct (*ṣalāḥ*) in associating with people and sincerity (*ikhlāṣ*) in the way he deals with his Lord.

He also said:

> The Book of God is founded upon five [virtues]: veracity (*ṣidq*), seeking the best [through God's guidance] (*istikhāra*), consultation (*istishāra*), patience (*ṣabr*) and gratitude (*shukr*).

His words:

[48:26] *...and made binding on them the promise to be mindful [of Him], for they were more worthy and deserving of it...*[10]

He said:

> [The promise to be mindful of God (*kalimat al-taqwā*)] is saying: 'There is no god except God (*lā ilāha illāʾLlāh*), for truly it is the summit of mindfulness of God.

Then he said:

> The best among people are the Muslims, the best among Muslims are the believers,[11] the best among believers are the scholars who act upon their knowledge, the best among those who act [upon their knowledge] are the fearful (*khāʾifūn*), and the best among the fearful are the sincere ones who are fully aware of God (*al-mukhliṣūn al-muttaqūn*), whose sincerity and awareness of God remains with them up until their death. Indeed, the likeness of these [latter] is that of a passenger on board a ship at sea. He does not know whether he will be saved from [the sea] or drown in it. Those for whom this was true were the Companions of the Messenger of God ﷺ according to His words: *and made binding on them the promise to be mindful of Him.*

His words:

[48:27] *...You will assuredly enter the Sacred Mosque in safety, God willing...*

He was asked, 'What is meant by making this exception [saying *God willing*] (*istithnāʾ*)?' He said:

> This is a way of teaching (*taʿlīm*) and disciplining (*taʾdīb*) [His] servants, [in order that they should feel] intense neediness (*shiddat al-iftiqār*) for Him at every moment and in every situation, and by way of emphasis (*taʾkīd*). If God makes an exception [by saying 'God willing'] while having full knowledge [of what is to happen], then it is not for one of his servants, who is deficient in knowledge, to determine upon something without making the exception of 'God willing'.[12]

---

9 That is to say his state in each present moment.

10 We have followed Abdel-Haleem's translation of *kalima* (lit. 'word') as 'promise'.

11 Tustarī is alluding again here to the difference between the nominal submission to God (*islām*) of the *muslim*, and the state in which one has faith (*īmān*), that of the *muʾmin*. See above, Tustarī's commentary on 14:24 in which the third level of *iḥsān* is mentioned. See also IT, p. lviii, n. 265 regarding the *ḥadīth* in which these three levels are discussed.

12 On the doctrine of 'exception' (*istithnāʾ*) in Islamic theology, see L. Gardet, 'In shāʾ Allāh', *EI²*, vol. III, p. 1196. On the *adab* of *istithnāʾ* see Rūmī, *Mathnawī*, Bk. I, lines 48–50.

His words, Exalted is He:

[48:29] ***...The mark is on their faces, from the effect of their prostrations...***

He said:

> The believer (*muʾmin*) in God is a face without a reverse side, [since he is] advancing towards Him without ever turning back from Him. This is the mark of the believers. ʿĀmir b. ʿAbd al-Qays said, 'It is almost as if the face of a believer is informing [us] of that which is hidden within him, and the same can be said of the face of the disbeliever.' This is what is meant by His words: *The mark is on their faces*. Ibn Masʿūd ﷺ said, 'The secret of the believer is a mantle over him'. But God, Glorified and Exalted is He, knows best.

49 Al-Ḥujurāt

His words, Exalted is He:

[49:1] ***O you who believe! Do not be forward in the presence of God and His Messenger...***

He said:

> Verily, God, Exalted is He, has instructed His believing servants in propriety (*adab*). The meaning is: 'Do not speak before he [the Prophet] speaks.' Then when he speaks, move forward towards him, hearkening and listening to him; ...*and fear God*, regarding the neglect of His rights, and the loss of reverence for Him. *Surely God hears* what you say, *and knows* what you do.

His words:

[49:2] ***...and do not raise your voices above the voice of the Prophet...***

> That is, 'Do not address him except when seeking to understand [from him].' Then He explains the honour of the one who reveres Him, and says:

[49:3] ***...they are the ones whose hearts God has tested for mindfulness of Him...***

> That is, He has made their intentions pure for Him.

His words:

[49:6] ***...If a reprobate comes to you with some tiding...***

He said:

> The reprobate (*fāsiq*) is a liar (*kadhdhāb*). The inner meaning of the verse is to teach (*taʾdīb*) a person who has been informed of someone's derogation of him, that he should not rush into exacting retribution on them, without having found out about [the matter] for himself.

His words:

[49:8] ***[that is] a favour from God and a blessing...***

He said:

> God has favoured them by that which He initially granted them,[1] and He has guided them to Him with various kinds of proximity (*qurb*) and intimacy (*zulf*).

His words:

[49:7] ***...God had endeared faith to you and made it beautiful to your hearts...***

He said:

> As a kindness (*ʿaṭf*) from Him, He singled out your hearts for His worship and endowed them with sincerity. [This is so] because being singled out (*istikhlāṣ*) is from His kindness (*ʿaṭf*), while [your] sincerity (*ikhlāṣ*) is His right (*ḥaqq*).[2] A servant cannot fulfil His right save through His kindness in granting him assistance through the means of faith (*asbāb al-īmān*), which are the irrefutable proofs and wondrous signs (*āyāt muʿjiza*).

His words:

[49:7] ***...He has made disbelief, mischief and disobedience hateful to you...***

---

1 That is, what He ordained for them in pre-eternity.

2 In other words we cannot consider selection to be a right; it is only due to His kindness, while on the other hand our sincerity is a right that we owe Him.

due to the fear of His abhorrent punishment.

His words:

[49:9] ***If two parties of believers fall to fighting, you [believers] make peace between them…***

He said:

The outward meaning of the verse is as those specialised in exegesis have explained.[3] However, in its inner meaning it refers to the spirit (*rūḥ*), intellect (*ʿaql*), heart (*qalb*), basic nature (*ṭabʿ*), desire (*hawā*) and lust (*shahwa*). If natural instinct, desire and lust take up arms against the heart, intellect and spirit, the servant must fight them with the swords of vigilance (*murāqaba*), the arrows of inspection (*muṭālaʿa*) and the lights of conformity (*muwāfaqa*), so that the spirit and the intellect gain the upper hand, and desire and lust are vanquished.

His words:

[49:12] ***…Shun much suspicion…***

He said:

That is, 'Do not discredit anyone [by holding] a bad opinion (*sūʾ al-ẓann*) about them without [knowing] the truth (*ḥaqīqa*) [of the matter].'[4] Indeed the Prophet ﷺ said: 'The most untruthful of reports is that of opinion (*ẓann*).'[5]

Then Sahl said:

Bad opinion comes from ignorance and pertains to the natural self (*nafs al-ṭabʿ*). The most ignorant person is the one who estranges his heart [from God] without being aware of it. Indeed, God, Exalted is He, has said: *And that suspicion of yours which you held about your Lord has ruined you, so you have become among the losers.* [41:23] Certainly, the servant is deprived of blessed provision and prayer at night because of bad opinion.

One night a man, one of [God's] servants, slept through [and missed] his customary rite (*wird*) and felt regret over it.[6] [He] was asked: 'Do you feel regret about [missing] that which you are wont to perform?' He replied, 'I do not feel regret because of that, but rather because of the sin through which I became deprived of that good [deed].'

Sahl was asked, 'What is the meaning of the Prophet's words ﷺ: "Be on your guard with people, [by holding a] bad opinion (*sūʾ al-ẓann*)."'[7] He replied:

The meaning of this is [that protection from people] is [gained by holding a] bad opinion of yourself, not of other people. In other words, accuse your own self for not treating them fairly in your dealings with them.[8]

His words:

[49:12] ***…and do not spy…***

---

3 According to the comment on this verse in *Tafsīr al-Jalālayn*, the verse is alluding to the fight between two clans, those of Ibn Ubayy and Ibn Rawāʿā. It is reported that the Prophet ﷺ was riding on a donkey and as it passed by Ibn Ubayy it urinated. Ibn Ubayy held his nose, whereupon Ibn Rawāʿā remarked, 'By God, the smell of the donkey's urine is sweeter than your musk.' Fighting then ensued between their two clans involving fists, sandals and palm branches.

4 For Tustarī's discussion of the benefits of *ḥusn al-ẓann* ('good opinion'), see above, the commentary on the poem included in his commentary on 2:260. See also IT, pp. lii–liii.

5 Bukhārī, *Ṣaḥīḥ*, 'Kitāb al-Nikāḥ', and 'Kitāb al-Adab'; Muslim, *Ṣaḥīḥ*, 'Kitāb al-Adab'.

6 The term *wird* (pl. *awrād*) is used to denote supererogatory devotions that may be observed at certain times of the day and night. With the formation of the Sufi 'orders' (*ṭuruq*, pl. of *ṭarīqa*) from the sixth/twelfth century on, certain *awrād* or sets of formulae became associated with a particular initiatory chain (*silsila*), and these *awrād* are given to disciples by a master at the time of their initiation.

7 Ṭabarānī, *al-Muʿjam al-awsaṭ*, vol. 1, p. 189.

8 One is then protecting oneself from wronging them, the serious implications of which are discussed by Tustarī in his commentary on 99:7. See also p. 300, n. 5.

He said:

That is, 'Do not search out the faults that God has covered for His servants, for you may well be afflicted by that [fault].

It was related of Jesus ﷺ that he used to say, 'Do not speak too much other than in remembrance of God, Mighty and Majestic is He, for your hearts will be hardened, and the heart that is hard is far from God. Do not regard the faults of people as if you were their masters, but look at your own works as if they were your slaves.[9] Know that people are either afflicted (*mubtalā*) or preserved (*muʿāfā*), so show mercy to those who are afflicted and ask God for preservation.'

His words:

[49:12] ***...or backbite one another...***

He said:

Whoever wants to be safe from backbiting must bar the door to [ill] assumptions (*ẓunūn*) in himself,[10] for whoever is safe from making ill assumptions, is safe from backbiting (*ghayba*), and whoever is safe from backbiting, is safe from calumny (*zūr*), and whoever is safe from calumny, is safe from slander (*buhtān*).

He said:

And Ibn ʿAbbās ﷺ said, 'The hypocrite (*munāfiq*) is guilty of backbiting, but the wicked (*fāsiq*) are not guilty of backbiting. This is because the hypocrites keep silent about their hypocrisy, whereas the wicked openly take pride in their wickedness.'

He said:

He [Ibn ʿAbbās] intended by this the sins (*maʿāṣī*) that they commit openly, whereas the sins which are kept a secret are a form of backbiting (*ghayba*).[11]

His words:

[49:14] ***...Say, 'You do not have faith; rather say, "We have submitted"...'***[12]

He said:

This means [they should admit], 'We [only] affirmed [the faith] from fear of being taken captive or killed; for faith (*īmān*) is in the truthful affirmation of the tongue (*iqrār al-lisān ṣidqan*), and certainty within the heart as a binding pact [with God] (*īqān fī'l-qalb ʿaqdan*), along with the realisation (*taḥqīq*) of these through the bodily members with sincerity (*ikhlāṣ*). Faith (*īmān*) has nothing to do with affiliations (*ansāb*); rather affiliations are only a part of Islam.[13] The Muslim is beloved of people but the believer is in no need (*ghanī*) of people.[14]

His words:

[49:17] ***They deem it to be a favour to you that they have submitted...***

Namely, that they affirmed as true that to which you were summoning them. *(Say) '...Rather it is God who has done you a favour in that He has guided you to faith, if you are being truthful,'* that is, if you are aware that it is God who blessed you with guidance from the beginning.

---

9 i.e., with the critical eye of the slavemaster. This tradition is also related in Imam Mālik's *Muwaṭṭaʾ*, 'Kitāb al-Kalām'; Ibn Abī Shayba, *al-Muṣannaf*, vol. 6, p. 340; and Bayhaqī, *Shuʿab al-īmān*, vol. 4, p. 263.

10 On holding 'false assumptions' or a 'bad opinion' as opposed to having a good opinion, again see above IT, p. lii.

11 This is an example of an esoteric interpretation of a tradition or *ḥadīth*.

12 The context which precedes and follows these words of 49:14, is that the desert Arabs claim to believe, but God tells the Prophet to tell them that they should not claim to believe or have faith, but rather they should say that they have submitted, for *faith has not yet entered into your hearts*.

13 Again, note the distinction being made both in the verse and in Tustarī's commentary between *islām* and *īmān*. See above, the commentary on 48:26 and IT, p. lviii, n. 265.

14 That is, he should be solely dependent on God.

Sahl said:

> I practised scrupulous piety (*wara*ʿ) for forty years and it happened that [my] attention was turned from me ⌜towards Him⌝[15] and He corrected me with His words: *They deem it to be a favour to you that they have submitted.*[16] But God Glorified and Exalted is He knows best.

15 The addition has been made on the basis of all three MSS: Z515, f. 105a, F638, f. 49a and F3488, f. 283a, which all have *waqaʿa minnī ilayhi iltifāt*.

16 Tustarī is here acknowledging that he had imagined it was he who was practising scrupulous piety, but then was made to realise that this was a divine favour. Compare the words of Bāyazīd (Abū Yazīd al-Bisṭāmī): 'At the beginning [of my wayfaring] I was mistaken in four things: I supposed that I remembered Him and knew Him and loved Him and sought Him. When I had become advanced [on the Way], I saw that His remembrance preceded my remembrance, His gnosis preceded my gnosis, His love came before my love, and that He sought me first, so that I would seek Him.' The saying of Bāyazīd is cited in Iṣfahānī, *Ḥilyat al-awliyā*ʾ, vol. 10, p. 34.

50 Qāf

His words, Exalted is He:

[50:1] ***Qāf...***

[With this word] God, Exalted is He, made an oath by His strength (*quwwa*) and omnipotence (*qudra*). In its outer meaning it refers to the mountain which surrounds this world, which is the first mountain God, Exalted is He, created. Then after it, He created Mount Abū Qubays, which is the mountain which rises above Ṣafā. Beyond this, by a distance of one year's journey, is a mountain behind which the sun sets, just as He said: *until it [the sun] disappeared behind [night's] veil* [38:32]. It has a face like a human face and a heart like the hearts of the angels in gnosis (*fi'l-maʿrifa*).[1]

His words:

[50:1] ***...By the glorious Qurʾān.***

He said:

This means that it is honoured above all other speech.

His words:

[50:8] ***As an insight and a reminder for every penitent servant.***

He said:

This means: ⌜as a lesson and source of evidence, guiding them to believe in the oneness of their Lord and to show gratitude to Him;⌝[2] *penitent* (munīb), that is, one who devotes his heart purely to God by turning his attention [wholly] to Him,[3] and by maintaining God's remembrance (*dhikr*) in the practice of his obligatory duties (*wājibāt*).

His words, Exalted is He:

[50:12] ***...as did the dwellers at al-Rass...***

That is, the well. And *al-Ayka* [50:14] is a wood. In its inner meaning, the people of Rass are the people of ignorance, and the *dwellers in the wood* [50:14] are the pursuers of lusts.

His words, Exalted is He:

[50:18] ***he does not utter a word but there is beside him a watcher, ready.***

He said:

That is, an attendant guardian who is never absent from him. The angels[4] do not know the good and evil that is within a person's conscience (*ḍamīr*) save when that person's heart acquiesces in it [either good or evil]. When there is a resolution [to do] something good, its effect will manifest a beautiful perfume within the breast (*ṣadr*) and thence from the breast to the bodily

1 Sic in both the printed edition and the MSS. On Mount Qāf see above p. 59, n. 29.

2 Added on the basis of all three MSS: Z515, f. 105 a, F638, f. 49b and F3488, f. 283b.

3 Translating *bi'l-tawajjuh ilayhi* as in all three MSS: Z515, f. 105a, F638, f. 49b and F3488, f. 283b, instead of *bi'l-tawḥīd ilayhi* in the published edition.

4 Translating *malāʾika* in the plural, according to the MSS, whereas the published edition has the singular, *malak*.

members; whereas when there is a resolution to do evil it manifests darkness and a rotten smell. In any event, God knows all of this from [the servant], so he should fear Him in accordance with His words, *Surely God has been watchful over you* [4:1].

His words, Exalted is He:

[50:21] ***And every soul will come accompanied by a driver and a witness.***

This means: the recording [angels] (*kataba*) who were with him in this world will lead him to the gathering place and will testify either for or against him. Then the servant says, 'Is not what You say the truth? Indeed, You have said: *And if you were to enumerate God's favours you could never number them* [14:34]'. And Your Prophet ﷺ said, 'None of you enters Paradise through his works, but only through His mercy.'[5] Then God says, 'My words are the truth, and my Prophet ﷺ has spoken truly, so therefore proceed to Paradise through My mercy.'

He said:

This is the meaning of His words, Exalted is He: *…and for them is forgiveness and a generous provision* [8:74].

His words, Exalted is He:

[50:22] ***…and your sight on this Day is acute.***

That is to say, your heart's vision (*baṣar*) will be penetrating (*nāfidh*), in its witnessing (*mushāhada*) of all its affairs and conditions [on this Day].

His words, Exalted is He:

[50:29] ***The word that comes from Me cannot be changed…***

That is, 'What is within My prior knowledge does not change, so that it would become contrary to My pre-existing knowledge concerning it.'

His words, Exalted is He:

[50:32] '***…[it is] for everyone who is oft-returning* (awwāb), *heedful* (ḥafīẓ) *of God…***'[6]

He said:

He is the one who turns back with his heart from evil suggestions to tranquil reliance (*sukūn*) on God, Exalted is He, and is the heedful one (*ḥafīẓ*), who guards his moments (*awqāt*) and states (*aḥwāl*), [while] keeping to His commandments and observing acts of obedience.

Ibn ʿAyniyya said, 'The one who is *oft-returning, heedful of God* is the person who does not get up from a gathering until he has asked for God's forgiveness for it, regardless of whether it was good or bad, due to the imperfection and deficiency that he sees in it.'[7]

His words, Exalted is He:

[50:37] ***Assuredly there is in that a reminder for him who has a heart* (qalb)…**

That is, whoever has an intellect (*ʿaql*) by which he acquires knowledge of the sacred law (*ʿilm al-sharʿ*).

His words, Exalted is He:

[50:37] ***…or gives ear.***

That is, he listens to Our reminder while being attentive [lit. present, (*ḥāḍir*)] and witnessing his Lord, not absent from Him.

5 Bukhārī, *Ṣaḥīḥ*, 'Kitāb al-Marḍā'', 'Kitāb al-Riqāq'; Haythamī, *Majmaʿ al-zawāʾid*, vol. 10, p. 357.

6 [It] being the reward of Paradise. On the word *awwāb* having the sense of 'repeatedly repenting', see above Tustarī's commentary on 17:25.

7 i.e., his conduct in it. In the *Glorious Treasure* of Ḥabīb ʿUmar b. Muḥammad b. Sālim (London), p. 37, two similar *ḥadīths* are cited. The first is related on the authority of Abū Hurayra, according to whom the Prophet ﷺ said, 'If a person sits in company which indulges in idle talk, and before standing says, "Glory be to You, praise be to You. I testify that there is no god but You; I ask Your forgiveness and I repent to you;" he is forgiven for his participation in that company.' The *ḥadīth* is recorded as sound by Abū Dāwūd, Nasāʾī, Ibn Ḥibbān and Tirmidhī.

Sahl was asked about the intellect (*ʿaql*) and he said:

Intellect is having good judgement (*ḥusn al-naẓar*) for yourself of the outcome of your affairs.

But God, Glorified and Exalted is He, knows best.

51 Al-Dhāriyāt

His words, Exalted is He:

[51:15] *Truly those who are mindful of God will be amid gardens and springs.*

He said:

> He who is mindful of God (*muttaqī*) [inhabits] in this world gardens of [God's] good pleasure (*riḍā*), and swims in well-springs of intimate companionship (*uns*). This is the inner meaning of the verse.[1]

His words, Exalted is He:

[51:17] *They used to sleep little of the night.*

He said:

> Neither heedlessness (*ghafla*) nor sleep ever, under any circumstances, diverts them from the remembrance [of God].

His words, Exalted is He:

[51:19] *and there was a share in their wealth [assigned] for the beggar and the deprived.*

He said:

> That is, [they give] alms both to those who ask for them and to those who do not ask.

Ḥasan al-Baṣrī said:

> In my time I came across people among whom [it was the custom for] the man to adjure his family never to turn away any supplicant. I also came across people among whom a man would leave his brother responsible for his family for forty years. [Moreover,] the members of his household would suffer a supplicant even if they were neither of jinn nor of humankind. Those who came before you only took from this world what was absolutely necessary. They would sell their own selves for the sake of kindness [to others]. May God have mercy on the person who lives the simplest of lives,[2] eating just a crust of bread, and wearing worn-out clothes, who is the lowliest of men,[3] strives hard in his worship, cries over the misdeed he commits, flees from punishment and seeks God's mercy up to the moment when death overtakes him, he being in that state.'[4]
>
> It was related that a man came to the Prophet ﷺ and said, 'O Messenger of God — may God make me your ransom! — what is the matter with me that I dislike death?' He said, 'Do you have wealth?' He replied, 'Yes.' So [the Prophet] said, 'Then give away your wealth.' [The man] replied, 'I am incapable of doing that, O Messenger of God.' [The Prophet said ﷺ],[5] 'Truly, a

1 The outer meaning would indicate that the gardens and springs are rewards in the Hereafter, but by saying 'in this world' Tustarī has, in its inner interpretation, extended the reward for mindfulness of God to life in the present.

2 lit. who can be sustained by one kind of sustenance (*jaʿala'l-ʿaysh wāḥidan*).

3 lit. he cleaves to the earth.

4 Iṣfahānī, *Ḥilyat al-awliyāʾ*, vol. 2, p. 149; Bayhaqī, *Kitāb al-Zuhd al-kabīr*, vol. 2, p. 65.

5 MSS Z515, f. 107a and F3488, f. 284b–285a have '...*yā rasūl Allāh*' followed by the statement about man's heart being attached to his wealth which therefore attributed the statement to the man, whereas F638, f. 50a, having *qāla nabī Allāh*, and the published edition, '...*yā rasūl Allāh.' Qāla*, are both assuming the statement to be a saying of the Prophet. This tradition appears with slight variation in Ibn Mubārak, *Kitāb al-Zuhd wa'l-raqāʾiq* (India, 1966), p. 224.

man's heart is with his wealth, so if he gives his wealth away, it will want to go along with it, but if he holds on to it, it will want to remain with it.'[6]

His words, Exalted is He:

[51:20] *On earth there are signs for those who know with certainty,*

He said:

That is, [signs] for the mystics (*ʿārifūn*) by which they find evidence for their gnosis (*maʿrifa*).

His words, Exalted is He:

[51:21] *and in yourselves too, do you not see?*

He said:

That is, [signs] in their forms; in their being endowed with the finest proportions (*taqādīr*); in their veins, which run through them like flowing rivers; and in His dividing them (*shuqūq*) without your experiencing any pain, after your being a mere drop.[7] Then He assembled you stage by stage. *Do you not see* this remarkable omnipotence (*qudra*), and hence believe in His unicity (*waḥdāniyya*) and His omnipotence (*qudra*)?

Furthermore, God, Exalted is He, has created within the soul of the son of Adam one thousand and eighty portents, three hundred and sixty of which are apparent and three hundred and sixty of which are hidden, but which you could see if He unveiled them to you. The [remaining] three hundred and sixty of them are obscure and are only known to a prophet or veracious person (*ṣiddīq*). If just one of these [latter portents] were to be revealed to the possessors of intellects (*ahl al-ʿuqūl*), they would attain sincerity (*ikhlāṣ*).

Truly God, Exalted is He, has veiled the hearts of those who are heedless (*ghāfilūn*) from His remembrance due to their pursuance of lusts, which [prevent them] from perceiving these portents. However, He has unveiled them to the hearts of those who have gnosis of Him (*ʿārifūn*), thereby causing them to attain it [sincerity].

His words, Exalted is He:

[51:22] *And in heaven is your provision, as [also] that which you are promised.*

That is, 'Apply yourself to worshipping Me and do not let the work of seeking your provision divert you from Us, for truly We are providing for you.'

Then He said:

God is content with your performing for Him just a day's worship at a time, so be content with Him for the provision you receive a day at a time.

He further said:

It also has another interpretation: *And in heaven is your provision*, that is, of remembrance and its reward.

His words, Exalted is He:

[51:24] *Has the story reached you, of Abraham's honoured guests?*

He said:

He [God] called them honoured (*mukramūn*) because he [Abraham] served them himself, and for seven days he had not eaten anything, as he was waiting for a guest. Then when God, Exalted is He, sent His angels to Him, he rejoiced at them and served them himself, but did not eat with them. This is the mark of true friendship (*khilla*),[8] that is, to feed others without eating oneself, and to cure another's illness when one is sick.[9]

---

6 Note that all three MSS have *in khallafahu* instead of *in akhkharahu*. The *ḥadīth* is listed in Daylamī, *Firdaws*, vol. 3, p. 205.

7 An allusion to 16:14; 35:11; 53:46; 75:37 and 76:2. Perhaps what is meant is the dividing of the cells.

8 Note, as mentioned above, p. 30, n. 94, Abraham's honorary title is '*Khalīl Allāh*' (Friend of God).

9 A practice which Tustarī carried out himself, for which see IT, p. xxi. MSS Z515, f. 107a and F638, f. 50b have: *wa yashfī*

His words, Exalted is He:

[51:50] ***[Say] 'So flee to God. Truly I am a clear warner to you from Him.'***

He said:

> That is, 'Flee from that which is other than God to God. Flee from disobedience to obedience, from ignorance to knowledge, from His punishment to His mercy, and from His wrath to His good pleasure.' Indeed, the Prophet ﷺ said, 'I take refuge in You from You.'[10] This in itself is a great branch of knowledge.

His words:

[51:54] ***So shun them, you will not be reproached.***

He said:

> Turn away from them, for you have striven with all your effort in conveying [the message]. But God, Glorified and Exalted is He, knows best.

al-ghayr min aḥadin wa yasqam, whereas the published edition has *wa yashfī al-ghayr min alamin wa yasqam*, which is what we have translated here.

10 Nīsābūrī, *al-Mustadrak*, vol. 3, p. 93; Tirmidhī, *Sunan*, 'Kitāb al-Daʿwāt'.

52 Al-Ṭūr

His words, Exalted is He:

[52:4] ***By the [Much]-frequented House***[1]

He said:

The outward meaning is in what Muḥammad b. Sawwār related in his chain of transmission from Ibn Masʿūd ﷺ, who stated that the Prophet ﷺ said, 'On the night I was taken up to the heaven, I saw the Much-frequented House (*Bayt Maʿmūr*) in the fourth heaven (and it is also related, the seventh). Each day seventy thousand angels make a pilgrimage to it, and never return' — to the end of the *ḥadīth*.[2]

In its inner meaning, it refers to the heart; the hearts of mystics are frequented (*maʿmūra*) by His gnosis (*maʿrifa*), His love (*maḥabba*) and intimacy (*uns*) with Him. It is to this [the mystic's heart] that the angels make pilgrimage, for it is the House of the Realisation of God's Oneness (*bayt al-tawḥīd*).

His words, Exalted is He:

[52:5] ***and the raised canopy***

This is the pleasing ⌜and pure⌝ act (*al-ʿamal al-murḍī ⌜al-zakī⌝*),[3] through which no reward is sought except God, Exalted is He.

His words, Exalted is He:

[52:26] ***[They will say,] 'Truly, before, when we were amid our families, we used to be ever anxious,'***

He said:

That is, in fear and trepidation of an ill decree (*sūʾ al-qaḍāʾ*) and the spiteful rejoicing of the enemy.

His words, Exalted is He:

[52:48] ***And submit patiently to the judgement of your Lord; you are under Our watchful eye...***

That is, 'Whatever pertaining to action (*fiʿl*) and power (*qudra*) appears in your character, [know that] it is He who has taken your whole being into His care (*riʿāya*), protection (*kilāya*), good pleasure (*riḍā*) and love (*maḥabba*), and guarded you from the Enemy.'

His words, Exalted is He:

[52:48] ***...Celebrate the praise of your Lord when you rise,***

He said:

This means: 'Perform the prescribed prayer with sincerity for your Lord when you rise for it.'

His words, Exalted is He:

[52:49] ***and glorify Him at night and at the receding of the stars.***

---

1 The '*Bayt Maʿmūr*' is traditionally said to be in heaven (according to various reports it is said to be the third, fourth, sixth or seventh heaven) directly above the Kaʿba, and is visited each day by seventy thousand angels, who circumambulate it and perform prayers there, but do not return.

2 Muslim, *Ṣaḥīḥ*, 'Kitāb al-Īmān'. This *ḥadīth* is among those which relate the *Miʿrāj*, the miraculous 'Night Journey' and Ascension of the Prophet. For references to traditional material on the *Miʿrāj* see above IC, p. 4, n. 15.

3 The addition is made on the basis of all three MSS: Z515, f. 107 b, F638, f. 50b and F3488, f. 286a.

He said:

> That is, 'Do not be negligent in remembering the One who is never negligent in His beneficence towards you, or in giving you His protection at all times, morning and evening.' But God, Glorified and Exalted is He, knows best.

53 Al-Najm

His words, Exalted is He:

[53:1] ***By the star when it sets,***

That is, [by] Muḥammad ﷺ when he returned from the heavens.[1]

His words, Exalted is He:

[53:2] ***your companion has neither gone astray nor has he erred,***

He said:

That is, he never ever strayed from the reality of the divine oneness (*ḥaqīqat al-tawḥīd*), nor ever followed Satan under any circumstances.

His words, Exalted is He:

[53:3] ***nor does he speak out of [his own] desire,***

[He said]:

That is, he never ever utters falsehoods (*bāṭil*).

Then he said:

His utterances were among the proofs (*ḥujaj*) of God, Exalted is He, so how could desire or Satan have any means of thwarting him?

His words, Exalted is He:

[53:8] ***Then he drew near and drew closer still,***

He said:

That is, he approached, drawing closer and closer.

His words, Exalted is He:

[53:11] ***The heart did not deny what he saw.***

⌜That is to say, what he saw⌝[2] at the witnessing (*mushāhada*) of his Lord, through the vision (*baṣar*) of his heart as a face-to-face encounter (*kifāḥ*).[3]

His words, Exalted is He:

[53:12] ***Will you then dispute with him concerning what he saw?***

What he saw from Us and through Us; and what he sees from Us and through Us is more excellent than what he sees ⌜from Us⌝ through himself.[4]

---

1 Sūra 53:1–15 are said to describe the *Miʿrāj*, miraculous Night Journey and Ascension, of the Prophet. Again, for references to traditional material on the *Miʿrāj* see above, IC, p. 4, n. 15.

2 The addition was made on the basis of all three MSS: Z515, f. 108a, F638, f. 50b and F3488, f. 286b.

3 There was a debate among Muslim theologians and mystics as to whether the Prophet's vision of God during his *Miʿrāj* was a vision of the eyes or the heart. See Schimmel, *Muḥammad*, pp. 162–4; Heribert Busse, 'Jerusalem in the Story of Muhammad's Night Journey and Ascension,' *Jerusalem Studies in Arabic and Islam* 14 (1991), pp. 1–40. Note that by using the expression 'vision of his heart' (*baṣar qalbihi*), Tustarī appears to adhere to the view that it was an inner vision of the heart. In our translation of Tustarī's commentary on 53:1–13, reference has been made in various ways to Böwering's translation in his *Mystical Vision*, pp. 150–1. For a discussion of this and other related passages in Tustarī's commentary, see ibid, pp. 149–53.

4 The addition was made on the basis of all three MSS: Z515, f. 108a, F638, f. 50b and F3488, f. 286b.

His words, Exalted is He:

[53:13] ***And verily he saw him another time,***

He said:

That is, in the beginning when God, Glorified and Exalted is He, created him as a light within a column of light (*nūran fī ʿamūd al-nūr*), a million years before creation,[5] with the essential characteristics of faith (*ṭabāʾiʿ al-īmān*), in a witnessing of the unseen within the unseen (*mushāhadat al-ghayb bi'l-ghayb*). He stood before Him in servanthood (*ʿubūdiyya*), *by the lote tree of the Ultimate Boundary* [53:14],[6] this being a tree at which the knowledge of every person reaches its limit.

[53:16] ***when there shrouded the lote tree that which shrouded [it].***

This means: ⌈that which shrouded⌉ the lote tree (*ay mā yaghshā al-shajara*)[7] was from the light of Muḥammad as he worshipped. It could be likened to golden moths, which God sets in motion towards Him from the wonders of His secrets. All this is in order to increase him [Muḥammad] in firmness (*thabāt*) for the influx [of graces] (*mawārid*) which he received [from above].[8]

[53:17] ***The eye did not swerve, nor did it go beyond [the bounds].***

He did not incline to the evidences of his self (*shawāhid nafsihi*), nor to witnessing them (*mushāhadatihā*), but was totally absorbed in the witnessing (*mushāhada*) of his Lord, Exalted is He, seeing (*shāhid*) the attributes [of God] that were being manifested [to him], which required firmness from him in that place (*maḥall*).

[53:18] ***Verily he saw some of the greatest signs of his Lord.***

That is, those of His attributes that became manifest through His signs. Though he saw them, he did not let slip [his gaze] from his witnessed Object (*mashhūd*) [of worship], and did not withdraw from the vicinity of his worshipped Object (*maʿbūd*), but rather [what he saw] only increased him in love (*maḥabba*), longing (*shawq*) and strength (*quwwa*).

God gave him the strength by which he could bear the theophany (*tajallī*) and supreme lights (*anwār ʿaẓīma*). This was out of his being favoured above the other prophets. Do you not see how Moses fell down in a swoon at the theophany. Yet twice as much did the Prophet ﷺ penetrate it (*jābahu*) in his contemplation, through a face-to-face encounter with the sight of his heart (*kifāḥan bi-baṣar qalbihi*), and yet remained firm due to the strength of his state, and his elevated station (*maqām*) and rank (*daraja*).[9]

---

5 The words *wa yuqālu* preceding *nūran* are absent from the MSS.

6 We have taken 'He stood before Him in servanthood' to be referring to the *Miʿrāj*, whereas Böwering has understood Muḥammad's standing in servanthood to be a reference to part of his creation — his reasons for this may well have been the other passage (in the commentary on 24:35), which speaks of Muḥammad's prostration before God from which the mighty column appeared. However, in our view, the main part of the commentary on verse 13 is describing the time before creation when the Prophet 'saw' God, depicted as a witnessing of the unseen within the unseen, whilst the words 'he stood before Him in worship', seems to be a movement towards the next verse. This is certainly how it appears from the MSS, since there is no break between that sentence and verse 14. Moreover, this is further confirmed by the reference in the commentary on the following verse to the light of Muḥammad shrouding the lote tree.

7 Significantly, the MSS have the addition of *ay mā yaghshā* before *al-ṣidra min nūr Muḥammad fī ʿibādatihi*, meaning that Tustarī is defining in his commentary what was shrouding the tree, namely an emanation from the light of Muḥammad in his worship.

8 See above, the commentary on 43:71, where Tustarī mentions the divine empowerment (*tamkīn*), granted to believers upon their encounter with God in Paradise, as a reward for their realisation of God's oneness in this life.

9 Later Sufis, such as Sulamī, Qushayrī and Maybudī contrasted the different responses of Moses and Muḥammad to the theophany. See, for example, Sulamī, *Bayān laṭāʾif al-miʿrāj*, trans. Colby, Nos 13, 15 and 45, and translator's comment to the latter p. 126. Some commentators contrasted the two prophets' experiences in order to illustrate the opposite stations of *talwīn* (vacillation) and *tamkīn* (firmness or stability) — the latter being the equivalent to Tustarī's *thabāt*. See the section on *talwīn* and *tamkīn* in Qushayrī's *Risāla*, pp. 232–5, trans. Knysh, p. 101; Sulamī, *Risāla al-Malāmatiyya* in Nasrollah Pourjavady, ed., *Majmūʿa* (Tehran, 1990), p. 403; French trans. Deladrière, p. 30; and Maybudī, *Kashf al-asrār*, vol. 2, p. 93.

His words, Exalted is He:

[53:40] ***and that his endeavour will be seen,***[10]

He said:

That is, his endeavour (*saʿī*) will be seen, and he will know that it is not worthy of God. He will see what his endeavour is entitled to,[11] and that if God's grace did not reach him, his endeavour would come to nought.

His words, Exalted is He:

[53:43] ***and that it is He who makes to laugh and to weep,***

He said:

That is, He made the obedient laugh with His mercy (*raḥma*) and destroyed the transgressors with His wrath (*sakhṭ*). He made the hearts of the mystics joyful with the light of gnosis of Him and made the hearts of His enemies grieve with the darkness of His wrath.

[53:44] ***and that it is He who brings death and gives life,***

He said:

He caused the hearts of His enemies to die through disbelief (*kufr*) and darkness (*ẓulma*), and He gave life to the hearts of His friends through faith (*īmān*) and the lights of gnosis (*anwār al-maʿrifa*).

[53:48] ***and that it is He who gives wealth and grants possessions***

He said:

Its outward meaning refers to worldly possessions, and its inner meaning is that He enriches [His servants] through obedience and impoverishes them through disobedience.

Ibn ʿUyayna said, *He who gives wealth and grants possessions* means: He gives satisfaction (*aqnaʿa*) and contentment (*arḍā*). But God, Glorified and Exalted is He, knows best.

10 This and the following verses are a continuation of the question that is begun in verse 36: *Has he [man] not been informed of what is in the scrolls of Moses…?*

11 i.e. he will see that it is worth nothing in the face of God. Or it could mean, he will see who (namely God) is entitled to his endeavour.

54 Al-Qamar

His words, Exalted is He:

[54:1] ***The Hour has drawn near and the moon has split.***

During the time of the Messenger of God ﷺ, when it was cleft into two segments, such that one segment disappeared behind Mount al-Ḥirāʾ. This was the first of the signs [of the approach] of the Hour.[1]

The following is related from Abū ʿAbd al-Raḥmān al-Sulamī:[2] 'Once I was with my father in town when the time for the Friday prayer came, so he took me by the hand and went with me to the Friday prayer. Then Hudhayfa b. al-Yamān rose to the pulpit, praised God and extolled Him, and said, "*The Hour has drawn near and the moon has split.* Is not the Hour drawing nigh? Has the moon not been cleft asunder? Is this world not fading into decline? Is it not so, that the race track is set today and the race will be on the morrow?" When we went outside again I said, "O Father, will people race each other tomorrow?" He replied "O my son! It's clear you don't realise [what he meant by] 'The race is on the morrow'. He is just saying that whoever works [righteousness] today will excel in the Hereafter."'[3]

His words, Exalted is He:

[54:17] ***And verily We have made the Qurʾān easy to remember. Is there anyone who will remember?***[4]

That is, 'We have made the Qurʾān easy to remember. If it were not so, tongues would not have been able to enunciate it. So will anyone take heed of this blessing (*niʿma*)?'

His words, Exalted is He:

[54:52] ***And everything they have done is in the scrolls,***

He said:

That is, in the books which the recording angels write.

[54:53] ***and every [matter] small and great, is recorded.***

That is, written in the book, which is then shown to them on the Day of Resurrection, [when they stand] before God.

The [following] saying is related from Abū Ḥāzim: 'Woe to you, O Aʿraj! The people of sin will be summoned on the Day of Resurrection with the call: "O people of such and such a sin!" and you will stand up with them. Then it will be called out: "O people of such and such a sin!" and you will stand up with them. Indeed, I see you, Aʿraj, standing with the people of every kind of sin.' But God, Glorfied and Exalted is He, knows best.

---

1 On this event see Lings, *Muḥammad*, p. 68.

2 The Kufan Qurʾān reciter and not the later celebrated Sufi author of *Ṭabaqāt al-ṣūfiyya* and *Ḥaqāʾiq al-tafsīr*. See Appendix below.

3 This tradition is to be found in Nīsābūrī, *al-Mustadrak*, vol. 4, p. 651. A section in brackets has been added by the editor of the Dār al-Kutub al-ʿIlmiyya edition of Tustarī's *tafsīr* on the basis of the *Mustadrak*. However, none of the MSS has this addition. Moreover, there is another discrepancy with the printed text, in that all the MSS (Z515, f. 109a, F636, f. 51b and F3488, f. 287b) appear to have *a-lā wa-inna al-dunyā qad ādanat biʾl-firāq*, instead of *a-lā wa-inna al-dunyā qad adbarat*.

4 The words of this verse are repeated in verses 22, 32 and 40.

55 Al-Raḥmān

His words, Exalted is He:

[55:4] ***and taught him [coherent] speech*** **(bayān).**[1]

He said:

This means: He has taught him [mankind] speech (*kalām*) which pertains to the spiritual self (*nafs al-rūḥ*), understanding of the intellect (*fahm al-ʿaql*), discernment of the heart (*fiṭnat al-qalb*), natural intuition (*dhihn al-khulq*) and knowledge of the natural self (*ʿilm nafs al-ṭabʿ*). God granted Adam ﷺ this [knowledge] through inspiration and then explained (*bayyana*) it to him.

His words, Exalted is He:

[55:7] ***...and has set up the balance,***

He said:

Its inner meaning refers to commandments and prohibitions governing the bodily members [of a person].

His words, Exalted is He:

[55:17] ***He is Lord of the two risings and Lord of the two settings.***

He said:

Its inner meaning refers to the rising of the heart and its setting, the rising of the tongue and its setting, and the rising of the profession of His oneness, [whose] setting is the witnessing (*mushāhada*) of Him. And He also says, *[I swear] by the Lord of the risings and the settings* [70:40], meaning the risings of the bodily members through sincerity (*ikhlāṣ*), and their settings through subservience to people (*ṭāʿa li'l-nās*) inwardly and outwardly.

His words, Exalted is He:

[55:19] ***He has loosed the two seas, and they meet.***[2]

He said:

One of these seas is the heart, which contains a variety of gems: the gem of faith, the gem of gnosis (*maʿrifa*), the gem of realising God's oneness, the gem of contentment (*riḍā*), the gem of love (*maḥabba*), the gem of longing (*shawq*), the gem of sorrow (*ḥuzn*), the gem of neediness [for God] (*faqr*), and other [gems]. The other sea is the self (*nafs*).

His words, Exalted is He:

[55:20] ***Between them is a barrier [that] they do not overstep.***

This is divine protection (*ʿiṣma*) and divinely-bestowed success (*tawfīq*).

His words, Exalted is He:

[55:46] ***But for whosoever feared the standing [before] their Lord, there will be two gardens,***

---

1 On the word *bayān*, see above p. 32, n. 105.

2 In his *Jāmiʿ al-bayān*, Ṭabarī presents a few possible interpretations of what the two seas might be, such as one sea being the Mediterranean Sea (Baḥr al-Rūm) and the other, the Persian Gulf (Baḥr al-Fārs). However, Ṭabarī prefers the view given in the majority of traditions that the two seas are the earthly and heavenly seas (*baḥr al-arḍ wa-baḥr al-samāʾ*).

Labīd[3] said:

> [Such a one] was on the point of [committing] a transgression, but then recalled the time when he will stand before God, Exalted is He, on the Day of Reckoning and refrained from that.
>
> I heard [the story of] a young man during the era of the caliphate of ʿUmar ﷺ who was endowed with beauty and had a striking appearance. ʿUmar ﷺ was impressed with the young man and sensed that much good [would come] from him. One day the youth encountered a woman to whom he took a fancy. However, as soon as he was on the point of committing an indecent act, the divine protection descended upon him and he fell down on his face in a swoon. The woman then carried him to his house. He had a father who was an old man and it was his wont when evening fell to sit in front of his door waiting for his son's return. When the old man saw him he also fell into a swoon. When he regained his senses he asked his son about his condition. So he recounted the story, but then suddenly yelled with one cry and fell down dead. After he was buried ʿUmar ﷺ stood up and recited over his grave: *But for whosoever feared the standing [before] their Lord, there will be two gardens*, upon which he [the young man] cried to him from the grave, 'God has given them to me and has granted me a third along with them.'[4]

His words, Exalted is He:

[55:56] *In them are maidens of restrained glances…*

He said:

> That is, they lower their gaze to all except their husbands. Thus whoever restrains his glances in this world from that which is forbidden and dubious, and from sensual delights and their attraction, will find that God grants him in Paradise maidens restraining their glances just as He has promised.

His words, Exalted is He:

[55:72] *Houris, secluded in pavilions.*

> That is, kept in seclusion in pavilions. It was related from Muḥammad b. Sawwār, on the authority of his chain of transmission, that Abū Mūsā al-Ashʿarī ﷺ related that the Prophet ﷺ said, 'Verily the believer will have in Paradise a pavilion made of white pearl, thirty miles in length, in which there are many inhabitants but they do not see one another.'[5]

3 Perhaps this is Abū ʿAqīl b. Rābiʿa Labīd (d. 40/661). The editor of the Dār al-Kutub al-ʿIlmiyya edition notes, however, that this tradition is attributed to Mujāhid in Aḥmad b. Ḥanbal's *Kitāb al-Waraʿ* (Beirut, 1983), p. 115.

4 A similar tradition is related in Bayhaqī, *Shuʿab al-īmān*, vol. 1, p. 468.

5 Muslim, *Ṣaḥīḥ*, 'Kitāb al-Janna'; Bukhārī, *Ṣaḥīḥ*, 'Kitāb Tafsīr al-Qurʾān'.

56 Al-Wāqiʿa

His words, Exalted is He:

[56:3] ***It will be abasing [some], exalting [others].***

He said:

This means: on the Day of Resurrection some people will be brought low by their false claims (*daʿāwā*), and some people will be raised high by their realities (*ḥaqāʾiq*).[1]

His words, Exalted is He:

[56:7] ***you will be three kinds* (azwāj).**

He said:

That is to say, three different groups (*firaq*).

[56:8] ***Those of the right [hand], what of those of the right [hand]?***

This means those who are given the book [of deeds] in their right hand.[2]

[56:9] ***And those of the left hand, what of those of the left [hand]?***

This means those who are given the book [of deeds] in their left hand.

[56:10] ***And the foremost, the foremost.***

He said:

They are those for whom God's election (*ikhtiyār*) and special friendship (*wilāya*) preceded them before they were even brought into existence. *The ones who are brought near [to God]* [56:11] are in stations of proximity (*manāzil al-qurb*), and [enjoy] the ease of intimacy (*rawḥ al-uns*). They are the ones who were the foremost (*sabaqū*) in this life. The prophets were the foremost in having faith in God; the veracious (*ṣiddīqūn*) and martyrs (*shuhadāʾ*) among the Companions and others were the foremost in having faith in the prophets.

His words, Exalted is He:

[56:13] ***a multitude from the former [generations],***[3]

He said:

That is, a group of those of old (*awwalūn*), and they are the people of gnosis (*maʿrifa*) [from the past].

[56:40] ***and a few from later ones.***

They are those who believed in Muḥammad ﷺ and in all the messengers and books.

His words, Exalted is He:

[56:25] ***They will not hear therein any vain talk or any sinful words.***

---

1 i.e. that which they have truly realised.

2 Tustarī discusses each person's being given the book of their deeds at the Resurrection, either in their right hand or their left, below, for example in his commentary on 69:19, 25 and 32.

3 These words occur again in verse 39.

He said:

> It is in no way a scene of frivolity (*laghw*), nor is it a place of sin (*ithm*), for it is a place which has been sanctified with [divine] lights for the holy (*muqaddasūn*) among His servants. Indeed, it is what has become manifest from them and upon them that makes them worthy of that station.

His words, Exalted is He:

[56:83] ***Why then, when it reaches the dying man's throat,***

That is, his soul reaches the throat, while he is in a state of bewilderment (*mutaḥayyir*), as he does not know what will become of him.

Similarly, it was related of Masrūq b. al-Ajdaʿ that he wept while he was dying and when his weeping intensified, he was asked, 'What makes you weep?' He replied, 'How can I not weep when it is a matter of an hour and then I do not know where I will be taken.'

[56:88] ***Thus if he be of those brought near,***

By which is meant the prophets, the martyrs and the virtuous (*ṣāliḥūn*), of whom some are superior in rank to others. Their stations in nearness [to God] are according to the degree of proximity of their hearts to the gnosis (*maʿrifa*) of God, Exalted is He.

[56:89] ***then repose and a goodly provision and a garden of bliss,***

in Paradise. Abū al-ʿĀliya said regarding this verse, 'Not one of these men would leave this world until he had been brought a sprig from the fragrant herb (*rayḥān*) of Paradise,[4] and given a whiff of it, then he would die, his spirit flowing into it [Paradise].'

[56:90] ***and if he be of those of the right [hand],***

He said:

> By which is meant those who realise God's oneness (*muwaḥḥidūn*). The outcome (*ʿāqiba*) will be theirs,[5] for they were God's faithful servants who delivered the trust (*amāna*),[6] namely, that which He has commanded and prohibited. Those who followed in excellence (*iḥsān*) did not commit any transgressions nor did they make any slips, so they became secure from the fear (*khawf*) and terror (*hawl*) which comes to [others].

4 Usually said to be basil, which indeed bears the name *rayḥān* in Arabic.

5 i.e. they will be the winners that day, the Day of Resurrection.

6 This is probably an allusion to 33:72: *We offered the trust to the heavens and the earth and the mountains, but they refused to carry it; and man carried it*. The trust (*amāna*) is traditionally interpreted to mean obedience (*ṭāʿa*) and carrying out the obligatory duties (*farāʾiḍ*) prescribed by religion, as may be seen in many of the traditions included by Ṭabarī in his *Jāmiʿ al-bayān*, and this is how Tustarī has understood it here. According to Qushayrī (*Laṭāʾif*, vol. 3, p. 173), *amāna* is upholding what is obligatory according to the principles (*uṣūl*) and applications (*furūʿ*) [of *fiqh*], or it is *tawḥīd* in faith (*ʿaqdan*) and keeping the limits (*ḥifẓ al-ḥudūd*) in endeavours (*jahdan*). Maybudī, however, interprets the trust to be love, for which see *Kashf al-asrār*, vol. 8, p. 101.

57 Al-Ḥadīd

His words, Exalted is He:

[57:3] ***He is the First and the Last…***

He said:

The greatest name of God is alluded to in six verses at the beginning of Sūrat al-Ḥadīd starting from the verse: *He is the First and the Last, the Manifest and the Hidden.* The significance (*maʿnā*) of the names (*asmāʾ*) is none other than gnosis (*maʿrifa*) of the One who is named (*musammā*), and the significance of worship (*ʿibāda*) is none other than gnosis of the One who is worshipped (*maʿbūd*).[1] The meaning of *the Manifest* (al-Ẓāhir) is the One who is manifest in His exaltedness (*ʿuluww*), omnipotence (*qudra*) and coerciveness (*qahr*). *The Hidden* (al-Bāṭin) is the One who knows the hidden thoughts (*ḍamāʾir*) and stirrings (*ḥarakāt*) that are concealed within hearts.

His words, Exalted is He:

[57:4] ***…He knows what enters the earth…***

He said:

[In] the inner meaning of the verse, *the earth* is the natural self (*nafs al-ṭabʿ*), and thus He knows, among the things which enter it [the natural self], that which is wholesome (*ṣalāḥ*) or corrupt (*fasād*) for the heart;[2] *and what issues from it,* in the way of diverse acts of obedience (*funūn al-ṭāʿāt*), the traces and marks of which are clearly seen upon the bodily members; *and what comes down from Heaven,* God's codes of fair conduct (*ādāb*) towards Him which [descend] to it; *and what ascends to it,* the beautiful scents and remembrance of Him that ascend to God.

His words, Exalted is He:

[57:6] ***He makes the night pass into the day…***

He said:

The inner meaning of the verse is that *the night* is the natural self (*nafs al-ṭabʿ*) and *the day* is the spiritual self (*nafs al-rūḥ*). If God, Exalted is He, wishes good for His servant, He reconciles and brings together his natural self and his spiritual self through the perpetuation of [His] remembrance (*dhikr*), and makes this manifest in the corresponding lights of humble submission (*khushūʿ*) [to God].[3]

His words, Exalted is He:

[57:7] ***Believe in God and His Messenger, and expend out of that which He caused to come down to you…***

---

1 Translating *biʾl-maʿbūd* on the basis of all three MSS: Z515, f. 111a, F638, f. 52b and F3488, f. 290a, instead of *fiʾl-ʿubūdiyya* in the published edition.

2 That is, reading *liʾl-qalb*, according to MS F638, f. 52b. The other MSS (Z5125, f. 111a and F3488, f. 290b) and the printed edition have *al-qalb*.

3 On this doctrine see above, IT, pp. xxxix–xl.

He said:

That is, what you inherited from your forefathers (*ābāʾ*), and your possessions (*mulk*). So give of what your natural selves enjoy from [this] world, in the cause of obeying Him and His Messenger. *For those of you who believe and expend* their whole lives in the ways that God commanded that they should expend them, *will have a great reward,* namely, to abide with the Everlasting (*al-Bāqī*) in His Garden, [enjoying] His good pleasure (*riḍā*).

His words, Exalted is He:

[57:11] *Who is he that will lend God a goodly loan* (qarḍan ḥasana)*...?*

He said:

God granted His servants His favour, and then He asked them to make Him *a goodly loan*. The *goodly loan* [for which He asks] is the witnessing of Him (*mushāhadat*), just as the Prophet ﷺ said: 'Worship God as if you see Him...'[4]

The following saying is narrated from Abū Ḥāzim: 'Verily, [in this world] there is little market for the merchandise of the Hereafter, so ask and hope for more slow seasons [to increase your stock], for when the day for spending arrives, you will not be able to build it up either by a little or a lot.

His words, Exalted is He:

[57:12] *[Mention] the Day when you will see the believing men and believing women, with their light shining forth before them and to their right...*

He said:

The light of the believer shines forth before him, and he inspires awe in the hearts of the people of conformity (*muwāfiqūn*) and the people of opposition (*mukhālifūn*) alike. The one who conforms reveres him and his standing (*shaʾn*), and the one who opposes holds him in awe and fears him. This is the light which God made for His friends and it does not appear in anyone unless he has submitted and humbled himself to Him. It belongs to the light of faith. Then He described the hypocrites, in their saying to them [the believers]:

[57:13] *...'Wait for us, that we may glean something of your light...'*

so that we can cross the Traverse (*al-Ṣirāṭ*) with you, for we are in darkness.[5] The angels will reply to them, *'Go back and seek light* by means of the intellects (*ʿuqūl*) you used to manage your affairs in your life in the world.' They turn back to the rear, but then God places a wall between themselves and their own intellects, and He veils from them the right choice, so they do not reach the path of guidance. Then when they end up crossing the Traverse they fall into Hell, abiding there forever.

His words, Exalted is He:

[57:15] *So on this day no ransom will be taken from you...*

That is, no ransom will be accepted for your souls.

Ibn Sālim said:

I served Sahl b. ʿAbd Allāh for sixty years and he did not change in terms of his practice of remembrance or anything else.[6] Then on the last day of his life a man recited the verse before him, *So on this day no ransom will be taken from you*, and I saw him tremble and sway to the point where he almost fell down. When he recovered his state of sobriety (*ṣaḥw*), I asked him about what had passed, saying, 'Nothing has happened like this during my time with you.' He

---

4 The *ḥadīth* continues: '...for if you see Him not He surely sees you.' This is part of the Gabriel *ḥadīth* which was discussed above, in IT, p. lviii, n. 265. On the levels of *islām*, *īmān* and *iḥsān*, see also Tustarī's commentary on 14:24.

5 On the Traverse (*al-Ṣirāṭ*) p. 135, n. 1.

6 A similar passage is cited in Sarrāj, *Kitāb al-Lumaʿ*, the beginning of which has the following variation, as translated by Böwering: '(Muḥammad b. Sālim) recalls: "I served Sahl for sixty years, yet I did not see him change while listening (*kāna yasmaʿu*) to (a repetitive formula of God's) commemoration (*dhikr*), to Qurʾān recital or any other recitation..."' See Sarrāj, *Kitāb al-Lumaʿ*, p. 292, Böwering, *Mystical Vision*, p. 72.

replied, 'Yes I know, my dear friend! Indeed I have become weak.' So I asked, 'What is the condition [that denotes] a strong state (*quwwat al-ḥāl*)?' He replied, 'There is no influx [from above] (*wārid*) that comes over him without his absorbing it through his strength. Whoever acts in this way will not be changed by the influxes [of grace] (*wāridāt*) that he receives, however strong they may be.'

He also used to say, 'My state during [ritual] prayer (*ṣalāt*) is the same as that before the commencement of the prayer.' This is because he would keep watch over his heart and keep God, Exalted is He, before his eyes with his innermost secret (*sirr*) before commencing the prayer, and consequently he would stand for prayer with the presence of his heart (*ḥuḍūr qalbihi*) and the collectedness of his spiritual energy (*jamʿ himmatihi*).[7]

His words, Exalted is He:

[57:16] ***Is it not time for those who believe to humble their hearts for the remembrance of God...?***

He said:

Is the time not ripe for them to feel humbled when they listen to the Reminder [the Qurʾān], and witness what is promised and what is warned of, in a contemplative witnessing of the unseen (*mushāhadat al-ghayb*)?

His words, Exalted is He:

[57:16] ***...so their hearts became hardened...***

He said:

That is, through the pursuit of lust.

His words, Exalted is He:

[57:20] ***Know that the life of this world is merely play and diversion...***

He said:

The world (*dunyā*) is a sleeping soul (*nafs nāʾima*), and the Hereafter is a soul awake (*nafs yaqẓāna*).

It was asked, 'What is the way to salvation from it [the life of this world]?' He replied:

The root of this [salvation] is knowledge (*ʿilm*) and its fruit is opposing one's desire (*hawā*) by avoiding what is forbidden (*manāhī*). Then it is the soul's endurance (*mukābadat al-nafs*) in fulfilling the divine commandments, [in a state of] purity (*ṭahāra*) from every kind of defilement (*adnās*). This will bring about ease in worship, and thereafter he will abide in the stations of the worshippers. Then God will let him experience that which His friends (*awliyāʾ*) and elect (*aṣfiyāʾ*) experienced, which is the rank of tasting (*madhāq*).[8]

He [Abū Bakr al-Sijzī] said, 'He [Sahl] then mentioned to us the following':

One day Abraham ﷺ, Friend of the Lord of Mercy, was in the desert on an extremely hot day, and he was afflicted with great thirst. He saw an Abyssinian man tending some camels, so he asked: 'Do you have any water?' He replied, 'O Abraham, what do you prefer: water or milk?' He said: 'Water.'

---

7 Böwering, *Mystical Vision*, p. 72, cites an almost identical passage from Sarrāj's *Kitāb al-Lumaʿ*, except that the explanation takes the form of a comment by Sarrāj: '"My state (*ḥāl*) during ritual prayer (*ṣalāt*) and before entering ritual prayer is one and the same"'. Sarrāj comments, 'He watched over his heart (*qalb*) and kept God before his eyes (*yurāqibu Allāh*) with his inmost being (*sirr*) before he entered the ritual prayer (*ṣalāt*). Then he performed the ritual prayer with the presence of his heart (*ḥuḍūr qalbihi*) and the collectedness of his energy (*jamʿ himmatihi*). He entered into ritual prayer with the intention (*maʿnā*) he had before the prayer, so that his state (*ḥāl*) during prayer was the same as his state before the prayer. Thus, his state before and after the auditive experience (*samāʿ*) was the very same thing.' See Sarrāj, *Kitāb al-Lumaʿ*, p. 293, trans. Böwering, *Mystical Vision*, p. 72.

8 Note that the verbal root *dh-w-q* may be used both for experiencing and tasting, and Sufis often use the term *dhawq* (here *madhāq*) for a mystical experience.

He [Sahl] continued:

> He then struck a rock with his foot upon which water gushed forth. Abraham ﵇ was amazed, so God said to Abraham, through inspiration, 'If that Abyssinian man had asked Me to remove the heavens and earth from existence I would have removed them.' So he [Abraham] asked, 'Why is that, O Lord?' He replied, 'It is because he does not desire anything from the world or the Hereafter except Me.'[9]

ʿĀmir b. ʿAbd al-Qays said,

> I have found the world to comprise four main properties (*khiṣāl*). As for two of these, namely, the [desire for] women and the [desire] to amass wealth, my soul (*nafs*) has renounced them willingly. However, as for the other two, there is no doing without them, though I try to keep them away from me as much as I can; these are sleep and food.[10]

His words, Exalted is He:

[57:23] ***So that you may not grieve over what escapes you (nor exult at what He has given you)...***

He said:

> In this verse there is guidance to the state of contentment in both adversity (*shidda*) and ease (*rakhāʾ*).

His words, Mighty and Majestic is He:

[57:27] ***...But as for monasticism, they invented it...***

He said:

> Monasticism (*rahbāniyya*) is derived from the word *rahba* which means fear. It refers to adherence to [a state of] fear without any earnest desire (*ṭamaʿ*). *We had not prescribed it for them*, that is, We did not demand that they worship Us in that way.[11]

His words, Mighty and Majestic is He:

[57:28] ***...and He will give you a twofold portion of His mercy...***

He said:

> That is, the ⌜secret of⌝ mercy (⌜*sirr*⌝*al-raḥma*),[12] and the essence of mercy (*ʿayn al-raḥma*). [Its] secret is the secret of gnosis (*sirr al-maʿrifa*). [Its] essence is the essence of obedience to God and His Messenger.

9 This is an example of *wasīla*, which Tustarī mentions in his commentary on 32:16. On *wasīla* see also 48:4 and p. 155, n. 4 and p. 196, n. 3.

10 Iṣfahānī, *Ḥilyat al-awliyāʾ*, vol. 2, pp. 90–1; Bayhaqī, *Shuʿab al-īmān*, vol. 5, p. 39; idem., *Kitāb al-Zuhd al-kabīr*, vol. 2, pp. 63–4.

11 Note that above in his commentary on 11:75 and 17:57, Tustarī, like other Sufis, strongly advocates the combining of fear (*khawf*) and hope (*rajāʾ*), while here he is using the word *ṭamaʿ* meaning 'desiring something eagerly' or 'earnestly'. In the Qurʾān the pairs *khawf* and *ṭamaʿ* are paired in 7:56; 13:12; 30:24 and 32:16. See also, p. 93, n. 13.

12 The word *sirr* appears in all three MSS: Z515, f. 111b, F638, f. 52b and F3488, f. 292b.

58 Al-Mujādila

His words, Exalted is He:

[58:10] ***Secret conversations are [the work of] Satan…***

He said:

> A secret conversation (*najwā*) is what the Enemy casts into the natural self (*nafs al-ṭabʿ*), just as the Prophet ﷺ said, 'There is a touch [of madness] (*lamma*) that comes from the angels and a touch [of madness] that comes from Satan.'

His words, Mighty and Majestic is He:

[58:9] ***…but talk secretly in righteousness and mindfulness of God…***[1]

He said:

> [Talk secretly] in remembering God, reciting the Qurʾān, and commanding what is right and forbidding what is wrong.

His words, Exalted is He:

[58:22] ***You will not find a people who believe in God and the Last Day loving those who oppose God and His Messenger, even were they to be their fathers…***

He [Sahl] said:

> No person whose faith is sound enjoys the company of the innovator (*mubtadiʿ*), nor does he comply with him, eat with him, drink with him or keep his company. Rather, he shows him hostility and loathing from himself. On the other hand, whoever fawns over an innovator will have the sweetness of [following] the Prophet's ways (*sunan*) removed from him by God, and whoever shows love for an innovator, seeking honour in this world and some ⌜worldy⌝ gain (*ʿaraḍan* ⌜*minhā*⌝),[2] will find that God humiliates him with that honour and impoverishes him through that wealth. Moreover, whoever jokes with an innovator will find that God removes the light of faith from his heart. As for the one who doubts this, let him try it for himself.

His words, Exalted is He:

[58:22] ***…[For] those, He has inscribed faith upon their hearts and reinforced them with a spirit from Him…***

He said:

> God has inscribed faith upon the hearts of His friends in lines (*suṭūran*). The first line is the profession of God's oneness (*tawḥīd*), the second, gnosis (*maʿrifa*), the third, veracity (*ṣidq*), the fourth, rectitude (*istiqāma*), the fifth, confidence (*thiqa*), the sixth, reliance (*iʿtimād*) and the seventh, trust (*tawakkul*). Furthermore, this writing is the work of God (*fiʿl Allāh*), not the work of the servant (*fiʿl al-ʿabd*). The work of the servant with regard to faith is in the outward aspect of Islam, and what outwardly appears from him, whereas its inner [reality] is the work of God, Exalted is He.

---

1 The first part of this verse reads: *O you who believe, if you do talk in secret, then do not talk in secret sinfully and in disobedience to the Messenger…*

2 lit. 'some gain or share from it [the world]'. All the MSS have *minhā* following the word *ʿaraḍan*: Z515, f. 112a, F638, f. 53b and F3488, f. 292b.

He also said:

The inscription on the heart is the gift of faith (*mawhibat al-īmān*) which God bestows upon them before creating them in loins and wombs. Then He reveals a glimpse of the light in the heart, and then He lifts the veil from it, so that through the blessing of that writing (*barakat al-kitāba*) and the light of faith (*nūr al-īmān*) they can behold things of the unseen (*mughayyabāt*).[3]

And he said:

The life of the spirit (*ḥayāt al-rūḥ*) is in the remembrance [of God] (*dhikr*), the life of remembrance is in the one who remembers (*dhākir*), and the life of the one who remembers is in the One who is remembered (*madhkūr*). God was pleased with them because of the sincerity they devoted towards Him in their works, and they were pleased with Him due to the abundant reward He granted them for their works.

[58:22] ***...They are the confederates of God...***

Confederates (ḥizb) means followers (*shīʿa*). They are the Substitutes (*abdāl*), and higher [in rank still] are the veracious (*ṣiddīqūn*).[4] *Truly it is the party of God who will be successful*, that is, they are the heirs to the secrets of their [the prophets'] sciences and are able to see (*mushrifūn*) the meanings of their beginning ⌜through to⌝ their end (*ibtidāʾihim* ⌜*ilā*⌝ *intihāʾihim*).[5]

3 That is according to MSS F638, f. 54a and F3488, f. 293a, which have *abṣirū bi-barakat al-kitāba*. However, Z515, f. 113b has *abṣirū bi-barakatihi al-kitāba...*, while Sulamī has *ḥattā abṣara* (sing.) *bi-barakat al-kitāb*. Böwering, however, has: 'so that they, by His blessing, may behold the hidden (*mughayyabāt*) writing, and light of faith (*nūr al-īmān*)'. See *Mystical Vision*, p. 220.

4 On the *abdāl* see above p. 89, n. 5.

5 All MSS have the addition of *ilā* between *ibtidāʾihim* and *intihāʾihim*: Z515, f. 113b, F638, f. 54a and F3488, f. 293a. MS Z515 only has *mushrifūn* instead of *mushriqūn*, and that is what we have translated here.

59 Al-Ḥashr

His words, Exalted is He:

[59:2] ***...Their homes were destroyed at their own hands and at the hands of the believers...***[1]

He said:

> That is, they ruined their hearts and invalidated their works by following innovations and abandoning the path of following the prophets. *And the hands of the believers*, that is, despite being side by side with the believers, witnessing them and sitting with them, they were deprived of their blessings. *So take heed, O you who have eyes,* that *God leads astray whomever He will* [35:8], through abandonment (*khidhlān*), *and guides whomever He will* [35:8], through His assistance (*maʿūna*), and you have no influence in the matter.

His words, Exalted is He:

[59:7] ***...And whatever the Messenger gives you, take it, and whatever he forbids you, abstain from it...***

He said:

> The principles of our school are three: consuming what is legitimate; following the example of the Messenger ﷺ in his character (*akhlāq*) and actions (*afʿāl*), and sincerity of intention (*ikhlāṣ al-nīya*) in all works.[2]

He then said:

> Impose upon yourselves three things, for the best of [all] that is in this world and the Hereafter is contained within them: keeping [your self] close to [lit. making it consort with, *suḥbatuhā*] His commandments and prohibitions by adherence to the Sunna; establishing within it the attestation of God's oneness, which [brings about] certainty (*yaqīn*), [and imposing upon it] knowledge (*ʿilm*), through which the spirit attains union (*fīhi ittiṣāl al-rūḥ*). The one who possesses these three [traits] is more knowledgeable about what is in the earth's core than about what is on its surface,[3] and he regards the Hereafter more than he regards this world. Furthermore, he is better known to the angels in heaven than he is on earth to his own family and relatives.

He was asked: 'What is the knowledge through which the spirit attains union?' [He replied]:

> It is the knowledge that God is taking care of it, and being contented [with that].[4]

His words, Exalted is He:

[59:9] ***...They give preference to others over themselves, even if they be in poverty* (khaṣāṣa)...**[5]

---

1 In its outer meaning the verse, and much of this *sūra*, is said to refer to the Jewish tribe of Banū al-Naḍīr, living in Medina, who had originally agreed with the Prophet that they would remain neutral, but later made an alliance with the Meccans and broke their agreements with the Muslims, even attempting to kill the Prophet. Eventually they were forced to leave Medina, some going to Syria and some to Khaybar.

2 Compare with the commentary on Sūra 9:71 above.

3 i.e. more knowledgeable of the inner world than the outer world.

4 Or alternatively the masculine pronoun might here be referring to an unspecified person rather than to the spirit, which we might translate: 'knowing that God is taking care of him...'

5 This verse describes the situation of those who were already resident in Medina, known as the Anṣāriyyūn (helpers), because they assisted and supported the Muslim Emigrants when they came to the city.

He said:

That is, in hunger (*majāʿa*) and poverty (*faqr*). The Arabs say a person is *makhṣūṣ* when he is poor (*faqīr*). Thus they gave preference to the good pleasure of God over their own desires. The act of giving preference to others over yourself (*īthār*) is the testimony (*shāhid*) of love.

The saying has been related from Wuhayb b. al-Ward: 'God, Exalted is He, says, "By My might, greatness and majesty, there is no servant who gives preference to My desire over his own desire, without My decreasing his worries, returning to him what he has lost, removing want from his heart, placing richness before his eyes, and trading in his interest through every trader. And by My might and majesty, there is no servant who gives preference to his own desire over My desire, without My increasing his worries, keeping him at a distance from what he has lost, removing richness from his heart and placing poverty before his eyes, and then I care not in which valley he may perish."'[6]

His words, Exalted is He:

[59:9] *...Whoever is saved from the avarice* (shuḥḥ) *of his own soul — they are the successful.*

He said:

That is, he who is saved from the covetousness (*ḥirṣ*) of his self and its miserliness (*bakhl*) in everything except God and His remembrance,[7] will abide with God, enjoying a good life, a good life.

His words, Exalted is He:

[59:14] *...You [would] suppose them to be together, but their hearts are disunited...*

He said:

The people of truth are united and the people of falsehood are forever divided. And even though they be united in body and agree outwardly, God has said: *You [would] suppose them to be altogether, but their hearts are disunited.*

His words, Exalted is He:

[59:18] *O you who believe, be mindful of God, and let every soul consider what it has sent ahead for tomorrow...*

He said:

God, Exalted is He, asks the servant concerning [these three]: that which he owes to his self (*ḥaqq nafsihi*), that which he owes to the knowledge (*ʿilm*) that is between him and his Lord, and that which he owes to the intellect (*ʿaql*). Let whoever has the ability fulfil what he owes to his self and what he owes to the knowledge which is between him and his Lord, by considering well the outcome of his affairs.

It was related of Ḥasan that he said, 'When a son of Adam [i.e. a human being] dies, the children of Adam [the other human beings] ask, 'What has he left behind?' But the angels ask, 'What has he sent ahead?'[8]

His words:

[59:19] *And do not be like those who forget God...*

while committing sins, ...*so that He makes them forget*. God [makes them forget] to apologise (*iʿtidhār*) and seek repentance (*tawba*).

He said:

Any servant who sins and does not repent, [will find] that sin leading him on to another sin, which will cause him to forget the former sin. On the other hand, any servant who does a good

---

6 Tirmidhī, *Nawādir al-uṣūl*, vol. 4, p. 25–6; Ibn al-Jawzī, *Ṣifat al-ṣafwa*, p. 220; Iṣfahānī, *Ḥilyat al-awliyāʾ*, vol. 8, p. 147.

7 Being miserly in relation to God may mean being reluctant to give of one's time, energy, wealth, etc. to other than God and His remembrance, and this is the only acceptable form of miserliness.

8 That is, they are asking what good or bad deeds he has put in store for himself in the Hereafter.

deed [will find] that leading him to another good deed, upon which his intellect will perceive the deficiency of the former good deed, so that he may repent for the deficiency in his past good deeds, even if they were pure and sound.

His words, Exalted is He:

[59:22] *(He is)...Knower of the unseen and the visible...*

He said:

The *unseen* (ghayb) is that which is secret (*sirr*) and the *visible* (shahāda) is that which is open [to all] (*ʿalāniyya*). He also said, Exalted is He: *(He is)...Knower of the unseen and the visible* [meaning]: He is the One who has full knowledge of this world and the Hereafter.

But God, Glorified and Exalted is He, knows best.

60 Al-Mumtaḥana

His words, Exalted is He:

[60:1] ***O you who believe, do not take My enemy and your enemy as friends…***

He said:

God, Exalted is He, has warned the believers not to take as friends other than those whom God and His Messenger have befriended. Indeed, God, Exalted is He, is not [even] pleased ⌜when one who is His friend⌝[1] depends upon [another who is] His friend, so how will it be when he depends on [one who is] His enemy? Furthermore, a person who engages his heart in that which does not concern him relating to his Hereafter gains an enemy, so how will it be concerning some other [affair that does not concern him]?

And a person who covets (*ṭamaʿa*) the Hereafter along with a desire for something lawful (*ḥalāl*) of this world is deluded (*makhdūʿ*), so how will it be for someone who desires something unlawful (*ḥarām*)?

Anyone's act that is not done in opposition (*mukhālafa*),[2] or with endurance (*mukābada*), or out of preferring others over oneself (*īthār*), will be an act of ostentation (*riyāʾ*).

He was asked the meaning of this. He replied:

Opposition is the abandonment of what is forbidden, and for sure, abandoning a particle of what God has forbidden is more meritorious than worshipping God, Exalted is He, for your whole life. To show endurance is to fulfil God's commandments, while to prefer others over oneself is to prefer God above all that is other than Him.

Furthermore, through opposition they were dispossessed of their selves, but through endurance they were dispossessed of their desires, so that their passions (*shahawāt*) were expressed through acts of obedience (*ṭāʿāt*); and by giving preference to others over themselves (*īthār*), they attained His love and good pleasure.

His words, Exalted is He:

[60:7] ***…and God is Forgiving, Merciful.***

He said:

He is Forgiving of your past sins through [accepting your] repentance (*tawba*), and Merciful, because He protects you from falling into the same kind of transgression during what remains of your life.

His words, Exalted is He:

[60:10] ***…And do not hold on to the [conjugal] ties of disbelieving women…***

1 All MSS (Z515, f. 115a, F638, f. 54b and F3488, f. 294b) have the addition of *man wāliya'Llāh*.

2 Opposition here has the positive meaning of opposing the lower self (*nafs*) as will be seen in Tustarī's explanation below. It will be recalled that in some contexts *mukhālafa* was used with a negative meaning, often when placed in contradistinction to conformity (*muwāfaqa*). See, for example, the commentary on 28:24.

He said:

> Do not agree with the people of innovations concerning anything which issues from their whims (*ahwāʾ*) or opinions (*ārāʾ*).[3]

3 Note the association which Tustarī has made between innovation (*bidʿa*) and people's whims or desires (*ahwāʾ*). This is also emphasised elsewhere in Tustarī's *Tafsīr*, for example in his commentary on 4:171 and 6:159.

61 Al-Ṣaff

His words, Exalted is He:

[61:2] ***You who believe, why do you say [you will do] what you do not do?***

[Sahl] said:

> Truly God warns His servants about making claims that they do not substantiate. Such claims require of [the servant] that from this day on he fulfil one of the rights of God, which is that he becomes free of (*barāʾa*), and repents from (*tawba*), every sin that he has committed.
>
> [The one who makes claims] says 'I will act tomorrow', but there is no one who makes a claim without overlooking the right of God from two points of view: both outwardly and inwardly. The one who makes claims (*muddaʿī*) has no fear; the one who has no fear is not safe (*āmin*); and the one who is not safe is one who has not acquainted himself with the recompense (*jazāʾ*).

He also said:

> Those who desire the Hereafter are many. However, there are but two [kinds of] servant whose sufficiency (*kifāya*) God takes care of: [one is] the simple servant who is nonetheless sincere in his quest, puts his trust in God (*mutawakkil*), and is true to Him; his Master will suffice him and take care of all of his affairs. The other is the servant who is knowledgeable about God, His days,[1] His commandments and His prohibitions; God will suffice him with all he needs in this world and, when he passes on to the Hereafter, ⌜he will have ease (*istirāḥa*)⌝.[2] God will pay no attention to any other than these two [kinds of servant], because the others claimed what they did not have.

Ibn ʿAyniyya said concerning this verse:

> Why do you speak about a matter which does not concern you, for you do not know whether you will do that or not.

His words, Exalted is He:

[61:8] ***They desire to extinguish the light of God with their mouths…***

> This means: with their tongues they denied the proof (*ḥujja*) of the Prophet ﷺ that appeared to them, and with their souls they turned away from it. But God bound (*qayyada*) some souls[3] to accept him, namely, those whom He brought into existence under the decree of eternal bliss, and He adorned some hearts with the lights of His gnosis (*maʿrifa*), and the secrets of its light by virtue of firm belief (*taṣdīq*). So they spent freely of their whole being (*muhaj*) and their possessions for Him, like al-Ṣiddīq and al-Fārūq, and the other honourable Companions, ﵃.[4]

---

1 On *ayyām Allāh* see above p. 128, n. 1.

2 The word *istirāḥa* appears after *idhā ṣāra ilāʾl-ākhira* in only MS F638, f. 55a. However, it makes more sense to include it, since firstly, Tustarī is contrasting this servant's situation in this world with his situation in the Hereafter, and secondly because Tustarī is making the point in general that God has nothing to do with the false claimants, not specifically in the Hereafter.

3 Through His pre-eternal decree — Böwering translates this as 'He foreordained some…'

4 Al-Ṣiddīq ('the Veracious') is the honorary title which was conferred on Abū Bakr, the first caliph, and al-Fārūq ('the one who distinguishes truth from falsehood') is an honorary title by which ʿUmar b. ʿAbd al-ʿAzīz, the second caliph of Islam, is known.

His words, Exalted is He:

[61:14] ***You who believe, be helpers of God…***

He said:

> That is, by accepting [that which comes] from Him, and heeding (*istimāʿ*) Him, and by obeying Him in what He has commanded you to do, and in what He has forbidden you from doing. But God, Glorified and Exalted is He, knows best.

62 Al-Jumuʿa

His words, Exalted is He:

[62:2] ***It is He who sent to the unlettered [folk] a messenger from among them…***

He said:

> *The unlettered* are those who believed in Muḥammad ﷺ and were connected to him through following (*ittibāʿ*) him and emulating (*iqtidāʾ*) him.[1] Whoever does not emulate him is not of his nation.

His words, Exalted is He:

[62:3] ***And [to] others from among them who have not yet joined them…***

> That is, those who came after him who believed in him and followed him, God will join with the first [generation of believers].

His words, Exalted is He:

[62:11] ***But when they see some opportunity for business or some amusement, they scatter off towards it…***

He said:

> God has informed [us] of the despicable nature and base aspiration of the one who is diverted from his Lord by something of this world or the Hereafter. For God made the way open for him and allowed him to call on Him in intimacy (*munājāt*), but he became preoccupied with that which is transient, and had no knowledge of the One who abides and will abide forever.

His words, Exalted is He:

[62:11] ***…Say, 'That which is with God is better than any amusement or commerce…'***

He said:

> By this is meant: the abundant gifts and lasting delight which God has kept in reserve for you in the Hereafter is better than that which He gives you of this world.

1 The term 'unlettered people' (*ummiyūn*) denotes a nation or community who had not previously had a revealed scripture of their own. *Ummī* can also mean 'he who has no [prior] knowledge of the scriptures', hence the term *ummī*, in relation to the Prophet Muḥammad, does not necessarily mean illiterate in the modern sense of that word.

63 Al-Munāfiqūn

His words, Exalted is He:

[63:1] ***...and God bears witness that the hypocrites truly are liars.***

He said:

> [This was] because they affirmed with their tongues what their hearts did not acknowledge. This is why He named them hypocrites. Whoever knows [the truth] with his heart and affirms it with his tongue, yet without any excuse does not perform with his bodily members (*bi-arkānihi*) that which God has made compulsory for him, is like Iblīs, may God curse him, who knew it [the truth] and affirmed it, but did not act upon His commandments.

He further said:

> Hypocrisy (*nifāq*) is of two kinds: [one is] a belief (*ʿaqd*) held in the heart which is contradicted outwardly on the tongue, just as He has said, Exalted is He: *They say with their tongues what is not in their hearts* [48:11]; the other is the hypocrisy of the natural self (*nafs al-ṭabʿ*) towards the person to whom it belongs, and this was referred to by the Prophet ﷺ when he said, 'The hidden association [idolatry] (*shirk*)[1] in my community is more hidden than the crawling of an ant across a boulder on a dark night.'[2]

His words, Exalted is He:

[63:9] ***O you who believe, do not let your wealth and your children distract you...***

> from performing your religious duties on time. For whoever is distracted from the remembrance of God or His service (*khidma*) by some phenomenon, or something for the sake of his lust (*shayʾan li-shahwatihi*),[3] [if then] he experiences [thereby] exultation (*nashāṭ*) in his devotions, he is deluded (*makhdūʿ*), save in [those religious duties] which God, Mighty and Majestic is He, accepts.
>
> It has been related that once [when he was ailing] Salmān was visited by Saʿd b. Abī Waqqāṣ. Salmān wept, so Saʿd asked him, 'What could be making you weep, O Abū ʿAbd Allāh, when our Master the Messenger of God ﷺ was content with you when he died, and you will meet your companions again and will drink from his pool?'[4] Salmān said, 'I do not weep out of fear of death or because of an avid attachment to the world, but rather because the Messenger of God ﷺ enjoined on us a commitment and said: "Let the provision that one of you takes from this world be like the victuals a rider [traveller] (*rākib*) takes [for his journey]."[5] I have all these cushions around me, but all the Prophet ﷺ had around him was his blanket, his washing vessel and a bowl for food.' Saʿd said: 'O Abū ʿAbd Allāh! Enjoin on us a pledge to which we can

---

1 That is, associating others with God, or ascribing partners to God.

2 Nīsābūrī, *al-Mustadrak*, vol. 2, p. 319; Tirmidhī, *Nawādir al-uṣūl*, vol. 4, p. 147; Mundhirī, *al-Targhīb*, vol. 4, p. 16.

3 That is, following MS F638, f. 55b, which has *aw shayʾan*, while the published edition has *shayʾan*. MSS Z515, f. 116b and F3488, f. 266b have *aw sababan*.

4 According to several *aḥadīth*, the Pool (*ḥawḍ*) is one of the blessings promised by God to the Prophet for his nation. In the section on the Pool in the *Kitāb Dhikr al-mawt* of Ghazālī's *Iḥyāʾ ʿulūm al-dīn*, he writes 'It is our hope that God (Exalted is He!) will grant us to know of it in this world and to taste it in the next, for one of its qualities is that whoever drinks of it shall never thirst again.' See trans. Winter, pp. 217–9, whence this extract was taken.

5 Ibn Māja, *Sunan*, vol. 2, p. 1374; Nīsābūrī, *al-Mustadrak*, vol. 4, p. 353.

> commit ourselves after you have gone.' He said: 'O Saʿd! Remember God, Exalted is He, when you have a concern that worries you, when you are making a judgement and when you are about to make an oath.'[6]

But God, Exalted is He, knows best what is correct.

6 Bayhaqī, *Shuʿab al-īmān*, vol. 7, pp. 305–6; Mundhirī, *al-Targhīb*, vol. 4, pp. 79, 112.

64 Al-Taghābun

His words, Exalted is He:

[64:2] ***...God is Seer* (baṣīr) *of what you do.***

⌜He said:

> ⌜He is Seeing (*baṣīr*)⌝[1] if the act is compatible with (*wāfaqa*) [a person's] nature (*ṭabʿ*) and disposition (*khilqa*).

His words, Exalted is He:

[64:14] ***O you who believe! Indeed among your spouses and your children are enemies to you, so beware of them...***

He said:

> Those among your spouses and children who induce you to the amassing of [the goods of this] world and reliance on them (*rukūn ilayhā*) are enemies to you. However, the one who prompts you to give of it and spend it [in a good cause], and guides you to be satisfied (*qanāʿa*), and to put your trust in God (*tawakkul*) is not an enemy to you.
>
> The saying is related from Ḥasan: 'O son of Adam! Do not be beguiled by the ferocious beasts around you, namely, your son, your wife, your relatives and your servant. As for your son, he is like a lion in his ferocity and force, and will certainly contend with you concerning what you possess. As for your wife, she is like a bitch with her growling and wagging of her tail, sometimes she is growling and at other times she is wagging her tail.[2] As for your relatives, by God, a *dirham* that falls to their share of your inheritance is dearer to them than your freeing of a slave. As for your servant, he is like a fox in trickery and theft. I say to you, son of Adam, fear God, and don't break your back for their benefit, for you only have a few steps till you reach your next home, which is four cubits by two cubits.[3] Once they have put you there, they will disperse from you, then carry out their intentions, beat the drums [in celebration], and break into guffaws of laughter, while you are being taken to account (*muḥāsab*)[4] for what is left in their hands.'

His words, Exalted is He:

[64:15] ***Your possessions and your children are only a test [for you]...***

He said:

> If God gives you wealth, you busy yourselves with how to keep it, and if He does not give you wealth, you busy yourselves with seeking after it. So when will you free yourself for Him?

---

1 Added on the basis of MS F638, f. 55b. In the margin there is an addition of two words that are supposed to follow *wāfaqa*, but we have not been able to decipher them. Sulamī has the same as has been translated above.

2 This misogynistic remark has to be seen in the context of the rest of the rhetoric of this statement, which is equally hyperbolic. Otherwise this would present a negative view indeed of the ties of kinship!

3 i.e. your grave.

4 The MSS all have *muḥāsab/muḥāsib*: Z515, f. 117a, F638, f. 56a and F3488, f. 297b, whereas the published edition has *tuḥāsabu*. The meaning, however, comes to the same.

65 Al-Ṭalāq

His words, Exalted is He:

[65:2] ***...By this is admonished whoever believes in God and the Last Day...***

He said:

> Only a believer accepts admonition. Moreover, an admonition only issues from a sound heart (*qalb salīm*) that is free of rancour (*ghill*), hatred (*ḥiqd*), and envy (*ḥasad*), and in which there is no ⸢self⸣ interest (*ḥaẓẓ* ⸢*li-nafsihi*⸣).[1]

His words, Exalted is He:

[65:2, 3] ***...God, He will make a way out* (makhraj) *for whoever is mindful of Him,* ❁ *and He will provide for him whence he never expected...***

He said:

> Mindfulness of God (*taqwā*) means disclaiming all power (*ḥawl*) and strength (*quwwa*) and all means (*asbāb*) other than [God]. By resorting to Him (*rujūʿ ilayhi*), [the servant] will find that God provides for him the means of acquitting himself of that which He has given him to do, without his circumventing it. [This He does by extending to him] His aid (*maʿūna*) and protection (*ʿiṣma*). Trust in God (*tawakkul*) is not admissible from anyone except those who are mindful of God, and mindfulness of God is not admissible except with trust in God.[2] For God, Exalted is He, said: *and He will provide for him whence he never expected.*

His words, Exalted is He:

[65:3] ***...And whoever puts his trust in God, He will suffice him...***

He said:

> That is, whoever entrusts his affairs to his Lord, will truly find that God, Exalted is He, suffices him in all that is necessary for him in both abodes.[3]

Abū al Ḥasan ʿUmar b. Wāṣil al-ʿAnbarī reported that he heard Sahl say:

> I entered the desert seventeen times without any provision (*zād*) in the way of food and drink, or a money bag, or a drinking vessel or a staff, and whenever I needed something to eat, I would find it ready prepared for me. On one occasion as I was approaching the desert, a man gave me two genuine dirhams, so I put them in my pocket and proceeded on my way. I had walked for a while but did not find anything so I became weak. I started to say to myself, 'What have you done that has resulted in that which you are accustomed to being withheld from you?' Then I heard a voice from the air (*min al-hawā*) say, 'Cast out what is in your pocket and what is in the unseen will come to you', upon which I remembered that I had those two dirhams in my pocket, so I took them out and threw them away. I had not walked for long before I saw before me two pieces of bread spread with honey between them, [as fresh] as if they had just that moment come out of the oven. So from then on I returned to my former state [of *tawakkul*].

---

1 lit. in which he has no share for himself. The addition of *li-nafsihi* is made on the basis of all three MSS: Z515, f. 117b, F638, f. 56a and F3488, f. 297b.

2 This statement was also made in Tustarī's comment on Sūrat al-Nisāʾ verse 81 above. The saying is also to be found in Iṣfahānī, *Ḥilyat al-awliyāʾ*, vol. 10, p. 192.

3 i.e. in this world and the next. On *tawakkul*, see above Tustarī's commentary on 4:81. See also IT, pp. lv–lvi.

66 Al-Taḥrīm

His words, Exalted is He:

[66:6] ***O you who believe! Guard yourselves and your families against a Fire...***

He said:

That is, by obeying God and following the ways of the Prophet ﷺ (*sunan*).

His words, Exalted is He:

[66:8] ***O you who believe! Turn to God in sincere repentance...***

He said:

Sincere repentance (*tawba naṣūḥ*) means that a person does not return [to sin], for he has become one of the company of lovers (*aḥibba*), and the lover does not embark upon anything which the Beloved dislikes.

And he said:

The mark of the one who is [truly] repentant (*tāʾib*) is that there is not a place on earth, nor a place under the sky, where he is not solely attached to the Throne and to the Owner of the Throne till the time when he leaves this world.[1] In these times, I do not know of anyone not requiring repentance,[2] for the Angel of Death will not visit any one of us without his saying [to the angel], 'Just allow me to do such-and-such a thing. Just let me do so-and-so. Let me breathe for just an hour more.'[3]

Then he said:

As for the one who is sincerely repentant (*tāʾib mukhliṣ*), even though it might be for only an hour, or even for one breath before his death, it will be said [to him], 'How quickly you have come forth with true [sincere repentance] (*ṣaḥīḥan*)! [Accordingly] we have come to you in the manner that you have come.'

His words:

[66:8] ***...on a day when God will not let the Prophet down...***

He said:

He will not let him down concerning his nation, and will not refuse his intercession. Indeed God, Exalted is He, addressed the Prophet ﷺ through inspiration saying, 'If you so wish I can place the affairs of your nation (*amr ummatik*) in your charge.' He replied, 'O my Lord, You are better for them than me.' So God, Exalted is He, said, 'Then I will not let you down concerning them.'[4]

His words, Mighty and Majestic is He:

[66:8] ***...They will say, 'Our Lord! Perfect our light for us...'***

---

1 lit. 'there is not a place where the earth bears him, nor a place where the sky shades him...' All the MSS (Z515, f. 118a, F638, f. 55b and F3488, f. 293b) have *taḥmilahu* instead of *tuqillahu* and *innamā* instead of *illā* in the published edition.

2 lit. 'I do not know that there should be anything less than repentance'.

3 In other words, asking the Angel of Death to allow us more time to make amends for our shortcomings.

4 This saying appears in Makkī, *Qūt al-qulūb*, vol. 1, p. 376, where God says to the Prophet ﷺ, 'If you so wish I can place the calling to account (*ḥisāb*) of your nation in your charge...'

He said:

> The state of utter neediness (*iftiqār*) does not leave the believers, either in this life or the next. When they are in Paradise they are in greater need for Him even though they are in the abode of honour, security and richness, because of their yearning for the encounter (*liqāʾ*) with Him. They say: *'Our Lord! Perfect our light for us*, and grant us an encounter with You.' This is because He is the Illuminator of [all] lights (*munawwir al-anwār*), and He is the Goal of every seeker.

67 Al-Mulk

His words, Exalted is He:

[67:1] ***Blessed be He in whose hand is all sovereignty…***

He said:

> That is, Exalted and Magnified is He above having likenesses, sons and rivals. *He in whose hand is all sovereignty* turns it over through His power (*ḥawl*) and strength (*quwwa*), granting it to whomever He will and removing it from whomever He will, and He is All-Powerful (*al-Qādir*) over it.

His words, Exalted is He:

[67:1, 2] ***…and He has power over all things,*** ❁ ***He who created death and life…***

He said:

> Death in this world is in disobedience, and life in the Hereafter is in obedience. It was for this reason that God, Exalted is He, addressed Moses ﷺ saying, 'O Moses, truly the first of my creatures to die was Iblīs, may God's curse be on him, because he disobeyed Me, and I count the one who disobeys Me as being from among the dead.'

Then he said:

> Death was created in the form of a handsome ram (*kabsh amlaḥ*). Whatever it passes by and [merely] catches a whiff of it, lives. It has been related in a tradition that the people of Paradise will fear death but the people of Hell will wish for death. It will be brought in the form of a handsome ram. Then it will be said, 'This is death, so behold what God is going to do with it.' Then it will be turned on its side and slaughtered. Thereupon God, Exalted is He, will [re]make it in the form of a horse which will be set free to graze in Paradise. Whoever among the inhabitants of Paradise sees it will enjoy its company, without realising that it is death.[1]

His words, Exalted is He:

[67:2] ***…that He may try you [to see] which of you is best in conduct…***

He said:

> That is, I keep him from error and I purify him. If he is correct [in conduct] but not sincere, he will not be accepted; ⌜while if he is sincere, but not correct [in conduct] he will not be accepted either⌝.[2] [He will not be accepted] until he is at the same time correct and sincere [in his conduct]. The one who is sincere (*khāliṣ*) is he who [lives] for God, Exalted is He, with the full intention (*irāda*) of his heart, while the one who is correct (*ṣawāb*) is he who is on the path of the Sunna and [lives] in accordance with the Book.

On another occasion he [Sahl] said:

> *that He may try you [to see] which of you is best in conduct*, that is, in putting your trust in Us, being satisfied with Us and journeying [to Us] after the renunciation of this world. Truly,

1 i.e. the people of Paradise would fear death if they were aware of it. But since death has been turned into a freely grazing horse, they do not recognise it. The tradition is listed in Mundhirī, *al-Targhīb*, vol. 4, pp. 316–8.

2 Added on the basis of all three MSS: Z515, f. 119a, F638, f. 56b, F3488, f. 299b.

mindfulness of God (*taqwā*) and certainty (*yaqīn*) may be compared to the two scales of a balance, while trust (*tawakkul*) is the pointer, by which it indicates any increase or decrease.[3]

Then it was asked of him : 'What is trust?'

He replied:

It is to flee from trust, that is, from claiming to have trust.[4]

His words, Exalted is He:

[67:2] ***...And He is the Mighty, the Forgiving.***

He said:

This means that He is the Unassailable (*al-Manīʿ*) in His rule, the Wise (*al-Ḥakīm*) in His management of His creation, and the Forgiving (*al-Ghafūr*) with regard to the deficiency and faults which are apparent in His servants' acts of obedience.

His words, Exalted is He:

[67:12] ***Assuredly those who fear their Lord in secret...***

That is, they fear their Lord in their innermost secret (*sirr*), and they keep their innermost secret pure from other than Him.

His words, Exalted is He:

[67:14] ***Would He who has created not know...?***

Does the One who created the heart not know what He deposited within it, [whether it be] the attestation of His oneness (*tawḥīd*) or denial (*juḥūd*). *He is the Subtle*, in His knowledge of the secrets concealed within the core of hearts (*lubb al-qulūb*), just as the Prophet ﷺ said, 'Truly within hearts there is a concealed secret (*sirr maknūn*) pertaining to knowledge, which belongs to God, Exalted is He'; *the Aware* — He informs you of what is [hidden for] you in the unseen (*fī ghaybik*).

His words, Exalted is He:

[67:15] ***It is He who has made the earth tractable for you...***

He said:

God, Exalted is He, created the souls (*anfūs*) in a humble state. Whoever abases (*adhalla*) his self (*nafs*) by opposing it, actually saves it from temptations, tribulations and trials. However, whoever debases (*adhalla*) his self and follows it, will be brought to humiliation and destroyed by it.

His words, Mighty and Majestic is He:

[67:22] ***Is he who walks prone upon his face, more rightly guided...?***

He said:

Is he who is bent over [in pursuit] of the desire of his lower self, due to its natural disposition, and who is without guidance from his Lord, better guided?

[67:22] ***...or one who walks upright on a straight way?***

He said:

By which is meant: or one who follows the laws of Islam, and emulates the prophets, ⌜adhering to it [the straight path] (*muqīman ʿalayhi*)⌝?[5] But God, Glorified and Exalted is He, knows best.

---

3 The saying is cited in Makkī, *Qūt al-qulūb*, vol. 2, p. 4.

4 Interestingly, the first part of this statement is cited in Makkī, *Qūt al-qulūb*, vol. 2, p. 9, where it is not attributed to Tustarī. In explaining the need to 'flee from *tawakkul*', Makkī mentions firstly the necessary abandoning of any dependence on the station of *tawakkul*, and secondly, that looking upon one's *tawakkul* is a flaw in that *tawakkul*, for the person should continuously have their attention upon the Guardian (*al-Wakīl*) alone. This complies with several of Tustarī's statements concerning the need not to feel complacent about one's state.

5 Added on the basis of all three MSS: Z515, f. 119b, F638, f. 57a and F3488, f. 300a.

68 Al-Qalam (or Nūn)[1]

His words, Exalted is He:

[68:1] ***Nūn. By the Pen, and by what they inscribe!***

He said:

> *'Al-Nūn'* is one of the names of God, Exalted is He, for if the opening letters of the *sūras*, *Alif Lām Rā*, *Ḥā Mīm* and *Nūn*, are joined together they make up the name *al-Raḥmān*.[2]
>
> Ibn ʿAbbās said: '*Al-Nūn* is the ink-well (*dawāt*) from which the Reminder (*dhikr*) [the Qurʾān] was written, and the Pen is that with which the Wise Reminder was written.'
>
> *By what they inscribe* — ⌜the Reminder which is written on the Preserved Tablet concerning the [divinely decreed] wretchedness (*shaqāwa*) or felicity (*saʿāda*) [of human beings].
>
> Ibn ʿAbbās has said in another report, '*Nūn* is the fish upon which rest the worlds (*arḍūn*),⌝[3] *what they inscribe* is the deeds of the children of Adam which the recording angels have written down.'[4]

ʿUmar b. Wāṣil said:

> *By what they inscribe* means: By the writing (*kitāba*) [i.e. the scripture] which God has undertaken [to provide] for His servants, which contains benefits (*manāfiʿ*) for people, and things that are in the best interests (*maṣāliḥ*) of His servants and their lands.

His words, Exalted is He:

[68:3] ***and assuredly you will have an unfailing reward,***

He said:

> That is, defined, apportioned (*maḥdūd maqṭūʿ*) and calculated (*maḥsūb*) for you.

His words, Exalted is He:

[68:4] ***and assuredly you possess a magnificent character.***[5]

He said:

> You have taken on the propriety taught by the Qurʾān (*taʾaddabta bi-adab al-Qurʾān*), and have not exceeded its bounds, which are in His words, Exalted is He: *Indeed God enjoins justice and virtue…* to the end of the verse [16:90],[6] and also in His words, *It was by the mercy of God that you were lenient with them* [3:159].

Then he said:

> Truly anger (*ghaḍab*) and harshness (*ḥidda*) come from the servant's dependence on his own strength (*quwwa*). However, when he gives up relying on his own strength, weakness will take

1 MS Z515 carries the former title, while MSS F638 and F3488 carry the latter title.

2 See the commentary on the *Basmala* [1:1], above.

3 According to cosmological legend, the earth (or as here, earths, *arḍūn*) rest on the back of a fish, or on the horns of an ox, which, in turn, rests on the back of a fish. See Anton M. Heinen, *Islamic Cosmology. A Study of as-Suyūṭī's al-Hayʾa al-samīya fī'l-hayʾa al-sunnīya* (Beirut/Wiesbaden, 1982), pp. 85–6.

4 The section between brackets has been added on the basis of all three MSS: Z515, f. 119b, F638, f. 57a and F3488, f. 300a.

5 These words are addressed to the Prophet.

6 The rest of the verse reads: …*and giving to kinsfolk, and He forbids lewdness, abomination and aggression. He admonished you so that you might remember.*

up residence in his soul, and this will generate mercy (*raḥma*) and benevolence (*luṭf*) from him, which is to take on the characteristics of the Lord, may His majesty be magnified.

God, Exalted is He, addressed David ﷺ through inspiration, saying, 'Take on My characteristics, for verily I am the Forbearing (*al-Ṣabūr*).' Whoever is given good character (*khulq ḥasan*) has been given the greatest station (*aʿẓam al-maqāmāt*), for all other stations are connected to the common folk (*ʿāmma*), whereas good character is connected with the [divine] attributes (*ṣifāt*) and qualities (*nuʿūt*).[7]

Sahl was asked one day about charismatic gifts (*karāmāt*) and he said:

What are charismatic gifts (*karāmāt*)? Truly charismatic gifts are phenomena which will not last beyond their designated time. The greatest charismatic gift, however, is to change a blameworthy trait within your character to a praiseworthy one.

His words, Exalted is He:

[68:44] ***So leave Me [to deal with] whoever denies this discourse...***

He said:

That is, leave him in My charge, for I will suffice you regarding his affair, so do not let your heart become preoccupied with him.

His words, Exalted is He:

[68:44] ***...We shall draw them on by degrees whence they do not know.***

He said:

We shall leave them with their heads bowed over, diverted in their preoccupation with it [the world] from the duties that they should perform for Us, such that they forget to show gratitude towards Us, so We shall seize them *whence they do not know*.[8]

His words, Mighty and Majestic is He:

[68:49] ***Had it not been for a grace from his Lord that reached him...***[9]

He said:

That is, if God had not kept for him his previous good deeds, which were a result of His preeternal election, and saved him, and had not the ⸢grace from his Lord (*niʿma min rabbihi*)⸣[10] reached him, ...*he would surely have been cast out onto a barren [shore], while he was blameworthy*. The barren shore (*ʿarāʾ*) is the plain [lit. earth, *ʿarḍ*] of the Resurrection, for nothing is cultivated or grown there. He had committed no other sin save that of busying his heart with planning (*tadbīr*) that which was not for him to plan, just as Adam ﷺ had done [before him].[11]

7 There is possibly an allusion here to the well-known *ḥadīth* of the Prophet, 'Take on the characteristics of God' (*takhallaqū bi-akhlāq Allāh*), listed in ʿAlī b. Muḥammad al-Jurjānī, *al-Taʿrīfāt* (Beirut, 1987), p. 216, and in ʿAbd al-Raʾūf al-Munāwī, *al-Tawqīf ʿalā muhimmāt al-taʿārīf* (Beirut and Damascus, 1990), p. 564.

8 Tustarī is here using a conventional form of interpretation where the commentator inserts a meaning that he considers to be implied without its actually having been mentioned in the verse.

9 This verse and the one that follows briefly allude to the story Jonah, which is narrated in a slightly extended form in 37:139–48. Jonah is also referred to in 10:98, which is why that *sūra* is named after him.

10 Added on the basis of MS F638, f. 57b. MSS Z515, f. 120a and F3488, f. 30a have *tadārakahu bi'l-ʿamal*, which is probably incorrect.

11 For the role of Adam's devising, planning or managing in his expulsion from Paradise see above Tustarī's commentary on 2:30 where Jonah's resorting to his own *tadbīr* is also mentioned.

69 Al-Ḥāqqa

His words, Exalted is He:

[69:1, 2] ***The sure Reality! ❁ What is the Reality?***

He said:

> Indeed, God, Exalted is He, has magnified the circumstances of the Day of Resurrection and the severity (*shidda*) of it by the inclusion of the letter *Hāʾ* in it [the word *al-ḥāqqa*].[1] Its meaning is: the Day when each person will encounter his good and bad deeds.

ʿUmar b. Wāṣil said:

> Its meaning is that on that day each group (*ṭāʾifa*) will be given its just reward (*yaḥiqqu*) for its works.

His words, Mighty and Majestic is He:

[69:17] ***…And on that Day eight of them will bear the throne of your Lord above them.***

He said:

> This means eight regiments of cherubim whose number no one knows except God. The Prophet ﷺ said, 'Indeed, God has allowed me to speak about one of the angels among the Throne Bearers. His feet are on the lowest earth, and upon his head rests the Throne. Between the lobes of his ears and his shoulders is the distance that a bird covers in flight during seven hundred years. This angel says, "Glory to God wherever I may be."'[2]

His words, Exalted is He:

[69:18] ***On that Day, you will be exposed and no hidden thing of yours will remain hidden.***

He said:

> You will be presented before God, Mighty and Majestic is He, and He will call you to account for your deeds, and not one of your deeds will be hidden from Him. That is all known [to Him], calculated for you in His prior knowledge. And He will ask [the servant] about all of it, saying to him, 'Did you not know about the hours [of the events of the Last Day] for My sake? Were you not placed in a position of [high standing] in assemblies [among people] for My sake? Did you not ask Me to marry you to such and such a bondswoman of Mine who was better than you and We married you to her? This is His questioning concerning the blessings He has bestowed upon you. So, how about His interrogation concerning the acts of transgression against Him?
>
> The saying has been related from ʿUtba al-Ghulām, 'Truly, the believing servant will be kept standing before God, Exalted is He, a hundred years for one sin.'

His words, Exalted is He:

[69:19] ***As for him who is given his book in his right hand, he will say, 'Here, read my book!***[3]

---

1 'Hāʾ 'rather than 'ḥā'. It is thus in all the MSS. This is probably a reference to the *tāʾ marbūṭa*. Since the word is originally *al-ḥāqq*, the addition of the 'hā' (i.e. the *tāʾ marbūṭa*) may have been in order to indicate the severity of the Day of Resurrection, thus it would read *ḥāqqah* were we to mark the *tāʾ marbūṭa*.

2 Haythamī, *Majmaʿ al-zawāʾid*, vol. 1, p. 80; Ṭabarānī, *al-Muʿjam al-awsaṭ*, vol. 2, p. 199 and vol. 6, p. 314.

3 What is meant is the book in which all his deeds are recorded. If it is given to the person in their right hand, it is full of good deeds, but if it is given in their left, it is full of bad ones.

That is, he says, 'Look here! Read my book, which is full of different kinds of acts of obedience.' And He says to them:

[69:24] ***'Eat and drink in enjoyment [as a reward] for what you did formerly in days gone by.'***

This is referring to fasting during the month of Ramadan and during the days of the full moon. It has been mentioned in a *ḥadīth* that on the Day of Reckoning, tables spread with food will be placed before those believers who devoted themselves to fasting (*ṣawwām*), from which they will eat. [Others] will say, 'O Lord, people are standing for the Reckoning who are not eating.' They will be told, '[These people] used to fast at length during the life of the world, while you ate your fill, and they would stay up at night in prayer while you took your rest.'

[69:25] ***But as for him who is given his book in his left hand, he will say, 'Would that I had not been given my book.'***

That is, because of the foul deeds (*aʿmāl khabītha*) and disbelief (*kufr*) contained within it, he wishes that he had never been resurrected and says:

[69:27] ***'O, would that it had been the final end!'***

That is, 'If only the first death had remained with me, and I had not been resurrected!'

[69:28] ***'My wealth has not availed me.'***

'The abundance of wealth I possessed, since I did not pay what was due from it to God, and I did not use it to strengthen ties of kinship.'[4]

[69:29] ***'My authority has gone from me.'***

That is, 'My proof and my excuse'.

[69:30] ***'Seize him, then fetter him',***

As soon as He says that, a hundred thousand angels will rush towards him. If just one of these angels took in his grasp the world and the mountains and seas it contains, he would be strong enough for that. [One of the angels] will take hold of his neck with his hands, and then he will enter the Hellfire (*jaḥīm*).

[69:32] ***'And [bind him] in a chain seventy cubits long.'***

Each cubit is equivalent to seventy fathoms (*bāʿ*), and each fathom is longer that the distance between Kufa and Mecca.[5] If you were to put one of its links on the summit of a mountain, it [the mountain] would melt, just as lead melts. This is what is related from Ibn ʿAbbās ﷺ. It is also related that ʿUmar ﷺ once said to Kaʿb, 'Frighten us, O Abū Isḥāq'. So he said, 'O Commander of the believers, if you performed acts of worship to the extent that you became like a pruned stick, and you had to your credit the works of seventy prophets, you would still think that you will not be saved from the command of your Lord and the Throne Bearers. When the Preserved Tablet is brought forward with the record of all the deeds, when Hell is displayed and Paradise is brought near, and humanity stands before the Lord of the Worlds, Hell will heave a sigh that will cause every one of the angels who are drawn near (*malak muqarrab*) and every prophet messenger (*nabī mursal*)[6] to fall down on their knees without exception, to the point that Abraham will cry "My soul! My soul!"[7] Then the just man (*rajul ʿādil*) and the oppressor (*rajul jāʾir*) will be summoned, [the name of each being called out] above the heads of the masses. When the just man is brought forward, his book will be raised up to him for him to receive in his right hand. There is no happiness, no joy, and no rapture that ever descended on a servant greater than that which will descend on him on that day. And he will say above the heads of the crowds what God, Exalted is He, related.[8] Then the oppressor will be brought forward and

4 On the prior right which a person's kith and kin have over the gifts he or she makes, see 33:6.

5 Clearly, a fathom in this context is more than 6 feet!

6 The word *nabī* is applied to all prophets while the word *rasūl* (pl. *rusul*) refers to those prophets who brought 'a message' or scripture.

7 An allusion to the *ḥadīth* of intercession, listed in Bukhārī, *Ṣaḥīḥ*, 'Kitāb Aḥādīth al-anbiyāʾ' and 'Kitāb al-Riqāq'.

8 i.e. the words of 69:19: *Here, read my book!*

his book will be thrust into his left hand, and there is no grief, no humiliation, and no distress that ever befell a man severer than that which will befall that man. He will then say above the heads of the crowds what God, Exalted is He, has related.[9] Then he will be seized and dragged on his face to the Fire and his flesh, bones and brains will be scattered about.'

Upon this ʿUmar ﷺ cried, 'That's enough for me! Enough!'[10]

Sahl said:

The chains and shackles are not for the sake of binding [the people], but rather for the sake of dragging them ever lower, forever after, as long as they reside there.

His words, Mighty and Majestic is He:

[69:44] ***And had he fabricated any lies against Us,***[11]

He said:

That is, if he said that which he had no permission [from Us] to say.

[69:45] ***We would assuredly have seized him by the right hand,***

That is, We would have ordered for him to be seized by the hand just as is the practice of kings.

[69:46] ***And We would assuredly have severed his life-artery*** **(wartīn),**

This being the aorta which is the main artery to which the heart is attached, and if it is cut the person dies.[12] We would cut it off as a result of his transgression against Us.

His words, Exalted is He:

[69:48] ***And assuredly it is a reminder for those who are mindful of God.***

He said:

That is, the Qurʾān is a mercy for those who are obedient.

His words, Exalted is He:

[69:50] ***And assuredly it is a [cause of] anguish for the disbelievers.***

He said:

That is, they see the reward that is had by the people who professed God's oneness, along with their ranks and noble stations.

But God, Glorified and Exalted is He, knows best.

9 i.e. the words of vv. 25–9, which were commented on above.

10 Nīsābūrī, *al-Mustadrak*, vol. 4, p. 634; Haythamī, *Majmaʿ al-zawāʾid*, vol. 10, p. 342; Ṭabarānī, *al-Muʿjam al-kabīr*, vol. 9, p. 360.

11 The subject here is the Prophet. Verses 38–51 comprise an oath given by God, in answer to the disbelievers, that the Prophet's speech is not that of a poet or soothsayer, but a revelation from the Lord of the Worlds.

12 See above, p. 86, n. 17 regarding *ḥabl al-warīd*, where *wartīn* is mentioned.

70 Al-Maʿārij

His words, Exalted is He:

[70:4] ***To Him ascend the angels and the spirit*** **(rūḥ)…**

He said:

> The angels ascend with the deeds of the children of Adam, as does the spirit, which is the intuition of the self (*dhihn al-nafs*).[1] They [the angels and the spirit] ascend to God, Exalted is He, in order to testify to the sincerity (*ikhlāṣ*) in his [a man's] deeds. They cover the distance to the Throne, which measures fifty thousand years, in the blinking of an eye. This is the inner meaning of the verse.

His words, Exalted is He:

[70:5] ***So be patient with comely patience*** **(ṣabran jamīlan).**

> That is, [with] contentment (*riḍā*) and without complaining (*shakwā*); for truly, complaints are a [form of] tribulation (*balwā*), and any claim to patience (*ṣabr*) that is accompanied by it [complaint] is merely a claim. [This notwithstanding], God, Exalted is He, has servants who complain through Him, from Him and to Him (*bihi minhu ilayhi*), as a proof of their restraining their natural self (*nafs al-ṭabʿ*) from turning its attention to anything other than the One for whose sake the patient show patience.[2]

His words, Exalted is He:

[70:6, 7] ***Lo! They see it as being far off,*** ❁ ***while We see it [to be] near.***

He said:

> This means that they see the death, resurrection and reckoning that are decreed for them as far away (*baʿīd*), due to the far-fetched nature (*buʿd*) of their hopes; *while We see it [to be] near*, for indeed everything in existence (*kāʾin*) is close and that which is distant does not even exist.[3]

Then he said:

> The scholars sought [the justification] for having scruples (*waswasa*), concerning the Book and the Sunna, but they could not find a basis for it except legitimate inquisitiveness (*fuḍūl al-ḥalāl*), and legitimate inquisitiveness is that the servant considers a time other than the time he is in. This, [however] is [on the basis of] hope (*amal*).[4] It is related from Ḥubaysh on the authority of Ibn ʿAbbās ﷺ that the Prophet ﷺ would pass water and then wipe himself with earth. So he [Ibn ʿAbbās?] said, 'O Messenger of God, there is water near you!', to which he replied, 'I do not know, it may be that I won't reach it.'[5] And [the Prophet ﷺ said to Usāma (b. Zayd)],[6]

---

1 Sic in the MSS and the published edition. Perhaps what is meant is the intuition of the spiritual self.

2 The prophet Jacob used the same words of this verse, when he said: *Yet comely patience* (ṣabr jamīl), and interestingly, in 12:86 he says, 'I complain of my anguish and grief only to God'.

3 Here is another indication that one should be living in the present and be a 'son of the moment' (*ibn al-waqt*), which is clarified by the statement of Tustarī which follows.

4 Because a hypothesis often assumes a future and a situation other than the one that a person is in.

5 Ibn Ḥanbal, *al-Musnad*, vol. 1, p. 303. Makkī, *Qūt al-qulūb*, vol. 2, p. 33.

6 All the MSS have *li-Usāma*: Z515, f. 122b, F638, f. 59a and F3488, f. 303b.

'Our nearness to [obtaining water] is two months away. Indeed, Usāma has far-reaching hopes (*ṭawīl al-amal*)!'

Sahl was asked, 'How does the world leave the heart?' He replied:

By the shortening of hope.

[Then] he was asked: 'What is it that shortens hope?' He replied:

It is cutting off from concerns (*humūm*) with what is guaranteed (*maḍmūn*), and finding reliance (*sukūn*) on the Guarantor (*al-Ḍāmin*).

His words, Exalted is He:

[70:19] ***Indeed man was created restless,***

He said:

This means that he is turned this way and that by the impulses of his lusts (*shahawāt*) and pursuance of his desire (*hawā*).

[70:20, 21] ***When evil befalls him [he is] anxious ۞ and when good befalls him [he is] grudging,***

He said:

If he experiences poverty (*iftaqara*) he grieves (*ḥazana*), but when he becomes wealthy (*athrā*) he withholds it from others (*manaʿa*).[7]

[70:22] ***except those who pray…***

That is, those who have cognisance of (*ʿārifūn*) the [true] proportions (*maqādīr*) of things, since they do not find joy (*faraḥ*) in anything other than God. They do not repose in anything other than Him and they do not fear[8] anything other than Him, their [only source of] anxiety being the possibility of separation from Him, just as He says, *and who are apprehensive of the chastisement of their Lord* [70:27].

The saying is narrated from the Prophet ﷺ: 'According to what the highest host in the highest ranks informed me, among the best of my nation are people who laugh out loud at the amplitude of the mercy of their Lord, and weep in secret out of fear of the severity of the punishment of their Lord. They remember their Lord morning and night in His blessed houses, and make supplications to Him with their tongues in hope and fear. They petition Him with their hands, lowering [their upturned palms] and raising them, and they long for Him constantly with their hearts. Their demands on people are light, but their demands on themselves heavy. They tread upon the earth [lightly] with their feet, as an ant would tread, without gloating, boasting or swaggering…' to the end of the *ḥadīth*.[9]

His words, Exalted is He:

[70:29] ***who guard their private parts;***

He said:

In its inner meaning [the verse refers to] all the bodily members, both exterior and interior. They preserve them from the manifestation of traces of the natural self (*nafs al-ṭabʿ*) in them.

[70:32] ***and those who are keepers of their trusts and their covenant,***

He said:

Its inner meaning refers to the trust (*amāna*) within the self, for it is God's secret with His servants.[10] He confides with them (*yusārruhum*) due to His knowledge of all the suggestions

7 lit. 'He prevents [others from benefitting from it]'.

8 That is, according to all three MSS (Z515, f. 122b, F638, f. 59a and F3488, f. 303b), which have *khawf*: The repetition in the published edition of the word *faraḥ* appears to be a misprint as it is only in the Dār al-Kutub al-ʿIlmiyya edition.

9 Nīsābūrī, *al-Mustadrak*, vol. 3, p. 19; Bayhaqī, *Shuʿab al-īmān*, vol. 1, p. 478. Compare Tustarī's statement that one should become as the earth for people, in his commentary on 9:71, above.

10 On *amāna* see p. 219, n. 6.

(*khawāṭir*) and aspirations (*himam*) which are within it [the self].[11] On the other hand, they confide in Him by showing their neediness for Him and seeking refuge in Him.

Furthermore, if the heart acquiesces in that which the evil whispering of the Enemy suggests to it, even though it may be the most insignificant thing, it will manifest itself in the breast, and from the breast to the body and thus will he have betrayed God's trust (*amāna*), His pledge (*ʿahd*) and faith (*īmān*).

[70:33] ***and who stand firm in their testimony,***

He said:

[They are those] who stand firm (*qāʾimūn*), upholding that to which they have testified, namely that there is no god except God, and who do not shirk with regard to it in any of their deeds, words or states. Neither do they fabricate anything. But God knows best.

11 *Himma* (pl. *himam*) can also mean 'desire', 'intention', 'concern', and 'spiritual aspiration or energy'.

71 Nūḥ

His words, Exalted is He:

[71:7] ***...And they persist [in their rejection], and act in great arrogance.***[1]

He said:

> Persistence in sin (*dhanb*) gives rise to ignorance, and ignorance gives rise to a transgression into falsehood (*bāṭil*). The transgression into falsehood gives rise to hypocrisy (*nifāq*) and hypocrisy in turn gives rise to disbelief (*kufr*).

[He] was asked, 'What is the sign of the hypocrite?' He replied:

> It is that he perceives something when he is reminded of it, but when he gets up to go, it is as if that thing never entered his heart. God, Exalted is He, has said: *Whenever it gives them light, they walk therein, and when darkness falls around them, they stand still* [2:20].

His words, Exalted is He:

[71:25] ***...they were drowned and then made to enter the Fire...***

He said:

> They were drowned in bewilderment (*ḥayra*) [beyond the reach of] guidance (*hudā*), and so they were made to enter the Hellfire. Hence, God made disgrace (*hawān*) binding upon them, and lodged them in the Abode of Misery (*dār al-shaqāʾ*).

1 The verse is part of Noah's complaint to God about his people, who continued to be resistant to the summons of God, even putting their fingers in their ears so that they would never hear it.

72 Al-Jinn

His words, Exalted is He:

[72:1] ***Say, 'It has been revealed to me that a company* (nafar) *of jinn listened, then said, "We have indeed heard a marvellous Qur'ān,***

He said:

> They were nine in number and had proceeded from Yemen. The word *nafar* refers to a number between three and ten. They came to the Prophet ﷺ while he was reciting Qur'ān in his prayer. They were among the best of their people in religion, and when they heard it, they were moved by it (*raqqū lahu*) and they believed in it. Then they returned to their people as warners, and said, '*We have indeed heard a marvellous Qur'ān,* ۞ *which guides to rectitude*' [72:1, 2], meaning, 'It guides [people] to follow the ways of Muṣṭafā ﷺ'.

Sahl said:

> Once I saw in the place that was home to the ʿĀd people of old, a city built of stone, within which there was a magnificent palace that that had been carved out of the rock, which was a refuge for the jinn.[1] I entered the palace to reflect [upon it], and I saw a large person standing in prayer facing the Kaʿba, wearing a long white woollen garment (*jubba*) which had a certain freshness (*ṭarāwa*) about it. I was impressed with its freshness, so I waited until he had finished his prayer and then I said: 'Peace be upon you.' He replied: 'And upon you be peace, Abū Muḥammad. Were you impressed with the freshness of my garment which has been on me for nine hundred years, and in which I met with Jesus son of Mary (peace be upon them both) and Muḥammad ﷺ, and believed in them both? Know, O Abū Muḥammad, that bodies [in themselves] do not wear out clothes, but rather, illegitimate sources of food, and persistence in committing sins.'
>
> Then I asked, 'Who are you?' He replied, 'I am one of those concerning whom God, Exalted is He, said, *Say, 'It has been revealed to me that a company of jinn listened…*'

Sahl was then asked, 'Do the jinn enter Paradise?' He replied:

> I have heard that in Paradise there are lands which the jinn inhabit, and where they eat and drink, and in the Qur'ān there is evidence of this as God said, Exalted is He: *[of modest gaze] who have not been touched by man or jinn before* [55:56].

His words, Exalted is He:

[72:18] ***'And [it has been revealed to me] that the places of prayer belong to God, so do not invoke anyone along with God'.***

He said:

> That is, 'Do not make a supplication to [anyone] along with God as a partner [to Him] (*sharīkan*)'; or in other words, 'There is no one who is a partner with Me in anything which would thereby prevent my servant from remembering Me.' Hence, it is the same with whatever belongs to God, Exalted is He, and no one has any means to resist Him or withhold [anything from Him].

1 The ʿĀd were an ancient Arab people to whom the prophet Hūd and other prophets were sent, but who for the most part rejected their message. They are mentioned some twenty-four times in the Qur'ān.

His words, Exalted is He:

[72:22] ***Say, 'Indeed none shall protect me from God, and I shall never find any refuge besides Him.'***

He said:

> He has commanded him [the Prophet] to [be in a state of] utter neediness (*iftiqār*) and to take refuge (*lujūʾ*) in Him, and then to manifest both of these [conditions] through his words, that thereby the disbelievers will be increased in error (*ḍalāl*), and the believers will be increased in guidance (*irshād*). And this is a maxim for sincerity (*ikhlāṣ*) in the profession of God's oneness (*tawḥīd*), since the truth (*ḥaqīqa*) of professing His oneness means looking towards God and none other, advancing towards Him (*iqbāl ʿalayhi*) and relying upon Him (*iʿtimād ʿalayhi*). However, this will not be accomplished save by turning away from everything other than Him, showing one's utter neediness for Him, and taking refuge in Him.

73 Al-Muzzammil

His words, Exalted is He:

[73:1] ***O you enfolded in your garment,***

He said:

The enfolded one (*al-Muzzammil*) is the one who is enfolded in [his] garments and clasps them about him. In its inner meaning, it is one of the Prophet's names (*al-Muzzammil*): 'O you, the one who is able to compose himself (*jāmiʿ nafsihi*) when God Himself is with him (*wa-nafsi'Llāhi ʿindahu*).'

His words, Exalted is He:

[73:6] ***Rising at night makes a deeper impression…***

He said:

That is, [rising for] the whole night, and the night worship that the servant performs makes a deeper impression on the hearing and heart [due to] [one's increased] attentiveness (*iṣghāʾ*) and understanding (*fahm*) [at that time]; *…and more upright with respect to speech,* that is, firmer in [spiritual] station (*athbatu rutbatan*). It is also said, more correct in speech because of being further away from ostentation.

Ḥasan said (may God have mercy on him), 'I met people who were able to perform acts [of worship] in secret, but preferred to do them openly. I also met people [whose custom was] that if one of them received guests, he would get up at night for prayer in order that none of his guests would notice him.' Luqmān used to say to his son, 'O my son! Do not be less than this cockerel which crows at night.'[1]

His words, Exalted is He:

[73:8] ***So mention the name of your Lord and devote yourself [exclusively] to Him with complete devotion.***

He said:

Recite 'In the name of God, the Compassionate, the Merciful' at the opening of your prayer, and the blessing of reciting this will connect you to your Lord and sever you from everything other than Him.

His words, Exalted is He:

[73:9] ***…there is no god but Him, so take Him as your guardian.***

That is, as Guarantor (*al-Kafīl*) of the help that He has promised you in [obeying] His command, and the protection He has promised you in [avoiding] what He has forbidden, along with divinely-bestowed success (*tawfīq*) in [showing] gratitude, patience in the face of tribulation, and a laudable end.

Then he said:

There is a Paradise and a Hellfire in this life. Paradise ⌜is safety (*ʿāfiya*),⌝[2] and safety is that God

---

1 i.e. 'Don't be afraid to be open about your prayers.' The tradition is listed in Bayhaqī, *Shuʿab al-īmān*, vol. 5, p. 41.

2 Added on the basis of all three MSS: Z515, f. 124b, F638, f. 60a and F3488, f. 306a.

takes care of your affairs, and Hellfire is tribulation (*balwā*). Tribulation is when He leaves you in charge of your self.[3]

He was asked, 'What is the (way to) relief (*faraj*)?' He replied:

Do not hope for relief while you still look to what is created. There is not a servant who desired God with a genuine resolve (*ʿazm ṣaḥīḥ*), without everything vanishing from his [consciousness] besides Him. Moreover, there is not a servant from whom everything has vanished besides Him, who does not deserve that God take charge of his affairs. [At the same time], there is not in this world a person who is [truly] obedient to God while he is [also] obeying his lower self, and no one becomes distanced from God except through engagement in that which is other than God.

Things only have access to someone who is idle (*fārigh*). However, evil suggestions (*waswasa*) will not reach a person whose heart is occupied with God; such a one is in [a state] of continuous increase. So protect yourself through [adhering to] the principle (*aṣl*).

He was asked, 'And what is that [principle]?' He answered;

It is submission (*taslīm*) to God's command, and freeing oneself (*tabarrī*) of all other than Him.

3 Compare this with Tustarī's commentary on 70:5, where he states that complaint can be a form of tribulation. The connection between these two statements is that in both cases we are not submitting to what God has destined for us, and His management of our affairs.

74 Al-Muddaththir

His words, Exalted is He:

[74:1, 2] ***O you enveloped in your mantle,* ❁ *arise and warn,***

He said:

> 'O you who are seeking succour from your own self in order to relieve your breast and heart. Arise through Us and shed from yourself all other than Us. Warn Our servants, for surely We have prepared you for the most honoured of positions (*ashraf al-mawāqif*) and the greatest of stations (*aʿẓam al-maqāmāt*).'

[74:4] ***and purify your garments,***

He said:

> That is, 'Do not wear your clothes in a state of disobedience (*maʿṣiyya*). Purify them from your selfish interests (*ḥuẓūẓ*) and wrap yourself around with them.'
>
> Similarly ʿĀʾisha ﵂ said, 'The Messenger of God ﷺ used to have a long shirt and he gave it to Abū Jahm in exchange for his Manbijī garment.[1] Someone said, "O Messenger of God, the shirt is better than the garment." He said, "Truly, I would look at it during prayer." He was distracted by the design of the shirt.'[2]

His words, Exalted is He:

[74:12] ***and [then I] assigned him ample means,***

He said:

> That is, to Walīd b. al-Mughīra,[3] to whom I [God] gave avarice and far-fetched hope (*ṭūl al-amal*).

His words, Exalted is He:

[74:56] ***...He is the [One who] is worthy of being heeded, and the [One who] is Master of forgiveness.***

He said:

> That is, He deserves to be heeded and not be disobeyed, and He is fit [and ready] to forgive the one who repents. Mindfulness of God (*taqwā*) means abandoning everything which is reprehensible (*madhmūm*). With regard to the command, it is abandoning procrastination (*taswīf*), and with regard to what is prohibited, it is giving up the very thought of it. In terms of codes of propriety (*ādāb*), it refers to noble characteristics; in the case of inducement (*targhīb*), it means keeping a secret; and in the case of intimidation (*tarhīb*), it means being wary of remaining in a state of ignorance.[4] Mindfulness of God means freeing oneself from [dependence] on all save God. Therefore, whoever observes these codes of conduct in mindfulness of God is deserving of forgiveness.

---

1 Probably a simple woollen cloak, which would also have been called an *anbijāniyya*, indicating, perhaps, that it came from the town of Manbij in Syria. See Yedida K. Stillman, *Arab Dress* (Leiden, 2000), p. 13.

2 Ibn Ḥanbal, *al-Musnad*, vol. 6, p. 46; Ibn Māja, *Sunan*, 'Kitāb al-Libās'.

3 Walīd b. Mughīra b. ʿAbd Allāh al-Makhzūmī (d. 1/623), was a leading figure among the Quraysh who did not accept Islam.

4 See above, Tustarī's commentary on 8:1, where the same was also said of the application of mindfulness of God (*taqwā*) in those two situations, i.e. inducement and intimidation.

It has been related that a man came to Jesus the son of Mary ﷺ and said, 'O Teacher of Good (*muʿallim al-khayr*), how can I become mindful of God in the way that I should?' He replied, 'It is very simple. Love God with all your heart, and work with a generous spirit and all your strength as much as you can. Have mercy on the souls of your own kind (*jins*), just as you have mercy on your own soul.' He asked, 'Who are my own kind, O Teacher of Good?' He replied, 'The sons of Adam. Furthermore, do not do to anyone else what you do not wish to be done to you.'

But God, Glorified and Exalted is He, knows best.

75 Al-Qiyāma

The following was read before Sahl and he affirmed the truth of it:

ʿUmar b. al-Khaṭṭāb ﷺ said, 'Whoever wishes to visualise (*yabṣira*) the Day of Resurrection should read Sūrat al-Qiyāma, for the resurrection of each one of you [occurs with] his death.

His words, Exalted is He:

[75:1, 2] ***Nay, I swear by the Day of Resurrection. ❁ And nay, I swear by the self-reproaching soul!***

The evil-inciting self (*nafs ammāra bi'l-sūʾ*) is [here in the form of] the blaming self (*nafs lawwāma*).[1] It is a companion (*qarīna*) to avarice (*ḥirṣ*) and [far-fetched] hope (*amal*).[2]

Then he said:

He [God] has simply forbidden you from obeying ⌜the Enemy [Satan]⌝,[3] from being deluded by the world, and from letting yourself be deceived by the lower self. God, Exalted is He, said, *Verily the soul is ever inciting to evil* [12:53]; and He said: *So do not let the life of this world deceive you* [31:33]; and He also said: *Truly Satan is an enemy to you* [35:6].

His words, Exalted is He:

[75:9] ***and the sun and moon are brought together.***

He said:

Its inner meaning is the following: the moon represents the light of the sight of the physical eye (*nūr baṣar ʿayn al-raʾs*) which pertains to the natural self (*nafs al-ṭabʿ*), and the sun represents the light of the sight of the eye of the heart (*nūr baṣar ʿayn al-qalb*) which pertains to the spiritual self (*nafs al-rūḥ*), and the intellect (*ʿaql*).[4] Do you not notice how He says:

[75:10] ***On that day man will say, 'Where is the escape?***

That is, the one who denies the Day of Resurrection says, when the two lights are brought together, 'Where is the deliverer from the punishment of God?'[5]

His words, Exalted is He:

[75:22, 23] ***Some faces on that day will be radiant, ❁ looking upon their Lord.***

---

1 The 'self which incites to evil' (*nafs ammāra bi'l-sūʾ*) and the 'self-reproaching or blaming self' (*nafs lawwāma*) are understood in Sufi 'psychology' to be two closely associated levels of the self at its lowest or least transformed stage. Later, through the practice of spiritual disciplines and through divine grace, the self may reach the level of being the 'self at peace' (*nafs muṭmaʾinna*), and, according to the doctrines of some Sufis, even beyond that to other levels and stages in the transformation of the *nafs*. On Tustarī's doctrines concerning the different levels of the *nafs*, see IT, pp. xli–xlii.

2 Note that almost the same characteristics were attributed to Walīd b. al-Mughīra, in the commentary on 74:12 above, except that in this case the word *ṭūl*, preceding *amal*, is absent from all three MSS: Z515, f. 125b, F638, f. 61a and F3488, f. 307a.

3 The word Allāh is absent from all three MSS, while the words *min al-ʿaduww*, absent from the published edition, have been added on the basis of all three MSS: Z515, f. 125b, F638, f. 61a and F3488, f. 307a. Thus we have read it as *innamā nahākum ʿan al-qabūl min al-ʿaduww*, that is, 'He has simply forbidden you from obeying (submitting or yielding) to the Enemy'.

4 MS F638 has the word *naẓar* in both places instead of *baṣar*.

5 See the commentary on 57:6 above, and 81:7 below, for Tustarī's recommendation that the natural self (*nafs al-ṭabʿ*) and the spiritual self (*nafs al-rūḥ*) should be brought together in this world.

He said:

Whoever was killed by his love [for Him], his recompense (*diya*) will be the vision of Him.[6]

Then he said:

The reward for works is Paradise, and the reward for the realisation of God's oneness (*tawḥīd*) is the vision of God, Mighty and Majestic is He.

It is related that Abū al-Dardāʾ ﷺ said, 'Travel for the sake of tribulation (*balāʾ*),[7] prepare for annihilation (*fanāʾ*), and make yourselves ready for the encounter (*liqāʾ*)!' Rābiʿa ﷺ used to say, 'My Lord, I love this world only that I might remember You in it, and I love the Hereafter only because I may see You there. Every hour that passes by while my tongue is not moist with Your remembrance is accursed. My Lord, do not bring upon me these two things for I will not be able to bear them: burning in Hell and separation from You.'

His words, Exalted is He:

[75:26] ***No indeed! When it [the soul] reaches the collarbones,***

That is, the throat (*ḥulqūm*);

[75:27] ***and it is said, 'Who is a magician [to restore him]?'***

That is, 'Is there a doctor who can cure [him]?' It has also been said that it means, 'Who will raise the soul of this disbeliever to heaven?'

[75:28] ***and he thinks that it is [the time] of parting,***[8]

He [God][9] is saying that he knows that it is the parting from this world.

[75:29] ***and [his] legs are joined together,***

He is speaking of the affairs of this world and the Hereafter. It has also been said that they are your legs when they joined together in your shroud. It has been related of Jacob ﷺ that when the [angel] bearing good tidings came to him, he [the angel] said, 'I have not been given permission to bring to you what I have come with, without saying: "May God make the pangs of death easy for you to bear"'. It was said to Aswad b. Yazīd when he was dying, 'Be of good cheer, for forgiveness is your lot.' He replied, 'But what about the shame [that we shall feel] before the One from whom forgiveness comes?'

It has been related that when Abū Bakr al-Ṣiddīq ﷺ was dying, he was visited by ʿĀʾisha ﷺ and she cited the following verse:

By your life, wealth does not enrich one
On that day when [the soul] reaches the throat and the breast is constricted [in death].[10]

Then he uncovered his face and said, 'That is not so [in my case], but the words for me are, *And the agony of death arrives with the truth* [50:19]. Look to those two [old] garments of mine, ⌜wash them⌝[11] and enshroud me in them, for the living have greater need for new clothes than the dead.'

---

6 The word *diya* is traditionally used for 'blood money' or 'blood wit' that can be claimed by a victim's family from the victim's killer.

7 Tribulation here being the tests and trials that purify the self.

8 The subject here is the person at the point of death.

9 Usually Tustarī's words, if they are being ascribed to him, are preceded by *qāla*, and in this comment and the one that follows, *yaqūlu* appears to refer to God.

10 This couplet, with some variants, appears in the *Dīwān* of Ḥāṭim b. ʿAbd Allāh al-Ṭāʾī (d. second half of sixth century C.E.) (Cairo, 1975), p. 210. In translating the version as it appears in Tustarī's *tafsīr*, the feminine of the verb has been taken to refer to the *nafs*. The verb *ḥashraja* is an old Arab verb meaning to come up to the throat, as the soul at the time of death, which is described in the verse that Tustarī is commenting on.

11 Translating *fa-'ghsilūhumā* added on the basis of all the MSS: Z515, f. 126a, F638, f. 61b and F3488, f. 307b.

76 Al-Insān[1]

His words, Exalted is He:

[76:5] ***Truly the righteous will drink from a cup whose mixture is camphor.***

He said:

> [These are] the righteous (*abrār*), who took on one of the characteristics of the ten [Companions] concerning whom the Messenger of God ﷺ bore witness that they would go to Paradise.[2]

He was asked, 'What are the most important characteristic moral traits that we should have?'

He replied:

> To show endurance (*iḥtimāl*) in the face of hardship (*maʾūna*), compassion (*rifq*) in every situation, and caution against inclining to one's lower passion if one is elevated [in rank].[3] Among these qualities is the attainment of the intellect (*iktisāb al-ʿaql*).
>
> Then there are another three which are necessary: attaining gnosis (*iktisāb al-maʿrifa*), and putting one's knowledge into practice (*istiʿmāl al-ʿilm*), clemency (*ḥilm*) and humility (*tawāḍuʿ*).
>
> Yet still there are a further three [characteristics] which are necessary to acquire, and which contain the precepts of worship (*aḥkām al-taʿabbud*), namely: serenity (*sakīna*), dignified bearing (*waqār*) and equity (*inṣāf*).[4]

He also said:

> The earth will not consume the body of anyone who keeps the following three qualities: refraining from harming people, bearing the harm that comes from them and doing good to them.

[76:7] ***...and they fear a day the evil of which will be widespread.***

He said:

> In the Hereafter, tribulations (*balāyā*) and hardships (*shadāʾid*) will befall the masses, and only a chosen few among the elect (*khāṣṣ al-khāṣṣ*) will receive deliverance.

His words, Exalted is He:

[76:11] ***...And [God] has granted them radiance and joy.***

He said:

> Radiance on their faces and gladness in the hearts.

His words, Exalted is He:

[76:18] ***from a spring therein named Salsabīl.***[5]

---

1 In both the Fātiḥ MSS, this *sūra* bears the title 'Hal atā', which are the first words of the *sūra*'s first verse.

2 There are various *ḥadīths* listing the ten named by the Prophet as being destined for Paradise. For example, in the *Sunan* of Abū Dāwūd, 'Bāb al-Sunna', they are listed as: the Prophet, Abū Bakr, ʿUmar, ʿUthmān, ʿAlī b. Abī Ṭālib, Ṭalḥa b. ʿUbayd Allāh, Zubayr b. al-ʿAwwām, ʿAbd al-Raḥmān b. ʿAwf, Saʿd b. Abī Waqqāṣ and Saʿīd b. Zayd. Other traditions do not mention the Prophet, but name Abū ʿUbayda b. al-Jarrāḥ.

3 Possibly elevated spiritually or in worldly status.

4 See Tustarī's commentary on 36:11 above, for his discussion of *inṣāf*.

5 The drink which the righteous will drink in Paradise. This spring is infused with ginger (vs. 17).

He said:

> It is related from al-Musayyib that he said, 'It is a spring situated to the right of the Throne, [which flows forth] from a reed-like ruby.'

Sahl said:

> God drew the attention of His believing servants to it (*Salsabīl*), and then He said, 'So, ask your Lord for the way to reach this spring.'

His words, Exalted is He:

[76:21] ...*Their Lord will give them a pure drink.*

Sahl said:

> God has informed[6] His servants of the impurity (*najāsa*) of intoxicating drinks (*khumūr*) in this world. This is why He differentiated between that which is pure and purifying (*ṭāhir wa ṭuhūr*), [namely], the wines of Paradise, and the wines of this world in their impurity. The wines of this world are sullied and they sully the one who drinks them with sins (*āthām*), whereas the wines of Paradise are purifying and purify the one who drinks them from every blemish (*danas*), thereby making him acceptable for the Holy Assembly (*majlis al-quds*) and the Glorious Spectacle (*mashhad al-ʿizz*).

[Once] while Sahl was performing the prayer of darkness (*ʿatma*),[7] he recited God's words, Exalted is He: *Their Lord will give them a pure drink*. Then he began moving his mouth as if he was sucking something. When he finished his prayer he was asked, 'Did you drink during the prayer?' To which he answered:

> By God, if I had not experienced its taste when I recited it as if I was drinking it, I would not have acted so.[8]

6 That is, translating *nabaha* according to all three MSS: Z515, f. 126b, F638, f. 61b and F3488, f. 308b, as opposed to *nahā* in the published edition.

7 i.e. the canonical night prayer (ʿ*Īsha*ʾ).

8 See above, the commentary on 2:25, for Sahl's tasting of the fruit of Paradise.

77 Al-Mursalāt

His words, Exalted is He:

[77:1] ***By those sent forth in succession;***

By this is meant the angels who are sent with the good (*maʿrūf*) of His command (*amr*).

He said:

In its inner meaning it refers to the spirits (*arwāḥ*) of the believers which are sent inspiration (*ilhām*) in accordance with the Book and the Sunna.

[77:3] ***by the sweeping spreaders;***

by which He causes virtuous deeds (*aʿmāl ṣāliḥa*) to appear.[1]

[77:4] ***by the decisive discriminators;***

[which discriminate] between truth (*ḥaqq*) and falsehood (*bāṭil*), and between the Sunna and innovation (*bidʿa*).

[77:5] ***By those that deliver the reminder,***[2]

This is the revelation (*waḥy*) through inspiration (*ilhām*) which the spiritual self (*nafs al-rūḥ*), the intellect (*ʿaql*) and the heart (*qalb*) cast upon the natural self (*nafs al-ṭabʿ*), and this is the hidden form of reminder (*dhikr khafiyy*).[3]

[77:6] ***as an excuse or as a warning.***

God has excused the suppression of that by which the Book and the Sunna is opposed; *or as a warning* to His creatures of His punishment. Furthermore, God, Exalted is He, swore by them to the reality of the Resurrection.[4]

His words, Exalted is He:

[77:15] ***Woe to the deniers of that Day!***

He said:

Woe on that day to those who make claims that have no truth [in them], for their claims will deny them publicly before [many] witnesses. This will occur at the time of exposure (*iftiḍāḥ*).

His words, Exalted is He:

[77:35] ***On that Day they will be speechless.***

He said:

Nobody will speak for himself by [presenting an] argument (*bi-ḥujja*), unless it be by the exhibiting of helplessness (*ʿajz*) and servanthood (*ʿubūdiyya*), and by refraining from infringements [of the Law] (*mukhālafāt*) and crimes (*jarāʾim*).

---

1 All three MSS (Z515, f. 127a, F638, f. 61b and F3488, f. 308b) appear to have *yuẓhiru* instead of *yuṭahhiru* in the published edition.

2 Exoteric or conventional commentaries interpret the deliverers of the reminder (*dhikr*) as the angels who delivered the revelation to prophets and messengers.

3 Thus Tustarī seems to be understanding two forms of revelation, one outer, taking the form of the revealed books delivered by the angels to prophets, and one inner, 'hidden (*khafiyy*)' revelation, which through inspiration (*ilhām*) is transmitted from the spiritual faculties in the human being to the natural self.

4 'Them' presumably referring to *those who are sent* in verses 1–5.

His words, Exalted is He:

[77:46] *'Eat and enjoy — for a short while, evildoers that you are'.*

He said:

> Whoever's only concern is with [satisfying] his stomach and private parts, has [already] manifested his ruin (*khasāra*), for He says [to such people], Exalted is He: *'Eat and enjoy — for a short while, evildoers that you are'.*

But God, Glorified and Exalted is He, knows best.

78 Al-Naba[ʾ1]

His words, Exalted is He:

[78:11] ***and [have We not] made the day for livelihood,***

That is, the lights of the heart and its illumination (*tanwīr*) through Our remembrance (*dhikr*), are the livelihood (*ʿaysh*) of the spiritual self (*nafs al-rūḥ*) and the intellect (*ʿaql*), as they are the livelihood of the angels. However, the other kind of livelihood is the way of the generality of people (*ʿawāmm*).

Then he said:

It is not [good] character for the believer to grovel (*tadhallul*) in times of poverty (*fāqa*), and it is distasteful for the poor to wear thread-bare clothes, and to carry the concerns related to their provisions (*arzāq*) in their hearts.[2] [The cure] at the root of these matters consists of three [things]: dependence on God, Majestic and Mighty is He; fleeing from people, and doing the least [possible] harm to others.

ʿĀmir b. ʿAbd al-Qays used to say when he rose in the morning, 'O God! Verily people have dispersed in pursuit of their needs, but I have only one need, which is that You forgive me.'[3]

His words, Mighty and Majestic is He:

[78:26] ***As a fitting requital,***

The Fire is a fitting punishment for association [idolatry] (*shirk*), because both of them are momentous (*ʿaẓīm*). There is no punishment ⌜greater than the Fire and no sin⌝ greater than association.[4]

His words, Exalted is He:

[78:33] ***and buxom maidens…***

He said:

Young and attractive concubines, *atrāb* means of equal age.

His words, Exalted is He:

[78:34] ***and a brimming cup.***

That is, continuously full.

Once, a wise man (*ḥakīm*) met another wise man in Mosul and said to him, 'Do you long for the dark-eyed houris?' He replied: 'Should I not long for them, when the light of their faces is from the light of God, Majestic and Mighty is He?' At this he [the wise man] fell into a swoon and was carried to his home. For a month afterwards people would visit him due to his sickness.

1 All the MSS give this *sūra* the title: "ʿAmmā yatasāʾalūn".

2 In other words the correct behaviour for the believer is not to burden others with displaying his poverty to the world at large, just as he should not burden his heart with concerns for his provision, since he should trust that God will provide for him. It is interesting that among the three guidelines that Tustarī puts forward to avoid the former situation, the inner is addressed first, i.e. depending on God.

3 Ibn Abī ʿĀṣim, *Kitāb al-Zuhd*, p. 225.

4 The addition is made on the basis of all three MSS: Z515, f. 127b, F638, f. 61a and F3488, f. 309b.

> Ibn ʿAbbās, ✿ said, 'If one of the maidens [of Paradise] were to spit into the seven seas, they would become sweeter than honey.'[5]

But God, Glorified and Exalted is He, knows best.

5 Mundhirī, *al-Targhīb*, vol. 4, p. 299.

79 Al-Nāziʿāt

His words, Exalted is He:

[79:4] ***By those that race forward,***

He said:

> This means the spirits of the believers which raced to be the first in [doing] good (*khayr*) and [acting in] conformity (*muwāfaqa*), and raced to be the first to respond to the Angel of Death out of longing (*shawq*) for their Lord. Subsequently, they departed with the most beautiful scent and the fullest joy.

His words, Exalted is He:

[79:16] ***When his Lord called out to him in the holy valley of Ṭuwa?***[1]

He said:

> Moses starved himself, emaciating himself (*ṭāwiyan*), devoting himself (*ʿābidan*) to God, Exalted is He. Then his Lord called him so that he would be closer to Him.

His words, Exalted is He:

[79:37, 38] ***as for him who was rebellious ۞ and preferred the life of this world,***

He said:

> That is, he forswore the rights (*ḥuqūq*) of God, was ungrateful for His blessings and preferred this world, following the craving of [his] lusts and pursuing his whims.

Then he said:

> Every person upon whom the sun has risen or set is ignorant (*jāhil*), except for the one who prefers God, Exalted is He, over himself, his spirit, his life in this world and his Hereafter.

He was asked, 'What is the sign of hatred (*bughḍ*) for this world?' He replied:

> It is that the afflictions (*maṣāʾib*) [of this world] are easy for a person to bear, even those which [affect] him personally or his children. So it is that Muslim b. Yasār said on the death of his son, 'O my son, my grief for you has distracted me from grieving over [my loss of] you. O God, I have transferred to him the reward [which You have granted] me concerning him.'[2] The second sign is that the happiness of this world becomes insignificant in his eyes, even though it gives him ease. The third sign is that there is nothing closer to him than God, Mighty and Majestic is He, as [is indicated by] the saying of ʿĀmir b. ʿAbd al-Qays, 'I never regarded anything without seeing God as closer to it than myself.'[3]

His words, Exalted is He:

[79:40] ***But as for him who feared the standing before his Lord, and restrained his soul from [pursuing its] desire,***

---

1 The Prophet is being asked if he has heard the story of Moses, which is here alluded to briefly. It is related more fully in 20:10–6; 27:7–9; and 28:31–5.

2 i.e. 'I hereby wish to transfer over to my son whatever reward which You give me for not grieving over my own suffering in the loss of my son.'

3 In other words, God was between him and every object. This saying appears in Tirmidhī, *Nawādir al-uṣūl*, vol. 4, p. 74.

He said:

> No one is safe from his desire except a prophet and some of the veracious (*ṣiddīqūn*), though not all of them. The only one who is safe from his desire (*hawā*) is the one who imposes propriety (*adab*) upon himself. The only ones who are purified in their propriety are the prophets ﷺ and some of the veracious; and it is the same case regarding character (*akhlāq*).
>
> One day Ibn al-Sammāk went out to meet his companions, who had gathered to see him, and said, 'I have already given you so many admonitions. Would you like my remedy for you?' They said, 'Yes'. He said, 'Oppose your desires (*ahwāʾ*)!'

But God, Glorified and Exalted is He, knows best.

80 ʿAbasa

His words:

[80:21] ***then He makes him die and buries him.***

He said:

> Its inner meaning is that He causes the pleasures (*ḥuẓūẓ*) which the lower self derives from lust, to die, *and buries him* [i.e. the pleasures] within him.

[80:22] ***Then, when He wills, He will raise him,***

> affiliated with wisdom (*ḥikma*), in a contemplative witnessing (*mushāhada*) of God, whilst being cut off from all other than Him.

His words, Exalted is He:

[80:25] ***We pour down water plenteously,***

He said:

> It is a pouring down of the subtlety of His meanings (*luṭf maʿānīhi*), represented by water. *Then We split the earth* [80:26] which is the heart, *in fissures* [80:26] and grow in it flowers of different colours, those of the spirit (*rūḥ*), intellect (*ʿaql*), faith (*īmān*) and gnosis (*maʿrifa*), just as the Messenger of God ﷺ said, 'Is not the Qurʾān the flower of hearts (*zahrat al-qulūb*)?[1] Does not faith cultivate wealth (*ghinā*)[2] in the heart, just as the rain causes the flowers to grow? Is it not so that avarice (*shuḥḥ*) causes hypocrisy (*nifāq*) to grow in the heart just as dew causes herbage to grow?'

His words, Mighty and Majestic is He:

[80:34] ***the day when a man will flee from his [own] brother,***[3]

> [such as] Abel from Cain, Muḥammad ﷺ from his uncle, Abraham ﷺ from his father, Lot ﷺ from his wife, and Noah ﷺ from his own son.

[80:37] ***every person that day will have a matter to concern him,***

> Which will distract him from everyone except his own self.

1 *Fī* preceding *qulūb* is absent from all three MSS: Z515, f. 128b, F638, f. 63a and F3488, f. 310b.

2 In Z515, f. 128b, F638, f. 63a, it appears to be *ghanī*, with two dots under the *alif maqṣūra*.

3 The following two verses (80:35 and 36) specify: *his mother, his father, his wife, his children.*

81 Al-Takwīr

Sahl said:

Muḥammad b. Sawwār related on the authority of Ibn ʿUmar ﷺ that the Prophet ﷺ said, 'Whoever wishes to behold the Resurrection as if he were seeing it with his own eyes should read: *When the sun is folded away* [81:1], *When the heaven is split open* [82:1] and *When the heaven is rent asunder* [84:1].'

His words, Exalted is He:

[81:14] *[then] a soul will know what it has presented.*

Every soul will be certain of the fact that whatever it strived to do will not be fitting for that assembly. Whoever is blessed by disclaiming any credit for himself will be saved, but whoever is tied to the [expectation of] reward for his deeds will be disappointed.

His words, Exalted is He:

[81:7] *and when souls are coupled.*

It has been said that the souls of the believers will be joined with the dark-eyed maidens of Paradise [houris], while the souls of the disbelievers will be joined with devils. The disbeliever (*kāfir*) and the devil (*shayṭān*) will be coupled together with a single chain. In this verse there is a cautioning against taking evil companions (*quranāʾ al-sūʾ*).

Sahl said:

The natural self and spiritual self will be joined together and will be mingled in [their partaking of] the bliss of Paradise inasmuch as they were allied in this world in keeping remembrance constantly (*idāmat al-dhikr*) and upholding a state of gratitude (*iqāmat al-shukr*).[1]

His words, Exalted is He:

[81:26] *So where are you going?*

⌜Where are you straying to (*ayna taʿdilūna*)⌝[2] away from His Book after [receiving] the explanation (*bayān*) that has come to you?

[81:27] *It is only a reminder for all the worlds,*

He said:

This Message [i.e. the Qurʾān] is especially for those among the worlds who are knowledgeable[3] and submit to the Sacred Law (*sharīʿa*). Do you not notice how God, Exalted is He, has said: *for those of you* ⌜O people of Mecca,⌝[4] *who wish to take the straight path* [81:28], following the way (*ṭarīq*)[5] to Him through faith (*īmān*) in Him. However, your rectitude (*istiqāma*) will not

---

1 See above, Tustarī's commentary on 57:6, and IT, pp. xxxix–xl.

2 Added on the basis of all the MSS: Z515, f. 129a, F638, f. 63a and F3488, f. 211a.

3 Translating *ʿāliman bi'l-ʿilm* according to all three MSS: Z515, f. 129a, F638, f. 63a and F3488, f. 311a, instead of *āliman bi'l-dhikr*.

4 The addition was made on the basis of all the MSS: Z515, f. 129a, F638, f. 63a and F3488, f. 311a.

5 All MSS have *ṭarīq* singular rather than *ṭuruq*, plural.

be sound for you, either in its root or in its branches, save in accordance with My pre-existing will (*mashīʾatī al-ṣābiqa*) [which prevails] over you.

But God, Glorified and Exalted is He, knows best.

82 Al-Infiṭār

His words, Exalted is He:

[82:5] ***[then] a soul will know what it has sent ahead and [what it has] left behind.***

> That is, what it has sent forward, the good or bad, and what it left behind in the form of an evil practice that it initiated (*sayyiʾa sannathā*) and whatever [part of that practice] was emulated [by others afterwards].[1]

His words, Exalted is He:

[82:6] ***O mankind! What has deceived you with regard to your Generous Lord?***

He said:

> That is, 'What has lured you away to other than Him, and severed you from Him, in spite of His graciousness (*luṭf*) and generosity (*karam*)?'

He was asked, 'What is it that cuts the servant off [from God]?' He replied:

> The servant belongs to God, and God is there for His servant. There is nothing closer to Him than the heart of the believer, and if anything else comes into his heart, that becomes a veil (*ḥijāb*) [for him]. Whoever looks upon (*naẓara*) God with his heart, will become distanced from all besides Him, and whoever seeks the means to [attain] His good pleasure (*marḍā*), will be made satisfied by God through His clemency (*ḥilm*).
>
> Furthermore, whoever surrenders his heart to God, Exalted is He, [will find that] God takes care of his bodily members so they remain in rectitude (*istiqāma*). Yet at the same time, their hearts' witnessing is in proportion to how much they safeguard their bodily members.

Then he said:

> Keep a check on your hearts. We are created and our Creator is with us. Do not tire in your works, for truly God watches over you wherever you are. Place your needs before Him and stand at His door.[2] Say: 'We are ignorant, but our Teacher (*ʿālimunā*) is with us. We are weak, but the One who gives us strength (*muqawwiyyunā*) is with us. We are helpless, but our All-Powerful One (*Qādirunā*) is with us.' Truly, whoever adheres to this will find that air, space, earth and sky will become of equal consequence [to him].[3]

ʿUmar b. Wāṣil, a student of Sahl, said, 'When [Sahl] would recite this verse, he [Sahl] would say:

> It is ignorance that has lured me away [from You] ⌜O Lord⌝,[4] due to Your withdrawing Your protection from me.

His words, Mighty and Majestic is He:

[82:13] ***As for the righteous, they will be in bliss*** **(naʿīm).**

---

1 This is according to the *ḥadīth* which states: 'Whoever establishes in Islam a good *sunna* (precedent or exemplary practice) will earn the reward for it and the reward for those who practise it after him, without their reward being reduced in any way. Similarly, whoever establishes a bad *sunna* will earn the punishment for it and for all those who practise it after him…' The *ḥadīth* is listed in Muslim, *Ṣaḥīḥ*, 'Kitāb al-Zakāt', and 'Kitāb al-ʿIlm'.

2 MS F638, f. 63b only has *qūmū* instead of *mūtū*, which latter would translate as 'die at His door'.

3 i.e he will attain detachment from all that is in the universe.

4 Added on the basis of all three MSS: Z515, f. 129b, F638, f. 63b and F3488, f. 311b.

He said:

> The *bliss* of the elect among His servants who are the righteous (*abrār*) is the encounter (*liqāʾ*) with Him and the witnessing (*mushāhada*) of Him, just as their bliss in this world was in the witnessing (*mushāhada*) of Him and proximity (*qurb*) with Him. But God knows best.

83 Al-Muṭaffifīn

His words, Exalted is He:

[83:1] ***Woe to the defrauders!***

He said:

> They are the hypocrites and those who take on their characteristics, stinting in their prayer. Thus did Salmān[1] [al-Fārisī] ﷺ say, 'The prayer is the balance (*mikyāl*); whoever deals faithfully will be rewarded his due, but as for whoever stints — you already know what God, Exalted is He, has said concerning the defrauders (*muṭaffifūn*): *Will you bid others to piety and forget yourselves...?* [2:44]. You vilify them for the slips they make that are typical of the faults of men, and yet you commit similar misdeeds and those which are more abominable still.'[2] No one looks upon the slips of [other] people except an ignorant wrongdoer, and no one [may] make known that which he has looked upon [of the faults of others] except God.[3] Indeed it has been related that God spoke to David ﷺ through inspiration the words, 'I complain of My servants to you, O David!' He asked, 'And why is that, my Lord?' He replied, 'It is because they sin in secret and repent in public, and truly I do not wish anyone to look upon the sin of my servant besides Me.'

ʿUmar b. Wāṣil said that he had asked Sahl about God's words, *Nay, on that day they will be veiled from their Lord* [83:15]. He replied:

> In this life they are veiled from the Commander (*al-Āmir*) and the Restrainer (*al-Zājir*). Thus it was related in a report, 'Happy is the one whose heart acts for him as an admonisher and whose intellect as a restrainer.' So if a person wants something from which God is absent, they [the heart and intellect] will hold him back from it.[4] — [But as for those mentioned in the verse], in the Hereafter they are veiled from the [divine] mercy, and from being able to behold God, Mighty and Majestic is He, and are deprived of His looking upon them with His good pleasure (*riḍā*) and satisfaction (*riḍwān*) when He questions them. Just as He has said, *But [first] stop them, for they must be questioned* [37:24] about [their] religion (*diyāna*), and they will not be able to shake off the evidence against them, so He will put them into the Hellfire.
>
> Then vantage points will be opened for the believers to watch them being burned in the Hellfire and tortured with different kinds of punishment. This will be a source of delight for them and they will laugh at them just as [the disbelievers] had laughed at the believers in this world. Then these vantage points will be blocked and they will be covered over, and with that God will erase their names, and their memory will leave the hearts of the believers. And He says:

---

1 The printed edition, as well as MSS, Z515, f. 130a and F3488, f. 312b all have Sulaymān; however MS F638, f. 63b has Salmān, and it is presumably Salmān al-Fārisī (d. 35/655) who is meant, and this is confirmed by Bayhaqī's *Shuʿab al-īmān* (see following note for reference).

2 This tradition is listed in Bayhaqī, *Sunan*, vol. 2, p. 291, and in Ibn Abī Shayba, *al-Muṣannaf*, vol. 1, p. 209. With a different wording the tradition is also listed in Bayhaqī, *Shuʿab al-īmān*, vol. 3, p. 147.

3 Translating *wa lā yahtiku sitr mā iṭṭalaʿa ʿalayhi illāʾLlāh*, according to all three MSS, Z515, f. 120a, F638, f. 63b and F3488 f. 312a, instead of *lā yahtiku sirr mā iṭṭalaʿa ʿalayhi illāʾl-malʿūn* in the printed edition.

4 All three MSS (Z515, f. 130a, F638, f. 63b and F3488, f. 312b) have: *ʿaqlihi* the second time instead of *qalbihi*. The sentence that follows is not clear either in the published edition or in the MSS, with Z515 and F3488 having *idhā arāda amr Allāh fīhi*...and F638 having *idhā arāda amran li-Llāh fīhi*...F638 only has *manaʿāhu ʿanhu* which seems to make more sense than *maʿnā ʿanhu*.

[83:36] ***Have the disbelievers been requited for what they did?***[5]

[Concerning these words Sahl also] said:

> In this verse there is a clear proof confirming that the vision [of God] (*rūʾya*) will be exclusively for the believers.

His words, Exalted is He:

[83:18] ***Nay, the record of the pious is in ʿIlliyyūn.***[6]

He said:

> The record in its outward meaning in both of the two verses [18 and 19] is a reference to the [record of] deeds, the good and the evil. In its inner meaning it refers to the spirits of the believers and the spirits of the disbelievers. The spirits of the believers are gathered at the lote tree beyond which none may pass, in the form of green birds which fly freely in Paradise until the Day of Resurrection, stamped (*marqūm*) with [seal] of [God's] good pleasure (*riḍā*) and satisfaction (*riḍwān*).[7] On the other hand the spirits of the disbelievers are gathered at Sijjīn beneath the lowest earth,[8] under the cheek of Satan, may God curse him, branded with hostility (*ʿadāwa*) and wrath (*ghaḍab*).[9]

5 The question in this verse may be what is asked by the believers as they watch, or it may be a rhetorical question from God.

6 ʿIlliyūn (or ʿIlliyīn) being the book in which the deeds of the righteous are recorded, though the word is also used to refer to the highest reaches of Paradise. On ʿIlliyyīn, see also Ghazālī's *Iḥyāʾ ʿulūm al-dīn, Kitāb Dhikr al-mawt,* trans. Winter, p. 137 and 237, n. A.

7 Compare a *ḥadīth* of the prophet cited by Ṭabarī in his commentary on 3:169, according to which in Paradise, the martyrs (*shuhadāʾ*) will live in the bodies of green birds who drink from the rivers of Paradise and eat of its fruits and betake themselves to (i.e. their nests are in) golden lamps beneath the shade of the Throne. A similar *ḥadīth* is listed in Muslim, 'Kitāb al-Imāra.'

8 Sijjīn is described in 83:7 and 8 as the book in which man's evil deeds are recorded. However, according to various traditions, it is also believed to be 'a rock beneath the seventh earth, under which the book of the unbeliever is placed', or 'a rock in Hell to which the spirits of the wicked are brought'. Again, see Ghazālī's *Iḥyāʾ ʿulūm al-dīn, Kitāb Dhikr al-mawt,* trans. Winter, p. 138, n. A.

9 All MSS (Z515, f. 130b, F638, f. 63b and F3488, f. 312b) have *ghaḍab* instead of *baghḍāʾ*.

84 Al-Inshiqāq

His words, Exalted is He:

[84:2] ***And heeds its Lord as it should.***[1]

That is, it hearkens to its Lord and responds by performing His command, as it is obliged to do.

[84:6] ***O man! Verily you are toiling laboriously toward your Lord…***

That is, you are striving towards your Lord through your works with great effort, *…and will encounter Him*, by your effort; so look upon your effort: does it merit Paradise and proximity with Him, or Hellfire and alienation from Him?

Once ʿUmāra b. Zādhān[2] said, '[Abū ʿAbd Allāh] Kahmas said to me in a whisper, "O Abū Salma, I committed a sin which I have been crying over for forty years now." I asked him, "What is that, O Abū ʿAbd Allāh?" He replied, "Once a brother of mine visited me and I bought him a grilled fish for a small coin. After he had finished eating, I got up [and went] over to the wall of my neighbour and took a piece of earth from it with which he proceeded to clean his hands. Consequently, I have been crying over that for forty years."'[3]

His words, Exalted is He:

[84:7, 8] ***Then as for him who is given his book in his right hand, ❁ he will receive an easy reckoning,***

That is, He forgives his sins and does not take him to account for them.[4] Similarly it is related in a tradition that God, Exalted is He, if He wishes to conceal [the sins] of a servant on the Day of Resurrection, will show him only those sins which are known to Him and His servant, and then forgive him for them.

[84:9] ***and will return to his family, joyful.***

[That is] in Paradise, with the fulfilment of the promised encounter (*liqāʾ*) and with the divine good pleasure (*riḍā*) that he has gained. Know for certain that God has servants who are not halted at the stopping places[5] [for questioning] and do not experience any of the horrors (*ahwāl*) of the Day of Resurrection, neither the reckoning (*ḥisāb*), nor the questioning (*suʾāl*), nor the Traverse (*ṣirāṭ*). This is because they are for Him and they [live] by Him, they have no cognition of anything other than Him, and they choose none other than Him.[6]

His words, Exalted is He:

[84:19] ***you will surely journey from stage to stage* (ṭabqan ʿan ṭabqin).**

He said:

Its inner meaning is that you will surely be raised rank upon rank (*daraja fawqa daraja*) in

---

1 It being the heaven which is mentioned in verse 1 as being rent asunder.

2 The editor of the Dār al-Kutub al-ʿIlmiyya edition notes that this is ʿUmāra b. Zādhān al-Ṣaydalānī, Abū Salma al-Baṣrī, who is mentioned in Mundhirī, *Targhīb* as having narrated traditions from Ḥasan al-Baṣrī.

3 The anecdote is related in Iṣfahānī, *Ḥilyat al-awliyāʾ*, vol. 6, p. 211.

4 Translating *yaghfiru* and *lā yuḥāsibu* as in all the MSS (Z515, f. 131a, F638, f. 64a and F3488, f. 313a), as opposed to *naghfiru* and *nuḥāsibu* in the published edition.

5 Translating *mawāqif* according to F638, f. 64a, instead of *muwāqafa*. F638 also has the addition of the words *wa-lā yuḥsharūna*.

6 Compare the tradition cited earlier regarding the friends of God in the commentary on 15:92 above.

Paradise, and will be changed from one state to another state (*ḥāl ilā ḥāl*), more eminent and satisfying than the previous one, as you were in the world, rising from rank to rank, higher and higher, through earnest desire (*ṭamaʿ*), fear (*khawf*), longing (*shawq*) and love (*maḥabba*).

85 Al-Burūj

His words, Exalted is He:

[85:3] ***and [by] the witness and the witnessed,***

He said:

> It has been said that the witness (*shāhid*) is the angel,[1] just as He has also said, *[and every soul will be accompanied by] a driver and a witness* [50:21].[2] That which is borne witness to (*mashhūd*) is the Day of Resurrection, ⌜for that is a day that is [indeed] witnessed (*wa dhālika yawmun mashhūdun*).⌝[3]

Ibn ʿAbbās ﷺ said, 'The witness is Muḥammad ﷺ, and that which is witnessed is the Qurʾān.' It has also been said that that which is witnessed is mankind. Sahl said:

> The witness is the spiritual self (*nafs al-rūḥ*) and that which is witnessed is the natural self (*nafs al-tabʿ*), for the natural self, along with the understanding of the intellect (*fahm al-ʿaql*) and the discernment of the heart (*fiṭnat al-qalb*),[4] will each have their witness, while God is the ever-present Witness (*al-Shahīd*) over everything.

His words, Mighty and Majestic is He:

[85:14] ***And He is the Most Forgiving, the Most Loving,***

He said:

> This means that He is the Most Forgiving (*al-Ghafūr*) towards sinners, and the Most Loving (*al-Wadūd*) in [His] forgiveness (*maghfira*). He makes Himself beloved and endearing to His servants through the abundance of blessings that He has granted them, [along with] His beautiful bounties (*jamīl ālāʾihi*) and beneficence (*iḥsān*).

His words, Exalted is He:

[85:22] ***in a Preserved Tablet.***[5]

He said:

> That which is preserved (*maḥfūẓ*) is the breast (*ṣadr*) of the believer. It [the Qurʾān] is protected from being reached by anyone who is not of its people (*ahlihi*),[6] for the people of the Qurʾān are the people of God and His elite. But God knows best.

---

1 Designated for each soul.

2 See above for Tustarī's interpretation of this verse.

3 Added on the basis of all three MSS: Z515, f. 131a, F638, f. 64a and F3488, f. 313b.

4 On this triad of terms, see above the commentary on 18:21; 19:61, 49:9 and IT, p. xl.

5 That which is in the Preserved Tablet (*lawḥ maḥfūẓ*) being here the Qurʾān, which is mentioned in the previous verse. See above 44:3 and p. 186, n. 1. On the Preserved Tablet see also IC, p. 5 and n. 22, and p. 27, n. 84.

6 Or perhaps this might be translated as 'anyone who is not worthy of it.'

86 Al-Ṭāriq

His words, Exalted is He:

[86:1, 3] ***By the sky and the night-visitor! (❁ The star of piercing brightness.)***

He said:

> The sky (*samāʾ*) linguistically means loftiness (*sumuww*) and elevation (*ʿuluww*). In its inner meaning it refers to the spirit of Muḥammad ﷺ, which subsists with the Lord of Might.[1] And the night-visitor (*ṭāriq*) is *the star of piercing brightness* [86:3], which refers to his heart, that is resplendent (*mushriq*) with the realisation of God's oneness (*tawḥīd*), the upholding of His Transcendence (*tanzīh*), constancy in practices of remembrance (*mudāwamat al-adhkār*), and in contemplative witnessing of the Compeller (*al-Jabbār*).

On another occasion he said:

> That which is *piercing* is the heart of the believer, that is, it is resplendent (*mushriq*), purified of uncertainty (*shakk*), doubt (*rayb*) and misgiving which the whispering of the Enemy and the natural self (*nafs al-ṭabʿ*) might stir up in it.[2]

His words, Exalted is He:

[86:4] ***Over every soul there is a keeper.***

> That is, over the natural self there is a keeper [which comes from] God's protection (*ʿiṣma*).

His words, Exalted is He:

[86:9, 10] ***on the day when [all] secrets are examined, ❁ whereat he will have no strength, nor any helper.***

He said:

> That is, He will reveal the intentions (*nīyāt*) with which they worshipped God by [performing] that which God made incumbent upon them, and [refraining] from that which He forbade them. Truly, [the value of] the deeds of all servants on the Day of Resurrection will wholly depend upon their aims (*maqāṣid*).[3]
>
> Rabīʿ used to say, 'The secrets which are concealed from [other] people belong to God and are clearly visible [to Him]. So seek out their remedy!' Then he added, 'What is their remedy? It is to repent and never return [to that sin].'[4]

---

1 Böwering has 'standing before the Lord of Might' which he understands to be a reference back to Muḥammad's pre-eternal time standing alone before God. See above the note to Tustarī's commentary on 7:172 and 53:13.

2 That is, translating *ḥarraka ʿalayhi* according to all three MSS: Z515, f. 131b, F3488, f. 314a (in F638, f. 34b, the *kāf* is just visible), instead of *jarat ʿalayhi* in the published edition.

3 In other words, on their intentions. Compare the famous *ḥadīth* on the importance of intention (*nīya*): 'Actions are but by intention and every man shall have but that which he intended. Thus he whose migration was for Allah and His Messenger, his migration was for Allah and His Messenger, and he whose migration was to achieve some worldly benefit or to take some woman in marriage, his migration was for that for which he migrated'. See Nawawī, *Forty Hadith*, pp. 26–7.

4 The implication is that the secrets are sins which are to be concealed from others. See above the commentary on 83:1. The tradition is listed in Bayhaqī, *Shuʿab al-īmān*, vol. 5, p. 459.

Then Sahl said:

> The weapon (*āla*) of the dervish is in three things: fulfilling his [religious] obligation[s] (*farḍ*), preserving his neediness [for God] (*faqr*), and keeping his secret (*sirr*).[5]

His words, Exalted is He:

[86:11, 12] ***By the heaven and its returning,*** ❁ ***and [by] the earth that cracks open,***

He said:

> In its outward meaning *it* [vs. 11] means [the sky] which repeatedly brings forth rain after rain; *and [by] the earth that cracks open* [outwardly means] through [the growth of] plants (*bi'l-nabāt*). In its inner meaning, [vs. 11] refers to the heart which returns to a state of regret (*nadam*) after sinning, while *the earth that cracks open* [inwardly refers to] the ⌜lower self⌝,[6] which is cracked open[7] through acts of conformity, in deeds and words.

His words, Exalted is He:

[86:16] ***and I [too] am devising a scheme.***

He said:

> In this world, His scheme (*kayd*) against them is His allowing them to descend, little by little (*istidrāj*),[8] and to remain in their delusion (*ightirār*); and in the Hereafter, it is the bitter regret they will be made to feel when they look upon the generous treatment (*ikrām*) and honour (*iʿzāz*) that those who professed His oneness [enjoy].

5 It is not entirely clear what is meant by 'secret' here, but, given the context, it probably has the same meaning as that referred to in the previous footnote.

6 The addition was made on the basis of all three MSS: Z515, f. 132a, F638, f. 64b and F3488, f. 314b.

7 i.e. subdued.

8 On *istidrāj* see above Tustarī's commentary on 2:41, and p. 20, n. 48 his commentary on 3:8 and p. 42, n. 10, 4:142 and p. 57, n. 26.

87 Al-Aʿlā

His words, Exalted is He:

[87:1] ***Glorify the name of your Lord Most High,***

He said:

> It [means] to proclaim His transcendence (*tanzīh*) above having rivals (*aḍdād*) and equals (*andād*). This is its outward meaning. In its inner meaning, it is to witness Him (*mushāhadatuhu*) through remembrance (*dhikr*) during the ritual prayer without witnessing anything else.

His words, Exalted is He:

[87:3] ***and [God] who determined and guided,***

He said:

> He destined for them wretchedness (*shaqāwa*) or felicity (*saʿāda*).[1] Then He took the people of felicity into His care and left the people of wretchedness to themselves.

He said:

> Guidance (*hudā*) comes in two forms, one being that which is made clear (*bayān*),[2] and the other, guardianship (*tawallī*) from God, Exalted is He. Do you not see how the suckling infant is guided to the means of its subsistence, the breast of its mother ⌜the moment it is born⌝,[3] due to God's caring for it, and inspiring it [with what to do].

His words, Exalted is He:

[87:14] ***Successful indeed is he who purifies himself,***

He said:

> That is, the one who fears God both in secret and in public has indeed triumphed (*fāza*) and attained felicity (*saʿāda*).

His words, Exalted is He:

[87:16] ***Nay, but you prefer the life of this world,***

He said:

> The believer should not be in this world other than as a man riding a piece of wood in the sea, crying the while, 'O Lord! O Lord! (*Yā Rabb! Yā Rabb!*), in the hope that He may save him from it. Every believing servant who has renounced this world, [will find that] God has placed in charge of him an angel, who will plant in his heart all kinds of wisdom (*ḥikam*), just as the people of this world plant different kinds of trees in their gardens.

---

1 Their wretchedness or felicity being on the basis of the ultimate end that is destined for them. See above, Tustarī's commentary on 7:172.

2 i.e. through the Revelation or the Sunna. On the meaning of *bayān*, see above, p. 32, n. 105.

3 The addition was made on the basis of all three MSS: Z515, f. 132a, F638, f. 64b and F3488, f. 314b.

88 Al-Ghāshiya

His words, Exalted is He:

[88:2] ***Some faces on that day will be humbled,***

That is, [they will face] humiliation (*dhalīla*), because God, Exalted is He, had ordered them to submit, become humble, and show neediness towards Him in this life, but they did not, so He brought them low in the Hereafter with everlasting humiliation (*dhilla bāqiya*).[1]

His words, Exalted is He:

[88:3] ***toiling, weary,***

That is, toiling in this world with innovations (*bidaʿ*)[2] and aberrations (*ḍalālāt*), weary in the Hereafter from the punishment in the lowest regions of Hell (*darakāt*).

[88:5] ***made to drink from a boiling spring,***

That is, from a spring of pus whose heat has reached its extreme, which He also called *ḥamīm ʾān* [55:44], meaning that it has reached its ultimate degree of heat.

His words, Exalted is He:

[88:8] ***Other faces on that day will be radiant with bliss,***

That is, [in] blessing (*niʿma*) and honour (*karāma*).

[88:9] ***pleased with their efforts,***

in the Hereafter.[3]

His words, Exalted is He:

[88:12] ***Therein is a flowing spring,***[4]

flowing [freely] (*muṭṭarada*), without [being impeded] by any furrow (*ghayr ukhdūd*).

[88:13] ***and therein are raised couches,***

That is, raised beds, upon each of which are seventy mattresses (*firāsh*) each as lofty as a high palace (*ghurfa*) of this world.[5]

Sahl said:

God, Exalted is He, mentioned these bounties to make it [Paradise] enticing for them. While He warns them that His punishment is in proportion to His authority (*sulṭān*), [He also informs them that] His generosity (*karāma*) is in proportion to His tremendousness (*ʿaẓīm al-shaʾn*) and authority (*sulṭān*). However, the hearts of the disbelievers in Mecca did not benefit from

---

1 MSS Z515, f. 132b, F638, f. 65a have *madhalla* whereas F3488, f. 315a and the published edition have *dhilla*.

2 All the MSS (Z515, f. 132b, F638, f. 65a and F3488, f. 315a) have simply *al-bidaʿ* instead of *anwāʿ al-bidaʿ* as in the published edition.

3 That is, in this world they should only have an eye on the shortcomings and inadequacy of their efforts.

4 That is, in the lofty garden (vs. 10) in which the blessed will find themselves in Paradise.

5 According to Winter's translation of Ghazālī's *Iḥyāʾ ʿulūm al-dīn*, *Kitāb Dhikr al-mawt*, p. 237, n. A., the word *ghurfa* (root *gh-r-f*) has been traditionally associated with the idea of 'exaltation'. See for example Tirmidhī, *Nawādir al-uṣūl*, vol. 3, pp. 93–4, and al-Murtaḍā al-Zabīdī, who in his *Itḥāf al-sāda al-muttaqīn bi-sharḥ asrār Iḥyāʾ ʿulūm al-dīn* (Cairo, 1894), vol. 10, p. 528, defines *ghuraf* (plural of *ghurfa*) as 'high palaces'.

this, even though He reminded them of His omnipotence (*qudra*), in order that they might take a lesson [from it].

Then He says, Exalted is He:

[88:17] ***Will they not consider the camels, how they are made?***

In its inner meaning it is a command for the believers to humble themselves before Him and declare their neediness for Him. He says: 'Consider the camels, how they have been created and how, notwithstanding their make up and their strength, they yield to a boy driving them without showing bewilderment (*taḥayyur*), and without choosing to do anything else.'[6] Thus, you are not incapable of being with your Lord as the camel is with its owner, and this is why the Messenger ﷺ said: 'Be for your Lord as the yielding camel',[7] meaning compliant (*miṭwāʿ*).[8]

But God, Glorified and Exalted is He, knows best.

6 The use of the word bewilderment (*taḥayyur*) is interesting here because the related word *ḥayra* can have the meaning of being confused in one's faith by doubt based on one's own reasoning (or lack of it). In Sufism, however, *ḥayra* and *taḥayyur* can have other more positive meanings. See, for example, Hujwīrī, *Kashf al-maḥjūb*, p. 401; trans. Nicholson, p. 275: 'Gnosis is continual amazement (*al-maʿrifa dawām al-ḥayra*)'. See also Ibn ʿArabī's explanations of *ḥayra*, translated by William Chittick in his *Sufi Path of Knowledge* (Albany, NY, 1989), pp. 3, 114, 211, 296 and 380; and several examples cited in Keeler, *Sufi Hermeneutics*, pp. 194, 251–3; and 258–9.

7 The editor of the Dār al-Kutub al-ʿIlmiyya edition notes that this may be an allusion to a *ḥadīth* which appears in Nīsābūrī, *al-Mustadrak*, vol. 1, p. 130: *Innaʾl-muʾmin kaʾl-jamaliʾl-anif.*

8 All the MSS (Z515, f. 132b, F638, f. 65a and F3488, f. 315b) have *miṭwāʿ*.

89 Al-Fajr

His words, Exalted is He:

[89:1] *By the daybreak,*

He said:

In its outward meaning, *daybreak* (fajr) refers to the dawn (*subḥ*).

[89:2] *and by the ten nights,*

His words:

[In its outer meaning] it refers to the [first] ten nights of Dhū al-Ḥijja, which are the Well-known Days.[1]

[89:3] *and by the even,*

[That is], Adam and Eve. It has also been said that it refers to all that God has created as opposites, such as the night and day, light and darkness, and death and life; *and the odd*: this [refers to] God, Exalted is He.

[89:4] *and by the night when it passes away!*

Night is the Night of the Assembly (*laylat al-jamʿ*): it passes away along with all that is in it.[2]

[89:1–4]

He said:

The inner meaning of [the verses] is [the following: *By the dawn* [89:1] refers to Muḥammad ﷺ, from whom the lights of faith, the lights of acts of obedience and the lights of the two worlds of existence gushed forth (*tafajjarat*); *and by the ten nights,* [89:2] [refers to] the ten Companions, regarding whom [the Prophet] testified [that they would] enter Paradise;[3] *by the even,* [refers to] the obligatory practice (*farḍ*) and the Sunna; *and the odd* [89:3], [refers to having] the intention of sincerity (*nīyat al-ikhlāṣ*) towards God, Exalted is He, in all acts of obedience, without regard for anyone else during them. *And by the night when it passes away* [89:4], [refers to] the Prophet's nation and the 'great blackness' (*sawād aʿẓam*), as [was mentioned by the Prophet when] he ﷺ said, 'On the night I was taken on the journey, I saw a great blackness from heaven to earth, so I asked, "What is this blackness, O Gabriel?" He replied, "This is your nation (*umma*), and there are belonging to you seventy thousand among them who will enter Paradise [directly] without reckoning (*ḥisāb*). They are not harmed by misdeeds (*khaṭāyā*),[4] they did not become

---

1 The tenth of the Hijrī month of Dhū al-Ḥijja marks the culmination of the Hajj and the commencement of ʿĪd al-Aḍḥā.

2 According to one of the traditions cited by Ṭabarī, *the night* here refers to the 'Night of Assembly', which is said to signify the assembly of Muzdalifa. Muzdalifa (also known as Mashʿar) is a place approximately halfway between Mina and Arafat, and it is where pilgrims performing the Hajj spend the night of the ninth to tenth of Dhū al-Ḥijja, after the Day of Arafat. From Arafat the pilgrims proceed to Muzdalifa where the sunset prayers are said. They then spend the night there and pray the dawn prayer. After sunrise they proceed to Mina, with the pebbles they have gathered in Muzdalifa, for the stoning at the Jamarāt, followed by the sacrifice marking the end of the Hajj and the beginning of ʿĪd.

3 Regarding these Companions, p. 259, n. 2 above.

4 The text has *lam tukallimhum*, by which may be meant: no misdeeds spoke out against them.

tainted in this life, and they are cognisant only of God."[5] Thus has God sworn an oath by him, his Companions and his nation.

That which is sworn to by the oath is:[6]

[89:14] ***Assuredly your Lord is ever watchful.***

This means: the path of every person leads to Him. He will then reward them for their deeds and they will either be saved or otherwise. And He [elsewhere] says that He will position a patrol (*raṣad*) of angels with ⌜hooks (*kalālīb*) and⌝[7] pikes (*ḥasak*) on the Traverse over Hell (*jisr jahannam*), who will question people concerning the religious obligations (*farāʾiḍ*).[8]

[89:15] ***And as for man, whenever his Lord tries him with honour and blessings, he says, 'My Lord has honoured me.'***

He said:

This means, there will be among the believers one who, when his Lord tests him with blessings, says, *'My Lord has honoured me* in the abundance (*saʿa*) and provision (*rizq*) that He has given me.' However, this is really a way of leaving him to degenerate further (*istidrāj*), and a source of delusion (*ightirār*).[9] Indeed, Ḥasan ﷺ once said, 'The servant remains in a good state as long as he is aware of that which corrupts his works. Among them [God's servants] is he whose [action] is made to appear beautiful to him, and among them is he who has been dominated by lust (*shahwa*).

[89:16] ***But when He tests him and restricts His provision for him…***

That is, He stints (*qatara*) His provision for him, *…he says, 'My Lord has humiliated me'* through poverty (*faqr*). But God says:

[89:17] ***'Not so!'…***

'I did not try him with wealth to honour him (*karāma*), nor did I try him with poverty to make him despicable to Me (*hawān*)'.[10]

It has been related that Fatḥ al-Mawṣilī, who was fasting on returning home to his family after the night prayer, said: 'Give me some supper.' They answered that they did not have anything to give him for supper. He asked, 'Why are you sitting in the dark?' They replied, 'We don't have any oil with which to light the lamp.'

He said:

Then he wept for joy and continued to do so until morning saying, 'O God! Does someone like me get left without supper and without light? O Master, which of my hands was responsible for this?'[11]

His words, Exalted is He:

[89:27] ***O soul at peace!***

---

5 Bukhārī, *Ṣaḥīḥ*, 'Kitāb al-Ṭibb', and 'Kitāb al-Riqāq'.

6 lit.: 'The answer (*jawāb*) to the oath is…'

7 Added on the basis of Z515, f. 133a, F638, f. 65b and F3488, f. 316a.

8 By *jisr jahannam* is meant the Traverse (*ṣirāt*), discussed above in p. 135, n. 1. The word *jisr* is used for the Traverse in Bukhārī, *Ṣaḥīḥ*, 'Kitāb al-Tawḥīd', and in Muslim, *Ṣaḥīḥ*, 'Kitāb al-Īmān'.

9 In other words, this person interprets the abundance and provision as being God's indication of his deserving it in some way. On *istidrāj*, again see references given on p. 278, n. 8.

10 Thus the blessing (*niʿma*) can be a form of *makr* from God, especially if one sees oneself as having deserved it, or being honoured by it. On *makr* see above p. 20, n. 47.

11 Cited in Bayhaqī, *Shuʿab al-īmān*, vol. 7, p. 230. See above the commentary on 29:1, 2, and 37:106, where Tustarī speaks of the benefits of suffering and privation. Overall, there appear to be two lessons in this tradition, one positive and one negative. The positive lesson is about the blessing of deprivation, which we have seen explained several times, while the negative lesson may be a warning about attributing blessings to one's own actions.

He said:

This speech addresses the spiritual self (*nafs al-rūḥ*), through which the natural self has its life, *at peace* is [its] affirming God's reward and His punishment.

[89:28] *Return to your Lord, pleased and pleasing.*

by way of the Hereafter, *pleased* with God through God, *pleasing*, due to its tranquil repose (*sukūn*) in God, Mighty and Majestic is He.

[89:29] *Then enter among My servants.*

That is, among the company of My friends (*awliyāʾ*), who are My servants in truth (*ḥaqqan*).

[89:30] *And enter My paradise.*

Sahl said:

Paradise is actually two paradises. One of them is the Garden itself, and the other is life with Life itself (*ḥayāt bi-ḥayāt*) and permanent subsistence with Permanent Subsistence itself. Similarly it has been related in a report that the angels say to those solely devoted to Him (*munfaridūn*) on the Day of Resurrection, 'Proceed to your resting places in Paradise',[12] to which they say, 'What is Paradise to us when we have devoted ourselves solely to [Him] because of a special understanding (*maʿnā*) which has been [granted] to us from Him? We do not want anything save Him — that is the only good life (*ḥayāt ṭayyiba*).' And God knows best.

12 The word *manāzil*, translated here as 'resting places', also has the meaning of rank, station or stopping place.

90 Al-Balad

His words, Exalted is He:

[90:1] ***I swear by this city,***

He said:

That is, Mecca.

[90:2] ***and you have free disposal of this city;***

This means: 'On the day of the conquest of Mecca, We made it legitimate for you, so that you could kill whomever you wished among the disbelievers', just as the Prophet ﷺ said: 'It was never made legitimate for anyone before, nor will it be made legitimate to anyone after me. However, it was made legitimate for me just for one hour in a day.'[1]

God, Exalted is He, swore by Mecca due to the fact that His Prophet resided there, as a way of honouring him and humiliating his enemies.

[90:3] ***and [by] the parent and offspring,***

He said:

Parent refers to Adam and *offspring* refers to Muḥammad ﷺ.[2]

[90:4] ***We certainly created man in travail* (kabad).**

That is, in [a state of] difficulty (*mashaqqa*) and hardship (*shidda*).

He [also] said:

Kabad also means erectness (*intiṣāb*) — that is, 'We have created him in the belly [of his mother] keeping him erect'. This resembles Mujāhid's saying: 'The child sits in the belly of its mother in a upright position corresponding to the uprightness of the mother,[3] and an angel is delegated, when the mother lies on her side, to raise up the child's head and if it was not for that it would drown in blood.'

His words, Exalted is He:

[90:10] ***and given him guidance [concerning] the two paths?***[4]

He said:

'We have clearly shown him the path of goodness that he may follow it, and the path of evil that he may avoid it', just as He said, *Verily We have guided him to the way, whether he be grateful or ungrateful* [76:3]. It has also been said [that it refers to] management and devising (*tadbīr*).[5]

---

1 Bukhārī, *Ṣaḥīḥ*, 'Kitāb al-Janā'iz'.

2 See above, IT, p. xxxii, Tustarī's commentary on 2:5 and p. 15, n. 17.

3 i.e. with its head upwards.

4 Verses 8–10 make up a rhetorical question: *Have We not given him two eyes ❁ and a tongue, and two lips ❁ and given him guidance concerning the two paths?*

5 Sic in both the published edition and all the MSS. Possibly it could mean either: He [God] showed them the way of submitting the management [of their affairs] to Him (this being the guidance); or it could be that the servant's being grateful or ungrateful means his either relinquishing everything to God's care or taking upon himself the management of his affairs.

His words, Exalted is He:

[90:11] *Yet why does he not attempt the obstacle?*

He said:

That is, 'Will he not cross the Traverse (*ṣirāṭ*) and the obstacle (*ʿaqaba*) which is before it?' In its inner meaning there are two obstacles. One of them is the sins that he has committed, which stand before him like a mountain and which he can only traverse by setting a slave free, or feeding someone who is either destitute (*miskīn*), or totally abject[6] from exertion (*jahd*) and deprivation (*fāqa*), or an orphan who is related to him, on a day of hunger (*majāʿa*) and hardship (*shidda*).[7]

The other obstacle is gnosis (*maʿrifa*), which the mystic is incapable of attaining, unless it be that, with [the assistance of] the power (*ḥawl*) and strength (*quwwa*) of God, he emancipates the slave of his soul from desire.

[90:14] *or to give food on a day of hunger,*

in order to uphold what is demanded by your faith, not by way of any oppression (*ẓulm*) or transgression (*ṭughyān*) that is for the pleasure of your natural self (*nafs al-ṭabʿ*).[8]

[90:15] *or [give food] to an orphan of kin* (dhā maqraba)

The orphan here refers to the heart (*qalb*), and its food is fidelity (*wafāʾ*). The destitute person (*miskīn*) refers to the mystic who is bewildered (*mutaḥayyir*) ⌜and grieving (*ḥazīn*)⌝.[9] His food consists of [divine] graces (*alṭāf*).[10] [Such a one] is in a state of proximity in 'the eyes of' God (*dhā maqraba ʿinda'Llāh*), but in a state of need and misery (*dhā 'l-matraba*) in the eyes of people [90:16].[11]

His words, Exalted is He:

[90:17] *(while being one of those who believe and who) enjoin one another to steadfastness and enjoin one another to compassion.*

He said:

That is, steadfastness (*ṣabr*) in keeping God's commandments, and in being compassionate with people.

The Messenger of God ﷺ was once asked, 'What is Islam?' He replied, 'It is patience (*ṣabr*) and magnanimity (*samāḥ*).' Then he was asked, 'What is faith?' He replied, 'Goodness in speech (*ṭayyib al-kalām*), and offering [others] food.'

Sahl said:

The best speech (*aṭyab al-kalām*) is the remembrance (*dhikr*) of God, Exalted is He.

[90:18] *Those are the people of the Right Hand.*[12]

---

6 lit. 'cleaves to the earth'.

7 This is probably an allusion to verse 14, which commands the giving of food *on a day of hunger*, which is how the word *masghaba* has been translated. In fact, MS F638, f. 66a has *yawm dhī masghaba ay majāʿa wa shidda*. If we take this to be correct, then the commentary is acting as an interpretation of the words *yawm dhī masghaba*, which occur in verse 14. There is also in the commentary an allusion forward to verse 15, the giving to an orphan of kin.

8 Perhaps what is meant by 'oppression' (*ẓulm*) here is the wronging of one's self, by giving, for example, in an ostentatious manner. The same verbal root (*ẓ-l-m*) is used concerning Adam and Eve in 7:23: *They said, 'Lord we have wronged ourselves'* (qālā, Rabbanā ẓalamnā anfusanā).

9 Added on the basis of all three MSS: Z515, f. 134b, F638, f. 66a and F3488, f. 317a.

10 That is, according to MSS Z515, f. 134b, F3488, f. 317a and the published edition. MS F638, f. 66a, however, has *fāqa* (deprivation).

11 The expression (*dhā matraba*) [90:16] is related to the expression *lazq al-turāb*, which Tustarī has used above, meaning literally 'cleaving or clinging to the dust'. Those who appear to others to be deprived and are outwardly so, are inwardly wealthy and close to God.

12 *Those* being the people who were described in the two previous verses as being among the ones who: *enjoin one another to steadfastness* [90:17] *and enjoin one another to compassion* [90:18].

That is, those who have kept themselves safe[13] from the horrors (*ahwāl*) of that Day.[14] They have no [sensory] perception other than of Him (*lā yuḥissūna dūnahu*), just as they were in this world; [thus they attain] life with Life itself (*ḥayāt bi-ḥayāt*), eternity with Eternity itself (*azaliyya bi-azaliyya*), and a mystery with Mystery itself (*sirr bi-sirr*).[15] But God, Glorified and Exalted is He, knows best.

13 lit. 'favoured themselves'. The printed text has *muyāminūn* whereas the MSS have *mayāmīn* (probably as the plural of *maymūn*) *ʿalā anfusihim*.

14 i.e. the Day of Judgement.

15 This resembles closely the commentary on 89:28, which spoke of: 'life with Life itself and permanent subsistence with Permanent Subsistence itself'.

91 Al-Shams

His words, Exalted is He:

[91:3] ***By the day when it reveals her [the sun],***

He said:

> This means: the light of faith removes the darkness of ignorance and extinguishes the flames of the Fire.

[91:4] ***and by the night when it enshrouds her,***

He said:

> This means: sins, and persistence in committing them, conceal the light of faith so that it does not shine within the heart, and does not manifest its effect in his qualitites (*ṣifāt*), just as the Prophet ﷺ said, 'Desire (*hawā*) and lust (*shahwa*) overwhelm knowledge (*ʿilm*), intellect (*ʿaql*) and lucidity (*bayān*).'[1] [This is due] to the pre-eternal decree of God, Mighty and Majestic is He.[2]

His words, Exalted is He:

[91:9] ***successful indeed will be the one who purifies it,***[3]

He said:

> He who is granted [the ability to consider] (*naẓar*) the matter of his final return (*maʿād*), succeeds.

[91:10] ***and he will indeed have failed who eclipses it.***

He said:

> The soul which is misled by God, Mighty and Majestic is He, such that it does not give the matter of its final return any consideration, will fail.

1 This tradition also appears in the context of 38:26 and under 2:106, and is listed in Iṣfahānī, *Ḥilyat al-awliyāʾ* (vol. 10, p. 88) not as a Prophetic *ḥadīth*, but a saying of al-Ḥārith b. Asad.

2 That is, reading *li-sābiq al-qadar* in MSS Z515, f. 134b and F3488, f. 317b, or *li-sābiqat al-qadar* in F638, f. 66b, as opposed to *li-sābiq al-qudra* in the printed edition.

3 *It* being a reference back to the soul, which was mentioned in verse 7: *By the soul and the One who proportioned it.*

92 Al-Layl

His words, Exalted is He:

[92:1] ***By the night as it enshrouds,***

He said:

In its inner meaning it refers to the natural self (*nafs al-ṭabʿ*).

[92:2] ***and [by] the day as it unveils,***

[It refers to] the spiritual self (*nafs al-rūḥ*).

[92:3] ***and [by] the One who created the male and the female,***

That is, by the One who created fear (*khawf*) and hope (*rajāʾ*), fear being the male and hope being the female.

[92:4] ***assuredly your efforts are dissimilar.***

There are some that are pure and some that are tainted with impurities (*aḥdāth*).

[92:5, 6] ***As for him who gives and is mindful [of God] ❁ And affirms the truth of the best [word],***

Abū Bakr al-Ṣiddīq ﷺ gave of his soul and wealth with all his effort, and was on his guard against acquiescing in his natural self. He affirmed *the truth of the best [word]* — the word which attests to the divine oneness (*kalimat al-tawḥīd*). It has also been said [that this means affirming the truth of] the reward (*jazāʾ*), or that it means sincerity (*ikhlāṣ*).

[92:7] ***We shall surely ease his way to [the abode] of ease.***

That is, the return to goodness (*khayr*).

[92:8] ***But as for one who is niggardly and deems himself self-sufficient,***

Abū Jahl[1] was niggardly in offering obedience to God and His Prophet; and *deems himself self-sufficient* — he [Abū Jahl] made it self evident that he considered himself to have no need of either [God or His Prophet].

[92:10] ***We shall surely ease his way to hardship,***

That is, We shall facilitate work[s] (*ʿamal*) for him — works that are as those of the people of the Fire. Do you not notice how He said directly after this:

[92:11] ***and his wealth shall not avail him when he perishes.***

in the Fire.

[92:13] ***Truly to Us belong the Hereafter and the first [life].***

The Hereafter is the spiritual self (*nafs al-rūḥ*), and *the first [life]* [i.e. this world] is the natural self (*nafs al-ṭabʿ*). He guides one person in the direction of [his] spiritual self and another in the direction of [his] natural self.

---

1 MSS: Z515, f. 134b and F3488, f. 318a have Abū Sufyān, but the printed edition has Abū Jahl, while F638, f. 66b has Abū Sufyān corrected to Abū Jahl, perhaps by a later hand. Abū Jahl is more likely since he remained till the end a bitter foe of the Prophet, whereas Abū Sufyān converted to Islam after the conquest of Mecca in 630.

His words, Exalted is He:

[92:17, 18] ***The [one who is] most mindful of God will be spared it, ❁ he who gives his wealth away to purify himself,***

He said:

> The one who is most mindful of God (*atqā*) refers to al-Ṣiddiq [Abū Bakr] ﵁, who was among people the one with the greatest awareness of God; for [other] people gave and were mindful of God, but he did not even see the ephemeral (*al-fānī*), keeping for himself [only] the Everlasting (*al-Bāqī*). Thus [when] the Messenger of God ﷺ asked [him], 'What did you leave for yourself?', he replied, 'God and His Messenger.'[2]

His words, Exalted is He:

[92:21] ***And verily [soon] he shall [himself] be pleased.***

He said:

> [*pleased*] with what is in store for him with Us, this being the position of [receiving God's] favour (*faḍl*), not the position of [receiving] a reward (*thawāb*); a mystery with Mystery itself (*sirr bi-sirr*), life with Life itself (*ḥayāt bi-ḥayāt*) and eternity with Eternity itself (*azaliyya bi-azaliyya*). But God knows best.

2 Bayhaqī, *Shuʿab al-īmān*, vol. 2, p. 106.

93 Al-Ḍuhā

His words, Exalted is He:

[93:1] ***By the forenoon,***

He said:

In its inner meaning it is the spiritual self (*nafs al-rūḥ*).

[93:2] ***and [by] the night when it is still,***

This means the natural self (*nafs al-ṭabʿ*) when it finds tranquil repose with the spiritual self (*nafs al-rūḥ*) in the constant remembrance (*dhikr*) of God, Exalted is He.[1]

His words, Exalted is He:

[93:4] ***and verily, the life to come will be better for you than first [life]***

He said:

What I have kept in store for you [Muḥammad], such as the Praiseworthy Station (*maqām maḥmūd*),[2] and the place of intercession (*maḥall al-shafāʿa*), is better than that which I have given you in the life of the world, such as prophethood and messengership.

His words, Exalted is He:

[93:6] ***Did He not find you an orphan and shelter you?***

He said:

Did He not find you alone and then gave you refuge with your Companions?

[93:7] ***And did He not find you erring and then guide you?***

He said:

He found you without knowledge of your own worth, so He made you aware of your great worth. He found you *erring* away from [understanding] the implications (*maʿānī*) of [God's] unadulterated affection (*maḥḍ mawadda*) for you, so He gave you to drink of the draught of His affection in the cup of His love. Then He guided you to gnosis (*maʿrifa*) of Him and invested you with the robe of His prophethood and His messengership, that He might guide [you] by them [these distinctions] to proximity (*qurb*) with Him, and to His unicity (*waḥdāniyya*).

He said:

It also has another interpretation: *And did he not find you*, that is, your natural self (*nafs al-ṭabʿ*) in need (*faqīra*) of the way of gnosis (*sabīl al-maʿrifa*).

[93:8] ***And did He not find you needy and enrich you?***

He said:

'He found your soul[3] in bewilderment (*ḥayrāna*), craving (*wāliha*) for gnosis of Us, in need (*faqīra*) of it. Then [He] strengthened your spiritual self (*nafs al-rūḥ*) and enriched it with the

---

1 The MSS (Z515, f. 135b, F638, f. 67a and F3488, f. 318b) all have *dhikr li'Llāh* as opposed to *dhikr ilā'Llāh*. Again we have here the idea of the natural self and the spiritual self coming together in the remembrance of God.

2 On the 'Praiseworthy Station' see above, p. 31, n. 104.

3 Or 'natural self' as in the preceding interpretation.

Qurʾān and wisdom (*ḥikma*).' Indeed, the Prophet ﷺ said, 'Richness (*ghinā*) is not having an abundance of possessions; richness is only a richness of the soul.'[4]

[93:9] ***So, as for the orphan, do not oppress him,***

'For you have tasted [the bitterness of] being an orphan (*yutm*).'

Then he said:

Another interpretation is the following: '⌜So be gracious to the orphan (*fa-ʾlṭuf biʾl-yatīm*)⌝,[5] for you know what it means for the heart of an orphan to receive benevolence (*luṭf*).'

4 Isḥāq b. Rāhwayh, *al-Musnad* (Medina, 1991), vol. 1, p. 332.

5 Added on the basis of all three MSS: Z515, f. 135b, F638, f. 67a and F3488, f. 318b.

94 Al-Inshirāḥ[1]

His words, Exalted is He:

[94:1] ***Did We not expand your breast for you?***

He said:

> 'Did We not dilate your breast for you, with the light of the Message (*risāla*), and make it a mine for the spiritual realities (*maʿdan li'l-ḥaqāʾiq*)?'

He [further] said:

> The first expansion takes place through the light of Islam, just as He has said, Exalted is He, *Whomever God desires to guide, He expands his breast to Islam* [6:125].

Then he said:

> Then He augments the degrees (*manāzil*) in addition [to this light], and the lights of [a believer] will be in proportion to the insights he has been granted.

[94:2] ***[and did We not] relieve you of the burden?***

He said:

> This means: 'We removed from you any acquiescence (*sukūn*) in other than Us, [that might arise] from the desire (*himma*) of the natural self, and We have made you peacefully reliant on Us, receiving [all] from Us, through Us.'

His words, Exalted is He:

[94:4] ***Did We not exalt your mention?***

He said:

> 'We linked your name with Our name in the call to prayer (*adhān*) and the profession of the divine oneness (*tawḥīd*).[2] Furthermore, a servant's faith is not accepted until he believes in you.'[3]

His words, Exalted is He:

[94:5] ***So truly with hardship comes ease,***

He said:

> God, Exalted is He, has magnified the state of hope (*rajāʾ*) in this verse out of His generosity (*karam*) and His hidden grace (*khafī luṭfihi*), and thus He mentions ease twice.[4] Indeed, the Prophet ﷺ said, 'Hardship (*ʿuṣr*) will not overwhelm the two eases.'[5] By this he meant: the discernment of the heart (*fiṭnat al-qalb*) and the intellect (*ʿaql*) are the two 'eases' which take control of the natural self, and return it to the state of sincerity (*ikhlāṣ*). This is [also]the inner meaning of the verse, namely that along with the hardship (*shidda*) of the natural self (*nafs*

---

1 All the MSS bear the title 'A-lam nashraḥ', these being the first words of the *sūra*.

2 The second part of the twofold attestation of faith, after the profession of the divine Unity, 'I bear witness that there is no god save God (*lā ilāha illā'Llāh*)', is the following: 'I bear witness that Muḥammad is the Messenger of God'. The second part of the twofold attestation of faith (*shahādatayn*), is likewise recited during the call to prayer (*adhān*).

3 As well as believing in the other prophets. The Muslim 'creed' comprises belief in God, His angels, His messengers, His books and the Resurrection.

4 For verse 94:6 also states: *Truly with hardship comes ease.*

5 Nīsābūrī, *al-Mustadrak*, vol. 2, pp. 329 and 575.

al-ṭabʿ), in its need for God Himself (*dhāt al-Ḥaqq*), Mighty and Majestic is He, [and] for the spiritual self (*nafs al-rūḥ*), ⌜[there comes] the ease (*suhūla*) of the spiritual self⌝,[6] the intellect (*ʿaql*) and the discernment of the heart (*fiṭnat al-qalb*), and this, in its inner meaning, [signifies] the confident abandonment (*taskīn*) of the heart of Muḥammad ﷺ to the [divine] succour (*iʿāna*) in fear. So He [God] said, 'Truly, We gave ascendancy (*sallaṭnā*) over your dense natural self, to the subtle [substances] (*laṭāʾif*) of your spiritual self, intellect, heart and understanding (*fahm*), all of which pre-existed as a momentous gift (*mawhiba jalīla*) before the creation appeared by a thousand years, and thus did they subdue the natural self.'[7]

[94:7] ***So when you are finished, toil,***

'[When you have completed] the prescribed prayer (*ṣalāt*), and you are seated, *toil* towards your Lord, and return to Him as you were before [the existence] of the natural self, before the appearance of the creation, alone with the One alone, a secret with a secret.' Hence, God granted him [Muḥammad] the likeness of his primordial rank in the world, just as the Prophet ﷺ said, 'Truly, I possess a moment (*waqt*) with God, during which I cannot attend to other than Him.'[8] This is the inner meaning of the verse. Its outer meaning is what is obvious.

Abū ʿAmr b. ʿAlāʾ related the [following story], saying, 'We fled from al-Ḥajjāj[9] to the desert, and lived there for a period of time going from neighbourhood to neighbourhood. One morning I was wandering through some neighbourhoods with a distracted mind, clouded heart and feeling downcast, when suddenly I heard an Arab shaykh [who was] passing by recite the following verses: [*khafīf* metre]

Impose patience upon your soul and every worry will vanish.
    For in patience there is a device [to undo every] deceit
Maybe the self detests something in which lies relief,
    Like the releasing of the cords binding a camel.

'The shaykh had not even completed the two couplets before I saw a knight calling out from afar, "Al-Ḥajjāj is dead!"' He [Abū ʿAmr] continued, 'Then I asked the shaykh about the word "relief" (*farja*). He replied, "*Furja* with a *ḍamm* on the letter *fāʾ* is an opening in a wall or in the *ʿūd* or something similar, whereas *farja* with a *fatḥa* on the letter *fāʾ* is relief after hardship and misfortunes."'[10] Abū ʿAmr then said, 'I did not know which I was happier about, the death of al-Ḥajjāj or the lesson from which I had benefitted.'

6 Added on the basis of MSS: Z515, f. 136a and F638, f. 67a.

7 See above the commentary on 7:172 regarding the presence of the spiritual self at the Covenant of *Alast*, from which the natural self was absent. See also IT, p. xl and n. 156.

8 See Munāwī, *Fayḍ al-qadīr*, vol. 4, p. 6.

9 Al-Ḥajjāj b. Yūsuf b. al-Ḥikam al-Thaqafī (d. 95/714).

10 According to Lane, while there may be that distinction, both *farja* and *furja* may be used to mean the relief from grief and misfortune.

95 Al-Tīn

His words, Exalted is He:

[95:4] *Verily We created man in the best of forms.*

He said:

That is, in the finest stature and form.

[95:5] *Then We reduced him to the lowest of the low,*

That is, We transform him from state to state until he is overtaken by old age (*haram*).[1]

[95:6] *except those who believe and perform righteous deeds...*

in their youth, for when they become weak and old, We command the angels to record for them deeds that they used to do in their youth; *for they shall have an unfailing reward*, that is, the rewards for their deeds will not cease, even though they are too weak to perform them. But God knows best.

1 Note that we have used the present tense here, since Tustarī is interpreting the verse to indicate an ongoing situation in human beings.

96 Al-ʿAlaq[1]

His words, Exalted is He:

[96:6, 7] ***Nay, but man verily is wont to transgress the bounds (❁ when he sees himself as self-sufficient)***

He said:

> That is, the [mere] sight of one's wealth (*ruʾyat al-ghinā*) brings about [a feeling] of independence (*istighnāʾ*), and the sense of independence gives rise to transgression (*ṭughyān*). Ḥasan [al-Baṣrī] ﷺ said, 'Short-sighted is the person who has had the world kept from him, yet does not realise that this is [a manifestation] of God's regard for him. Moreover, short-sighted indeed is also the person who has had the world placed at his disposal, and does not fear that this may be a form of ruse (*makr*) that God is devising against him.'[2]

Then [Tustarī] said:

> By God, the world has not been made available to a servant without him transgressing as a consequence, no matter who they happened to be. Then he recited His words, Exalted is He, *Nay, but man verily is wont to transgress the bounds ❁ when he sees himself as self-sufficient.*

His words, Exalted is He:

[96:14] ***Is he not aware that God sees?***

He said:

> Nothing can be behind His back.[3] He is behind all that is behind.

His words, Exalted is He:

[96:17] ***Let him, then, call upon his council.***[4]

He said:

> This means his tribe.

[96:18] ***We shall call the Zabāniya.***[5]

> This means the keepers of Hell whose feet are on earth and heads in the heaven of this world. They are called Zabāniya from the word *zabn*, meaning the act of pushing away, for they push the people of Hell back on their tracks, using their arms and feet.
>
> When Abū Jahl heard the mention of the Zabāniya he fled to his people, upon which they asked him, 'Have you become afraid of him [the Prophet]?' He replied, 'No, but I fear the Zabāniya for I don't know who they are.'

---

1 Two of the MSS, F638 and F3488, bear the title 'Iqraʾ', this being the first word of the *sūra*.

2 Compare the commentary on 29:1, 2; 37:106; and 89:17 above.

3 Lit. 'There is no behind to Him'.

4 This is a reference to Abū Jahl, who had tried to obstruct the Prophet when he was at prayer. When the Prophet responded harshly to this, Abū Jahl threatened him by pointing out to him that he could summon the largest council of men to support him.

5 The function of the Zabāniya, known as the Guardians of the Inferno or the Angels of Hell, is described in Ghazālī's *Iḥyāʾ ʿulūm al-dīn, Kitāb Dhikr al-mawt*, trans. Winter, pp. 196, 205, 206, 220 and 225.

97 Al-Qadr

His words, Exalted is He:

[97:1] ***Lo! We revealed it on the Night of Great Merit.***

He said:

> On the Night of Great Merit [the descent of] mercy upon His servants was decreed.

His words, Exalted is He:

[97:4, 5] ***(The angels and the Spirit descend by the leave of their Lord) with every command. ۞ Peace…***

> That is, safety from the cutting off (*qaṭʿ*)[1] of the states [lit. moments, *awqāt*] of those who have gnosis of Him (*ʿārifūna bihi*), and those who preserve with Him the limits of the ordinances concerning the commands and prohibitions.

But God, Glorified and Exalted is He, knows best.

1 All three MSS (Z515, f. 137a, F638, f. 68a and F3488, f. 320b) have *qaṭʿ* instead of *ẓulma* in the printed edition.

98 Al-Bayyina

His words, Exalted is He:

[98:5] ***And they were only commanded to worship God, devoting religion purely to Him***

He said:

> All knowledge is concerned with acts (*ḥarakāt*),[1] until the person attains sincerity (*ikhlāṣ*). Then when he reaches sincerity, he will attain profound peace (*ṭumaʾnīna*).[2] For the one whose knowledge [has become] certainty (*yaqīn*) and whose works are [done in] sincerity, will find that God removes from him three things: anxiety (*jazaʿ*), ignorance (*jahl*) and action (*ʿamal*), and will grant him patience (*ṣabr*) in exchange for anxiety, knowledge in exchange for ignorance, and the abandonment of choice in exchange for action — but this will only be the case for those who have full awareness of God (*muttaqūn*).[3]

He was asked, 'And what is sincerity (*ikhlāṣ*)?' He replied:

> It is responding (*ijāba*), and whoever does not respond has no sincerity.[4]

He also said:

> Sincerity has three facets: worshipping purely for God (*ikhlāṣ al-ʿibāda li'Llāh*), acting purely (*ikhlāṣ al-ʿamal lahu*) for Him, and [keeping one's] heart purely for Him (*ikhlāṣ al-qalb lahu*).[5]

His words, Exalted is He:

[98:8] ***…This is [the reward] for him who fears his Lord.***[6]

He said:

> Fear (*khashiya*) is [experienced] privately, within [lit. is secret, *sirr*], whereas humble submission (*khushūʿ*) is shown openly (*ʿalāniyya*). As for the one whose bodily members are in a state of humble submission, Satan will not approach him.

He was asked, 'What is humble submission (*khushūʿ*)?' He replied:

> It is standing before God and being steadfast (*ṣabr*) in that.[7]

He [continued]:

> The perfection of fear [of God] (*khashiya*) is the abandonment of sins, [those that are committed] both in secret and openly.

---

1 Tustarī may be indicating here knowledge of outward conduct according to *fiqh*, such as the manner of ablution, the movements of prayer, etc.

2 That is, peaceful assurance in heart and mind. On *ṭumaʾnīna* see Tustarī's commentary on 2:260 and p. 30, n. 92.

3 That is, reading *ʿamal* instead of *ʿilm* according to MSS F638, f. 68a and F3488, f. 320b.

4 See the commentary on 39:11 above, and IT, pp. lvi–lvii.

5 This translation has attempted to take into account the other meaning of *ikhlāṣ*, namely being 'purely for', 'freed for' something.

6 The rewards that are mentioned in the first part of this verse are: *Gardens of Eden beneath which rivers flow, wherein they shall abide for ever. God is pleased with them and they are pleased with Him…*

7 That is, maintaining a state of awareness of the presence of God at all times. *Ṣabr* in this context has the meaning of endurance and perseverance, rather than patience as we would usually understand that word in English.

99 Al-Zalzala

His words, Exalted is He:

[99:6] ***On that Day, mankind shall issue forth in separate groups (to be shown their deeds).***

He said:

> Each person will be [made to] follow whatever he used to depend upon.[1] Whoever depended upon God's favour (*faḍl*) will follow His favour. Whoever depended on his [own] works will follow his works. Whoever depended on intercession (*shafāʿa*) will follow the intercession.

His words, Exalted is He:

[99:7] ***Whoever has done an atom's weight of good will see it,***

He said:

> When this verse was sent down, the Messenger of God ﷺ gave a sermon in which he said, 'Nay indeed, this world has an array of goods that are ready to hand which are consumed by the righteous (*barr*) and the wicked (*fājir*) alike. Nay indeed, the Hereafter is truly an appointed hour in which the All-powerful King will make the decree. Nay indeed, all of goodness in its entirety[2] is in Paradise. Nay indeed, all of evil, in its entirety is in the Hellfire. So be aware, since you have already been cautioned by God, and know that you will be shown your deeds, *Whoever has done an atom's weight of good will see it,* ۞ *but whoever has done an atom's weight of evil will see that.* [99:7, 8]'[3]
>
> Abū al-Dardāʾ said, 'Perfection in the mindfulness of God (*taqwā*) is that the servant fears God to the point that he fears Him even concerning a mere atom's weight, such that he leaves aside some of the things he considers to be legitimate, for fear of the possibility of its being forbidden. This will act as a screen between him and [doing] what is forbidden.'[4]

Sahl said:

> Do not consider any sin to be insignificant, even if it be small, for truly it has been said by some, 'There are four things which come after a sin which are more serious that the sin itself: persistence [in sin], rejoicing [at it] (*istibshār*), deeming it insignificant (*istiṣghār*) and taking pride in it (*iftikhār*).'
>
> Ibn Masʿūd said, 'The believer sees his sins as if he were at the foot of a mountain that he fears will fall on top on him, whereas the disbeliever sees sin as a fly which alights on his nose. Then he says, "It's like this", with a gesture of his hand [as if it will] fly off.'

Then Sahl said:

> O assembly of Muslims! Indeed you have succeeded in professing on your tongue and believing with certainty in your heart that God is One, that there is none like Him, and that there is a Day for you on which He will resurrect you and on which He will question you about the [deeds

1 That is, each person will be made to follow along in a group according to that upon which they had depended in this world.

2 lit. in its minutest details (*bi-ḥādhafirihi*).

3 Iṣfahānī, *Ḥilyat al-awliyāʾ*, vol. 1, pp. 264–5.

4 Ibn Mubārak, *Kitāb al-Zuhd* (Beirut, 1997), vol. 1, p. 17. See the similar recommendation above in a tradition cited on the authority of ʿĀʾisha in the commentary on 25:70.

> you did which were of an] atom's weight. If they were good, He will reward you for them but if they were bad, He will punish you for them if He so wills. Therefore, realise this through action.

He was asked, 'How can we realise this through action?' He answered:

> Through five things which are essential for you: to consume what is lawful, to clothe oneself in what is lawful, to safeguard your bodily members, to fulfil the rights [of others] over you as you have been commanded and to refrain from all harm to other Muslims, so that your [good] deeds are not spent in the retribution (*qiṣāṣ*) due to others [because of your harm to them in this world] on the Day of Resurrrection.[5] Then seek assistance in all of this from God so that He brings them to completion for you.

He was asked, 'How do these conditions (*aḥwāl*) become sound in the servant?' He replied:

> There are ten things which are essential. Five are things from which he must desist, and five are things to which he must adhere: he must leave behind the whisperings of the Enemy [i.e. Satan] and abide by the intellect in what it restrains him from; he must give up concern for the affairs of this world and leave them to its people;[6] and he should preoccupy himself with the Hereafter and aid its people;[7] he must give up following his [base] desire (*hawā*) and fear God in every situation; he must give up disobedience and occupy himself in [acts] of obedience; he must abandon ignorance and acting upon ignorance (*iqāmat al-jahl*), until he judges his actions,[8] and he must seek knowledge and act upon it.

He was asked, 'How can we uphold this and act upon it?' He replied:

> There are four essentials [prerequisites]: he should not tire himself with those things which will only turn to dust,[9] neither should he desire them. Furthermore, he should not fraternise with those whose end is [no more than] dust,[10] nor should he have any desire for [their company].

He was asked, 'How can that [be achieved]?' He said:

> By the servant's knowing that he is a servant and his Master has full knowledge of his state and is witnessing [him]. It is He who has power over his joy and his grief, and is compassionate with him.

5 In the *Kitāb Dhikr al-mawt* of his *Iḥyāʾ ʿulūm al-dīn*, Ghazālī cites the following *ḥadīth* on the authority of Abū Hurayra: '... The bankrupt of my nation is he that shall come forward on the Day of Arising with the Prayer, the Fast and the Tithe, but having insulted this man, and abused that man, and having consumed another's wealth, and shed another's blood, and struck yet another. Each one of these shall be given a portion of his good works, and should these be exhausted before his obligation is discharged, then he shall be assigned some of their sins, which shall be heaped upon him. Then he shall be cast into Hell.' Trans. Winter, p. 200.

6 i.e. worldly people.

7 i.e. others whose concern is with the Hereafter.

8 i.e. whether they are good or bad. Or it could mean he rules over, or is in command of his actions.

9 lit. 'that which has no other end than to become dust', i.e. the transient things of this world.

10 i.e. those who are only interested and involved in the material things of this transient world and have no regard for their spiritual destiny or the Hereafter. The image is a powerful one.

100 Al-ʿĀdiyāt

His words, Exalted is He:

[100:6] ***Verily man is ungrateful* (kanūdun) *to his Lord,***

He said:

> [The word] *kanūd* means the ungrateful. He is the one who has broken the Covenant (*khālafa al-ʿahd*),[1] avoids the truth (*jānaba al-ṣidq*) and is on intimate terms with his [lower] desire, at which point God makes him despair of acquiring any righteousness (*birr*) and mindfulness of God (*taqwā*).[2]

[100:7] ***And verily to that He is a witness,***

> Meaning God is witness to his actions, his states and his secrets.

[100:8] ***And verily he is avid in [his] love of wealth* (khayr).**

He said:

> The wealth (*khayr*) which is intended here is of three kinds: love of the lower self (*ḥubb al-nafs*), love of the world (*ḥubb al-dunyā*) and the love of [base] desire (*ḥubb al-hawā*). It is called 'good' (*khayr*) due to the conception of it that is held by its adherents. However [in reality] the good is only in three things: self-sufficiency with regard to, and independence from, people; [recognising one's] utter neediness (*iftiqār*) for God, Mighty and Majestic is He; and fulfilling His commandments.

But God knows best.

---

1 It is not clear which covenant is meant here, but it could be read in the general sense as God's Covenant, rather than specifically the Covenant of *Alast*.

2 In other words God removes from him any aspiration to improve his situation.

101 Al-Qāriʿa

His words, Exalted is He:

[101:1, 2] ***The Crashing Blow! ❁ What is the Crashing Blow?***

He said:

> God strikes His enemies a crashing blow through His punishment.

[101:3] ***What will show you what the Crashing Blow is?***

> This is a way of magnifying it due to its severity (*shidda*). Everything in the Qurʾān which is preceded by the words: *What will show you?* is something about which He has not yet provided information, just as He said: *And what will explain [it] to you? The Hour may well be near* [33:63]; He had not informed [the Prophet] of it up until His words: *What will show you what the Crashing Blow is?* Then He informed [him] about it.

His words, Exalted is He:

[101:4] ***A day [when] people will be like scattered moths.***

> This means that they will bump into each other because of the awe (*hayba*) [they experience] before God, Mighty and Majestic is He. It has been said: the blow (*qaraʿ*) is threefold: the blow which strikes bodies is the arrow of death; the blow which strikes works is God's questioning them; and the blow which strikes hearts is the fear of alienation.

But God, Glorified and Exalted is He, knows best.

102 Al-Takāthur

His words, Exalted is He:

[102:3] ***Nay indeed! You will come to know.***

Sahl said:

> The one who turned away from Me shall come to know that he will not find any like Me. Then he cited the following verse [in the *wāfir* metre]:
>
> > You'll remember Me if you try out someone other than Me,
> > And you will realise I was for you a treasure.

His words, Exalted is He:

[102:5] ***No indeed! If you were to know with certainty,***

> Certainty (*yaqīn*) is the fire, affirmation on the tongue is the wick (*fatīla*) and the deed is its oil (*zayt*).[1] Certainty begins with unveiling (*mukāshafa*), then [comes] visual beholding (*muʿāyana*) and witnessing (*mushāhada*).

His words, Exalted is He:

[102:7] ***You will certainly see it with the eye of certainty*** **(ʿayn al-yaqīn).**

He said:

> The eye of certainty (*ʿayn al-yaqīn*) is not an aspect of certainty, but it denotes the thing itself and its entirety (*kulliyya*).[2]

[102:8] ***Then on that Day you will assuredly be questioned about the comforts [of the world].***

He said:

> Not an hour of the night or day passes by the jinn and men among creation that does not contain a right (*ḥaqq*) which God holds over them, and which it is incumbent on them [to fulfil], whether they know it or are ignorant of it. And He ascertains their states on the Day of Resurrection.

Then he [Sahl] recited: *Then on that Day you will assuredly be questioned about the comforts [of the world].*

1 These all being parts of the lamp. See above Tustarī's commentary of Āyat al-Nūr (The Light Verse), 24:35.

2 Or perhaps, 'the wholeness [of its vision]', as in our translation of this word as it occurred in Tustarī's commentary on 2:40. On *ʿayn al-yaqīn* see also IT, pp. xlviii–xlix and n. 209.

103 Al-ʿAṣr

His words, Exalted is He:

[103:1] ***By Time!*** **(wa'l-ʿaṣr)**[1]

That is: 'By the Lord of time (*Rabb al-dahr*).'[2] It has also been said [that He meant] 'By the afternoon ⌜prayer⌝.'[3]

[103:2] ***Verily man is in [a state of] loss,***

This means: all the days of Abū Lahab were wasted.

[103:3] ***except those who believe and perform righteous deeds…***

That is, they perform their religious obligations (*farāʾiḍ*) as prescribed for them; *and enjoin one another to the truth*, that is, to God, Mighty and Majestic is He; *and enjoin one another to patience* [in carrying out] His commandments.[4]

He was asked, 'What is patience (*ṣabr*)?' He replied:

⌜It is contentment (*riḍā*) and true [inner] verification of the truth (*taṣdīq al-ṣidq*).

Then he was asked if there was anything more excellent (*afḍal*) than patience, and he replied:⌝[5]

There is no better act than patience, and no greater reward than the reward for patience. There is no provision [for the way] (*zād*) except mindfulness of God (*taqwā*) and there is no mindfulness of God without patience. There is no aid to patience for God's sake save God, Mighty and Majestic is He.[6]

Then he was asked, 'Is patience included among works?' He answered:

Yes indeed. Patience is to action as is the status of the head to the body, the one is useless without the other.

Then he was asked, 'What is the time-span (*ajl*) of patience?' He replied:

Its time-span is as long as it takes to wait for relief (*intiẓār al-faraj*) from God.[7]

[After this] he was asked, 'What is the basis of patience?' to which he replied:

It is striving [with] the self (*mujāhadat al-nafs*) to maintain acts of obedience and perform them according to their rules (*aḥkām*) and limits (*ḥudūd*), and struggling to avoid acts of transgression (*maʿāṣī*), whether big or small.

---

1 The word *ʿaṣr* has both the general meaning of an 'era', 'epoch' or 'period', or 'the late hours of the afternoon', apart from its other meaning, derived from the verb *ʿ-ṣ-r*, of 'pressing out', as in the juice of grapes, olives, etc.

2 According to Lane, the word *dahr* signifies time, usually of a long or unlimited duration, or from the beginning of the world to its end. *Dahr* is also sometimes, especially but not exclusively, associated with fate as a source of good and ill that happens to man, and therefore it is traditionally linked with God, as in Tustarī's speaking of God as the Lord of *dahr*. See also M. Watt, 'Dahr' *EI*², vol. II, p. 94.

3 The addition is made on the basis of all three MSS: Z515, f. 139a, F638, f. 69a and F3488, f. 322b.

4 Again, it should be borne in mind that *ṣabr* also has the meaning of being 'steadfast' or 'staunch' as well as 'patient'.

5 The section in brackets has been added on the basis of all three MSS: Z515, f. 139b, F638, f. 69a and F3488, f. 322b.

6 A similar saying of Tustarī is cited in Iṣfahānī, *Ḥilyat al-awliyāʾ*, vol. 10, p. 198.

7 On the virtue of waiting for relief (*intiẓār al-faraj*) see the commentary on 2:197 and 12:87 above.

He was asked, 'What are the people who practise patience like?' He replied:

> People of patience are of two kinds: one kind practise patience for the sake of this world, until they acquire what they desire for themselves from it, this is a blameworthy form of patience. The other kind practise patience for the sake of the Hereafter, seeking its reward and fearing its punishment.

Then he was asked, 'Is there only one kind of patience for the sake of the Hereafter, or are there different kinds?' To which he replied:

> Patience for the sake of the Hereafter has four stations (*maqāmāt*), three of which are obligatory (*farḍ*) and one of which is a superogatory virtue (*faḍīla*). [The first three are:] patience [or steadfastness] in obedience to God, Mighty and Majestic is He; patience in [refraining from] His disobedience; and patience in the face of afflictions (*maṣāʾib*) from Him.[8]

(Or he said):

> Patience in [observing] His commandments, Mighty and Majestic is He; patience in [observing] His prohibitions and patience with the acts of God, Mighty and Majestic is He. These are the three levels which are obligatory. The fourth level is a supererogatory virtue and it is patience in the face of the acts of His creatures.
>
> God, Exalted is He, has said, *And if you retaliate, retaliate with the like of what you have been made to suffer; and yet if you endure patiently, verily that is better for the patient* [16:126], [with these words He has set forth both] the ruling allowing for equal [treatment] and the superiority of showing patience. Then He said, *So be patient, and your patience is only through God* [16:127] — there is no one to assist in it except Him.

Once a man met with Uways al-Qaranī ﷺ and he heard him say, 'O God, I apologise this day for every hungry stomach and naked body. Truly, I do not have in my home any food except what is in my belly and I do not have anything from this world except what is on my back.' He [the man] said, 'On his back was just a cloth with which he covered himself.'[9]

He [Sahl] said:

> A man came to him [Uways] and said to him, 'O Uways, how is your state this morning?' (Or he may have said), 'How is your state this evening?' He replied, 'I praise God in every situation. You should not ask about the state of a man who, when entering upon the morning, assumes that he will not live till the evening, and who, when entering upon the evening, assumes that he will not live till morning. Truly, death and its remembrance does not leave the believer with any cause to rejoice. Truly, the portion due to God, Mighty and Majestic is He, from a believer's wealth does not leave him owning a [piece of] silver or gold. Truly, commanding right and forbidding wrong does not leave the believer with any friends. We command them to do good, and they abuse us with regard to our women's honour, and find wicked people to assist them in this, to the point where, by God, they even impute terrible things to me. But I swear by God, I will not give up performing God's right regarding them.' Then he went his way.[10] This was the station in patience reached by Uways.

But God knows best.

---

8 This saying is cited in Makkī, *Qūt al-qulūb*, vol. 1, pp. 351–2, but is attributed to Ḥasan al-Baṣrī.

9 Bayhaqī, *Shuʿab al-īmān*, vol. 1, p. 524; Ibn al-Jawzī, *Ṣifat al-ṣafwa*, vol. 3, pp. 53–4.

10 Bayhaqī, *Kitāb al-Zuhd al-kabīr*, vol. 2, p. 219; Ibn al-Jawzī, *Ṣifat al-ṣafwa*, vol. 3, p. 53.

104 Al-Humaza

His words, Exalted is He:

[104:1] ***Woe to every backbiter* (humaza), *[who is] a slanderer* (lumaza),**

Humaza means a 'backbiter' (*mughtāb*), [a word which is used] when a person maligns someone in their absence; *lumaza* means a person who defames (*ṭāʿin*), [that is] he defames someone when he sees them. [The verse] was revealed with reference to al-Wālid b. al-Mughīra.[1]

[104:2] ***who amasses wealth and counts it over.***

He said:

He exploited his wealth for his worldly life.

[104:3] ***He thinks that his wealth will make him live forever.***

He said:

That is, [he thinks] it will make him live forever in the abode of permanent subsistence (*dār al-baqāʾ*). It has also been said: [he thinks] it will make him live forever, [saving him from] death.

His words, Exalted is He:

[104:6] ***[It is] the fire of God, kept kindled,***

That is, it will not die down through consuming the skin and flesh, but [will go on burning] until its heat reaches the very hearts.

Fire is of four kinds: the fire of lust (*shahwa*), the fire of wretchedness (*shaqāwa*), the fire of alienation [lit. being cut off, *qaṭīʿa*], and the fire of love (*maḥabba*). The fire of lust consumes acts of obedience (*ṭāʿāt*), the fire of wretchedness consumes the profession of God's oneness (*tawḥīd*), the fire of alienation consumes hearts, but the fire of love consumes all fires.[2]

It has been related of ʿAlī b. al-Ḥusayn ﷺ that once he entered a cave with some of his companions and found a woman alone there.[3] He asked her who she was, and she answered, 'I am one of God's bondswomen. Get away from me so that this love (*ḥubb*) does not leave me!' Then ʿAlī ﷺ asked her, 'What is love?' She replied, 'It is too hidden (*akhfā*) to be seen and too evident (*abyan*) to be concealed. Its concealment within a person's interior is like the concealment of fire within a stone. When you strike it can be seen but when you leave it alone it remains hidden.[4] Then she started to recite the following:

---

1 Al-Walīd b. al-Mughīra was one of the chiefs among the Quraysh and head of the Makhzūm clan. It was he who decided in a council among the Quraysh that the best way to discourage people from following Muḥammad was to call him a sorcerer (*sāḥir*).

2 This comment would be presenting a quite different perspective from that which prevails in Tustarī's comments on the Fire in its eschatological meaning, unless it is simply a comment of the 'keynote' type.

3 The MSS (Z515, f. 140b, F638, f. 71a and F3488, f. 324a) appear to have *mafāza*, meaning a waterless desert place, instead of *maghāra*, meaning cave. However, given the poem that follows, cave seems appropriate.

4 Ibn al-Jawzī, *Dhamm al-hawā* (Cairo, 1962), p. 346; Maḥmūd b. ʿUmar al-Zamakhsharī, *Rabīʿ al-abrār wa-nuṣūṣ al-akhbār* (Qum, 1989), vol. 4, p. 23; Dāwūd al-Anṭākī, *Tazyīn al-aswāq fī tafṣīl ashwāq al-ʿushshāq* (Beirut, 1987), p. 40; Sarrāj al-Qārī, *Maṣāriʿ al-ʿushshāq* (Beirut, 1969), vol. 1, p. 175, vol. 2, p. 217.

Verily the lovers are preoccupied with their Master,
Like the young men of the Cave, they know not how long they tarried![5]

5 On the Companions of the Cave, see the commentary on Sūra 18 above.

105 Al-Fīl

His words, Exalted is He:

[105:1] ***Have you not considered the way in which your Lord dealt with the Men of the Elephant?***[1]

He said:

> 'Do you not know how your Lord dealt with your enemies while you had not yet appeared in this world? Thus will He treat your enemies while you are amongst them, and will avert their scheming (*makr*) from you.'

His words, Exalted is He:

[105:3] ***(And did He not unleash upon them) flights of birds?***

> ʿIkrima said regarding these words of God, Exalted is He, 'They are birds that came from the direction of the sea, and had heads like the heads of vipers.' It was said also, 'They had heads like those of predatory beasts.' Their likeness had never been seen before that day nor has it been seen since. They proceeded to pelt them [the Men of the Elephant] with stones to infect their skin with smallpox. This was the first day on which a person infected with smallpox was seen. But God, Exalted is He, knows best what is correct.

1 This *sūra* alludes to an event which took place in 570 C.E., the year of the Prophet's birth, when Abraha, the Christian ruler of Yemen, led an army to attack the Kaʿba, wishing to destroy Meccan power and divert the pilgrims to his newly-built cathedral in Sanaa. His troops were supported by at least one elephant, and tradition relates that when the elephant reached the borders of the Meccan territory, it kneeled down and refused to move forward. Flights of birds then came and pelted the army from the air with small pebbles, killing them all.

106 Quraysh

His words, Exalted is He:

[106:1] ***For the security of the Quraysh,***

He said:

This means: for the safety sought by the Quraysh for their two journeys.[1]

[106:2] ***[their security during] the winter journey,***

to Shām [Syria], *and* the journey of *the summer*, to Yemen. We destroyed the army of Yemen thus. It is as if He were saying to the Prophet ﷺ, 'Remind the Quraysh of the blessing that I bestowed on them before I sent you to them.'

[106:3] ***let them worship the Lord of this House,***

That is, of Mecca.

[106:4] ***who has fed them against hunger…***

for many years; …*and secured them from fear* of the Negus.

But God knows best.

1 The Qurʾān alludes to the two annual migrations of the Quraysh, which Tustarī explains in his commentary on the next verse.

107 Al-Māʿūn[1]

His words, Exalted is He:

[107:1] ***Have you seen him who denies the Judgement?***

He said:

That is, the reckoning on the Day when people will be judged.

[107:2] ***That is he who repels the orphan,***

That is, he turns him away from that which is his right.

[107:3] ***and does not urge the feeding of the needy.***

That is, he does not feed the needy. This was revealed with reference to ʿĀṣim b. Wāʾil.[2]

[107:4, 5] ***So woe to those who pray ❁ but are heedless of their prayers,***

He said:

They are the hypocrites who are negligent about the [prescribed] times for the prayers, and observing the requirements and obligations [of prayer]. This is a severe warning indicating that not everyone who has the appearance of being obedient and stands alongside the worshippers is actually an obedient person whose works are accepted. In the Psalms (*zabūr*) of David ﷺ [are the words]: 'Ask those who attend at the temples with their bodies, keeping the positions of the worshippers, while yet their hearts are occupied with the world, whether they value Me lightly, or are they trying to deceive Me?'

In another tradition it is reported: 'A person does not obtain any [benefit] from his prayer save that in which he was mindful (*ʿaqala*).'[3]

His words, Exalted is He:

[107:6] ***those who make a pretence [at worship],***

He said:

This refers to the hidden form of association [idolatry] (*shirk*), for the hypocrites would perform their prayers well at the mosques, but when they were out of the sight of the Muslims, they would become lazy in performing them. Do you not notice how firstly He confirmed that they were among those who pray, then He threatened them with a warning.[4]

Know that association [idolatry] (*shirk*) is of two kinds: the association regarding God as such,[5] Mighty and Majestic is He, and the association in a person's dealing[s] (*muʿāmala*).[6] The

---

1 MS Z515 uses the title 'al-Dīn', while MSS F638 and F3488 use the title 'A raʾayta'.

2 Al-Wāḥidī in his *Asbāb al-nuzūl* (Louisville, KY: Royal Aal al-Bayt Institute for Islamic Thought and Fons Vitae, 2008) presents two opinions, one shared by Muqātil and al-Kalbī, who like Tustarī are of the view that this verse is referring to ʿĀsim b. Wāʾil al-Sahmī, and another on the authority of Ibn Jurayj, who states that it is a reference to Abū Sufyān. Another view, presented in *Tafsīr al-Jalālayn*, is that it was either ʿĀsim b. Wāʾil or Walīd b. al-Mughīra.

3 Several similar traditions are cited in Makkī, *Qūt al-qulūb*, vol. 2, p. 169.

4 The words of verse 5 are: *Woe to those who pray*.

5 Translating *dhāt Allāh*, which here is unlikely to have the meaning of the supreme essence of God.

6 Perhaps what is at issue here are the two aspects of Islamic law, that which deals with belief (*uṣūl*) and that which deals with our actions and dealings with others (*furūʿ*).

association concerning [God] Himself is unforgivable. But as for the association in a person's dealing[s], ⌜this is subject to a stern threat (*waʿīd shadīd*), and it is subject to the divine will (*mashīʾat Allāh*).

He was asked about the meaning of 'association regarding his dealings', and he replied:⌝[7]

It is as in the case of someone [who] makes the pilgrimage and prayers in the knowledge that other people will praise him for it. This is hidden association. In a tradition it is related, 'Devote your works solely to God, for God accepts only what is sincere in a deed. And do not say, "This is for God" [for example] when you tie the bonds of kinship (*raḥm*); that is for kinship, there is nothing in it for God. ⌜Neither will it expiate [for you] any misdeed (*maẓlama*).⌝'[8] Indeed, when Muʿādh requested of the Prophet ﷺ, 'Counsel me, O Messenger of God.' He [the Prophet ﷺ] said, 'Be sincere to God and a small amount of deeds will suffice you.'[9]

His words, Exalted is He:

[107:7] *and refuse common kindnesses* (māʿūn).

He said:

[The word] *māʿūn* refers to household necessities (*matāʿ al-bayt*). It has also been said that it refers to almsgiving (*zakāt*), and that it means wealth in the Abyssinian tongue.

---

7 The section in brackets was added on the basis of all three MSS: Z515, f. 141b, F638, f. 70b and F3488, f. 325a. However, both Z515 and F3488 are missing the first mention of *shirk fī dhātihi ʿazza wa jalla wa shirk fī muʿāmalatihi.*

8 The section in brackets was also added on the basis of all three MSS: Z515, f. 141b, F638, f. 70b and F3488, f. 325a. The tradition is cited in Bayhaqī, *Shuʿab al-īmān*, vol. 5, p. 336; Mundhirī, *al-Targhīb*, vol. 1, p. 23; Daylamī, *Firdaws*, vol. 5, p. 271 and other sources.

9 Tirmidhī, *Nawādir al-uṣūl*, vol. 1, p. 91; Bayhaqī, *Shuʿab al-īmān*, vol. 5, pp. 342–3.

108 Al-Kawthar

His words, Exalted is He:

[108:1] ***We have assuredly given you Abundance [al-Kawthar].***

He said:

> When al-Qāsim died in Mecca and Ibrāhīm in Medina, the Quraysh said that Muḥammad ﷺ had become heirless.[1] He was angered by this. Then the verse came down, *We have assuredly given you Abundance*, [that is], 'We are consoling him and compensating him with *Abundance* (*al-Kawthar*).'[2] '[*Al-Kawthar*] is a pool from which you can give whomever you wish a drink, with My permission, and refuse whomever you wish a drink from it, with My permission.'[3]

[108:2, 3] ***So pray to your Lord and make your sacrifice to Him ۞ Indeed it is your antagonist who is cut off,***

> from the good of both abodes.[4]

---

1 lit. 'cut off' (*abtar*).

2 The MSS are at variance concerning the form of the verb here: MSS Z515, f. 142a has *tuʿazzīhi*. While F3488, f. 352b has *taʿziya*, and F638, f. 70b has *yuʿazzīhi*. However Z515 uses the first person plural form of the verb that follows (*nuʿawwiḍuhu*), and the sentence that follows relates to God in the first person (*idhnī*), so it is logical to suppose that the first person might also apply to the first verb.

3 *Al-Kawthar*, which literally means 'abundance', is also the name for a river or pool in Paradise, or alternatively the river which feeds the Pool (*al-ḥawḍ*), at which the believers, on entering Paradise, will quench their thirst. See al-Ghazālī, *Iḥyāʾ ʿulūm al-dīn, Kitāb Dhikr al-mawt*, trans. Winter, pp. 217–8. Note that Tustarī identifies *al-Kawthar* itself with *al-ḥawḍ*.

4 That is, the good of this world and of the Hereafter. Having used the word *abtar* in his commentary on verse 1 in its meaning of 'being without an heir', Tustarī now interprets the word *abtar* more literally as 'cut off'.

109 Al-Kāfirūn

His words, Exalted is He:

[109:1] ***Say, 'O disbelievers!***

He said:

> The mentioning of the [command] *Say,* is merely in response to the request put [to the Prophet ﷺ] by the disbelievers, 'Worship our god for a month and we will worship your God for a year.' At their saying this, God, Exalted is He, sent down this *sūra*. He said, *Say, 'O disbelievers!* They returned with, 'What is the matter with you, O Muḥammad?' He replied [with God's words]:

[109:2] ***I do not worship what you worship,***

> now.

[109:2] ***and you do not worship what I worship,***

> now.

[109:4] ***nor will I worship what you worship,***

> in the future.

[109:5] ***nor will you worship what I worship,***

> in the future.

[109:6] ***(You have your religion and I have a religion).***[1]

> *You have* your choice (*ikhtiyār*) for *your religion and I have* my choice for *a religion*. Then [this verse] was abrogated by the verse of the sword [9:5].[2]

1 The whole verse has been added in for clarity here.

2 9:5 reads: *Then, when the sacred months have passed, slay the idolaters wherever you find them and take them, and confine them, and lie in wait for them at every place of ambush. But if they repent and establish prayer and pay the alms, then leave their way free. God is Forgiving, Merciful.*

110 Al-Naṣr

His words, Exalted is He:

[110:1] ***When the help of God comes along with victory,***

He said:

When the help of God comes for your religion, and victory for your religion.

[110:2] ***and you see people entering God's religion in throngs,***

and you see people, the people of Yemen,[1] *entering God's religion in throngs*, in multitudes (*zumaran*) — the tribe with its families, and the whole people. So, help your spirit (*rūḥ*) against your lower self (*nafs*) by preparing for the Hereafter, for it [the spirit] comes from it.[2] The lower self desires the world because it comes from that, but the spirit desires the Hereafter because it comes from that. Gain ascendancy over the lower self and open for it the door to the Hereafter by glorifying [God] (*tasbīḥ*) and seeking forgiveness for your nation. From then on, he [the Prophet ﷺ would seek forgiveness and glorify God] a hundred times in the morning and a hundred times in the evening. Furthermore, he would strive in worship night and day to the point where his feet swelled up, his eyes became red, and his cheeks became pale. He would smile little and weep and ponder a lot.

It has been narrated from Ibn ʿAbbās ﷺ that he said, 'When this *sūra* was revealed, the Companions of the Prophet ﷺ were gladdened by it, but Abū Bakr wept profusely. So the Messenger of God ﷺ asked him "What makes you weep?" He said, "The parting of your soul has been announced for you O Messenger of God."[3] The Prophet ﷺ said to him, "You have spoken the truth." Then he said: "O God, grant him understanding of the religion, and teach him [the science of] interpretation (*taʾwīl*)."[4] This is also a teaching in religion and glorification for his nation. Indeed Rabīʿ b. Khaythum ﷺ said, 'Reduce your speech except in nine [areas]: [in saying], "Glory be to God!", "Praise be to God!", "There is no god except God", "God is Great", and in the recitation of the Qurʾān, commanding what is right, forbidding what is wrong, asking for goodness and seeking refuge from evil.'[5]

---

1 This verse is said to refer to the conquest of Mecca by Muḥammad, when tribes assembled from all over Arabia, including those of the Yemen, who had converted to Islam or pledged their allegiance to the Prophet. See Lings, *Muḥammad*, pp. 299ff.

2 On this doctrine, see IT, p xxxix.

3 The editor of the Dār al-Kutub al-ʿIlmiyya edition notes that this interpretation of the verse was not, according to the *ḥadīth* collections, attributed to Abū Bakr, but was from Ibn ʿAbbās himself, and he refers to the *Ṣaḥīḥ* of Bukhārī, 'Bāb tafsīr Sūrat al-Naṣr', and 'Bāb al-manāqib'.

4 Bukhārī, *Ṣaḥīḥ*, 'Bāb waḍʿ al-māʾ ʿinda'l-khalāʾ'; Ibn Ḥanbal, *al-Musnad*, vol. 1, p. 335; Ibn Abī Shayba, *al-Muṣannaf*, vol. 6, p. 383. The word *taʾwīl*, a verbal noun derived from the second form of the verbal root *a-w-l*, occurs several times in the Qurʾān with the meaning of interpretation, especially in the twelfth *sūra* (Sūrat Yūsuf) where it is found seven times, but also in 3:7, where it has particular significance (for which see Tustarī's commentary on 3:7 above). In Qurʾānic exegesis, the word *taʾwīl* was often used synonymously with *tafsīr* to mean simply 'interpretation', as in the title of Ṭabarī's *Jāmiʿ al-bayān fī taʾwīl āy al-Qurʾān*. However, later the word *taʾwīl* also took on a more specific meaning when it was applied either to the esoteric interpretation of the Qurʾān that was practised by Sufis, or to the metaphorical interpretations of Muʿtazilīs, Ismāʿīlīs and philosophers. On *taʾwīl*, see I. Poonawala, 'Taʾwīl', *EI²*, vol. x, pp. 390–2, and Henri Corbin, *Avicenne et le récit visionnaire: étude sur le cycle des études avicenniens* (Paris, 1979), pp. 32ff., passim.

5 Iṣfahānī, *Ḥilyat al-awliyāʾ*, vol. 2, p. 109.

[110:3] ***He is ever ready to relent.***

He accepts repentance over and over again, each time the servant repents to Him. And know that our Lord is too generous not to be with you, [assisting you] against your lower self. He [also] said: *Truly God loves those who repent* [2:222]. If you oppose your lower self, He will be 'on its side' with a pardon and if you are on its side in opposition to God's commandments and prohibitions, He will be against you. Whoever conforms to God's commandments against his lower desire will be delivered, whereas whoever accedes to his lower desire in opposition to God's commandments will be ruined. Indeed, the commandments of God, Exalted is He, are bitter whereas the desire of the lower self is sweet. Its similarity is none other than the likeness of delicious foods which contain within them the [bitterness] of aloes (*ṣabr*); whereas medicine is drunk despite its bitterness, because of the benefits that have been placed within it. One of the righteous used say, 'Ah, the pity, even if You [do] forgive them! For among them, there is one who is wary of the withdrawal [of forgiveness], and another who weeps out of shame, even if he is pardoned.'

111 Al-Masad

His words, Exalted is He:

[111:1] ***Perish the hands of Abū Lahab, and may he perish too!***

He said:

That is, may his hands be ruined [lit. lost], *and may he perish too!* The first loss is the loss of his wealth and the other loss is in the loss of his soul. The meaning of loss is mentioned in what comes after this.

He says:

[111:2] ***His wealth will not avail him, nor what he has gained.***

[*His wealth will not avail him,*] in the Hereafter when he is brought to the Fire, *nor what he has gained*, that is, his sons, ʿUtba, ʿUtayba and Muʿtab.

There is also another interpretation which is that the first *Perish* is like a supplication against him, while the second is describing the loss that will befall [him] according to that which has been pre-eternally destined [for him]. [This curse] is the response to Abū Lahab's saying to the Prophet ﷺ 'May you perish!'[1] when he gathered them together and invited them to the profession of God's oneness, and warned them of the punishment with His words, *And warn the nearest of your kinsfolk* [26:214].

His words, Exalted is He:

[111:3] ***He will [soon] enter a flaming fire,***

Abū Lahab will be enveloped by the Fire in the Hereafter; *a flaming fire*, that is, it has no smoke.[2]

[111:4] ***And his wife…***

Umm Jamīl, *…[will be] the carrier of firewood.* It has been said that this means 'the scandal mongerer' (*nammāma*). ʿIkrima said, 'She used to carry thorns and throw them down in the path of the Prophet ﷺ.'

[111:5] ***with a rope of palm-fibre round her neck.***

That is, in the Fire it will be an iron chain like the iron pulley with which she will be dragged into it. She will be known by this distinguishing mark (*ʿalāma*) in Hell, just as she was well-known for hostility towards the Prophet ﷺ. But God, be He glorified, knows best what is correct.

1 Bukhārī, *Ṣaḥīḥ*, 'Kitāb al-Tafsīr'.

2 Because of the intensity of the heat.

112 Al-Ikhlāṣ

Sahl was asked about sincerity (*ikhlāṣ*).[1] He said:

> It is insolvency (*iflās*),[2] that is to say, the one who knows that he is insolvent has realised the truth [of his situation].

He [further] said:

> With these four verses God falsified all disbelief (*kufr*), and all [vain] desires (*ahwāʾ*). It was called the Sūra of Purity [of Faith] because it contains the declaration of God's transcendence (*tanzīh*), Exalted is He, above all that is not fitting for Him.

His words, Exalted is He:

[112:1] ***Say: 'He is God, One,***

> He has neither equal (*kufʾ*) nor likeness (*mathal*).

[112:2] ***God, the Self-Sufficient, Besought of all.***

He said:

> *The Self-Sufficient, Besought of all* (al-Ṣamad) is the Master (*al-Sayyid*) who is resorted to for all needs (*ḥawāʾij*) and exigencies (*ʿawāriḍ*). The meaning of [*al-Ṣamad*] is the One who is resorted to (*al-Maṣmūd ilayhi*).

Then he said:

> *The Self-Sufficient, Besought of all* is the One who has no need of food and drink.

[112:3] ***He neither begot,***

> such that He appoints heirs, *nor was begotten*, for in that case His sovereignty (*mulk*) would be something temporal (*muḥdath*). It is also a confirmation of His unicity (*waḥdāniyya*), and a disavowal of His dependence on causes (*asbāb*), and a refutation (*radd*) of the disbelievers.

[112:4] ***nor is there anyone equal to Him.'***

> It means: no one is comparable to Him — [taking the word *kufūʾ*] as having been brought forward [in the verse].

1 See above, p. 49, n. 42 on the meaning of *ikhlāṣ*. See also IT, pp. lvi–lvii for Tustarī's emphasis on the importance of sincerity. For other references to *ikhlāṣ* thoughout the *Tafsīr* see the index.

2 The word *iflās* can nowadays be used for bankruptcy or insolvency. It means being stripped of everything one owns.

113 Al-Falaq

His words, Exalted is He:

[113:1] ***Say, 'I seek refuge in the Lord of the Daybreak,***

He said:

> Truly God, Exalted is He, commanded him [the Prophet] in these two *sūras* [113 and 114] to take refuge (*iʿtiṣām*) in Him, seek help (*istiʿāna*) from Him, and show [his] need (*faqr*) for Him.

He was asked, 'What is showing [one's] need?' He replied:

> It is the [substitution of one] state by another (*huwa'l-ḥāl bi'l-ḥāl*), for the natural disposition (*ṭabʿ*) is dead [in and of itself] and its life is in displaying this.[1]

He also said:

> The best form of purification (*ṭahāra*) is that the servant purifies himself from [the illusion of] his own power (*ḥawl*) and strength (*quwwa*).[2] Every act or saying that is not accompanied by the words: 'there is no power or strength save in God', will not have God's support, Mighty and Majestic is He. Furthermore, every saying which is not accompanied by the proviso,[3] will incur a punishment for [the person who said it], even if it was an act [or saying] of righteousness. And for every affliction (*muṣība*) which is received without being accompanied by the saying of 'return' (*istirjāʿ*),[4] the afflicted person will not be given steadfastness when facing it [affliction] on the Day of Resurrection.

He said:

> According to Ibn ʿAbbās ﷺ, *al-falaq* means the morning (*ṣubḥ*) while according to al-Ḍaḥḥāk it refers to a valley in the Hellfire. [On the other hand], according to Wuhayb[5] it refers to a chamber in Hell, and according to Ḥasan it refers to a well in Hell.
>
> It has also been said that He intended by it all people (*jamīʿ al-khalq*). Or it has been said that it refers to the rock from which water springs forth.[6]

[113:2] ***from the evil of that which He has created,***

> from man and jinn. This is because Labīd b. Aʿṣam al-Yahūdī cast into the well of Banū Bayāḍa a spell against the Prophet, who used to frequent it. [One day as] he headed towards [the well] the spell [cast against him] possessed him and the Prophet ﷺ became affected by it, so God sent down the two *sūras* of seeking refuge (*muʿawwidhatayn*),[7] and the Angel Gabriel ﷺ informed him of the magic spell. Then he sent two men among the Companions to [the well] and they

1 Presumably what is meant here is that by displaying or acknowledging its neediness, life in the remembrance of God will be substituted for the death of our natural state.

2 The word *ṭahāra* is used in Islamic law to signify ritual purity.

3 lit. 'exception' (*istithnāʾ*), that is, the proviso of saying 'God willing', on which see above 48:27 and p. 198, n. 12.

4 *Istirjāʿ* being the utterance of the words: 'Truly, we belong to God and truly to Him we will return' (*innā li'Llāhi wa-innā ilayhi rājiʿūn*), which words are customarily said on hearing of the death of someone.

5 Wuhayb b. al-Ward (d. 153/770).

6 Most of these explanations of *al-falaq* may be found in Ṭabarī's *Jāmiʿ al-bayān*, as well as the opinion that it is a prison (*sijn*) within Hell, or that it is one of the names of Hell.

7 Sūras 113 (*al-Falaq*) and 114 (*al-Nās*).

took it [the knot] out of the well. They brought it to the Prophet ﷺ, upon which he started to untie the knot reciting the verses the while, so that the Messenger ﷺ was cured without delay after having completed the two *sūras*.

After this occurrence, Labīd used to go to the Prophet ﷺ but he did not see any trace of [his spell] on the face of the Prophet ﷺ, neither did he mention to him [what he had done].[8]

[113:3] ***and from the evil of darkness when it gathers,***

That is to say, when night falls, or it has been said that it means when the darkness intensifies. It has also been said [that it means]: when night first encroaches on [lit. 'penetrates,' *dakhala*] the day, [that is], when night is just beginning, devils among the jinn are released and anyone who is afflicted in that hour will not recover.

Sahl [also] said regarding *and from the evil of darkness when it gathers*:

Its inner meaning refers to remembrance, when regard for the self enters it, thereby screening it from sincerity towards God in the remembrance [purely] of Him.

[113:3] ***and from the evil of the women-blowers,***

That is, the sorceresses who blow on knots.

[113:5] ***and from the evil of the envier when he envies.'***

This means the Jews who envied the Prophet ﷺ to the point that they practised sorcery against him.[9] Ibn ʿAbbās said: In this verse [is a reference to] the lower self of a human being [lit. son of Adam] ⌜and his eye (*wa ʿaynuhu*)⌝.[10]

8 Bukhārī, *Ṣaḥīḥ*, 'Kitāb al-Ṭibb'.

9 In his commentary on this verse, Ṭabarī includes, among others, the opinion that what is meant by *the one who envies* is the Jew, and the tradition he cites adds that it was merely on account of envy that the Jews did not believe [in Muḥammad's message]. However, Ṭabarī himself opts for the opinion that the Prophet is being commanded to seek refuge from the evil of anyone who envies, and he discounts the view that it is specifically intended to refer to the Jews.

10 Added on the basis of F638, f. 72a, or, according to Z515, f. 144b and F3488, f. 328a, his eyes (*ʿaynayhi*). Presumably what is meant is the evil eye, which is aroused by envy, and indeed Ṭabarī includes in his commentary on this verse a tradition of Qatāda which glosses the words, *and from the evil of the envier when he envies*, with the words, 'from the evil of his eye or his [lower] self'.

114 Al-Nās

His words: Exalted is He:

[114:4] ***From the evil of the slinking whisperer,***

Sahl was asked, 'What is 'a whispering' (*waswasa*)? He replied:

> Everything besides God, Exalted is He, is a whispering. Truly, when the heart of a person is with God, Exalted is He, it speaks from God, Exalted is He, but if it is with other than Him, it speaks from other than Him.

Then he said:

> Whoever desires this world will not be saved from whispering. The position of whispering in relation to the servant is that of the evil-inciting self (*nafs ammāra bi'l-sūʾ*) when it mentions [a suggestion] to the natural disposition (*ṭabʿ*).[1] The whispering of the Enemy (*ʿaduww*)[2] within the breasts is as in His words, '*who whispers in the breasts of people — ❁ whether they be of jinn or mankind* [114:5, 6], meaning within the breasts of jinn and men alike. The whispering of the lower self is within the heart, for God, Exalted is He, has said: '*We know what his soul whispers to him. We are closer to him than his aorta.*' [50:16]
>
> Knowledge (*maʿrifa*) of the lower self (*nafs*) is more elusive [lit. hidden, *akhfī*] than knowledge of the Enemy (*ʿaduww*), while knowledge of the Enemy is more apparent (*ajlā*) than knowledge of the world.[3] The way to capture the enemy is through knowing him, for when you know him you have captured him, but if you do not know that he is the enemy then he has captured you.
>
> The similitude of the servant, the Enemy and the world is that of the hunter, the bird and the grain. The hunter is Satan (*Iblīs*), the bird is the servant and the grain is this world. There is not a [single] gaze (*naẓar*) that is not coveted by Satan.[4] If you have been fasting [continuously] and wish to stop fasting he will say to you, 'What will the people say? You, who are known for fasting, have given up fasting.' If you respond with, 'What do I care about people?' he will say to you, 'You have spoken rightly, so stop fasting for they will put the matter of the cessation of your fast down to good judgement and sincerity.'[5] Likewise, if you are known for seclusion and you leave your seclusion, he will say, 'What will people say? You have left your seclusion.' If you

---

1 See the explanation concerning the process of evil incitement or 'whispering' (*waswasa*) in the human being in the commentary on 7:20 above.

2 i.e. Satan.

3 Perhaps what is meant by the latter statement is that the danger of the Enemy (i.e. Satan) to the soul is more apparent than the danger that the world poses to it.

4 MS F638, f. 72a has *shayāṭīn* (pl.) instead of *shayṭān* in the other MSS and the printed edition. A tradition of the Prophet states, 'The gaze (*naẓar*) is among the arrows of Iblīs.' See Qurṭubī, *Tafsīr*, vol. 12, p. 227, While a comparable *ḥadīth* listed in Iṣfahānī, *Ḥilyat al-awliyāʾ*, vol. 6, p. 101 and Tirmidhī, *Nawādir al-uṣūl*, vol. 3, p. 181, specifies 'a gaze or look at the beauty (*maḥasin*) of a woman.' See also Tustarī's discussion about lowering one's gaze in the commentary on 24:30 above.

5 Note that Tustarī is really showing the subtlety of the Satanic 'whisperings' here, because firstly Iblīs has the appearance of encouraging him not to stop fasting, almost in the guise of religious conscience, but he does so by attempting to appeal to the person's concern for what others will think of him, i.e. his reputation, and Tustarī shows in his comment on this situation that the evil is not actually the giving up of fasting or seclusion, but the concern for fame and reputation. On the latter, see Tustarī's commentary on 16:67 above.

respond by saying, 'What do I care about people?' He will say, 'You have spoken rightly, so give up your seclusion, for they will put the cessation of your seclusion down to good judgement and sincerity.' In this way in all your affairs he turns you back to people, to the point where it is as if he commands you to humility (*tawāḍuʿ*) for the sake of attaining fame with people.[6]

It was related that there was a man among the devout worshippers (*ʿubbād*) who never used to get angry, so Satan came to him and said, 'If you get angry and then show patience your reward will be greater.' The devout worshipper understood him,[7] and asked, 'How does anger come about?' He said, 'I will bring you something and will say to you "Whose is this?" to which you should say, "It's mine." To which I will say, "No it's not, it's mine."' So, he brought him something and the devout worshipper said: 'It's mine!' to which Satan said: 'No it's not, it's mine!' But the worshipper said, 'If it's yours, then take it away.' And he did not get angry. Thus did Satan return disappointed and aggrieved. He wished to engage his heart so he could get what he wanted from him, but he [the worshipper] found him out and warded off his deception.

Then Sahl said:

You must have sincerity (*ikhlāṣ*) to keep you safe from whispering. Beware of devising and self-management (*tadbīr*) for it is a sickness of the lower self. Incumbent on you is emulation (*iqtidāʾ*),[8] for emulation is the basis of [good] works. Beware of conceit (*ʿujb*) for even before accomplishing its most elementary stage, you will have entered Hell. Incumbent on you are satisfaction (*qunūʿ*) and contentment (*riḍā*), for [your] livelihood is in these two. Beware not to conspire against others, apart from yourself,[9] for this will cause you to forget yourself. Incumbent upon you is silence, for you know the [beneficial] states that are within it.[10] Incumbent upon you is the abandonment of lusts, so that you may thereby cut yourself off from the world. Incumbent upon you is the night vigil, so that your self dies to the inclination of its natural disposition (*maylat al-ṭabʿ*), and your heart comes to life.

When you perform the prayer, do it as if you were bidding farewell.[11] Fear God and He will give you security. Aspire towards Him and He will give you hope. Put your trust in Him and He will suffice you. Incumbent upon you is seclusion (*khalwa*), that all flaws (*āfāt*) may be removed [lit. severed] from you. Indeed, Ibn ʿAbbās said, 'If it wasn't for fear of whisperings, I would remove to a country where I have no friends. Does anything corrupt man besides man?'

Then Sahl said:

The mingling of a friend of God with people is a disgrace (*dhull*), whereas his solitude (*tafarrud*) is a source of honour (*ʿizz*). I have never seen friends of God, Exalted is He, who were not solitary beings (*munfaridūn*).

ʿAbd Allāh b. Ṣāliḥ was a man with a glorious past and a great talent. He used to flee from country to country until he came to Mecca where his sojourn was long. So I [Sahl] remarked to him, 'Your stay has been long there,' to which he replied: 'Why shouldn't I stay here when I have not seen any place in which mercy and grace descends as it does here. The angels unceasingly circumambulate the House [Kaʿba] morning and night in diverse forms. Truly, there are many ⌜great⌝ wonders here.[12] If I related all I have seen, the hearts of people who do not believe would be too weak [to accept it].'[13] I said, 'I ask you in God's name to tell me something about

---

6 Which would indeed be ironic!

7 i.e. he perceived what Satan was attempting to do, but gave the appearance of being aroused by him.

8 That is, the good example of the Prophet and pious predecessors, perhaps also of spiritual masters. On this teaching see above, IT, pp. liiiff.

9 MS F638, f. 72a only has beware of 'depending upon' (*iʿtmād ʿalā*), instead of 'conspiring against' (*iʾtimār*), but that does not work with *ghayraka*, because it is not a matter of not relying on other than ourselves, but not relying on other than God!

10 On the virtue of silence, see the commentary on 10:62 above.

11 That is, as if it were your last prayer. This saying is attributed to the Prophet in Tustarī's commentary on 25:20.

12 The word *kabīra* appears before *kathīra* in MS F638, f. 72b.

13 That is translating *ḍaʿufat ʿanhu* according to all three MSS (Z515, f. 145b, F638, f. 72b and F3488, f. 329a) instead of

it.' He said: 'There is not a friend of God, Exalted is He — [that is], one whose friendship is genuine — who does not attend here on the night before Friday. One night I saw a man here called Mālik b. al-Qāsim al-Jabalī and I saw on his hand traces of food (*ghamr*), so I said, "For sure you must recently have been eating." He replied, "May God forgive me, I haven't eaten anything for a week.[14] However, I fed my mother and hastened here to make the dawn prayer in congregation." Between Mecca and the place that he came from is a distance of seven hundred parasangs.[15] Can you believe this?' I replied, 'Of course.' He said: 'Praise be to God who has shown me a [true] believer, a [true] believer!'[16]

Ibn Sālim said:

Once I was at Sahl's house. After the ʿ*Aṣr* prayer two men came to him and started to converse with him. I said to myself. 'They have stayed long with him and I do not see them returning anytime soon.' So, I went home to prepare dinner for them. When I returned to him I did not find anyone with him. I inquired about them [lit. about their state] and he replied, 'One of them prays the *Maghrib* prayer in the East and the other in the West.[17] They came to me as visitors.'

Once Sahl visited [the house of] a devout man of Basra, and saw a nightingale in a cage there. He asked, 'Whose is the nightingale?' He replied: 'This boy's.' It was one of his sons. He [Sahl] took a dinar out of his sleeve and said, 'My boy, which is dearer to you, the dinar or the nightingale?' He replied, 'The dinar.' So he paid him the dinar and set the nightingale free.

He [Ibn Sālim] continued:

The nightingale sat on the wall of the house until Sahl left and then it flew up and fluttered along above Sahl's head until he entered his house. He had a lotus tree in his house, and so the nightingale took up residence in the lotus tree and remained there until [Sahl's] death. When they lifted up his bier it proceeded to [fly up] and flutter above his bier while the people wept until they brought him to his grave. There it perched nearby until he was buried and the people had departed from his grave. It remained in a state of commotion above his grave until its death, after which it was buried beside him.

But God, Glorified and Exalted is He, knows best.

The End

ṣaghurat ʿanhu in the printed edition.

14 His asking forgiveness here being lest what he is about to say should be in some way a claim.

15 A parasang (Ar. *farsakh*, Pers. *farsang*) is an old Iranian measurement of distance equivalent to the league, that is, probably the distance that infantrymen can walk in one hour, so between 3 and 5 miles. Thus, when ʿAbd Allāh says that all the friends of God attend on the eve of Friday, he means from far and wide, and the story which follows provides another example of a charismatic gift attributed to true friends of God.

16 Ibn al-Jawzī, *Ṣifat al-ṣafwa*, vol. 4, p. 254.

17 That is, they were able to return to their homes away in the East and West respectively, by just after sunset (the time for the *Maghrib* prayer, when they had been for some time with Sahl after the ʿ*Aṣr* prayer, which is prayer after the mid-afternoon.

Appendix of Names Cited[1]

ʿAbd Allāh b. ʿUmar b. al-Khaṭṭāb (d. 73/693). A Companion of the Prophet and a prominent narrator of *ḥadīth*. He was known for his piety, noble character and scrupulous observance of the precepts of Islam, and numerous anecdotes are related about his exemplary conduct. He is said to have been offered the caliphate three times after the death of his father, the Caliph ʿUmar. He refused on each occasion, however, apparently wishing to remain aloof from politics, and apply himself instead to study and devotion.

ʿAbd al-ʿAzīz b. Rafīʿ al-Asadī, Abū ʿAbd Allāh al-Makkī al-Ṭāʾifī (d. 130/747) A narrator of *ḥadīth* from among the generation of Followers, he was accredited with trustworthiness (*thiqqa*) and is cited in the text as having narrated from ʿAbd Allāh b. ʿUmar.

ʿAbd al-Wāḥid b. Zayd (d. ca 177/793–4). A leading preacher and mystic of Basra who was a student of Ḥasan al-Baṣrī. Having established the first Sufi refuge and retreat (*ribāṭ*) at ʿAbbādān on the present day border of Iran/Iraq, he travelled to Fars and Jerusalem to preach, and became known for his miracles and the efficacy of his prayers.

Abū al-ʿĀliya, Rufayʿ b. Mihrān al-Riyāḥī (d. 92/710). A prominent narrator and Qurʾān reciter from among the generation of Followers in Basra.

Abū ʿAmr b. ʿAlāʾ (d. 154/771). An important Basran philologist and reciter of the Qurʾān.

Abū Bakr al-Ṣiddīq (d. 13/634). The first of the four caliphs who succeeded the Prophet, he was known as al-Ṣiddīq, meaning the true or veracious — some say this title was given to him because he was, to begin with, the only person to have affirmed as true the Prophet's account of his Night Journey and Ascension. A merchant of Mecca who knew Muḥammad before he was called to prophethood, Abū Bakr is often said to have been the first male convert to Islam. He remained a close friend and trusted advisor of the Prophet throughout his mission, and it was he alone who accompanied him on his flight from Mecca to Medina. He also fought at his side in many battles. His daughter ʿĀʾisha was married to the Prophet at a young age. As caliph, Abū Bakr had to deal with the rebellions of the apostasy (*ridda*), and also oversaw the conquest of Syria. He is buried next to the Prophet in Medina.

Abū al-Dardāʾ, ʿUwaymir al-Khazrajī (d. 32/652–3). A celebrated Companion of the Prophet. A merchant, he embraced Islam some time after the Battle of Badr and subsequently renounced commerce in order to devote himself to worship and the remembrance of God. He was one of the few who collected revelations in writing during the Prophet's lifetime and later came to be regarded as an authority on the Qurʾān. The caliph ʿUmar appointed him as a judge (*qāḍī*) in Damascus, where he died.

---

1 Sources used for the biographical appendix: Muḥammad b. Aḥmad al-Dhahabī, *Siyar aʿlām al-nubalāʾ* (Beirut, 1982); ʿAbd al-ʿAzīz b. Aḥmad Dihlawī, *Bustān al-muḥaddithīn*, trans. Aisha Bewley as *The Garden of the Hadith Scholars* (London, 2007); *EI²*; *EIr;* Ghazzālī, *Iḥyāʾ ʿulūm al-dīn;* Feras Hamza and Sajjad Rizvi (eds.), *An Anthology of Qurʾanic Commentaries* (Oxford, 2009); Muḥammad Ibn Saʿd, *Ṭabaqāt al-kabīr*, vol. 5 trans. Aisha Bewley as *Men of Madina*. 2 vols. (London, 2000); Jāmī, *Nafaḥāt al-uns;* Karāmustafa, *Sufism;* Abū Saʿīd al-Kharrāz, *Kitāb al-Ṣidq*, trans. A. J. Arberry as *The Book of Truthfulness* (Oxford, 1937); Alexander Knysh, *Islamic Mysticism: A Short History* (Leiden, 2000); Schimmel, *Mystical Dimensions;* Khayr al-Dīn Ziriklī, *al-Aʿlām* (Beirut, 1979).

Abū Ḥāzim, Salama b. Dīnār al-Madanī (d. 140/757). A scholar and jurist of Medina. Said to be of Persian origin, he is held to have lived a devout and ascetic life and is counted among the second generation of Muslims.

Abū Hurayra al-Dawsī al-Yamānī (d. ca 58/677–8). A close Companion of the Prophet and one of the most prolific narrators of *ḥadīth*, owing to his exceptional diligence in keeping the company of the Prophet. He is said to have entered Islam at the time of the conquest of Khaybar (7/629). In Medina, he joined the 'People of the Bench' (*Ahl al-Ṣuffa*), living a life of poverty and piety. After the death of the Prophet, he was appointed as a tax collector by ʿUmar b. al-Khaṭṭāb, and later acted as deputy to the governor of Medina, the Umayyad Amir Marwān b. al-Ḥakam.

Abū Jahl, ʿAmr b. Hishām (d. 2/624). One of the most virulent enemies of the Prophet. Known in his time as Abū al Ḥakam, he was given the epithet 'Abū Jahl' meaning 'father of ignorance' by the Muslims. He was killed in the Battle of Badr.

Abū Lahab b. ʿAbd al-Muṭṭalib (d. 2/624). A half brother of the Prophet Muḥammad's father ʿAbd Allāh, and the wealthiest of his uncles. On the death of Muḥammad's closest uncle and protector, Abū Ṭālib, Abū Lahab became head of the clan, and initially promised to take on the protection his nephew. However, this was only a nominal protection, which later changed to opposition. Abū Lahab died shortly after the Battle of Badr. Though not having fought in this battle himself, he had sent someone in his place to oppose the army of the Prophet. He and his wife (Umm Jamīl) are mentioned in Sūrat al-Masad (111:1 and 4) as being destined for Hell.

Abū Mūsā al-Ashʿarī, ʿAbd Allāh b. Qays (d. ca 42/662). A military leader and Companion of the Prophet who was appointed governor of Basra during the reign of 'Umar. He was later selected as an arbitrator at Ṣiffīn (37/657) to adjudicate between ʿAlī and Muʿāwiya, after which he retreated from the public sphere.

Abū Saʿīd al-Khuḍrī (d. ca 64/683–4 or 74/693–4). He was a Companion of the Prophet and one of his lieutenants, fighting in twelve battles. A prolific narrator of *ḥadīth*, he related a vast number to Ibn ʿAbbās and Ibn al-Musayyib and was recognised as a legal authority in Medina.

Abū Sufyān b. Ḥarb b. Umayya (d. ca 32/653). Chief of the Banū ʿAbd Shams clan of Quraysh, he was a staunch opponent of the Prophet's mission before converting to Islam at the time of the conquest of Mecca, fighting alongside the Muslims in subsequent battles. He died in Medina.

Abū Yaʿqūb, Yūsuf b. Hamdān al-Sūsī (d. end third/ninth century). A Sufi from Sūs in Khūzistān and the master of Abū Yaʿqūb al-Nahrajūrī. He lived in Baghdad and Basra and died in al-Ubulla.

ʿAdī b. Thābit al-Anṣārī (d. 116/734). A Shīʿī scholar who died in Kufa.

Aḥmad b. Muḥammad b. Sālim (d. 356/967). An important disciple of Sahl al-Tustarī, often confused with his father, Muḥammad b. Sālim. After the death of Tustarī, Aḥmad and his father remained in Basra and established the circle of disciples which formed the nucleus of a group of mystics that came to be called the Sālimiyya. Abū Ṭālib al-Makkī frequented this circle, referring to Aḥmad b. Sālim as 'our shaykh', and Makkī's *Qūt al-qulūb* played a key role in the propagation of a great number of Tustarī's sayings and teachings.

ʿĀʾisha bint Abī Bakr (d. 58/678). The daughter of the caliph Abū Bakr and the third wife of the Prophet. The Prophet died and was buried in her house. She was known for her extensive knowledge of *fiqh*, medicine, history and poetry and was a prolific narrator of *ḥadīth*s. She died in Medina and is buried in Baqīʿ cemetery.

ʿAjjāj, ʿAbd Allāh b. Ruʾba al- (d. ca 97/715). An influential Arabian poet of the early Umayyad period. He was renowned for his compositions in the *rajaz* meter.

ʿAlī b. Abī Ṭālib (d. 40/660). The cousin and son-in-law of the Prophet, married to his daughter Fāṭima. He was one of the first to embrace Islam and held the office of caliph after ʿUthmān, during an especially turbulent period in Islamic history. He is also considered to be first Imam by Shīʿī Muslims. Known for his austerity and worldly detachment, he holds an important position in Sufi literature and is often referred to as 'the Gate of Knowledge'. He was assassinated in Kufa by a member of the Khārijī sect.

ʿAlī b. Ḥusayn b. ʿAlī b. Abī Ṭālib (d. 94/712). Better known by his honorary title 'Zayn al-ʿĀbidīn' or 'Adornment of the Worshippers.' An ardent worshipper and authority on *ḥadīth*, he was known for his piety and abstinence. He lived through the martyrdom of most of his family, remaining sorrowful until his death. He is buried in Baqīʿ cemetery in Medina.

Aʿmash, Sulaymān b. Mihrān al-Asadī al- (d. 148/765). A Kufan traditionist who was famous for his recitation of the Qurʾān. He transmitted numerous exegetical *ḥadīth*s, especially traditions relating the circumstances of revelation (*asbāb al-nuzūl*).

ʿĀmir b. ʿAbd al-Qays (d. ca 41–60/661–80). One of the generation of Followers, he learnt the Qurʾān from Abū Mūsā al-Ashʿarī. He lived in Basra and then moved to Damascus where he died.

ʿAmr b. Dīnār al-Jumāhī (d. 126/743–4). A traditionist of Mecca who studied *ḥadīth* and the recitation of the Qurʾān under Ibn ʿAbbās.

Anas b. Mālik, Abū Ḥamza (d. 91–3/709–11). A celebrated Companion and prolific traditionist, his mother presented him as a servant to the Prophet at an early age. He remained in the service of the Prophet until the latter died, after which he took part in the wars of conquest. He lived to an advanced age, narrating a great number of *ḥadīth* that are recorded in the collections of al-Bukhārī and Muslim.

ʿAqīl b. Abī Ṭālib (d. ca 50/670). The elder brother of ʿAlī b. Abī Ṭālib, who was 20 years his junior. He converted to Islam after the Battle of Badr, when he was taken prisoner by the Muslims and then ransomed by the uncle of the Prophet, al-ʿAbbās. He was noted for his eloquence and knowledge of genealogies and the history of Quraysh. He died and is buried in Medina.

Aswad b. Yazīd al-Nakhaʿī (d. ca 80/699). A Kufan scholar and ascetic from the generation of Followers who was taught by ʿAbd Allāh b. Masʿūd.

ʿAwn b. ʿAbd Allāh b. ʿUtba b. Masʿūd (d. 115/733). A narrator of *ḥadīth* from among the generation of Followers, he was also known as a preacher, an expert on genealogy and a poet. Of Medinan origin, he later settled in Kufa.

Ayyūb al-Sakhtiyānī b. Abī Tamīma (d. 131/748). A Basran scholar and authoritative transmitter of *ḥadīth*. He was a pupil of Anas b. Mālik and associated with Ḥasan al-Baṣrī. Renowned for his piety, he is said to have been meticulous in his practice of the Sunna. A number of miracles are recorded of him.

Bilāl b. Rabāḥ (d. 17–21/638–42). He was the muezzin of the Prophet in Medina and is held to have been the second adult convert to Islam. Initially the slave of the Qurayshī elder Umayya b. Khalaf, he endured severe persecution by his master on account of his faith, until he was freed by Abū Bakr. He became a loyal Companion of the Prophet and migrated with the early Muslim community to Medina. After the death of the Prophet he moved to Syria, where he died. His tomb in Damascus remains a popular place of pilgrimage.

Bishr b. al-Ḥārith al-Ḥāfī (d. ca 227/841–2). A prominent figure in early Sufism, he was born in Marw in Khurasan and initially engaged in the study of *ḥadīth* before devoting himself to pious renunciation. Tales surrounding his life appear frequently in classical Sufi treatises. He died in Baghdad.

Ḍaḥḥāk, Ibn Muzāḥim al-Hilālī al- (d. 102/720). A famous traditionist from Balkh known for his knowledge of Qurʾānic exegesis. It is said that he transmitted a *tafsīr*, which had been dictated to him by Saʿīd b. Jubayr in Kufa, and which was later used as a source by Ṭabarī.

Fatḥ Abū Naṣr b. Shakhraf al-Marwazī (d. 273/887). An early mystic of Khurasan, he spent sixteen years in Baghdad and was praised by Aḥmad b. Ḥanbal. It is said that he died in a state of intense longing for the meeting with God.

Fatḥ b. ʿAlī al-Mawṣilī (also known as Abū Naṣr b. Saʿīd), (d. 220/835). A well-known Sufi and ascetic who knew Bishr al-Ḥāfī in Baghdad. It is said that on the day of ʿĪd al-Aḍḥā, seeing all the sacrifices that were being made, he said to God that he had nothing to sacrifice but himself, and pointing to his throat died instantly.

Ḥajjāj b. Yūsuf al-Thaqafī al- (d. 95/714). A provincial governor under the Umayyad dynasty, notorious for his ruthlessness and severity in suppressing rebellion.

Ḥammād b. Salma b. Dīnār al-Baṣrī (d. 167/783). He was a mufti in Basra and transmitter of *ḥadīth*.

Ḥammād b. Yazīd b. Dirham al-Azdī al-Jahḍamī (d. 179/795). A scholar who is said to have memorised four thousand *ḥadīth*s.

Ḥasan al-Baṣrī al-(d. 110/728–9). An important personality in the early religious history of Islam, he was a famous ascetic and preacher among the second generation of Muslims, as well as a jurist and authority on *ḥadīth*. He was born in Medina and in his youth joined the campaign for the conquest of eastern Iran. He then settled in Basra, where his teaching attracted a large circle of followers. He was not afraid to criticise some of the rulers of his time. His sermons emphasised the imminence of death and the Day of Judgement, and the need for detachment from the world and worldly possessions. Thus many of his sayings are cited in the works of Sufism. He died and is buried in Basra.

Ḥubaysh, probably Zirr b. Ḥubaysh (d. 81–3/700–3). A transmitter of *ḥadīth* amongst the generation of Followers in Kufa, who was known for his knowledge of the Qurʾān.

Ḥudhayfa b. al-Yamān al-ʿAbasī (d. 36/656–7). One of the earliest converts to Islam, he fought alongside his father in the Battle of Uḥud and was known for his asceticism. He was later made governor of Madāʾin in Fars during the caliphate of ʿUmar. The Prophet is said to have entrusted him with the secret knowledge of all the events preceding the Day of Judgement. A number of *ḥadīth* are related on his authority.

Ibn ʿAbbās, ʿAbd Allāh (d. 68/687–8). A cousin and close Companion of the Prophet and a prolific transmitter of *ḥadīth*. He is regarded as one of the greatest scholars of the first generation of Muslims and the founder of the discipline of Qurʾānic exegesis. He held classes on different subjects on which he was well-versed, including Qurʾān, matters of law, the expeditions of the Prophet, pre-Islamic history and Arabic poetry. Interpretations of the Qurʾān attributed to him were collected and have been preserved in numerous manuscripts. He fought alongside ʿAlī at the Battle of Ṣiffīn, and died and was buried in the city of Ṭāʾif.

Ibn Abī Dhiʾb, Muḥammad b. ʿAbd al-Raḥmān (d. 158/775). A major narrator from the second generation of Muslims and a scholar in his own right. A contemporary of the Imam Mālik b. Anas, he compiled his own collection of *ḥadīth* and was an authoritative source of legal opinions in Medina. He died and was buried in Kufa.

Ibn Abī al-Jaʿd, Sālim (d. 99–101/717–19). A Kufan narrator of *ḥadīth* from the generation of Followers.

Ibn Ḥayyān, probably Muqāṭil Ibn Ḥayyān (d. 150/767 or 153/770). *Ḥadīth* authority of Khurasanian origin from among the second generation of Muslims.

Ibn Masʿūd, ʿAbd Allāh b. Ghāfil al-Hudhalī (d. 32/652–3). One of the closest Companions of the Prophet and a source of many *ḥādīths*, including some relating details of the Prophet's Night Journey and Ascension (*Miʿrāj*). Of Bedouin origin, he is said to have been either the third or sixth convert to Islam. He heard the Qurʾān from the mouth of the Prophet himself and is thought to have been the first to have recited it in public. He is known both for his reading and exegesis of the Qurʾān. He settled in Kufa, where he acted as an administrator during the rule of the caliph ʿUmar and a portion of that of the caliph ʿUthmān, then he travelled to Medina where later died. It was through the Kufan traditionists that much of his knowledge of the Qurʾān and *ḥadīth* was transmitted.

Ibn al-Sammāk, Muḥammad b. Ṣabīḥ (d. 183/799–800). A preacher and ascetic of Kufa who lived in the time of Hārūn al-Rashīd and studied under Sufyān al-Thawrī.

Ibn ʿUyayna, Sufyān al-Hilālī (d. ca 198/813–4) A scholar of *ḥadīth* born in Kufa and raised in Mecca, he was a notable imam and a student of Ibn Shihāb al-Zuhrī (d. 122/742).

ʿIkrima (d. ca 105/723–4). A distinguished member of the generation of Followers and a respected narrator of *ḥadīth*. A slave of Ibn ʿAbbās, he was later manumitted by the latter's son ʿAlī, and came to be known as a *mawlā* of Ibn ʿAbbās. He was the main transmitter of the latter's commentary on the Qurʾān. He travelled widely and died in Medina.

Jābir b. ʿAbd Allāh, al-Khazrajī al-Anṣārī (d. 78/697). A Companion of the Prophet, he accompanied him on many expeditions. Although only a child at the time, he is counted among the seventy men of Aws and Khazraj who gave the Prophet their oath of allegiance at ʿAqaba. After the death of the Prophet he was appointed by ʿUmar as leader of his clan. He fought alongside ʿAlī at the Battle of Ṣiffīn, and spoke out strongly in defence of the city of Medina when it was threatened by the forces of Yazīd b. Muʿāwiya. Respected by *ḥadīth* scholars, he related a large number of Traditions. He is also held in particularly high regard by the Shīʿa.

Junayd, Abū al-Qāsim b. Muḥammad al- (d. 298/910). The most eminent of the Sufis of Baghdad and one of the most influential figures in the development of Sufism. A nephew and disciple of Sarī al-Saqaṭī (d. 253/867), he associated in his youth with al-Ḥārith al-Muḥāsibī (d. 243/857). He was also an authority on theology and law, which he studied with Abū Thawr (d. 240/855). In his mystical writings he elucidates the doctrines of *tawḥīd* (the oneness of God), *fanāʾ* (annihilation of the self in God) and *baqāʾ* (subsisting through God). It may have been due to his insistence that the sobriety of *baqāʾ* should follow the overwhelming intoxication of *fanāʾ*, and also perhaps because of his caution concerning the exposure of such doctrines to the uninitiated, that he came to be regarded as the founder of the 'sober school' of Sufism.

Kaʿb al-Aḥbār, Ibn Matīʿ al-Ḥimyarī (d. 33/652 or 34/654). A Jewish rabbi of Yemeni origin who converted to Islam during the caliphate of ʿUmar. He is the earliest authority for Haggadic and Talmudic traditions in Islam.

Kahmas b. Ḥasan al-Tamīmī (d. 148/766). An ascetic and scholar of *ḥadīth* from Basra, who is said to have placed particular emphasis on rigour in subduing the *nafs*. He later settled in Mecca, where he died.

Kharrāz, Abū Saʿīd Aḥmad b. ʿĪsā al- (d. 277/890). An eminent Sufi of Baghdad, he was a close companion of Bishr b. al-Ḥārith and Sarī al-Saqaṭī. He travelled widely during his life, and eventually left Baghdad, probably due to the persecutions against Sufis being carried out by the Ḥanbalī *qāḍī* Ghulām al-Khalīl. He is credited with being one of the first to produce a systematic presentation of the theory of Sufi experience in writing.

Labīd, Abū ʿAqīl b. Rabīʿa (d. 40/661). A well-known poet of the Banū ʿĀmir b. Ṣaʿsaʿa, who converted to Islam (possibly in the year 9/630–1). He later emigrated to Kufa where he died. One of his poems is included in the famous collection of pre-Islamic poetry known as the *Muʿallaqāt*.

Labīd b. al-Aʿsam al-Yahūdī (d. *unknown*). A Jewish magician who is said to have been employed by the leaders of Quraysh in an attempt to cast a spell on the Prophet. Some commentators are of the view that he is referred to in Sūra 113 of the Qurʾān.

Luqmān (d. *unknown*). A sage-like figure, regarding whom opinion is divided as to his status as a wise man or prophet. A chapter of the Qurʾān bears his name, wherein he is presented as a model of filial piety and wise conduct. Legends surrounding his wisdom appear both in Islamic and pre-Islamic literature, with many fables attributed to him being passed down through the generations.

Maḥārab b. Dithār (d. 116/734). Kufan jurist, *qāḍī* and *ḥadīth* transmitter.

Mālik b. Anas al-Aṣbaḥī (d. 179/795). The founder of one of the four principal schools of Islamic law. Born in Medina, he is included in Bukhārī's 'Golden Chain' of authoritative *ḥadīth* transmitters, and is the author of the well-known early work of law, *al-Muwaṭṭaʾ*. He is reported to have taught Shāfiʿī, Sufyān al-Thawrī and Ibn al-Mubārak.

Mālik b. Dīnār al-Nājī (d. 131/748–9). An ascetic of Basra and noted early calligrapher of the Qurʾān through which he made a living. He is said to have associated with Mālik b. Anas, Ḥasan al-Baṣrī, Ibn Sīrīn and Rābiʿa al-ʿAdawiyya. He lived an ascetic life, and a great number of anecdotes are recorded about him, including the attribution of several miracles.

Maʿrūf Abū Maḥfūẓ b. Fīrūz (or Fīrūzān) b. ʿAlī al-Karkhī (d. 200/815). A pious ascetic and preacher of Baghdad. Born of Christian or Sabian parents of Persian origin, he studied with Farqad al-Sabakhī (d. 132/749), through whom he is linked to the circle of Ḥasan al-Baṣrī. Through hearing one of Karkhī's sermons Sarī al-Saqaṭī is said to have converted to mysticism. Karkhī's tomb on the banks of the Tigris is visited and supplication made there is said to be propitious for obtaining rain.

Masrūq b. al-Ajdaʿ (d. 63/682). One of the generation of Followers from Kufa, he was a jurist and respected transmitter of *ḥadīth* who studied under ʿAbd Allāh b. Masʿūd.

Muʿādh b. Jabal al-Khazrajī (d. ca 18/639–40). An early convert to Islam who was noted for his memorisation of the Qurʾān and his extensive knowledge of *fiqh*. He was appointed governor of Yemen by the Prophet and died in Syria.

Mubarrad, Abū al-ʿAbbās Muḥammad b. Yazīd al- (d. ca 286/900). A leading scholar amongst the Basran grammarians and a prolific author. He was called to the court of the ʿAbbāsid caliph al-Mutawakkil in 245/860 and after the assassination of the latter, moved to Baghdad where he died.

Muḥammad b. Aḥmad b. Sālim (d. 297/909). A companion and disciple of Sahl al-Tustarī who remained with him all his life (according to the sources for either thirty or sixty years), and whom Tustarī is known to have addressed in Persian as his 'friend' (*dūst*). A native of Basra, he remained there with his son Aḥmad b. Sālim after the death of Tustarī, establishing the circle of disciples there who came to be known as the Sālimiyya. Muḥammad b. Sālim was an important transmitter of anecdotes about Tustarī's life and of his teachings, who is cited in many works of Sufism.

Mujāhid b. Jabr al-Makkī (d. 100/718 or 104/722). A Follower who was known as a Qurʾān reciter and an authority on Qurʾānic exegesis. He is said to have been a disciple of Ibn ʿAbbās, but also studied with other Companions such as ʿAlī b. Abī Ṭālib and Ubayy b. Kaʿb. He is said to have gone to great lengths to discover the meaning and circumstances of each revealed verse. Numerous comments in his name are cited in later *tafsīr* works, and an individual commentary in his name has been preserved in a single manuscript.

Muslim b. Yasār (d. 107 or 108/725–6). A jurisprudent and pious man, knowledgeable in *ḥadīth*. Originally from Mecca, he settled in Basra where he became a mufti.

Qatāda b. Diʿāma al-Baṣrī (d. ca 117/735). Blind from birth, he was a Follower and an authority on Qurʾānic exegesis and well-known for his excellent memory and knowledge of genealogies and historical traditions. He was a pupil of Ḥasan al-Baṣrī and Ibn Sīrīn. He is thought to have espoused the doctrine of the Qadariyya, i.e. free will, and to have given the Muʿtazilīs their name, though it is said that he later renounced their doctrine.

Quss b. Saʿīda b. ʿAmr b. ʿAdī al-Ayyādī (d. 23 before the Hijra/599). An Arab sage and preacher who lived in the period of the Jāhiliyya, before Islam. His eloquence is proverbial, and he is also said to have predicted the imminent coming of the Prophet.

Rabīʿ b. Anas al-Bakrī (d. 139/756). A Basran interpreter of the Qurʾān and narrator of *ḥadīth* from among the second generation of Muslims.

Rabīʿ b. Khuthaym (or 'Khaytham') al-Thawrī al- (d. ca 63/682–3). A narrator of *ḥadīth* and disciple of Ibn ʿAbbās. Known as an ascetic in Kufa, he was afflicted with a form of palsy throughout his life, on account of which he had to be carried to the congregational prayers. He thus became a symbol of patience in adversity.

Rābiʿa al-ʿAdawīyya, bint Ismāʿīl (d. 185/801–2). A famous woman mystic of Basra. Born into a poor family, she was kidnapped and sold into slavery. Later, she regained her freedom and lived a life of devotion and celibacy. An important figure in early Sufism, she placed great emphasis on divine love, producing a number of eloquent prayers and poems to this effect. She had many disciples, including Sufyān al-Thawrī and Shaqīq al-Balkhī. In the works of Sufism she is accredited with miraculous powers.

Saʿd b. Abī Waqqāṣ al-Murrī (d. 50/670 or 55/674–5). An early convert to Islam and one of the ten Companions to have been promised Paradise by the Prophet. Noted for his political and military achievements, he led the Muslims to a decisive triumph in the Battle of al-Qādisīya against the Persians in the year 16/637.

Saʿīd b. Jubayr al-Asadī (d. 95/713–4). A legal scholar, traditionist and Qurʾān reciter of the second Muslim generation who studied under Ibn ʿAbbās and Ibn ʿUmar. He was killed by al-Ḥajjāj for his part in the rebellion of Ibn al-Ashʿath.

Saʿīd b. al-Musayyib al-Makhzūmī (d. 93–4/711–2). He was a leading authority on *ḥadīth*, law and Qurʾānic exegesis among the second generation of Muslims, and one of those included under the honorific title of 'The Seven *Fuqahāʾ* of Medina.' He knew a number of the Companions including the caliphs ʿUmar, ʿUthmān and ʿAlī and was married to the daughter of Abū Hurayra. Renowned for his knowledge and piety, his commitment to his moral ideals in the face of political pressure caused him to be flogged by the authorities on two occasions.

Sālim b. ʿAbd Allāh b. ʿUmar al-Khaṭṭāb (d. 106/725). Grandson of the caliph ʿUmar, he was a reliable transmitter of *ḥadīth* who was known for his knowledge and scrupulousness. He died in Medina and is buried in Baqīʿ cemetery.

Salmān al-Fārisī (d. 35/655–6 or 36 /656–7). One of the most famous among the Companions of the Prophet. Of Persian origin and a convert to Christianity, he is said to have travelled to Arabia on the advice of a Christian monk, in order to search for the Prophet who was to restore the religion of Abraham. On this journey he was sold as a slave to a Jew of Medina by his Bedouin guides. Having converted to Islam and bought his freedom, he is reputed to have advised the Prophet to dig a ditch (*khandaq*) to protect the city of Medina from the siege of the Meccan army. Also known by the Persian title Salmān the Pure (Salmān-i pāk), he is regarded as a model of piety by Sufis, and venerated by Shīʿīs for his devotion to the Prophet and his family. His tomb in Madāʾin is a popular place of pilgrimage.

Sāriya (d. *unknown*). A general under the Caliph ʿUmar who led the Muslims in battle against the Persians. ʿUmar is famously said to have perceived an impending attack by the Persians and from his pulpit in Medina, shouted a warning to Sāriya, who miraculously heard his voice despite the geographical distance.

Shaqīq b. Ibrāhim Abū ʿAlī al-Balkhī (d. 194/809–10). An early mystic and ascetic of Khurasan, who associated with Ibrāhīm al-Adham (d. 161/777–8). Having studied Ḥanafī law and theology, he worked as a merchant before converting to the spiritual life, allegedly after an encounter with a Buddhist monk. He is one of earliest mystics to have stressed the importance of *tawakkul* (complete trust in, and reliance on God), which he himself practised with particular rigour. He is also said to have been the first mystic to have discussed the mystical states.

Shaybān al-Rāʿī (d. 158/775) An ascetic shepherd from Lebanon, said to have associated with Sufyān al-Thawrī.

Shuʿabī, ʿĀmir b. Sharāḥīl al- (d. 103/721). A Follower and transmitter of *ḥadīth*, he narrated from a great number of the Prophet's Companions and was a teacher of Abū Ḥanīfa.

Sijzī, Abū Bakr Muḥammad b. al-Ashʿat al- (also known as Muḥammad b. al-Ashʿat al-Iṣṭakhrī) (fl. third/ninth century). A contemporary and close disciple of Sahl al-Tustarī, who received permission to transmit the latter's *Tafsīr* in the year 275/888. He is mentioned in twelve passages of the *Tafsīr*, indicating his standing as one who was intimate with Tustarī and his teachings. In the *Tafsīr*, he also mentions meetings with other contemporaries from Baghdad, including Junayd and Abū Saʿīd al-Kharrāz. After the death of Tustarī in 283/896, Sijzī settled in Baghdad.

Suddī, Ismāʿīl b. ʿAbd al-Raḥmān al- (al-Suddī al-Kabīr), (d. 127/744). An interpreter of the Qurʾān and transmitter of *ḥadīth*s from such prominent figures as Anas b. Mālik and Ibn ʿAbbās. Abū Jaʿfar al-Ṭabarī and other commentators cite numerous exegetical traditions on his authority.

Suddī, Muḥammad b. Marwan al- (al-Suddī al-Ṣaghīr), (d. 186/801 or 2). An early traditionist of Kufa who lived in Baghdad.

Sufyān al-Thawrī, Ibn Saʿīd b. (d. 161/778). A renowned scholar of *ḥadīth*, Qurʾān interpretation and jurisprudence, and founder of the Thawriyya school of law. Born in Kufa, he travelled widely during his life, transmitting *ḥadīth*s in Khurasan, the Hijaz, Syria and Yemen. He figures prominently in Sufi literature, particularly in anecdotes concerning his position as an ascetic. He was among the devout men who eschewed government service under the Umayyad regime. He is buried in Basra.

Sulamī, Abū ʿAbd al-Raḥmān b. Ḥabīb b. Rubayʿa (d. ca 70/689–90 or 72/691–2). A Kufan Qurʾān reciter from among the generation of Followers, he was also a transmitter of *ḥadīth*.

Ṭāwūs b. Kaysān al-Khawlānī (d. 106/724–5). Regarded as one of the leading scholars of the generation of Followers in Mecca. He studied under Ibn ʿAbbās and was particularly knowledgeable in matters of law, *ḥadīth* and the recitation of the Qurʾān.

Thawbān b. Yuḥdad (d. 54/673–4). One of the freed slaves of the Prophet, whom he continued to serve devotedly until the latter's death. Several *ḥadīth* are narrated by him.

ʿUbāda b. al-Ṣāmit b. Qays al-Khazrajī (d. ca 34/654–5). A Companion of the Prophet who took part in the battles of ʿAqaba and Badr and was also present at the conquest of Egypt.

ʿUmar b. ʿAbd al-ʿAzīz b. Marwān (r. 99–101/717–20). An exceptionally pious Umayyad caliph, sometimes referred to as 'the fifth rightly-guided caliph.' He was known for his moral integrity and concern to implement the *sharīʿa* in his governance, particularly in those areas that had been neglected by former leaders. He died in Aleppo in the year 102/720.

ʿUmar b. al-Khaṭṭāb (d. 23/644). One of the closest Companions of the Prophet and the successor to Abū Bakr as caliph. He is credited with some of the largest expansions of Muslim rule and the development of its accompanying administrative structures. He also played an important role in the collection of the Qurʾān during the caliphate of Abū Bakr, encouraging the latter to initiate the process with the aid of Zayd b. Thābit, the former scribe of the Prophet. He was assassinated whilst leading the prayer in 23/644.

ʿUmar b. Wāṣil, Abū al-Ḥasan al-ʿAnbarī (fl. third/ninth to fourth/tenth century). Pupil and close disciple of Tustarī. He is one of the transmitters of Tustarī's *Tafsīr*, and and is cited as a source of information and anecdotes about him by Sulamī and Qushayrī. He is also said to have transmitted *ḥadīth*s. He assisted at Tustarī's deathbed and attended his burial in Basra, after which he settled in Baghdad, possibly joining the Ḥanbalī traditionists of that city. He may have died on his return from a pilgrimage to Mecca in 312/924, when his caravan was ambushed.

Usāma b. Zayd b. Ḥāritha b. Kalbī al-Ḥāshimī (d. ca 54/674). The son of an Abyssinian freedwoman and a close Companion of the Prophet, who had a special fondness for him when he was a child, so that he is known by the name Ḥabīb b. Ḥabīb Rasūl Allāh. He rode behind the Prophet when, in the year 8/632, he entered Mecca, and entered the Kaʿba with him, and he was one of those who prepared the Prophet for burial. He served the first three caliphs but refused to pay homage to ʿAlī.

ʿUtba al-Ghulām, Ibn Abān b. Samʿa al-Anṣārī (d. ca 153/770–1). An ascetic and pious man of Basra who associated with Ḥasan al-Baṣrī. He was known as 'al-Ghulām' or 'the young man-servant' due to his seriousness and endeavour. He was martyred in northern Syria.

Uways al-Qaranī, Ibn ʿĀmir al-Murādī (d. 37/657). A Yemeni who converted during the lifetime of the Prophet and was greatly praised by him although they never met. Tradition relates that such was Uways' love for the Prophet that when he heard that he had lost a tooth in the Battle of Uḥud, he pulled out one of his own teeth. The Prophet commanded that after his death, when Uways came to visit Medina, his mantle should be given to him, and he should be asked to pray for the Muslim community. He is said to have died fighting alongside ʿAlī in the Battle of Ṣiffīn.

Walīd b. al-Mughīra al- (d. *unknown*). Chief of the Banū Makhzūm tribe of Quraysh and a judge in the time of the Jāhiliyya. He was a leading figure amongst the Quraysh who did not accept Islam and the father of the famed warrior and Companion, Khālid b. al-Walīd.

Wuhayb b. al-Ward al-Makkī (d. ca 153/770–1). A Follower and scholar of *ḥadīth* who led a life of abstinence and worship. He is said to have taught Ibn ʿUyayna and Ibn al-Mubārak.

Zayd b. Arqam al-Khazrajī al-Anṣārī (d. ca 65/684–5). A Companion who fought in seventeen battles together with the Prophet and later alongside ʿAlī in the Battle of Ṣiffīn.

Zayd b. Aslam al-ʿAdawī al-Ṭūsī (d. 136/753–4). A Medinan traditionist and jurist who is said to have taught Mālik b. Anas and narrated from ʿĀʾisha. He is also said to have composed a commentary on the Qurʾān.

Zuhrī, Muḥammad b. Muslim b. ʿUbayd Allāh b. Shihāb al- (d. 124/742). A prominent scholar and renowned authority on *ḥadīth* among the third generation of Muslims in Medina.

Bibliography

Primary Sources

Abdel Haleem, Muhammad, trans. *Qur'an*. New York: Oxford University Press, 2008.

Abū Dāwūd, Sulaymān b. al-Ashʿath al-Sijistānī al-Azadī. *Sunan*, ed. Muḥammad Muḥyī al-Dīn ʿAbd al-Ḥamīd. Beirut, 1988.

Abū Nuʿaym al-Iṣfahānī. See Iṣfahānī.

ʿAjlūnī, Ismāʿīl b. Muḥammad al-. *Kashf al-khafāʾ wa muzīl al-ilbās ʿammā ishtahara min al-aḥādīth ʿalā alsinat al-nās*, ed. Aḥmad al-Qalāsh. Beirut, 1979.

ʿAlī b. Abī Ṭālib. *Nahj al-balāgha*. See Sharīf al-Raḍī, Muḥammad b. al-Ḥusayn.

Alkāʾī, Hibat Allāh b. al-Ḥasan al-Ṭabarī al-. *Karāmāt al-awliyāʾ*, ed. Aḥmad Saʿd al-Ḥamān.Riyadh, 1991.

Anṣārī, Abū Ismāʿīl ʿAbd Allāh al-. *Ṭabaqāt al-ṣūfiyya*, ed. ʿAbd al-Ḥayy Ḥabībī. Kabul, 1961.

———. *Manāzil al-sāʾirīn*, edited with introduction and French translation by Serge de Laugier de Beaurecueil. Cairo, 1962.

———. *Ṣad maydān*, text and French translation in Serge de Laugier de Beaurecueil, 'Une ébauche persane des Manāzil as-Sāʾirīn: Le *Kitāb-e Ṣad maydān* de ʿAbdullāh Anṣārī'. *Mélanges Islamologues d' Archéologie Orientale* 2 (1954), pp. 1–90.

Anṭākī, Dāwūd al-. *Tazyīn al-aswāq fī tafṣīl ashwāq al-ʿushshāq*. Beirut, 1986.

ʿAsqalānī, Aḥmad b. ʿAlī b. Ḥajar al-. *Lisān al-mīzān*. Beirut, 1971.

ʿAṭṭār, Farīd al-Dīn. *Tadhkirat al-awliyāʾ*, ed. M. Istiʿlāmī. Tehran, 1967–8.

ʿAẓīmābādī, Muḥammad Shams al-Ḥaqq al-. *ʿAwn al-maʿbūd: sharḥ Sunan Abī Dāwud*, ed. Khālid ʿAbd al-Fattāḥ Shibl. 10 vols. Beirut, 1998.

Baqlī, Rūzbihān b. Abī Naṣr. *ʿArāʾis al-bayān fī ḥaqāʾiq al-Qurʾān*. 2 vols. Lucknow, 1315/1898.

Bayhaqī, Aḥmad b. al-Ḥusayn al-. *Kitāb al-Zuhd al-kabīr*. Edited by ʿĀmir Aḥmad Ḥaydar. Beirut, 1987. Also edited by Taqī al-Dīn al-Nadwī. Kuwait, 1983.

———. *Sunan al-kubrā*, ed. Muḥammad ʿAbd al-Bāqī ʿAṭā. Beirut, 1994.

———. *al-Jāmiʿ li-shuʿab al-īmān*, ed. Muḥammad al-Saʿīd Basyūnī Zaghlūl. Beirut, 1996.

Bukhārī, Muḥammad b. Ismāʿīl al-. *Al-Jāmiʿ al-ṣaḥīḥ*. Edited by Ludolf Krehl and Theodoor W. Juynboll. Leiden: Brill, 1862–1909. Arabic text and translation in Muhammad Muhsin Khan, *The Translation of the Meanings of Sahih al-Bukhari*. 9 vols. Riyadh: Darussalam, 2004.

Dāwūdī, Shams al-Dīn Muḥammad al-. *Ṭabaqāt al-mufassirīn*. MS Ṭalʿat, mag. 283.

Daylamī, Abū al-Ḥasan ʿAlī b. Muḥammad al-. *ʿAṭf al-alif al-maʾlūf ʿalaʾl-lām al-maʿṭūf*, ed. Jean-Claude Vadet. Cairo, 1962. Translated into French by Jean-Claude Vadet as *Le traité d' amour mystique d' al-Daylami*, Geneva, Droz and Paris, 1980. Translated into English by Joseph Norment Bell as *A Treatise on Mystical Love*. Edinburgh, 2005.

———. *Sīrat-i Ibn-i Khafīf*. Translated into Persian by Rukn al-Dīn Yaḥyā b. al-Junayd al-Shīrāzī, ed. Annemarie Schimmel. Tehran, 1984.

Daylamī, Abū Shujāʿ Shīrawayh b. Shardār al-. *Firdaws bi-maʾthūr al-khiṭāb*, ed. Muḥammad al-Saʿīd Basyūnī Zaghlūl. Beirut, 1986.

Dhahabī, Muḥammad b. Aḥmad al-. *Siyar aʿlām al-nubalāʾ*, ed. Shuʿayb Arnaʿūt. Beirut, 1982.

Dihlawī, ʿAbd al-ʿAzīz b. Aḥmad. *Bustān al-muḥaddithīn*, translated from the Persian into Arabic by Mohammed Akram Nadwi, and from Arabic into English by Aisha Bewley as *The Garden of the Hadith Scholars: Bustān al-Muḥaddithīn*. London, 2007.

Ghazālī, Abū Ḥāmid Muḥammad al-. *Iḥyāʾ ʿulūm al-dīn*. Damascus, 1417/1997.

———. *Kitāb al-Adhkār waʾl-daʿawāt*. Translated by Kojiro Nakamura as *Al-Ghazālī: Invocations and Supplications (Kitāb al-Adhkār waʾl-daʿawāt), Book IX of the Revival of the Religious Sciences (Iḥyā ʿulūm al-dīn)*. Cambridge, 1990.

———. *Kitāb Dhikr al-mawt wa mā baʿdahu*. Translated with an introduction by Timothy J. Winter as *Al-Ghazālī: The Remembrance of Death and the Afterlife (Kitāb Dhikr al-mawt wa-mā baʿdahu), Book XL of the Revival of the Religious Sciences (Iḥyā ʿulūm al-dīn)*. Cambridge, 1989.

———. *Kitāb Riyāḍat al-nafs* and *Kitāb Kasr al-shahwatayn*. Translated with introduction by Timothy J. Winter as *On Disciplining the Soul and on Breaking the Two Desires, Books XXII and XXIII of the Revival of the Religious Sciences (Iḥyā ʿulūm al-dīn)*. Cambridge, 1995.

———. *Kīmiyāʾ al-saʿādat*, ed. Ḥusayn Khadīwjam. Tehran, 1985.

———. *Ayyuhāʾl-Walad*, trans. Tobias Mayer as *Al-Ghazālī: Letter to a Disciple (Ayyuhāʾl-Walad)*. Cambridge, 2005.

Ḥāfiẓ, Shams al-Dīn Muḥammad. *Dīwān-i Ḥāfiẓ*, ed. Parvīz Nātil Khānlarī. Tehran, 1980–1.

Ḥājjī Khalīfa. *Kashf al-ẓunūn*, ed. C. Flügel. 4 vols. Leipzig, 1835.

Harawī, ʿAlī al-. *Kitāb al-Ishārāt ilā maʿrifat al-ziyārāt*, ed. Janine Sourdel-Thomine. Damascus, 1953. Translated by J. W. Meri as *A Lonely Wayfarer's Guide to Pilgrimage*, Princeton, 2004.

Haythamī, ʿAlī Abū Bakr al-. *Majmaʿ al-zawāʾid wa manbaʿ al-fawāʾid*, ed. ʿAbd al-Raḥmān b. al-Ḥusayn al-ʿIrāqī. Cairo, 1933–4.

Hujwīrī, ʿAlī ʿUthmān Jullābī al-. *Kashf al-maḥjūb*, ed. Maḥmūd ʿĀbidī. Tehran, 2004. Translated by Reynold Alleyn Nicholson as *Kashf al-maḥjūb: The Oldest Persian Treatise on Sufism*, London, 1911.

Ibn Abī ʿĀṣim, Aḥmad b. ʿAmr. *Kitāb al-Zuhd*, ed. ʿAbd al-ʿAlī ʿAbd al-Ḥamīd Ḥāmid. Cairo, 1988.

Ibn Abī Ḥātim, ʿAbd al-Raḥmān al-Rāzī. *ʿIlal al-ḥadīth*, ed. Muḥibb al-Dīn al-Khaṭīb. Beirut, 1985.

Ibn Abī Shayba, Abū Bakr ʿAbd Allāh b. Muḥammad. *al-Muṣannaf*, ed. Kamāl Yūsuf al-Ḥūt. Riyadh, 1988.

Ibn ʿArabī, Muḥyī al-Dīn Abū Bakr Muḥammad. *al-Futūḥāt al-Makkiyya*, ed. Nawwāf al-Jarraḥ. Beirut, 2007.

Ibn al-Athīr, ʿIzz al-Dīn ʿAlī b. Muḥammad. *al-Lubāb fī tahdhīb al-ansāb*. Cairo, 1348–87/1929–67.

Ibn al-Farrāʾ, Abū Yaʿlā. *al-Muʿtamad fī uṣūl al-dīn*, ed. Wadīʿ Zaydān Ḥaddād. Beirut, 1974.

Ibn Ḥanbal, Aḥmad. *al-Musnad*. Cairo, 1895. Edited by Aḥmad Muḥammad Shākir et al. Cairo, 1995.

———. *Kitāb al-Wara*ᶜ, ed. Zaynab al-Qārūṭ. Beirut, 1983.

Ibn Isḥāq, Muḥammad. *Kitāb al-Mubtada*ᵓ *wa'l-mab*ᶜ*ath wa'l-maghāzī*, known as *Sīrat Ibn Isḥāq*, ed. M. Ḥamīd Allāh. Rabat, 1976. Translated into English by Alfred Guillaume as *The Life of Muḥammad: A Translation of Ibn Isḥāq's Sīrat Rasūl Allāh*. London, 1955.

Ibn al-Jawzī, Abū al-Faraj ᶜAbd al-Raḥmān al-Baghdādī. *Talbīs Iblīs, Naqd al-*ᶜ*ilm wa'l-*ᶜ*ulamā*ᵓ, ed. Muḥammad Munīr Dimashqī. Cairo, 1950.

———. *Ṣifat al-ṣafwa*, ed. Maḥmūd Fākhūrī and Muḥammad Qalᶜajī. Beirut, 1979.

———. *Dhamm al-hawā*, ed. Muṣṭafā ᶜAbd al-Wāḥid. Cairo, 1962.

Ibn Khaldūn. *Kitāb al-*ᶜ*ibar*. Beirut, 1961.

Ibn Māja, Muḥammad b. Yazīd Abū ᶜAbd Allāh al-Qazwīnī. *Sunan*, ed. Fūᵓād ᶜAbd al-Bāqī. Beirut, 1995.

Ibn Mubārak, ᶜAbd Allāh. *Kitāb al-Zuhd wa'l-raqā*ᵓ*iq*, ed. Ḥabīb al-Raḥmān al-Aᶜẓamī. Beirut, 1971. Reprint Beirut, 1997.

Ibn al-Nadīm, Muḥammad b. Isḥāq. *Fihrist*, ed. C. Flügel. 2 vols. Leipzig, 1871–2.

Ibn Saᶜd, Muḥammad. *Ṭabaqāt al-kabīr*. Vol. 5 translated by Aisha Bewley as *Men of Madina*. 2 vols. London, 2000.

Ikhwān al-Ṣafā. *Rasā*ᵓ*il Ikhwān al-Ṣafā*ᵓ *wa khullān al-wafā*ᵓ, ed. Buṭrus al-Bustānī. 4 vols. Beirut, 1957.

Iṣfahānī, Abū Nuᶜaym al-. *Ḥilyat al-awliyā*ᵓ. Cairo, 1932–8.

Isḥāq b. Ibrāhīm b. Rāhawayh al-Ḥanẓalī. *al-Musnad*, ed. ᶜAbd al-Ghafūr al-Balūshī. Medina, 1991.

Ismāᶜīl Pāšā al-Bāghdādī. *Hadīyat al-*ᶜ*ārifīn, asmā*ᵓ *al-mu*ᵓ*allifīn wa āthār al-muṣannifīn*, ed. Muallim Kilisli Rifat Bilge and Ibnülemin Mahmud Kemal Inal. Istanbul, 1951–5.

ᶜIyāḍ b. Mūsā, Abū al-Faḍl al-Qāḍī. *Kitāb al-Shifā*ᵓ *bi-ta*ᶜ*rīf ḥuqūq al-muṣṭafā*. Damascus, 1972.

Jāmī, Nūr al-Dīn ᶜAbd al-Raḥmān. *Nafaḥāt al-uns min ḥaḍarāt al-quds*, ed. M. ᶜĀbidī. Tehran, 1991.

Jīlānī, ᶜAbd al-Qādir al-. *al-Ghunya li-ṭālibī ṭarīq al-ḥaqq*. Cairo, 1322/1904.

Jurjānī, ᶜAlī b. Muḥammad b. ᶜAlī al-. *al-Ta*ᶜ*rīfāt*, ed. Ibrāhīm al-Abyārī. Beirut, 1987.

Kalābādhī, Abū Bakr Muḥammad b. Isḥāq al-. *Kitāb al-Ta*ᶜ*arruf li-madhhab ahl al-taṣawwuf*, ed. Arthur J. Arberry. Cairo, 1934. Translated by Arthur J. Arberry as *Doctrine of the Sufis*.Cambridge, 1935.

Khargūshī, Abū Saᶜd. *Tahdhīb al-asrār*. MS Ahlwardt, 2819.

Kharrāz, Abū Saᶜīd al-. *Kitāb al-Ṣidq*. Translated by Arthur J. Arberry as *The Book of Truthfulness*. Oxford, 1937.

Khaṭīb al-Tibrīzī. *Mishkāt al-maṣābīḥ*. Translated by James Robson. Lahore, 1975.

Makkī, Abū Ṭālib al-. *Qūt al-qulūb fī mu*ᶜ*āmalat al-maḥbūb*, ed. Bāsil ᶜUyūn al-Sūd. 2 vols. Beirut, 1997. Translated into German with introduction and commentary by Richard Gramlich as *Die Nahrung der Herzen*. Stuttgart, 1992–5.

Mālik b. Anas (Imām Mālik). *Kitāb al-Muwaṭṭa*ᵓ. English translation by Muhammad Rahimuddin. Damascus, 2003.

Maqdisī (al-Muqaddasī), ᶜAbd Allāh Muḥammad b. Aḥmad al-. *Aḥsan al-taqāsīm fī ma*ᶜ*rifat al-aqālīm*, ed. M. J. de Goeje. Leiden, 1877.

Maybudī, Abū al-Faḍl Rashīd al-Dīn. *Kashf al-asrār wa ʿuddat al-abrār*, ed. Ali Asghar Hekmat et al. Tehran, 1952–60.

Munāwī, Muḥammad ʿAbd al-Raʾūf al-. *al-Tawqīf ʿalā muhimmāt al-taʿārīf*, ed. Muḥammad Riḍwān al-Dāya. Beirut and Damascus, 1990.

——— and ʿAbd al-Salām Suyūṭī. *Fayḍ al-qadīr: sharḥ al-Jāmiʿ al-ṣaghīr min aḥādīth al-bashīr al-nadhīr*. Cairo, 1938.

Mundhirī, ʿAbd al-ʿAẓīm b. ʿAbd al-Qawī al-. *al-Targhīb wa'l-tarhīb*, ed. Ibrāhīm Shams al-Dīn. Beirut, 1996.

Nasāʾī, Aḥmad b. Shuʿayb Abū ʿAbd al-Raḥmān al-. *al-Sunan al-kubrā*, ed. ʿAbd al-Ghaffār al-Bandārī. Beirut, 1991.

Nawawī, Abū Zakariyya Yaḥyā b. Sharaf al-. *An-Nawawī's Forty Ḥadīth*. Arabic text and translation by Ezzeddin Ibrahim and Denys Johnson-Davies. Lebanon, 1980.

———. *Forty Ḥadīth Qudsī*. Arabic text and translation by Ezzeddin Ibrahim and Denys Johnson-Davies. Lebanon, 1980.

Nīsābūrī, Muḥammad b. ʿAbd Allāh Abū ʿAbd Allāh al-Ḥākim al-. *Mustadrak ʿalā al-Ṣaḥīḥayn*, ed. Muṣṭafā ʿAbd al-Qādir ʿAṭā. Beirut, 1996.

Nūrī, Abū al-Ḥusayn al-. *Maqāmāt al-qulūb*, edited with introduction by Paul Nwyia in *Mélanges de l'Université Saint-Joseph* 44 (1968), pp. 117–54.

Qārī, Jaʿfar b. Aḥmad Sarrāj al-. *Maṣāriʿ al-ʿushshāq*. Beirut, 1969.

Qifṭī, Abū al-Ḥasan ʿAlī b. Yūsuf al-. *Taʾrīkh al-ḥukamāʾ*, ed. J. Lippert. Leipzig, 1903.

Quḍāʿī, Muḥammad b. Salāma b. Jaʿfar Abū ʿAbd Allāh al-. *Musnad al-Shihāb*, ed. Ḥamdī b. ʿAbd al-Majīd al-Salafī. Beirut, 1986.

Qurṭubī, Muḥammad b. Aḥmad b. Abī Bakr al-. *al-Jāmiʿ li-aḥkām al-Qurʾān, al-maʿrūf bi-Tafsīr al-Qurṭubī*, ed. Aḥmad Baraddūnī. Beirut, 1985.

Qushayrī, Abū al-Qāsim ʿAbd al-Karīm b. Hawāzan al-. *Kitāb al-Miʿrāj*, ed. ʿAlī Ḥusayn ʿAbd al-Qādir. Cairo, 1964.

———. *al-Risāla al-Qushayriyya fī ʿilm al-taṣawwuf*. Cairo, 1966. Translated into English by Alexander D. Knysh as *Qushayri's Epistle on Sufism*. Reading, 2007.

———. *Laṭāʾif al-ishārāt*, ed. Ibrāhīm Basyūnī. Cairo, 1968–71.

Rūmī, Jalāl al-Dīn al-Balkhī. *The Mathnawī*. Edited with translation and commentary by Reynold A. Nicholson. 8 vols. London, 1925–40.

Sakhāwī, Shams al-Dīn Abī al-Khayr Muḥammad b. ʿAbd al-Raḥmān al-. *al-Maqāṣid al-ḥasana fī bayān kathīr min al-aḥādīth al-mushtahira ʿala'l-alsina*, ed. ʿAbd Allāh Muḥammad al-Ṣādiq. Beirut, 1979.

Samʿānī, ʿAbd al-Karīm b. Muḥammad al-. *Kitāb al-Ansāb*. Facsimile edition. Leiden, 1912.

Samʿānī, Shihāb al-Dīn Aḥmad al-. *Rawḥ al-arwāḥ fī sharḥ asmāʾ al-Malik al-Fattāḥ*, ed. Najīb Māyil Harawī. Tehran, 1989.

Sarrāj, Abū Naṣr ʿAbd Allāh b. ʿAlī. *Kitāb al-Lumaʿ fī'l-taṣawwuf*, ed. with English synopsis by Reynold Alleyne Nicholson. London and Leiden, 1914.

Shaʿrānī, ʿAbd al-Wahhāb b. Aḥmad al-. *Ṭabaqāt al-kubrā, al-musammā Lawāqiḥ al-anwār al-qudsiyya fī manāqib al-ʿulamāʾ waʾl-ṣūfiyya*, ed. Aḥmad ʿAbd al-Raḥīm al-Sāyiḥ and Tawfīq ʿAlī Wahbah. Cairo, 2005.

Sharīf al-Raḍī, Muḥammad b. al-Ḥusayn. *Nahjul balagha: Sermons, Letters, and Sayings of Imam Ali*. Qum, 1981.

Shāṭibī, Ibrāhīm b. Mūsā al-. *al-Muwāfaqāt fī uṣūl al-aḥkām*, ed. M. Ḥasanayn Makhlūf. Cairo, 1922.

Suhrawardī, Shihāb al-Dīn Yaḥyā. *Qiṣṣat al-ghurbat al-gharbiyya*, in Shihāb al-Dīn Yaḥyā Suhrawardī, *Oeuvres philosophiques et mystiques*, ed. H. Corbin. Tehran/Paris, 1952–77.

———. *Kitāb al-Maṣārī waʾl-muṭāraḥāt*, in Shihāb al-Dīn Yaḥyā Suhrawardī, *Opera Metaphysica et Mystica*, ed. H. Corbin. Istanbul, 1945.

Sulamī, Abū ʿAbd al-Raḥmān al-. *Ṭabaqāt al-ṣūfiyya*, ed. Johannes Pedersen. Leiden, 1960.

———. *Bayān laṭāʾif al-miʿrāj*. Arabic text edited with English translation and annotation by Frederick S. Colby, published as *Subtleties of the Ascension*. Louisville, KY, 2006.

———. *Risālat al-malāmatiyya*, ed. Abū al-ʿAlāʾ ʿAfīfī, edited and reprinted by Nasrollah Pourjavady, *Majmūʿa-yi āthār-i Abū ʿAbd al-Raḥmān Sulamī*. Tehran, 1990. French translation by Roger Deladrière as *Sulami*: *La lucidité implacable* (*Épître des hommes du blâme*). Paris, 1991.

———. *Ḥaqāʾiq al-tafsīr*. MS British Museum Or. 9433. Edited by Sayyid ʿImrān. Beirut, 2001. Comments attributed to Jaʿfar al-Ṣādiq, edited with introduction by Paul Nwyia in 'Le tafsîr mystique attribué à Jaʿfar Ṣâdiq'. *Mélanges de l'Université Saint-Joseph* 43 (1967), pp. 179–230. Comments of Ibn ʿAṭāʾ al-Adamī, edited by Paul Nwyia in *Trois oeuvres inédites de mystiques musulmanes*: *Šaqīq Balḫī, Ibn ʿAṭā, Niffārī*. Beirut, 1973. Comments attributed to Ḥallāj, edited by Louis Massignon in Paul Nwyia, *Essai sur les origines du lexique technique de la mystique musulmane*. Paris, 1922. These extracts have been edited and reprinted in Nasrollah Pourjavady, *Majmūʿa-yi āthār-i Abū ʿAbd al-Raḥmān Sulamī*. 2 vols. Tehran, 1990.

———. *Ziyādāt ḥaqāʾiq al-tafsīr*, edited with an introduction by Gerhard Böwering. Beirut, 1995.

Suyūṭī, Jalāl al-Dīn al-, and Jalāl al-Dīn al-Maḥallī. *Tafsīr al-Jalālayn*, ed. ʿAbd al-Qādir al-Arnāʾūṭ and Aḥmad Khālid Shukrī. Damascus and Beirut: Dār Ibn Kathīr, 1998. Translated by Feras Hamza. Louisville, KY: Royal Aal al-Bayt Institute for Islamic Thought and Fons Vitae, 2008.

Ṭabarānī, Abū al-Qāsim Sulaymān b. Aḥmad al-. *al-Muʿjam al-ṣaghīr*, ed. Muḥammad Shukūr Maḥmūd al-Ḥājj Amrīr. Beirut/Amman, 1985.

———. *al-Muʿjam al-awsaṭ*, ed. Ṭāriq b. ʿAwaḍ Allāh and ʿAbd al-Muḥsin al-Ḥusaynī. Cairo, 1995.

———. *al-Muʿjam al-kabīr*, ed. Ḥamdī ʿAbd al-Majīd al-Salafī. Mosul, 1983–90.

Ṭabarī, Abū Jaʿfar Muḥammad b. Jarīr al-. *Jāmiʿ al-bayān ʿan taʾwīl āy al-Qurʾān*. Published under the title *Jāmiʿ al-bayān ʿan tafsīr al-Qurʾān*. Cairo, 1321–8/1904–10. Edited by Maḥmūd Muḥammad Shākir and Aḥmad Muḥammad Shākir. Vols. 1–16 (incomplete). Cairo, 1955–69. Abridged English translation with introduction of vol. 1 by John Cooper as *The Commentary on the Qurʾān by Abū Jaʿfar Muḥammad b. Jarīr al-Ṭabarī*. Oxford, 1987.

———. *Tārīkh al-rusul waʾl-mulūk*, ed. Muḥammad Abū al-Faḍl Ibrāhīm. Cairo, 1960–9. English translation of vol. 1 by Franz Rosenthal as *The History of al-Ṭabarī I*: *From the Creation to the Flood*. Albany, 1989. English translation of vol. 3 by William M. Brinner as *The History of al-Ṭabarī III*: *The Children of Israel*. Albany, 1991.

Ṭāʾī, Ḥāṭim b. ʿAbd Allāh al-. *Dīwān*, ed. ʿĀdil Sulaymān Jamāl. Cairo, 1975.

Thaʿlabī, Abū Isḥāq Aḥmad b. Muḥammad al-. *Qiṣaṣ al-anbiyāʾ al-musammā biʾl-ʿArāʾis al-majālis*. Cairo, n.d. English translation by William M. Brinner as *ʿArāʾis al-majālis fī qiṣaṣ al-anbiyāʾ or: Lives of the Prophets as recounted by Abū Isḥāq Aḥmad b. Muḥammad b. Ibrāhīm al-Thaʿlabī*. Leiden and Boston, 2002.

Tirmidhī, Abū ʿĪsā Muḥammad b. ʿĪsā al-. *al-Jāmiʿ al-saḥīḥ wa huwa sunan al-Tirmidhī*, ed. Aḥmad Muḥammad Shākir. Cairo, 1937–65.

Tirmidhī, al-Ḥakīm Muḥammad b. ʿAlī al-. *Bayān al-farq bayn al-ṣadr wa'l-qalb wa'l-fuʾād wa'l-lubb*, ed. Nicholas Heer. Cairo, 1958. Translated into English by Nicholas Heer in Nicholas Heer and Kenneth L. Honerkamp, *Three Early Sufi Texts*. Louisville, KY, 2003.

———. *Kitāb Nawādir al-uṣūl fī maʿrifat aḥādīth al-rasūl*, ed. Muṣṭafā ʿAbd al-Qādir ʿAṭāʾ. Beirut, 1992. Edited by ʿAbd al-Raḥmān ʿUmayra. Beirut, 1993.

ʿUmar, Aḥmad Mukhtār and ʿAbd al-ʿĀl Mukarram. *Muʿjam al-qirāʾāt al-Qurʾāniyya*. Cairo, 1997.

Wāḥidī, ʿAlī b. Aḥmad. *Asbāb al-nuzūl*. Translated by Mokrane Guezzou. Louisville, KY: Royal Aal al-Bayt Institute for Islamic Thought and Fons Vitae, 2008.

Washāʾ, Abū Ṭayyib Muḥammad b. Isḥāq b. Yaḥyā al-. *Ẓarf al-ẓurafāʾ*, ed. Fahmī Saʿd. Beirut, 1985.

Zabīdī, al-Murtaḍā al-. *Itḥāf al-sādat al-muttaqīn bi-sharḥ asrār Iḥyāʾ ʿulūm al-dīn*. Cairo, 1894.

Zamakhsharī, Maḥmūd b. ʿUmar Jār Allāh al-. *Rabīʿ al-abrār wa-nuṣūṣ al-akhbār*, ed. Salīm al-Nuʿaymī. Qum, 1989.

Secondary Sources

Abdel-Kader, Ali Hasan. *The Life, Personality and Works of al-Junayd*. London, 1976.

Abrahamov, B. 'The *bi-lā kayfa* Doctrine and its Foundation in Islamic Theology.' *Arabica* 42 (1995), pp. 165–79.

Arberry, Arthur John. *Pages from the Kitāb al-Lumaʿ*. London, 1947.

———. 'A Biography of Dhul-Nūn Al-Miṣrī.' In *ʿArshī Presentation Volume*, ed. M. Rām and M. D. Aḥmad. New Delhi, 1965.

Arnaldez, R. 'Maʿrifa.' *EI²*. Vol. vi, pp. 568–71.

Azarnoosh, Azartash. 'Abjād', trans. R. Gholami. *Encyclopedia Islamica*. Vol. i, p. 339.

Böwering, Gerhard. *The Mystical Vision of Existence in Classical Islam: The Qurʾānic Hermeneutics of the Ṣūfī Sahl at-Tustarī (d.* 283/896). Berlin and New York, 1980.

———. 'Sufi Hermeneutics and Medieval Islam.' *Revue des études islamiques* 55–7 (1987–8), pp. 255–70.

———. 'The Light Verse: Qurʾānic Text and Sufi Interpretation.' *Oriens* 36 (2001) pp. 113–44.

———. 'The Scriptural Senses in Medieval Ṣūfī Qurʾān Exegesis.' In Jane Dammen McAuliffe et al., eds. *With Reverence for the Word: Medieval Exegesis in Judaism, Christianity, and Islam*, pp. 346–65. Oxford and New York, 2003.

Busse, Heribert. 'Jerusalem in the Story of Muhammad's Night Journey and Ascension.' *Jerusalem Studies in Arabic and Islam* 14 (1991), pp. 1–40.

Calder, Norman. 'Tafsīr from Ṭabarī to Ibn Kathīr: Problems in the Description of a Genre, Illustrated with Reference to the Story of Abraham.' In G. R. Hawting and A. K. Shareef, eds. *Approaches to the Qurʾān*. London and New York, 1993.

Caspar, Robert. *A Historical Introduction to Islamic Theology: Muhammad and the Classical Period.* Translated by P. Johnstone. Rome, 1998.

Chabbi, Jacqueline. 'Abdāl.' *EIr*. Vol. III, pp. 173–4.

Chittick, William. *Sufi Path of Knowledge*. Albany, 1989.

Cooperson, Michael. *Classical Arabic Biography: The Heirs of the Prophets in the Age of al-Maʾmūn.* Cambridge, 2000.

Chodkiewitz, Michel. *Seal of Saints: Prophethood and Sainthood in the Doctrine of Ibn ʿArabī.* Cambridge, 1993.

Fahd, T. 'Djafr.' *EI²*. Vol. II, p. 375.

Fowden, Garth. *The Egyptian Hermes: A Historical Approach to the Pagan Mind*. Cambridge, 1996.

Gaafar, M. K. I. 'The Sufi Doctrine of Sahl al-Tustarī, with a Critical Edition of his *Risālat al-ḥurūf*.' PhD thesis. Cambridge University, 1966. (See also Jaʿfar).

Garrido Clemente, Pilar. 'El *Tradado de las Letras* (*Risālat al-ḥurūf*) del Sufí Sahl al-Tustarī.' *Anuario de Estudios Filológicos* 29 (2006), pp. 87–100.

———. 'Estudio, Traducción y edición de las obras de Ibn Masarra de Córdoba: la Ciencia de las Letras en el Sufismo.' PhD thesis. University of Salamanca, 2007.

Gardet, L. 'In shāʾ Allāh.' *EI²*. Vol. III, p. 1196.

Geoffroy, Eric and Farhad Daftary. 'Umm al-kitāb.' *EI²*. Vol. X, p. 854–5.

Gimaret, Daniel. Théories de l'acte humaine en théologie musulmane. Paris and Leuven, 1980.

Goldziher, Ignaz. 'Abdāl.' *EI²*. Vol. I, p. 94.

Gutas, Dimitri. *Greek Wisdom Literature in Arabic Translation: A Study of the Graeco-Arabic Gnomologia*. New Haven CT, 1975.

———. *Greek Thought, Arabic Culture: The Graeco-Arabic Translation Movement in Baghdad and Early ʿAbbāsid Society (2nd–4th/8th–10th centuries)*. London, 1998.

———. *Greek Philosophers in the Arabic Tradition*. Aldershot, 2000.

Ḥabīb ʿUmar b. Muḥammad b. Sālim. *The Glorious Treasure: On the Knowledge Required of a Muslim and Supplications for Different Occasions.* Translated by Mohammad Ahmad Mbaye. London: Sheba Press, 2006.

Hamza, Feras and Sajjad Rizvi, eds. *An Anthology of Qurʾanic Commentaries*. Oxford, 2009.

Heinen, Anton M. *Islamic Cosmology. A Study of as-Suyūṭī's al-Hayʾa as-samīya fī'l-hayʾa as-sunniya.* Beirut and Wiesbaden, 1982.

Holmyard, Eric John. *Alchemy*. Baltimore, 1997.

Homerin, Th. E. 'Soul.' *EQ*. Vol. 5, p. 80.

Izzi Dien, Mawil Y. and Paul E. Walker. 'Wilāya.' *EI²*. Vol. XI, pp. 208–9.

Jaʿfar, Muḥammad Kamāl Ibrāhīm. *Min al-turāth al-Tustarī al-ṣūfī: dirāsa wa taḥqīq*. Cairo, 1974–. (See also Gaafar).

Kamada, Shigeru. 'A Study of the Term *sirr* (secret) in Sufi *Laṭāʾif* Theories.' *Oriens* 19 (1983), pp. 7–28.

Karamustafa, Ahmet T. *Sufism: The Formative Period*. Edinburgh, 2007.

Keeler, Annabel. *Sufi Hermeneutics: The Qurʾān Commentary of Rashīd al-Dīn Maybudī*. Oxford, 2006.

———. 'Sufi *tafsīr* as a Mirror: Qushayrī the *murshid* in his *Laṭāʾif al-ishārāt*.' *Journal of Qurʾanic Studies* 7 (2006), pp. 1–21.

———. 'Joseph, in Exegesis.' *EIr*. Vol. xv, Fasc. 1, pp. 34–41.

Kinberg, Leah. 'Muḥkamāt and Mutashābihāt (Q. verse 3/7). Implication of a Qurʾānic Pair of Terms in Medieval Exegesis.' *Arabica* 35 (1988), pp. 143–72.

Kingsley, Peter. *Ancient Philosophy, Mysticism and Magic, Empedocles and the Pythagorean Tradition*. Oxford, 1995.

Knysh, Alexander. *Islamic Mysticism: A Short History*. Leiden, 2000.

Kraus, Paul. 'Jābir Ibn Ḥayyān.' In *Mémoires de L'Institut d' Égypte*. Cairo, vol. 44 (1942), vol. 45 (1943).

Lagarde, Michel. 'De l'ambiguité dans le Coran.' *Quaderni di Studi Arabi* 3 (1985), pp. 45–62.

Lalani, Arzina. *Early Shīʿī Thought: The Teachings of Muḥammad al-Bāqir*. London, 2004.

Landolt, Hermann. 'Walāyah.' *The Encyclopedia of Religion*, ed. Mircea Eliade. Vol. 14, pp. 9656–62. 16 vols. New York, 1987.

Lazarus-Yafeh, Hava. *Studies in al-Ghazzālī*. Jerusalem, 1975.

———. 'Uzayr.' *EI*[2]. Vol. x, p. 960.

Lewisohn, Leonard, ed. *The Heritage of Sufism*. 3 vols. Oxford, 1999.

Lings, Martin. *Muḥammad*. Cambridge, 2005.

Lory, Pierre. *Les Commentaires ésotériques du Coran d' après ʿAbd al-Razzâq al-Qâshânî*. Paris, 1980.

———. *Alchimie et mystique en terre d' Islam*. Lagrasse, 1989.

———. 'Walī.' *EI*[2]. Vol. xi, p. 109.

Macdonald, D. B. 'Ilhām.' *EI*[2]. Vol. iii, p. 1119.

——— and Wilferd Madelung. 'Malāʾika.' *EI*[2]. Vol. vi, p. 216.

Madelung, Wilferd. 'The Origins of the Controversy Concerning the Creation of the Qurʾān.' In idem, *Religious Schools and Sects in Medieval Islam*, pp. 504–25. London, 1985.

———. "ʿIṣma.' *EI*[2]. Vol. v, pp. 182–5.

Marmura, Michael E., ed. *Islamic Theology and Philosophy*. Albany, 1984.

Martin, Richard C. 'Anthropomorphism.' *EQ*. Vol. 1, p. 103.

———. 'Createdness of the Qurʾān.' *EQ*. Vol. 1, p. 467.

———. et al. *Defenders of Reason in Islam: Muʿtazilism from Medieval School to Modern Symbol*. Oxford, 1987.

Massey, Keith. 'Mysterious Letters.' *EQ*. Vol. 5, 412–4.

Massignon, Louis. *Essai sur les origines du lexique technique de la mystique musulmane*. Paris, 1922. Translated into English by Benjamin Clark as *Essay on the Origin of the Technical Language of Islamic Mysticism*. Paris, 1997.

———. *La passion d' al-Hosayn-ibn-Mansour al-Hallâj, martyr mystique de l'Islam*. 2 vols. Paris, 1922. Translated by Herbert Mason as *The Passion of al-Ḥallāj, Mystic and Martyr of Islam*. 4 vols. Princeton, 1982.

Mayer, Tobias. 'Theology and Sufism.' In T. J. Winter, ed., *The Cambridge Companion to Classical Islamic Theology*. Cambridge, 2008.

McAuliffe, Jane Dammen. 'Qurʾānic Hermeneutics: The Views of Ṭabarī and Ibn Kathīr.' In Andrew Rippin, *Approaches to the History of the Interpretation of the Qurʾān*. Oxford and New York, 1988, pp. 46–62.

———, Barry D. Walfish and Joseph W. Goering, eds., *With Reverence for the Word: Medieval Scriptural Exegesis in Judaism, Christianity, and Islam*. Oxford and New York, 2003.

Meri, Josef W. *The Cult of Saints among Muslims and Jews in Medieval Syria*. Oxford, 2002.

Morris, James W. 'Surrender and Realisation: Imam ʿAli on the Conditions for True Religious Understanding.' *Ruḥ ad-Din* 1 (2000), pp. 17–29.

Nagel, Tilman. *The History of Islamic Theology: From Muhammad to the Present*. Translated by Thomas Thornton, Princeton, 2000.

Nakamura, Kojiro. 'Makkī and Ghazālī on Mystical Practices.' *Orient* 20 (1984), pp. 83–91.

Nasr, Seyyed Hossein. *An Introduction to Islamic Cosmological Doctrines*. London, 1978.

———. *Islamic Science: An Illustrated Study*. London, 1976.

Nwyia, Paul. *Exégèse coranique et langue mystique*. Beirut, 1970.

Patton, Walter M. *Aḥmad b. Ḥanbal and the Miḥna*. Leiden, 1897.

Picken, Gavin N. 'The Concept of Tazkiyat al-Nafs in Islam in the Light of the Works of al-Ḥārith al-Muḥāsibī.' PhD thesis. University of Leeds, 2005.

Poonawala, Ismail. 'Taʾwīl.' *EI*[2]. Vol. x, pp. 390–2.

Pourjavady, Nasrollah. '*Nahj al-khāṣṣ* (atharī az Abū Manṣūr-i Iṣfahānī).' *Taḥqīqāt-i Islāmī*, Year 3, no. 2 (1988–9), pp. 94–149.

———. "ʿAhd-i Alast: ʿAqīda-yi Abū Ḥāmid al-Ghazzālī wa jāygāh-i tārīkh-i ān.' *Maʿārif* 7 (1990), pp. 3–47.

———. 'Parvāna u ātash: sayr-i taḥawwul-i yik tamthīl-i ʿirfānī dar adabiyyāt-i Fārsī.' *Nashr-i Dānish*, Year 16, no. 2 (1999), pp. 3–15.

———. 'Bāzmānda-yi kitāb-i *al-Ishārah wa'l-ʿibārah-i* Abū Saʿd Khargūshī dar kitāb-i *ʿIlm al-qulūb*.' *Maʿārif* 15 (1999), pp. 34–41. Republished in Pourjavady, *Pazhūhishhā-yi ʿirfānī: just-u-jū dar manābiʿ-i kuhan*. Tehran, 2006.

———. 'Laṭāʾif-i Qurʾānī dar majālis-i Sayf al-Dīn Bākharzī'. *Maʿārif* 18 (2001), pp. 3–24.

———. *Du mujaddid*. Tehran, 2002.

———. *Bāda-yi ʿishq*. Tehran, 2008.

Radtke, Bernd. 'The Concept of *Wilāya* in Early Sufism.' In Leonard Lewisohn, ed., reprinted as *The Heritage of Sufism*, vol. 1, pp. 486–96. Oxford, 1999.

——— and John O' Kane. *The Concept of Sainthood in Early Islamic Mysticism*. Richmond, 1996.

Robinson, Neal. *Discovering the Qurʾān: A Contemporary Approach to a Veiled Text*. 2nd edn. Washington, D.C., 2003.

Rosenthal, Franz. *The Classical Heritage in Islam*. Translated from the German by Emile and Jenny Marmorstein. London, 1992.

Rubin, Uri. 'Pre-existence and Light: Aspects of the Concept of *Nūr Muḥammad*.' *Israel Oriental Studies* 5 (1975), pp. 62–119.

Sands, Kristin Z. *Ṣūfī Commentaries on the Qurʾān in Classical Islam*. London and New York, 2006.

Schimmel, Annemarie. *Mystical Dimensions of Islam*. North Carolina, 1975.

———. *And Muhammad is His Messenger*. North Carolina, 1985.

Seale, Morris S. *Muslim Theology*. London, 1964.

Sezgin, Fuat. *Geschichte des Arabischen Schrifttums*. Leiden, 1967.

Smith, Margaret. *Studies in Early Mysticism in the Near and Middle East*. London and New York, 1931.

———. *Rābiʿa the Mystic and her Fellow Saints in Islam*. Cambridge, 1984.

Stillman, Yedida K. Arab Dress: From the Dawn of Islam to Modern Times. Leiden, 2000.

Streck, M. [A. Miguel]. 'Ḳāf.' *EI*[2]. Vol. IV, pp. 400–2.

Swartz, Merlin L. *A Medieval Critique of Anthropomorphism*: *Ibn al-Jawzī's Kitāb Akhbār aṣ-ṣifāt*. Leiden, 2002.

Syamsuddin, Sahiron. '*Muḥkam* and *Mutashābih*: An Analytical Study of al-Ṭabarī's and al-Zamakhsharī's Interpretations of Q. 3:7.' *Journal of Qurʾanic Studies* 1 (1999), pp. 63–79.

Tortel, Christiane. *Paroles d' un soufi*: *Abû'l-Ḥasan Kharaqânî* (960–1033). Paris, 1998.

Vajda, G. 'Isrāʾīliyyāt.' *EI*[2]. Vol. IV, pp. 211–2.

Van Ess, Josef. *Die Gedankenwelt des Ḥārit al-Muḥāsibī*. Bonn, 1961.

———. *Theologie und Gesellschaft im* 2. *und* 3. *Jahrhundert Hidschra*: *eine Geschichte des religiösen Denkens im frühen Islam*. Berlin, 1991–5.

———. *The Flowering of Muslim Theology*. Translated by Jane Marie Todd. Boston, 2006.

———. 'Tashbīh wa Tanzīh.' *EI*[2]. Vol. X, p. 341.

Walzer, Richard. *Greek into Arabic*. Oxford, 1962.

Watt, Montgomery. 'Early Discussions about the Qurʾān.' *Muslim World* 40 (1950), pp. 21–40 and 96–105.

———. 'Dahr.' *EI*[2]. Vol. II, p. 94.

———. *The Formative Period of Islamic Thought*. Edinburgh, 1973.

———. *Free Will and Predestination in Early Islam*. London, 1948.

———. 'The Origin of the Islamic Doctrine of Acquisition,' *Journal of the Royal Asiatic Society of Great Britain and Ireland* (1943), pp. 234–47.

Wensinck, A. J. 'Isrāfīl.' *EI*[2]. Vol. IV, p. 211.

———. 'Waḥy.' *EI*[2]. Vol. XI, p. 53.

Wild, Stefan. 'The Self-Referentiality of the Qurʾān: Sura 3:7 as an Exegetical Challenge.' In McAuliffe et al., eds., *With Reverence for the Word*, pp. 422–36.

Williams, W. 'Aspects of the Creed of Aḥmad ibn Ḥanbal: A Study of Anthropomorphism in Early Islamic Discourse.' *IJMES* 36 (2002), pp. 441–63.

Winter, Timothy J., ed. *The Cambridge Companion to Classical Islamic Theology*. Cambridge, 2008.

Ziriklī, Khayr al-Dīn. *al-Aʿlām*. Beirut, 1979.

Index I: Qurʾānic Citations

Index II: People and Places

N

P

Q

R

S

T

U

W

Y

Z

Index III: Subjects and Technical Terms

Arabic terms are followed by English equivalents (in parentheses) and cross referenced to other related Arabic as well as relevant English terms and subjects. English terms are followed by Arabic equivalents used in the *Tafsīr* (in parentheses) and cross referenced only to other related English terms and subjects. When two Arabic equivalents are derived from the same verbal root they are separated with a forward slash, e.g. decree, divine (*qaḍāʾ*, *qadar / taqdīr*, *ḥukm*). Items that are cross referenced are separated by semi-colons. Where the same Arabic or English word is used with more than one meaning, this is indicated in the cross reference either by an equivalent in parentheses, e.g. *See also* desire (*irāda*), as opposed to desire (*hamm*), or with the use of a comma followed by a clarifying word, e.g. *See also* secret, innermost, as opposed to secret, inner truth. In some cases, when the reader might find both / all entries useful, the entry is listed without clarification. Colons are used to indicate a subheading, e.g. *See also* prayer: at night. Analytic subheadings appear only under English entries, whereas subheadings under Arabic terms consist solely of constructs, e.g. under *rūḥ* (spirit), the subhead *ḥayāt al-* for *ḥayāt al-rūḥ* (life of the spirit). In words where the *tāʾ marbūṭa* would be used, this is not indicated in the subheadings, e.g. under *muʿāyana* (visual beholding), the subheading *al-abṣār* refers to *muʿāyanat al-abṣār* (beholding with the eyes). Occasional cross references are made between Indexes II and III, and this is clearly indicated prior to the reference of the word, e.g. *See also* Index II, Muḥammad.

A

abandonment (*khidhlān*, *tark*), by God, xxxiii, xxxiv, 17, 18, 50, 51, 67 and n22, 122, 151, 226. *See also* protection: withdrawal of

ʿabd pl. *ʿibād*, *ʿubbād* (servant), xiii, 10, 12. *See also ʿubūdiyya*; servant(s); slave(s)

abdāl (Substitutes), 89 and n5, 225. *See also awtād*; *quṭb*

ʿābid pl. *ʿubbād*, *ʿābidūn* ([devout] worshipper), xlvi, 130, 194, 321. *See also ʿibāda*; *taʿabbud*; worshipper(s)

  aʿbad (most devout of people), 64

abjad, xviii and n32. *See also* letter(s)

ablution, 11, 90 and n9, 135, 247–8, 298 n1. *See also* purification; prayer

abrār sing. *barr* (righteous), xxxvii, 79, 259, 271, 299. *See also birr* (righteous); righteous

abstinence (*ṣawm*, *zuhd*), xxi, xxx, lviii, 57, 103, 117, 119, 140, 188, 226. *See also* fasting; hunger; renunciation; silence

accounting (*ḥisāb / muḥāsaba*) at Resurrection, xxxvi, 35, 87, 109, 112, 113 and n5, 122, 236, 238 n4, 244, 274

  calling one's self to account (*muḥāsaba*), 87, 112

acquiescence (*sukūn / musākana*), in God, lv, lx, 184, 187. *See also* reliance, on God

acquiescence (*sukūn / musākana*), in other than God, xxxv, xlii, xlvi, 16 and n26, 17, 37–8, 49, 80, 127, 134, 184, 204, 249, 289, 293. *See also* reliance, on other than God

action, acting, act(s) (*ʿamal* pl. *aʿmāl*) 55, 104, 125. *See also* deed(s)

  nobility of, 101

  on one's knowledge, 55, 97, 102

  for other than God, 91

  purely for God, lvii, 298

  wrong, Joseph protected from, 50 and n48

ādāb sing. *adab* (spiritual proprieties, codes of fair conduct), xvi, xxxviii, xlixff, 59, 72, 76, 78, 81, 101, 110, 134, 135, 143, 153, 196, 197 n5, 220, 242, 255. *See also* propriety(ies)

ʿadhāb (torment, punishment), 69. *See also* punishment; torment(s)

ʿ*aqaba* (obstacle before Traverse, 90:11), 286
ʿ*aql* pl. ʿ*uqūl* (intellect), xxviii, xxxvi, xl, xlvi, xlvii n205, lvii, lix, 18, 25, 42, 51, 54, 59, 83, 96, 100, 104, 107, 113, 120, 135, 157, 160, 163, 166, 174, 181, 194, 201, 205, 208, 227, 261, 263, 267, 288, 293. *See also* intellect(s)
  fahm al- (understanding of the intellect), xxxix, xl, xliv n184, 116, 120, 168, 181, 216
ʿ*ārif* pl. ʿ*ārifūn* / ʿ*urafāʾ* (mystic, possessor of mystical knowledge, gnosis), xiii, xxxvii, xl, xliii, 24, 31, 58, 108, 172, 175, 208, 248, 297. *See also maʿrifa*; mystic(s)
  al-muḥibbūn (loving mystics), 40
arrogance (*istikbār, baṭar*), xlix n189, 61, 96, 119, 250. *See also* conceit; pride, hubris
  behaving arrogantly in the earth, 74 and n19
asbāb sing. *sabab* (secondary causes, means), 25 n77, 98, 101, 237, 317. *See also* cause(s)
  al-īmān (means of faith), 200
  madhmūma (blameworthy means), 145
aṣfiyāʾ (elect, choicest ones), of God, 222. *See also* choice: election
ashqiyāʾ (the wretched), 183. *See also shaqāwa*; wretchedness
aṣl pl. *uṣūl* (fundamentals), of religious knowledge or theology, 9 n39, 88, 90, 117, 151, 173, 254
asmāʾ (names), of God, xviii, 220. *See also* name(s), of God
aspirant(s) (*murīd* pl. *murīdūn*), xxix, xlix, l. *See also* seeker(s)
aspiration (*himma*), li, liii–liv, 40, 76, 92, 249 and n11, 301 n2
  base, 233
ʿ*Aṣr* (afternoon prayer), 35 and n126. *See also* prayer
assistance (*maʿūna*), from God, 14, 90, 128, 226. *See also* aid
  withdrawal of, 57
association, of partners with God (*shirk*), 98, 177, 234, 263, 310–1. *See also* idolatry
  hidden form of, 310
  two kinds of, 310
astray, going / led (*ḍalāl* / *ḍalāla* / *iḍlāl*), 1, 14 n14, 61, 65 n11, 66, 68, 116, 119, 126, 131, 168, 184, 189, 212, 226. *See also* error(s), erring
ʿ*aṭf* (inclination, kindness, sympathy)
  from God, 50, 200. *See also* attributes, of God: kindness, gentleness
  towards purest love of God, 40
attestation, of faith (*shahāda*), 45 and n27, 110, 293 n2
attributes, for spiritual wayfarers, lix. *See also* character
  of lordliness, 32
attributes (*ṣifāt*), of God, general, xviii, xxiv and n84, xxvii, xxxi, xxxvii, xlvii n205, xlviii, lix, 12, 13, 20, 32, 78, 118, 142 n3, 213, 243. *See also* volition; will, of God
  beyond attributes, lx, 78
  manifest through His signs, 213
  Qurʾān contains, xxxi
attributes (*ṣifāt*), of God, particular. *See also* oneness
  authority (*sulṭān*), 280
  beneficence (*iḥsān, birr*), xxi, 14, 11, 59, 211, 276
  clemency (*ḥilm*), 183, 270
  coerciveness (*qahr*), 220
  compassion (*raḥma, ishfāq*), 9 and n40, 14
  divinity (*ilāhiyya*), xxxvii, 32
  dominion (*jabarūt*), 114, 145
  of essence (*dhāt*) of God, xlvii n205, xlviii, 20, 142
  exaltedness (ʿ*uluww*), 190, 220, 240
  generosity (*karam, karāma*), xl, 34, 48, 85, 155, 172, 173, 270, 280, 293
  gentleness, compassion (*rifq*), 23, 259
  glory (*majd*), xxxi, 8, 12
  grace, graciousness (*faḍl, luṭf*), xxi, xl, 12, 14, 50, 85, 270
  ineffability, xxx, lx
  ipseity (*huwiyya*), xxxvii, 32
  justice (ʿ*adl*), 27, 44
  kindness (*raʾfa*), 23
  light (*nūr*), xlvii, 42, 47. *See also* light(s), of / from God
  lordliness, lordship (*rubūbiyya*), xlvii, lv, 10, 32, 42, 46 and n33, 47, 55
  loving compassion (*ḥanān*), xlvii n205
  magnificence (*bahāʾ*), xxxi, 8
  majesty, sublimity, greatness (ʿ*aẓama*), xxxii, 107, 186 n3, 190
  mercy (*raḥma*), 6 n28, 8, 9 and n40, 18, 27, 68, 113, 152, 172, 180, 187, 214
    secret and essence of, 223
  munificence (*inʿām*), 11
  omnipotence (*qudra*), xxiii n73, xxxiv, xliv, xlvii n204, lv, 10 n4, 46, 50, 56, 74 and n16, 76 n26, 79, 90, 102, 150, 175, 176, 190, 204, 208, 220, 281
  power (*ḥawl*), 204
    and strength (*ḥawl wa quwwa*), 13, 114, 190, 197, 240

resplendence (*sanāʾ*), xxxi, 8, 176
self-sufficiency and being besought of all (*ṣamadiyya*), xxxvii, 32, 317
sovereignty (*mulk*), 317
speech (*kalām*), xxxvii, 189
strength (*quwwa*). *See above* power, and strength
transcendence (*tanzīh*), xxx, lviii, lx, 197 n6, 277
tremendousness (*ʿaẓm al-shaʾn*), 280
unicity (*waḥdāniyya*), 33, 136, 208, 291, 317. *See also* oneness
wrath (*ghadab*, *sakhṭ*), 6 n28, 100, 209, 214
wisdom (*ḥikma*), 59, 102
word, creative (*kalam*), 108 n5
workmanship (*ṣanʿa*), 102
authority (*sulṭān*), 3 n14, 83, 116, 120
of / from God, 114, 280
intoxication of, xlv, 109
awe, dread (*rahba*, *hayba*, *khashiya*), 13 n9, 19, 23, 101 n8, 116, 136, 158, 221, 302. *See also* fear; mindfulness
awliyāʾ (friends, of God). *See walī* (friend)
awtād (mainstays), in the spiritual hierarchy, 72 and n6, 89. *See also abdāl*
awwāb (repeatedly repenting, penitent), 113, 205. *See also tāʾib*; *tawwāb*; repentant
āya pl. *āyāt* (sign, revelation, verse), 36, 37, 176 and n7, 188, 200. *See also* signs, of God
ʿayn (eye, essence)
al-karam (essence of generosity), 172
al-qalb (eye of the heart), 257
al-raḥma (essence of mercy), 223
al-raʾs (physical eye, lit. eye of the head), 257
al-yaqīn (eye of certainty). *See yaqīn*: *ʿayn al-*; certainty
ʿaysh (livelihood, way of life, sustenance, subsistence), xl, 120, 160, 184, 207 n2, 263. *See also* life, way of
of angels, prophets, veracious, liii, lvii, 25, 160
patience as, 23
remembrance as, lvii, 160
trust as a means of, lv
understanding as, 120
ayyām Allāh (days of God), knowledge of, 128 and n1, 231
azaliyya bi-azaliyya (eternity, with Eternity itself), xxxvi n143, 287, 290
ʿaẓama (majesty, sublimity, greatness), of God, xxxii, 107, 186 n3, 190. *See also* attributes, of God
al-ʿAzīz (Almighty), 175. *See also* name(s), of God
Azrāʾīl, 173 and n20. *See also* Angel of Death; angel(s)

B

Badr, Battle of, 49 and n43, 57 n22, 81, 82 n5, 323, 324, 325, 331
backbiting (*ghayba*), 110, 202, 306
bakhl (miserliness), 227 and n7
balāʾ / *balwā* / *balīya* pl. *balāyā* (affliction, tribulation, trial, calamity), 18, 49, 108, 129, 136, 139, 149, 165, 166, 198, 258. *See also ibtilāʾ*; affliction
baqāʾ (subsistence, remaining with, in God), 14, 327. *See also* subsistence (*baqāʾ*)
maʿaʾl-Bāqī (subsistence with the Permanently Subsistent One), xxxvi, 184
dār al- (abode of permanent subsistence), 306
and *fanāʾ*, lix and n269, 47 n36
al-Bāqī (the Everlasting, the Permanently Subsistent), xxxvi, 221, 290. *See also* name(s), of God
baraka pl. *barakāt* (blessing), 153, 225 and n3. *See also niʿma*; blessing(s)
baʾsāʾ (misfortune, suffering), 39, 149. *See also balāʾ*; affliction
baṣar (vision, sight, insight, perception), xlix, 213, 257. *See also baṣīra*; *ʿiyān*; *naẓar* (sight); *rūʾyā*; beholding; vision
ʿayn al-qalb (sight of the eye of the heart), 257
al-qalb (heart's insight, vision), 19, 133, 205, 212 and n3, 213
al-Baṣīr (the Seeing, 'Seer'), God as, 236. *See also* name(s), of God
baṣīra pl. *baṣāʾir* (insight), xlviii, 4, 11, 21, 116, 121. *See also baṣar*; insight(s)
al-yaqīn (insight of certainty), 29
Basmala, xxiv, xxxi, xliv n189, 8, 9, 13 n6, 242 n2. *See also* Qurʾān
bāṭil (false, falsehood), 153, 212, 250, 261
bāṭin (inner)
as inner aspect, sense of the Qurʾān, xxvi, xxvii, 2, 48 n40. *See also* meaning(s)
as inner self, 86, 129. *See also* self
ṭarīq al- (inner path), 189
al-Bāṭin (the Hidden), 220. *See also* name(s), of God
bayān (coherent speech, 55:4), 216. *See also* speech

C

D

E

F

H

al-warīd (aorta, 'jugular vein'), 86 and n17
ḥadd (limit), xxvii, 2. *See also* meaning(s)
ḥadhr (wariness), xxi, li, 47, 76. *See also taqwā*
Hajj (the Pilgrimage), 6, 7, 24 n68, 77, 132 and n9, 282 n1. *See also* Pilgrimage
al-Ḥakīm (the Wise), 241. *See also* name(s), of God
ḥāl pl. *aḥwāl* (state, state of being, situation), l, lvi n256, 39 n155, 86, 87 n19, 89, 93, 95, 113, 119, 140, 148, 149 n5, 166, 181, 198, 205, 222, 205, 222, 275, 318. *See also waqt*; state(s)
quwwat al- (strength of state), 222
ḥāl (present moment), 39 and n155
ḥalāl (lawful, licit, permissible), xxvi, 4, 36, 41, 68, 82, 140, 160, 229. *See also ḥarām*; lawful; command(s)
al-fuḍūl al- (legitimate inquisitiveness), 247
ḥamd (praise), lvii, 10, 143. *See also* praise
hamm (concern, anxiety), 61, 97
al-dunyā (for the world), 67
hamm (desire), 71. *See also hawā*; desire (*hamm*)
ḥanān ([loving] compassion), xlvii n205. *See also* attributes, of God
of John the Baptist, 119 n1
hand(s), of God. *See* God: hands of
happiness, predestined, in this life and eternal (*saʿāda*), xxxvi, 76 and n28, 154. *See also* felicity; bliss, predestined; wretchedness
ḥaqāʾiq sing. *ḥaqīqa* (spiritual realities), xlvii n204, 79, 218, 293
al-waḥdāniyya (realities of unicity), 116
ḥaqīqa (inner) realisation, 138. *See also* realisation
ḥaqīqa (truth, reality), 9, 146, 193, 201. *See also ḥaqq* (truth); truth
al-īmān (truth, realisation, of faith), 84, 134
al-maʿrifa (reality, of gnosis), 113
Muḥammadiyya, xxxii n128. *See also* Light, Muḥammadan
al-ṣidq (truth of veracity), 159
al-tawakkul (reality, of trust), lv, 56
al-tawḥīd (truth, of God's oneness), 252
ḥaqq pl. *ḥuqūq* (right, duty), lvii, 85 n11, 143, 200, 227, 303. *See also* duty; right(s)
al-Ḥaqq (the Truth), i.e. God, lvii, 8. Passim in Arabic original
being led by, to, 171
ḥaqq (truth, reality), 39, 171, 261. *See also* truth; reality
ahl al- (people of truth), 21
khalīṣat al- (purest reality), 40
maʿrifat Allāh / *maʿrifathi* (knowledge of God as He should be known), 150, 173
taḥqīq al- (realisation of truth), 191
ṭarīq al- (path of truth), 139
al-yaqīn. *See yaqīn*: *ḥaqq al-*
ḥarakāt sing. *ḥaraka* (activity, movement, commotion), 128, 171, 197
wa-sukūn (activity and stillness, repose), 27 n81, 66, 93 and n11, 135. *See also sukūn* (stillness)
ḥarām (unlawful, forbidden, illicit), xxvi, li, 4, 41, 80, 140, 160, 198, 229. *See also* forbidden
ḥarf pl. *ḥurūf*. *See* letter(s)
harm, avoidance of, to others (*kaff al-adhā*), li, lii, 45, 56, 84, 137, 149, 160
ḥasad (envy), 72
hawā pl. *ahwāʾ* (desire, whim), xxvii, xl, 6, 18, 19, 22, 29, 38, 41, 75, 78, 96, 113, 128, 131, 168, 173, 175, 177, 196, 201, 222, 237, 248, 266, 288, 300, 301, 317. *See also hamm* (desire); *shahwa*; desire (*hamm*)
ḥawḍ. *See* Pool
ḥawl (power). *See also quwwa*; power (*ḥawl*); power and strength
wa quwwa (and strength), xxxiii, xxxiv, xxxvii, lv, 2 , 12, 13, 14, 28, 37, 55, 114, 145, 148, 154, 180, 190, 197, 213, 237, 240, 286, 318
ḥayāʾ (shame), 135. *See also* shame
ḥayāt (life), 110, 120, 128, 171, 194. *See also ʿaysh*; life (*ḥayāt*)
bi-ḥayāt (life, with Life itself), xxxvi n143, 284, 287, 290
ṭayyiba (good life), xxxvi
al-rūḥ (life of the spirit), lviii, 225
hayba (awe), 302. *See also rahba*; *taqwā*; awe
ḥayra / *taḥayyur* (bewilderment), 122, 250, 281 and n6. *See also dahsha*; bewilderment
al-Ḥayy (the Living), 175 and n2. *See also* name(s), of God
ḥaẓẓ pl. *ḥuẓūẓ* (share, portion, [self] interest, pleasure), 15, 69 and n29, 75 and n21, 93 and n10, 134, 237, 255, 267
heart(s) (*qalb* pl. *qulūb*, *fuʾād* pl. *afʾida*), xv, xvi n11, xxi, xxvii, xxviii, xxx, xxxii, xxxv, xxxvii, xxxviii, xxxix, xl, xli, xlii–xliii, xliv, xlvi, xlvii n205, xlviii, l, li, lii, lv, lvi, lvii, lviii, lix, 2, 3, 4 and n20, 8, 14, 16 and n26, 17, 19, 20 and n54, 25, 28, 29, 30, 32, 34, 37, 38, 39 and n155, 41, 42, 45, 48, 49 and n44, 50, 54, 55, 62, 65, 66, 68, 69 n29, 72, 73 n12, 78, 81 and n1, 83, 85, 86 and n17, 97, 100 n4, 101 and n8, 104, 105, 106,

I

iḍṭirāb (disturbance, perturbation), 128. *See also ḥarakāt*; *wārid*

ifḍāl (giving bounty, being gracious), 148. *See also faḍl* (divine favour); *niʿma*; grace / graciousness

iflās (insolvency), 317 and n2

iftikhār (taking pride in), 80, 299

iftiqār (neediness, utter neediness), for God, xxxiv, liv, 28, 37, 49, 118, 147, 159, 239, 252, 301. *See also faqr*; poverty
- *shiddat al-* (intense neediness), 198

ightirār (delusion, conceit), 75, 278, 283. *See also* delusion

ignorance (*jahl*), xxi, xli, xlv and n192, l, li, lii, lvi, 39, 41, 53, 55, 56, 59, 60, 64, 81, 96, 101, 106, 108, 117, 122, 138, 155, 189, 198, 201, 204, 209, 255, 270, 288, 298, 300
- darkness is, 48
- death is through, 189
- and disobedience, 105, 110
- persistence in sin gives rise to, 250
- is root of evil, 170
- and satiety, 72

iḥsān (beneficence, of God, goodness, benevolence), xlvii n205, 11, 29, 109, 147, 219, 276

iḥsān (excellence, in faith), lv, lviii n265, 52 n54, 56, 103 and n5, 166 n12, 198 n11, 219, 221 n4. *See also islām*, both entries; *īmān*; faith

iḥtimāl (endurance), 259. *See also ṣabr*; *mukābada*; patience

ījāb (willing compliance), 7, 109, 145 n10, 181

ijāba (response / responding), lvii, 91, 170 and n3, 298

ijmāʿ (consensus), 59. *See also* consultation

ijtihād (striving, toiling), 26, 66 n16. *See also jahd*; *jihād*; striving

ikhbāt (humility), 115, 134. *See also khushūʿ*; *khuḍūʿ*; humility; humble

ikhlāṣ (sincerity), xxx, xxxviii, xl, li, lv, lvi, lvii, lix, 22 n61, 49 n42, 51, 55, 71, 78, 83, 86, 88, 91, 101, 103, 120, 122, 138, 150, 153 and n4, 158, 159, 160, 163, 170, 181, 194, 196, 198, 200, 202, 208, 216, 226, 247, 252, 282, 289, 293, 298 and n5, 317 and n1, 321. *See also* sincerity

ikhtibār (testing), 129. *See also balāʾ*; *ibtilāʾ*; *miḥna*; *imtiḥān*; test(s)

ikhtilāf (dissension), 39. *See also mukhālafa*; opposition

ikhtiyār (choice / choosing, power of disposal), human, 28, 93, 112, 313. *See also* choice

ikhtiyār (choosing, election), by God, liii, 61, 218. *See also* choice

ikrām (generous treatment, honouring), 74, 278. *See also karam*

ilāhiyya (divinity), xxxvii, 32. *See also* attributes, of God

ilhām (inspiration), xxviii, xl, 106, 261 and n3. *See also waḥy*; inspiration

ʿilm pl. *ʿulūm* (knowledge), xliii, xxi, xxii n72, xxiv, xliii, xlv, xlvii and n204, xlviii, xlix, li, 6, 18, 19, 25, 37, 41, 48, 59, 77, 89, 100, 102, 110, 135, 150, 166, 175, 194, 198, 216, 222, 226, 227, 259, 268 n3, 288. *See also maʿrifa*; knowledge (*ʿilm*, *maʿrifa*); gnosis
- *bāb al-* (gate of [God's] knowledge), xxiii n73, 10 n4
- *funūn al-* (multifarious dimensions of God's knowledge), 107
- *ʿindī* (knowledge directly bestowed by God), xlvii, 42
- *istiʿmāl al-* (putting knowledge into practice), 259
- *ladunnī* (knowledge from the divine presence), xlvii, 37 n147, 42
- *rāsikhūna fi'l-*, xxvii, 41–2
- *al-sharʿ* (knowledge of the sacred law), 205

iltijāʾ (taking refuge), in God, 96. *See also iʿtiṣām*; refuge

imām (guide, leader), 111, 120

īmān (faith), xx n50, xxxii, lii, lvii, 20 n54, 28, 43 n13, 52 n54, 77, 82, 88, 96, 103 and n5, 118, 126, 158, 166 and n12, 167, 198, 202, 213, 214, 221 n4, 225, 249, 267, 268. *See also iḥsān*; *islām*, both entries; faith
- *asbāb al-* (means of faith), 200
- *ḥaqāʾiq al-* (realities of faith), xlvii n204, 194
- *ḥaqīqat al-* (true faith), lii, 84
- *bi'Llāh* (faith in, or through God), xlviii, 19
- *li'Llāh* (faith for the sake of God), xlviii, 19
- *mawhibat al-* (gift of faith), xlii, 225
- *nūr al-* (light of faith), 225
- *ṣidq al-* (true faith), 134
- *sirr al-* (mystery of faith), xlii, 132

immortality, xxxv, 16, 18

imtiḥān (testing), 49. *See also miḥna*, *balāʾ*; *ibtilāʾ*; *ikhtibār*; test(s); trial(s); tribulation(s)

ināba (contrition), l, 84, 91, 168. *See also nadam*; regret

independence (*istighnāʾ*). *See also* wealth
- of God, liv. *See also* attributes, of God; name(s), of God; *al-Ghanī*
- sense of, in humans, 296

al-lisān (affirmation of the tongue), 202
iqtidāʾ (emulation, imitation), liii–liv, 25 and n73, 86, 121, 131, 170, 181, 184, 189, 233, 321. *See also* emulation
irāda (volition), of God, xxiii, 10 and n4, 51 n50. *See also* volition; will, of God
irāda (will, wish, aspiration, intention), 120, 135, 240. *See also murīd*; *murād*; aspirant(s)
ʿĪshāʾ (night prayer), 35 n129, 72 and n8. *See also* prayer: ritual
ishāra (allusion), xvii, xxviii, xlv, 33, 150. *See also* allusion
ishtighāl (preoccupation, distraction), from God, 115
islām, *īmān* and *iḥsān*, 52 n54, 103 and n5, 166 n12. *See also īmān*; *iḥsān* (excellence)
islām (submission, surrender), lv, 56, 97, 158, 202 n13, 221 n14. *See also istislām*; *taslīm*; submission; peace (*salām*)
  and *īmān*, 198 n11
Islam, religion of, xii, xiii, 93, 114 n13, 121 n13, 129, 202, 270 n1, 289 n1, 314. *See also* religion; faith; submission; peace
  definition of, 47
  expansion of breast for, 66
  honouring elderly in, 74
  laws of, 22, 57, 71, 103, 241
  light of, 293
  locus of, is breast, xliii, 43
  outward aspect and reality of, 224
  path of, 164
  prayer to be kept in, 154
  Prophet's definition of, 286
  religion of, 11, 43, 84
  taqwā at level of, 166
ism pl. *asmāʾ*, xviii, 107, 220. *See also* name(s)
ʿiṣma (divine protection, from error or sin), xxxiii, xxxiv, 2, 14, 42, 49, 50 n48, 62, 72, 95, 96, 116, 128, 148, 151, 165, 216, 237, 277. *See also maʿūna*; *wilāya* (God's patronage); help; protection
Isrāʾ (Night Journey of the Prophet), xxviii, 4 n15, 20 *See also Miʿrāj*; Night Journey
Israelites, 78 n40. *See also* Index II, Children, of Israel
Isrāfīl, 5 and n22, 100 n2, 173 n20. *See also* angel(s); Preserved Tablet
Isrāʾīliyyāt, 121 n13
istidrāj (God's giving respite, lulling people into false sense of security), 3 n12, 20 and n48, 42 n10, 57 n26, 278 and n8, 283 and n9. *See also makr*
istighfār (seeking forgiveness), of God, 24, 91. *See also maghfira*; *ghufrān*; forgiveness (*maghfira*)
istighnāʾ (independence, wealth, lack of need), liv, 296. *See also ghinā*; wealth
istimāʿ (listening, heeding), 143, 232. *See also* Qurʾān: listening to
istinbāṭ (eliciting meanings from the Qurʾān), xi, 37 n143. *See also tafsīr*; *taʾwīl*; interpretation
istiqāma (rectitude), xxxv, 53, 117, 155, 160, 178, 224, 268, 270. *See also* rectitude
istirāḥa (ease), in Hereafter, 231. *See also* Hereafter; Paradise
istislām (complete submission, self-surrender), lv and n245, 51. *See also islām* (submission); *taslīm*
istiṭāʿa (ability), 114
istithnāʾ (making an exception or a proviso), 198 and n12, 318 and n3
īthār (altruism, preferring others [over oneself]), 229
ithm (sin), 28, 219. *See also dhanb*; *maʿṣiya*; sin(s)
iʿtimād (reliance), 173, 224, 252. *See also sukūn* (tranquil repose); acquiescence; reliance
iʿtiṣām (taking refuge), in God, 318. *See also iltijāʾ*; *lujūʾ*; refuge
ittibāʿ (following), Muḥammad, 184, 233. *See also iqtidāʾ*; Sunna; emulation: of Prophet
ittiṣāl (conjunction, union, spiritual attainment), xlix, 19, 20 n53, 138, 226. *See also* union
ʿiyān (direct witnessing), xlix and n209, 30, 32, 43 n6. *See also* vision; witnessing, direct
  ʿiyān al- (immediate vision of direct witnessing), xxxvii, 31
ʿizz (honour), 38. *See also karam*; *ikrām*

J

jabarūt (Dominion), 114, 145
al-Jabbār (the Compeller), 92, 277. *See also* name(s), of God
jafr, xviii and n32. *See also* letter(s)
jahd (exertion, striving, endeavour), 67, 219 n6, 286. *See also jihād*; *ijtihād*; *saʿī*; striving
  aṣḥāb al- (people who strive [for the good]), 122
jāhil (ignorant), 111. *See also jahl*; ignorance
Jāhiliyya ('Period of Ignorance', prior to Islam), 8 and n34, 30 and n95, 329, 331
jahl (ignorance), xlv, li, lvi, 39, 48, 59, 105, 122, 138, 170, 198, 298, 300. *See also* ignorance
Jahmites, xxxi n123

L

of God, 24, 34, 149 n6, 238, 307
loving mystics (*ʿārifūn muḥibbūn*), 40
those who love each other for God's sake (*mutaḥābbūn fi'Llāh*), 120 and n9
lower self. *See* self, lower
lubb pl. *albāb* (pith, inner substance), xxxviii
lujūʾ (taking refuge), in God, 252. *See also iltijāʾ*; refuge
lust(s) (*shahwa* pl. *shahawāt*), xli, xlii, xliii, l, 18, 36, 96, 132, 133, 147, 168, 177, 179, 180, 193, 201, 204, 208, 222, 234, 248, 265, 267, 283, 288, 306, 321. *See also* desire (*hamm*)
luṭf (benevolence, grace, graciousness), 85, 136 n5, 243, 267, 270, 292. *See also birr* (beneficence); *faḍl* (divine favour)
al-rubūbiyya (grace of Lordship), 32

M

mā shāʾa'Llāh (what God wills), 117 n11
maʿād (final return), 288
maʿbūd (the One worshipped), xxxvii, 213, 220. *See also ʿibāda*; worship
madhāq (tasting), rank of, 222
madhhab (school of thought, method), 90
madhkūr (the One remembered), i.e. God, lviii, 133, 225. *See also dhikr* (remembrance); *dhākir*; remembrance
maghfira (forgiveness), 24, 132, 276. *See also ghufrān*; *istighfār*; forgiveness, both entries
maḥabba (love), xxxvii, xlii, 24 n69, 124, 145, 159, 182, 210, 213, 216, 275, 306. *See also ḥubb*; *wudd*; *widād*; love
majesty (*ʿaẓama*), of God, xxxii, 77, 190. *See also* attributes, of God
majlis al-quds (Holy Assembly), 260. *See also* Night, of Assembly; Resurrection
makhdūʿ (deluded), 234. *See also ightirār*; *khidāʿ*; delusion
makr (ruse, scheming, delusion, illusion, plotting), 20 and n47, 28, 42 n10, 74, 90 n9, 96, 138, 145, 154, 283 n10, 296, 308. *See also* ruse; *istidrāj*
makrūh pl. *makrūhāt* (reprehensible according to Islamic law), 36 and n141
malakūt (heavenly, celestial dominions, heavenly kingdom), xxxiii, xxxix, 70, 171
malāmatiyya ('School of Blame'), 188 n2
al-Malik (the King), 18, 175. *See also* name(s), of God
manʿ (hindering, impediment, withholding), by / from God, 99, 146
maʿnā / *maʿnan* pl. *maʿānī* (meaning, significance, a 'particular thing', understanding) 25, 220, 222 n7, 272 n4, 284. *See also* meaning(s)
manāzil sing. *manzil* / *manzila* (degrees, stations, resting places), liii, lvi n256, 74, 189, 218, 284 n12, 293. *See also maqām*; station(s)
al-Manīʿ (the Forbidding), 241. *See also* name(s), of God
maqām maḥmūd (Praiseworthy Station, accorded to Muḥammad), 31, 291
maqām pl. *maqāmāt* (station, rank, level), xxxvii, l n213, liv, lvi n256, lix, 32, 67, 77, 144, 189, 213, 305. *See also manāzil*; station(s)
aʿẓam al- (greatest station), 243, 255
maqt (abhorrence, by God), 67, 168, 176
maʿrifa (knowledge, cognicence, recognition), 26, 39 and n158, 131, 171, 183. *See also ʿilm*
maʿrifa pl. *maʿārif* (gnosis), xiii, xxvi, xli, xlii, xliii, xliv, xlvii n204, lv, 1, 6 and n25, 19, 20, 21, 24 n69, 25, 39, 43, 48 and n41, 56, 73 n9, 96, 103, 113, 126, 129, 131, 138, 145, 158, 176, 182, 195, 196, 204, 208, 210, 216, 218, 219, 220, 224, 231, 259, 267, 281 n6, 286. *See also maʿrifa* (knowledge); gnosis
ahl al- (people of gnosis), xliii, 73, 149, 192
anwār al- (lights of gnosis), 214
nafs al- (self of gnosis), xxxix, xli, 96
nūr al- (light of gnosis), xlii, 132, 184
sabīl al- (way of gnosis), 291
sirr al- (light of gnosis), 223
marriage, 27, 53 n2, 277 n3
Moses', 124
martyr(s), liii, 82, 150, 171–2 n10, 218, 219, 273 n7
mashīʾa (will), God's, xxiii and n73, 10 and n4, 13 n11, 89, 269. *See also irāda* (volition); will, of God
mashīʾa (will), human, 135
maʿṣiya pl. *maʿāṣī* (sin, transgression, disobedience), 53, 104, 122, 170, 202, 304. *See also* sin(s)
maskana (lowliness, deprivation), 38 and n150. *See also miskīn*; poverty; poor
mathal pl. *amthāl* (like, likeness, similitude, parable), xxvi, 6, 21, 25 n72, 317. *See also* similitude(s)
maṭlaʿ (point of transcendency), xxvii, 2. *See also* meaning(s)
maʿūna (aid, assistance, help), from God, xxxiii, xxxiv, 2 n6, 10, 14, 57, 108, 117, 126, 128, 171, 197, 226, 237. *See also taʾyīd*

Munkar and Nakīr, 73 and n10, 193. *See also* angel(s)
muqarrab ([the] one brought nigh), xxxii, liv, 78
muqarrabūn (people of proximity), liv, 33, 47, 78, 155
murād pl. *murādūn* ([divinely] sought), xxix, xxxii, liv, 66 and nn14 and 16, 77. *See also* *murīd*; aspirant(s)
murāqaba (vigilance, heedfulness), 14, 61, 125, 128, 160, 194, 201. *See also rāqib*; heedful
murīd pl. *murīdūn* (seeker, aspirant), xxix, xxxii, liv, 66 and nn14 and 16, 67, 77. *See also murād*; aspirant(s)
musākana (acquiescence), 16 and n26, 17, 37, 49, 80 n47. *See also sukūn* (tranquil repose); acquiescence
mushāhada (contemplative witnessing of the unseen), xxxvii, xli, lvii, 19, 52, 77, 88, 101, 106, 122, 159, 180, 205, 212, 213, 216, 271, 279, 303. *See also mukāshafa*; *naẓar* (sight); *ʿiyān*; witnessing; unveiling; vision
  al-ghayb (witnessing the unseen), 222
  al-Rabb (witnessing the Lord), xxxii, 77
mushtāq pl. *mushtāqūn* (longing, yearning), 33, 48, 58. *See also shawq*; longing
muṣība (affliction), 318. *See also balāʾ*; *ibtilāʾ*; *miḥna*; affliction
muskir (intoxicating drink), 105. *See also sukr*; intoxicant(s)
muslim f. muslima (Muslim, in state of submission to God), 23, 86 n13, 146 n13, 198 and n11. *See also islām* (submission); Islam; submission
  ḥaqqan (true Muslim), 146 n13
Muslim(s), xxiii, xxxi n123, liii, 11 n8, 54, 121 n13, 146 n13, 158, 181, 198, 226 n1, 299, 300, 310
  compared to believer (*muʾmin*), 198 n11, 202,
  defined, 47
  as midmost nation, 178 n8
  seeking knowledge an obligation for every, 86
mustanbaṭ pl. *mustanbaṭāt* (understanding elicited from the Qurʾān), 37 and n143. *See also* *istinbāṭ*; interpretation; meaning(s)
mustaslim (self-surrender), 165. *See also islām* (submission); *istislām*
mustawḍaʿ (deposit). *See also* deposit(s)
  from God, within man, 63
mutafarridūn (those isolated for God), 4. *See also* *munfaridūn*
mutafarrisīn (people of spiritual perception), 105. *See also firāsa*; perception, 'spiritual'
mutaḥayyir (bewildered), 286. *See also ḥayra*; *dahsha*; bewilderment
mutashābih, pl. *mutshābihāt*. *See muḥkam*
mutawassimīn (those who take note), 105
Muʿtazilīs (Muʿtazilites), xxxi n123, 197 n6, 314 n4, 329
muṭīʿ (obedient), 53. *See also ṭāʿa*; obedience
muttaqī pl. *muttaqūn* (those mindful of God), liii, lvi, 13 and n9, 26, 50, 56, 121, 128, 133, 198, 207, 298. *See also taqwā*; mindful
  mawadda (love, affection), 137, 291. *See also* *ḥubb*; *maḥabba*; *wudd*; love
muwāfaqa (conformity), 89, 101, 114, 189, 201, 229 n2, 265
muwāfaqāt (acts of conformity), 171
muwāfiqūn (people of conformity), 147, 221
muwaḥḥidūn (those who realise God's oneness), 219. *See also tawḥīd*; oneness
muwāzana (weighing up), 113. *See also* *muḥāsaba*; reckoning; accounting
mystery(ies) (*sirr* pl. *asrār*), xxxvii, xli, xliii, 41, 120, 195. *See also* secret(s), inner truth(s)
  of faith (*sirr al-īmān*), xlii, 132
  unseen, xlvii, 20, 145
  unseen, in the Qurʾān, xxvii
  with Mystery itself (*sirr bi-sirr*), xxxvi n143, 287, 290
mystic(s) (*ʿārif* pl. *ʿārifūn* / *ʿurafāʾ*), xi, xiii, xvi, xvii, xviii, xix n42, xxvi, xxxi and n125, xxxvii, xxxviii n149, xli, xlii, lvi n256, lix, lx, 8 n35, 19 n44, 31, 32 nn 105 and 107, 34, 39 n155, 58, 64 n6, 73 n12, 89 n5, 92, 113 n10, 120 n7, 148 n6, 150 n9, 166 n13, 176 n8, 188 n3, 208, 210, 212 n3, 286. *See also* gnosis
  adornment of, is worship, 108
  and the Book, 175
  hearts of, xlii, 58, 175
  joyful with light of gnosis of God, 214
  loving (*al-ʿārifūn al-muḥibbūn*), 40

N

nabī pl. *anbiyāʾ* (prophet), 25 n72, 46 n34, 82, 196, 245 and n6. *See also nubuwwa*; *rusul*; prophet(s)
nadam / *nadāma* (remorse, regret), l, 84, 139, 278. *See also ināba*; regret
nafl pl. *nawāfil* (supererogatory act), 113
nafs pl. *anfus* / *nufūs* (self, lower self), xxxv, xxxviii–xlii, xxxviii nn147 and 150, xl n155, xli n172, xlix, lix, 6, 16 nn23 and 27, 17 n30, 55,

O

Q

R

rūḥ pl. *arwāḥ* (spirit), xxxviii, xxxix, lix, 23 n63, 81, 120, 163, 168, 171 and n9, 172, 186, 201, 247, 267, 314. *See also nafs al-rūḥ*; spirit; self, spiritual
badhl al- (exertion of the spirit), 158 and n8
ḥayāt al- (life of the spirit), lviii, 225
ittiṣāl al- (spirit's attainment of union), 226
Rūḥ al-Quddūs (Holy Spirit). *See* Spirit [Holy]
rūḥ (soul), 178. *See also* soul
rukhṣa. *See* concession
ruse, plotting, scheming (*makr*)
of enemies against Prophet, 308
of God, 20 and n47, 28, 42 n10, 74, 90 n9, 138, 145, 154, 296
rushd (right course, guidance), 65, 90, 192. *See also hudā*; guidance
rusul sing. *rasūl* (messengers, of God), xlvi, 194, 245 n6. *See also* messenger(s)
rūʾyā (vision, of God in heavenly kingdom), xxxix, 171, 273. *See also* vision

S

saʿāda (felicity, bliss, eternal happiness), xxxvi, 71, 76, 154, 242, 279. *See also* felicity
Sabbath, 75
sābiq (foremost), 162, 218
ṣabr (patience, forbearance, steadfastness, fortitude), liv, lvi, lix, 23, 25, 28, 51, 95, 108, 139, 149, 158, 167 and n2, 171, 192, 198, 247 and n2, 286, 298, 304, 315. *See also* patience
al-Ṣabūr (the Forbearing), 243
sacrifice, 312
for Eid after Hajj, 132. *See also* Hajj
of Ishmael, 62, 165 and n4, 192
prayer as, for mindful of God, 133
ṣadaqa (charity), 135, 149, 161. *See also zakāt*; almsgiving
ṣadr pl. *ṣudūr* (breast), xxx, xxxviii, xliii, 2, 17, 204, 276. *See also* breast
safety (*salāma*, *ʿāfiya*, *taʾalluf*), liv, 32 and n110, 42, 47, 57, 96, 110, 129, 149, 198, 297, 309
seeking / asking for, 28, 49, 67, 149
Ṣaffārid, 61 and n6
Saḥāba. *See* Companions
ṣaḥw (sobriety), 221
saʿī (endeavour), 172 n11, 214. *See also jahd*; *jihād*; *mujāhada*; striving
saint(s), xix, xx n52, 3 n14, 32, 89 n5, 124 n5, 176 n7. *See also* friend(s): of God
sakar (intoxicant, wine), 109. *See also muskir*; intoxicant(s); intoxication
sakhāwa (liberality), 66
sakhṭ (wrath, of God), 214. *See also* attributes, of God: wrath
sakīna (serenity), 259. *See also sukūn* (tranquil repose); *ṭumaʾnīna*; acquiescence, in God
sakīna (spirit of peace), 196
salaf (pious predecessors), 131
salām (peace), xiii, 56, 77. *See also* peace (*salām*)
salāma (safety, security), 28, 67, 96, 149. *See also ʿāfiya*; safety
ṣalāt (prescribed, ritual, prayer), 7, 33, 135, 149, 150, 222 and n7, 294. *See also* prayer: ritual
ṣalawāt (blessings, prayers), 23, 132. *See also* blessings
ṣāliḥ pl. *ṣāliḥūn* (virtuous), 25 n72, 82, 153, 159, 219. *See also* virtuous
imām ṣāliḥ (virtuous guide), 111
Sālimiyya, xxii and n68, xxiii, 324, 328
Salsabīl, 259 and n5
salvation, xxxv, lii, 1, 90, 142 n4, 149 n6, 155, 222
path of 47, 189
samāʿ (listening, auditive experience), 114, 222 n7. *See also* Qurʾān: listening to
al-Ṣamad (Self-Sufficient, Besought of all), 71, 317. *See also* name(s), of God
ṣamadiyya (God's being eternally Self-sufficing and Besought of all), xxxvii, 32. *See also* attributes, of God
Sāmānids, 61
ṣamma (resolve), li, 76
sarīra pl. *sarāʾir* (innermost secret), 26, 105, 130. *See also sirr*; secret, innermost
Satan, xxxv, xli, 13, 17, 29, 30, 31, 32, 34, 35, 37 n147, 49, 55, 82, 122, 127, 133, 134, 153, 161, 170, 212, 224, 257, 273, 298, 300, 320–1. *See also* Iblīs; Enemy
tempts Adam, 16
whispering, evil suggestions of (*waswasa*), xxxv, lvi, 16, 67, 71, 320 and n5
satisfaction (*qanāʿa* / *qunūʿ*), 37, 38 n149, 48, 214, 321
satr (veil), 72. *See also ḥijāb*; veil(s)
ṣawm (fasting, abstinence), 119, 149. *See also zuhd*; abstinence; fasting
ṣawwām (those who fasted), 245
al-Sayyid (Master, divine name), 317. *See also* name(s), of God
scholar(s), the learned (*ʿālim* pl. *ʿulamāʾ*), xvi, xxii n68, xlv, xlvi, liii, 7, 41 and n3, 47, 58 n27, 62, 86, 103, 104, 109, 148, 159, 162, 194, 247. *See also* learning; knowledge (*ʿilm*, *maʿrifa*)
religious, Tustarī's criticism of, xix n41

T

U

V

W

Colophon

~

Tafsīr al-Tustarī is set in Minion Pro, an Adobe typeface designed by Robert Slimbach and released in 2000. Minion Pro is inspired by classical, old style typefaces of the late Renaissance, a period of elegant and highly readable type designs. It combines the aesthetic and functional qualities that make text type highly readable for computerized typesetting needs. The type was modified to create additonal glyphs needed for the composition of this work.

~

Printed on acid-free, Glatfelter offset 50 # extra bulk off-white paper made by the Glatfelter corporation of York, Pennsylvania. It provides superior opacity, print clarity, and meets the requirements of ANSI/NISO Z39.48-1992 (Permanence of Paper). It was printed by the Friesens Corporation of Altona, Manitoba, Canada and perfect bound in Mohawk Loop Linen cover.

~

The Fons Vitae Qurʾānic Commentary Series
Directly available from Fons Vitae

Tafsīr al-Jalālayn by Jalāl al-Dīn al-Suyūṭī and Jalāl al-Dīn al-Maḥallī

Tafsīr Ibn ʿAbbās by Ibn ʿAbbās (attrib.), Muḥammad al-Fīrūzābādī (attrib.)

Al-Wāḥidī's Asbāb al-Nuzūl by ʿAlī Aḥmad b. al-Wāḥidī

Tafsīr al-Tustarī by Sahl b. ʿAbd Allāh al-Tustarī

The Immense Ocean (al-Baḥr al-Madīd) by Aḥmad ibn ʿAjība
A Thirteenth-Century Quranic Commentary on the
Chapters of the All-Merciful, the Event, and Iron

Spiritual Gems The Mystical Qurʾān Commentary ascribed
by the Ṣūfis to the Imām Jaʿfar al-Ṣādiq